The Structure of Community Power

The Structure
of
Community Power

Edited by
MICHAEL AIKEN
University of Wisconsin
and
PAUL E. MOTT
University of Pennsylvania

RANDOM HOUSE   *New York*

Copyright © **1970** *by Random House, Inc.*
All rights reserved under International and Pan-American Copyright Conventions. Published in the United States by Random House, Inc., New York, and simultaneously in Canada by Random House of Canada Limited, Toronto.
Library of Congress Catalog Card Number: 70–97904
Manufactured in the United States of America.
Printed and bound by The Kingsport Press, Inc., Kingsport, Tenn.
Book design by Quentin Fiore.
First Edition
987654321

Dedicated to
Amos H. Hawley and Morris Janowitz

Preface

In 1959 the editors were both graduate students in the same department of sociology and neighbors on the same street. We also shared an interest in political sociology. During numerous front porch conversations, the prototypes for the outline of this book and our articles in it were developed.

The field of community power was then in ferment. The great surge of enthusiasm and effort resulting from Hunter's methodological breakthrough had begun to wane in the face of the counterarguments of political scientists, particularly those of the pluralist persuasion. We were trying, as others were, to make sense out of the welter of conflicting findings and stoutly defended positions. We thought then, as now, that the findings made sense if the emerging concepts and theorems from complex organizations were applied to them. The intervening years have not dissuaded us of this conviction. The organization of the present volume reflects it; we hope that the further development of this approach will provide a meaningful scheme for organizing existing and future work in community power systems and that it reveals lacunae where greater theoretical and empirical effort should be made. In any case the outline of this reader reflects a plan of action for us.

Both authors wish to acknowledge their intellectual indebtedness to Amos H. Hawley and Morris Janowitz by dedicating this book to them. In their defense it should be noted that they tried their best to train us; any inadequacies of the approach taken here are our own.

We are also grateful to a number of people and organizations for their help in making our research and this volume possible. Aiken received financial assistance from The Center for Vocational and Technical Education and The Institute for Research on Poverty: a part of that assistance was used for his contribution to this book. The Office of Research Administration at the University of Michigan and the Wharton School of Finance and Commerce at the University of Pennsylvania provided Mott with grants to facilitate his research in Cibola and other communities: a part of that research is reported here. We are also grateful to Miss Kathleen Kilpatrick who typed much of the manuscript and provided valued grammatical and bibliographic advice.

M.A.
P.E.M.

Contents

ix

Part IV. Locating Centers of Power

Part V. Interaction Among Centers of Power: Community and Subgroup Interactions

Part VI. Comparative Studies of Community Power

Part I.
The Meaning of Power

Power, Authority, and Influence

Paul E. Mott

When we say that a population is organized, we mean that the energies of the members are to some degree being utilized for collective activities. The degree of this social ordering varies and so we often observe that some of these patterns of order are being violated, that new patterns are being created, and that much behavior is not ordered at all. But regardless of flux or occasional chaos, it is obvious that the behavior of the members is to some degree controlled. From the very beginning of work in the field of sociology its practitioners have sought answers to the questions: What produces this order among people? What are the sources of social control? Political sociologists have been as interested in this question as have other specialists in the field, but, as the name of their specialty implies, they have been most interested in studying social power, influence, and authority as sources of social control. They conceive of human organization as a system of influence or power in which every act is seen as an attempt to affect the behavior of others, to control it. Social control, then, is treated as a product of acts and not the acts themselves; it is a dependent variable.

The initial purposes of this essay are:

1. to define social control,
2. to define power, influence, and authority,
3. to show how the latter concepts are related to social control and to each other.

Despite (or perhaps, because of) the importance of these concepts, there is little agreement about how to define them, much less measure them. The term "social power" denotes quite different things to different

social scientists. Further, what one writer calls "power" another calls "influence" and vice versa. Some forgo distinguishing between these two concepts, while others draw very fine distinctions between them. However, there has been a relatively high level of agreement about the meaning of the concept of authority; it is usually defined as either legitimized power or legitimized influence, depending on what definitional choices a particular social scientist has made concerning the latter concepts.

What follows is one attempt to construct a scientifically useful conceptual framework out of the plethora of definitions. The major concepts and their many definitions are reviewed and sorted out in the development of a conceptual framework. Then, this framework is tested for its capacity to generate new hypotheses and fresh interpretations of existing research findings. There is no notion that this framework is *the* framework. It is only our most optimistic wish to join the dialogue and facilitate movement in the direction of developing a generally serviceable framework.

Social Organization and Social Control

To provide a basis for later discussions, we note in passing some relevant features of the model of social organization used here: organizations are developmental rather than equilibrating, open rather than bounded. They do fulfill a vast array of the needs and purposes of the members, but at any given moment, there are important human needs they are not structured to fulfill. Organizations do not create systems of social control because it is imperative that "they" do so;

An original article written for this volume.

they *are* systems of social control, but they are also systems for the dissolution of control.

Social control is the achievement of modifications, or limitations of behavior of a group(s) or person(s) as a consequence of the actions— direct or indirect—of others.

When an organization is observed, we see much ordered behavior. This ordering indicates that control has been achieved. We also see many instances of varying degrees of disorder; patterns of order are broken, attempts of varying success may be made to reestablish the old patterns. Out of the conflict new patterns of order may be achieved; control is established. Some order results from purely personal decisions, but most of it is the product of human interaction. Social control is the product of acts and not the acts themselves. *In the ensuing discussion we will use the concept of social control tentatively as a dependent variable.*

What are the determinants of social control, the forces and actions that create and destroy it? Few questions are of more fundamental importance to sociological and political theory. It is easier to list the acts that create or destroy control than it is to delineate the forces behind such acts. The repertoire of verbs denoting these acts is very large: for example, forcing, persuading, consenting, coercing, demanding, and agreeing. Social control is the organizationally relevant consequence of this repertoire of behavior.

A second feature of our definition of social control should be noted. It says that the behavioral change is a consequence of the actions of others. It does not say that it is an intended consequence because it may very well be that control is achieved as an unintended consequence.[1] Much more attention has been paid to intended achievements of control than to unintended ones, yet the latter are very frequent in their occurrence and crucial from a theoretical point of view. For example, one of the most sophisticated approaches used to locate elites and analyze how they operate is often called decision sociometry. A representative sample of the universe of community decisions is taken and the researchers trace the patterns of interactions about these decisions in order to locate those people who had the most to say about the decision made. These are designated the decision-making elites. Yet while the researchers may have found the people who *made* the decision, they may have missed completely those who *shaped* the decision. What we are suggesting here is an adaptation of standard reference group mechanisms. Decision-shapers are those persons whose attitudes and opinions weigh heavily in the calculations of decision-makers. There need not be any interaction over specific issues between these two categories of people. The decision-makers may attempt an empathetic dialogue; making a decision that they think is compatible with the interests of decision-shapers. They may be right, partially right, or wrong. This decision process can occur at various levels of consciousness and with varying speed and accuracy. For some decision-makers it is an unconscious, swift, and accurate process. These people can feel that they were the most influential in the making of given decisions and others may agree, including the decision-shapers, because they are all unaware of how the decisions were shaped.

From the point of view of the decision-shapers this effect may have been intended or unintended, but the fact remains that the decision was shaped by them and an amicable pattern of social control has resulted. Put in a very general way: human beings very often adjust their behavior to harmonize or conflict with others, not because they were made to do so, but because it is personally profitable or convenient for them to do so. A serviceable model for studies of community power must embrace these unintended achievements of social control and the often unplanned interactions that led to them.

Social Power

When the term "social power" is used, even our common cultural definitions conjure up in us a sense of its centrality and importance for understanding human behavior and organization. That is the problem: we know intuitively that power is central and important, but what is it? The more we attempt to define it, the more complex it becomes. A political scientist once described power as "one of those awful big tent concepts under which a three ring circus—at least—is going on." He is not the first to despair of its complexity. His resignation becomes all the more apparent whenever attempts are made to measure this seemingly multivariate concept. Some give up; others create "indicator" measures (e.g., perceived reputation for power); few who tackle the task boldly come away well satisfied with their products.

All definers of social power agree that it is some form of energy, but there the agreement ends. Below is given a sample of the spectrum of definitions of social power. There are many more, but they are essentially thematically minor variations of those listed.

> *Goldhammer* and *Shils:* A person has power "to the extent that he influences the behavior of others in accordance with his own intentions."

> *Weber:* Power is the probability that one actor within a social relationship will be in a position to carry out his own will, despite resistances, regardless of the basis on which this probability rests.

> *Bierstedt:* Power is latent force.

> *Dahl: A* has power over *B* to the extent that he can get *B* to do something that he would not otherwise do.

> *Blau:* Power is the ability of persons or groups to impose their will on others despite resistance through deterrence either in the form of withholding regularly supplied rewards or in the form of punishment, inasmuch as the former as well as the latter constitute, in effect, a negative sanction.

> *Lasswell* and *Kaplan:* Power is "participation in the making of decisions."[2]

The first of these definitions views power as a class of the acts themselves—forcing persuading—while most of the others define power as the potential or capacity to act. Some definitions stress the personal or individual character of power; others see it as an organizational property which individuals share only by virtue of their positions in these organizations. In many definitions the element of coercion is integral: people are forced to perform certain ways against their wills. Some see power as related to the degree of participation in decision-making. Assuming that the various emphases in these definitions identify many of the parameters of defining power, they provide us with a number of questions to answer in shaping our definition: Is social power an organizational or a personal property? Is it potential or kinetic energy? Is the element of coercion essential to the definition of social power? Is power located exclusively or even primarily in the decision-making structure?

Is Social Power an Organizational or Personal Property?

To answer this question, another is asked: Is there any significant organizational property or properties that must be accounted for in our system of definitions because it helps to produce social control? The work of ecologists, particularly Amos Hawley,[3] and of cultural determinists, particularly Leslie White, [4] suggests that the answer to this question is yes.

White conceives of organizations as energy-binding systems; the very process of organizing involves the binding in of energy. Anyone who has ever seen a highly organized team play a poorly organized one has witnessed this phenomenon in its simplest form. A trained tug-of-war team represents the effectively pooled energies of its individual players; their pooled energies are available for collective use. The jailed criminal has seen operationally this directed energy which characterizes organization when a milling mob transforms into the organization that is intent on lynching him. Every organization, then, creates a collective pool of some or all of the energies of its members, which is then available for collective use. Some organizations, like communist cell organizations, maximize this pool of energy by demanding the total allegiance and energy of their members. The Roman Catholic Church prevents the dilution of its collective energy by denying its priests many other organizational memberships, e.g., by imposing the norm of celibacy. But most organizations settle for less.

The creation of human systems of co-ordinated action is the major means of binding in energy. The amount of this energy and the efficiency with which it is utilized can be increased or decreased by changes in levels of technology. The use of power-driven steel plows instead of wooden plows greatly increases the ratio of energy produced to human energy inputs. It also permits the cultivation of more land by fewer people, thus increasing the amount of energy available per person.

Access to this pooled energy tends to be unevenly distributed among the members of the organization. The operation of any of several factors can cause this unevenness of access. One source lies in the creation of transitive connections in an organization. The simplest connection between persons or groups is an unmediated or direct one (connexity). Transitivity exists when two in-dividuals or groups who wish to interact *must* use a third party as the connecting link. Examples of transitivity are abundant. Our interactions with judges must ordinarily be mediated by lawyers. A hierarchy or chain of command contains a series of transitive links. Telephone and elevator operators are trans-itive links.

These links can act like simple switches, permitting the utilization of energy in the system or preventing it, and, thereby, con-trolling it. Strikes by subway or railroad workers, elevator operators, telephone em-ployees, or other types of communications specialists are extremely serious because they can greatly reduce the abilities of the mem-bers of an organization to utilize their pooled, coordinated energies.

In laboratory experiments by Bavelas and others,[5] various communication networks were set up among small numbers of isolated people using telephone circuits. Most of the nets contained transitive links. Each group was given sample problems to solve and the results showed the disproportionately im-portant role of the people in transitive positions in controlling the problem-solving process.

Transitive connections can be used for subtler purposes than the simple switching phenomena described above. They can be used to control the persons or groups they link by forcing them to alter their messages as a condition of transmission. In many villages the social scientist must secure the approval and cooperation of the village headman before he is allowed to interview the members of the village. The headman uses his position as a device for social control making sure that the scientist does nothing that is inimicable to his interest. In sum, access to the available collective energy in an organization is generally lodged more heavily in its transitive links than elsewhere.

The last example given leads us to another source of the unequal distribution of access to pooled energy: the control and use by individuals or groups of resources needed by others. If a person or group controls such a resource, he can control the behavior of others—intentionally or unintentionally—as a condition of access to the resource. In other words, he can utilize the energies of others for his own purposes. Thus, potential ability to utilize the energies of others by the holder of a resource is increased:

1. the more vital is the resource to the population,
2. the greater is the monopoly of the resource,
3. the more central is the position of the person or group in the controlling organization.

Blau points out, conversely, that this ability to control can be reduced by: (1) devaluing the resource or finding a substitute for it, (2) finding a less adequately controlled source, or (3) increasing control over another resource needed by the controllers.[6]

A third source of unevenness of access to the pooled energies of others is the varying reputations for access to pooled energy that is attributed to individuals and groups. It does not matter whether or not these reputa-tions are grounded in real access, as long as they exist they can enhance or reduce the abilities of the holders of reputations to control others. The current controversy over the validity of reputational techniques to assess elite status thus has largely missed this point.[7] Reputation is stuff; it is a resource. Thus we do find in many validating studies some correspondence between reputation for access to collected energies and actual access.[8] But, as we have seen, there are other factors of at least as great significance that are related to the disproportionate ability to use the energies of others. Thus we also find in the same validating studies some lack of correspondence between lists of reputational elites and lists of people with actual access to pooled energy.

Our purpose is not to give a complete listing of these sources but rather to show the relationships among organization, binding in energy, and social control. There are inherent in organizations features that have fundamental and powerful influences on social control. This inherent capacity must, therefore, find a central place in any conceptual framework for community power studies. We propose to cast our lot with those who use the term "social power" to denote this latent energy in human systems. The concept of social power does not refer to all forms of latent energy, but only to usable energy sources that have value to members of the population.[9]

Among those who define power as an inherent property of organization is the sociologist Talcott Parsons.[10] But Parsons goes further than we have here by suggesting that this capacity serves a function: to get things done in the collective interest. Power does result from the summing of human energy (aided by technology), but does it always or only serve collective purposes? The answer must be that sometimes it does, but sometimes it does not. We do create organizations, i.e., sum power, to achieve collective purposes, for example, an army. But we have also seen that this capacity can operate to achieve unintended as well as intended effects. Those of us who have held jobs remember the many ways we modified our behavior vis-à-vis our supervisors:

politeness, deference, and occasionally hiding information from them that reflected negatively on ourselves. We did this because supervisors "have more power" in the sense that they have greater access to our pooled energies than we do. They can tell us how to use these energies and sanction us for our performance. In this instance because of the presence of power differences, no "collective purpose" was served when information on the effectiveness with which we had functioned was concealed. In sum, power exists, whether or not it serves collective purposes. We can now deal rapidly with our other questions.

Is Social Power Potential or Kinetic Energy?
The groundwork for answering this question has already been laid in the previous section. If pooled energy is inherent in organization, then unless it is instantly converted to acts, some must be stored and available as latent energy. As we saw earlier, this energy is stored unevenly throughout the organization and even in this form can have effects, e.g., social control. This latent energy is, therefore, socially significant and must be contended with. We cast our lot with those who denote as social power the latent, socially valued energy inherent in organizations.

Is the Element of Coercion Essential to the Definition of Social Power?
So far we have hewed fairly close to Bierstedt's definition of social power in that he also conceives of it as a latent organizational property.[11] But he chooses to stress heavily the coercive aspect of power. In fact, he uses it to distinguish between power and influence: power is coercive while influence is persuasive; power requires submission, but we submit voluntarily to influence.

It is difficult to understand how that which is latent can coerce. "To coerce" is a verb: A coerces B. If this is power, it is no longer latent. But if it is no longer latent, then in Bierstedt's terms, it is no longer social power. If he means that social power is potentially coercive, then at least the problem of contradiction disappears. But does social power have to be potentially

coercive to the exclusion of all other potentialities? To put it another way, is it potentially operative only against the wills of
others?

We agree that pooled energy can be and
is used to coerce others, but, with Parsons,
we agree that it can also be used to serve
collective purposes. Power simply *is*. It is
not inherently directed; it is directed by
people and in a multiplicity of ways, not all
of them are coercive. This is the fundamental
insight of the plant and animal ecologists in
their use of the concept of dominance. The
effects of dominant elements in an eco-
system are not directed, they simply exist.
Other, less dominant elements may have to
take the actions of the dominant elements
into account in their own activities. They
may be coerced, then again they may not.

To conform with our own earlier statements about the relationship between social
power and control, we say:

1. Social power is latent energy locked in
   by human organization.
2. It is not directed energy in and of
   itself. Others direct it in a variety of
   ways, coercive or otherwise.
3. As latent energy it must be "taken
   into account" by those who need it or
   value its particular forms. In this process of "taking into account" the
   persons or groups may feel coerced
   or they may not.

Where Bierstedt would say that "power is
required to inaugurate an association. . . ,"[12]
we would say that individual energies are
required to inaugurate an association, but
association is required to create social
power. Where Bierstedt would say, "With
out power there is no organization . . . ,"[13]
we would say that without organization there
is no social power.

**Is Power Located Exclusively or Even Pri-
marily in the Decision-Making Structure?**
To the extent that the concept of "decision-
making structure" is an organizational concept, it follows that these structures contain

social power. The amount of that power will
vary with the organizational characteristics
of the structure: its degree of integration, the
energetic involvement of the members, and so
on. Of course the attribution of organizational
properties to these structures may be empirically invalid in some cases. But setting that
distinct possibility aside, the real question for
us here is not whether these structures have
any power, but whether or not they are
the primary loci of power. An earlier
example will now serve its double purpose.
We distinguished earlier between decision-
makers and decision-shapers. The former
are in the decision structure, but the latter
are not, yet the latter have greater access to
social power. Decisions may be shaped by
the perceived attitudes and opinions of
specific persons, but they may also be shaped
by predominant values and norms. Values,
norms, customs, or traditions are not
synonymous with power, but they are highly
relevant to understanding decision processes
as long as they are determinants of the
actions of people who have unusual access
to social power. Kaufman and Jones said it
more simply: the members of an elite may be
carried along by forces at work in the community as well as directing those forces.[14]
We join those who question the assumption
that power is synonymous with participation
in decision-making. The decision structure
may be the dependent variable and the configuration of organizational power in which
it is embedded the independent variable.[15]

In summary: social power is defined as
usable and socially valued latent energy
locked in human organizations. Every individual has his own quantum of power—
physical, persuasive, etc.—and every group
has some measure of social power. Groups
are centers of power. Some groups are
centers of greater power than others, depending on the number of people, the degree of
their organization, the relative level of their
technology, the social value of resources
they control and the degree of their control
of them, the transitiveness of their structural
position, etc. All of these determinants are
measurable; therefore, we can measure the

relative social power of groups in organizations on *each* of these several dimensions, which are, in turn, measures of the potential ability of each group to shape the actions of others. Constructing a summary index of social power is another, more difficult, but not insoluble matter. It may, however, be both sufficient and useful to use several rankings of groups on these dimensions separately.

Aside from obtaining the various power scores of groups and ranking them, we can also describe the configurations of power in an organization at any given moment. In other words, we can examine the sociometric relationships among the major centers of power and between the major and the secondary centers. We shall assume that the configurations of power in an organization— whether centralized or decentralized, integrated or fragmented—is a useful concept for analyzing many of the phenomena of interest to students of community organization and functioning. Hypotheses that utilize this concept will be discussed after the concepts of authority and influence have been discussed.

Authority

As was mentioned earlier, there has been considerable agreement among social scientists as to the meaning of the concept of authority.[16] In general, it has been defined as legitimated exercises of power, or influence, or simply legitimated power. We find such definitions inadequate because they obscure two fundamentally different processes. The first is the process of legitimizing certain acts by members of centers of power; this process is the one most obviously implied by the definitions mentioned above. The second is the process of creating centers of power by legitimate authorization. These two processes are radically different from each other and deserving of separate attention. The second process is examined here first.

Reinhold Niebuhr has discussed the distinction between what is legitimate and what is legal.[17] What is legitimate conforms to the moral order; what is legal may not.

To Niebuhr, the relationship between the moral order and the law is transcendental: the law should be uplifted by the moral order. We can see, from Niebuhr's point of view, that the actions of a group, which is a center of power, may be legalized but not legitimated. There is a world of difference between these two conditions: a lynch mob can be legalized (deputized), but few would agree that it is legitimated.

The political scientists Elmer Schattschneider and Robert MacIver were among the few who disagreed with the prevailing definition of authority. Schattschneider once referred to organization as "the mobilization of bias."[18] In so doing he was agreeing in a very general and succinct way with MacIver, who conceived of authority as the established right to lead people.[19] Where did this established right originate? Like Niebuhr, he saw it as a derivation of the moral order and end-values of the population. When "authorized" groups are created they represent an attempt to implement these end-values. A required measure of consent has been given for the new authorities to perform their prescribed activities: both this prescription and the method of giving it are legitimated.

The method of consent does not necessarily require the active concurrence of a majority of the population; that is a legitimated method used in some societies to resolve certain classes of problems. Legitimated techniques vary from approval by one person, a divine-right monarch, to requirements of unanimous consent. Sometimes these techniques do not involve decisions by varying numbers of people, but rather the correct reading of culturally-valued external signs, such as those denoted in systems of magic.

The processes of legitimizing existing centers of power are quite different from the processes of creating new legitimate centers of power. Unlegitimated centers of power may become legalized and ultimately legitimated, but as any stepparent knows, this process is not an easy one. Many who have used coercive power to achieve hegemony over a population have failed to identify themselves as instruments of the end-values of that population. Faced with this problem, many conquerors solve it by enslaving, liquidating, or learning to live in an uneasy binational truce with the captive population. Some even find themselves culturally compromised by their captives. The major conclusion of modern studies in persuasion is that attitudinal change is very difficult to accomplish. The three most effective methods have traditionally been: (1) to effect, over generations, a change in the end-values of the population, (2) to obtain legitimation from accepted conveyors of legitimacy, and (3) to accept a seemingly subordinate position within a legitimated organization. The last method is often used by revolutionary groups when they infiltrate or join legitimated political organizations. Human history is marked with warlords who obtained a cloak of legitimacy from the accepted religious organizations. Businessmen have variously sought legitimacy through honorific titles, modifications of religious dogmas and social philosophies, and extensive public relations and philanthropic activities.

The monumental task of changing the end-values of a population has been attempted throughout history, but it has found its highest expression in modern totalitarian revolutionary organizations. The core of their strategy is a combination of violence, overt or threatened, and an all-embracing ideology which must be inculcated in the population. The ideology provides: (1) a coherent framework for explaining all behavior, (2) a series of explanations designed to delegitimize the existing authority system and its ideology, and (3) a legitimation of their own organization.

There is one additional distinction that should be noted between legalized and legitimated centers of power. In theory, at least, authority systems are designed to implement collective values, but legalized power systems need not be. Agencies of government are expected to serve these collective purposes and it is generally considered a perversion when they do not. Such legalized centers of power as business organ-

izations are spared such requirements; they can pursue their self-interests, which internally may be the product of competing individuals and groups pursuing their self-interests. While the facts often do not fit this ideal-typic distinction, it is worth preserving: first, because it is consistent with the aforementioned processes, and, second, because popular semantic confusion of legitmacy and legality may help to explain one form of alienation. If people treat these terms synonymously, they set higher standards of moral behavior for self-oriented organizations than the latter measure up to. The result is often a total disaffection with such systems.

Authority is consent legitimately given to groups or individuals to direct certain activities and to utilize certain resources to achieve collective purposes.

Authorization refers to the process of granting authority. Authorization is related to our definition of social power in that it creates or allocates power to make it available for selected purposes.

Social Influence

Thus far we have mentioned only one dynamic property of organizational life—the self-adjustments made by individuals or groups to put themselves in satisfactory positions vis-à-vis other centers of power. No directed, conscious effort to achieve this result is made by persons in the other centers of power; it occurs as a result of the usual actions of the members of the other centers of power.

But not all effects are unintended, a great many are the results of direct and conscious effort. Forcing, persuading, consenting, coercing, demanding, and so forth were samples of kinds of behavior mentioned in the discussion of social control. This class of actions we subsume under the concept of social influence.

Social influence is the attempt to utilize the energies of others to achieve a desired objective.

Influence is action: it is influencing. It is suppressing, hiding, and refusing to act as well as directing, threatening, persuading, and so on. It does not include the self-adjusting responses to power that we discussed earlier since no desired effect is consciously sought in those instances by the center of greater power. Influencing is purely social; it is interaction among persons who are attempting to achieve certain objectives. Influencing and self-adjustment are the major dynamic links between social power and authority on the one hand and social control on the other. If control is the achievement of order, influencing includes those attempts to achieve it; social control is a product of many forces, *successful* influencing is one of them.

Social Power, Influence, and Social Control

The amount of social control a group achieves and the amount of power to which it has access are directly, but weakly related. Community studies have shown that some people do not achieve their potential amount of social control. Similarly, some people or groups exert either far less or far greater influence than their power base would permit. An examination of these imperfect relationships should reveal some interesting questions for further research.

The total amount of power to which a group or person has access and can use depends *primarily* on position, reputation, and personal traits. Positional power is the maximum amount of power that could be utilized by virtue of positions in organizations. This access can derive from authority given, transitive positions controlled, and the other organizational sources of power discussed earlier. As such, this concept is similar to Weber's notion of class as opposed to status accesses to power.[20]

There is one special type of position that must be noted. Ordinarily, when we discuss high positional access, we think of positions in very large organizations controlling highly valued resources. High positions in such organizations undoubtedly give the occupants access to very great amounts of latent energy. But when that position is coupled with the right to "represent" or speak for the values of the population, even greater power can be obtained readily. Values themselves have no power; they are mere symbols, however complex. They gain the appearance of power when they are the bases for action by men and groups who have access to power. Some values identify certain positions as more estimable than others, say banker or corporation president. People in these positions often find that they exert influence beyond their original valued positions because they can easily gain access to secondary positions of considerable importance: e.g., the city council, cabinet positions, heads of government task forces, and commissions.

Reputation for power can give its possessor access to power; as we said earlier, reputation is a resource. Numerous studies have shown that a reputation for power can intimidate others, causing them to perform well below their usual standards. In an autokinetic effect experiment, Sherif showed that the judgments of subjects were influenced by other participants to whom great prestige had been attributed.[21] The same mechanisms appeared in Whyte's study of the Norton gang. Each gang member's bowling performance correlated with his respect status in the gang when the gang bowled together, but when the members bowled separately there was no correlation between performance and respect status.[22]

Finally, personal traits can provide access to power. A person may be without a significant positional base for power, but still have great access to power because of the brilliance of his ideas, his knowledge of people and organization, or his persuasive abilities. *He achieves access indirectly by influencing persons with positional power.* The mathematician John Von Neumann, serving as a consultant to various governmental agencies, tapped great sources of power through the application of his theory of games to problems of military strategy.

There are other, relatively minor attributes that affect access to power, but the present catalogue is sufficient for our major purpose here, which is to discuss discrepancies between the amount of social power in an organization and the amount of social control achieved by its members.

One reason for these discrepancies stems from the fact that the holders of power may be quite satisfied with the control they achieve from the self-adjusting actions of others. We have already seen that two major ingredients to the achievement of control are self-adjustment to power and successful influencing. There is a direct relationship between social control achieved and total power: self-adjusting behavior by others usually increases as the ratio of the total power of a unit to the total power of all units in the organization increases. To achieve this effect, no unusual actions by the center of power are required. However, the amount of influencing is not so easily related to this ratio. Influencing requires directed attempts to utilize the energies of others and the holders of power may or may not elect to engage in influencing. Ideally for them, conditions should be created whereby the more obvious and heavyhanded forms of influence need never be used because they often generate resistance and counter-organization. The leaders of very powerful organizations may attain most or all of their objectives vis-à-vis the less powerful via the self-adjustment mechanism. In this case, the minor gains achieved by influencing would often be outweighed by the ill-will generated by the attempt.

This last point leads to the interesting speculation that reliance on measures of frequency and intensity of overt influencing as indicators of actual power may exclude the very powerful altogether. It may be that the very powerful groups eschew a method that is the mainstay of groups with lesser power. It may be the latter who must rely on tactics, influencing, and other overt methods to achieve their ends. We have at least one datum to confirm this supposition. When we asked the Director of Community Relations of a very large corporation if his office *routinely* fought tax increases in the communities where its factories were located, he said, "We are a wealthy company: we can afford to pay our way within reason. It isn't worth the ill-will it would cause. Of course if it's an unreasonable grab, we fight it!"

Personal traits also play a crucial role in a person's willingness to engage in influencing. Studies in community influence have shown that not all of those people who have positional access to power engage in community affairs: the players come from a larger pool of eligibles. Browning and Jacob administered Thematic Apperception Tests to former businessmen and found that those who were active in politics had higher needs for sociability than those who were not.[23] Courage and intelligence are other obvious personal characteristics that play a crucial role in willingness and ability to influence.

Interest in an issue or objective and the ability to recognize that interest are also factors in willingness to influence. Community studies usually have shown that few holders of power are involved in all community issues; e.g., Meyerson and Banfield show that the fairly powerful real estate group failed to act in a Chicago housing decision because it was too late in recognizing that its interests were involved.[24]

A final factor in the ability to control concerns the types and amounts of power to which a group has access. We can imagine two organizations with equal amounts of total power; however the power of one derives almost exclusively from position, while the other has fairly equal portions of all three types of access to power: position, reputation, and personal characteristics of the members. It is conceivable that the latter may achieve more control than the former. The possession of certain skills is essential to getting a maximum control pay-off from given inputs of influence. For example, the amount of positional power may have gone up or down between successive Presidents of the United States, but degree of control achieved by each need not vary directly with it. Some Presidents have a greater knowledge of the workings of government, of the numbers and types of influence levers available to them, of the personalities of the participants, of the techniques of persuasion, and they are more willing to use their knowledge and skills than other Presidents. A simpler example of the importance of reputation and skill is the strategy of bidding and bluffing in poker. A player may win despite poorer cards (resources) than the other players because of his skill and reputation.

Let us summarize some of the major points made above:

1. As the ratio of group power to total power of all groups in the organization increases, social control achieved by the group *tends* to increase.
2. As this ratio increases, social control resulting from self-adjusting behavior by others will increase directly.
3. As the ratio increases, the frequency of influence attempts may or may not increase.
4. As this ratio increases, the proportion of successful attempts to influence will increase directly.

Access to Power and Types of Influence

The above discussion suggests that we might profit from an examination of variations in degree of consistency of power statuses, particularly on the positional and reputational scales, and from an identification of the associated techniques of influence. Several methods were proposed earlier for the determination of positional access; see p. 8. A single measure that should be an adequate indicator is to rank order *organizations* in the community in terms of the amount of wealth they infuse into the local economy. While it is customary to select the managers or owners (or mayors) of these enterprises, it is of primary importance to learn how their *organizations* influence local affairs. The head of a large business organization may engage in no direct influencing himself, but still have on his payroll a number of people who are specialists in community influence.[25]

There is less need for innovation to obtain a rank ordering of reputational access.[26] We do suggest that the panels selected be asked to rank order organizations

on one list and people on another, that the organizational list be converted to a list of people by substituting the names of their leaders, and that the panel produce a single list by force-ranking the two lists. Then the list can be divided into three parts using normal distribution criteria, resulting in a tabulation similar to that in Table 1.

TABLE 1.

		AMOUNT OF POSITIONAL ACCESS		
		High	Medium	Low
AMOUNT OF	High	1		2
REPUTATIONAL	Medium			
ACCESS	Low	3		4

Some of the categories may seem immediately less interesting, but certainly the numbered categories where consistency is least or greatest are very interesting. We expect, for example, that self-adjusting behavior is highest to individuals and their organizations in category 1 followed by 3, 2, and 4. This can be determined by cataloging the reactions of others to stimuli emanating from categories 1 and 3 compared to categories 2 and 4.

The techniques or strategies of influence used by the people in each category are a function of issues, arenas, and objectives. But given a particular issue, arena, and set of objectives, the strategy selected is determined by at least four criteria: (1) its normative acceptability to the strategist, (2) its costs in terms of resource and energy expenditures required, (3) its costs in terms of the reactions of others, and (4) its probability of success. Suppose, for example, a person who is high in both positional and reputational power wishes to prevent a theatrical production from being performed in his town because he considers it immoral; he is unlikely to picket the theatre because it is a normatively unacceptable strategy and too costly. It is far easier for him to use his influence with his fellow patrons of the arts on the theatre owner and the sponsoring group. Picketing and demonstrations are costly strategies with uncertain probabilities of success; they are a part of the sparse repertoire of strategies available to those who have little positional or reputational power.

We expect, for instance, that use of suppression of issues is greatest for members in category 1. The probability of success for this and related strategies is easily highest in this category. The occupants of category 3 (in some communities the labor leaders and heads of large construction firms would appear in this category) have some obvious choices. They can settle for the self-adjusting behavior of others, but since their reputational status is low, they are unlikely to be satisfied with that. Strategies that *improve* their reputational status—public relations techniques, charitable activities—may have a high value. Category 1 groups may use the same techniques, but to maintain rather than improve their positions. More likely, category 3 groups will lead from their positional strengths and use their resource power to threaten, bargain, bribe, buy, withhold, form coalitions, and so forth. Category 4 (perhaps including the more radical Negro rights organizations or consumer groups) lacks much access to power, and, therefore, we would expect either withdrawal or the use of mass organizational techniques: mass demonstrations, boycotts, violence, and so forth. The people in category 2 lack resources other than their reputations. For them, success must hinge on the use of their personal abilities, their contacts and their image: charm, persuasiveness, wisdom, and similar abilities become more important here.

We wonder also about the sociometry of influencing by the persons in each category. Who interacts with whom? What are the patterns of coalition formation? Is there a logical natural history to the development of coalitions? What are the relationships of the persons in each category to the infrastructure of the community?

There is a parallel set of problems worthy of study in bureaucratic organizations. There authority status is not an accurate measure of positional access to power.

Corporate vice-presidents can have similar authority statuses, but radically different resource statuses. What are the differences in influencing techniques used by people of similar authority, but differential access to resources? What techniques are used by those whose resources are inadequate for the authority granted or whose resources far exceed their authority?

Summary

In studying organizations we find much social order or ordered behavior; we observe patterns of behavior appearing, developing, and disappearing. Organizations do not create social control but are in themselves systems of social control as well as systems for the dissolution of control. Social control is the achievement of modifications, or limitations of behavior of a group(s) or person(s) as a consequence of the actions—direct or indirect—of others. Social control is the product of acts and not the acts themselves. Behavioral changes in groups or individuals are consequences—intended or unintended, conscious or unconscious—of the actions of others.

A fundamental property of organization is social power. Social power is potential energy which is created in the actual process of organizing or pooling individual energies; energy which can be used. However, access to this energy tends to be unevenly distributed among members of the organization. Control of transitive or connecting links provides greater access to power than other types of linkages, i.e., control of individuals or groups through whom communications must be made. Other factors contributing to the uneven distribution of access to pooled energy are the control of resources needed by others and the reputations for access to pooled energy attributed to individuals or groups.

The pooling of human energy does not always result in collective purposes being served. Power is not directed energy in and of itself; individuals or groups direct it in a variety of ways, coercive or otherwise. However, as latent energy it must be taken into consideration by those who need or value it; they must accommodate or adjust their actions to the fact of its existence.

Decisions may be shaped by the perceived attitudes and opinions of specific persons who are not actually involved in the decision-making and they may also be shaped by predominant values, norms, customs or traditions. Thus power is not necessarily located primarily in the decision-making structure.

Authority is consent legitimately given to groups of individuals to direct certain activities and to utilize certain resources to achieve collective purposes. Authorization is related to social power in that it allocates power for selected purposes.

Social influence is the attempt to utilize the energies of others to achieve a desired objective. It is the interaction among persons who are attempting to achieve certain objectives. Influencing and self-adjustment (accommodation) are the major links between social power and social control. As the ratio of a group's power to the power of all the groups in the organization increases, the social control achieved by the group tends to increase. As this ratio increases, social control resulting from self-adjusting behavior by others will increase directly, but the frequency of attempts at influencing may or may not increase. As this ratio increases, the proportion of successful attempts to influence will increase directly.

Notes

1. This position seems to be stressed almost exclusively by human ecologists in their concept of dominance. See, A. H. Hawley, *Human Ecology: A Theory of Community Structure* (New York: Ronald Press, 1950).
2. H. Goldhammer and E. Shils, "Types of Power and Status," *American Journal of Sociology*, 54, 2 (September, 1939), 173. M. Weber, *Theory of Social and Economic Organization*, trans. by A. M. Henderson and T. Parsons (New York: Oxford University Press, 1947), p. 152. R. Bierstedt, "An Analysis of Social Power," *American Sociological Review*, 15, 6 (December, 1950), 733. R. A. Dahl, "The Concept of Power," *Behavioral Science*, 2 (July, 1957), 201–215. P. M. Blau, *Exchange and Power in Social Life* (New York: Wiley, 1964), p. 117. H. D. Lasswell and A. Kaplan, *Power and Society* (New Haven: Yale University Press, 1950), p. 74.
3. A. H. Hawley, "Community Power and Urban Renewal Success," *American Journal of Sociology*, 68 (January, 1963), 422–431. Also in this volume.
4. L. A. White, *The Science of Culture* (New York: Grove Press, 1949).
5. A. Bavelas, "Communication Patterns in Task-Oriented Groups," *Journal of the Acoustical Society of America*, 22 (1950), 725–730. G. A. Heise and G. A. Miller, "Problem-Solving by Small Groups Using Various Communication Nets," *Journal of Abnormal and Social Psychology*, 46 (1951), 327–335. H. Guetzkow and H. A. Simon, "The Impact of Certain Communication Nets Upon Organization and Performance in Task-Oriented Groups," *Management Science*, 1 (1955), 233–250.
6. Blau, *op. cit.*, pp. 118–120.
7. L. J. R. Herson, "In the Footsteps of Community Power," *American Political Science Review*, 55, 4 (December, 1961), 817–830. A. Wildavsky, *Leadership in a Small Town* (Totowa, N.J.: Bedminster Press, 1964). L. V. Blankenship, "Community Power and Decision-Making: A Comparative Evaluation of Measurement Techniques," *Social Forces*, 43 (December, 1964), 207–216. Also in this volume.

   The exception to this statement is in W. A. Gamson, "Reputation and Resources in Community Politics," *American Journal of Sociology*, 72 (September, 1966), 121–131. Also in this volume.
8. See for example, the Wildavsky and Blankenship articles, *op. cit.*
9. Blau, *op. cit.*, p. 117.
10. T. Parsons, "Voting and the Equilibrium of the American Political System," in E. Burdick and A. J. Brodbeck (eds.), *American Voting Behavior* (New York: Free Press, 1959), pp. 80–120.
11. Bierstedt, *op. cit.*, pp. 730–738.
12. *Ibid.*, p. 735.
13. *Ibid.*, p. 735.
14. H. Kaufman and V. Jones, "The Mystery of Power," *Public Administration Review*, 14, 3 (Summer, 1954), 205–212. Also in this volume.
15. This is a general proposition that we will discuss in greater detail later.

16. See for example: Bierstedt, *op. cit.*, pp. 730–738. Goldhammer and Shils, *op. cit.*, pp. 171–182. T. Parsons, "Authority, Legitimation, Political Action," in C. J. Friedrich (ed.), *Authority* (Cambridge: Harvard University Press, 1958), pp. 197–221. H. D. Lasswell, *et al.*, *The Comparative Study of Elites* (Stanford: Stanford University Press, 1952). D. Katz and R. L. Kahn, *The Social Psychology of Organizations* (New York: Wiley, 1966).

A different, if minority, view is offered by R. M. MacIver, *The Web of Government* (New York: Macmillan, 1947), p. 87; W. Buckley, *Sociology and Modern Systems Theory* (Englewood Cliffs, N.J.: Prentice-Hall, 1967), p. 180.

17. From a speech given by R. Niebuhr on "Grace and Law" at Purdue University in 1949.

18. E. E. Schattschneider, *The Semisovereign People* (New York: Holt, Rinehart and Winston, 1960), p. 30.

19. MacIver, *op. cit.*, p. 87.

20. M. Weber, "Class, Status, and Party," in H. H. Gerth and C. W. Mills, (trans. and eds.), *From Max Weber: Essays in Sociology* (New York: Oxford University Press, 1946), pp. 186–193.

21. M. Sherif, "An Experimental Approach to the Study of Attitudes," *Sociometry*, 1 (1937), 90–98.

22. W. F. Whyte, *Street Corner Society: The Social Structure of an Italian Slum* (Chicago: University of Chicago Press, 1955), pp. 14–18.

23. R. P. Browning and H. Jacob, "Power Motivation and Political Personality," *Public Opinion Quarterly*, 28 (Spring, 1964), 75–90.

24. M. Meyerson and E. C. Banfield, *Politics, Planning and the Public Interest* (New York: Free Press, 1955).

25. P. E. Mott, "The Role of the Absentee-Owned Corporation in the Changing Community," a paper read at the annual meeting of the American Sociological Association, 1967. This article appears in this volume.

26. C. M. Bonjean's refinement of this technique, reported in "Community Leadership: A Case Study and Conceptual Refinement," *American Journal of Sociology*, 68 (May, 1963), 672–681, seems most appropriate since it provides a method for locating concealed reputational leaders. This article appears in this volume.

Part II.

Historical Perspective and Community Power Structure

Introduction

Studies of community power are often ahistorical. But, as the articles in this section show, the history of a community is an important prologue to understanding its current circumstances. What changes have occurred in its leadership patterns, in its social, economic, and cultural organization? Are there relationships among these types of changes? For example, communities differ in their stages of industrialization; some industrialized long ago, while others are currently industrializing, and still others never will. Each faces different problems, harbors different populations, and, perhaps, demands different styles and organizations of leadership. And each should exhibit these differences over time if they have moved through the stages of industrialization. The Census of the United States is an accounting sheet of these changes: the presence in one city of a high proportion of Southeast Europeans, their children or grandchildren, and of semiskilled workers suggests one stage in industrialization; the absence in a second city of these characteristics suggests another. Tracing the socioeconomic compositions of such communities back through earlier censuses yields valuable information about their life cycles.

In the first article in this part, "'Yankee City' Revisited: The Perils of Historical Naïveté," Thernstrom provides a description of the erroneous interpretations included in W. Lloyd Warner's study of Yankee City (Newburyport, Massachusetts). By careful historical analysis, Thernstrom suggests that the Industrial Revolution came to Yankee City in the middle of the nineteenth century with the coming of textile mills, not thirty years later with the shoe industry. This meant that the former, homogenous, and stable community structure of the preindustrial era was shattered long before the shoe industry became the dominant industry of Yankee City. Increased ethnic and religious diversity became a part of Yankee City's life at an earlier date, bringing with it new dimensions of community structure. This fact, of course, reflects only one aspect of Thernstrom's concern both in this article and in his book, *Poverty and Progress.*[1] Warner's ignorance of, or at least inattention to, the history of Newburyport has cast doubt on many of the findings of his study of Yankee City.

The next two articles in Part II are concerned with historical patterns in the recruitment of formal leaders, i.e., the mayors of New Haven and Chicago. The first, "From Oligarchy to Pluralism: The Patricians and the Entrepreneurs," is taken from Dahl's *Who Governs?* The thesis of Dahl's book is that historically the political structure of New Haven has changed from one of oligarchy to one that currently is pluralistic. He attempts to document these historical changes through examination of the social backgrounds of those elected to formal political office, the Mayor and Board of Aldermen, although his emphasis is clearly on the former. Dahl suggests that there are four categories of mayors: (1) the "patricians," highly educated and often legally trained men who served as mayors from 1784–1842; (2) "the entrepreneurs," recruited from the larger commercial and industrial firms during the period 1842–1899; (3) "the ex-plebes," largely working-class men whose political base was that of ethnic politics; and (4) "the new men," a type suggested by New Haven's most recent mayor, who may be characterized more by his professional administration than by his reliance on ethnic politics.

In the second article on leader recruitment, "From Commercial Elite to Political Administrator: The Recruitment of the Mayors of Chicago," Bradley and Zald do a similar analysis of Chicago and find the pattern there to be somewhat different from that of New Haven. Owing to the absence of truly patrician families in Chicago, the first mayors were recruited from commercial leaders. By the turn of the century these were followed, after a brief transitional period, by widely known social notables and politically involved businessmen, not by "ex-plebes" as in New Haven, although some might have had such origins. After 1930, most of the mayors could qualify as "ex-plebes," but the most important characteristic of the political regime was the Democratic party machine.

Such dissimilar results from these two studies raise more questions than they answer about how historical processes affect the recruitment of formal political leaders. A recent historical study of the mayors of Nashville adds more complications.[2] The early mayors of Nashville (1806–1832) looked more like those of Chicago than those of New Haven. The recent pattern of mayoral recruitment in Nashville (1909 to present) indicates a trend toward mayors having full-time political careers (like those in New Haven and Chicago), but these mayors were found to be neither from social and economic elite families nor from any given class, religion, or ethnic group. Zald and Anderson identify three tentative generalizations about the historical patterns of mayoral recruitment: (1) a trend toward increased formal education of mayors; (2) a trend toward the office of mayor becoming part of a political career rather than part time service (i.e., a trend toward the professionalization of the office of mayor); and (3) the low prestige of local politics making it an unattractive political alternative for social and economic elites. The flight of middle-class people to the suburbs removes them and their votes as factors in central city elections. This gives added emphasis to the last generalization. The general conclusions of Zald and Anderson are further supported by a recent study of the recruitment of mayors in four Wisconsin cities: Madison, Racine, Kenosha, and Green Bay.[3] The only factor that was common to the historical recruitment of mayors in these cities was a general trend to mayors now being full-time political administrators.

One of the conclusions that can be drawn from these studies is that the role of mayor in "nonreformed" cities is becoming a full-time role, one that is often part of a political career. This role, like many roles in local governmental administrations such as that of the city manager in "reformed" city governments, is becoming more professionalized: a process that will contribute materially to greater autonomy not only for the mayors of cities, but for other political roles also. Another conclusion that can be drawn from these few studies is that no matter what the life cycle of the city has been —i.e., oligarchic control, industrialization, the arrival of immigrants, the eventual political ascendancy of such groups, a trend toward pluralism such as in New Haven or recent industrialization such as in many Southern communities—there is an inevitable trend towards professionalization of local governmental administrative roles. The professionalization of political dominants is one more factor contributing to their increasing autonomy.

The paucity of studies, the regional variations in the cities studied, and variations in such factors as population size, age of city, and the like, make any additional generalizations about mayoral recruitment particularly hazardous. At the same time, these studies clearly suggest that this is an interesting area for further inquiry.

The other two selections in this part examine historical changes in the patterns of elite participation in community activities. In the first of these, "The Role of Economic Dominants in Community Power Structure," Schulze argues that there has been an historical trend toward bifurcation of the power structure, i.e., a drift toward withdrawal of economic dominants from active and overt participation in the public life of Cibola (Ypsilanti, Michigan). He finds that since 1900 economic dominants have been less likely to serve as village president or mayor or in other public offices, elective and appointive. Further, since 1920 they have been less likely to serve on the Board of Directors of the Chamber of Commerce. He argues that the increasing interdependence of local firms with large, nonlocal units, the trend toward absentee control of local plants, and the consequent dissolution of networks of interlocking directorates of local firms have created a structure in which there are fewer incentives for economic dominants to participate in the local community. "Withdrawal" may have been an unfortunate semantic choice for Schulze, since he really means decreased participation in the formal associational and political life of the community by incumbents in certain structural roles rather than complete withdrawal from all forms of participation in local community affairs. In "Role of the Absentee-Owned Corporation in the Changing Community," included in Part III of this reader, Mott suggests that Schulze's research procedures may have overlooked some of the newer ways in which corporation elites participate in the local community.

In the last article in this part, "Economic Dominants and Community Power: A Comparative Analysis," Clelland and Form present their findings from a replication of the Schulze study made in the nearby city of Wheelsburg. They provide general support for the bifurcation hypothesis, but there is evidence of greater community participation by economic dominants in Wheelsburg than in Cibola. They suggest that the differences in participation by economic dominants in Cibola and Wheels-

burg may be due to Wheelsburg's being a relatively economically independent community while Cibola is a satellite of a large metropolitan community. In a concluding note they speculate that differences in political structures or in the history of the introduction of absentee control into the community may also account for differences in participation. In studies of Northville[4] and Cornucopia,[5] there is general support for the bifurcation hypothesis, but these four studies hardly provide sufficient information to explain satisfactorily some of the more specific differences in the findings of Schulze and Clelland and Form.

These studies raise a whole series of questions that are extremely important for the understanding of the relationship between economic structure and the community leadership patterns. For example, how do variations in the economic base of the community affect leadership patterns?[6] In what range of community issues are economic elites—both in absentee-controlled and local firms—likely to become involved? What new mechanisms of corporate participation in local community affairs have evolved?[7] Do regional variations in the patterns of absentee versus local economic control undermine the Schulze thesis? What is particularly important about some of these questions is that the answers will have important implications for linking theories of organizational behavior with those of community structure and process, a trend that is already beginning to be reflected in the literature of these two fields.

Notes

1. S. Thernstrom, *Poverty and Progress: Social Mobility in a Nineteenth-Century City* (Cambridge: Harvard University Press, 1964).
2. M. N. Zald and T. A. Anderson, "Secular Trends and Historical Contingencies in the Recruitment of Mayors: Nashville as Compared to New Haven and Chicago," *Urban Affairs Quarterly*, 4 (June, 1968), 53–68.
3. T. J. Weirath, "Mayoral Recruitment in Four Wisconsin Cities: An Investigation into Historical Sociology" (Unpublished Masters' thesis, University of Wisconsin, 1966).
4. T. C. Smith, "The Structuring of Power in a Suburban Community," *Pacific Sociological Review*, 3 (Fall, 1960), 83–88.

5. R. M. French, "Cornucopia in Transition" (Unpublished Ph.D. dissertation, University of Wisconsin, 1967). Also see his article on Cornucopia in the next section.
6. M. N. Goldstein, "Absentee Ownership and Monolithic Power Structures: Two Questions for Community Studies," in B. E. Swanson (ed.), *Current Trends in Comparative Community Studies* (Kansas City, Mo.: *Community Studies*, Inc., 1962), pp. 49–59.
7. Compare P. E. Mott, "The Role of the Absentee-Owned Corporation in the Changing Community," in this volume.

"Yankee City" Revisited: The Perils of Historical Naïveté[*]

Stephan Thernstrom

It is easy enough to nod agreement at E. H. Carr's remark that "the more sociological history becomes, and the more historical sociology becomes, the better for both."[1] But in truth, unhappily, the mutually-enriching dialogue between history and sociology that Carr calls for has barely begun; so far, communication between the two disciplines has largely been in the form of a monologue, with history on the receiving end. Sociologists and social anthropologists have been eager to suggest how their brethren in the most traditional and least theoretical of the social sciences might broaden their horizons and deepen their insights into man's behavior in the past. It is clear, from a number of recent books and articles, that this advice has not gone entirely unheard.[2] What seems to have been neglected, however, is that if historians have much to learn from their colleagues in sociology, the converse of this proposition is also true. Carr's remark cuts both ways. Sociological work based on erroneous historical assumptions can be as superficial as sociologically primitive history, and it is no less common.[3] Close scrutiny of an influential specimen of contemporary social research which is particularly vulnerable to this charge may help to clarify why an accurate sense of historical perspective is indispensable to students of modern society.

One of the richest and most inviting sources of knowledge about modern American life is the *genre* that includes such books as *Black Metropolis, Caste and Class in a Southern Town, Streetcorner Society, Elmtown's Youth,* and *Middletown.* Maurice Stein has recently urged the relevance of these works to the student of 20th-century America in his stimulating study, *The Eclipse of Community: An Interpretation of American Studies.*[4] Stein, himself a sociologist, is surely correct in urging that the community studies conducted by American sociologists and anthropologists in the past 50 years are an exceptionally rich source of knowledge about the history of American civilization. But these works must be approached with a large measure of caution and critical reserve, for too many of them have been built upon shaky historical foundations. In particular, W. Lloyd Warner's famous "Yankee City" series well illustrates the distortions that historical ignorance and naïveté can produce.

The "Yankee City" series, five bulky volumes reporting on field research conducted in "an old New England community" in the 1930's, made W. Lloyd Warner the most influential American student of social stratification.[5] The first Yankee City publication, *The Social Life of a Modern Community* (1941), was widely praised, and the subsequent volumes and a

Reprinted from the American Sociological Review, 30 (April 1965), 234–242, by permission of the author and the American Sociological Association. Copyright 1964 by the American Sociological Association.

[*]I am indebted to the Joint Center for Urban Studies of the Massachusetts Institute of Technology and Harvard University for supporting this research, and to Oscar Handlin, P. M. G. Harris and David Riesman for constructive criticism. Some of the materials included here are drawn from Chapter 8 and the Appendix to my book, *Poverty and Progress: Social Mobility in a Nineteenth Century City,* Cambridge: Harvard University Press, 1964, and are reprinted with the permission of Harvard University Press. Detailed citations to the historical evidence alluded to below will be found in the book.

host of other books by Warner and his students served to establish members of "the Warner school" as leading interpreters of American community life. In recent years, it is true, the techniques of social analysis pioneered in the Yankee City study have been severely criticized, but the abundant literature on the Warner school does not include a detailed analysis of the mistaken historical assumptions out of which so many of Warner's errors grew.[6] Future investigators of social stratification in American communities will no doubt avoid the methodological blunders tellingly exposed by Mills, Lipset and Bendix, Pfautz and Duncan, and other sociological critics; that glaring misinterpretations and distortions can stem from failure to utilize relevant historical data is less widely understood.

What follows is in no sense a full and balanced appraisal of the five Yankee City volumes or of Lloyd Warner's contributions to an understanding of American society. Such an appraisal would pay Warner the tribute he deserves as a pioneer in his field —for having gathered a wealth of interesting material about a subject that had been too little studied, and for having inspired an enormous amount of further research and controversy. It would applaud certain fruitful insights and note that Warner had the gift for social portraiture of a lesser social novelist; portions of the Yankee City volumes display some of the virtues of the novels of John P. Marquand, a writer who dealt with the same New England community. Such an assessment would be more appreciative, in short, and perhaps it is overdue. That, however, is a different task than the one undertaken here, and a larger one. These critical observations focus on what Warner failed to see about the community he studied so intensively in the 1930's and particularly on what he failed to see because of his misconceptions about the community's history.

That community was Newburyport, Mass., a city whose social and economic history I have been studying for the past five years. Like many another sociological field worker, Warner made evaluation and

criticism of his work more difficult by obscuring the identity of the community studied with a pseudonym. The usual justification for this step is that it protects the identity of local informants. Whatever the merits of this argument, it seems clear that a latent function of this device is to lend an aura of typicality to the community in question: "Yankee City" is manifestly a place of more universal significance than Newburyport, Mass., "Jonesville" is more truly American than Morris, Ill. To say this is not to endorse the familiar criticism that cities like Newburyport were "unrepresentative" of the larger society. With respect to the problems that interested Warner, Newburyport was much more "representative" than his critics have allowed—though it is admittedly difficult to discern this from Warner's distorted and idealized description of the city.[7] The point is rather that Warner *assumed* Newburyport's representativeness without any critical examination of the issue, and that he made it difficult for others to think critically about the question by disguising the identity of the community.

The Uses of the Past

The Yankee City project was carried out on a scale that can only be described as prodigious. It still ranks as the most intensive, exhaustive, and expensive survey ever made of a small American city. The five published volumes occupy more than 1700 pages, with 208 tables, charts, and maps. The field work extended over a period of several years, and required the labor of some 30 research assistants. The amount of data collected was staggering. Warner at one point refers to "the millions of social facts" recorded; the study is replete with comments like this: "All of the types of social structures and each of the thousands of families, thousands of cliques, and hundreds of associations were, member by member, interrelated in our research." "Social personality cards" were compiled for all 17,000 members of the community, and interviews with local citizens occupied thousands of hours. Aerial photographs were made of Newburyport and environs; detailed questionnaires were administered at gas stations and lunch stands along the highway to discover what transients had stopped in the city and why; the plots of plays performed by students and various social organizations were collected and subjected to content analysis (which yielded the illuminating conclusion that they all "clearly conformed to the standards of the local group"). An observer was stationed at the movie house to "see who attended the pictures and with whom they attended," and newsstands were closely scrutinized to see how actual purchases conformed to professed reading preferences. (One must sympathize with the haunted "upper upper" of Warner's Newburyport seeking furtively to pick up his monthly *Esquire* under the cool stare of a Radcliffe graduate student in sociology.) Death itself brought the citizen no more than partial respite from surveillance: "All the names of those persons buried in the several cemeteries were gathered and compilations were made of the members of several ethnic groups."[8]

Virtually every aspect of Newburyport life was probed by the Yankee City team—every aspect but one. Early in the first volume of the series the authors casually commented: "To be sure that we were not ethnocentrically biased in our judgment, we decided to use no previous summaries of data collected by anyone else (maps, handbooks, histories, etc.) until we had formed our own opinion of the city."[9] This was a remarkable and revealing utterance. To consult the historical record would be to fall victim to the biases and preconceptions of the historian, a man necessarily "unscientific," "culture-bound," "ethnocentric."

How, then, were Warner and his associates to form their "own opinion" about the Newburyport past? At times Warner was inclined to speak as if the past was simply irrelevant. He was contemptuous of the historical school in anthropology; the merely "ethnological or temporal aspects of social behavior" were of much less interest to him than "the scientific problems of explanation of the facts by classification and their interpretation by the formulation of laws and principles."[10] "The facts," in this context, meant the facts visible in the present.

It was quite impossible, however, for the Yankee City researchers to avoid making assumptions about what Newburyport had been like prior to their arrival on the scene; the reasons they gave for selecting Newburyport as a research site included a host of historical assumptions. They sought a small community which was "above all a well-integrated community." It was to be self-contained, as insulated as possible from "disruptive" influences emanating from large cities undergoing "rapid social change." Its population was to be "predominantly old American," and it was to have "developed over a long period of time under the domination of a single group with coherent tradition." Newburyport, Warner took for granted, was such a city, one whose "Puritan tradition" remained "unshattered," one whose "social superstructure remained very much what it had been at the end of the War of 1812."[11]

How did Warner decide that Newburyport met this rather unusual set of specifications? He found out "scientifically," by direct observation of the image of the past held by present members of the community. This seemed a plausible procedure for men determined to "use the techniques and ideas which have been developed by social anthropologists in primitive society in order to obtain a more accurate understanding of an American community."[12] Warner came to Newburyport after three years of observing a tribe of Australian aborigines, a people without a written history. In a community without written records, the dead exist only in the minds and deeds of the living; there history survives only as tradition, ritual, myth, "remembered experiences . . . . newly felt and understood by the living members of the collectivity."[13]

Rarely is the student of a primitive community able to find sources that allow him to penetrate beneath this tissue of myths; much of the past is irrevocably lost. The modern social investigator, however, need not remain entirely at the mercy of such subjective data. He may ask not only "what is remembered of things past?" but also "what was the actual past?"[14] The historical record available to him, it need hardly be said, is not pure, disembodied Truth; even the simple factual information it contains was gathered by men whose interests and passions colored their perceptions, men who were "culture-bound." The point to be underscored, though, is that this record may be read in a way that allows us to discriminate, at least to some degree, between the mythic past and the actual past.

Warner eventually became aware of this crucial distinction. The last of the Yankee City volumes, published long after the others (1959), includes a lengthy and perceptive analysis of the image of the Newburyport past presented in the pageants staged during the tercentenary celebration of 1935. By utilizing historical sources Warner was able to detect and interpret some interesting discrepancies between the real past and the "history" portrayed in the pageants, which was what community leaders "now *wished* it . . . were and what they wished it were not. They ignored this or that difficult period of time or unpleasant occurrences or embarrassing group of men and women; they left out awkward political passions; they selected small items out of large time contexts, seizing them to express today's values."[15]

Regrettably, however, a similar indictment must be returned against the first four volumes of Warner's own study. "Where truth ends and idealization begins cannot be learned," the authors of *The Social System of the Modern Factory* tell us.[16] This was not a limitation imposed by the absence of historical evidence; it was the result of Warner's own methodological commitments. In this instance and in many others his interpretations rested on assumptions about the past which were demonstrably false. Warner's unwillingness to consult the historical record and his complete dependence on materials susceptible to anthropological analysis—the acts and opinions of living members of the community—served to obliterate the distinction between the actual past and current myths about the past. Thus,

the Yankee City investigators' determination to escape the ethnocentric biases of culture-bound history led them to accept uncritically the community's legends about itself—surely the most ethnocentric of all possible views.

The ahistorical predilections of Warner and his associate produced a number of glaring misconceptions about the character of the community they studied. The static old "Yankee" city whose "social superstructure remained very much what it had been at the end of the War of 1812" was largely a creation of Warner's imagination. Every investigator admittedly sees the community he studies from a particular, limiting perspective; a degree of subjectivity is perhaps inescapable in treating a complex social object. But, whatever the bounds of legitimate subjectivity, the Yankee City series far exceeds them. As late as the 1930's, according to Warner, the "Puritan tradition" of Yankee City remained "unshattered," for the community's population was happily still "predominantly old American." But in point of fact the population of Newburyport had ceased to be predominantly "old American" more than half a century before the Yankee City team began its labors! The effects of mass immigration, the high birth rate of the newcomers, and the heavy migration of old residents from the community produced radical changes in the composition of the Newburyport population during the 1850–1880 period. By 1885, first- and second-generation immigrants constituted almost half of the city's population; their descendants and later immigrants together made up the overwhelming majority of the Newburyport population at the time of the Yankee City study. Furthermore, only a small minority of the "Yankee" families remaining in the community in 1880 were actually from old Newburyport families. A comparison of local city directories for 1849 and 1879 provides a precise measure of the extent of this devastating change: little more than a *tenth* of the family names recorded in the directory of 1879 could be located in the first local directory 30 years before. The economic and social transformation the community underwent midway in the 19th century, when it became a bustling manufacturing city, effectively shattered the social structure of preindustrial Newburyport. The Federalist ethos lingered on in a few old families, but the dominant values in this city of mobile newcomers bore no resemblance to Warner's description. It is true that the community's economic growth slowed after the Civil War, and that its total population was little larger in 1930 than it was in 1855, but to infer from these facts that Newburyport was a static, old Yankee community sealed off from the larger society was utterly mistaken.[17]

These misconceptions about the community become more comprehensible when we realize that the key concepts of the study —class and ethnicity—were both based entirely on the opinion of Warner's local respondents, and were defined so as to render difficult any systematic study of the relations between subjective opinion and objective social reality. An "ethnic," for example, was said to be a Newburyport resident who "considered himself or was considered by" others to be an "ethnic" and who "participated in the activities" of an "ethnic" association; any citizen who did not fulfill these two criteria, amazingly, Warner classified a "Yankee." Thus, a community in which immigrants, their children and grandchildren were an overwhelming majority could become, in Warner's mind, a city whose population was "predominantly old American."[18]

Not only did the Yankee City investigators accept uncritically the opinions of informants living in the community at the time; they tended to accept the opinion of informants from a particular social group with very special biases—Yankee City's "upper uppers." This group fascinated Warner; he devoted an inordinate amount of space to them, despite the fact that they constituted less than 2 per cent of the Newburyport population. The upper uppers were the few dozen prominent old Yankee families who presumably had enjoyed high status in the community for more than a century. In fact Warner overestimated the continuity and rootedness of even this tiny elite, as they themselves were wont to do; while each of

his vivid "composite drawings" of upper uppers depicted a family that had resided in the community for several generations, Warner's own questionnaires showed that at the time of the study fewer than 60 per cent of this group had been born in or near Newburyport, and that almost a quarter of them had been born outside of New England entirely.[19] These were the Yankee City families whose sense of subtle prestige distinctions was translated into Warner's famous theory that the community was stratified into six discrete prestige classes; this was the "single group with a coherent tradition" whose eagerness to equate Newbury port history with their own history led Warner to believe that the community's "social superstructure . . . remained very much what it had been at the end of the War of 1812" and to attribute the apparent stability of the Newburyport social order to the fictitious dominance of the "Yankee."[20]

Industrialization and the Blocked Mobility Theory

The American class system was becoming "less open and mobility increasingly difficult for those at the bottom of the social heap," Warner wrote in 1947. "The evidence from Yankee City and other places in the United States," it seemed to him, "strongly" indicated that both manual laborers and their children enjoyed fewer opportunities to rise than was common in the 19th century; on the expanding frontier and in the idyllic craft structure of the 19th-century city, social mobility had been "certain," but the spread of the factory system had degraded the worker and had blocked the "ladder to the stars."[21] On the basis of his interpretation of "the industrial history" of Newburyport in *The Social System of the Modern Factory*, Warner concluded that the "traditional" American open class structure was becoming increasingly rigid; the "blue print of tomorrow" drawn up in Yankee City included the growing likelihood that America would soon see "revolutionary outbreaks expressing frustrated aspirations."[22]

The historical event that inspired these

dark forebodings was the strike which closed all the shoe factories of Newburyport in 1933 and eventually resulted in management recognition of the shoe worker's union. Warner portrayed this strike as a dramatic success, and argued that such a radical departure from the community's tradition of social peace and labor quiescence required elaborate explanation. The initial field interviews, Warner admitted, revealed that Newburyport citizens tended to think of the strike as a struggle over economic grievances provoked by the depression: "Each man, owner, and worker, and townsman, spoke his own brand of economic determinism." But Warner found these answers superficial; there had been depressions, wage cuts and the rest in the city before, he observed, yet this was the first "successful" strike. There had to be some "secret" as to "why the Yankee City workers struck and . . . why men in other cities strike." That secret, Warner decided, lay "beyond the words and deeds of the strike"; it could only be ferreted out by probing deeply into the evolution of the community's productive system.[23] A knowledge of history, he now seemed to concede, could supply deeper insight into an event in the present.

Warner began his excursion into the Newburyport past with a hymn to the Golden Age of the craftsman, when every youngster became an apprentice and every apprentice a master. The local youth was gradually trained in the complex skills of his calling, and eventually became "an inextricable member of the honorable fraternity of those who made, and who knew how to make, shoes." In this system, presumably, "workers and managers were indissolubly interwoven into a common enterprise, with a common set of values."[24] To strike was unthinkable. The workman held a respected place in the community, and there was little social distance between him and the men for whom he worked. Economic power was concentrated at the local level, and the age-graded skill hierarchy of the craft assured maximum social mobility opportunities.

One day, however, the serpent "mechanization" entered this Eden:

The machine took the virtue and respect from the worker, at the same time breaking the skill hierarchy which dominated his occupation. There was no longer a period for young men to learn to respect those in the age grade above them and in so doing to become self-respecting workers. The "ladder to the stars" was gone and with it much of the structure of the "American Dream."[25]

The shoe industry, Warner argued, underwent a technological revolution that shattered the craft order and destroyed local economic autonomy. The Newburyport laborers' sudden decision that a union was necessary to defend their rights was an inescapable consequence of this revolution. The growth of giant factories controlled by absentee owners opened up a vast social gulf between worker and manager. The steady encroachment of the machine rendered all manual skills useless; there resulted a sharp "break in the skill hierarchy." The status of all laboring jobs became equally degraded, and opportunities to rise into supervisory and managerial posts were eliminated. The "secret" behind the upsurge of union support in 1933 was thus a series of fundamental changes in the productive system, which separated the shoe workers from the community, blocked the mobility opportunities they had once enjoyed, and inspired a new sense of labor solidarity and class consciousness.

This portrait of a community in crisis, of course, represents a stunning reversal of the image of Newburyport presented in earlier volumes of the Yankee City series. The reader may well wonder if there were *two* Yankee Cities; the research for *The Social System of the Modern Factory* might almost have been conducted in another community. The placid New England town Warner selected for investigation because of its extraordinary continuity and stability suddenly became the site of a study in social disorganization and class conflict.[26]

Warner's new interest in historical change and his determination to present a dynamic analysis of the impact of larger social forces on Yankee City was commendable. Unhappily, however, his account of the evolution of Newburyport from "the simple folk economy of the earliest community" to the 1930's grossly distorted the city's actual history; it is a classic example of the old American habit of judging the present against a standard supplied by a romantic and sentimental view of the past. The sweeping conclusions about the American class structure he drew from this case study are not in accord with the Newburyport evidence, nor do they square with the findings of recent mobility studies conducted in other communities.

As an attempt to explain the shoe strike of 1933, *The Social System of the Modern Factory* can be quickly dismissed. This strike did not in fact represent as radical a departure from community traditions as Warner believed. "Everyone in management and labor agreed that the strike could not have happened" in the good old days, Warner reports, but strikes *had* taken place in Newburyport—in 1858, in 1875, and a good many times since.[27] The strike of 1933 was distinctive only in that it was more successful than previous strikes, and not very much more successful at that. As Handlin pointed out, the union asked for a closed shop and a 10 per cent wage increase, but it won simple recognition and no raise. And within three years the union had lost out in one of the two factories still open.[28] The events of 1933, therefore, were not unprecedented, and massive changes in the community need not be invoked to explain them.

Even if this be doubted, Warner's explanation of the strike is wholly unsatisfactory, because the causes to which he attributed the supposedly drastic changes of the 1930's were fully operative in Newburyport several decades before the events they presumably explain. Once upon a time, the Newburyport economy was organized along craft lines; labor was content, social mobility was "certain," to strike was unthinkable. Warner was exceedingly vague as to the actual dates of this idyllic craft age, but he assumed that memories of it were alive in the minds of the strikers of 1933, and one chart made it appear that craft and apprenticeship relations prevailed in local shoe

production until "approximately World War I."[29] The vagueness is not accidental, for the craft order portrayed in this volume was but a Never Never land conjured up by the author. Not a shred of evidence pertaining to Newburyport itself is cited in support of this account; none could be. If one goes back as far as 1800, one can indeed find evidence of a well-integrated craft order in Newburyport, but its outstanding features were not equality and mobility but hierarchy, religiously-sanctioned elite rule, and institutionalized deference of the lower classes.[30] And, in any case, the craft order had virtually disappeared in Newburyport and industrial cities like it long before the 19th century drew to a close without producing a powerful union movement, much less "revolutionary outbreaks expressing frustrated aspirations."

Well before 1880 the Newburyport economy was dominated by large textile and shoe firms. Production was highly mechanized in both industries; all of the textile mills and some of the shoe factories were already controlled by absentee owners.[31] Factory laborers found no inviting "ladder to the stars" before them; in the substantial sample of workers and their sons I studied for the 1850–1880 period, there was not a single instance of mobility into the ranks of management or even into a foreman's position! Since Warner failed to present any quantitative evidence to substantiate his assertions about the supposed decline in mobility rates, no detailed comparison of mobility rates in Newburyport in the 1850–1880 period with those in the 1930's can be made.[32] Extensive comparisons between my own findings concerning the intra-generational and inter-generational occupational mobility of unskilled laborers in 19th-century Newburyport and mobility rates in several other 20th-century American communities, however, provide no support at all for Warner's claim that to rise "from the bottom of the social heap" has become increasingly difficult in modern America. Instead, both types of upward mobility seem to have become somewhat less difficult over the past century.[33]

Nor is Warner's stress on the importance of absentee ownership confirmed by the history of the community. Several of the Newburyport plants were controlled by outside capitalists in this early period; this was a common pattern in many American industries from the very beginning of industrialization. And, more important, labor-management relations in the firms still in local hands were not in fact characterized by the happy solidarity Warner attributed to them, local mythology to the contrary notwithstanding. Whether the Yankee Protestant mill-owner lived on High Street or in Boston could have mattered little to his Irish-Catholic employees, whose willingness or unwillingness to strike was governed by more tangible and impersonal considerations.

The clue to these errors, I believe, lay in the fact that Warner's new-found appreciation of history did not lead him to any critical awareness of what constituted historical *evidence*. Though he cited a few secondary historical accounts that were tangentially relevant to his analysis, Warner derived the main outlines of his romantic interpretation of "the industrial history of Yankee City" from his informants in the community in the 1930's. That this set of myths flourished in the city is indeed a social datum of great interest (though one might well be skeptical about how widespread these attitudes really were, given Warner's initial admission that most local residents viewed the strike as a simple and familiar contest over wage grievances). To comprehend the function of myths like these in the social struggles of the present, however, is impossible when they are taken for an accurate description of past social reality and used as the foundation for an ambitious theory of social change in industrial society.

The distortions that pervade the Yankee City volumes suggest that the student of modern society is not free to take his history or leave it alone. Interpretations of the present require a host of assumptions about the past. The real choice is between explicit history, based on a careful examination of the sources, and implicit history, rooted in ideological preconceptions and uncritical acceptance of local mythology.

Notes

1. Edward Hallett Carr, *What is History?* New York: Knopf, 1962, p. 84.
2. For a useful discussion of the impact on history writing of some recent developments in the social sciences, see two essays by H. Stuart Hughes: "The Historian and the Social Scientist," *American Historical Review*, 66 (October, 1960), pp. 20–46; "History, the Humanities, and Anthropological Change," *Current Anthropology*, 4 (April, 1963), pp. 140–145. Both of these have been reprinted in Hughes' book, *History as an Art and as a Science*, New York: Harper and Row, 1964.
3. For a powerful critique of ahistorical social science, see Barrington Moore, Jr., *Political Power and Social Theory: Six Studies*, Cambridge: Harvard University Press, 1958, esp. Ch. 4. For an excellent case study written from a similar point of view, see E. R. Leach, *Political Systems of Highland Burma: A Study in Kachin Social Structure*, Cambridge: Harvard University Press, 1954. Carl Degler's "The Sociologist as Historian: A Look at Riesman, Whyte and Mills," *American*

Quarterly, 15 (Winter, 1963), pp. 483–497, raises some of the issues considered below, though I believe Degler's substantive conclusions to be mistaken.
4. Maurice Stein, *The Eclipse of Community: An Interpretation of American Studies*, Princeton: Princeton University Press, 1960; Harper Torchbook paperback edition, 1964.
5. The five Yankee City volumes were published as follows: Vol. I, W. Lloyd Warner and Paul S. Lunt, *The Social Life of a Modern Community*, New Haven: Yale University Press, 1941; Vol. II, W. Lloyd Warner and Paul S. Lunt, *The Status System of a Modern Community*, New Haven: Yale University Press, 1942; Vol. III, W. Lloyd Warner and Leo Srole, *The Social Systems of American Ethnic Groups*, New Haven: Yale University Press, 1945; Vol. IV, W. Lloyd Warner and J. O. Low, *The Social System of the Modern Factory*, New Haven: Yale University Press, 1947; Vol. V, W. Lloyd Warner, *The Living and the Dead: A Study of the Symbolic Life of Americans*, New Haven: Yale University Press, 1959. A one-volume abridgement of

the series has recently been published by Yale University Press under the title *Yankee City* (1963). For a guide to other publications by Warner and his students, and to the critical literature as of 1953, see Ruth Rosner Kornhauser, "The Warner Approach to Social Stratification," in Reinhard Bendix and Seymour M. Lipset, *Class, Status and Power: A Reader in Social Stratification*, Glencoe, Ill.: The Free Press, 1953, pp. 224–254.

6. See, however, the penetrating reviews by historians Oscar Handlin and Henry F. May. Handlin reviewed Vols. I and II of the Yankee City series in the *New England Quarterly*, 15 (September, 1942), pp. 554–557; Vol. III in the *New England Quarterly*, 18 (September, 1945), pp. 523–524; and Vol. IV in *The Journal of Economic History*, 7 (June, 1947), pp. 275–277. May reviewed Vol. IV for the *New England Quarterly*, 21 (June, 1948), pp. 276–277.

7. For a discussion of Newburyport's representativeness and the controversy provoked by Warner's claims, see Thernstrom, *op cit.*, pp. 192–206.

8. Warner and Lunt, *The Status System of a Modern Community*, p. 13; *Social Life of a Modern Community*, p. 90. These are but a few examples to suggest the monumental scale of the Yankee City venture. For a full account of "The Field Techniques Used and the Materials Gathered," see *Social Life*, pp. 38–75.

9. *Social Life*, p. 400.

10. *Ibid.*, Ch. 2.

11. *Ibid.*, pp. 1–5, 38–39; Warner and Low, *The Social System of the Modern Factory*, p. 2.

12. *Social Life*, p. 14.

13. Warner, *The Living and the Dead*, p. 4.

14. Cf. Robert Bierstedt, "The Limitations of Anthropological Methods in Sociology," *American Journal of Sociology*, 54 (January, 1948), pp. 22–30; Handlin, review of Vols. I and II of the Yankee City series, *op. cit.*

15. *The Living and the Dead*, p. 110.

16. *Social System of the Modern Factory*, p. 139.

17. See Thernstrom, *op. cit.*, pp. 84–86, 167–168, 195–196.

18. Warner and Srole, *The Social Systems of American Ethnic Groups*, p. 29. In his excellent study of Burlington, Vt., Elin L. Anderson found a similar myth, particularly among the upper classes. Anderson was unwilling to accept their claims without investigation, and discovered that in fact the "pure" Yankee stock made up less than a third of the population; *We Americans: A Study of Cleavage in an American City*, Cambridge: Harvard University Press, 1937, Ch. 3. For a similar finding in another Vermont community, see the unpublished study by Martin

and Margy Ellin Meyerson described in David Riesman, *Faces in the Crowd: Individual Studies in Character and Politics*, New Haven: Yale University Press, 1952, p. 274.

19. *Social Life*, p. 209. "Composite drawings" of "fictive persons" play a crucial role in the Yankee City volumes. They occupy much space, and are often referred to in support of subsequent analyses. In these narrative sketches of local residents, "no one actual individual or family in Yankee City is depicted"; instead, "the lives of several individuals are compressed into that of one fictive person." Warner did not hesitate to "exclude all material which might identify specific persons in the community, and . . . included generalized material whenever necessary to prevent recognition. The people and situations in some of the sketches are entirely imaginary." *Social Life*, p. 129.

These sketches often seem illuminating. But have they any value as evidence? As the example cited in the text indicates, the method gives free rein to any biases and preconceptions the social scientist brings to his subject. Warner assures us that all the liberties taken with the original evidence were checked to see that "the essential social reality" was not impaired. This is a commendable effort, but is it an adequate substitute for the ordinary safeguards which the historian imposes upon himself by guiding the critical reader to the body of evidence on which he bases his interpretation? *Quis custodiet ipsos custodes?* Warner's desire to "protect" his subjects and to tell his story "economically" is understandable, but he paid a rather heavy price to satisfy these requirements. All too rarely in the Yankee City series is the ordinary reader able to check the assertions of a composite drawing against data of genuine probative weight.

20. *Social Life*, p. 5; *Modern Factory*, p. 2. John P. Marquand's savage lampooning of Warner as the "Malcolm Bryant" of *Point of No Return* should not be allowed to obscure the fact that the two men viewed the community from a very similar perspective. Marquand appears to have felt that Warner betrayed the confidence placed in him by Marquand himself and other upper-class respondents. Whatever the merits of this accusation, Warner's image of the community seems to have been shaped by this group to a striking degree.

21. *The Social System of the Modern Factory*, pp. 182–185, 87–89.

22. *Ibid.*, Ch. 10.

23. *Ibid.*, pp. 4–7.

24. *Ibid.*, p. 87.

25. *Ibid.*, pp. 88–89.

26. A possible explanation of this startling shift

in Warner's image of the community would be that events in Newburyport since the publication of the early volumes had given the Yankee City researchers a different perspective. The actual chronology of the series, however, does not support this suggestion. The strike took place in 1933; the volumes stressing the harmony of social relations in what was supposedly "above all a well-integrated community" (*Social Life*, p. 38) appeared in the early 1940's; the factory study, whose dark fears of "revolutionary outbreaks expressing frustrated aspirations" (*Modern Factory*, p. 185) were allegedly inspired by the 1933 strike, was published in 1947. A better explanation may be that Warner, though he never replied to his critics overtly, was stung by the charge that the Yankee City he portrayed was static, "trendless," and thus entirely unrepresentative of changing industrial America. Certainly this criticism could never be made of *The Social System of the Modern Factory*, for here Warner pursued trends with a vengeance, elaborating not only the national but the "world implications" of the dramatic changes he now perceived taking place in Newburyport.

27. *Modern Factory*, p. 5.
28. Handlin, *op. cit.*
29. *Modern Factory*, chart i, p. 65.
30. See Thernstrom, *op. cit.*, pp. 34–42, for a discussion of the craft order of preindustrial Newburyport. In the Middletown volumes, Robert and Helen Lynd offered a more con-

vincing sketch of the craft order and a more sophisticated version of the blocked mobility theory. For some critical reflections on their analysis, see *ibid.*, pp. 214–216.
31. It is ironic that Warner, in discussing the idyllic craft order in shoe manufacturing, alludes to the efforts of the Knights of Crispins to preserve stringent apprenticeship requirements and to prevent the use of "green hands" in the post-Civil War decade. Not only had the Knights everywhere lost this crucial struggle more than half a century before the "successful" Newburyport strike; it was precisely in Newburyport that the craft order was so weak as to permit capitalists from the great shoe center, Lynn, to set up "runaway shops" as a means of avoiding "Crispin trouble."
32. In *The Social Systems of American Ethnic Groups* Warner did attempt to supply quantitative data about social mobility in Newburyport, and his effort to analyze historically the occupational and residential mobility patterns of local ethnic groups was not completely unfruitful. But because he believed that the essence of class was *prestige*, Warner was too predisposed against objective indices to use them properly. See Thernstrom, *op. cit.*, pp. 236–238, for a detailed critique of the mobility study reported in *The Social Systems of American Ethnic Groups*.
33. See Thernstrom, *op. cit.*, pp. 202–203, 216–221.

From Oligarchy to Pluralism:
The Patricians and the Entrepreneurs

Robert A. Dahl

The Patricians

In the course of the past two centuries, New Haven has gradually changed from oligarchy to pluralism. Accompanying and probably causing this change—one might properly call it a revolution—appears to be a profound

alteration in the way political resources are distributed among the citizens of New Haven. This silent socioeconomic revolution has not substituted equality for inequality so much as it has involved a shift from cumulative inequalities in political resources—to use an expression introduced a moment ago—to noncumulative or dispersed inequalities. This point will grow clearer as we proceed.

The main evidence for the shift from oligarchy to pluralism is found in changes in the social characteristics of elected officials in New Haven since 1784, the year the city was first incorporated after a century and a half as colony and town.

In the first period (1784–1842), public office was almost the exclusive prerogative of the patrician families. In the second period (1842–1900), the new self-made men of business, the entrepreneurs, took over. Since then, the "ex-plebes" rising out of working-class or lower middle-class families of immigrant origins have predominated. These transformations reflected profound alterations in the community, in the course of which important resources for obtaining influence were fragmented and dispersed. Wealth was separated from social position by the rise of industry, and public office went to the wealthy. Later, popularity was divorced from both wealth and social position by the influx of immigrants, and public office went to the ex-plebes, who lacked wealth and social position but had the advantage of numbers.

It is theoretically possible, of course, that the "real" decision-makers differed from the official decision-makers; if this were so, the real decision-makers might even have come from different social strata than the official decision-makers. However, for reasons I shall discuss later, it is highly unlikely that a set of real decision-makers from different social strata controlled either the patricians or the entrepreneurs. With the ex-plebes, the case is more plausible. We shall return to this question [see p. 222, this volume].

With this reservation in mind, let us now examine the changes that have taken place in the origins, occupations, and styles of life of the leading elected officials, the mayor and the aldermen, over the past century and three-quarters. Ever since 1784, the mayor of New Haven (Table 1) has been elected by his fellow citizens. At first, however, once elected, he held office on the pleasure of the General Assembly of the state, which until 1818 was a staunchly Federalist body and hence willing to let Federalist mayors remain in office indefinitely. In 1826 this quaint practice, more congenial to Federalism than the new Democracy, was superseded by annual elections. The members of the Common Council, including the aldermen, were elected annually in a town meeting. Since the 1870s, the mayor and aldermen have been elected for two-year terms.

During the period of patrician government, the typical mayor came from one of the established families of New Haven, went to Yale, was admitted to the bar, retained some connection with Yale, and spent most of his life in public affairs. Yet there were interesting nuances. Roger Sherman, the

TABLE 1. *The mayors of New Haven, 1784–1960*

PARTY	ELECTED	MAYOR	OCCUPATION	
	1784	Roger Sherman	U.S. senator, signed Declaration of Independence	
Dem.-Rep.	1793	Samuel Bishop	judge of probate	
Fed.	1803	Elizur Goodrich	professor of law	
Dem.-Rep.	1822	George Hoadley*	president, Eagle Bank	
Fed.	1826	Simeon Baldwin	judge, congressman	
Dem.-Rep.	1827	William Bristol	judge, state senator	
Fed.	1828	David Daggett	professor of law, U.S. senator	The patricians: law and the professions
Dem.	1830	Ralph Ingersoll	lawyer, congressman, state attorney	
Dem.	1831	Dennis Kimberly	lawyer, major general, U.S. senator	
Dem.	1832	Ebenezer Seeley	?	
Whig	1833	Noyes Darling	judge	
Whig	1834	H. C. Flagg	lawyer, editor	
Whig	1839	S. J. Hitchcock	lawyer, law teacher	

TABLE 1. *The mayors of New Haven, 1784–1960*

PARTY	ELECTED	MAYOR	OCCUPATION	
Whig	1842	P. S. Galpin	carpet manufacturer and insurance	
Whig	1846	Henry Peck	Durrie and Peck	
Whig	1850	A. N. Skinner	headmaster, classical boarding school	
Whig	1854	Chauncey Jerome	clock manufacturer	
Dem.	1855	A. Blackman	attorney	
Whig	1856	P. S. Galpin	secretary, Mutual Security Insurance Company	
Dem.	1860	H. M. Welch	founder and president, New Haven Rolling Mill, president, First National Bank	
Dem.	1863	Morris Tyler	wholesale boot and shoe dealer	
Rep.	1865	E. C. Scranton	president, Second National Bank	
Dem.	1866	L. W. Sperry	Sperry and Co. (meat-packing)	
Rep.	1869	William Fitch	E. T. Fitch and Co., coach spring manufacturer	The entrepreneurs: business and industry
Dem.	1870	H. G. Lewis	president, New Haven Wheel Co.	
Dem.	1877	W. R. Shelton	president, American Needle and Fish Hook Co.	
Rep.	1879	H. B. Bigelow	Bigelow and Co., machinery manufacturing	
Dem.	1881	J. B. Robertson	vice president, National Life and Trust Co.	
Ind. Dem.	1883	H. G. Lewis	president, New Haven Wheel Co.	
Dem.	1885	G. F. Holcomb	Holcomb Brothers and Co.	
Dem.	1887	S. A. York	judge of probate, lawyer	
Rep.	1889	H. F. Peck	president, Peck Brothers and Co., brass goods manufacturers	
Dem.	1891	J. B. Sargent	president, Sargent and Co., hardware manufacturing	
Rep.	1895	A. C. Hendrick	general inspector, Board of Fire Underwriters	
Rep.	1897	F. B. Farnsworth	president and treasurer, McLagon Foundry Co.	
Dem.	1899	C. T. Driscoll	lawyer	
Rep.	1901	J. P. Studley	judge, Court of Common Pleas	
Dem.	1908	J. B. Martin	lawyer	
Rep.	1910	F. J. Rice*	real estate	
Rep.	1917	S. C. Campner†	lawyer	
Dem.	1919	D. E. Fitzgerald	lawyer	
Rep.	1925	J. B. Tower	president, Geom. Garage Co., treasurer, J. R. Rembert Co.	The ex-plebes
Rep.	1928	T. A. Tully	assistant secretary, printing business	
Dem.	1931	J. W. Murphy	business agent, Cigar Workers, A.F.L.	
Rep.	1945	W. C. Celentano	secretary-treasurer, Celentano Funeral Home Inc.	
Dem.	1953	R. C. Lee	director, Yale News Bureau	

*Died in office.
†Succeeded to office on Rice's death in 1916, elected in 1917.

most distinguished of all New Haven mayors, was one of the few prominent New Haven Federalists who rose to eminence from modest beginnings. Like most New Englanders of the time, he could trace his New World ancestry back to 1634. His father was a farmer near Newton, Massachusetts, and it was there that Roger first learned the shoemaker's trade with which he began his career in New Haven; he then started a store, acquired real estate, and was admitted to the bar. By 1764 his fellow citizens in New Haven thought well enough of him to send him to the colonial legislature, and from that time onward political life was his real career. He was in the senate of both colony and state for two decades; during the same period he was a judge of the Superior Court; he was a delegate to the Continental Congress; he signed the Declaration of Independence; during his tenure as mayor of New Haven he was sent first to the Constitutional Convention at Philadelphia and then to the United States Senate. In addition to his public life, he was treasurer of Yale College for more than a decade, a sure sign (if any were needed) of his acceptance by the established families of New Haven; in 1768, Yale awarded him an honorary master of arts.[1]

Elizur Goodrich was more typical of the patrician mayors. He could trace his ancestry to Dr. Thomas Goodrich, who had been Bishop of Ely in 1534; his forebears settled in Wethersfield in 1643. His father had graduated from Yale in 1752, was a Congregational minister, a fellow of the Yale Corporation, and at one time a strong candidate for the presidency of the University. Elizur himself went to Yale, was admitted to the New Haven bar, became judge of probate, a position he held for seventeen years, and was judge of the county court for twelve years. He was sent to the United States Congress and in one of John Adams' historic "midnight" appointments (when Adams sought to pack the courts and the federal service against the incoming Jeffersonians) was appointed collector of customs at New Haven. When Jefferson removed him in order to award the office to

Samuel Bishop, an aged Republican whose son Abraham was a loyal and active Jeffersonian, some eighty New Haven merchants purporting to own "more than seven-eighths of the navigation of the port of New Haven" promptly dispatched a letter of protest. Jefferson was not moved. But Goodrich's friends rewarded him by making him a professor of law at Yale, and two years later mayor of New Haven, a position he held for the next nineteen years.[2] The careers of Simeon Baldwin, David Daggett, and Ralph Ingersoll were much the same: Yale families, Yale education, the bar, public life.[3]

The patricians had all the political resources they needed: wealth, social position, education, and a monopoly of public office; everything, in fact, except numbers—and popularity with the rank and file. It is puzzling to know which is the more in need of explanation: their domination over public life or their ultimate downfall.

As for their domination, New Haven, and for that matter the colony and the state of Connecticut, had been ruled for a century and a half by an elite, the "Standing Order," consisting of Congregational ministers, lawyers, and men of business, of whom the ministers had historically furnished most of the leadership. Like Connecticut itself, New Haven was a kind of Congregational theocracy in the trappings of primitive democracy. David Daggett described the operation of the system in 1787, and mourned its decline. "The minister, with two or three principal characters," he said, "was supreme in each town. Hence the body of the clergy, with a few families of distinction, between whom there was ever a most intimate connection, ruled the whole State."[4]

Among the English upper classes, perhaps the leaders of eighteenth-century New England would not have cut much of a figure. By the standards of English society they were at best of middling status, and in religion more akin to the lower middle classes of England. Perry Miller is doubtless right in saying that "what New England took to be the real England was lower-middle class England."[5] But New Englanders were, after all, living in New England; there the patrician families knew no social superiors. By almost any test it seems safe to infer that the elite of New Haven, like the Standing Order in Connecticut, completely dominated the political system. They were of one common stock and one religion, cohesive in their uniformly conservative outlook on all matters, substantially unchallenged in their authority, successful in pushing through their own policies, and in full control of such critical social institutions as the established religion, the educational system (including not only all the schools but Yale as well), and even business enterprise. Both they and their opponents took their political supremacy as a fact. By 1800 they were so thoroughly accustomed to the habit of ruling that their response to the emerging challenge of Jeffersonian republicanism was a kind of shocked disbelief: a response immediately followed, however, by energetic efforts to stamp out the new political heresy root and branch.

The capacity of the elite to continue its dominant position in New Haven politics through the first half-century of city government was probably a result of several factors. New Haven, though one of the largest towns in Connecticut, was essentially a small town where everyone knew everyone else by appearance, name, position, origins, and social rank. In 1787, the total population of the city was about 3,400. Not more than 800 of these could have been men eighteen years of age or older.[6] Even as late as 1820, the population was barely over 7,000, of whom about 1,600 were males of twenty-one years and older. Voting took place in town meetings where, under a "Stand-Up" Law enacted with great political shrewdness by the representatives of the Standing Order in the General Assembly of the state in 1801, a man had to reveal his choice within full view of the elite. Only a man of unusual courage was likely to display his opposition to the candidates preferred by church, wealth, and, in effect, state. (There was a beautifully contrived system for voting in town meetings on candidates for the upper chamber of the General Assembly. In theory it allowed a voter to cast a paper ballot for any twelve out of twenty nominees; in fact one had to reveal his support of candidates not on the approved list of twelve. So opponents of the Standing Order, lacking the courage of public opposition, took to casting blank ballots for one or more of the twelve nominees of the elite.)[7]

Even the pressures of small-town life and open voting seem insufficient to account for the dominance of the elite, however, for the top group was a remarkably tiny one. In 1811, when the city could not have contained many more than 5,000 people, President Timothy Dwight of Yale, who was surely in a position to know, listed only thirty-two professional men in the whole city: six clergymen, sixteen lawyers, nine physicians, and one surgeon. (Table 2) If we add to that number the proprietors of "29 houses concerned in foreign trade" and seven manufacturers, we must come very near to the number of men eligible for membership in the religious, social, and economic elite. A large intermediate social group, a sort of middle class, consisted of dry goods merchants, grocers, owners of lumber yards, and the like, numbering well over a hundred persons; probably most of these looked to the elite for leadership. Even so, there were over two hundred artisans in the city, men more predisposed than their social superiors to egalitarian political faiths and to evangelistic dissenting religions like Baptism or Methodism.[8]

TABLE 2. *Distribution of occupations in New Haven, 1811 (probably incomplete)*

The professions	32
Foreign commerce and manufacturing	36
Retail and wholesale firms	122
Artisans	222
Total	412

SOURCE: Dwight, *Statistical Account of New Haven*, pp. 32–33.

However, many of the artisans were doubtless prevented from voting by the state's property qualification for voting, which required a freehold estate equivalent to the value of $7 a year, or a personal estate of $134. It is difficult to know how many potential voters were disfranchised by this requirement, but at the beginning of the period the number seems to have been rather large. In the first city election in 1784, out of 600 adult males only 343 were qualified to vote. A quarter of these failed to take the oath, so that 249 out of the 600 men in the city actually voted in the town meeting to elect the first mayor. (A few days later in a meeting called to elect lesser officials only about 100 men showed up.)[9]

Even so, had grievances run deep enough, the fact that popular elections were the only legitimate means to public office almost certainly would have resulted in more conflict and opposition than the records reveal. The elite seems to have possessed that most indispensable of all characteristics in a dominant group—the sense, shared not only by themselves but by the populace, that their claim to govern was legitimate. If the best families regarded public life as a prerogative, they must also have looked upon it as an honorable career; like the ministry, politics must have carried with it very high prestige. Hence it is reasonable to conclude that until the winds of Jacksonianism blew in from the West, a man of nonpatrician origins must have regarded it as an act of unusual boldness, if not downright arrogance, to stand for public office. Given the perspectives of the time, who after all were more entitled to rule than those who had founded and governed town and colony, city and state for nearly two centuries and who, besides, embodied the highest achievements of a Congregational society? In a community of Calvinists, the idea of an elect was certainly not strange. And who had a better right to be elected than the elect?

The whole social system, in short, was a hierarchy in which the patricians stood at the apex. In this respect New Haven was closer to Europe across the Atlantic than to the frontier across the Hudson. The outlook that must have prevailed in such a society is difficult to recapture today, but perhaps nothing better symbolized it than two practices. First, until 1765 Yale College, the educational institution for that tiny

minority of Congregational ministers and lay leaders who provided the leadership, catalogued her students not alphabetically but according to their social standing; second, it was the custom in Congregational churches to assign seats according to the age, family background, or wealth of the occupant.[10]

Yet the elect did meet with opposition, and once their legitimacy as rulers began to be doubted, they were too few in number to maintain control over public office in a political order where office could be contested in elections. As an examination of the list of mayors (Table 1) reveals, the Federalist-Congregationalist-patrician class was occasionally challenged successfully even during this early period. Although opponents to the regime came from various sources, they all seem to have shared a common hostility to the patrician oligarchy. Religion played an important part. For just as dissenters in England were prone to join the opposition to Tories and later Conservatives, so dissenters in New Haven (and in Connecticut generally) resented that Congregationalism was the established church, and that members of other religious bodies were discriminated against in a variety of annoying ways. When Congregationalism became the religion of a minority, the end of patrician rule was in sight. And even by 1787 only about 26 per cent of the New Haven population was actually enrolled in one of the three Congregational churches.[11]

Religious dissent helps to account for the occasional maverick who "betrayed his class" and went over to Jefferson or Jackson. The Republicans of Connecticut first organized themselves in 1800 at the New Haven home of Pierrepont Edwards, a leading lawyer, federal district judge, and member of one of the most aristocratic families in New England.[12] Henry W. Edwards, Pierrepont's son and also a highly successful lawyer, was not only a Jeffersonian but later became one of the leading Jackson men in the state.[13] It is difficult to account for this open hostility to the Standing Order unless one recalls that it was the Edwards' common ancestor, Jonathan, who set the whole Congregational establishment of New England on its ear after 1734 when he tried to demonstrate, as Perry Miller has put it, "that they had ceased to believe what they professed, and that as a result the society was sick. He did not merely call them hypocrites, he proved that they were."[14] He attacked the mighty, and as often happens it was the mighty who won. It seems not fanciful to suppose that his eleventh and last son, Pierrepont, born only a few months before the Connecticut River barons drove him in defeat from Northampton, felt less than charity and deference toward the class that destroyed his father, even though that class was his own.

The social origins of Ralph Ingersoll were, as I have already indicated, as impeccable as those of Baldwin and Daggett; he was of a family of lawyers, his father having gone to Yale and thence into the law. Young Ingersoll followed his father's path, began his political life as a Federalist, and was a leader of the bar of Connecticut for many years. But the Ingersolls were Episcopalians, and Ralph Ingersoll moved (with his father) into the Toleration party that seized control of the state from the ruling Federalists in 1818; he ended up as a Jacksonian Democrat and a leader of the Democratic party.[15]

The Bishop family was something else again. In their case religion was perhaps less important than class and ideological factors. The origins of Samuel Bishop are somewhat uncertain, but he was not one of the elect. His son Abraham, appointed collector of customs on his father's death, had been sent to Yale and became a wealthy man, but he remained throughout his life a strong Jeffersonian, a bitter opponent of the Federalist-Congregationalist oligarchy, possibly a bit of a scapegrace, and something of an outcast. The elect accused him of atheism and French Jacobinism, but he was a skilled polemicist who gave as good as he got, and charged his enemies with conspiracies against republican institutions and religious freedom.[16] At times bitterness must have covered the small town like a dank fog.

The Bishops reflected still another source

of strength available to the opposition. After 1800 the national government was firmly in the hands of the Jeffersonians; in 1818 the Federalist monopoly over the government of the state was finally and forever destroyed. For Republicans these changes in state and national politics meant patronage, political organization, and even a certain legitimacy. New Haven Federalists could fume about Samuel Bishop's appointment, but they could not reverse it. Where before only the Federalist-Congregationalist elite had an effective political organization, now their opponents began to develop one. And where the Federalists were once the party of experience, increasingly they were the party of the has-beens while the Republicans were men of national reputation and extensive political experience.

Sooner or later, leaders who knew how to mobilize sheer numbers were bound to prevail over the old oligarchy. Five factors helped in that triumph: the secret ballot, the spread of the suffrage, the growth in population, mobilization of the voters by the political parties, and ideology. Of these, the last two were probably far and away the most important.

It was not until 1826 that the secret ballot began to be used in town meetings.[17] Property restrictions prevailed throughout the whole period of patrician rule although their effect (except to ease the task of Democrats in generating resentments against the oligarchy) seems to have declined, probably because of economic growth and rising property values—and, according to one authority, because "party leaders had often secured the enfranchisement of landless residents by conferring upon them titles to worthless swamp tracts or scrubby acres unfit for cultivation."[18] When property was finally eliminated as a voting requirement in 1845, the effect on the turnout at elections was negligible not only in New Haven (Figure 1) but in the whole state.[19]

Meanwhile, New Haven was rapidly ceasing to be a small village. Between 1820 and 1860 the population grew at the rate of about 4.3 per cent a year. (Figure 2). The adult population was getting too big to be

FIGURE 1. *Total votes cast in New Haven in elections for governor, as percentages of males 21 years old and over, 1813–1850*

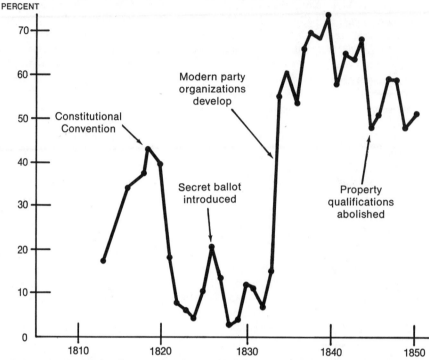

SOURCE: All population data used in tables and figures are, unless otherwise noted, from the U.S. Census with linear interpolations between census years.

managed by the old techniques. Once political organizations were developed for mobilizing voters at elections, the patricians were bound to be swamped by sheer numbers.

Before the extensive development of political parties more or less in their modern form, voting turnout was sporadic. (Figure 3) Evidently it depended heavily on the intensity of issues. Thus in contests for state offices there was a gradual increase in the total turnout as the opposition began to challenge the Standing Order. In New Haven, the number of voters rose from 225 in 1813 to 550 for the critical election to the state constitutional convention in 1818 (a major defeat for the Federalist oligarchy) and to 648 in the referendum on the constitution itself. After 1820, when the Federalists were clearly a moribund group in the state, turnout drastically declined. But from 1834 a wholly new phenomenon appeared. Where voting had oscillated before with the in-

tensity of campaigning and organization, now the development of two nation-wide political parties, the Democrats and the Whigs, with highly developed grass-roots organizations at the town and ward level brought the big swings to an end, and except for small oscillations and long-run changes, voting participation became relatively stable. A competitive, two-party system was now at work; and while New Haven voters continued to support Whig candidates in state and presidential elections pretty generally until the end of the Civil War, clearly the old basis for monopolistic control over public affairs was now permanently at an end.

The old oligarchs seem to have been crippled by their very ideology, which justified their own tight rule and left no place for the new competitive party system with its slogans and programs directed toward the ordinary voter. With the rising

FIGURE 2. *Population and electorate of New Haven, 1820–1960*

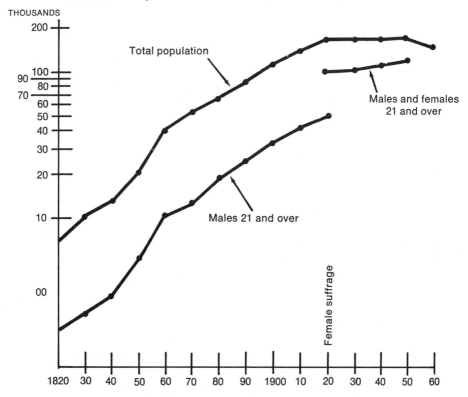

threat of Jeffersonian opposition, their public utterances became one long complaint against novelty, innovation, and the spread of democratic ideas, and their public actions reflected a rigidity ill-suited to competitive politics. The rules of the game were, of course, changing rapidly, and it is not surprising that someone like David Daggett, who continued to wear the white-topped boots and long white stockings of the previous age, should find the change uncongenial and even incomprehensible.

Quite possibly it was this ideological rigidity that finally made the displacement of the old oligarchs a peaceful one, for when the various critical tests of strength came, it must have been obvious even to them that they now commanded such a small following that subversion and revolt were impossible. They had begun by fighting back, as they did when Collector of Customs Elizur Goodrich was removed by Jefferson and

Samuel Bishop appointed instead. Beaten on this front, they turned to darker plans. These eventuated in the ill-famed convention at Hartford in 1814, which with its secrecy, its hint of secession, and the unhappy arrival of its commissioners in Washington just when news of the American victory at New Orleans and the peace treaty of Ghent had been received, proved to be the graveyard of Federalism in America. Thereafter the old Federalists whose memories carried them back to the days of unchallenged dominion grew feeble and died off one by one, leaving younger conservatives with different memories and traditions, a generation of men who learned politics according to the new rules and who found in the Whig party an instrument better suited to the competitive game of politics. By 1840, the patricians had either withdrawn from politics in order to turn their attention to economic affairs, or they had come to terms with the new order.

FIGURE 3. *Votes cast in New Haven in elections for governor, 1813–1850*

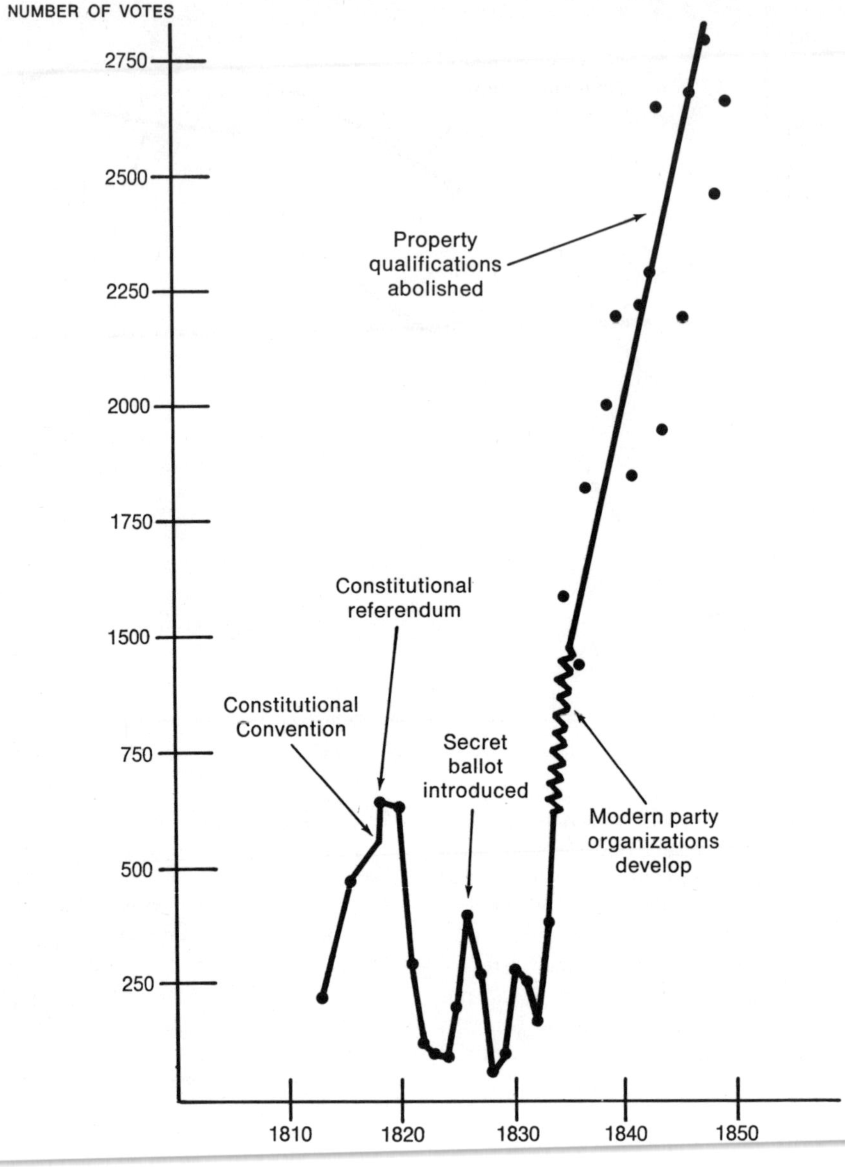

NUMBER OF VOTES

And so ended a period when social status, education, wealth, and political influence were united in the same hands. There was never again anything quite like it.

The Entrepreneurs

In 1842, Philip Galpin was elected mayor. He was a carpet manufacturer and secretary of a newly organized company specializing in fire and marine insurance. "No New Haven corporation," a local historian wrote of Galpin's "large and successful" insurance company in 1887, "can quote from its directory more well known names."[20]

Galpin ushered in a period during which wealthy entrepreneurs dominated public life almost without interruption for more

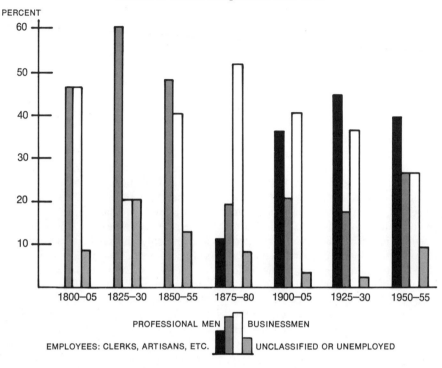

FIGURE 4. *Percentage of members of Boards of Aldermen and Finance in various occupations, 1800–1955*

than half a century. Mayor after mayor was a successful manufacturer, and businessmen virtually crowded all other occupations from the Board of Aldermen and the newly established Board of Finance. (Figure 4)

The emergence of the new (but assuredly not idle) rich as occupants of public office reflected an important splitting off of wealth and political influence from social standing and education in New Haven. With the growth of manufacturing a new kind of man rose to the top in the local economic order. Typically he came from the same stock as the patricians; like almost any New England-er he could trace his forebears back to the early colonial period or even to the May-flower. But he frequently came from humbler origins, quite probably from poverty, turned his hand to hard physical work at an early age, had little opportunity for formal education, got in on the ground floor of some new enterprise, and one day found himself a man of substance. He was,

in short, the epitome of the self-made man.

As is often the case, behind these self-made men lay the work of others. In origins, in time, and in life-style, Eli Whitney was a transitional man who stood somewhere between the patricians and the new industrialists. Whitney's father was a Mass-achusetts farmer who, according to tradition, mortgaged the farm in order to send Eli to Yale. As every American school child knows, Eli went to Georgia to study law and teach on a plantation, and there in 1793 he invented the cotton gin. Less of a business-man than an inventor, he was largely cheated out of the fruits of his invention, and he returned to New Haven where in 1800 he began to manufacture firearms with produc-tion methods that made possible a large output of highly standardized interchange-able parts. In this way he helped to lay the foundation for the mass production methods that became commonplace during the nineteenth century.[21]

The contest for mayor was frequently a struggle between two leading businessmen. In 1856, after a long interval out of office, Philip Galpin ran again as a Whig and defeated one of the most eminent entrepreneurs in New Haven, James Brewster, who ran on the ticket of the newly formed Republican party. For Brewster, who lost the election by a mere few hundreds votes, it must have been nearly the only setback in his entire adult career. Although he was the seventh generation from Elder William Brewster, one of the Mayflower pilgrims, Brewster himself began in social obscurity and hardship. His father, a farmer in Preston, Connecticut, died when James was still a boy in school, and at sixteen the youth was apprenticed in Massachusetts to learn carriage-making. When he was twenty-two he moved to New Haven, began a mechanic's shop, and in the natural course of his trade undertook to make a few of the light new carriages just then replacing the heavy old wagons. Out of these efforts grew one of the largest firms in New Haven. Later Brewster helped to organize the New Haven and Hartford Railroad, of which he was president for a few years. When he ran for mayor against Galpin at nearly seventy years of age, he was a leading figure in the local business world.[22]

The story of Chauncey Jerome, who was elected mayor between Galpin's first and last terms, is much the same as the others—except for the ending. His father was "a blacksmith and wrought-iron maker in very poor circumstances and Jerome's early life was an extremely hard one." At nine, Jerome went to work making nails in his father's shop in Canaan, Connecticut, and at eleven, when his father died, he sought work on local farms. In due course he became a carpenter; in winter, when work was slack, he made dials for grandfather clocks. When he was thirty, he set up a small clock manufacturing shop of his own in Plymouth, moved to the South, failed there in the depression of 1837, and about twenty years later returned to Windsor, Connecticut to manufacture brass clocks, which were rapidly making obsolete the old-fashioned

kind with works of wood. After a fire in Bristol destroyed his main factory and nearly wiped him out in 1845, Jerome concentrated his manufacturing in New Haven, where his use of mass production methods and interchangeable parts in the tradition of Eli Whitney revolutionized the whole clock industry. For a few years his was the biggest clock factory in America, turning out 200,000 clocks a year. But in 1855, only a year after he was elected mayor, the firm failed. Jerome was left a pauper and died in poverty and obscurity.[23]

Jerome's clock company was taken over by James E. English, who, according to a local historian writing in 1887, "more than any other person who has been a citizen of New Haven—unless we except Roger Sherman—is commonly regarded as pre-eminently a self-made man."[24] English was probably New Haven's leading entrepreneur. He had been born into a relatively obscure New Haven family and at twelve began working on a farm. After a few years that included some schooling, he was apprenticed to a contractor to learn the carpenter's trade. He became a journeyman carpenter, then a contractor, ventured into the lumber business, began buying and building vessels, and shipped many of Jerome's clocks to distant markets. When Jerome's clock company failed, owing him large sums, English took it over and under the name of the New Haven Clock Company turned it into a financial success. He was also one of the founders of the First National Bank and the Connecticut Savings Bank. English, who regarded himself as a Jeffersonian Democrat, was successively honored by his fellow citizens as a selectman, member of the City Council, representative and senator in the state legislature, U.S. representative, governor, and U.S. senator.[25] His partner during one of his early enterprises was Harmanus M. Welch, also a Democrat, who followed Galpin as mayor in 1860; Welch later organized the New Haven Rolling Mill and was for a time president of the First National Bank.

English and Welch serve to remind us that the Democrats were quite as anxious as the Republicans to nominate industrialists. It would be highly misleading to read back into that period recent differences in the leadership of the two national parties, for in social origins, occupations, and achievements (even in outlook) the nominees of both parties were indistinguishable. (Table 3) Neither party could be regarded as the party of the patricians, and though the Democrats may have had a little more success with the immigrant workers, particularly the Irish, it was assuredly not a working-class party with a working-class program or ideology.

TABLE 3. *Occupations of candidates for mayor, 1856–1899*

OCCUPATION	DEMOCRATIC	REPUBLICAN
Business		
Manufacturing	8	8
Insurance	1	1
Banking	—	3
Wholesale	1	—
Total	10	12
Law	2	—
Unidentified	4	4
Total	16	16

If any evidence were needed as to the Democrats' willingness to endorse industrialists, examine the case of J. B. Sargent. The son of a storekeeper and manufacturer in Leicester, Massachusetts, Sargent had operated a store in Georgia and then a commission firm in New York that soon became one of the country's leading hardware outlets. Among other things, he distributed the products of a hardware firm in New Britian owned by a one-time carpenter named Peck who manufactured hardware and brass goods in New Britain and New Haven. In due course, Sargent secured a tenth of the Peck firm's stock and a few year's later acquired the entire business. In the middle of the Civil War, Sargent moved his firm to New Haven, bought the Pavilion Hotel from James Brewster, brought down several hundred of his New Britain workers and their families, housed them in the hotel, managed a $9,000 loan from the State Education Fund, contracted for the entire year's output of the Hartford and New Haven brickyards, and rushed eight build-

ings to completion in record time. The firm made everything, from locks to casket hardware, imported additional workers from Italy, and a century later was still the seventh largest employer in New Haven.[26] J.B. was a Democrat, and as such enjoyed four years in office before being defeated by a Republican. It was appropriately ironic that J.B., who had followed the Peck family into the hardware business and then into New Haven itself, became mayor of New Haven in 1891 hard on the heels of H. F. Peck, a Republican, after losing his job in New Britain when Sargent took over his father's firm, H. F. Peck had come to New Haven, where he ultimately became president of his father's New Haven firm and enjoyed a career in public life as a member of the City Council, Board of Aldermen, Board of Finance, Board of Education, and as mayor. Although they were in opposite parties, the two men never ran for office against each other.

Why this enthusiasm in both parties for the new men of industry? Perhaps the best answer is another question: Who else was a more likely candidate than one of the successful entrepreneurs?

The patricians had been almost totally displaced from the center of public attention; in fact most of the voters probably could not even distinguish between the patricians and the new rich. Moreover the whole emergent style of life in politics and business was against them. In the course of the century politics had taken on some of the flavor of the lower middle classes, with their enthusiasms, emotionalism, and evangelistic religions; frequently the decorum of the preceding period now gave way to buffoonery, dignity was undone by the horselaugh, and the deadly seriousness of the Puritan was replaced by ballyhoo.

Even the new style of economic life seems to have been unsuited to the patricians, none of whom seems to have turned into an important entrepreneur. Tradition drew the patricians toward the professions, commerce, and banking. The three Trowbridge brothers, who could claim descent not merely from one but from two original settlers of the Connecticut Colony, entered their father's countinghouse, which engaged in a prosperous trade with the West Indies, bringing in rum and sugar and exporting farm products and manufactured goods. All three went into banking: T.R. was a director of the Mechanics Bank, Henry became a director and vice-president of the New Haven Bank, and E.H. helped organize the Elm City (later the Second National) Bank.[27] The respectability the patricians enjoyed made them useful on boards of directors, but they were not entrepreneurs.

Quite possibly the patricians had a distaste for manufacturing; many of them seemed to think that industry would attract ignorant artisans and thus disrupt the settled order of society. Quite possibly also the entrepreneur had to be a touch too ruthless and aggressive. Perhaps to understand industry and manufacturing, to see and seize the new opportunities, to realize the deficiencies of old methods, and to put together a new business, took a man moving up from hard, concrete experience with poverty, artisans, and machines. There may even have been a kind of failure of imagination, an ingrained habitual incapacity to forget the past and look to the revolutionary future of factories and mass production methods that were already transforming the present. Whatever the reasons, manufacturing and entrepreneurship were evidently not careers for the genteel.

Who else, then, should occupy public office if not the industrialists? Not the urban workers, who though they more and more outnumbered all the rest were immigrants lacking in status, political know-how, and economic resources. And what is perhaps the most important of all, in a society where each generation of workers was enormously more prosperous than its parents in a seemingly endless expansion of gains, there was no distinctive working-class outlook that could be formed into an ideology and program different from that already expressed in middle-class ideals. As for the middle classes, the matter was probably quite simple: why nominate and elect a grocer as mayor if you can have a manufacturer or bank president?

What is perhaps most interesting of all in retrospect is the fact that the chief elective public offices must still have enjoyed very high prestige. The patricians had perhaps helped to leave that much of a legacy; their prestige had brushed off on politics; the new rich evidently accepted that valuation and by their readiness to stand for the highest public offices must have helped to continue the tradition.

The entrepreneurs had brought about something of a division between two important political resources, wealth and social standing. To be sure, outside the most rarefied circles, where long memories kept old differences alive, social standing followed wealth by a generation or so. Yet entrepreneurs had erected a structure of business in which achievement was to a substantial extent independent of family origins. Henceforth those who had wealth comprised a set of people who overlapped only in part the set with highest social standing. Modern industry—which has often been represented as a development that produced a convergence of political resources in the same hands—helped, at least in New Haven, to fragment and disperse political resources to different groups in the community. The process was not, however, a matter of equalizing the distribution of political resources; rather it created what might be called dispersed inequalities.

The monopoly that leading entrepreneurs enjoyed over the chief elective offices of New Haven depended to a considerable extent on a third resource that need not always go with wealth or social standing, namely, popularity. The popularity of the businessman as an elective official in turn required a wide belief on the part of the rank-and-file voter in the peculiar virtues and meritorious attainments of the businessman, a certain measure of respect, and perhaps even some sympathetic identification.

Like the patricians before them, the entrepreneurs suffered from one acute political vulnerability—they necessarily lacked numbers. This weakness was now to be exploited by another band of new men, the ex-plebes, who made up in popularity with their fellow citizens what they frequently lacked in wealth and social standing. As the ex-plebes took over the center of the

political stage, the entrepreneurs followed the patricians into the wings.

Notes

1. *Encyclopedia of Connecticut Biography* (New York, American Historical Society, 1917), *1*, 6–7.
2. *Ibid., 1*, 88.
3. For brief biographies of Daggett and Baldwin, see *ibid., 1*, 73–74 and 74–75. For Ingersoll, see Edward E. Atwater, *History of the City of New Haven* (New York, W. W. Munsell, 1887).
4. Richard J. Purcell, *Connecticut in Transition, 1775–1818* (Washington, American Historical Association, 1918), p. 310.
5. Perry Miller, *Jonathan Edwards* (New York, William Sloan, 1949), p. 109.
6. Timothy Dwight, *A Statistical Account of the City of New Haven* (New Haven, 1811), pp. 57–58. Reprinted from New Haven City Year Book, 1874.
7. Purcell, *Connecticut in Transition*, pp. 194 ff.
8. Dwight, *Statistical Account of New Haven*, pp. 32–33.
9. Atwater, *History of New Haven*, p. 231.
10. Purcell, *Connecticut in Transition*, p. 73.
11. *Ibid.*, p. 44.
12. *Ibid.*, p. 232. See also Rollin G. Osterweis, *Three Centuries of New Haven, 1638–1938* (New Haven, Yale University Press, 1953), p. 197.
13. Jarvis M. Morse, *A Neglected Period of Connecticut's History, 1818–1850* (New Haven, Yale University Press, 1933), pp. 70–73 and passim.
14. Miller, *Jonathan Edwards*, pp. 108–09.
15. Atwater, *History of New Haven*, p. 247. For Ingersoll's Episcopalian background, see

Purcell, *Connecticut in Transition*, p. 335.
16. *Dictionary of American Biography* (New York, Scribner's, 1946), *2*, 294–95.
17. Charles H. Levermore, *The Republic of New Haven, A History of Municipal Evolution* (Baltimore, Johns Hopkins University, 1886), p. 258.
18. Morse, *A Neglected Period*, p. 323.
19. Total votes cast in presidential elections before and after the elimination of property requirements were (in thousands): 1836, 77.1; 1840, 113.9; 1844, 129.2; 1848, 124.7; 1852, 133.5. See W. Dean Burnham, *Presidential Ballots* (Baltimore, Johns Hopkins Press, 1955), p. 318. As percentages of the total population of the state, assuming a linear increase in population between census years, the presidential votes were: 1836, 25%; 1840, 37%; 1844, 39%; 1848, 35%; and 1852, 35%.
20. Atwater, *History of New Haven*, p. 339.
21. *Dictionary of American Biography, 20*, 157–60.
22. Atwater, *History of New Haven*, pp. 558–59 and Carleton Beals, *Our Yankee Heritage, The Making of Greater New Haven*, 2nd ed. (New Haven, Bradley and Scoville, 1957), pp. 130–39, 147–50, 166, 207, 222.
23. *Dictionary of American Biography, 3*, 27–28, and Beals, *Our Yankee Heritage*, pp. 129 ff.
24. Atwater, *History of New Haven*, p. 577.
25. *Ibid.*, and Beals, *Our Yankee Heritage*, p. 185.
26. Beals, *Our Yankee Heritage*, pp. 206–09.
27. Atwater, *History of New Haven*, p. 577.

From Commercial Elite to Political Administrator: The Recruitment of the Mayors of Chicago[1]

Donald S. Bradley and Mayer N. Zald

The urbanization and industrialization of American life have had a profound impact on the operations of political institutions and the elements of political power. This political transformation has occurred not only on the national scene but in the structure of local politics as well. There have been changes in the strength and structure of local political, social, and economic elites and in the political coin necessary to win office. While this statement is almost a truism, it is difficult to find valid data which concisely summarize the changes in social structure, politics, and the linkages between them. Indexes of political transformation that reveal underlying changes in community structure and composition are needed.

Our study follows the lead of R. A. Dahl who uses an analysis of the salient features of the life histories of mayors in New Haven, Connecticut, as evidence for shifts in the distribution and differentiation of political resources from 1789 to 1961.[2]

Dahl finds that the social and occupational backgrounds of New Haven mayors fall into three main groupings: (1) "the patricians," well-educated, legally trained men from well-established New Haven families, who dominated the political field from 1784–1842; (2) "the entrepreneurs," heads of the largest and most prominent New Haven industrial and commercial firms who, whether or not they had high social standing, consistently were elected to the office of mayor from 1842–99; and (3) the "ex-plebes," men from working-class and ethnic backgrounds who capitalized on an

arithmetic of ethnic composition and were able to be the major figures in politics from 1899 on. Dahl sees such a man as Richard Lee, mayor since 1953, as possibly the first of "the New Men"; men who build on an ethnic base but also have a wider base of support through advocating such good-government policies as community redevelopment.

To explain these shifts in recruitment Dahl focuses on the relative advantages and disadvantages possessed by the various groupings within the community for gaining important political positions. He does not deal with the motivation to participate in politics. In order to understand the historical shifts in local political elites it is necessary to deal with changes in both the distribution of the resources of political power and the value of political participation for the various social groups, for these are separate aspects of recruitment to political office.

We have used the social characteristics of Chicago mayors as the basis for an analysis of the changes in the political and social structure of Chicago. As compared with New Haven, Chicago has had a more dynamic and restless growth. While New Haven had an established and cohesive elite at the time of its incorporation as a city, the groups that were to make up Chicago's elite migrated there as it grew into a transportation and trading center; where New Haven grew slowly and incorporated a few major ethnic groups, Chicago grew rapidly and assimilated a multitude of diverse immigrant groups. Thus, we were led to

Reprinted from The American Journal of Sociology, *71 (September 1965), 153–167, by permission of the authors and The University of Chicago Press. Copyright 1965, 1966 by The University of Chicago.*

TABLE 1. *Mayors of Chicago and the Years in Which They Were Elected,* by Chronological Periods*

PERIOD	MAYORS
Commercial elite (1837–68)	Ogden, 1837; Morris, 1838; Raymond, 1839 and 1842; Lloyd, 1840; F. C. Sherman, 1841, 1862, and 1863; Garrett, 1843 and 1845; A. Sherman, 1844; Chapin, 1846; Curtiss, 1847 and 1850; Woodworth, 1848 and 1849; Gurnee, 1851 and 1852; Gray, 1853; Milliken, 1854; Boone, 1855; Dyer, 1856; Wentworth, 1850 and 1860; Haines, 1858 and 1859; Ramsey, 1861; Rice, 1865 and 1867
Transition mayors (1869–75)	Mason, 1869; Medill, 1871; Colvin, 1873; Hoyne, 1875†
Personalized politics versus party machine (1876–1930)	Heath, 1876‡ and 1877; Harrison I, 1879, 1881, 1883, 1885, and 1893§; Roche, 1887; Cregier, 1889; Washburne, 1891; Hopkins, 1893; Swift, 1885; Harrison II, 1897, 1899, 1901, 1903, and 1911; Dunne, 1905; Busse, 1907; Thompson, 1915, 1919, and 1927; Dever, 1923
Political administrators (1931–65)	Cermak, 1931; Kelly, 1933‖, 1935, 1939, and 1943; Kennelly, 1947 and 1951; Daley, 1955, 1959, and 1963.

*Terms were for 1 year 1837–62, two years 1863–1905, four years from 1907 on.
†Hoyne never took office. Colvin refused to yield seat because of change in election procedure.
‡Special election.
§Harrison assassinated, Hopkins elected at special election.
‖Cermak assassinated, Kelly elected at special election.

expect a rather different pattern of recruitment to the office of mayor. Our central purpose is to present an analysis of the changes in recruitment in Chicago. In order to highlight the differences between the two communities, comparison with New Haven will be reserved for the conclusions.

From a host of biographical sources we gathered information on the social background and political careers of each of the thirty-nine Chicago mayors. By comparing the backgrounds of each of these individuals, we established patterns of common characteristics. The mayors grouped into four periods, which we have labeled according to their most salient characteristics.[3] Changes in the patterned characteristics from one period to another are interpreted in terms of shifts in the social, economic, and ideological conditions of the city. The names and dates of election of the mayors, arranged by the periods to which we have assigned them, are presented in Table 1. In Table 2 we present summaries of the social and occupational backgrounds and of the political background and careers of the mayors of each period.

I. The Elite of Commercial Expansion: 1837–68

In 1830 Chicago was only a small trading post with a population under 100. As the frontier was pushed further west, Chicago rapidly became a transportation and trading center. The businessmen who were most prominent in this economic development commanded respect, prestige, and economic resources; they dominated the political scene and, to some extent, other institutional areas of community life. From 1837, the date of Chicago's incorporation, to 1868 the mayor, whether Whig, native American, Democrat, or Republican, was likely to be a leading businessman, highly active in political affairs and active in the affairs of his religious denomination.

A. Social, Occupational, and Political Characteristics

The speculative fever that characterized the economic development of Chicago at this time led most of the leading citizens to participate in several kinds of economic

TABLE 2.* *Summary of Social, Occupational, and Political Characteristics, by Chronological Periods*

	COMMERCIAL ELITE (N = 19)	TRANSITION MAYORS (N = 4)	PERSONALIZED POLITICS VS. PARTY MACHINE (N = 12)	POLITICAL ADMINIS- TRATORS (N = 4)
Social and occupational background:				
Occupations:				
Multiple occupational practice†	10	—	1	1
Real estate and building	2	—	2	—
Grain and meat processing and packing, and merchandising	5	—	—	—
Wholesale and distribution, Chicago area	—	—	4	1
Law and judiciary	2	1	3	—
Newspaper	—	1	—	—
Career government service	—	—	—	2
Other	—	2	2	—
Education:				
Less than ten years	5‡	—	—	—
High school	3§	1	5	3
College	1	2	1	—
Legal training	4‖	—	5	1
No information	6	1	1	—
Religion:				
Protestant	17	2	6	—
Catholic	—	—	3	3
Other	—	—	—	1
No information	2	2	3	—
Age at arrival in Chicago:				
0–15	1	—	1	3
15–29	10	1	7	1
30+	8	3	2	—
No information	—	—	2	—
Membership in social elite of modal mayor # (impressionistic rating)	Yes (social elite not highly organized)	Yes	Yes**	No
Economic standing of modal mayor at times of first election (impressionistic rating)	Highest	A level below the highest	A level below the highest	Medium-medium high

*The detailed table which this table summarizes has been deposited as Document No. 8387 with the ADI Auxiliary Publications Project, Photoduplication Service, Library of Congress, Washington 25, D.C. A copy may be secured by citing the document number and remitting $1.25 for photoprints or $1.25 for 35-mm. microfilm. Advance payment is required. Make checks or money orders payable to Chief, Photoduplication Service, Library of Congress.

†These men were involved in several lines at once. Almost all speculated in land, two combined this with banking, one was a medical doctor, a contractor, and in banking. Several were also active in railroads.

‡Includes "very little," "village school," "district school," and "public school."

§Includes one "superior education for his time."

‖Two of these four lawyers were "self-educated."

#No social registry before 1880.

**Catholics not in social registry.

TABLE 2. *(continued) Summary of Social, Occupational, and Political Characteristics, by Chronological Periods*

	COMMERCIAL ELITE $(N=19)$	TRANSITION MAYORS $(N=4)$	PERSONALIZED POLITICS VS. PARTY MACHINE $(N=12)$	POLITICAL ADMINIS-TRATORS $(N=4)$
Political background and experience:				
Party affiliation:				
Democrat	11	—	5	4
Republican	4	2	7	—
Whig	3	—	—	—
Other	1	2	—	—
Mean age at election (years)	36	57	48	54
Mean length of residence before election (years)	13	23	28	49
Political experience prior to election:††				
Alderman	9	—	4	1
Other positions:				
From local system	8	2	9	3
Non-local	2‡‡	—	—	—
No previous position or no information	5	2	3	—
Over-all judgment of prior political experience of modal mayor	High	Low	Moderate	High
Number of mayors serving different lengths in office (including two and more terms):				
1 year	10	§§	—	—
2 years	8	2	6	1
3 years	—	1	1	—
4 years	1	—	2	—
5–7 years	—	—	—	—
8 or more years	—	—	3	3
Later political office (aside from being re-elected mayor):††				
Alderman	4	—	—	—
Other local-based elections	10	—	2	—
No information or no other known position	7	4	10	4
Summary judgment: Amount of office-holding after mayoralty	High	Low	Low	Low

††A mayor could have been both an alderman and held other positions. Therefore, some mayors have been recorded twice.
‡‡Two of the first group of mayors had been members of their state legislatures before moving to Chicago.
§§See Table 1, n. †.

enterprise at the same time. More than half of this first group of mayors was engaged in between two and four occupations. For instance, a man might be a practicing lawyer, a land speculator, and a forwarding agent.

The first nineteen mayors represent the commercial, transportation, and building interests related to the growing economy. Real-estate speculation and investment were sources of income for at least eight of the first nineteen mayors; eight were associated with the merchandising and trading activities of the city; at least six were active in the development of railroads; three were in banking and building; and four were practicing lawyers. Almost all were extremely prominent in the business world. As Pierce observed, "Indeed, only two of the twenty-seven men running for the office between 1848 and 1869—Isaac L. Milliken, a blacksmith [and self-taught lawyer] and Timothy Wait, a barkeeper—had not attained enviable standing in the business life of the city."[4] Like most of the early migrants to Chicago all but three of these nineteen men came from New York or New England and all were born in the United States.[5]

Although we do not have complete information on the religious and educational background of this group, the available evidence indicates that it was almost entirely Protestant or non-religious. Furthermore, several of this group were instrumental in the organization of their denominations in Chicago. Raymond, Lloyd, Sherman, and Boone were either founders or prominent supporters of their respective congregations. By and large these men did not have extended formal education. Only three—Curtiss, Boone, and Wentworth—can indisputably be said to have had a college education. Although Morris and Milliken were qualified lawyers, their educational backgrounds are in doubt, for a college degree was not one of the requirements for admission to the bar.

The political careers of these mayors reveal extensive political participation. As a group, they had held substantially more offices than the group which immediately follows them. All but five of the commercial elite had anywhere from one year (Lloyd) to twelve years (Wentworth) of experience in some type of public office. After the mayoralty all but two (Ramsey and Rice) went on to serve in other positions.

Although these men were active in politics, none dominated the mayoralty for long periods, as we find happening later in the century. Even though there were no legal restrictions on the number of consecutive terms that one could serve, of the nineteen mayors only four held office for two consecutive terms and none for more than that. On the one hand, long terms in office would not have been consonant with the maintenance of economic and other interests. On the other hand, given the size of the community in its early days, the office of mayor may have had mainly honorific rather than central career importance.

The small size of the community also means that most of these men must have had extensive business dealings with each other and have known one another quite well. This homogeneity of background did not always result in a common approach to the policies of city administration. In fact, Dyer and Chaplin were members of the same firm, but they ran on opposite party tickets. Although some differences in viewpoint may have existed, in Chicago, as in other new commercial towns,[6] the views of the commercial elite were stamped on the administration of the city.

The evidence presented above suggests that these first mayors were part of a "multi-institutional" elite; active in political office both before and after being mayor, heading the largest economic enterprises, and active in school and religious activities, these mayors were the leading figures in the community. They attained their position, not by virtue of family background, but through economic achievement.

B. Changes in Community Structure

The population of Chicago grew from 4,000 in 1837 to 29,000 in 1850 to 120,000 in 1860. As the town grew, forces developed to displace the original commercial elite from their position of both economic and political dominance. Before discussing those forces we must account for a peculiarity in the recruitment of the early mayors: Of the mayors from 1837 until 1870 all but Rice arrived in Chicago between 1833 and 1837. What accounts for the "entrenchment" of these early arrivals?

A partial explanation is found in the depression of 1837, which ruined many of the businessmen who had made fortunes during the preceding speculative era. The "panic" also served to change the character of the people who continued to come to Chicago; the speculator and the bankrupt merchant left—1838 is one of the few years in Chicago's history that reveals a decline in population—and in their place came the laboring immigrant. Those who stayed and consolidated their positions found themselves in economic ascendancy with the return of prosperity; those who came later found themselves competing against an entrenched and active group of commercial leaders who also were active in politics and dominated the political scene.

Several factors led to the eventual economic and political decline of the commercial elite, however. First, the original business leaders were eclipsed by later arrivals who built large industrial, trading, and meat-packing firms. Second, requirements developed that made the office of mayor less desirable for the businessman. Third, political resources became available to other groups within the community.

The original commercial entrepreneurs of the city had a dominant position during the 1840's, but in the 1850's and 1860's they began to be economically obscured by later arrivals.[7] By the end of the 1860's they had lost their position of economic supremacy. Such firms as Wadsworth, Dyer, and Chapin were obscured by the growth in Chicago of Armour and Company; the Chicago Packing and Provision Company; and Libby, McNeill, and Libby; and others. The new leaders of business did not replace the old commercial elite in politics, however; in part because they did not choose to run for office.

The office of mayor became a less desirable sideline occupation for a businessman as the scope of competing firms was enlarged and more energy and time were required to maintain a commanding position in the business community. Also, to be mayor in an era when the pioneer work of building the physical plant and establishing an order for the growing city was complete was a less valuable financial investment than it had been in the early days when various city improvements in transportation, sanitation, and waterworks could not but benefit economic interests founded on real-estate and commercial holdings.

At the same time, the growth in the physical size of the city and the expansion of public services made the elected officials responsible for more duties, requiring full-time attention to public office. The increase in municipal expenditures from approximately $45,000 in 1848–49 to over $6,000,000 in 1868 indicates the tremendous growth in municipal complexity. Duties formerly performed by private enterprises were taken over by the administrative authorities of the city.[8] This extension of city services and the increased responsibility of the mayor for the performance of these functions made the office an all-engaging activity.

Furthermore, the proliferation of public services extended governmental responsibility into areas where it conflicted with the interests of some segments of the business community. The business leader in office found it increasingly difficult to resolve his business interests and his public responsibilities, and businessmen found they could buy advantages from the developing ward bosses of the city council. All of these developments—the increased attention demanded by commercial and public activity, the decreasing necessity for active political involvement, and the conflict of interest between the two roles—tended to make the mayoralty less desirable to the leading business notables.

At the same time there was a decline in the political resources of the economic dominants. Specifically, there was a lower popular estimation of the virtues and attainments of the businessman. The commercial elite had dominated the political scene despite rapid changes in the community composition. The city census of 1843 listed almost 30 per cent of Chicago's population as foreign-born, and by 1850 this figure had risen to 52 per cent. Until 1870, in spite of its numerical superiority and with only minimal residence requirements for voting, the foreign-born population of the city continued to support the Yankee businessman year after year.[9] The only explanation of this support seems to be that they believed they too would be the beneficiaries of the rapidly expanding wealth of the city.[10] The rise of labor consciousness, growing public concern over the extent of graft and spoils in public office, and the growing awareness of a divergence of business and public goals all worked to undercut the ideological legitimation of the commercial elite.

II. Transition Mayors: 1869–75

In 1869, with the election of Rosewell Mason, a change occurred in the social background of the mayors. Supported by radical labor and pledged to the restoration of official morals, Mason no longer typifies the commercial elite. During this short period an interlude occurs between a business-dominated political scene and one controlled by charismatic and party leaders.

This period is characterized by political unorthodoxy, conflict between public moralists and advocates of personal liberty, a high degree of party irregularity, and the formation of successful independent parties. Both the disarray of the regular parties and and the need for total unity following the fire of 1871 required men who could build a coalition outside of normal channels. The mayors of this period were generally older men with few local political commitments who had high standing in the community.

The type of individual chosen to serve during this period of transition and political conflict had less commitment to the economic growth of Chicago than did the entrepreneur

of the preceding period. It is true that Mason and Colvin represented large transportation concerns, but they were managers rather than owners; all of the nineteen previous mayors had been more or less self-employed. Furthermore, the organizations employing them (Mason was employed by the Illinois Central Railroad and was a well-known civil engineer and Colvin was the resident agent of the United States Express Company) were oriented to a much wider area than just that of Chicago.

That the mayoralty was not the prerogative of the leaders of commerce in this period is also indicated by the election of Joseph Medill (editor and owner of the *Chicago Tribune*) and Thomas Hoyne (lawyer and jurist). Although wealthy, Medill did not hold a position in the commercial, industrial, or financial activities of the city comparable to that of the previous mayors. Wentworth, the figure of the first group of mayors most analogous to Medill, in that he owned a newspaper, was also active in real estate, banking, and railroad development. Medill, on the other hand, was completely committed to managing and editing the *Tribune*. Apparently, Hoyne had no active connection with the business community.

The average age of the transition mayors was older than either the preceding or the following groups of mayors. At the time they became mayor the mean age of the first nineteen mayors was forty-one while that of transition mayors was fifty-seven. Of the first nineteen, only two (Dyer and Rice) exceeded the age of the youngest of the second group (Medill). The transition mayors were older in average age than the subsequent two groups (forty-eight and fifty-four, respectively).

Although these mayors were older than their predecessors they had more limited local political involvements. Hoyne and Medill were active in state and national politics, but neither took the usual route to becoming mayor, that is, via the aldermanic position. Moreover, neither Mason nor Colvin had any prior political experience in the city and at the end of their terms of office they discontinued political participation.

How can we account for the selection of these mayors? The disarray in politics had led to the rise of independent parties such as the reform-minded Citizens' Ticket and the labor and ethnic-based People's Party. The "Union-Fireproof" ticket (headed by Medill) was a response to the fire. For finding a candidate that was acceptable to the diverse parties and elements of the community, who could be more acceptable than highly respected older men who had not become identified with the local political issues?

After the election of 1879 the Republicans were convinced that they could elect one of their own candidates and that a bipartisan coalition was not necessary. Thus, party politics returned to their more usual course, the reform elements of the Citizens' Ticket went over to the Republicans, and many of the ethnic elements of the People's Party returned to the ranks of the Democratic party. The transition period was ended.

III. Personal Machine Versus Party Machine: 1876–1930

Disunity, self-interest, and apathy characterized the business, labor, and middle-class elements of Chicago during this period. A lack of clear numerical preponderance and a high degree of social mobility prevented a clear victory by any one class or ethnic group. Whereas in other major cities strong machines developed, political factions controlled the various regions and groups of Chicago. The distribution of political resources in the community was such, however, that when the city-wide office of mayor was at stake it took more than these local allegiances to elect a candidate. Because of its "payoff" in patronage and political influence, the office of mayor was the focal point of activity for the politicians of all factions of both parties.

Given these conditions, there seemed to be two chief routes of ascent to the office of mayor during this period: through long and careful service to the party and through charismatic or vote-getting abilities. On the

one hand, a potential mayor could extend the range of his influence until he became head of one of the party factions or he could be chosen because he epitomized party loyalty and respectability in reform periods. On the other hand, there were the two Harrisons and Thompson—upper-class notables who came to power because they could at the same time mobilize party support and, through personal qualities, appeal widely to the diverse groups of the community.

A. Social, Occupational, and Political Characteristics

Even though commerce and industry were growing rapidly, the period from 1880 to 1930 did not see the election of any businessman from the major industrial companies, department stores, or banks which came to dominate the Chicago economy. Legal practice, wholesaling, and real-estate management were the major business connections of the twelve mayors elected during this period. A larger proportion of these than of the previous mayors had legal training (five out of twelve as compared to six out of twenty-three); and, whereas many of the first group of mayors had been involved in shipping and milling grain or were in general merchandising, only one of these mayors was a merchant. Three of the mayors in this period were practicing lawyers and judges; five were involved primarily in the distribution of coal, paint and wood, and machinery; three were wealthy real-estate owners and operators; and one, Cregier, was a mechanical engineer and former city engineer. Both real estate and law permit an easy transition to and from public office; thus running for public office was more feasible for many of these men than for the heads of major companies.

Even the men whose businesses demanded much time differ from those who were mayors in previous eras. In several instances the political activities of these businessmen seem to be more important than their business careers. For instance, Hopkins was active in Democratic politics from his arrival in 1880 organizing several annexation movements. He was one of the organizers and early presidents of the Cook County Democratic Club; chairman of the Democratic County Committee in 1889; delegate to the Democratic National Conventions of 1892, 1900, and 1904; and ofttime chairman of the Democratic State Committee. Although he held office for only a short time, he had much more than a passing interest in politics. The same prolonged involvement is true of Busse and Swift. Not only were the mayors of this period not the leaders of the business community but politics and party work were a major part of their lives. Furthermore, five of them were identified with the large Irish and German populations of the city.

All but three of the mayors between 1880 and 1931 had obtained enough social standing and financial success to be listed in the social directories of their periods. Their educational attainment was considerably greater than that of the previous mayors. Of the twelve mayors between 1880 and 1931 six had received college educations, and of the remaining six we know that five graduated from high school. (Of the nineteen mayors of the first period only four had a college education.)

Most of these men had long service in their party, and several were heads of factions. Hopkins, Swift, Busse, and Dunne all worked up to power from unpromising beginnings. Using position in the business world and ethnic communities, each gradually extended the range of his influence over party workers and supporters until each became head of one of the party factions. Once in a position to concoct schemes and negotiate treaties, each was able to parlay his political strength into the mayoralty. The success of these mayors in the party was dependent on political generalship, and their election success was a result of the superior working of their respective party organizations.

Heath, Roche, Cregier, and Dever also spent considerable time in the service of their parties. They differed from the former group, however, in their positions within the parties. None was the head of a party

faction; rather each was a party supporter. They were chosen as candidates because of their party loyalty and because of their respectability. They pacified the occasional reform or businessman groups that organized to fight the party bosses.

Although the Yankee businessman and the members of first-generation ethnic groups sought and obtained office, the most successful candidate was the charismatic social leader. During this fifty-five-year period, the two Harrisons and Thompson held the office of mayor for a total of thirty-one years and when not in office were a force to be reckoned with. In a sense the history of the mayoralty of this period is the story of these three individuals. Although quite different in their administration of public office, the Harrisons and Thompson were successful because they could appeal to a wider variety of groups than could their opponents.

Chosen to run initially for minor posts because of their silk-stocking respectability and financial standing, both the senior Harrison and Thompson showed remarkable ability as campaigners. While Harrison, and especially his son, were less raucously flamboyant than Thompson (and were never as involved in scandals), all three had oratorical skills, a sense of showmanship, and an ability to adapt to their audience. Their personal following enabled them to jump to the top of their parties without serving long apprenticeships. Because of their city-wide following they were relatively independent of the political fiefs making up the respective party organizations.

B. Changes in Community Structure

Between 1876 and 1931 Chicago developed into a great central manufacturing center and one of the principal agricultural clearing houses in the country. From virtually complete destruction in the fire of 1871, Chicago became the showplace of the 1893 Columbian Exposition. These radical rearrangements in the economic and physical structure were paralleled by extensive migration to the city and a reordering of its population composition. In the 1890's extensive numbers of Poles, Bohemians, Russians, and Italians arrived, following the Germans, Irish, and Scandinavians. By 1920, 70.6 per cent of the population was either foreign-born or of foreign parentage. Finally, in the early 1900's the influx of Negroes increased.[11] The high rate of economic growth, the extent of vertical mobility, and the rapid movement of large numbers of people to and from the city prevented stable political organizations and traditional groupings.[12]

Of the groupings that arose out of this economic development, the most effectively organized and *potentially* the most influential was the business element. Able to control newspapers, campaign funds, propaganda, and the services of political leaders, they could play—when they cared to act together—an important role in the political game. They seldom, however, chose either to act, or, when they did act, to do so in concert. There was conflict between commerce and industry and railroads and real-estate operators and public utilities. There was also conflict within each of these groups and between them and the public, which felt that its interests had been subordinated to narrow economic goals. Both factors, the lack of group solidarity and the lessening of social legitimation, prevented the business elite of the community from exerting control over the political scene.[13]

The numerically most powerful group, labor, was not notably successful in political participation. Organized in the 1870's and 1880's under the pressures of an expanding labor force, recurring unemployment, rising food prices and falling wages, and the injustices of child labor, the labor movement was beset by strife resulting from the issue of radicalism versus trade unionism. General prosperity between 1887 and 1892 brought quiet to the labor front and a degree of rapprochement within the labor movement. The insecurity of this rapprochement led the leaders who feared the effects of politics upon the unity of their trade-union organizations, to discourage union participation in political contests. Even when this policy was abandoned, as it was in the mayoralty campaign of 1919, lack of solidarity made labor's efforts in politics unsuccessful.

At the same time, the very diversity of ethnic groups prohibited any one group from dominating the scene. The cleavages in the ethnic composition of the community presented natural lines along which political power could be organized. Capitalizing on the neighborhood segregation of their countrymen, and their own ethnic identification, political bosses appeared who were supreme in their own bailiwicks. Chicago politics became more and more controlled by several party organizations able to distribute patronage and to obtain large campaign funds.[14]

The diversity in the community structure did not totally exclude businessmen from political participation; the time had passed, however, when an individual could be elected merely on the basis of his standing within the business community. Thus, Harrison was able to defeat a movement in 1881 to nominate in his stead candidates of the highest prestige in the business world, such as Levi Z. Leiter, George L. Dunlap, and Cyrus McCormick, and he defeated the Republican John M. Clark, a leather manufacturer, who had the backing of five hundred leading businessmen.

Although the first-ranking businessmen were not elected, several considerations lead to the conclusion that ethnic identification, while important, was not sufficient to insure election to the office of mayor. Such identification had to be paired with some business success. Roche, Hopkins, Dunne, and Dyer were all only one or two generations removed from Ireland. (Of these four, three were sufficiently wealthy to be listed in the elite directory for the mid-1880's, a precursor to the Social Register.) Busse, an influential leader of the Republican party and quite prosperous, represented the large German population in Chicago. Even when business success was paired with factional strength and ethnic identification, however, the flamboyant appeal of Thompson and the Harrisons could dominate such candidates.

The election of Anton Cermak as mayor in 1931 brought an end to the Thompson era and represented the ascendancy of a party machine that was unparalleled in the history of the city. From a position at the beginning of the depression in which the balance between the two major parties in Chicago was fairly even (seven of the last twelve mayors had been Republicans), the political complexion changed such that by 1936 the Democrats were in complete control of all the governmental agencies within the territorial limits of the city of Chicago. Henceforth, the Democratic party machine was the decisive force in the selection of elected officials. No longer could the competition between the two parties or the divergent factions within them be used as a lever for political success. The route to public office was now limited to ascendancy through the party's ranks.

IV. Political Administrators: 1931–65

In many other cities the economic crisis and the community disorganization that resulted from the depression led to the introduction of political reforms and the election of rabidly antimachine candidates. In Chicago, however, the effect of the depression was to weld together the political resources of the community into the all-powerful Democratic machine. Thus, at a time when the Tammany Hall machine of New York and the Republican machine of Philadelphia were meeting severe reverses, Chicago was embracing an organization of unparalleled strength.[15] Consequently, that individual able to rise to the top of the organization or chosen by the machine to run for the office was elected to the mayoralty. Under such conditions the mayors of this period had to be, above all else, strongly connected to the local Democratic party structures.

A. Social, Occupational, and Political Characteristics

The four men who held office between 1931 and 1965 started from rather modest beginnings. They had little formal education —only Daley had college training; the others had a high school diploma or less— and started near the bottom of the occupa-

tional hierarchy—Cermak in the coal mines of Illinois, Kelly as an axeman for the Sanitary Department, Kennelly as a laborer in a warehouse, and Daley as a stockyard cowboy.

With the exception of Kennelly, the mayors after 1931 started fairly low in the party organization and served in a variety of elective positions (Cermak spent thirty-three years in elective office) before becoming mayor. Even Kennelly, who has been characterized as an outsider, had a long history of political involvement as a commissioner to the Lincoln Park Board and as a member of the Chicago Park District.

None of these four mayors was among the top leaders in the industrial, commercial, or financial activities of the city (although Cermak's banking and real-estate holdings placed him at the head of his ethnic community of Lawndale). They were not social notables, and none of them appeared in the elite directory of his time.[16] They had demonstrated administrative and managerial abilities, however. For instance, Kelly had been head of a large public-service agency, president of the South Park Board of Commissioners, and heir apparent to the machine; Daley had been the Illinois Revenue Director and Clerk of Cook County. All had shown ability to organize and direct large organizational structures. They were political rather than economic entrepreneurs.

The religious and ethnic identification of most of the Democratic mayors from Hopkins on reflects the domination of the party by Irish Catholics. With the exception of the Harrisons and Cermak, all of the Democratic mayors from 1893 to the present have been first or second-generation Irish Catholics.

Cermak, the only foreign-born Chicago mayor and, besides Busse, the only mayor to fall outside of the old-stock American, English, Scottish, or Irish groups, was able to obtain success as spokesman of the "wet" vote and the other ethnic groups making up the Democratic party. His organization and consolidation of the party, however, enabled the Irish to gain consolidated control after Cermak's death.[17]

A long and intimate participation in the life of Chicago became increasingly important for political success. Each of the ten mayors from Swift to Daley had resided in the city for more than twenty-eight years. Of these, five had been born and raised and a sixth raised in the city. The requisite sensitivity to the issues and social arrangements of the community, the necessity of an extensive network of informal social and business connections, and the lengthy party apprenticeship made residence in Chicago an imperative for political leadership.

B. Changes in Community Structure

What led to the rise of the political administrators? We must look at the motives for participating in politics. Judging from the social standing of a number of the aldermen and mayors of the pre-1930 period, political participation was accepted as a legitimate activity for the well-to-do. The activities of the "gray wolves" and the "boodle boys" during the era of the Harrisons, the open protection of a wide-open city during the Thompson period, the breaking of scandal after scandal, and the general circus atmosphere under which the political campaigns were run all led to the destruction of any social prestige that had been attached to office-holding and cast political participation in a negative light.[18] Many social and business leaders refrained from mingling in the rough and tumble of politics. Private welfare and philanthropy offered a much more respectable way of performing one's civic duties.[19] Busily engaged in building up their fortunes, fearful of alienating the populace with an unpopular political stand, and finding it much more profitable to buy the political favors they needed, the business and social elite stood at the sidelines of the political game. Furthermore, movement to the suburbs removed many of them from political scene.[20]

Even those of the economic and social elite who stayed and wished to participate would have had to do so through the party organization, for the party machine, with its mobilization of the working-class vote, financial resources, and hard core of party

workers, could afford to pick its candidate from within the organization.[21] The ward committeemen constituted the core of the party machinery. They controlled the selection of candidates for public office as well as the operation of the election machinery that elects the candidates. In order to become boss of the party one had to have the backing of the principal ward bosses of the inner city. It is not surprising, therefore, to find the ward bosses giving support to a leader whose identifications were with the inner-city wards.

Once chosen and in office, however, the mayor possessed a great deal of the coin upon which the machine is built—patronage. This resource made the mayor independent of the ward bosses and the ward bosses dependent upon him. This partially accounts for the coincidence of the mayor and the party boss being one and the same. The mayor, however, never gained complete independence—witness Kennelly's defeat when he tried to run without the support of the regular party organization in 1955—but must always have some measure of support from the ward bosses.[22] Faced with the necessity of centralized leadership, the ward bosses have chosen to follow individuals with working-class backgrounds, intimate knowledge of Chicago and the party organization, Irish Catholic identification,[23] and demonstrated administrative ability. The popular and charismatic qualities that had enabled the Harrisons and Thompson to dominate the political scene during the 1890's and 1920's would in 1950 only hinder their political aspirations. The kind of leader produced by the organization was, above all else, a political executive.

V. Conclusions

Our conclusions can best be stated by comparison and contrast with those presented by Dahl for New Haven:[24]

1. In New Haven a long and settled history prior to incorporation led to the selection of mayors from among the patrician families—families of long and established

social standing; these mayors had had legal training and extensive education. In comparison, Chicago's first mayors were drawn from its commercial leaders, regardless of family background, who were caught up in the growth and speculative investment of the community. This came about partly because Chicago's "old" families were almost non-existent but also because the commercial elite represented the driving force in the new community.

2. After 1842, New Haven's patricians gave way to the leading entrepreneurs, whether recruited from the commercial or from the industrial elite, who were to hold sway until 1900. Chicago's commercial elite were followed in the 1860's and 1870's by the transition mayors, men picked as a compromise because of the disunity and chaos of party alignments. While not unsuccessful in their occupational or social pursuits, they represented neither the commercial elite nor the local politically active.

3. In New Haven, the entrepreneurs were succeeded around 1900 by the ex-plebes, representatives of the city's recent new arrivals. In Chicago, beginning about 1880, two types of men were recruited, social notables with wide popular following and highly politically involved businessmen: men who had status in the business community, but were not from the largest firms or factories; men who had both business, political, and ethnic (Irish or German) connection. While the "ex-plebe" or at least the ethnic, label might fit some of them, ethnic politics seem not to have been as dominant a feature in their election as in that of New Haven's mayors. The diversity of ethnic groups and of the community prohibited giving the simple label of ex-plebe to these men, or to the period, until 1930.

4. Finally, with Cermak, the dominance of the Democratic party machine began. While the new mayors are "ex-plebe," the driving force in community politics becomes the machine, and the style of the mayor becomes that of the political administrator. The machine and city politics had become a full-time career. While a business career

parallel to a political one is not impossible in this era, it becomes more and more unlikely.

Dahl suggests that politics and recruitment to the mayoralty may be in a period of transformation in New Haven. Ethnicity is declining as a major criterion of political success; instead Dahl hypothesizes, the "new men" will be those who, by a concern with the fate of the city, expand their political base to the self-interested downtown businessmen and the social-welfare professional. The "new men" expand their support from ethnic organizations by becoming the leaders and initiators of programs of physical and social city renewal.

The parallel with Chicago is difficult to find. As Banfield notes, in a community as diverse as Chicago there is little development of the conditions for consensus supporting a widespread attack on city problems. In such a situation the mayor is more a referee than a combatant in the resolution of the issues facing the city.

There is a parallel of another sort, however. Even though the patronage available to Chicago mayors allows the machine to function with less concession to reform than in other cities, as in other cities there has been a transformation of the posture of its political administrator. Thus, to quote the political slogan of Mayor Richard J. Daley, "Good government is good politics."

With the assimilation of foreign immigrants, the rise of social-security measures, the introduction of civil service, and the transformation of the occupational and educational structure, the only significant source of political support in the traditional patronage-welfare exchange is the Negroes, and even they are becoming increasingly concerned with the ideological dimensions of politics.

Given this transformation of the urban setting, the present mayor of Chicago, like those in Philadelphia, New Haven, and Detroit, must represent the process of collective betterment and not the process of machine greed. A new ethos of "the good of the community" becomes dominant and shapes the administration of the mayor.

Notes

1. We are indebted to the Center for Social Organization Studies and its director, Morris Janowitz, for criticism and financial support. A small grant from the Social Science Research Committee, Division of Social Sciences, University of Chicago, helped in the early stages of the study. A critical reading by R. W. Hodge was also of great help.

   This paper was based on a more detailed manuscript prepared by Donald Bradley (Working Paper No. 10, Center for Social Organization Studies, University of Chicago, 1963 [Mimeographed]).
2. Robert A. Dahl, *Who Governs? Democracy and Power in an American City* (New Haven, Conn.: Yale University Press, 1961), pp. 1–81.
3. We recognize that precise dating of periods is risky, but it helps organize reporting of the shifts in recruitment. More important than the dates are the underlying trends.
4. Bessie L. Pierce, *A History of Chicago* (3 vols.; New York: Alfred A. Knopf, Inc., 1937, 1940, 1957), II, 305. This work was an indispensable aid to our study.
5. *Ibid.*, I, 174.
6. See Richard C. Wade, *The Urban Frontier: Pioneer Life in Early Pittsburgh, Cincinnati, Lexington, Louisville, and St. Louis* ("Phoenix Book" [Chicago: University of Chicago Press, 1964]), esp. chap. iii, pp. 72–101.
7. Pierce, *op. cit.*, II, 77–117.
8. *Ibid.*, p. 344.
9. With the incorporation of the city in 1837, in addition to an age requirement and a residence requirement of at least six months, there was a requirement that the voter have the status of householder or have paid a city tax of not less than three dollars. The property qualifications were eliminated in 1841 and the naturalization requirements were clarified in 1843, when it was explicitly stated that persons could vote whether naturalized citizens or not. This was not changed until 1871 when naturalization was made a condition of registration (A. A. Lavery [ed.], *Smith-Hurd Illinois Annotated Statutes* [Chicago: Bendette Smith Co., 1944], p. 28).
10. Ethnic politics began to play some role quite early. The charge was made that "the Irish entirely controlled" a local election of 1840 (Ogden to Edwin Crowell, August 31, 1840, *Ogden Letter Books*, II, 494).
11. Helen R. Jeter, *Trends of Population in the Region of Chicago* (Chicago: University of Chicago Press, 1927). See also Paul F. Cressy, "The Succession of Cultural Groups in Chicago" (unpublished Ph.D. disserta-tion, University of Chicago, 1930); Pierce, *op. cit.*, III, 20–64; Charles E. Merriam, *Chicago: A More Intimate View of Urban Politics* (New York: Macmillan Co., 1929), pp. 134–77.
12. See Merriam, *op. cit.*, and Lincoln Steffens, *The Autobiography of Lincoln Steffens* (New York: Harcourt, Brace & Co., 1931), pp. 422–29, for a description of the political system at this time.
13. There is some evidence to suggest that the Republican party was more influenced by the business element of the city than was the Democratic party. Every one of the Republican mayors elected during this period could be found listed in the executive directory of their time, in contrast to the Democratic candidates, only one of whom was listed.
14. Merriam, *op. cit.*, pp. 97–98.
15. Harold F. Gosnell accounts for the ascendancy of the Chicago machine by referring to an "unfavorable press situation, a lack of leadership, and the character of the party division at the beginning of the depression" (*Machine Politics: Chicago Model* [Chicago: University of Chicago Press, 1937]).
16. This lack of representation of the "silk stocking" element is also reflected in the city council. Of the thirty-four aldermen on the council in 1900, five were listed in the *Chicago Social Directory* for that year. By 1935, of the fifty men who sat on the council, not one was listed. This lack of representation of the "better class" has continued so that in 1965 there is still no alderman to be found in the listed elite of Chicago.
17. Alex Gottfried, *Boss Cermak of Chicago: A Study of Political Leadership* (Seattle: University of Washington Press, 1962).
18. The following volumes give colorful, if at times overly journalistic, accounts of the history of Chicago's political and social reputation: John Bright, *Hizzoner Big Bill Thompson, an Idyll of Chicago* (New York: J. Cape & H. Smith, 1930); Fletcher Dobyns, *The Underworld of American Politics* (New York: privately printed, 1932); Lloyd Lewis and Henry Smith, *Chicago: The History of Its Reputation* (New York: Harcourt, Brace & Co., 1929); Merriam, *op. cit.*; William H. Stuart, *The Twenty Incredible Years* (Chicago: M. A. Donahue & Co., 1935).
19. Much of the motivation dynamics operating in Chicago is similar to that found by Lynd and Merrill in Middletown (Robert S. Lynd and Helen Merrill, *Middletown: A Study in Modern American Culture* [New York: Harcourt, Brace & Co., 1929], p. 421).
20. William R. Gable, "The Chicago City Coun-

cil: A Study of Urban Politics and Legislation" (unpublished Ph.D. dissertation, University of Chicago, 1953), p. 10.
21. It should be noted that, while the socially
and economically advantaged moved out of
the city and into the suburbs, their places
were taken by the migrants from the agrarian
areas of the North and South (chiefly
southern Negroes and whites), immigrants
from Puerto Rico and other Latin American
countries, and occasional immigrants from
Europe. Thus the often-predicted changing
class character of urban politics and the
resulting decline in machine dominance has
been postponed in Chicago. See Part V of
Edward C. Banfield (ed.), *Urban Government: A Reader in Administration and Politics* (Glencoe, Ill.: Free Press, 1961); especially relevant in this regard are Samuel
Lubell, "The New Middle Class" (pp. 301-
8) and Frank J. Sorauf, "The Silent Revolution in Patronage" (pp. 308-17).
22. Our analysis draws heavily on Edward C.

Banfield's *Political Influence* (Glencoe, Ill.:
Free Press, 1961).
23. A comment on the success of the Irish: both
in the city council and in the party hierarchy,
the religious similarity between the Irish and
the other nationality groups (the principal
ethnic groups in the Democratic party, in
descending order of importance, were the
Poles, Italians, Bohemians, Lithuanians,
Slovaks, and Greeks) and the fact that in a
city which has no one single ethnic group
in a clear majority, the Irish upset the community balance least, made the Irish Catholics the most logical and acceptable candidates. As one investigator quotes a politician:
"A Lithuanian won't vote for a Pole, and
a Pole won't vote for a Lithuanian. A
German won't vote for either of them, but
all three will vote for a 'Turkey' [Irishman]"
(Martin Meyerson and E. C. Banfield, "A
Machine at Work," in Banfield [ed.], *op.
cit.*, p. 136).
24. Dahl, *op. cit.*, pp. 11-64.

The Role of Economic Dominants in Community Power Structure[*]

Robert O. Schulze

That persons occupying positions of economic importance are among the key wielders
of local influence and control has long been
one of the most commonplace assumptions
of American sociologists and one of the
most consistent findings of research concerned with American communities and
community power structures.[1] With very
few exceptions, however, most studies
relevant to the role of economic dominants
in community control structures have focused
on current power configurations. Relatively

little research attention has yet been devoted
to historical shifts in local power structures
associated with metropolitan and bureaucratic drift of American life.[2] Likewise,
while most relevant studies have indicated
that a considerable number of persons of
significant local influence are men of
economic substance, they have not revealed
the pattern of community involvement (nor
changes in that pattern) of the economically
most-powerful considered as a category.
Thus, we have heard a good deal about the

Reprinted from the American Sociological Review, *23 (February 1958), 3-9, by permission of the
author and the American Sociological Association. Copyright 1958 by the American Sociological
Association.*

*Expanded version of paper read at the annual meeting of the American Sociological Society,
August, 1957. I wish to thank Morris Janowitz and Melvin Reichler, both of the University of
Michigan, for their helpful comments on this paper.

activities and influence of the "X" family and its equivalents in American communities, but rather less about the "Y" families, and almost nothing at all about the ratio of "Xs" to "Ys" either currently or over time.

This paper reports some findings of an investigation of the power structure of a middle-sized American community—findings concerned primarily with the historical role of the economic dominants in that community's power structure.[3] Although the study has among its numerous limitations those inevitable in any piece of single-community research, it is hoped that it might be theoretically and methodologically suggestive for research in other communities, especially those which—like the subject of this study—have become satellites in a society increasingly dominated by giant metropolitan centers and large national corporations.

The rudimentary theory underlying this research may be briefly summarized. The basic assumption was that as the functional relationship of the community to the larger society changes, so does the nature and form of its control structure, and so, too, does the role of its economic dominants in that structure.

It was hypothesized that in the community *relatively* self-contained and uninvolved in the larger social and economic system, the community with few and scattered commitments beyond its borders, local power would tend to be structured as a pyramid and heavily concentrated at the apex. More specifically, it was surmised that those persons who exercised major control over the community's economic system would tend to be the same persons who exercised preponderant control over its socio-political system, and that this latter control would be reflected, at least in part, by their active leadership and participation in the political and civic life of the community.

With increasing urbanization and as the community passed beyond what Lloyd Warner has called "the period of local capitalism"[4] however, it was suggested that the economic dominants would begin to withdraw their interest and active attention

from the local socio-political system. Although the major economic units would have grown in size and potential influence, it was hypothesized that several factors would militate against the effective exercise, the actual "cashing-in" of their power in the community. The most significant of these would be the fact that the local community would have become ever less important to the survival and prosperity of its dominant economic units. As the activities of these units became increasingly directed toward—and by—populations and groups other than the local ones, the relevance of local community organizations and the impact of local political influences on the major economic units would accordingly diminish. As this occurred, the local power structure would in effect, bifurcate—with those who exercised primary direction over its socio-political system no longer being essentially the same set of persons who exercised primary control over its economic system.[5]

An effort was made to test this general theory in Cibola, a Midwestern industrial community of some 20,000 inhabitants, located approximately 30 miles from Metro City, one of the nation's largest metropolitan centers. Founded in 1823, Cibola grew rather slowly until World War II. Between 1940 and 1950, however, its population increased over 50 per cent, a shift symptomatic of countless other changes to which the community has lately been subject. One of the principal changes has been the gradual absorption of its major industrial plants by large, absentee-owned corporations, a trend sharply accelerated during the World War II period.

In our research, we attempted to reconstruct Cibola's economic dominants from the time of its founding in 1823 until 1955, and to determine the general nature and extent of their overt involvement in the political and civic life of the community.

The economic dominants for the various historical periods were operationally-defined as those persons who: (a) occupied the top formal roles in the largest industries and banks in the community; or (b) were members of the boards of directors of two or more of these industries and banks, thus serving formally to "interlock" the dominant economic units; or (c) were the largest property-owners in the community.[6]

Insofar as local involvement was reflected by occupancy of formal offices in the political and civic organizations in the community, the research tended clearly to support the basic hypothesis. *The historical drift has been characterized by the withdrawal of the economic dominants from active and overt participation in the public life of Cibola.* Tables 1, 3, and 4 are presented to illustrate this withdrawal.

Table 1 indicates that prior to the turn of the century, fully four-fifths of Cibola's economic dominants held public office in the community, while since 1900, the proportion has declined to approximately one-quarter.[7] Likewise, as shown in Table 3, the proportion of economic dominants who have held the top political office in Cibola has sharply diminished. Not indicated in either

of these two tables is the fact that *none* of the most recent type of economic dominant—the managers of the absentee-owned corporations—has held any public office (elective or appointive) in the community.

There was some evidence that in the early decades of this century the arena of active local involvement of Cibola's economic dominants shifted from politics to the important voluntary associations. Even in this area, however, an appreciable subsequent diminution of active participation has been apparent—perhaps best reflected by the declining number of dominants holding responsible office in the community's most influential association, the local Chamber of Commerce.

It is suggested that the withdrawal of the economic dominants was primarily a consequence of the changing relationship of the community's economic system to that of the larger society. Prior to about 1900, three aspects of Cibola's economic life were

TABLE 1. *Number and Per Cent of Economic Dominants in Public Office, 1823–1954 Periods*

PERIOD	NUMBER OF ECONOMIC DOMINANTS	NUMBER OF ECONOMIC DOMINANTS IN PUBLIC OFFICE	PER CENT OF ECONOMIC DOMINANTS IN PUBLIC OFFICE
1823–1860	12	10	83
1860–1900	21	17	81
1900–1940	43	12	28
1940–1954	31	7	23

TABLE 2. *Changes in Number of Economic Dominants and Number of Available Offices, 1823–1954 Periods*

PERIOD	PERCENTAGE CHANGE IN NUMBER OF ECONOMIC DOMINANTS	PERCENTAGE CHANGE IN NUMBER OF PUBLIC OFFICES IN CITY GOVERNMENT
From 1823–1860 to 1860–1900 periods	plus 75	plus 80
From 1860–1900 to 1900–1940 periods	plus 105	plus 183
From 1900–1940 to 1940–1954 periods	minus 28	minus 30

especially notable: (a) all of its economic dominants were local residents; (b) all of its dominant economic units were locally-owned; and (c) the majority of its dominants were associated in extensive economic networks *within* the community.

Our research established that in the pre-1900 period, almost 70 per cent of the economic dominants had known business or financial ties—as partners, co-officers or co-directors—with other dominants in the community. Thus, throughout most of Cibola's history, its "average" economic dominant was not only a local resident, or merely the head of a single major economic unit; he was also directly and indirectly linked with a considerable number of other major economic units and dominants within the community.

Combined, these factors provided most economic dominants with deep, branching roots in Cibola. The business and financial links, in particular, afforded many of them a basis for shared concern in the local community. The economic networks served to weld together blocs of dominants, giving them frequent and specific occasion for interpersonal contact. By the same token, the very diversity of the "average" dominant's local economic commitments meant that there was always a variety of areas and methods in which local political considerations could impinge upon his pecuniary and related interests. The evidence suggests that these considerations were closely associated with the high incidence of involvement by economic dominants in the socio-political system of the community.

TABLE 3. *Number and Per Cent of Economic Dominants in Office of Village President or Mayor, 1823–1954 Periods*

PERIOD	NUMBER OF DOMINANTS IN OFFICE OF VILLAGE PRESIDENT OR MAYOR	PER CENT OF DOMINANTS IN OFFICE OF VILLAGE PRESIDENT OR MAYOR	PER CENT OF "POLITICALLY-ACTIVE" DOMINANTS IN OFFICE OF VILLAGE PRESIDENT OR MAYOR*
1823–1860	5	42	50
1860–1900	7	33	41
1900–1940	2	5	17
1940–1954	1	3	14

*"Politically-Active": All those economic dominants who had held *any* public office.

TABLE 4. *Number of Economic Dominants in Offices of the Chamber of Commerce, 1920–1955**

PERIOD	MEDIAN NUMBER OF MEMBERSHIPS PER YEAR ON BOARD OF DIRECTORS	NUMBER SERVING AS PRESIDENT
1920–1927	6	3
1927–1934	3	2
1934–1941	3	0
1941–1948	2	1
1948–1955	1	0

*The Cibola Chamber of Commerce was founded in 1920. From that date until 1953, the number of directors was fifteen; in the latter year, the number was increased to eighteen. Directors serve two-year terms and are eligible for reelection.

The period since 1900, and more particularly, since 1930, has been marked by the increasing absorption of the local economic system into the larger industrial complex, especially that of Metro City. While several complex social factors were patently involved, the following three seem most closely related to the eventual withdrawal of the economic dominants from active participation in the political-civic life of Cibola: (a) the establishment by a growing number of locally-owned industrial units of direct supplier relationships with a small number of large, non-local manufacturing plants; (b) the subsequent introduction into the local economic system of an increasing number of branch plants of large absentee-owned corporations; and (c) the concomitant dissolution of the extensive networks of inter-locking director and officerships which had formerly served to link significant numbers of local economic dominants within the community.

Consequently, the overt direction of the political and civic life of Cibola has passed almost wholly into the hands of a group of middle-class business and professional men, almost none of whom occupies a position of economic dominance in the community. That this has in fact been the case was suggested in another aspect of our research by the finding that only two of Cibola's seventeen current economic dominants were perceived by the local voluntary association heads to have been among the eighteen most influential leaders in the community.[8] And both of these two, by the way, were heads of relatively small, locally-owned economic units.

Patently, these data reveal changes only in the level of overt and manifest involvement of the economic dominants in the local power structure. It may be suggested, of course, that covertly—"behind-the-scenes" —the economic dominants continue to exercise considerable direction and control of community affairs. However, the findings of another part of our research strongly suggest that things may, in fact, be what they seem.

In an effort to view the community power structure "in action," we endeavored to determine the patterns and processes of local decision-making in a series of recent community episodes (including a successful campaign to change the structure of municipal government from a mayor-aldermen to a city manager form, and an ambitious but unsuccessful annexation effort).[9] Our findings in this aspect of the research forced us to conclude that the recent economic dominants —and especially those representing the growing number of large, absentee-owned corporations—appear indeed to have dissociated themselves from active involvement in Cibola's power structure.

These episodes reflected a growing adherence on the part of the absentee-owned corporations in Cibola to a "hands-off" position with regard to local political decision-making. And while it cannot be conclusively documented within the limits of the present paper, this evolving policy is graphically suggested by presenting excerpts from interviews with several executives in the larger economic units.

The general manager of the second largest manufacturing plant in the community, commenting on our findings that but two of the top ten officials in his plant actually resided in Cibola, stated:

> That's a sore spot with me. I've always felt that if I'm going to work in a town, I ought to live there. But there's no consensus on that by a long ways. It's been discussed at the highest levels in our corporation—I know because I've been on the company's community relations committee ever since it was set up. The company has decided that it won't encourage its executives to live in the communities where they work if they don't already or if they don't want to. . . . The company doesn't feel its people—at least its executives—have to live in a town in order to have good community relations. Just about the opposite, as a matter of fact. You're always subject to a hell of a lot of local pressures if you're there. If they know where you are, you're always a target. So maybe it's better not to be in a position to be asked to do something than to have to say, "No."

In discussing the paucity of both formal and informal contacts between corporation officials and local leaders, the assistant general manager of the largest industrial plant in Cibola said:

> No, I've almost never gone downtown for lunch "with the boys." I sometimes get my hair cut in [Cibola], but outside of that I don't show my face any more than I feel I absolutely have to. . . . The people at the Chamber of Commerce seem to fall all over themselves trying to do anything we want— but the point is, we don't really *want* anything there except for the people to have a good opinion of us. But mostly due to this placating attitude of the town's leaders, I'm afraid to say much or be around much.

The corporations were interested, to be sure (as the title of one company's "kit for divisional executives" indicated) in "Making Friends for [U.S. Motors] in the Local Community," but a growing number of them were coming to regard "making friends" and "getting involved" as inconsonant. The general manager of another large plant summed up his attitude:

> One sure way to give [our firm] a black eye would be for me to get myself into things so deeply in town that no matter what I did, I'd end up alienating a lot of people.

And another:

> You've got to remember that what I do doesn't affect us just here. The guy who represents our company in this area could affect our reputation a lot of other places as well. . . . Why, if I went out and got myself [involved] in local politics, you'd see a new boy in these shoes so damned fast it'd make your head swim.

Meaningful participation in the decision-making processes of a community such as Cibola was mainly regarded by these corporations as entailing risks to their operations as to their positions in the larger social system—risks which could not be offset by any palpable advantages which might accrue to them through playing significant roles in the local power structure. They were clearly cognizant, for example, of the possibility that involvement by their executives in local affairs might induce conflicting loyalties.

Likewise, their executives recognized that decisive involvement in critical community decisions posed the threat of alienating significant superiors and publics at the extra-community level, thus endangering their larger occupational and public relations objectives. It seems tenable that it was the very sensitivity of the large corporations to socio-political determinations at the regional and national levels which militated against their involvement in these matters at the level of the local community.

The central finding of the Cibola study— the bifurcation of the community's power structure, stemming from the withdrawal of the economic dominants from active direction of the political and civic life of the community—appears quite generally to corroborate the investigation of Peter Rossi and his associates of the changing patterns of political participation in a middle-sized industrial community in New England.[10] Likewise, our findings seem to be consistent with C. Wright Mills' observations regarding the altered position of large economic units in the power structures of local communities.[11] On the other hand, the Cibola findings do not appear consistent with Hunter's research in Regional City, nor, especially, with that of Pellegrin and Coates in Bigtown.[12]

In addition to the obvious and perhaps significant differences in the sizes of the several communities involved, it will be noted that Hunter and Pellegrin and Coates studied the structures and dynamics of community power in Southern cities, while Rossi's and the present research concern New England and Midwestern communities, respectively. In correspondence with the writer, Pellegrin has suggested that the disparate findings may be largely the function of regional differences: the historical tradition of paternalism being perhaps stronger in the South than in the North. It has also been suggested that economic dominants may become involved in community power structures independent of the desires of their economic units to guide or influence local decision-making. Thus, for example, to the extent that economic dominants represent the wealthier interests in the community and are a major source of voluntary donations to local charities and similar activities, they may be coopted into decision structures by those actively "in charge" in order to reinforce the latter's control positions and to guarantee a continued source of contributions. Likewise, to the extent that the economic dominants represent the upper prestige levels in a community, they may be drawn into the control structure by the active community leaders in an effort by the latter to legitimize their own prestige positions.

It should be noted, however, that both of the foregoing hypothetical instances cast the economic dominants in the role of rather reluctant participants in local power structures. In such situations, it would be *other* members of the community, not the economic dominants nor the dominant economic units themselves, who would have most stake in the latter's local involvement. And this, in turn, would have, perhaps, significant

ramifications for the kinds of roles which the economic dominants played in community power structures and for the degree of interest and local concern with which they acted out these roles.

Whatever the reasons for the apparent differences in the nature and extent of economic dominant involvement in local power structures—and the delineation of these reasons should certainly be one objective of future research—the Cibola study appears to document the absence of any neat, constant, and direct relationship between *power as a potential for determinative action*, and *power as determinative action, itself*. It suggests, likewise, the need to re-examine the role of economic dominance in community power structures in view of the continued drift of American society, on the one hand, toward the concentration of population in suburban and satellite communities, and, on the other, toward the continuing expansion of huge economic bureaucracies.

Notes

1. In addition to the well-known works of the Lynds, Warner, Hollingshead, Mills, and Hunter, see Roland J. Pellegrin and Charles H. Coates, "Absentee-Owned Corporations and Community Power Structure," *American Journal of Sociology*, 61, 5 (March, 1956), pp. 413–419; George Belknap and Ralph Smuckler, "Political Power Relations in a Mid-West City," *Public Opinion Quarterly*, 20, 1 (Spring, 1956), pp. 73–81; A. Alexander Fanelli, "A Typology of Community Leadership Based on Influence and Interaction Within the Leader Subsystem," *Social Forces*, 34, 4 (May, 1956), pp. 332–338; Robert E. Agger, "Power Attributions in the Local Community," *ibid.*, pp. 322–331; Peter Rossi, "Historical Trends in the Politics of an Industrial Community," paper presented at the 51st annual meeting of the American Sociological Society, September, 1956.
2. Rossi's study is a notable exception.
3. Robert O. Schulze, *Economic Dominance and Public Leadership: A Study of the Structure and Process of Power in an Urban Community*, microfilmed Ph.D. dissertation, University of Michigan, 1956. (University Microfilms, Publication No. 21,359.)
4. W. Lloyd Warner and J. O. Low, "The

Factory in the Community," in William Foote Whyte (ed.), *Industry and Society*, New York: McGraw-Hill, 1946, p. 35.
5. It is not suggested that the decline in the economic dominants' leadership and participation in community decision-making processes stems wholly from their diminishing concern with local affairs. With their attenuation of local involvement, it is obvious that effective contact and meaningful communication between economic dominants and diverse elements of the community population are likewise reduced, contributing to what has been referred to as the loss of "multi-class leadership" by the top business groups in American communities. In such a situation, economic dominants—when they occasionally may want to influence community decisions—may find that their local leadership base has so shrunken that their effectiveness is impaired. Somewhat illustrative of this was the case of Cal Lamkin, the general manager of a large industrial plant in the community studied. Long inactive in local political and voluntary associational affairs, Lamkin was eventually prevailed upon to stand for election to the board of directors of the local Chamber of

Commerce. To the considerable embarrassment of the Chamber's officials, however, Lamkin failed to muster sufficient votes to win a seat on the board. Cf. Wilbert E. Moore, *Industrial Relations and the Social Order*, New York: The Macmillan Company, 1951, pp. 547–553. Although presented in causal terms somewhat different from those suggested in this paper, the best known and perhaps most sanguine statement of the American business elites' loss of multi-group leadership is contained in Kenneth Galbraith, *American Capitalism and the Concept of Countervailing Power*, Boston: Houghton, Mifflin, 1952.

6. Specific criteria for classification as an economic dominant in each historical period were based on such measures as number of employees (industries), capital worth (banks), and assessed valuation of holdings (property-owners). Various source data were utilized in the determination of these measures, including county tax records, city directories and histories, newspapers, records of individual companies and of the Chamber of Commerce and the State Historical Collections, plus such standard references as *Poor's Register of Directors and Executives* and *Polk's Bank Directory*.

7. It might be suggested that the declining proportion of economic dominants in public office was a function of the fact that the number of dominants increased at a greater rate than the number of available offices, and therefore, that the declining proportions are spurious. This was not the case. Changes in the number of economic dominants throughout the four periods were very closely paralleled by proportionately similar changes in the number of available public offices. (See Table 2.)

8. The heads of 143 voluntary associations in Cibola were asked a series of five questions intended to elicit their perceptions of the most influential leaders in the community. On the basis of their total "nominations," the eighteen most-frequently cited persons were designated as the "public leaders" of Cibola. See Robert O. Schulze and Leonard U. Blumberg, "The Determination of Local Power Elites," *American Journal of Sociology*, 63, 3 (November, 1957), pp. 290–296.

9. In these reconstructions, a variety of source materials was utilized, including intensive interviews with the seventeen current economic dominants, the eighteen persons perceived by the 143 local voluntary association heads as the community's most influential leaders, and a selected number of informants. In addition, relevant newspaper files, Chamber of Commerce records and reports, and city council minutes were reviewed.

10. Rossi, *op. cit.*

11. C. Wright Mills, *The Power Elite*, New York: Oxford University Press, 1956.

12. Floyd Hunter, *Community Power Structure*, Chapel Hill: University of North Carolina Press, 1953; Pellegrin and Coates, *op. cit.*

Economic Dominants and Community Power: A Comparative Analysis[1]

Donald A. Clelland and William H. Form

Introduction

Three avenues to the study of American community power structure have received widest attention during the last decade. The earliest approach studied a single set of community influentials who allegedly made the major community decisions.[2] Adherents of this method have generally concluded that business leaders are the "ruling elite" or at least *primi inter pares* in the community power structure. The second method discerned the power structure

Reprinted from The American Journal of Sociology, *69 (March 1964), 511–521, by permission of the authors and The University of Chicago Press. Copyright 1964 by The University of Chicago.*

by examining how specific persons and groups behaved in specific community issues and decisions.[3] Those using this technique have generally found a pluralistic system of decision-making. The third avenue has investigated the forces changing the character of persons holding positions of potential power.[4] Irrespective of approach, an ideological question has been persistent—whether the community is governed informally by an economic elite or whether the dominant pattern is political pluralism, a situation where decision-makers represent groups with differing interests.

One instructive way of posing this controversy is to ask what types of relationships characterize the stratification orders in American communities in the past and in the present.[5] More specifically, the sociological question is: To what extent has private economic power been translated directly into community or public power? Although R. O. Schulze did not formally place his research within the Weberian framework, operationally he did study the question we have posed by tracing historically the place of economically powerful figures in the public life of Cibola.[6] The study reported here attempts to replicate his investigation in a different type of community, which we shall call "Wheelsburg."

Schulze's findings upheld his hypothesis that as a city grows from an isolated, self-contained entity to an urbanized community "increasingly involved and interrelated in the large social complex," its sociopolitical power structure changes from a monolithic one dominated by persons possessing great economic power to a bifurcated structure comprising "two crucial and relatively discrete power sets, the economic dominants and the public leaders."[7] Economic dominants were defined as "those persons who occupy the top formal statuses in the major economic units within the community area,"[8] and public leaders (or top influentials) as those who, in the opinion of community "knowledgeables," exercise major influence and leadership in community affairs.[9]

Schulze tentatively explained the dissociation of economic dominants from local political-civic affairs by the following three trends:

(a) the establishment by a growing number of locally-owned industrial units of direct supplier relationships with a small number of large, non-local manufacturing plants; (b) the subsequent introduction into the local economic system of an increasing number of branch plants of large, absentee-owned corporations; and (c) the concomitant dissolution of the extensive networks of interlocking directorates and officerships which had formerly served to link significant numbers of local economic dominants within the community.[10]

These trends have also occurred in Wheelsburg, but to a more limited degree. The greatest variation between Cibola and Wheelsburg is in the first factor, because in Wheelsburg many local supply plants were established to serve the local automobile firms.

Comparison of the Communities

The two communities differ significantly in a number of ways. For most of its history Cibola was a small independent town. It is now a satellite city of approximately 20,000 inhabitants located just beyond the Standard Metropolitan Area of a large midwest industrial center containing more than 3,000,000 people. The five largest of its eight major industrial plants were absentee-controlled. Cibola is an extreme example of a city that "has felt the full impact of the metropolitan drift of American life."[11] A period of rapid expansion began during World War II with the establishment just outside the city's boundaries of a gigantic war-production plant which employed over 40,000 workers at its peak. After the war the economic instability of absentee-owned companies occupying this plant caused wide and rapid fluctuations in the local labor force. Consequently, during the 1940's the community experienced rapid fluctuation and high turnover in population. At the time of Schulze's study employment at the main plant had leveled off at 9,500 as it became tied securely to the motor vehicle industry.

Wheelsburg is located about 60 miles west of Cibola. It is an independent city of over 100,000 dominating a metropolitan area with a population of approximately 180,000. Like Cibola, its economy is based primarily on motor vehicle production. In fact, the same motor vehicle company is the largest single employer in both communities. In Wheelsburg the company employs nearly 15,000 workers. However, significant sections of Wheelsburg's labor force are employed in state government and in a nearby state university. Wheelsburg's period of most rapid industrial and population growth occurred earlier than Cibola's, between 1900 and 1920. This growth largely reflected the success of locally owned automobile and supplier plants. Since 1920 Wheelburg's growth has been moderate and steady even with the large invasion of absentee-owned companies. Such companies came earlier to Wheelsburg, but entered and grew more gradually than in Cibola.

Currently, thirteen of the twenty non-financial dominant economic units are absentee-controlled.[12] Unlike Cibola, (a) Wheelsburg's major firms have been fairly stable operations, (b) the vast majority of its labor force has always been employed within the city limits, (c) very few of its economic dominants have lived beyond the city's contiguous suburbs, and (d) the city is removed from the influence of a large competing metropolis. Wheelsburg, then, is a much more stable and "normal" type of community setting in which to test Schulze's hypothesis.

Following Schulze's method closely, we tested his main hypothesis by (1) reconstructing the formal participation patterns of economic dominants over the past century in the political and civic activities of the community; (2) ascertaining the representation of current economic dominants among public leaders, that is, in the "reputational" power structure; and (3) analyzing the role of current economic dominants in specific community issues and programs.

Economic Dominants as Political and Civic Leaders

In Wheelsburg, as in Cibola, the proportion of economic dominants who occupied high local governmental offices declined dramatically over the century. Data in Tables 1 and 2 reveal that in both communities prior to 1900 the economic dominants were highly represented in local government. The comparable percentages in each table are virtually identical. Although the twentieth century ushered in a sharp decline in the proportion of economic dominants holding public office in both communities, this decline was sharper in Wheelsburg than in Cibola. Moreover, in both cities, but especially in Wheelsburg, the offices held by economic dominants have been increasingly appointive rather than elective. Indeed, no economic dominant has served as mayor since 1899, or as councilman since 1932.

The trend of these developments in Wheelsburg may be seen more clearly by examining the data in terms of twenty-year periods. A precipitous decline in public officeholding by economic dominants occurred in the 1900–1920 period, with relatively little change thereafter. However, there has been a continuing change in the type of office held. In each succeeding twenty-year period, fewer of the economic dominants who held office were elected. Increasingly, they have come to hold advisory and honorary positions in local government. Since it is probably fair to assume that the power potential of appointive offices is less than that of elective offices, the shift of economic dominants from the latter may be taken as evidence of continuing loss of formal political power.

Schulze suggests that after 1900 the arena of local involvement of the economic dominants shifted from politics to voluntary associations. The Wheelsburg data confirm his observation. Thus data in Table 3 show that at the beginning the economic dominants were highly represented among the members and officers of the Chamber of Commerce, and that their representation declined at a later era. Apparently the Wheelsburg

TABLE 1. *Economic Dominants Serving in Public Office in Wheelsburg and Cibola*

	No. of	Per Cent			
PERIOD	ECONOMIC DOMINANTS	IN PUBLIC OFFICE	IN ELECTIVE OFFICE	ON GOVERNING BODY	IN HIGHEST PUBLIC OFFICE
1823–60:					
Wheelsburg*	—	—	—	—	—
Cibola	12	83	83	75	50
1860–1900:					
Wheelsburg	44	73	64	57	30
Cibola	21	81	67	57	33
1900–1940:					
Wheelsburg	80	25	11	4	0
Cibola	43	26	16	12	5
1940–59:					
Wheelsburg	71	14	0	0	0
Cibola	31	23	13	10	3

*Wheelsburg was not incorporated until 1859.
SOURCE: Cibola data, see Schulze, "The Bifurcation of Power [in a Satellite City," in *Community Political Systems*, ed. Morris Janowitz (Glencoe, Ill.: Free Press, 1961),] pp. 37–38.

TABLE 2. *Offices Held by Politically Active Economic Dominants in Wheelsburg and Cibola**

	No. of POLITICALLY ACTIVE ECONOMIC DOMINANTS	Per Cent		
PERIOD		IN ELECTIVE OFFICE	ON GOVERNING BODY	IN HIGHEST PUBLIC OFFICE
1823–1860:				
Wheelsburg	—	—	—	—
Cibola	10	100	90	60
1860–1900:				
Wheelsburg	32	88	78	41
Cibola	17	88	71	41
1900–1940:				
Wheelsburg	20	45	15	0
Cibola	12	64	45	18
1940–1959:				
Wheelsburg	10	0	0	0
Cibola	7	57	43	14

*"Politically active" refers to economic dominants holding any appointive or elective office.
SOURCE: Cibola data, see Schulze, "The Bifurcation of Power . . .," *op. cit.*, pp. 37–38.

economic dominants were even more powerful in the Chamber than their Cibola counterparts, for one of their number was president during nineteen of the first twenty years of the organization's existence. During the past two decades their representation in the Chamber has declined, but not so sharply as in Cibola. An historical analysis of the proportion of officerships held by Wheelsburg economic dominants in other civic organizations (major service clubs, community chest, and the board of trustees of the leading local hospital) reveals patterns of withdrawal similar to that evident in Table 3. While it is difficult to estimate the power potential of these officerships, current public leaders or top influentials regard the Chamber of Commerce as the single most influential organization in the city. Yet, as indicated above, direct control of this

TABLE 3. *Economic Dominants as Board Members of Chamber of Commerce*

PERIOD	MEDIAN NO. OF MEMBERSHIPS PER YEAR ON BOARD OF DIRECTORS*		NO. SERVING AS PRESIDENT	
	Wheels-burg	Cibola	Wheels-burg	Cibola
1901–6	8	—	3	—
1906–13	9	—	4	—
1913–20	9	—	4	—
1920–27	10	6	3	3
1927–34	9	3	2	2
1934–41	9	3	2	0
1941–48	4	2	0	1
1948–55	3	1	3	0
1955–59	5	—	0	—

*The number of directors varied from 15 to 18 in Cibola and from 15 to 21 in Wheelsburg.
SOURCE: Cibola data, Schulze, "The Bifurcation of Power . . .," *op. cit.*, p. 49. Since the Cibola Chamber was founded in 1920, there are no data for earlier periods.

organization by economic dominants has probably declined over the years.

In both Wheelsburg and Cibola economic dominants reduced their incumbency in public offices at the turn of the century. A similar withdrawal from civic leadership positions began about 1940.[13] A comparative analysis of the economic development of the two communities corroborates some of Schulze's explanations and contradicts others. The evidence fails to support Schulze's position that the growth of absentee ownership and the dissolution of local business ties (interlocking directorates) among the economic dominants account for their withdrawal from public office. In both communities these phenomena occurred *after* the withdrawal; in Cibola, the first absentee-controlled plant was established in 1932, and in Wheelsburg as late as 1940 two-thirds of the major economic units were locally owned. Moreover, 80 per cent of the Wheelsburg economic dominants maintained local business ties with other economic dominants as late as 1940. A third factor which Schulze associated with withdrawal, namely, the growth of direct supplier relationships to non-local industries by locally owned plants, must also

be discarded, for in Wheelsburg no such growth took place and yet the pattern of withdrawal was similar to that of Cibola. Moreover, in Wheelsburg this withdrawal does not seem to have been forced by the growing political power of ethnic groups as was the case in many American cities.[14] There has never been a large ethnic proletariat in Wheelsburg, nor have local politics ever been heavily based on ethnic lines or class conflict.

What factors, then, are associated with the sharp decline in political participation by economic dominants (i.e., the bifurcation of political and economic power structure) since the turn of the century? At the broadest level of explanation, the increased involvement of the community and its economic units in state and nationwide social economic systems was, no doubt, an important factor. More specifically, in Wheelsburg, the end of the period in which political and economic power tended to coincide was marked by the rise of a new breed of economic elite, namely, managers and owners of the new automobile and supply plants. Younger, wealthier, operating larger businesses, more directly involved in the day-to-day operation of their businesses, introducing a wide variety of new products, these men did not participate in local politics probably largely because they lacked the time and because they probably found that business was much more exciting. A growing separation of wealth and social honor may have been a second factor, but the new economic elite was partly based on old local wealth and the majority were entrepreneurs rather than simply managers of companies financed by non-local capital. However, in the absence of ethnic and class cleavage in the community, it is doubtful that the new economic dominants, many of whom were classed Horatio Alger success models, lacked the popularity needed for election. They probably did not choose to run.

On the other hand, later withdrawal from civic leadership positions seems to be associated with the introduction of absentee-owned plants and the related decrease in common local business ties (interlocking directorates) among the economic dominants. The importance of the latter factor is underscored in Wheelsburg where economic dominants not only have more local economic linkages but also comprise a larger proportion of the local civic leaders.[15]

The so-called pattern of withdrawal needs to be interpreted within a broad context of the local participation. In Wheelsburg, the historical pattern has been for the economic dominants to become officers of new organizations as they emerged in the community, then to retain membership, and later to withdraw from active participation. Thus when the Chamber of Commerce was created, dominants were its earliest officers; when the service clubs arose they again became officers; when the Community Chest arrived they became its sponsors and officers; and they sponsored the largest hospital and dominated its board. This pattern of domination and later "withdrawal" is subject to various interpretations. We are inclined to believe that it demonstrates two related phenomena: (a) assumption of officerships in new organizations validated not only their importance to the community but the power and status of the original officers, namely, the economic dominants, and (b) the policies, direction, and administration of the new organizations were set and institutionalized by the original officers. After this initial period the organizations needed only informal and non-official guidance from the dominants and not their active officeholding. In other words, a change in officers did not necessarily mean a change in policy or loss of power and control by dominants.[16]

Community Influence of Economic Dominants

In order to assess the community influence of current economic dominants in Wheelsburg, two procedures were used. First, their reputational influence was investigated by assessing their representation in the list of public leaders (community influentials as determined by the method outlined in

n. 9). Second, their "actual" influence was probed by examining their role in a number of community issues or projects.

In 1958–59, thirty-nine individuals were found to be economic dominants, and coincidentally, thirty-nine people were designated as public leaders. The names of twelve persons (31 per cent) appeared on both lists. This overlap is considerably higher than that found in Cibola where only two of seventeen economic dominants were among the community's eighteen public leaders. Moreover, eight of the top fifteen public leaders in Wheelsburg, including the top four, as rated by the public leaders themselves, were economic dominants. Although major absentee-owned corporations were "underrepresented" among the economic dominants who were also public leaders, "U.S. Motors" (the absentee-owned industrial giant in the community) was represented by three executives (two of whom were not defined as economic dominants). From these observations we cannot conclude that two discrete power sets are found in Wheelsburg.

In order to substantiate the basic dissimilarities between the economic dominants and public leaders in Cibola, Schulze examined their patterns of political and civic participation. He found that the economic dominants had held only about half as many governmental offices as the public leaders. The same was true in Wheelsburg, although both groups were less active. Somewhat surprisingly, economic dominants were as well represented as the public leaders in the five most influential associations. Table 4 reveals a similar situation of high participation by both economic dominants and public leaders in Wheelsburg's most influential associations. However, the Cibola situation of wide differences between public leaders and economic dominants in the number of officerships held in these associations was not in evidence. Table 5 reveals that a higher proportion of economic dominants in Wheelsburg (from both locally and absentee-owned companies) have in the past held office in the five most influential organizations. Differences are small between

TABLE 4. *Membership of Current Public Leaders and Economic Dominants in the Most Influential Associations**

| ASSOCIATION | Public Leaders | PER CENT BELONGING TO ASSOCIATION Economic Dominants | | Total |
		Local	Absentee	
Chamber of Commerce:				
Wheelsburg	87	96	100	97
Cibola	78	100	87	94
Rotary:				
Wheelsburg	49	38	40	38
Cibola	50	70	14	47
Kiwanis:				
Wheelsburg	18	13	7	10
Cibola	44	30	0	18
Lions:				
Wheelsburg	5	8	0	5
Cibola	11	0	0	0

*In Cibola the five most influential associations were determined by polling the voluntary association heads, public leaders, and economic dominants. The four associations listed above and the Junior Chamber of Commerce were named by all of the groupings questioned. These organizations were also designated by Wheelsburg public leaders as highly influential. Since few public leaders or economic dominants were young enough to be eligible for membership in the Junior Chamber of Commerce in either city, and none were members, this association was omitted from the table.
SOURCE: Cibola data, Schulze, "The Bifurcation . . .," *op. cit.*, p. 47.

TABLE 5. *Officerships of Public Leaders and Economic Dominants in Five Most Influential Community Associations*

| | PUBLIC LEADERS | | ECONOMIC DOMINANTS | | | | | |
| | | | Local | | Absentee | | Total | |
	Wheels-burg	Cibola	Wheels-burg	Cibola	Wheels-burg	Cibola	Wheels-burg	Cibola
Per cent having served as president of at least one of the five associations.	31	61	25	20	20	0	23	12
No. of presidencies occupied in the five associations	17	14	8	2	3	0	11	2
Per cent *currently* serving as officer or board member in at least one of the five associations*	18	44	4	10	27	30	13	18
No. of officerships or board memberships *currently* held in the five associations	7	12	1	1	4	2	5	3

*"Currently" refers to the year of research: 1954 for Cibola, 1958–59 for Wheelsburg.
SOURCE: Cibola data. Schulze, "The Bifurcation of Power . . .," *op. cit.*, p. 48.

the two communities in the proportions currently holding such offices. In short, both Tables 4 and 5 document no deep bifurcation in associational participation between Wheelsburg's economic dominants and public leaders. The relatively high rate of participation by absentee-owned corporation executives is especially notable.[17]

One of the reasons for the failure of economic dominants to participate in the civic life of Cibola was that they regarded the city mainly as the locus of their work life and not their community life.[18] Moreover, their private economic interests were primarily non-local. This may not be surprising since the city's largest economic units were absentee-owned and oriented toward a national market. However, Table 6 indicates that a much more extensive network of economic ties exists in Wheelsburg than in Cibola.[19] Despite a high degree of absentee ownership in Wheelsburg, a fairly extensive network of economic ties unites the interests of the economic dominants

TABLE 6. *Number of Known Local Economic Ties Among Public Leaders and Economic Dominants*

	PUBLIC LEADERS	ECONOMIC DOMINANTS	
		Local Firm	Absentee Firm
Public leaders:			
Wheelsburg	23	31	8
Cibola	4	3	2
Local-firm dominants:			
Wheelsburg	—	47	11
Cibola	—	15	0
Absentee-firm dominants:*			
Wheelsburg	—	—	2
Cibola	—	—	2

*In neither Wheelsburg nor Cibola were there any economic ties between absentee-firm dominants from *different* corporations. In the case of two absentee firms in Wheelsburg, a second person in addition to the general manager was defined as an economic dominant because he held a directorship in a local bank as well as an officership in the absentee-owned firm.
SOURCE: Cibola data supplied by Robert O. Schulze in an unpublished manuscript.

and the public leaders. These ties may explain the higher rate of civic participation by its economic dominants and their closer social integration to public leaders.

As a final demonstration of the bifurcation of Cibola economic dominants and public leaders, Schulze analyzed the decision-making process on two important community issues. The economic dominants refused to become involved in resolving either of them, leaving the public leaders autonomous but perhaps without a solid power basis for community action.

In Wheelsburg, an analysis of eleven community issues[20] revealed that eight of the economic dominants who were also public leaders were among those mentioned as influential in initiating and resolving these issues. Economic dominants, including some representing absentee-owned corporations, either initiated or co-initiated programs of action for six of the eight issues in which they were involved. Although this evidence suggests that economic dominants have not withdrawn from community decision-making and that they are not just ceremonial leaders, apparently they do not form a monolithic power elite. Different individuals became involved in different issues, doing so in the process of playing their own "games."[21]

Not all of the broad community issues in which economic dominants were involved were controversial. Some of them may more properly be called "projects." The major issues in Cibola seemed to involve a higher degree of conflict in the political arena. Perhaps this conflict reflected the inertia of partisan party politics which existed in the community as late as 1947. In addition, both of the major issues in Cibola—adoption of a new city charter and annexation—were the direct results of rapid urbanization and industrialization, processes which had occurred at a more gradual rate in Wheelsburg. There, political life seemed less marked by conflict, for local government not only was non-partisan but it traditionally and customarily responded to the needs of business.[22] It is highly probable that the lack of political conflict and the tendency for community decision-making to be channeled to the private rather than public sphere are interdependent. In Wheelsburg there was little evidence of basic differences in values among the economic dominants, the public leaders, and the elected officials. If representation of conflicting interests or values is chosen as the indicator of pluralism in the power structure, Wheelsburg (and most American communities) will be judged less pluralistic than if a weaker test of pluralism, such as the participation of separate individuals in different issues, is used.[23]

Thus, the social climate of the decision-making roles of the economic dominants in the two cities is not identical. Whether Wheelsburg dominants would become involved in highly conflictful issues should they arise is not known. Certainly they hestitated to publicize their involvement in controversial issues.[24] One large firm, for example, refused to become overtly involved in an annexation issue despite the fact that its economic interests were involved. However, it made its position known. What covert influence this might have had cannot be accurately appraised. Yet, since executives of the absentee-owned corporations were less likely to become involved in community decision-making than economic dominants from locally owned enterprises, possibly Wheelsburg's pattern of influence is evolving toward the type found in Cibola. On the other hand, both economic dominants and public leaders work hard to solve issues without conflict, and controversial issues probably arise less often in gradually expanding cities such as Wheelsburg than in cities which have grown very rapidly and have experienced extreme economic fluctuations, such as Cibola. Further research is required to determine the power roles of economic dominants in cities differing in size, social composition, economic composition, and economic history.

Conclusions

Comparative analysis of the roles of economic dominants in power structures of a satellite and an independent city reveals that in both communities the formal political and economic power structures which were once melded have tended to become bifurcated over time. This process seems to have paralleled the integration of local economic units into national markets and the process of governmental centralization. The economic dominants, once highly active leaders in civic associations, have tended to reduce their participation in this area, especially in the satellite community. This withdrawal coincided roughly with the rapid extension of absentee ownership in both cities. Currently, the nearly complete bifurcation of economic dominants and public leaders (top influentials) found in the satellite city was not as evident in the independent city, where an extensive network of economic ties bound the two groups together. Moreover, unlike the economic dominants in the satellite city, those in the independent city have not abandoned their decision-making role in community issues.

While the evidence cited in this research is not conclusive, it points to variable patterns of relations between economic dominants and public leaders in different types of communities. Apparently the absence of local party politics, a history of local industries becoming absentee-owned rather than the introduction of branch plants from outside the community, the institutionalization of local political controls, and the absence of ethnic, class, or other cleavages which contribute to partisan politics reduce the withdrawal rate of economic dominants from participation in community associations and local power arrangements. The time is ripe for many rapid comparative studies of a wide range of communities to determine more precisely the factors responsible for the bifurcation of persistence of ties between economic dominants, civic leaders, and community influentials.

Notes

1. We are grateful to Professor James B. McKee for a critical reading of the manuscript.

2. The tradition of Robert S. Lynd and Helen Merrill Lynd, *Middletown in Transition* (New York: Harcourt, Brace & Co., 1937); C. Wright Mills, *The Power Elite* (New York: Oxford University Press, 1956); Floyd Hunter, *Community Power Structure* (Chapel Hill: University of North Carolina Press, 1953), and many others.

3. E.g., Robert A. Dahl, "Equality and Power in American Society," in *Power and Democracy in America*, ed. William V. D'Antonio and Howard J. Ehrlich (Notre Dame, Ind.: University of Notre Dame Press, 1961); Nelson W. Polsby, "The Sociology of Community Power: A Reassessment," *Social Forces*, 37 (March, 1959), 232–36; Linton C. Freeman, *et al.*, "Local Community Leadership," *Syracuse College Paper No. 15* (Syracuse, N.Y.: Syracuse University, 1960); Edward C. Banfield, *Political Influence* (New York: Free Press of Glencoe, 1961); and many others.

4. Robert A. Dahl, *Who Governs?* (New Haven, Conn.: Yale University Press, 1961); Constance Green, *Holyoke, Massachusetts* (New Haven, Conn.: Yale University Press, 1939); Thorstein Veblen, *Absentee Ownership* (New York: Viking Press, 1939); and the works of R. O. Schulze cited in n. 6.

5. In the framework of Max Weber as explicated in "Class, Status and Power," in *From Max Weber: Essays in Sociology*, ed. and trans. Hans H. Gerth and C. Wright Mills (New York: Oxford University Press, 1946).

6. Robert O. Schulze, "Economic Dominance and Public Leadership: A Study of the Structure and Process of Power in an Urban Community" (microfilmed Ph.D. dissertation, University of Michigan, 1956); "The Role of Economic Dominants in Community Power Structure," *American Sociological Review*, 23 (February, 1958), 3–9; "The Bifurcation of Power in a Satellite City," in *Community Political Systems*, ed. Morris Janowitz (Glencoe, Ill.: Free Press, 1961), pp. 19–80.

7. "The Bifurcation of Power . . .," *op. cit.*, pp. 21–22.

8. *Ibid.*, p. 21. For Schulze's operational criteria for determining economic dominants and public leaders see *ibid.*, Appendixes A and B, pp. 73–75. Essentially the same criteria were utilized to identify the dominant economic units (and consequently economic dominants themselves) in the two cities. Number of employees, capital worth, and assessed valuation were used as measures.

However, since Wheelsburg is a much larger city than Cibola, the minimum figures for cutoff points were necessarily larger. In Cibola the only dominant economic units were manufacturing plants, banks, and savings and loan companies. In Wheelsburg a wider variety of economic units was included in the dominant group, e.g., department stores, utilities, and insurance companies. In addition to the heads of the major economic units, all who were on the board of directors of two or more of the major economic units were also identified as economic dominants.

9. As suggested by Hunter, *op. cit.* The "knowledgeables" who were interviewed in two studies differed somewhat. Schulze's knowledgeables were the heads of local voluntary associations. This research relied on the nominations of fourteen high-ranking officials from seven institutional sectors of the community (mass communication, business, union, welfare, education, government, religion). David A. Booth and Charles A. Adrian compared the results of the method used by Schulze with the simpler method we employed, and found almost identical results (see their "Simplifying the Discovery of Elites," *American Behavioral Scientist*, 5 [October, 1961], 14–16).

10. Schulze, "The Role of Economic Dominants . . .," *op. cit.*, p. 6.

11. Schulze, "The Bifurcation of Power . . .," *op. cit.*, p. 24.

12. An absentee-controlled company is defined as one having a majority of its board of directors living outside of the local community. In both Cibola and Wheelsburg, slightly less than 50 per cent of the dominant economic units were absentee controlled—five of eleven units in Cibola and thirteen of twenty-seven units in Wheelsburg. In both cities, all of the financial units (three and seven, respectively) were locally owned.

13. "Withdrawal" is probably an apt phrase, because no evidence is available to suggest that there was community pressure on the economic dominants to reduce their community involvement. However, individual economic dominants were constantly changing. Their withdrawal consisted not so much in dropping civic leadership positions as in the failure of new economic dominants to seek such positions.

14. E.g., in New Haven, from the late nineteenth century until recently, local politics were controlled primarily by "ex-plebes," individuals on the rise from the ethnic proletariat, who gained office through "the skills of ethnic politics." From 1842 to 1898, New

Haven politics were dominated by the leading entrepreneurs. It may be significant that the period of dominance by economic dominants is almost identical in New Haven, Wheelsburg, and Cibola (see Dahl, *Who Governs?* [*op. cit.*] chap. iii and iv).

15. Sixty-five per cent of the economic dominants in the 1940–59 period were associated as officers, partners, or directors in at least one other business with other economic dominants.

16. Lest the concentration on "withdrawal" be overwhelming, it should be noted that almost half the economic dominants in the 1940–59 period held civic leadership positions in Wheelsburg and that their participation in the Chamber of Commerce was increasing.

17. Although managers of the largest absentee-owned corporation did not dominate the local scene as extensively as in the case of Bigtown, they did have representatives on most of the local bodies to co-ordinate knowledge of what was going on in the city. For data on Bigtown see Roland J. Pellegrin and Charles H. Coates, "Absentee-owned Corporations and Community Power Structure," *American Journal of Sociology*, 61 (March, 1956), 413–19.

18. A large proportion lived in other communities in the metropolitan area and may have participated in the associational life of these other communities.

19. "Economic ties" are instances in which a pair of individuals serves as officers or directors of the same firm. Each pair is counted as one economic tie. For example, if four public leaders serve on the board of directors of a bank, there are six economic ties (pairs).

20. These issues were selected and recapitulated by the public leaders in interviews. They included hospital expansion drive, downtown development, establishment of a metropolitan planning agency, improvement of airport terminal facilities, establishment of a tricounty planning agency, annexation of a school district to the city, widening of a city street, ban on Sunday shopping, proposed shift of location of city hall, proposed sale of bonds by the city to finance construction of parking facilities, and proposed annexation of a suburban shopping center. Our inspection of newspapers and other documents reveals that these indeed represent nearly the full range of community issues during the last five or six years. One or two others might be added by other local interests such as organized labor (see William H. Form and Warren L. Sauer, "Community and Labor Influentials: A Comparative Study of Participation and Imagery," *Industrial and Labor Relation Review*, 17 [October, 1963], 3–19).

21. Norton E. Long, "The Urban Community as an Ecology of Games," *American Journal of Sociology*, 64 (November, 1958), 251–61.

22. Form and Sauer, *op. cit.*

23. For a fuller discussion of this problem see Marshall N. Goldstein, "Absentee Ownership and Monolithic Power Structures: Two Questions for Community Studies," in *Current Trends in Comparative Community Studies*, ed. Bert E. Swanson (Kansas City, Mo.: Community Studies, Inc., 1962), pp. 49–59.

24. The same attitudes were revealed in interviews conducted by Rossi in Mediana. This does not mean that economic dominants had withdrawn from local influence systems because, as Rossi points out, "this is the age of community projects" (Peter H. Rossi, "The Organizational Structure of an American Community," in *Complex Organizations*, ed. Amitai Etzioni [New York: Holt, Rinehart & Winston, 1961], p. 301).

Part III.

Factors Influencing Configurations of Power

Introduction

The previous selections have drawn our attention to the importance of historical processes for shaping community power. Implicit within these articles were a number of suggestions about structural factors that can affect power distributions. For example, the Schulze, Clelland and Form, and Dahl selections in Part II each suggested that the industrialization process is likely to result in structural differentiation in communities and lead to the fragmentation and subsequent dispersion of power centers.[1]

The articles that follow can be classified roughly as being concerned with three (although very broad and by no means mutually exclusive) types of structural characteristics of communities—political, social, and economic—and their effects on the arrangement of power. We have arranged the following articles according to these categories, although some, such as that by Rossi, could be placed in more than one category.

The first essay, "Configurations of Power" by Mott, is the most general in that it is concerned with several types of social factors that shape the distribution of community power. Mott describes a model of community which conceives of a community as a collection of centers of power. How these centers of power are configured vis-à-vis each other is a function of several social and economic factors which he discusses. Finally, he suggests how the extant systems of political authority may be related consistently to the underlying configurations of power found in communities.

One factor which affects the shape of power in a community is the extent to which one or more groups control its major resources. Some of the early community elite studies were done in company towns where a tightly knit economic elite monopolized resources and dominated community affairs. For example, the Middletown studies provide an early illustration of this correspondence and of the decentralization of power that attends the demonopolization of key resources.[2] The second article in this part, "The Politicians," which was taken from *Politics, Planning and the Public Interest* by Meyerson and Banfield, illustrates how an elite which controls vast resources can dominate community affairs. The elite in this study is not an economic one; it is a political machine. Therefore, this article serves to illustrate an additional point: in large cities where extensive public services are demanded, the political elite may command resources superior to those of the more factionalized economic groups in the community. The trend favoring the political elite helps to explain the increasing autonomy of political leaders that has been found in many communities.

Still another political factor that may explain how power is configured is the degree to which political parties are competitive. Walton, for example, found that cities with competitive political parties were more likely to be in communities with dispersed centers of power.[3]

In the next article, "Power and Community Structure," Rossi develops a number of hypotheses which relate aspects of both the political structure and the social structure to variations in the configuration of community power. He suggests that communities with partisan electoral procedures and professionalized administrators are more likely to be found in communities with decentralized decision-making arrangements. Further, a predominantly homogeneous middle-class community will opt for "reform" or "good government" political mechanisms which are in turn likely to affect the less formal political structure of the community. Rogers also suggests that the degree of heterogeneity of the population is important, especially in terms of ethnic, religious, and occupational diversity.[4]

In "Status and Power in the Industrial Community: A Comment on Drucker's Thesis," included in this part, McKee suggests that racial, religious, and ethnic groups provide bases for the creation of new centers of power in communities. But more importantly, he argues that labor unions may become the vehicle for mobilizing the working class for political action. He argues that labor unions as well as racial, religious, and ethnic groups capture resources and thus become real or potential centers of power in communities.

A number of research works and speculative articles have suggested that the nature of the economic structure of a community may have profound effects on its configurations of power. Each of the remaining five articles in this part is concerned with how varying aspects of the economic organization of a community are related to the distribution of community power.

The first of these is a seldom read, but often quoted, study by Mills and Ulmer, "Small Business and Civic Welfare." Part of the reason for its few readers has been its inaccessibility; it is included in this volume in its entirety in the hope that it will receive the attention it deserves. The study was published in 1946 as a report of the Smaller War Plants Corporation to the Special Committee to Study Problems of American Small Business. Its thesis is that small-business cities, economically pluralistic cities with many small, locally-owned firms, have higher levels of civic welfare (a polyglot idea reflecting advantages of education,

health, and medical care, economic well-being, and community services) than do big-business cities, those that have a few, large, absentee-controlled firms. The relevance of this study to our concerns is that it examines the intervening process between type of industrial structure and the level of civic welfare which Mills and Ulmer believe is the degree of "civic spirit" or widespread participation in civic affairs. Since Mills and Ulmer completed their study long before the lexicon of community power studies was developed, their terminology may seem antiquated, but it is apparent that there is an equivalency between what they call a high degree of "civic spirit" and what is currently referred to as pluralistic, decentralized, or dispersed power structures. They suggest that the presence of an independent middle class is an important structural basis for the development of such "civic spirit" in the small-business cities, and they also suggest some of the structural barriers in big-business cities to widespread citizen participation. Mills and Ulmer conducted their study in six anonymous cities. The identity of these communities is important since some recent work suggests that big-business cities in the Midwest do have lower levels of civic welfare—more people who are poor, unemployed, and poorly educated—than small-business cities, even today, but that the pattern is just the opposite among cities located in the South and Northeast.[5] Therefore, the editors attempted to obtain the true identity of these cities, but without official success.* Through a process of elimination based on information provided in the Mills and Ulmer study, the probable identity of the cities is as follows:

A Big-Business   Flint, Michigan
B Small-Business Battle Creek, Michigan

* The files of the Mills and Ulmer study are now located in the Archives of the United States in Washington, D.C., along with a yellowed, handwritten note from Mills identifying the names of the cities, but bearing a request and an admonition that their identities should never be revealed, since there are materials in the file the disclosure of which could allegedly be prejudicial to some of the subjects of the study. On a recent visit to the Archives of the United States, after over a year of unanswered correspondence, Aiken was denied the information once again by a minor official who honors the request of C. Wright Mills even though almost a quarter of a century has passed since the study was completed. There is a certain irony in the spectacle of this representative of the establishment zealously protecting one of its major detractors.

C Big-Business Pontiac, Michigan
D Small-Business Kalamazoo, Michigan
E Big-Business Rome, New York
F Small-Business Nashua, New Hampshire

The next article, entitled "Local Industrial Structures, Economic Power, and Community Welfare," is by Fowler and includes findings from a study of 30 New York communities and is seemingly in direct contradiction to the findings of Mills and Ulmer. Deriving hypotheses from Mills and Ulmer's study, he finds that big-business cities (high absentee-control and high concentration of employment) have slightly *higher* levels of welfare (which he measured with an index of General Social Welfare). He also utilized a novel, although problematic, measure of pluralistic or dispersed power structures which includes: low concentration of employment, a high degree of industrial unionism, a high proportion of the "old" middle class, heterogeneity of population (ethnicity, race, and religion), and a low percent of Republicans. While the Mills and Ulmer thesis would argue that pluralistic power structures would have *higher* levels of civic welfare, Fowler finds just the opposite; the cities with more concentrated power structures, using his measure, have slightly higher welfare levels. The Fowler article is important for two reasons. First, it attempts to put the Mills and Ulmer thesis in perspective, although the differences between the two studies may be a function of regional differences between Midwestern and Eastern cities. Second, and more important, it develops a measure of how community power is configured: the measure assumes that if these five characteristics are present in communities, then power is decentralized. However, the differences between Mills and Ulmer and Fowler have not been resolved; they still await a definitive examination.

The remaining three articles in Part III are concerned with still other aspects of the economic structure of communities—the absentee-controlled firm and the local power structure. In the first of these, "Absentee-owned Corporations and Community Power Structure," Pellegrin and Coates argue that Bigtown is a community in which the large, absentee units can have decisive effects on community decisions, when and if they choose to act. They argue that the participation of such officials is irregular and instrumentally oriented, that is, they act only when it is in the self-interest of the corporation. There have been a large number of studies which have discussed the participation of managers of absentee-controlled firms in the community, and most have concluded that absentee managers have only limited involvement in community activities.[6] Pellegrin and Coates are often cited as an exception to this finding. However, there is more controversy than substance to this argument. The generalization that is most defensible is that the heads of absentee-controlled firms are undoubtedly involved in some community decisions, but they carry on negotiations in very discreet, unobtrusive ways and only get involved in issues that are of direct self-interest to their corporation. A careful reading of Clelland and Form's replication in Wheelsburg of Schulze's study provides support for this generalization.[7]

The most direct type of support for this generalization is Mott's restudy of Cibola, "The Role of the Absentee-Owned Corporation in the Changing Community," which is published here for the first time. He provides evidence for this generalization and describes new organizational roles which make the participation of the top management of absentee-controlled firms less essential. At the same time it is clear that large economic units do play an important role in community decision-making, at least in those in which their self-interests are directly involved.

The last paper in this part is French's "Economic Change and Community Power Structure: Transition in Cornucopia," a longitudinal study of a community that became the site for the location of a large automobile assembly plant. French studies the decision-making structure before the plant entered the community and then again two years later. He found that the arrival of the plant in the community brought about further dispersion of community power, a process already underway, probably because previous changes in the community's economic structure. French's study also reveals corporate involvement in community affairs when their self-interests are involved, but little participation otherwise. While French's study is not the first longitudinal study of community power, it is the first to examine the impact of the location of a large, absentee-owned firm on the community decision-making structure.[8]

The inclusion of a disproportionate number of articles in Part III relating the economic structure of a community to its configuration of power is not intended to imply that economic factors are the most

important. Rather there seems to be a paucity of articles that discuss other factors. In an attempt to counterbalance this situation, the reader's attention is called to essays in Part VI of this reader: Walton's "A Systematic Survey of Community Power Research" and Aiken's "The Distribution of Community Power: Structural Bases and Social Consequences." While Walton and Aiken do not always arrive at the same conclusion, these two articles do suggest the range of structural factors that can have an influence on community power configurations. The reader's attention is also called to an article, by Clark, at propositional development in which a series of hypotheses linking community attributes to the distribution of power are listed and briefly discussed.[9]

Notes

1. R. O. Schulze, "The Role of Economic Dominants in Community Power Structure," in this volume; and his "The Bifurcation of Power in a Satellite City," in M. Janowitz (ed.), *Community Political Systems* (New York: Free Press, 1961), pp. 19–80; D. A. Clelland and W. H. Form, "Economic Dominance and Community Power: A Comparative Analysis"; and R. A. Dahl, "From Oligarchy to Pluralism: The Patricians and the Entrepreneurs," both in this volume.
2. R. S. Lynd and H. M. Lynd, *Middletown* (New York: Harcourt, Brace & World, 1929); and their *Middletown in Transition* (New York: Harcourt, Brace & World, 1937).
3. J. Walton, "Differential Patterns of Community Power Structure: An Explanation Based on Interdependence," *Sociological Quarterly*, 9 (Winter, 1968), 3–18; and his "A Systematic Survey of Community Power Research," in this volume.
4. D. Rogers, "Community Political Systems: A Framework and Hypothesis for Comparative Studies," in B. E. Swanson (ed.), *Current Trends in Comparative Community Studies* (Kansas City, Mo.: Community Studies, Inc., 1962), pp. 31–48.
5. These comments from recent work are based on a continuing research project of M. Aiken at the University of Wisconsin in which a number of aspects of the community economic structure have been measured for the 513 nonsuburbs in the size rank 10,000–249,999 and with at least 20 percent of the labor force engaged in manufacturing in 1960. A preliminary, unpublished report was prepared in 1967 at the University of Wisconsin.
6. Schulze, "The Role of Economic Dominants in Community Power Structure," in this volume; and his "The Bifurcation of Power in a Satellite City," *op. cit.*; M. K. Jennings, *Community Influentials: The Elites of Atlanta* (New York: Free Press, 1964); T. C. Smith, "The Structuring of Power in a Suburban Community," *Pacific Sociological Review*, 3 (Fall, 1960), 83–86; and M. N. Goldstein, "Absentee Ownership and Monolithic Power Structures: Two Questions for Community Studies," in B. E. Swanson (ed.), *op. cit.*, pp. 49–59.
7. Clelland and Form, *op. cit.*, in this volume.
8. W. V. D'Antonio and W. H. Form, *Influentials in Two Border Cities* (Notre Dame: University of Notre Dame Press, 1965), is one example. Also G. M. Belknap and R. H. Smuckler, "Political Power Relations in a Mid-West City," *Public Opinion Quarterly*, 20 (Spring, 1956), 73–81; with which compare D. A. Booth and C. R. Adrian, "Power Structure and Community Change," *Midwest Journal of Political Science*, 6 (August, 1962), 277–296.
9. T. N. Clark, "Power and Community Structure: Who Governs, Where, and When?" *Sociological Quarterly*, 8 (Summer, 1967), 291–316. See also his "Community Structure and Decision-Making," in T. N. Clark (ed.), *Community Structure and Decision-Making: Comparative Analyses* (San Francisco: Chandler, 1968), pp. 91–120.

Configurations of Power

Paul E. Mott

No organization, and that includes communities, can be understood without employing the concepts of social power, influence, and authority. Human organizations are dynamic affairs and power is responsible for much of that dynamism as human groups strive to take each other's power into account in their own actions: they align themselves in the force fields of power. This adjustive ordering is greatly augmented by the exercise of influence. Communities, like all human organizations, contain power and centers of power.

Like other human organizations, communities can gain, lose, or maintain energy; they are not bound by the physical law of entropy. As the total power in a community increases or decreases, so too does the amount of power in some, or all of the centers of power within it. Competition among the holders of power is a zero-sum game only under very special circumstances: unchanging total power and social isolation. Perhaps in the dwindling number of independent agrarian communities the conditions for the zero-sum game do exist. But for most communities they do not because many forces in them generate activities that change their total amount of power. Conflict and stress are everpresent conditions in human affairs; no verisimilitude can be created without allowing for them. The very nature of the human organism is such that when people attempt to interact they must misunderstand as well as understand. The very natures of man and community are such that the latter can never, at any given time, be organized to satiate all of the pressing needs of all of the former. Stress and conflict, whether peacefully or forcefully resolved, are inevitable. In situations of stress or conflict the parties involved can, and usually do, seek to accumulate energy—

social power—for increased social power increases the probabilities of successful resolution of the issue at hand.[1] When the English landed gentry found its power waning during the Industrial Revolution, it responded by trying to increase its power by improved use of its landholdings. That was no zero-sum game and the result was the emergence of two great centers of power, one based on land, the other on manufacturing, and the increasingly powerful position of Great Britain in European affairs.

Other factors that result in increases or decreases in the total amount of power available to an organization were discussed earlier: (1) population size, (2) the degree of mobilization of the population, (3) accumulation of valued resources, and (4) gain of control over important transitive connections.[2]

These and other factors also give rise to different configurations of power. Organizations vary in the degree of centralization of the power that is lodged in them and in the degree of social integration that exists among these centers of power. Any social factor that affects the number of subgroups in an organization by definition affects the degree of decentralization of power. The number of centers of power is likely to increase as: (1) the population increases, (2) the ethnic composition becomes more heterogeneous, (3) functional specialization increases, (4) the number of self-conscious social classes increases, and (5) as in-migration increases. Thus the probability of finding very few centers of power is most likely in small communities with low in-migration, little specialization, and an homogeneous socioeconomic and ethnic composition.

Communities vary also in the degree of integration of the power holders. Again a variety of factors can operate to produce

An original article written for this volume.

85

these conditions: degree or value consensus in the community, awareness of threat, proximity, and tradition and ideology. Jennings and Bouma among others have identified many of these factors in their respective studies of Atlanta elites and the machinations of real estate boards.[3] Speaking of decision structures, Jennings' observations apply equally well to our notion of configurations of power: they may be highly stratified, loose, fragmented, integrated, unintegrated, highly variable, or quite permanent.

In sum, social scientists have identified many factors that lead to greater or lesser subgroup formation and varying degrees of social integration. These factors, some of them mentioned above, must be treated as independent variables by community power specialists in order to delineate the expected number, types, and degrees of integration of centers of power. The assumption of a single elite is dangerous because it exists only under a special set of infrequently occurring circumstances.[4] Diagram 1 summarizes the relationships suggested. Of the many features that power configurations might have, we shall discuss two of them in the next sections: their degree of centralization and integration.

Degree of Centralization of Power

Community organizations contain varying numbers of subgroups, each with their own sum of power. We can show this social power as a continuum, ranging from complete centralization in a single subgroup to total and equal decentralization among all subgroups. It is theoretically convenient to identify five points along this continuum: centralized, fairly centralized, balanced, fairly decentralized, and decentralized.[5]

Centralized

The theoretical endpoint of centralized social power describes a condition that cannot easily exist for long periods of time in large organizations: all access to social power is controlled by a single subgroup or individual in an organization. Concentration camps are perhaps the closest approximation to this extreme with total societies being a somewhat distant second. In smaller units—families and subunits of business and governmental organizations—approximations to this centralized situation can be found.

For this situation to exist, the following organizational characteristics must be

DIAGRAM 1.

SOCIOECONOMIC FACTORS*

Large	←	Population size	→	Small
Heterogeneous	←	Ethnic composition	→	Homogeneous
High	←	In-migration	→	Low
High	←	Economic diversification	→	Low
Many, self-conscious	←	Social classes	→	Few, not self-conscious

CONTINUUM OF CONFIGURATIONS OF POWER

Numerous centers of considerable power which are likely to be relatively unintegrated ←————————————————→ Few centers of power which are likely to be relatively integrated

*This listing of factors is not exhaustive of all of those discussed in the literature; it is restricted to those for which the author feels there is ample empirical evidence.

present. There are only two important
roles: elite and nonelite. The elite discourages specialization, subgroup formation,
and all other means of decentralizing power.
Communication patterns are simple: little
that is not of functional significance is discussed laterally, information but not advice
is sent upward, orders but no requests for
advice are sent downward. Overt value consensus is high and the values, not surprisingly, are those of the elite.

Fairly Centralized
In the situation of fairly centralized social
power, the greatest access to power is
possessed by a single person or subgroup,
but now other units also have some access to
power. In many authority systems, although
by no means all of them, this condition
prevails, e.g., business, governmental, and
military organizations. It is also the most
common distribution of access to power in
the family where the parents usually manage
to retain the greater share, at least when the
children are young. This may be the most
common distribution of access to power in
human organizations.

Specialization and subgroup formation
are permitted and often encouraged or
expected. This condition decentralizes access
to power and changes the nature of intergroup communication. Lateral communication is abundant and its content is difficult
for the elite to control. Information flows
upward, but without the impetus of coercion
its flow is blocked occasionally below the
elite. Suggestions, recommendations, and
advice are also sent to the elite: a condition
which they foster, since it is their design to
use the specialists as advisors. The elite
reserves to itself the making of final decisions
on major matters, but it often finds it useful
to carry on a dialogue with the subelite
about the criteria for its decisions. Value
consensus is relatively high, but not as high
as it is in a centralized organization. Homogeneity of views on technical issues is
sometimes not desired because it limits the
options available to solve technical problems.

The power configurations of some
American communities are undoubtedly

fairly centralized, but they must be primarily
smaller communities where the pressures
for decentralizing power are not at work.
Small, one-company towns are often fairly
centralized. Muncie, Indiana, at the time of
the Lynds' first visit, displayed a pattern of
heavy domination by the Ball family.[6]
Among the major American cities, Dallas is
purported to have a fairly centralized power
structure. Washington, D.C., is an example
of a city in which power has been fairly
centralized (the Congressional District Committee), but which is currently undergoing
some decentralization.

Balanced
At the theoretical midpoint of balanced
social power, over a long period of time,
one key unit has access to the same amount
of power as all of the other units combined.
To some extent, therefore, it must mitigate
its methods of influencing to include the
politics of bargaining and coalition formation. But since the odds are heavily in favor
of this unit—it must be a party to every
winning coalition—neither the bargaining
costs nor the problems of finding a willing
coalitional partner are usually too high. The
interests of the members of the key power
unit are likely to shape those of many other
units to a considerable extent. However, the
members of the other units do have greater
opportunities to express their self-interests
than are found in fairly centralized configurations of power.

Examples of this precise midpoint are
difficult to find. A parliamentary organization where one-half of the votes are possessed
by a single, cohesive political party is an
obvious example. Perhaps General Motors
represents an approximate balance between
corporate headquarters and the various
divisions.

Fairly Decentralized
Access to power is so broadened in a fairly
decentralized situation that no subgroup has
sufficient access to dominate the others. The
subgroups do not have equal or nearly equal
access to power; some may have several

times as much access as others, but not enough unilaterally to dominate the others. These subgroups can and do represent their special interests. Any collective action requires some means, preferably peaceful, of resolving conflicts among the interests represented. The politics of bargaining and coalition formation are common; arenas are created in which these interest groups can meet and bargain. The minority is forced to capitulate when the power of the majority coalition is sufficient to reduce the life-chances of the minority. Sometimes such decisions are formalized by rules which stipulate when a successful majority has been achieved. Value consensus is minimal, reflecting the centrifugal forces of specialization of interest and function that prevail.

Most of the recent community studies have found this condition of fairly decentralized power. Interestingly, community power specialists are finding as many centers of power or elite structures as they look for. Jennings found political, economic, reputational, and civic staffer elites in Atlanta—all with some members who had played active roles in the three major community decisions he studied.[7] Schulze and Pellegrin and Coates have found it useful to distinguish centers of power based on absentee-owned corporations versus indigenously-owned enterprises.[8]

As social power is decentralized within the organization, the styles of influencing also change, because men of power must increasingly take into account other men of power: a situation that does not trouble the elite of a centralized organization. This general proposition suggests a number of sub-propositions.

As the ratio of a subgroup's access to power to the total power available in the organization decreases:

1. the scope of issues that can be suppressed decreases,
2. the effective use of coercion declines,
3. the effective use of bargaining increases,
4. the effective use of the techniques of persuasion increases,

5. the effective use of rational argument increases.

Further, as this ratio decreases, the costs of intergroup interaction increase. By "costs of interaction" we mean the resources that a group must give up to open a channel of interaction or to get what it wants from the ensuing interaction. These costs are relatively low in centralized groups and relatively high in less centralized groups. Only the highly integrated, totally decentralized group constitutes a possible exception to this rule.

Thus the leader of a subgroup in a fairly decentralized organization finds himself in a special position. He cannot coerce; he must bargain. He cannot order; he must form coalitions with others whose interests are served by coalition formation, and he must handle his partners with tact. He must use rational arguments increasingly in order to get what he wants. He cannot conveniently suppress all issues that seem inimical to his interests: that ability is restricted to the subgroups of his own coalition.

Just as the styles of influence change, so too the scope of involvement in organizational affairs changes. The scope of issues of interest to any subgroup is *approximated* by the ratio of its power to that of the total community. As this ratio approaches unity, the scope of issue involvement of the subgroup increases to embrace virtually all community issues. Since this ratio is normally very small in fairly decentralized power configurations, subgroups are likely to be involved only in those issues that affect their interests.[9] Any greater involvement probably reflects the workings of tradition, habit, *noblesse oblige*, personality factors, and so forth. Therefore, as the issues change, different combinations of groups and individuals become involved in them. Miller has proposed that if you know the values of the elites and their relative power you can predict the outcomes of community issues.[10] This proposal assumes they perceive the issue and that the coalitional strategy they use is successful, but it does reflect an approximate, if overly simplified, view of the dynamics of influencing in fairly decentralized power configurations.

Decentralized

At the theoretical endpoint of decentralized social power all subgroups have identical amounts of power or access to power. Some small groups are of this type. The participant-determining groups that adherents to certain "human relations" approaches advocate, T-groups and Likert-styled management teams, are examples. A committee of specialists charged with solving a problem by contributing the knowledge of their various specialities can have this type of power distribution. Perhaps some small towns or tribal groups approximate this situation. Metropolitan areas often have this distribution in regard to one type of power: each community in the area is equal in a legal sense and therefore independent of the authority of the other communities. The problem of the central city has been that its high ratio of positional access to power of the total metropolitan power makes a great many problems and issues important to it, but it lacks the authority to do anything about them without the concurrence of the smaller communities. The smaller communities, on the other hand, feel very strongly the force field of the central city and they must make self-adjustments. The consequent insecurity of their position often makes them all the more resistant to the influencing of the officials from the central city.

Total decentralization of access to all forms of power is rarely found, however. Increases in population or specialization, the emergence of transitive connections, or the uneven distribution of skills and motivations are usually accompanied by some centralization of access to power.

Integration of Power Configurations

By the term "social integration" we mean that all of the parts of an organization are bound together functionally and normatively so as to function as a unified whole. The sources and types of integration are commonly agreed upon by sociologists: integrated communication nets among the parts, functional interdependence, and homogeneity of values.[11]

In centralized organizations integration of a sort is high: all units are aligned to the elite and function to support it. Many other forms of integration are discouraged. But as access to power decentralizes, meaningful breaks in patterns of integration can occur. Few business or governmental organizations can boast high levels of integration, although their degree of integration is relative, in some instances fairly high and in others low. If some subgroups are fairly uncolligated, the character of influencing must expand from order-giving, coercion, and value indoctrination to include a greater emphasis on bargaining with the relatively separated subgroups. Labor-management relations are an obvious example of this situation.

Variations in degree of integration can have interesting effects on balanced organizations. Since they are difficult to find, our discussion of them must lean more on theory than on empirical observation. Justice Holmes once wrote a dissenting opinion in which he denied the right of the federal government to exercise a certain type of regulation over the states. He said that he would not deny the right of the states to experiment, since that was of benefit to all of the people. He envisaged a society that was at once balanced and integrated: a society in which forty-eight experiments in solving a particular problem might take place. The nation would benefit from the results. By holding the federal government in a balanced position he hoped to maximize experimentation, yet have available a very powerful unit that could cull the learning from the state experiments and ensure the implementation of the results.[12] In the highly integrated balanced system, such rational problem-solving is feasible.

Unless these techniques of experimentation, rational problem-solving, and selection for general use of those experiments that seem most successful are used, the balanced organization will function quite differently. If, for example, a permanent coalition is maintained by major powerholders, then unless the problems of the minority are dealt with, integration will decline. In the poorly integrated, balanced situation, the styles of influencing are likely to be bargaining and coalitional. The rational, programmatic approach to problem-solving is likely to give way to interest-group politics similar to those found in fairly decentralized systems, except that the coalitions are likely to be more stable in the balanced situation.

Centrifugal forces show their effects readily in fairly decentralized organizations which can vary greatly in their integration. In fact, it is difficult, though certainly not impossible, to maintain a highly integrated organization in which access to power is decentralized. In less integrated systems coalitions are more ephemeral, communication networks are less stable and the combinations of subgroups found in the coalitions shift with the problems confronting them. If the coalition is fairly permanent, the minority may find itself without much

hope of getting positive action on its programs.

As we said above, many communities have fairly decentralized access to power and they vary in their levels of integration. In some the elites work in fair concert with one another; in others the situation is loose and amorphous.

The level of integration weighs very heavily on styles of influencing in decentralized organizations. If integrated, the group is highly goal-oriented and only those forms of influencing that promote goal achievement are desired. Influencing that fulfills personal motives without implementing group objectives is sanctioned negatively. Usually, systematic methods of interaction for problem-solving are present or under development. In unintegrated situations common goals are rare and so is joint

DIAGRAM 2.

CONFIGURATION OF ACCESS TO POWER	INTEGRATION	MAJOR TYPES OF INFLUENCE USED	ISSUE INVOLVEMENT
Centralized	High	Coercive, orders given, value indoctrination, suppression, requested information sent upward	Influence extends to all issues perceived. Suppressive influence used on some; those that interest the elite are considered
	Low	Same as above	Same
Fairly centralized	High	Same as above, although less emphasis on coercion, more on advising, recommending	Primarily issues of interest to elite, others are sent up for consideration however
	Low	Same as above, plus bargaining, persuasion, coalition formation	Elite issues, issues of interest at lower levels sometimes solved at the lower levels covertly
Balanced	High	Bargaining, coalition, programmatic problem-solving	All issues of interest to any subgroup are raised and considered
	Low	Bargaining, coalition	Interests may be raised but not all are considered. Elite interest required for success
Fairly decentralized	High	Bargaining, coalition	Issue spectrum equals the interest spectrum of interest groups
	Low	Bargaining, coalition, intransigence	Groups are activated only by those issues that they perceive as affecting them
Decentralized	High	Rational consensus	Any issue that relates to the group goals is of interest to all members
	Low	Intransigence, bargaining	Only a few issues can muster enough support to make the effort of raising them worthwhile

problem-solving. For example, metropolitan efforts to solve transportation problems must overcome enormous inertia. Each unit seeks primarily to protect its own unit of power: all else is secondary. Diagram 2 summarizes these points schematically.

Configurations of Power as Independent Variables

The concept of configurations of power has been used in a number of studies to predict variations in other organizational phenomena. The "human relations" school of industrial studies has used three power configurations—centralized, fairly decentralized, and decentralized—to explain differences in the morale, self-actualization, initiative, and productivity of the workers. Swanson has used the entire range of degrees of centralization of power as the key independent variable in predicting the acceptance of forms of Protestantism in Reformation Europe.[13] In this section an additional application of the concept is considered: configurations of power and community authority systems.

An interesting set of findings about the relationships between the economic and social characteristics of communities and their political institutions has developed. Sociologist Peter Rossi was among the first to call attention to the possibilities in this area.[14] He proposed that the more homogeneous the class structure, the more likely it was to have a monolithic power structure. Other hypotheses were proposed but underlying them was the assumption that certain social factors operate to create more or fewer centers of power, a position that was summarized earlier in Diagram 1. The line of reasoning was as follows: if political organization is the mobilization of values, then, to the extent that the elites of a community are free to determine the character of their political systems, they create systems that are compatible with their configuration of power, if that configuration is generally seen as legitimate. If it is not perceived as legitimate, some elites may attempt to create authority systems that

countervail the effects of less valued parts of the arrangement of power. Such structures are designed to permit those styles of influencing that are compatible with the extant, valued configuration of power. If there are numerous centers of considerable power, then two interrelated consequences usually follow. Each center of power becomes a base for the development of subcultures. Disagreements about values and norms can become quite marked in this situation. If these elites are dependent upon each other for the achievement of some of their objectives, then some form of arena must be created in which the various elites can assemble to bargain with each other, e.g., a council, parliament, or stock exchange. There the politics of coalition formation can be exercised freely. Such an arena is unnecessary in organizations where power is centralized and value consensus exists: an administrative apparatus designed to implement the wishes of the elite is more appropriate.

This line of reasoning suggests that it may be possible to link the social and economic characteristics of a community to its political practices. Herson proposed that social scientists relate certain political practices to the ranges of political concentration: (1) ranges in executive power varying from city-manager, short-ballot communities, to weak mayor, long-ballot communities, and (2) ranges in party organization from one- to multi-party communities or boss-dominated machines, to systems of factions within parties.[15]

The usefulness of these ideas was quickly tested in a number of studies. Kessel found that the mayor-council form of government was most common in very large and very small cities, in cities where the industrial base was most diversified and where the percentage of adult foreign-born was highest.[16] Council-manager plans were most common in medium-sized communities with a narrow economic base and fewer foreign-born. Only the finding that the mayor-council system is found in small towns conflicts with the proposals made by Rossi and Herson. But the percentage of small towns with the mayor-council form really increases significantly for towns with fewer than 25,000 people: towns that cannot afford a professional city-manager and probably don't have enough work for him to do anyway. If the town clerk is the underpaid, unlettered equivalent of the city-manager, maybe *he* is the bureaucracy. Others have produced data to support or elaborate Kessel's findings.[17] These findings are summarized in Diagram 3.

Diagram 3.

Social and Economic Characteristics	Mayor-Council	Council-Manager
Population size	Largest, smallest	Medium
Population growth	Low	High
Percent foreign-born	High	Low
Percent completing high school	Low	High
Percent in white-collar occupations	Low	High
Diversity of economic base	High	Low

In a parallel study of suburban government, Schnore and Alford found that the council-manager form was preferred in all but the smallest suburbs.[18] It was also the prevalent form of government in the rapidly growing suburbs with the most educated white-collar population.

The expected pattern does emerge: large populations, multiple social classes, and ethnic and economic diversification are all factors that contribute to value dissension and to the decentralization of power and that necessitate parliamentary (council) forms of government. The opposite set of conditions results in value consensus and a lack of seriously competing elites, which indicates the need for a bureaucracy that implements the popular values.

Using the same line of reasoning, it is expected that a partisan system of election from wards is preferred in communities with decentralized configurations of power. The existence of differentiation, economic and cultural, finds conscious expression in competition among identifiable parties; the parties vie for the right to control community authority systems. Nonpartisan elections either obscure such differences or demonstrate that differences do not exist. The system of election by wards facilitates representation in the arenas of political action of many of the elites in a decentralized arrangement of power. An at-large election defeats this purpose; it tends to result in the election of well-known people, people with famous names, or people with the proper ethnic name. Accordingly, it has been found that nonpartisan, at-large election systems are usually instituted in the same cities that elect the council-manager form of government.[19] Eighty-five percent of council-manager cities use the nonpartisan ballot and 81 percent of them elect their council at-large.[20] One-half of mayor-council cities use partisan elections and forty-one percent elect their councilmen from wards.[21] These last findings also confirm our hypothesis, but they should not be heavily emphasized because all three devices—council-manager government, nonpartisan ballot, and at-large election—are not independent of each other. They are part of a package advocated by municipal reformers: a package that is usually presented *in toto* to the voters. We suggest only that this package is most likely to be accepted in those communities where socioeconomic factors prevent a decentralized configuration of power.

We add our own variation to this collection of data. Following our general hypothesis, we expect some predictable socioeconomic differences between communities that vote to accept council-manager plans and those that reject it. The results of such decisions are published annually in the *Municipal Yearbook*. The list for 1956 was sampled (cities accepting = 124; cities rejecting = 60) and 1950 census data for the selected cities were examined. Cities rejecting council-manager plans were compared to those accepting these plans and were found to have more foreign-born residents and nonwhites (p ≤ .05 for these and the other findings listed here), with smaller percentages of people earning in excess of $10,000, smaller percentages of professional and managerial workers, higher percentages of service and operative workers, and an industrial base primarily in the manufacturing and construction industries.[22] While these findings do support the general hypothesis relating socioeconomic factors to community authority systems, they do so in limited fashion. Like so many of the studies mentioned above, the differences, if significant statistically, nonetheless are small. Other factors are at work which dilute the magnitude of the differences: these factors will be examined below because they should tell us more about systems of power and authority.

As noted earlier, the general hypothesis assumes that people are free to choose how to organize to express their values. They often are not. Kessel has noted some of these impediments.[23] State laws often limit home rule; for example, California requires that its cities adopt the council-manager plan. Small towns are limited by their available resources to inexpensive systems of authority, usually a mayor-council-clerk plan. And sometimes an ineffective form of government is retained due to inertia and custom. As a result, the best predictor of what form of government a community uses is the geographic location of the community; the more westerly and southerly its location, the more likely it is to have the council-manager form of government.[24]

So great is the effect of regionalism that Wolfinger and Field would have us discount the findings supporting our hypothesis. Yet the fact persists that this hypothesis is supported nationally despite the powerful effects of regionalism, state laws, financial limitations, and tradition. Rather than discount the evidence, we should refine our hypothesis to take into account the effects of these additional social factors.

But before we do that, we must consider another source of problems for our general hypothesis. All of the studies mentioned above, including our own, treat the types of authority systems as discrete, categoric phenomena. Yet beneath similar labels there is considerable variation in practice. For example, consider the label "council-manager": several cities so denoted may

have radically different functional arrangements. In some the council is strong and the city manager is little more than a civil administrative officer, one iron filing among fields of political force; in others the manager is in control, guiding a council by giving it the information he wants to give it and getting the decisions he wants from it. Most council-manager plans undoubtedly lie along a continuum between these two extreme points. Similarly a mayor-council plan can vary from the strong mayor–weak council plan (Chicago) to the weak mayor–strong council system found in many American communities. The label can be misleading and even unimportant; what occurs in fact represents the workings of the underlying configuration of power, which molds the form to shape it to the realities of power. Diagram 4 summarizes our view.

Therefore, while the form "council-manager" may predominate in the Southwest, practice may conform to the underlying configuration of power in each Southwestern community. This hypothesis has not been tested; it is a difficult one to test. To do so would require going beyond the labels in the *Municipal Yearbook* to detailed observation in each community of the actual distributions of power among the members of the city council and vis-à-vis the city manager. We suggest that it would be fruitful to add measures of the concepts discussed in this section to the protocols of future comparative studies of community power systems.

Finally, we must take into account, as Wolfinger and Field would have us do, that the organizations we are studying are not static.[25] Like other organizations, communities are open systems subject to external as well as internal pressures and problems. They experience sudden increases in migration, acquire new industries, and generally are impacted upon through the media and other means by the larger society. These changes can disturb and even change existing configurations of power.[26] They initiate a chain reaction that will at least change the styles of influence, but if they are powerful enough they may result in a change

DIAGRAM 4.

SOCIOECONOMIC FACTORS

Large	←———	Population size	———→	Small
Heterogeneous	←———	Ethnic composition	———→	Homogeneous
High	←———	In-migration	———→	Low
High	←———	Economic diversification	———→	Low
Many, self-conscious	←———	Social classes	———→	Few, not self-conscious

↓   CONTINUUM OF CONFIGURATIONS OF POWER   ↓

Decentralized—Fairly decentralized	Balanced	Fairly centralized—Centralized
Numerous centers of considerable power which are likely to be relatively unintegrated	The power of one center approximately equals the sum of power of all other centers	Few centers of power which are likely to be relatively integrated

↓   REALITIES OF POWER IN TYPES OF COMMUNITY AUTHORITY SYSTEMS   ↓

1. Commission

| Commissioners equal | Commissioners vary a little in their power | One commissioner has about as much power as all of the rest | One commissioner dominates the others or the commission, as a whole, dominates the community |

2. Mayor-council

| Weak mayor—council in which all are equal | Weak mayor—council in which the members vary a little in their power | Mayor has about as much power as the sum of council's power | Strong mayor—weak council |

3. Council-manager

| Council members equal; manager has about as much influence as a member of council | Power differences among members, but no one can dominate | Manager has about as much power as the sum of council's power | Manager dominates a weak council |

in the form itself. The choice among forms is usually limited to what is known and fashionable. Since the mid-1930s the council-manager form has been the most publicized and fashionable type of municipal government. But even if a community adopts it, it is theoretically crucial that we note *how* it adopts it, i.e., what modifications it makes in the model charter. As Weber notes, it is the modifications from the ideal type that tell us something about the underlying reality of the organization.

Communities and Complex Organizations: Comparable Studies of Power?

Community power studies are now entering their second phase of development: the idiosyncratic single community study will increasingly be replaced by comparative studies of two or more communities. It is our feeling that the theoretical payoff from these studies will be considerably augmented if advantage is taken of the theorems from comparative organizational research. Communities are organizations: a fact that is too often overlooked because we are most immediately aware of the differences between, say, Atlanta and the Department of Agriculture. But some of the most obvious differences begin to disappear as our familiarity with these two types of organizations increases. There are at least two major stumbling blocks to understanding the similarities between communities and complex organizations—professional specialization and the concept of bureaucracy. About the former little need be said because we are aware that social scientists have enough trouble keeping up to date in their chosen fields much less two or more fields. The comment on bureaucracy does need further explanation. This construct has been *the* organizing concept for the field of complex organizations and, as such, it is a limiting one. For example, few governmental organizations can properly be labelled "bureaucratic": their configurations of authority and power are seldom fairly centralized as is required by Weber's model. Sometimes the legally prescribed authority structure is hierarchical, but even then this structure is readily remolded by the underlying realities of power. And it is no simple matter of a small, if interesting, deviation from the ideal type: the structure of power and authority in many government organizations is fundamentally and often purposely different from Weber's model. The National Aeronautics and Space Administration, the Department of Agriculture, and the Department of Health, Education and Welfare, for example, are not bureaucratic organizations; they have fairly decentralized power configurations—multiple centers of power. These centers of power vary in their degree of integration with each other (the degree of integration varies among units within the organizations as well as between organizations). The structure of decision-making is expectedly parliamentary —committees are rife—and the techniques of influencing are more likely to be bargaining and coalition formation than ordering and coercing. Each organization has bureaucracies within it, but then so do communities. Thus in business, governmental,. and labor organizations we actually find the same extensive variations in the degrees of centralization of power and authority and in the patterns of influence that we find in communities.

The Structure of Community Power

But it still seems difficult to compare a community with a complex organization. Consider, for example, the application of the concept of coordination to these two

types of organization. The processes and consequences of coordination in business organizations are obvious to the observer, but to this same observer the concept often seems inapplicable to communities. Communities are loose and amorphous; they are Topseys that just grew. The parts function without seeming reference to the whole; harmonious relationships are accidental or spontaneous and unplanned developments. The concept of communication can be similarly viewed; obvious in corporations, confused or virtually nonexistent in communities.

Can we develop a model of community that lends itself to comparison with complex organizations and yet is valid for the study of communities themselves? The findings of Crain and Rosenthal give us some leads to the answers to this question.[27] They find that the higher the average educational level of a community, the more likely are the citizens to attempt to influence the decision-making processes and the more likely are those processes to be immobilized by their efforts. What interests us here is the exception to this finding—the effect of the top stratum in the more educated communities. Here the trend is reversed because the citizens participate in the decision process through consistent roles in stable organizations and facilitate that process. We have already seen that the highly educated prefer city-manager, bureaucratized, service-oriented government. Their preferences are remarkably similar to the organizational preferences of scientists.[28] The latter like to make their own decisions in a facilitative environment: one that can be approached rationally and that efficiently fulfills their requests. They are most productive under these circumstances. The highly educated citizen apparently values participation in the decision-making process and accordingly participates in associations that have stable, rational relationships with the leaders of the fairly centralized governmental bureaucracy. The will of all is, in effect, determined during these exchanges and the bureaucracy makes the needed changes in practices. This preference for a combination of community associations and a fairly centralized, rational bureaucracy is a significant modification of the classic democratic arrangement, but it is considered legitimate by the highly educated.

But what about the communities with a less well educated citizenry? There is little problem in communities with the least well educated residents. They consider classic representative democracy to be legitimate. The decision-making process is somewhat insulated from effective action by many pressure groups because the political leaders are protected by the extensiveness of the delegation of authority the population has made to them. It is in the communities with upper middle levels of education that conflict is most difficult to resolve. Here too the council-manager plan is the most common one, but it seems unlikely that the residents have the same perceptions of it as their better educated contempories have. What proportions of the residents of these two types of communities work in the middle and upper levels of bureaucratized organizations or in the professions? Probabilities favor the communities of the highly educated: they are more likely than the less educated to understand these organizations, to be less fearful of them, and to know how to use them. Conflict over solutions to problems may be much more difficult to resolve in communities where education is middling because: (1) the citizens do not develop bureaucratized patterns of interaction with their government, (2) they resort to more widely known pressure group techniques, which are often ad hoc, media and referenda oriented, and (3) without the insulation of stewardship, the city government has difficulty developing a consistent, positive program amidst this field of pressure groups.

This study suggests a model of community that meets our criterion. Three types of groups—economic, political, associational —make their customary appearance in the political process. To these we add another category, the solo individual who without any organizational base participates in the influence processes.[29]

Groups and categories of these types can vary on many dimensions, some of which are particularly relevant to the influence process: (1) involvement in the influence process, (2) permanence, (3) degree of internal centralization of power, and (4) adequacy of the skills of the members to the tasks they perform.

The key question is: How are these groups linked together, if at all, to form the core of the community influence process? We answer that they are linked together in much the same way that the parts of other complex organizations are linked. Virtually all parts of organizations perform activities that are experienced by other parts of the organization and which affect each other's internal activities. It is these interfaces, actual or desired, that are the grist for more formalized linkages, for coordination among the parts and for the appropriateness of the skill levels of the personnel to the demands of the coordinative plan. The internal coordination of each unit is less relevant for total organizational effectiveness except as it is translated into interface relations. The internal productive activities of a company are not in themselves relevant to the community influence process except at their interfaces, e.g., productive activity yields wages which are spent in the community or the factory pollutes the air or a river. The model of community as an organization for the exchange of influence is one that focuses primarily on the nature of the interfaces among the units affecting this process—the interstitial organization of groups.

Now let us link this conception with our earlier ones of configurations of power and interunit integration to develop some modal types of community influence structure. The interfaces can vary in the extent to which included activities are integrated with each other. They can be stable, coordinated, and consistent or the opposite; they can be segmented, yet ordered and devoid of conflict, e.g., the silent trading between certain Pacific island groups; they can be segmented, chaotic, and conflict-ridden. They can also vary in the extent to which interface activities are hierarchicalized. Dominance of political elites by economic elites means that at the interfaces occupants of political roles take their orders from occupants of economic roles.

This last illustration describes one modal community arrangement; fairly complete interpenetration of community units resulting in an hierarchicalized and fairly integrated structure of interfaces. The Lynds' first impression of Muncie, Indiana, is illustrative—fairly centralized and integrated.

The organization of power, authority, and influence in the communities of the well-educated, described by Crain and Rosenthal, represents an interesting modality. They suggest that the interfaces were integrated— the elites were interpenetrated—and stable, consistent patterns of mutual influencing had emerged. The core of the community influence structure is a fairly centralized governmental administrative structure surrounded primarily at the apex by community groups, which influence it through expected roles in expected ways. This model conforms fairly closely to our notion of the balanced-integrated organization, described earlier (see p. 89 and Diagram 2). The types of influencing Crain and Rosenthal describe for this type of community fit our theoretically derived expectations: bargaining, coalition-formation, reasoning, and programmatic problem-solving.

The communities of those with a little less education conform more nearly to our balanced-segmented model. The fairly centralized political apparatus is still present, but its interfaces with other groups are less integrated. Ad hoc, ephemeral pressure groups are more common, the modes of interaction are less often regulated by norms, conflict is higher, and intransigence is a more common experience here than it is in the balanced-integrated community.

Since the educational level of our society is steadily increasing, and since education and all it entails is a serviceable independent variable predicting to the adoption of the council-manager form of government, perhaps the balanced organization of influence and power will become increasingly prevalent in the future. But most recent studies suggest that the fairly decentralized con-figuration of power, varying in degrees of integration, is currently the largest mode. In this form of organization there are many centers of power with rather limited interpenetration. Joint activity in the interfaces is only likely to take place as relevant problems or issues appear. In the integrated instance, groups are represented in an arena, which is, in effect, a common interface to all the major groups in the community. There interface problems are discussed and resolved by stable legitimated methods. In the segmented instance, the stable, legitimated methods are, by definition, not present. Solutions are sought in ad hoc groups and intergroup conflict and hostility are more common. Fairly decentralized business and governmental organizations are more likely to exhibit segmented characteristics because they are usually devoid of the compensating parliamentary mechanisms that are ordinarily found in communities. In cities where the institutions of total community interface— courts, councils, mediation facilities—are weak and power is decentralized, the more combative forms of influence are likely to be used frequently. In communities where some groups are denied access to these arenas, intergroup conflict and hostility are also likely.

Summary

Power is an integral part in the functioning of any type of human organization. Increases or decreases in power due to changing socio-economic conditions will result in a lesser or greater number of subgroups—centers of power—which will array themselves into a variety of structures or configurations of power with varying degrees of integration with each other. The factors leading to more or fewer subgroups and varying degrees of social integration must be treated as independent variables to delineate the expected numbers, types, and degrees of integration of centers of power in communities.

As organizations contain varying numbers of subgroups, each with their own sum of power, levels of social power are conceived as lying along a continuum ranging from complete centralization in a single subgroup to total and equal decentralization among all the subgroups. Five theoretical points are identified along this continuum: centralized, fairly centralized, balanced, fairly decentralized, and decentralized. In the centralized organization one group has almost complete access to power, while at the decentralized end of the spectrum it is visualized that all subgroups have identical amounts of power or access to power. As social power is decentralized, the scope of relevant issues that will be discussed and styles of influencing change. As the ratio of a subgroup's access to power to the total power in an organization decreases, the issues that can be suppressed decrease and the effective use of coercion declines, while the use of bargaining, persuasion and rational argument increases. Also as the ratio decreases the costs of intergroup interaction increase. A corollary is that the scope of issues of interest to any subgroup is approximated by the ratio of its power to that of the total organization.

Social integration, which exists when all parts of an organization are bound together functionally and normatively so as to function as a unified whole, is also changed with the decentralization of power. Styles of effective influencing are affected by the level of integration. Thus in a balanced organization where integration is relatively high, programmatic problem-solving will be emphasized; however, where integration is low, influencing can degenerate to intransigence and interest group politics.

Based on the assumption that certain social factors operate to create greater or fewer centers of power, the concept of configuration of power may be used to link the social and economic characteristics of a community with its political institutions. If political organization is the mobilization of values, then to the extent that elites of a community are free to determine the character of their political systems, they will create systems that are compatible with their valued configurations of power. Large populations, multiple social classes, and ethnic and economic diversification are factors contributing to value dissension and to the decentralization of power which together necessitate parliamentary forms of government. A more homogeneous class structure is more likely to have a monolithic power structure resulting in a bureaucracy that implements popular demands.

Governmental, business, and labor organizations have the same extensive variations in degrees of centralization of power and authority as are found in communities. Communities should then be viewed as complex organizations and theorems from comparative organizational research applied. To understand how community power groups are linked to form the core of the community influence process, a model can be derived which focuses on communities as organizations for the exchange of influence and emphasizes the interfaces among the units affecting the influence process. Interfaces can be seen to vary in the extent to which included activities are integrated with each other—i.e., the degree of integration or segmentation—and the extent to which interface activities are hierarchicalized.

Notes

1. R. L. Kahn, "Introduction" in R. L. Kahn and E. Boulding (eds.), *Power and Conflict in Organizations* (New York: Basic Books, 1964), p. 3.
2. T. N. Clark, "Power and Community Structure: Who Governs, Where, and When?" A paper read at the annual meeting of the American Sociological Association, 1965. W. H. Form and W. L. Sauer, "Organized Labor's Image of Community Power Structure," *Social Forces*, 38 (May, 1960), 332–341. S. Keller, *Beyond the Ruling Class: Strategic Elites in Modern Society* (New York: Random House, 1963), pp. 65–76. P. H. Rossi, "Power and Community Structure," *Midwest Journal of Political Science*, 4 (November, 1960), 390–401. Also in this volume.

3. M. K. Jennings, *Community Influentials: The Elites of Atlanta* (New York: Free Press, 1964). D. H. Bouma, "Analysis of the Social Power Position of a Real Estate Board," *Social Problems*, 10 (Fall, 1962), 121–132. Also in this volume.

4. J. Q. Wilson, *Negro Politics: The Search for Leadership* (New York: Free Press, 1960). D. Rogers, "Community Political Systems: A Framework and Hypothesis for Comparative Studies," in B. E. Swanson (ed.), *Current Trends in Comparative Community Studies* (Kansas City, Mo.: Community Studies, Inc., 1962), pp. 31–48. J. Porter, "Elite Groups: A Scheme for the Study of Power in Canada," *Canadian Journal of Economic and Political Science*, 21 (November, 1955), 498–512. A. Wildavsky, *Leadership in a Small Town* (Totowa, N.J.: Bedminster Press, 1964). R. A. Dahl, "A Critique of the Ruling Elite Model," *American Political Science Review*, 52, 2 (June, 1958), 463–469. R. O. Schulze, "The Role of Economic Dominants in Community Power Structure," *American Sociological Review*, 23 (February, 1958), 3–9. Also in this volume.

5. G. E. Swanson, *Religion and Regime: A Sociological Account of the Reformation* (Ann Arbor: University of Michigan Press, 1967).

6. R. S. Lynd and H. M. Lynd, *Middletown* (New York: Harcourt, Brace & World, 1929).

7. Jennings, *op. cit.*

8. R. O. Schulze, "The Bifurcation of Power in a Satellite City," in M. Janowitz (ed.), *Community Political Systems* (New York: Free Press, 1961), pp. 19–80. R. J. Pellegrin and C. H. Coates, "Absentee-Owned Corporations and Community Power Structure," *American Journal of Sociology*, 61 (March, 1956), 413–419. Also in this volume.

9. Dahl, *op. cit.* N. W. Polsby, "The Sociology of Community Power: A Reassessment," *Social Forces*, 37 (March, 1959), 232–236. E. Barth and S. D. Johnson, "Community Power and a Typology of Social Issues," *Social Forces*, 38 (October, 1959), 29–32. Also in this volume. J. Q. Wilson, *op. cit.*, p. 13. C. V. Willie, "Community Leadership in Washington, D.C." A lecture presented at the Washington Center for Metropolitan Studies, Washington, D.C., October 14, 1964. Mimeo.

10. D. C. Miller, "The Prediction of Issue Outcome in Community Decision-Making," *Proceedings of the Pacific Sociological Society, Research Studies of the State College of Washington*, 25 (June, 1957), 137–147.

11. W. S. Landecker, "Types of Integration and Their Measurement," *American Journal of Sociology*, 56 (January, 1951), 332–340.

12. Weaver v. Palmer Bros. Co., 270 U.S. 402 (1926).

13. Swanson, *op. cit.*

14. Rossi, *op. cit.*

15. L. J. R. Herson, "In the Footsteps of Community Power," *American Political Science Review*, 55, 4 (December, 1961), 817–830.

16. J. H. Kessel, "Governmental Structure and Political Environment: A Statistical Note About American Cities," *American Political Science Review*, 56 (September, 1962), 615–620.

17. E. C. Banfield and J. Q. Wilson, *City Politics* (Cambridge: Harvard University Press and M.I.T. Press, 1965), pp. 169ff. R. E. Wolfinger and J. O. Field, "Political Ethos and the Structure of City Government," *American Political Science Review*, 60, 2 (June, 1966), 315. R. R. Alford and H. M. Scoble, "Political and Socioeconomic Characteristics of American Cities," *1965 Municipal Yearbook* (Washington, D.C.: International City Managers' Association, 1965), pp. 82–97.

18. L. F. Schnore and R. R. Alford, "Forms of Government and Socioeconomic Characteristics of Suburbs," *Administrative Science Quarterly*, 8, 1 (June, 1963), 1–17.

19. E. C. Lee, *The Politics of Nonpartisanship: A Study of California City Elections* (Berkeley and Los Angeles: University of California Press, 1960), pp. 25 *et passim*. Banfield and Wilson, *op. cit.*, pp. 88 *et passim*. Wolfinger and Field, *op. cit.*, p. 313.

20. *Ibid.* p. 312.

21. *Ibid.*

22. P. E. Mott and D. Nager, "Acceptance of City-Manager Government and Socioeconomic Characteristics of the Community" (Unpublished manuscript).

23. Kessel, *op. cit.*, pp. 619–620.

24. Wolfinger and Field, *op. cit.*, p. 316.

25. *Ibid.*, p. 326.

26. The classic example: Muncie, Indiana, where the Ball family controlled the community to a degree suggesting the centralist configuration of power: see Lynd and Lynd, *op. cit.* But with the addition of a new industry, the Ball family saw its power erode and found itself sharing it with others: see R. S. Lynd and H. M. Lynd, *Middletown in Transition* (New York: Harcourt, Brace & World, 1937).

27. R. L. Crain and D. B. Rosenthal, "Community Status as a Dimension of Local Decision-Making," *American Sociological Review*, 32, 6 (December, 1967), 970–984.

28. N. Kaplan, "The Relation of Creativity to Sociological Variables in Research Organizations," in C. W. Taylor and F. Barron (eds.), *Scientific Creativity: Its Recognition and Development* (New York: Wiley, 1963),

pp. 195–204. W. Kornhauser, *Scientists in Industry: Conflict and Accommodation* (Berkeley: University of California Press, 1962). D. C. Pelz and F. M. Andrews, "Organizational Atmosphere, as Related to Types of Motives and Levels of Output," *Analysis*

Memo No. 9, Study of Scientific Personnel (Ann Arbor: Institute for Social Research, 1961).
29. For one of the best discussions of the role of the solo individual, see Wildavsky, *op. cit.*

The Politicians

Martin Meyerson and Edward C. Banfield

The City Council, the body which would have to pass upon any sites proposed by the Authority, consisted of 50 aldermen, with the mayor as presiding officer. The aldermen were elected for four-year terms from wards of roughly 25,000 to 65,000 registered voters, only about a third of whom usually voted in aldermanic elections. (The number who voted in mayoralty elections was about twice as great.) Nominally the office of alderman was non-partisan. Actually, however, no one could win an election without the support of a powerful organization and (with some rare exceptions) the only powerful political organizations in the wards were the Democratic and Republican parties. An alderman who did not have the support of

his party "machine"* ordinarily had no hope of reelection.

The Democratic "machine" had ruled Chicago since 1923. Catholics were in control of it; since 1930, with a few exceptions, they had held the major city offices: the mayor, city treasurer, county clerk, more than half of the county commissioners, and two-thirds of the aldermen were Catholics.[1] And among the Catholics it was those of Irish extraction who were dominant in politics: one-third of the Council, including most of its leaders, were Irish-Catholics. The other aldermen were mostly of Polish, Italian, Bohemian, Lithuanian, Slovak, or Greek extraction (in descending order of importance, these were the principal nation-

*Although written almost two generations ago, Lord Bryce's description of machines applies both in general and in detail to the Chicago machines of the present day. See *The American Commonwealth*, 1917 ed., Macmillan, New York and London, Vol. II, Ch. LXIII for Bryce's account of the circumstances which give rise to machines.

"The elective offices are so numerous that ordinary citizens cannot watch them, and cease to care who gets them. The conventions come so often that busy men cannot serve in them. The minor offices are so unattractive that able men do not stand for them. The primary lists are so contrived that only a fraction of the party get on them; and of this fraction many are too lazy or too busy or too careless to attend. The mass of the voters are ignorant; knowing nothing about the personal merits of the candidates, they are ready to follow their leaders like sheep. Even the better class, however they may grumble, are swayed by the inveterate habit of party loyalty, and prefer a bad candidate of their own party to a (probably no better) candidate of the other party. It is less trouble to put up with impure officials, costly city government, a jobbing State legislature, an inferior sort of congressman, than to sacrifice one's own business in the effort to set things right. Thus the Machine works on, and grinds out places, power, and opportunities for illicit gain to those who manage it." *Ibid.*, p. 110.

ality groups in the Democratic party) or of German extraction (these were Republicans).[2] A few aldermen were Jews (unlike the Poles, Italians, and other ethnic minorities, the Jews did not usually endeavor to be recognized as a group on the party slate or in the award of patronage).[3] Two were Negroes. The numerical importance of the Irish in the Council was to be accounted for not so much by their numbers in the electorate as by the fact that in wards where no one ethnic group had a clear majority they made the most acceptable compromise candidates. As one politician explained to an interviewer, "A Lithuanian won't vote for a Pole, and a Pole won't vote for a Lithuanian. A German won't vote for either of them—but all three will vote for a 'Turkey' (Irishman)."*[4]

A few of the aldermen aspired to higher political office, especially (among those who were lawyers) to judgeships, but most of them were in the business of being aldermen as other men are in the business of selling shoes. Being an alderman was supposed to be a full-time occupation, but the salary was only $5,000, so most aldermen supplemented their salaries by selling something—most often insurance or legal service (more than half of them were lawyers). Being an alderman was, of course, very good for business.

Ordinarily, even if he were so inclined, an alderman could not concern himself deeply with the larger issues of city government or take a city-wide view of important problems. If he wanted to stay in office, he had to devote all of his available time and attention to the affairs of the groups that made up his ward. He was in the Council to look after the special interests of his ward and to do favors for his constituents: to get streets repaired, to have a playground installed, to change the zoning law, to represent irate parents before the school authorities, and so on, In addition to activities of this kind, he had to take an interest in the social life of his ward—to appear at weddings, funerals, and neighborhood occasions, and to say a few well chosen words and make a small donation when called upon. If he had any time left, he might think about the problems of the city as a whole. But whatever he thought, he was expected to work for his ward first.

From a formal standpoint, the 50 aldermen governed Chicago.† The Council made appropriations for all municipal purposes, it awarded franchises to and regulated the rates of public utility companies, it passed on appointments presented by the mayor, and (within the authority given it by the state) it could create new city departments at will. The mayor could send or read messages to the Council, he could vote when there was a tie (or when more than one-half of the aldermen had already voted for a measure), and he had a veto (including an item veto over appropriations acts) which could be overridden by a two-thirds vote. In principle, each alderman was the independent agent of his ward. From a formal standpoint, then, the Council was a good deal like a league of independent nations presided over by a secretary-general.

In fact, however, there existed two sets of informal controls by which the aldermen's independence was very much limited and qualified. One set of controls was the leadership of the Council itself. Half a dozen of the most powerful Democratic aldermen— the "Big Boys," they were sometimes called —working usually with the mayor, effectively

---

*A candidate's ethnicity was often a decisive asset or liability; in mixed wards he was most fortunate if his name was such that he could be represented as belonging to more than one ethnic or nationality group. Thus, Alderman Benjamin M. Becker's ward committeeman introduced him to voters of German extraction as of German extraction, stressed to voters of Swedish origin that Becker's wife had lived in Sweden and must have Swedish blood herself, pointed out to Catholics that Becker was a graduate of the DePaul University College of Law and a teacher there (thus implying that he was a Catholic), and presented him to Jews as a Jew. If the Catholics were fooled, no great injustice was done, for Becker's predecessor as alderman for many years was Dr. Joseph Ross, a Catholic whom the Jews assumed was a Jew.[5]

†The city could exercise only those powers doled out to it by the state legislature, however, and so it might be more accurate to say that the city was governed by the state. See Barnet Hodes, "The Illinois Constitution and Home Rule for Chicago," 15 *Chicago Law Review* 78, (1947).

controlled the whole Council when matters of interest to them or to the mayor were at stake. They did this in part by controlling committee assignments. Unless an alderman could get on an important committee, his power in the Council was small. And unless he cooperated with the chairmen of the important committees and especially with the chairman of the Finance Committee (whose salary was $8,500, who was provided a limousine with a police chauffeur, and who had an office second only to the mayor's in splendor), he could not hope to get anything done for his ward. Any measure that required an appropriation had to go to the Finance Committee, and so, as one alderman explained, the chairman of that committee "sits at the gate of accomplishment for any alderman. . . ."[6] Indeed, if an alderman fell foul of the Finance Committee chairman or of any of the "Big Boys" he might be punished by having some city service to his ward reduced or suspended. On the other hand, even if he were a Republican, he could expect generous treatment from the leadership if he "played ball."

The other set of informal controls operated through the party or machine. An alderman had to stay in favor with his ward committeeman—i.e., the party leader in his ward—or else be the committeeman himself. The ward committeeman made all of the important decisions for the party within the ward. The committeeman was elected in the primary every four years (usually he could keep an opponent off the ballot by raising technical objections to his petitions) and so his power rested in part upon a legal foundation. From a legal standpoint, he was entitled to receive and disburse party funds, to manage campaigns, and to represent the leaders of the party within the ward. In fact he was commonly the "boss" of the ward; the party organization in the ward "belonged" to him. He decided who would run on the party's ticket within the ward, he appointed and dismissed precinct captains at will, and he dispensed patronage. As a member of the City and County Central Committees of his party, he participated in selecting its candidates for all city, county,

and state offices and for Congress. (Half of Illinois' 26 Congressional districts were in greater Chicago.) In each of the party governing bodies his vote was in proportion to the total primary vote for his party in the last election; this of course gave him an incentive to "turn in" the biggest vote possible.

No salary went with the office of committeeman, but most of the committeemen held one or more public jobs and some of them ran businesses which were profitable because of their political connections.

William J. Connors, Democratic boss of the 42nd ward (the district described by Zorbaugh in *The Gold Coast and the Slum*),[7] may be taken as reasonably representative of at least some other ward committeemen. In 1950 Connors, who was in the insurance business, was on the public payroll in two capacities: as a state senator and as a bailiff of Municipal Court. His way of running his ward was described as follows:

> That Connors provides well for his workers is undeniable. Not only does he have a great many jobs to distribute, but he is a source of funds if any of his men need to borrow. He supports them when they are in difficulty with the law, as sometimes happens, and takes an interest in their family affairs. His relationship with them is that of a benevolent despot. He holds the power to withdraw their source of livelihood and to banish them from active work in the party and from their power positions in the community. He is the sole dispenser of the campaign funds from the party superstructure and the candidates. He may establish the assessments of the jobholders at any rate he desires without consulting them. He makes the party commitments to the county and city organs without a canvass of the captains' opinions and then demands complete obedience to these decisions. He may move a captain from one precinct to another at his discretion and is, of course, the sole source of patronage distribution.
>
> The committeeman generals his workers much like a military leader might. He plots the strategy of the campaign, estimates the difficulties that may be encountered, and decides the amount and allocation of money to be spent. He shifts captains from one point to another when called for. He attempts to

"build" good precincts over a long period of time. Such building requires several years and may involve extensive trials and changes. Jobs are distributed not only on the basis of the effectiveness of the captain but in regard to the total effects such distribution may have. It happens occasionally that a strong Democratic captain has a smaller number of jobs allotted to him than one who is attempting to build up a Democratic precinct in the face of strong Republican competition. Thus in one precinct which casts a heavy Democratic vote, there are only two jobs besides the captain's, while another precinct that turns in only a slight Democratic majority is staffed by nine jobholders in addition to the captain.

The committeeman respects the unity of the precinct organization and the authority of the captain and his workers. As long as the captain's activities are successful and his conduct does not threaten the party's vote-getting power, Connors does not interfere with the internal structure. The captain selects his own assistants and nominates his choices to receive public jobs. He assumes the responsibility for building an effective precinct organization. He decides how party funds allocated to him will be distributed and to a certain extent how they will be obtained. He and his men must share the responsibility of contributing whatever additional money is necessary beyond that sent from the party's headquarters. Connors respects the autonomy of the captain in this area of personal influence. Captains may or may not distribute campaign literature, pay cash for votes, engage in fraudulent activities, or arrange precinct meetings of the voters. The only important check on the captain's conduct is the final tabulation of votes at each election.[8]

Any ward committeeman who cared to could have himself nominated alderman. If he chose not to run for the office himself (like Connors, he might prefer to be on the public payroll in another capacity), he made sure that the candidate was someone who would work closely with him in ward affairs and offer no challenge to his control of the organization. "Naturally," an alderman once explained, "he (the ward committeeman) doesn't want to get a man who will build himself into a power so he can take the organization away from the committee-man. If the alderman doesn't do what the ward committeeman wants him to do, then the committeeman will dump him at the next election."[9] Some committeemen treated their aldermen as errand boys, others paid little attention to them, and still others treated them as friends, partners, and collaborators.[10]

If an alderman became powerful enough, he might unseat his committeeman and become the ward boss himself. But even in this case he could not be independent of the machine. The leaders of the Central Committee could bring him into line by withholding patronage or discharging public employees from his ward, by denying him financial support from the party's general coffers at election time, or by allowing an investigation of graft and corruption to take place in his ward. If it saw fit, the Central Committee could destroy a ward organization—and thus a ward committeeman—by these means, but it could do so, of course, only at the cost of impairing, at least temporarily, the effectiveness of the machine. Since its purpose was to win elections, a major concern of the machine was "harmony." Only if a committeeman failed to support the party's slate was he likely to be disciplined severely. If they wanted a favor from him, party leaders would offer him a favor—usually patronage—in return.

To increase their power *vis-à-vis* the Central Committee leadership, ward committeemen formed factional alliances or "blocs." Usually these alignments were on a geographical basis—thus, for example, there were South Side and West Side blocs of ward committeemen.

In order to maintain itself and to accomplish its purposes, any organization must offer incentives of the kinds and amounts that are necessary to elicit the contributions of activity it requires. It must then use these contributions of activity so as to secure a renewed supply of resources from which further incentives may be provided—it must, in other words, maintain what Chester Barnard has called an "economy of incentives" or else cease to exist.[11]

In Chicago a political machine distributed "gravy" to its officials, its financial backers, and to the voters. In this way it induced them to contribute the activity it required—to ring doorbells on election day, to give cash, and to go to the polls and vote for its candidates—and in this way it gained possession, through its control of the city or county government, of a renewed supply of "gravy."

As the word "gravy" suggests, the incentives upon which the machines relied were mainly material. Some prestige attached to being a ward politician; there was "fun" in playing the political "game"; there was satisfaction in being "on the inside"; and sometimes there was even an ideological commitment to an issue, the party, or a candidate. But these non-material incentives were not ordinarily strong enough to elicit the amount and kind of activity that a machine required from its workers. "What I look for in a prospective captain," a ward committeeman told an interviewer, "is a young person—man or woman—who is interested in getting some material return out of his political activity. I much prefer this type to the type that is enthused about the 'party cause' or all 'hot' on a particular issue. Enthusiasm for causes is short-lived, but the necessity of making a living is permanent."[12]

The "material return" that the party offered a worker was generally a job on the public payroll. Committeeman Connors, for example, had at his disposal in 1952 an estimated 350 to 500 jobs and the total public payroll to Democratic workers in his ward was conservatively estimated at $1,320,000.[13]

Although jobs were the most visible of the material returns the party gave its workers, other opportunities to make money may have been more valuable. An alderman or committeeman who was a lawyer, an insurance man, or a tavern owner could expect to profit greatly from his association with the party. Whether he was profiting lawfully or unlawfully it was often impossible to tell. Alderman Sain and his ward committeeman, County Commissioner John J. Touhy, for example, were partners in an insurance business. "We handle a lot of business, no question about it," Touhy once blandly told a reporter. "I assume its just good business in the ward to carry insurance with us."*[14]

Even with the voters the machine did not make its appeal on the basis of issues or ideology. It offered them certain non-material incentives—chiefly the friendship and protection of its precinct captains—but in the main with them, as with the party workers, it relied upon "gravy." Just as it gave its workers jobs and opportunities to make money in exchange for their services, so it gave its loyal voters "favors"—special services and preferential treatment at the hands of its members and dependents who held city or county jobs—in exchange for their votes.

The party's agent in exchanging friendship and favors for votes was the precinct captain.† In 1950 a representative captain described his work as follows:

> I am a lawyer and prosecuting attorney for the City. I have spent 19 years in precinct work and have lived and worked in my present precinct for three and a half years.
>
> I try to establish a relationship of personal obligation with my people, mostly small

---

*Some years earlier the *Chicago Daily News* compiled a list of the ordinances introduced by Sain over a five-month period and then inquired of the people who were specially benefited by these ordinances whether they had recently bought insurance of the firm of Touhy and Sain. It turned out that many of them had. (September 24, 1940.)

†In a vivid account by David Gutmann, the Chicago precinct captain is described as a "salesman." "Mr. Dolin [the precinct captain] is a go-between between his party, which has services and favors to sell the public in exchange for the public's votes, and the public, or at least the segments of it which are willing to exchange their votes for services—often enough to swing a close election. In this relationship the vote stands for currency, the party is the manufacturer or the supplier, the public is the consumer, and Mr. Dolin the door-to-door salesman. . . . To the party the vote has 'commodity' or exchange value, in that it represents a fraction of the total sum of votes needed by the party to gain exclusive control over the 'tons' of patronage whereby it holds power, and to gain access to the financial resources of the community." David Gutmann, "Big-Town Politics: Grass-Roots Level," *Commentary*, 17:1, February 1954, p. 155.

shopkeepers and eighty per cent Jewish. I spend two or three evenings a week all year round visiting people, playing cards, talking, and helping them with their problems. My wife doesn't like this, but it is in my blood now. I know ninety per cent of my people by their first names.

Actually I consider myself a social worker for my precinct. I help my people get relief and driveway permits. I help them on unfair parking fines and property assessments. The last is most effective in my neighborhood.

The only return I ask is that they register and vote. If they have their own opinions on certain top offices, I just ask them to vote my way on lower offices where they usually have no preferences anyway.

I never take leaflets or mention issues or conduct rallies in my precinct. After all, this is a question of personal friendship between me and my neighbors. I had 260 promises for Korshak in this primary.

On election day I had forty or fifty people to help me because this was a "hot" campaign. All they had to do was to get out their own family and friends. I used to lease an apartment near the poll where I gave out drinks and cigars, but I don't do this any more.

I stayed inside the poll most of election day, especially during the vote counting. If something went wrong, you could have heard me yell all over the precinct. Actually there isn't as much fraud now as there used to be.

Abner (the PAC candidate) was not really a threat in my precinct. He had seven workers but they contacted only their friends. No one feels obligated to them and they worked only during the campaign. Abner's campaigners were naive. They expected to influence people by issues, and they relied on leaflets and newspaper publicity which is not effective. Besides, Abner (Negro) is not hard to beat in a white precinct. I just carried a picture of both candidates around with me.

I can control my primary vote for sure because I can make the party regulars come out. I don't encourage a high vote here, just a sure vote. In the general election there is much more independent voting, and I can't be sure of control.[15]

In the conservation areas, especially, the precinct captain was often active in the neighborhood improvement association and a leader in efforts to keep "undesirable people" out of the neighborhood. An interviewer who spoke to 30 precinct captains in 1951 found that 16 of them had been approached by voters who wanted help in preventing Negroes and Jews from moving into the neighborhood. Some of these captains invented slogans and ran campaigns on an issue such as: "The ———— neighborhood is a good clean neighborhood. Let's keep it that way!" A captain was likely to learn about it almost immediately if a landlord rented to an "undesirable"; very often the captain would go to the landlord to urge in the name of civic pride that he discriminate and to point out that property values would decline if he did not.

In heavily Democratic precincts the owners of rooming houses sometimes consulted with their precinct captains about new roomers and assisted the party workers with their canvass at election time. In some cases these owners refused to permit Republican workers to enter their buildings. The loyalty of the rooming house owner to the Democratic party was not a matter of ideology: the owner who did not cooperate with the precinct captain could expect a visit from the city building inspector the next day.[16]

In addition to the services of party workers and voters, the machine needed cash. (It usually cost about $40,000 to elect an alderman.) This it raised by assessing the salaries of people who owed their jobs to the party, from the proceeds of ward-sponsored affairs such as picnics, boxing matches, and golf days, and in contributions from individuals and organizations who wanted to be on good terms with the party or, perhaps, even to help its candidates win.[17] These were all considered legitimate sources of revenue. In some wards, however, money was raised by promising favors or threatening injury to business interests, especially to those interests—e.g., taverns, hotels, and nightclubs—which were subject to inspection and licensing laws. Business people who wanted favors—a change in the zoning law, a permit to operate a tavern, a tax adjustment, and so on—were expected to pay for them in cash. In some wards there was even said to be a fixed schedule of prices for such favors. Whether the money so received went to support the party or to support personally the ward committeeman, the alderman, and their cronies was seldom clear; indeed, in many wards no real distinction could be made between the coffers of the party and the pockets of the boss: the ward organization "belonged" to the boss.*

The most profitable favors were of course those done for illegal enterprises. In giving protection to gambling joints, unlawful taverns, and houses of prostitution some politicians joined with racketeers to form a criminal syndicate.† A by-product of their activity was the systematic corruption of the police force; in one way or another officers were either bribed or discouraged from doing their duty. "After you find out how many places are protected by the ward politicians," a patrolman of long service told an investigator, "you just stay out of the way so you won't be around when something happens."[18]

The machines were most effective in delivering votes in the precincts where they were most corrupt. In general, these were in the "skid-row" districts and the slums, where votes were cheapest and illegal activities most numerous. The "river wards" in the decaying center and on the West Side of the city were the most solidly organized and the most corrupt. Here "social absenteeism"—the departure of socially articulate leaders of the community—had reached such a point that the machine politicians had the field to themselves.‡ It was almost un-

thinkable that an alderman in one of these wards might lose at the polls because he took an unpopular stand on an issue. If he lost, it was because his committeeman "dumped" him, because the committeeman sold out to the opposition, or because the opposition managed to build a more powerful machine, but it was not because the voters disliked his stand on any issues. These "river wards" were in sharp contrast to the so-called "newspaper wards" particularly on the North Side where voters usually split the ticket in the way a newspaper advised. The aldermen in the "river wards" could afford to be contemptuous of the newspapers; in their wards editorials were words wasted.

Although corruption in varying degrees was widespread in both parties, it was by no means universal in either. Some Democratic and some Republican wards were probably almost entirely "clean" and even in wards which were not "clean" there were aldermen and other officials who were not parties to the "deals" that were made in the back rooms. The honest aldermen, however, got little credit or encouragement from the voters. Many people seemed to think that all politicians were corrupt and that if an alderman did not use his office for personal profit it was because he was a fool. When a North Side alderman bought his boy a football suit and helmet the other children in the neighborhood said, "Look at the alderman's son," suggesting ill-gotten funds. The alderman himself drove a two-year-old Dodge instead of the Cadillac that he could

---

*If he thought the transaction was likely to be profitable, the ward boss might sell the services of his organization to the opposition. He might be criticized for doing this, but he was not likely to be unseated; after all, the organization "belonged" to him.

†". . . the criminal syndicate," according to Aaron Kohn, chief investigator for the Emergency Crime Committee of the City Council, "can be described as consisting of political officials, having the power and responsibility to enforce the laws, who maliciously withhold that power in exchange for money and support from hoodlums, vice operators, professional gamblers, and other community enemies, to aid them in their political ambitions." Independent Voters of Illinois, *The Kohn Report; Crime and Politics in Chicago,* Chicago, 1953, p. iii. However, after two months inquiry a grand jury in the Spring of 1954 gave up its efforts to uncover specific links between crime and politics in Chicago. "If an alliance exists," the jurors said, "it might be disclosed with funds to conduct undercover work. . . ." *Chicago Sun-Times,* May 1, 1954.

‡See the discussion of social absenteeism in Morris Janowitz, *The Community Press in an Urban Setting,* The Free Press, Glencoe, Illinois, 1952, p. 214. Janowitz notes that social absenteeism contributes to the decay of the ideological element in politics, thus creating "a new kind of hoodlumism in politics" and making possible sudden shifts from one party to another which have no significance in terms of the traditional political allegiances.

well afford, but even this did not convince his constituents that he was honest.*[19] This widespread cynicism tended, perhaps, to give the aldermen a low conception of their calling and to encourage irresponsibility on their part.

Some of the honest men, the Mayor among them, did less than they might have done to put a stop to corruption. The fact was that they needed for themselves or for their party the support of the powerful bosses in the corrupt wards. So, for that matter, did many other interests, both liberal and conservative, in city, state, and nation.

———

During his 14 years as Mayor, Edward J. Kelly had been the undisputed boss of the Democratic Party in Chicago and in Cook County. Through an alliance with Patrick A. Nash, chairman of the County Central Committee, Kelly controlled all patronage and thus the whole machine. As an admiring alderman once remarked, "Kelly walked around with 9,000 jobs stuck in his back pocket."[20]

As Mayor and as boss of the machine, Kelly was in full control of the Council. He saw to it that his men had all of the important committee posts and if a Democratic alderman dared to oppose one of his measures he would call the man's committeeman to demand that he be made to conform.

In 1947, faced with a hard campaign—public opinion was aroused by corruption in the school system—Kelly retired. Jacob Arvey, a West Side lawyer who had been his chief lieutenant and who succeeded him as chairman of the County Central Committee, maneuvered successfully to have the party nominate as Kelly's successor a candidate who would stand for reform and who would not disturb the balance of power among the factions then struggling to inherit Kelly's power.

Martin H. Kennelly had the qualifications that were wanted. He was of Irish extraction and a Catholic, he was a successful business-man (he had been in the trucking and warehouse business all his life), he had never been prominent in politics although he had been active in one wing of the Democratic Party and a generous contributor to it, and he was favorably known as the head of the city Red Cross drive. All of this, of course, made him a good reform candidate. But from the standpoint of the factional leaders who were fighting for control of the party, it was perhaps an even greater advantage that he was not allied to any of them and that he clearly had no inclination to participate in the struggle for control of the machine. Indeed, Kennelly is supposed to have accepted the nomination on the explicit understanding that he would not be expected to act as a machine leader or to take directions in policy matters from the machine.

Kennelly made a campaign pledge that he would respect the independence of the City Council and after his election, when the leaders of the Council met to choose the committee heads, he made a point of being on vacation in North Carolina. Kelly had always attended meetings of the important committees of the Council; Kennelly did not even attend meetings of the Finance Committee. Moreover, Kennelly in effect declined to take a place on the County Central Committee and he seldom attended party conferences.[21] He even extended the merit system to cover a large number of minor jobs in the city government. Whether from expediency, prejudice, or principle, the new Mayor apparently believed that the aldermen should run the city with as little direction from him as possible.

Without the Mayor's help, Arvey, the chairman of the County Central Committee, could not hold the remnants of the Kelly organization together. Thomas D. Nash, committeeman for the 19th ward, formed a coalition of several South Side Democratic and Republican ward bosses to take control of the Council away from the Kelly-Arvey forces, and shortly after Kennelly's election, the alderman of Nash's ward, John J.

---

*As this study went to press a committee of the Chicago Bar Association filed charges against this very alderman after the *Sun-Times* had accused him of fee-splitting in zoning cases.

Duffy, was elected chairman of the powerful Finance Committee over the Kelly-Arvey candidate.

For many years Duffy had had to defer to Kelly. "Kelly was a good mayor," he once told an interviewer, "but he became too powerful—the same thing happened to him that ruined Hitler and Mussolini. Kelly said, 'If you don't run the organization and its members, they'll run you.' He argued that you have to be the boss to be successful. Kennelly is a different type. He says it's the responsibility of the Council to make decisions. We get together and we throw out our views—exchange them—and we learn a lot from listening to each other."[22]

Some of the aldermen who did not, like Duffy, gain power thereby were not so sure that it was an advantage to have a weak mayor. "What he (Kennelly) is trying to do," one of them said, "is introduce a new philosophy into Chicago government of letting the legislative branch take care of itself. The trouble with that is we have been so used to being led around that we haven't gotten used to working out our own problems. Take when Mayor Kelly was in; when I needed something I could say, 'We have to have this,' and in twenty-four hours we would have it. Today, it takes a lot longer to get something. Maybe his position is right, but it will take a lot longer to catch on."[23]

Critics of the Kennelly administration, including the liberals, most of whom had voted for him, were often exasperated by the Mayor's way of doing things. They criticized him for acting like a discussion leader instead of a politician. "Kennelly's idea of a beautiful world," one of the public housing leaders once said, "is to sit around a table and have the opposing parties come to an agreement for which he would take the credit without ever having opened his mouth."[24]

The way the Council worked under Kennelly at the time of the public housing site selection struggle was described by Thomas Drennan, a seasoned observer of City Hall who was the *Sun-Times'* political columnist:

"As finance committee boss in control of over $200,000,000 a year for city expenditures" Drennan wrote, "Duffy has been able to set up some order among the rambunctious lads in the council.

"But this is limited mainly to deciding who gets to the jam pot first—and how much he gets. This also stops the overly-playful ones from setting fire to the aldermanic house.

"A select number of the 'big boys' are entrusted with enforcing Duffy's policies. They include Alds. Francis Hogan; Clarence Wagner; Harry Sain; William J. Lancaster and P. J. Cullerton. Important, too, because of their seniority are Alds. George D. Kells and Dorsey Crowe.

"When Edward J. Kelly was mayor and aldermanic brats were punished by the baseball-bat-in-the-woodshed system, those in this group used to dine daily in the Bismarck Inn, across from the LaSalle Street entrance to the City Hall. The place featured a 75-cent lunch.

"But things have changed. Since Kennelly got in, the group may be found in the same hotel's Walnut Room where the à-la-carte lunch items run into three figures.

"These aldermen, good Democrats all, are the 'works' in operating the city's business. Through their control of key subcommittees created by Duffy, they pass on every vital measure—especially those involving spending of public money on contracts.

"So far Duffy has been able to use these lieutenants to 'deliver' the City Council for legislation wanted by Kennelly. Some liberal measures had to be crammed down their throats on the grounds of expediency. But despite long delay—the building code revision, for instance—they eventually went along.

"The rest of the aldermen, with about six exceptions, usually fall in line because of Duffy's influence with key department heads, one of whom, Lloyd M. Johnson, is superintendent of streets and electricity. He decides which streets should be repaired and maintained and how often the garbage will be collected in the wards—important decisions to an alderman."[25]

Most of these aldermanic leaders represented, it should be noted, lower middle-class wards on the South Side—wards which were mainly in conservation areas. Duffy himself came from a South Side ward where there was much vacant land and a small colony of upper-class Negroes. Wagner, his close friend and chief lieutenant, probably could expect to win only one or two more elections, so rapidly was the Negro population increasing in his ward. Horan's situation was similar. Lancaster did not come from the South Side, but his ward was a conservation area and his allegiance had been shifting from Arvey's West Side Bloc. The aldermen from these South Side wards and allied areas were a minority but possessed most of the power that was exercised in the Council, for they were its leaders.

Notes

1. William R. Gable, "The Chicago City Council: A Study of Urban Politics and Legislation," Unpublished dissertation, Department of Political Science, University of Chicago, Chicago, 1953, p. 13.
2. John P. White, "Lithuanians and the Democratic Party, A Case Study of Nationality Politics in Chicago and Cook County," Unpublished Ph.D. dissertation, Political Science Department, University of Chicago, Chicago, 1953, p. 25.
3. *Ibid.*, p. 28.
4. *Ibid.*, p. 64.
5. Interview document.
6. Interview document.
7. Harvey W. Zorbaugh, *The Gold Coast and the Slum*, University of Chicago Press, Chicago, 1929, p. 287.
8. Leonardo Neher, "The Political Parties in Chicago's 42nd Ward," Unpublished dissertation (Department of Political Science, University of Chicago, Chicago, 1952, pp. 65–66.
9. W. R. Gable, *op. cit.*, p. 74.
10. James A. Rust, "The Ward Committeeman in Chicago," Unpublished dissertation, Department of Political Science, University of Chicago, Chicago, 1953, p. 56.
11. Chester I. Barnard, *The Functions of the Executive*, Harvard University Press, Cambridge, 1938, Ch. XI. Barnard discusses the special case of the political organization on pp. 156–57.
12. H. Dicken Cherry, "Effective Precinct Organization," Unpublished dissertation, Department of Political Science, University of Chicago, Chicago, 1952.
13. Leonardo Neher, *op. cit.*, p. 76.
14. *Chicago Daily News*, August 27, 1949.
15. Quoted in Fay Calkins, *The CIO and The Democratic Party*, University of Chicago Press, Chicago, 1952, pp. 67–68.
16. H. D. Cherry, *op. cit.*, pp. 67–68.
17. Neher, *op. cit.*, p. 92.
18. Independent Voters of Illinois, *The Kohn Report; Crime and Politics in Chicago*, Chicago, 1953, p. 10.
19. Interview document.
20. Interview document.
21. W. R. Gable, *op. cit.*, p. 121.
22. Interview document.
23. Quoted by Gable, *op. cit.*, p. 121.
24. Interview document.
25. *Chicago Sun-Times*, April 4, 1950.

Power and Community Structure[*]

Peter H. Rossi

This paper deals with some structural characteristics of local communities which are relevant to their power structures and decision making processes. The ideas presented constitute a theory both in the sense of a conceptual scheme and in the sense of a set of propositions, albeit only loosely interrelated. The theory has its origins both in the growing body of literature on the power structures of local communities and in the field experiences of the author.

The immediate impetus to the construction of this theory was a growing dissatisfaction with the non-cumulative character of the field to which it purports to apply. Case study after case study of communities has appeared within the past few years, each contributing its part to a body of knowledge best characterized by the statement, "It is different here than elsewhere."[1] The author often inserts a particular comparison somewhere into his paper: Hunter's Regional City, Schulze's Cibola, Rossi's Mediana, and so forth. Each author owns his own town, defending it from the erroneous and somewhat heretical conceptualizations of others much the way a feudal lord defends the integrity of the local patron saint against the false counterclaims of nearby realms.

One firm generalization emerges from the literature: the power structure of local communities and the decision making processes to be found therein show a significant range of variation. This range can be only partly dependent on the differences in research technology employed by each researcher, for the same researchers have found different patterns in different communities. No firm generalizations emerge, however, concerning the sources of these variations.

There are two main reasons for the failure of generalizations of this sort to emerge. First, with few exceptions, comparative studies are rare. Most studies are concerned with establishing a pattern within one particular community, setting it off at best against one other community. Studies in which a large number of communities are systematically contrasted with comparable committees are the sources from which desired generalizations will emerge. The empirical relationships between power structures and other community social structures will provide the data.

The second main reason lies in the inadequacy of social theory. Despite the many community studies which have been undertaken since the classic Booth study of London, we are still lacking a conceptual scheme specifying with some degree of clarity what are the important elements in community structure. Indeed, the operational form that Hunter gave to the conception of community power structure will probably remain as his greatest contribution.[2] Before Hunter only the Lynds[3] paid attention to this feature of social structure, and this interest of the Lynds did not start a tradition because they were unable to communicate the techniques by which they singled out the "X" family as the dominant center in Middletown. After Hunter laid out his quasi-sociometry, community studies experienced a revival, all centered around some modification of his device.

Reprinted from the Midwest Journal of Political Science, *4 (November 1960), 390–401, by permission of the author and Wayne State University Press. Copyright 1960 by Wayne State University Press.*

[*]A revised version of a paper delivered at the 1959 Annual Meeting of the American Sociological Association, Chicago, Illinois, September, 1959. Preparation of this paper and some of the author's research cited was supported by a grant from the Social Science Research Council, hereby gratefully acknowledged.

Of course without a conceptual scheme, comparative studies are difficult to plan and to achieve. What should the researcher and his team look for? He now knows that to define the powerful he can employ some modification of Hunter's balloting. The census and other published sources provide additional ways of classifying communities, but these provide at best only indirect indicators of social organization, and the researcher must still have a rationale for choosing among the possible indicators. Researchers are therefore forced to collect their own data. To do so obviously requires some *a priori* conceptions as to what is important. The vicious circle is closed: comparative community studies are one of the important sources of ideas concerning the structural concomitants of variations in power and decision making, but properly to conduct such studies requires some framework for the collection of such data.[4]

Gaps in the Conception of Community Structures

To characterize communities we need some sort of framework which can guide observations, alerting the researcher to the crucial elements in the structure of the community. What form should such a conceptual scheme take? Should we construct some grand scheme which would be the all around best way of characterizing communities or should we work piecemeal, building one scheme for one problem and another scheme for another? It is my conviction that the latter path will prove most fruitful: namely, the construction of schemes which are specific to the particular substantive problem at hand. Thus the best way of characterizing communities for the purpose of understanding fluoridation controversies in principle may be different from the best way for understanding some other community process.

Even if one were to grant the soundness of this notion of specific theories for specific purposes, there still remains a considerable problem in the construction of such theories. Although we have made much progress through the work of the human ecologists in

classifying cities according to their economic functions and their relations to their environments, we have done little with the internal social organization of communities. In this last respect, perhaps the best known structural characteristic of communities is along stratification lines. A large enough body of research and thinking has gone into the definition of stratification both on the purely nominal level and on the operational level for the researcher to have a fairly clear idea of how to use this term, how to measure stratification systems, and how to locate the positions within such systems of particular individuals or groups. Similar amounts of thinking and effort have not been expended on invention of an appropriate methodology for studying other kinds of organized relationships among the members of a community. Although on the abstract level sociometric devices might seem useful tools in the study of large communities, on the empirical level they prove impractical.

The gap in the conception of community structure is most serious in the area of social organization. This paper is intended to fill in part of this conceptual hiatus by constructing a scheme for classifying the political structures of local communities. The scheme purports to be useful specifically for understanding variations in power structures. Hopefully it may also turn out to be of some utility in the study of closely related community characteristics.

A Conceptual Scheme for the Political Structure of Local Communities

The purpose of the scheme to be described here is to account for the variations in power structures to be found among American local communities. It may also prove of some utility in other areas, for example, community conflicts. The general thesis underlying the scheme is a simple one: the pattern taken by the power structure of a community is a function of the kind of political life to be found therein. My reasons for postulating this relationship are also simple and somewhat obvious: the political institutions of a community are the ultimate locus of the decisions that are binding on the total community. Hence much of the power exercised is focused on the governmental institutions of the local community.

For our present purposes, it is useful to regard the political life of a community as occurring at two different levels, interrelated but to some degree independent. On the one hand, there is a set of governmental institutions manned by officials and employees with defined functions and spheres of authority and competence. On the other hand, there is the electorate, the body of citizens with voting rights, organized to some degree into political parties. We expect that phenomena appearing on each of these levels independently influence the forms taken by community power structures.

On the institutional level, there are several characteristics of local government that are of some consequence. First, communities vary according to the degree to which the roles of officials are *professionalized*. In many communities, mayors and city councilmen and often other officials are employed in their official capacities only part time and lack the opportunity to become fully engrossed in these roles. At the other extreme, some communities employ professionally trained officials—city managers, school superintendents, etc.—who are full time employees expecting to remain in their occupation—although not in any particular post—for long periods of time. In communities where local officials exercise their functions on a part time basis and where the qualifications for incumbency are not exacting, the incumbents are less likely to segregate their official roles from their other roles and hence extra-official considerations are more likely to play roles of some importance in their decisions. Thus the informal cabal which ran Springdale, as described by Vidich and Bensman,[5] hardly distinguish between their roles as city fathers and their roles as businessmen and professionals. At the other extreme are the professional politicians who run Chicago, whose independence is curbed very little.

A second important structural characteristic of local government refers to the rules by which officials are selected. Two aspects of electoral rules are significant. Electoral rules can either retard or facilitate the development of enduring political alignments in the community, and the latter are important determinants of the forms of decision making. In this respect, the crucial differences lie between communities which have non-partisan and communities which have partisan elections. Non-partisan electoral rules discourage the development of enduring political alignments by reducing the advantages to candidates of appearing on slates, whereas partisan elections facilitate cooperation among candidates and the drawing of clear lines between opposing slates of candidates. It should be noted in this connection that primaries are in effect non-partisan elections in communities which are predominantly Democratic or Republican.[6]

Another structural characteristic which tends to reduce the importance of political organizations is the rule concerning the number of officials elected by popular vote. Short ballots on which only a few candidates compete for the major offices tend to reduce organizational importance by lowering the benefits to candidates of cooperation with each other.

These structural characteristics of the governmental institutions of the local community underlie the ability of these institutions to develop an independence of their own and also indicate the extent to which conflicts within the community are manifested in the political realm or in some other fashion.

Moving now to the level of the electorate and its organization, there are two important dimensions to be considered. First, we must consider the political homogeneity of the electorate, roughly defined as the extent to which the community is divided equally or unequally among the contending political factions of the community. The more unequally the community is divided, the less likely are open political struggles to be the major expressions of clashes of interest and the more likely is decision making to be a prerogative of a "cozy few."

Borrowing from Gerhard Lenski, a second characteristic of the electorate might be called "political crystallization": the extent to which the lines of political cleavage within the community coincide with major social structural differentiations. In this connection the crucial modes of social structural differentiation are along class and status lines. The more political lines coincide with class and status lines, the more likely are community clashes to take a political form. These are important lines of differentiation within communities because they are likely to endure over time.[7] Political differences which coincide with class and status differences are for these reasons likely to be reinforced by the double factors of differential association and connection with important interests.

If we now consider the entire set of community characteristics distinguished here, we see that they may be conceived of as indicators of two more abstract attributes of communities: first, the institutional indicators express the degree of segregation of political institutions from other community institutions; second, the indicators relating to the electorate reflect the extent to which partisan politics is a crucial arena for the important decision making within the community.

It is important to note that these characteristics of communities can be easily translated into operational forms. The city charter can tell us how officials are elected and whether their jobs are full or part time. Election statistics and survey research can tell us the degree of political homogeneity and political crystallization.

Two broad hypotheses can be formulated at this point. (1) The more segregated are political roles from other roles played by incumbent officials, the more independent the governmental structure of a community from other institutional structures. (2) The more heterogeneous the electorate and the greater the degree of political crystallization, the more important the governmental institutions as loci for important decision making.

Implications for Community Power Structures

The studies of community power structures have universally found the upper levels of the occupational hierarchy to occupy prominent power positions. In no city—even heavily working class Stackton—have proprietors, managers, and professional men played insignificant parts. Often enough some members of these groups do not play as prominent a part as others, even though they are as wealthy and as important in the economic life of the city, but in all cities members of these groups were to be found in some kind of inner circle.

The disagreement among researchers concerns two important matters. First, there is disagreement over the pattern of power, with some researchers preferring the monolith as their model and others preferring polyliths or more complicated forms. Second, there is disagreement over the roles played by public officials and voluntary associations. Hardly anything could be written about Chicago, Stackton, or Philadelphia without reference to the mayor's office and other top level public officials. In contrast, in Regional City and some of the towns studied by C. P. Loomis and his research workers, public officials and often labor leaders appear as minor and insignificant personages. It should be noted that these two kinds of disagreements among researchers are related. A monolithic model for a power structure generally goes along with a very subordinate role for voluntary associations and public officials. Thus, in Hunter's Regional City public officials are explicitly viewed as the handmaidens of the elite group, and labor leaders are scarcely worth mentioning.

A polylithic power structure tends to mean a number of small monoliths each centering around a particular sort of activity. Thus in industrial Stackton, the civic associations and community service organizations were the preserves of the business community, whereas local government was safe in the hands of professional politicians resting on the mass base of the Democratic Party and its heavy support from among ethnic groups of relatively recent arrival from abroad. Indeed, respondents rarely reported that any one individual was powerful in all spheres of community life.

To some degree the disagreements among researchers on the forms taken by the power structures in communities and the place to be accorded public officials and associational leaders are functions of the different research techniques employed. Some approaches preclude the finding of polylithic power structures. However, in much larger part, the differences among researchers are functions of "reality," representing major ways in which communities *in fact* differ. My general thesis is that these differences are functions of the differences among communities in their political structures.

If we look carefully at the studies of community power structure we may discern the following types:

(1) *Pyramidal.* Lines of power tend to have their ultimate source in one man or a very small number of men. Decision making tends to be highly centralized, with lower echelons mainly carrying out major policy decisions made by the small group at the apex.
Examples: Middletown, Regional City

(2) *Caucus rule.* Lines of power tend to end in a relatively large group of men who make decisions through consensus. Decision making tends to be a matter of manufacturing consent among the "cozy few" who make up the caucus. Typical power structure in the small town or dormitory suburb.
Examples: Springdale, Mediana

(3) *Polylith.* Separate power structures definable for major spheres of community activity. Typically, local government in the hands of professional politicians backed by the solidary strength of voluntary associations, with the community service organizations in the hands of the business and professional subcommunity.

(4) *Amorphous.* No discernible enduring pattern of power. Logical residual category. No examples.

Note that the first two types of power structures are very similar, differing only in the number of decision makers who share power among themselves. The major differentiation is between the first two types wherein lines of power tend to converge and the last two types wherein lines of power tend to diverge.

The divergence of power lines has its source in the existence of the possibility for occupational groups other than business and professional to occupy positions of importance within major community institutions. This occurs typically when there is political crystallization in a community which is heterogeneous class wise or status wise. When the lower status or class levels have a political party representing them which has a chance to get into office, there is the possibility that public office can become one of the important sources of power.

The conditions under which the political parties have a vigorous life are defined by the structural features described earlier. Under partisan electoral laws, when officials are professionalized, when either the majority of the electorate favor the underdog party or when the parties are balanced in strength, then the political institutions and public officials assume a position of importance within the power structure of the community.

Another way of putting this thesis is to say that the leaders of the dominant economic institutions ordinarily wield power, but they are forced to take others into account when popular democratic rules allow the lower levels of the community an opportunity to place their representatives in public office. The elements of the community political structure we have distinguished here are those which facilitate the development of governmental independence from the business and professional community.

The general hypothesis may now be stated more precisely, as follows: *in communities with partisan electoral procedures, whose officials are full time functionaries, where party lines tend to coincide with class and status lines and where the party favored by the lower class and status groups has some good chance of getting elected to office, community power structures tend to be polylithic rather than monolithic.* Since these characteristics of community political structures are to some unknown degree independent of one another, different combinations of such characteristics can appear empirically. The patterns in such communities cannot be deduced from this hypothesis since we do not specify the weights to be assigned to each characteristic.

There are further expectations implied in the general hypothesis. Some examples follow:

(1) Homogeneous middle class communities, for example, dormitory suburbs and the like, will tend to have monolithic power structures, since the class basis for countervailing political power does not exist.

(2) In communities where the lower class party has a clear majority there will be moves on the part of the business and professional community to introduce structural changes in city government to undermine this majority, as for example, nonpartisan elections, short ballot, and the like.

(3) In polylithic communities, city government and private community organizations try to limit the sphere of each other's operations by moving more and more functions into their own spheres of authority.

(4) In communities with monolithic power structures, conflicts tend to take on the character of mass revolts in which small incidents are magnified out of proportion because there are no regularized means for the expression of conflict.[8]

(5) Historically, the development of voluntary civic associations may be interpreted as a reaction to the loss of local political power by high status groups. Since these community organizations were not governed by the mass vote of the lower class groups, high status groups could keep control over them.

Additional similar propositions may be generated from the basic hypothesis set forth in this paper. Although I believe that such propositions will be upheld in general by empirical data, I am also sure that considerable modifications will be made in them.

Conclusions

To sum up, I have presented in this paper a conceptual scheme which provides a way of classifying the political structures of local communities. I have also tried to spell out how these political features may modify the power structures to be found in such communities. The utility of the scheme obviously requires for testing empirical data generated by comparative community studies. Though I have no doubt that the hypotheses presented here will at best suffer considerable modification when confronted with such data, I hope they will serve the purpose of providing some impetus for comparative community studies.

Notes

1. An early bibliographic review was published by the author as "Community Decision Making" in *The Administrative Science Quarterly*, 1 (March, 1957), 415–443. An incomplete list of more recent studies follows: Warner Bloomberg, *The Structure of Power in Stackton* (Unpublished Ph.D. dissertation, University of Chicago, 1960). James S. Coleman, *Community Conflict* (Glencoe, Illinois: Free Press, 1957). William H. Form, "Organized Labor's Place in the Community Power Structure," *Industrial and Labor Relations*

Review, 12 (July, 1959), 526–539. William H. Form and William V. D'Antonio, "Integration and Cleavage Among Community Influentials in Two Border Cities," *American Sociological Review*, 24 (December, 1959), 804–814. Orrin E. Klapp and Vincent L. Padgett, "Power Structure and Decision Making in a Mexican Border City," *American Journal of Sociology*, 65 (January, 1960), 400–406. Delbert C. Miller, "Decision Making Cliques in Community Power Structure," *American Journal of Sociology*, 64 (November, 1958), 299–310. Delbert C. Miller, "Industry and Community Power Structures," *American Sociological Review*, 23 (February, 1958), 9–15. Roland J. Pellegrin and Charles H. Coates, "Absentee Owned Corporations and Community Power Structure," *American Journal of Sociology*, 61 (March, 1956), 413–419. Nelson W. Polsby, "Three Problems in the Analysis of Community Power," *American Sociological Review*, 24 (December, 1959), 796–803. Nelson W. Polsby, "The Sociology of Community Power: A Reassessment," *Social Forces*, 37 (March, 1959), 232–236. Edwin H. Rhyne, "Political Parties and Decision Making in Three Southern Counties," *American Political Science Review*, 52 (December, 1958), 1091–1107. Peter H. Rossi, "Industry and Community," National Opinion Research Center, Report No. 64, October, 1957 (mimeo.). Peter H. Rossi and Phillips Cutright, "The Political Organization of an Industrial Community," in Morris Janowitz and Heinz Eulau (eds.), *Community Political Systems* (Glencoe, Illinois: Free Press, 1960, forthcoming). Peter H. Rossi and Robert A. Dentler, *The Politics of Urban Renewal* (Glencoe, Illinois: Free Press, 1960, forthcoming). Robert O. Schulze, "The Role of Economic Dominants in Community Power Structure," *American Sociological Review*, 23 (February, 1958), 3–9. Arthur J. Vidich and Joe Bensman, *Small Town in Mass Society* (Princeton, New Jersey: Princeton University Press, 1959).

2. Floyd A. Hunter, *Community Power Structure* (Chapel Hill, North Carolina: University of North Carolina Press, 1952).

3. Robert S. and Helen M. Lynd, *Middletown in Transition* (New York: Harcourt Brace and Company, 1937).

4. An important exception to this characterization are the studies undertaken at Michigan State University by C. P. Loomis, W. Form and others.

5. Vidich and Bensman, *op. cit.*

6. Non-partisan elections operate to the benefit of the highly organized political minority. Hence, usually, non-partisan elections operate to the benefit of the white collar groups in industrial communities and to the benefit of the Democratic Party in middle class suburbs.

7. On a large space scale—i.e., for regions and nations—regional differences would also play important roles, but since the micro-regional differences in the American city tend to be wiped out quickly by residential mobility, they play only a minor role within communities.

8. See Coleman. *op. cit.*

Status and Power in the Industrial Community: A Comment on Drucker's Thesis

James B. McKee

Professor Drucker's provocative thesis of the employee society includes the hypothesis that large-scale organization is "the qualitatively, socially, and morally decisive realm" in the industrial society.* This does not ring entirely strange in our ears, for we have long

Reprinted from The American Journal of Sociology, 58 *(January 1953), 364–370, by permission of the author and The University of Chicago Press. Copyright 1953 by The University of Chicago.*

*[Peter F. Drucker is a political scientist by training and currently teaches in the Graduate School of Business Administration, New York University. He has written numerous books about the political and economic organization of American society. Among some of his better known works are *The New Society* and *Concept of the Corporation*—Editor's note]

been accustomed to such ideas as bureaucracy, management rights, the managerial revolution, and the separation of ownership and control.

But Drucker has extracted from the mass of now somewhat familiar data and ideas an image of the employee society focused on two basic elements: *stratification* and *power*. He has located their source in the large corporate organization:

> This employee society is a hierarchical system—a system in which everybody is related to people through his relationship to a strictly impersonal, strictly objective, strictly abstract thing, the "organization," the "corporation," the "government agency," etc. It means, second, that this is a society which is based on, and ruled by, status. . . .
>
> A new ruling group has emerged in our society—management. It is a ruling group which derives its authority and its responsibilities squarely from function, that is, from its status relationship to the organization.

Thus, the strictly impersonal status pattern of the organization becomes that of society; the management of large-scale organization becomes the new ruling elite. The new society emerges in the image of the corporation.

The theory of the employee society is the logical culmination of a quarter-century of social theorizing about a complex of problems. It links the factory studies of industrial sociology with the economic analysis of corporate ownership and control; it encompasses such seemingly unlike thinkers as [Elton] Mayo and [James] Burnham. For here in a single theory we find the conception of corporate and factory organization of social life, the managerial revolution, and the bureaucratically stratified society.

One significant trend of this theorizing has been its anti-Marxism. We are informed that the economic determinism in which Marxian social theory is rooted is as much in error as is the classical image of economic man. Yet can we not detect here the makings of a new determinism which differs from Marxism in conceptual but not in psychological orientation?

Marx saw stratification as a series of social classes determined by economic relationships; the protagonists of the new society see it as a stratified hierarchy determined by bureaucratic status. For Marx's monopoly capitalism the new thinkers substitute large-scale organization; for the imperative logic of capitalistic development we get the impersonal dynamics of administrative bureaucracy; and, instead of the proletarian revolution, the managerial one.

Marx analyzed an economic system and constructed his view of society from it. Similarly, the new thinkers have projected their analysis of organization and factory into conception of society. The logical process is the same: one views a society from inside a limited set of relationships and projects it outward to the larger society. The conceptualization may be brilliant, the insights numerous, and the explanation cogent and fairly inclusive. But it is a biased perspective, nonetheless. It is one way, and a significant one, to look at industrial society. Yet what we see, we see from our vantage point; and the vantage point of plant and bureaucracy gives a different perspective of industrial society than does the vantage point of community, or family, or something else.

Industry and Community

Drucker notes that the relationship of management to the other groups in society is a major research problem and mentions the family and education as two phenomena whose function in the new society needs further analysis. It is perhaps not insignificant that he does not even mention the community. The drift of theoretical and research interests in sociology in recent years, especially toward industry and bureaucracy, has pushed such older concepts into the background. Industrial sociologists seem to accept the assertion by Elton Mayo that industrialism has rendered the community anomic and that the bonds of association and sentiment between men can be reestablished only within the plant. As a consequence, industrial sociology has been almost entirely in-plant research, and family and community have been relegated to a residual category of individual influences on morale and productivity.

Yet here and there in the literature one gets clues that the community is not yet ready for the sociological limbo. C. W. M. Hart's perceptive analysis of Windsor,[1] with its data on the role of the union in the community, and Charles Walker's study of a steel town,[2] with its clues to the meaning and value of the community for the worker, suggest that the interaction between community, corporation, and union poses significant problems for sociological research.

While the economic enterprise is essential if there is to be a community, the community as an organized system of social relations is essential to the enterprise. It provides the source of socialized persons from which the enterprise draws its personnel; it provides and protects the system of legal rights and moral values on which economic action is based; and it provides the full social life, the intricate organization of roles and actions, values and motivations, which characterize the fully socialized personality. As long as man is more than economic man, as long, that is, as he is *social* in all that we have meant by the term, the corporation must live with and within the community.

But that is the very issue: how to live with it? The economic elite of any given era —whether landed gentry, feudal merchants, capitalist entrepreneurs, or managerial executives—has been concerned with its relation to the community. The need for harmony in the relationship between the economic structure and the community is an old but vital theme.

The community is made up of the same persons who participate in the economy, but as members of the community, with its complex of groups and institutions, their behavior expresses other values and goals than those found in the economic organization. Such behavior will either conflict with the economic structure, especially with its system of rewards, or will complement and support it.

Thus, when we focus on an industrial community, even one dominated by a single industry and a single plant, we are forced to recognize that the values and goals, the sentiments and bonds, around which men organize their social life are not derived entirely from the industrial bureaucracy. Rather, the organization of industrial life is clearly a consequence of the interaction among the more significant social units.

Dimensions of Status

Take the problem of status. Drucker simplifies the stratification of society by reducing it to a single dimension, that of employeeship. The varied pattern of status and role which the sociologist long has struggled to represent adequately now becomes not so much inaccurate as irrelevant, for it is only the social relationships derived from large-scale organization which constitute the "socially decisive" realm.

In Lorain, Ohio, a steelmaking city of 50,000, a steel mill provides more than half of the local jobs. If one proceeds to view the status system of Lorain by the dimension of employeeship, there are at least three functional strata. The upper stratum consists of the managers of the industrial, banking, and utility firms, the owners and operators of the larger local business enterprises, and a small group of upper professionals. The middle stratum consists of the small retail merchants, the white-collar and supervisory employees, and the lower professionals. The third stratum, numerically the largest, is the working class, most of whom are steelworkers. These three strata could, of course, be divided into substrata.

But in the social life of Lorain this is not the only important dimension of status; there are also race, ethnicity, and religion. The original settlers of Lorain were from New England, and their descendants constitute an "old-stock American" group. When the steel mill was established, it brought immigrant labor into the community; the major groups were the Polish, the Hungarians, the Italians, the Germans, and the various Slavic groups from what is now Czechoslovakia and Yugoslavia. About 65 per cent of the local people are either the foreign-born or their children. Furthermore, they are not randomly distributed throughout the three functional strata but are grouped in the second and third, the lower-middle and working-class strata, especially in the latter, constituting more than three-fourths of the steelworkers.

Besides the above, there is another status group made up of Negroes, Mexicans, and Puerto Ricans. This is the lowest in prestige, occupying most of the lowest-paid jobs. It is, in effect, a fourth stratum.

Sixty-five per cent of the community is Catholic, and another 6 per cent is Orthodox; less than 30 per cent is Protestant. Neither are the religious groups randomly distributed throughout the status system. The Catholics are concentrated in the lower strata, especially in the working class, where they number more than three out of four steelworkers. The Protestants are concentrated in the higher strata; they are the managerial and business class and are largely old-stock Americans. These ethnic, religious, and racial clusterings in the functional strata are significant in the organization of the community and the distribution of power.

The functional positions of corporate organization provide one strategic dimension of status, but the organization of the community provides others. However, what is most important sociologically is not the several status dimensions but the pattern by which they intersect one another. Ethnic groups cluster around functional positions and are blocked from others. Thus, ethnicity, religion, and race take on cultural definitions in the community that reflect their access to or monopoly over levels of functional positions. Here we see that managerial status not only means a high functional position but also contains ethnic and religious definitions. An individual at the managerial level acts not only in terms of the expectations of the managerial role but also as a person who is white, Protestant, and old-stock American, attributes which enter into his personality and influence his behavior, especially toward individuals from other levels.

Drucker points out that large-scale organization creates a status system that is a graded series of employee positions, impersonally relating people by virtue of their function in the organization. But at this point employeeship as a stratification system faces a problem: What determines access to these graded positions? What are the criteria of selection? It is here that the other dimensions of status become relevant. They are, as it turns out, strategically decisive for the life-chances of individuals.

It is, of course, quite clear that any specific set of status dimensions is not necessary to the impersonal organization of the corporation. And the theorists of the new society may believe that the role of race, religion, and ethnicity in providing access to preferred positions is only a passing phase in our culture, a historical phenomenon. But perhaps not.

In the first place, it is in the heavy-industry towns that ethnic status is decisive for class position. Assimilation is effectively blocked as long as race, religion, and ethnicity are significant channels to class and also security systems against the hazards of impersonal bureaucracy. Furthermore, assimilation may not be a unidimensional process. In Lorain assimilation has proceeded rapidly in cultural aspects such as speech, dress, manners, style of life, interests, etc., but ethnic *identification*, with its bonds of sentiment and loyalty, is still very much evident.

Second, even if assimilation were to remove these status criteria, the need for some criteria to determine life-chances would produce new status dimensions. Some of these are already apparent: education, for one, family, the subtle and not so subtle cultural differences that emerge at class levels, and personality models that reflect group and class attitudes.

Power in the Community

But status in the industrial community is also closely related to social power. Though American sociologists have given a central place to the analysis of status, they have seriously neglected the study of social power.

Our conceptual frameworks have rarely made provision for the analysis of the power relations which are structured into social organization. Now we seem ready to recognize the sociological importance of power and to conceive of it as the process of decision-making.

In the employee society management faces all the old problems of power in defining the relation of the enterprise to the community, to which is added a new one: the emergence of a competing power group. The rise of industrial unionism brought a new institution into the local community, disrupting the older institutional pattern. By crystallizing interests and values in the community into a new power bloc, the union adds another dimension to the shifting patterns of the new society.

Hart noted in his study of Windsor that the local labor leaders took only a minor part in the collective-bargaining process, which became instead a function of top-level leadership. Consequently, in order to hold the political support of their constituency, the local leaders turned their attention to community issues. In Lorain, also, the local labor leaders have only a minor part in the process of collective bargaining, which takes place in Pittsburgh. And, as in Windsor, the CIO in Lorain has also extended the scope of its activities to include the community. Active in politics and civic affairs, they have become a new and important power bloc in the community.

The union is undoubtedly most influential in Lorain's municipal politics. Until the formation of the Political Action Committee, municipal politics was a competition between the Republican and Democratic parties for control of the vote of the 65 per cent of the community's voters who were either foreign-born or the children of the foreign-born (i.e., the nationality vote). In national elections the Democratic party was able to command the support of the majority of these lower-middle-class and working-class citizens. But in local elections ethnic identification frequently superseded class identification. The numerous nationality organizations bargained with the two parties

for patronage and for places on the party slate. Ethnic rivalry and jealousy prevented either party from creating a solid nationality vote. Thus, by skillfully exploiting ethnic rivalry, the Republican party was able to control the city administration on behalf of the community's upper stratum.

This pattern was seriously altered by the organization of PAC. The CIO mobilized political support for candidates of both parties, but mostly Democratic, by appealing to their members as workers rather than as ethnics. They submerged the ethnic rivalries which permitted upper-stratum control and thus enabled the Democratic party to become the dominant party in municipal politics.

Yet the success of the CIO in local politics is not based strictly on a labor vote. Rather, a coalition of four groups is politically dominant: the nationality groups, the Democratic party, the CIO, and the Catholic church. These are the significant social identifications of the lower strata in the community and constitute a pattern of over-lapping memberships. The large nationality groups are Catholic and provide the membership and the leadership of the Democratic party and the CIO.

The function of the CIO has been to provide the mechanism by which lower-status groups could be effectively united for political power in the community. To religious and ethnic identification has been added class identification. The Democratic party has become the party of the lower strata, a working-class, nationality group, Catholic party. Political leadership and authority are now held by representatives of these status groups.

The CIO has also used its political power to wrest control of the educational system from the upper stratum. However, this pattern of power is in contrast to municipal politics: the individuals who have sought leadership here, and whom the CIO has successfully supported, have been distinguished more on the basis of their policy toward the functioning of the school system than by their status and social identification.

The success of the CIO in altering the

power structure in municipal politics and the educational system comes from its ability as a mass organization to influence the voting pattern in local elections. But its participation in the decision-making process in the community's civic welfare structure is not premised on voting power, for civic welfare is not democratically organized.

Typical of American communities, civic welfare is a "voluntary" program in Lorain. The Community Chest supports a group of social agencies; it is nongovernmental but depends on widespread community support. Thus, it is semiprivate, semipublic.

Until the end of the 1930's the Community Chest operated in the name of the entire community but was effectively controlled by the upper stratum. The leaders of the nationality groups were rigidly excluded from participation, even from door-to-door solicitation. The prestige of civic leadership was a monopoly of the community's upper stratum.

The unrepresentative character of Community Chest leadership too overtly reflected the social cleavage that ran along ethnic and religious lines in the community. Consequently, community support was difficult to mobilize; the lower-status groups contributed little, if anything. This produced a series of financial crises which finally culminated in the recognition by the Chest's leaders that they would have to find some means of mobilizing community support or disband, and the latter was seriously considered. Then the Catholic church and the professional social workers proposed the inclusion of organized labor as an alternative. The leaders of the Chest reluctantly accepted.

A participant now, the CIO leadership has mobilized working-class support for the Chest, and in the past decade the latter's budget has tripled. Working-class contributions solicited by CIO personnel in the plants have made the difference. And at the same time the Chest has been generally accepted as an institution representative of the entire community.

The Legitimation of Power

Yet labor does not dominate decision-making in civic welfare; their representation is still a small minority. Apparently they have no need for a greater voice, for they have not brought to the decision-making process a new set of interests, a new program, or a new ideology. They do not have a specific labor program but they have accepted the community welfare program at face value.

Paradoxically, the CIO was anxious to be included in the leadership of civic welfare and would not mobilize working-class support until they were; yet, once included, they have not sought to alter the civic welfare program in any significant degree. The paradox disappears when one realizes that the primary function of the civic welfare program is not to meet any significant proportion of the community's social needs but to provide a legitimacy for its elite of status and power. The CIO in Lorain wants to be regarded as concerned with the welfare of the whole community, not merely with the interests of labor, and views its participation in the Community Chest as demonstrating this concern.

Consequences of Shifts in Power

Thus, the emergence of organized labor has brought about an alteration in the traditional pattern of power relations in the community. The carefully controlled monopoly over decision-making once held by the upper stratum of the community has broken down, and channels of influence for low-status groups have been created. The significance of this is readily apparent to students of society.

For one thing: the alteration of power relations has disturbed the community's status system. Prestige and leadership go with social power. Thus, members of low-status ethnic groups have been able to achieve the careers of leaders largely in politics, local government, and the union. Ranking low in class position and in status identification, they nevertheless constitute a new elite in the community. That in itself is an attack upon the status system. Social power rather than assimilation has enlarged the opportunities of these low-standing members of the community. In some ways, power may be more significant than assimilation in changing the distribution of life-chances in the industrial community. And, by virtue of this, inconsistencies appear in the status pattern created in the corporate image. Furthermore, there may be future consequences. Penetration into higher-status levels through government, politics, labor, and the professions threatens to break down the convergence of functional and ethnic status which have traditionally patterned the community's social relations.

In the second place, the union, in uniting the lower strata for political action, is decisive in shifting control of the community from the upper stratum, including the managerial group. Municipal government and education are two loci of decision-making in Lorain where management does not control.

Indeed, no one group can now be called a ruling group in industrial society. This is so for two reasons. First, there is no single locus of decision-making but rather a number of loci, each differently structured. Within the corporation is one, within the community are several, and there are other significant ones within the larger society. Second, a number of groups may have varying effects upon decision-making in a given locus. Hence the pyramidal model of the social order, with power and authority located at the apex, is inaccurate and misleading.

Thirdly, the organization of political power in the community provides a striking and contradictory contrast to the system of power and authority within the corporation. The latter is a status hierarchy in which power and authority are located at the top; decision-making is a function of management, a basic "managerial right." Participation in decision-making seems hopelessly unlikely to the employee at the bottom of the hierarchy. To be sure, labor unions have somewhat modified this pattern by forcing a share in managerial decision-making. But, to do so, the workers have had to create organizational entities which are separate from the corporate structure itself, a fact management is quick to point out.

In the community decision-making is more democratically structured. This is not to assert that what goes on in the community always fully epitomizes democracy. But it is to assert that a share in decision-making in the community is now more easily attained by citizens of low-status. To gain such a position in the corporation, the worker has to violate the prevailing value system, which asserts the rights and authority of management. In the community his political action is more consistent with the dominant political values.

One more point: the organization of the corporate bureaucracy includes a value system which accounts for the power and authority of management, but the community's value system provides no such validation of the existing power relations. However power may be distributed in the community, whatever the relative influence of union and corporation, the legitimation of power remains a strategic need. The CIO in Lorain, and in other communities, has participated actively in the civic welfare program thereby demonstrating that they, too, are unselfishly concerned with the community's welfare and thus to legitimize their very real power in community decision-making.

The problem is undoubtedly more acute for the union. As a new institution it is less accepted outside its own ranks and still has the aura of a special interest group. Management, on the other hand, inherits the upper-class tradition of community service. Furthermore, it also inherits a paternalistic ideology of trusteeship which the public relations experts translate into contemporary speech: the "responsibility of wealth" now becomes the "social responsibility of the corporation." Participation in civic affairs as an adjunct of a managerial career becomes the explicit policy of many corporations. Thus does management seek the legitimation of corporate power.

Yet the persistently unflattering, even hostile, images of management and union among various publics indicate that no effective formula for the legitimation of their power in the community and in the larger society has been found.

The Conceptual Problem

These, of course, are only a few of the issues revealed by the study [of] status and power in the industrial community. There are many others. Whether we can identify and analyze them, however, depends as much on our conceptualizing ability as on our research skills. This, probably, is what Drucker meant in remarking that we need more adequate conceptual tools. New ideas on how to organize the concepts into models which can be empirically tested are equally needed.

Perhaps the greatest hindrance to such conceptual reorganization is our professional commitment to "fields" of sociological study: community, urban, industrial, family, ecology, and so on. These have been, and remain, valuable ways of dividing sociological labor. But so committed have we become to these compartmentalizations that most of our research proceeds within boundaries which they set.

As a consequence important areas of behavior which do not fit these traditional categories are neglected. Is the union's activity in the community a problem in urban or industrial sociology? With jurisdictional rights unclear, both have ignored it. Yet it is not sufficient that one or the other, or both, include it within their existing frameworks. The industrial sociologist would add material on a new function of the union; the urban sociologist would discuss the influence of the union on community life. Neither touches the real problem, which is not union or community but the social consequences upon organized behavior when the two structures intersect.

To analyze industrial society, sociologists must locate decisive areas of industrial life, which are the points where the major structural units intersect and penetrate one another. Community, corporation, and union are three such units; the currently unstable process of interaction provides a significant object of research for those who wish to understand the nature of industrial society.

Notes

1. [C. W. M. Hart], "Industrial Relations Research and Social Theory," *Canadian Journal of Economics and Political Science*, XV (February, 1949), 53–73.

2. [Charles Walker], *Steeltown: An Industrial Case History of the Conflict between Progress and Security* (New York: Harper & Bros., 1950).

Small Business and Civic Welfare

C. Wright Mills and Melville J. Ulmer

Part I. Introduction and Summary

The American economy became increasingly concentrated during the war as big business made substantial gains—gains superimposed upon an already extremely high level of economic concentration. A few gigantic corporations are now responsible for the bulk of America's entire industrial production and employment. In 1944, 2 percent of the manufacturing concerns in the United States employed 60 percent of the industrial workers.

How does this concentration of economic power affect the general welfare of our cities and their inhabitants? This is one aspect of the concentration problem which has received little attention, despite its obvious importance. Does economic concentration tend to raise or depress the levels of civic welfare?

Economic concentration can never be justified if it tends to develop cities in which there exist, for example, overcrowding, a high infant death rate; low per capita public expenditures for education, health, and recreation; low per capita installation of electricity, gas, telephones, etc.

This exploratory report is designed to shed light on the effects of economic concentration on civic welfare. It is based on a study of six American cities. They were selected in such a way as to provide contrasts in industrial organization and to make possible an evaluation of the effects of big and small business on city life.

The tentative conclusion suggested by this study is that big business tends to depress while small business tends to raise the level of civic welfare.

The Results in Brief

At first glance, civic welfare may appear to be a highly difficult topic to measure, or even to discuss objectively. Yet, there does exist a considerable amount of concrete, factual data bearing directly on the subject. Thus it was found that the chance that a baby would die within 1 year after birth was considerably greater in big- than in small-business cities; in fact, the chance was almost twice as great in one big-business city than in the comparable small-business city. Public expenditures on libraries (per capita) were 10 times greater and on education (per student) were 20 percent greater in 1 of the small-business cities studied than in the comparable big-business city; slums were more prevalent—in one case nearly 3 times more prevalent—in big- than in small-business cities.

These facts are cited here merely to indicate the nature of the standards employed. The broad conclusions suggested by the study are that—

(1) The small-business cities provided for their residents a considerably more balanced economic life than did big-business cities;

(2) The general level of civic welfare was appreciably higher in the small-business cities;

(3) These differences between city life in big- and small-business cities were in the cases studied due largely to differences in industrial organization —that is, specifically to the dominance of big business on the one hand and the prevalence of small business on the other.

Reprinted from Senate Document Number 135, Serial Number 11036, 79th Congress, Second Session, Report of the Smaller War Plants Corporation to the Special Committee to Study Problems of American Small Business, United States Senate. Washington, D.C.: Government Printing Office, 1946.

The more "balanced" economic life provided in small-business cities was noted in several ways. First of all, industrial stability was much more pronounced. In small-business cities employment was more diversified; not only did a relatively large number of industrial firms operate in a number of different manufacturing lines, but a much greater proportion of workers were engaged in wholesale, retail, and other distributive pursuits. On the other hand, the entire pay roll of big-business cities was largely dominated by one or a few great industrial firms.

This economic dominance of a few big absentee-owned corporations in the big-business cities studied resulted in relative insecurity and instability. The mere decision of one corporation to move its local plant to some other area would be sufficient for economic collapse in a big-business city. Moreover, it has been contended by some economists* that production and employment are typically less stable in monopolistic or quasi-monopolistic industries. In any event, it was found that in the big-business cities studied, fluctuations in employment, wages, and even in the number of business enterprises were considerably greater, on the average, than in the small-business cities.

Second, it was found that retail facilities were more satisfactory in small-business cities. They were more abundant, more efficiently managed, and offered greater variety. In the big-business cities, it was discovered, retailers hestitated to make substantial investments because of the business hazards incident to the economic instability referred to above. Thus, the residents of big-business cities often had to go elsewhere to buy.

Third, the gap between the incomes of the few very rich and those of the poor appeared to be greater in big-business cities, although available evidence on this point is not conclusive. In small-business cities it appeared that a larger proportion of the population earned medium or high incomes.

The final and most important test applied to big- and small-business cities was the measurement of the general level of civic welfare. The measure employed was that developed by an eminent social scientist. It gives weight to most of the important measurable factors which bear on the welfare of a city's residents, including, for example, numerous items relating to health, housing, sanitation, incomes, education, and recreation among others. A few of these factors—for example, infant mortality and slums—were cited above. The over-all measure of civic welfare, summarizing all of these figures, showed that in each case the small-business city studied rated materially higher than did the comparable big-business city.

In the concluding chapter of this report certain tentative reasons are advanced for the generally higher level of civic welfare found in the small-business cities. It was found that in these cities, civic spirit was more pronounced, more widely shared, and more active. The economically independent middle class was more abundant in the small-business cities. For several reasons cited later, it was the independent middle class which usually took the lead in the voluntary management of civic enterprises. In the small-business cities they operated with the relatively widespread cooperation of labor groups.

In the big-business cities, on the other hand, the independent middle class was not only small but for the most part was not truly independent. In these cities the giant corporations were the real powers. Local executives of these corporations had little interest in civic enterprises as such, except insofar as such enterprises might impinge upon the profit opportunities of the corporation. The nominally independent middle class in these cities—directly or indirectly—was compelled to follow the dictates of the corporation executives. Whatever civic activities were undertaken by labor in these cities were instituted not in cooperation with other groups in the city but usually in conflict with them.

*National Resources Committee, *The Structure of the American Economy, 1939*; and Theodore Kreps, "Some Price Problems" in W. L. Thorp (ed.), *Economic Problems in a Changing World*, 1939.

In short, in small-business cities the environment was favorable to the development and growth of civic spirit. The interests of the potential leaders of civic enterprises were generally mutual and locally rooted. In big-business cities, civic spirit was stunted or distorted. The potential leaders of civic enterprise were either powerless to act or were motivated by interests outside the city —particularly the home office of the giant corporation. These differences were reflected in the contrasting levels of general civic welfare found in big- and small-business cities.

The Approach

For purposes of this report a big-business city is defined as one in which (a) a few large firms employ all or most of the workers; (b) ownership of most of the industrial facilities lies outside the city; (c) business activity is concentrated in one or a very few industrial lines. Conversely, a small-business city is one in which (a) most of the workers are employed by a large number of small firms; (b) the bulk of the industrial facilities are locally owned; (c) business activity is diversified in several different industrial lines.

In accordance with these definitions three pairs of cities in the United States were selected for study in this report. The members of each pair were so selected* that they had several basic factors in common— general geographical location, population size, percentage of foreign-born and Negroes in the population, etc. In the case of two of these pairs, however, the members differ sharply in one important respect. One of each pair is clearly a big-business city; the other is distinctly a small-business city. In the case of the third pair, there is also a differentiation with respect to big- and small-business industrial organization, but it is not as sharp as in the case of the other two, and thus they constitute an intermediate check.

To these cities were applied standards of evaluation generally recognized by sociologists as suitable for the purpose. The figures used to measure the levels of civic life were obtained from official Government sources,

from authoritative sociological studies, and from direct field investigation of the cities selected by a sociologist. Also obtained in the field by the sociologist was a considerable amount of information concerning non-quantitative factors in city life, such as the attitudes of civic leaders, the role in city life played by executives of the great absentee-owned industrial plants, and so forth.

Finally, it should be noted that the big-business cities studied here were chosen to represent the local manifestations of a national trend—the trend toward industrial concentration, absentee ownership, the dominance of giant corporations. Similarly, the small-business cities were selected to represent the typical community of small, locally owned, competitive enterprises.

It is obviously impossible to state whether or not the conclusions derived in this report are applicable to all big-business and all small-business cities in the United States. An answer to this question would require a field study covering most of the cities in this country. Among big-business cities as well as among small-business cities, there must be many deviations from the patterns found in this survey. It is left for studies of the future to show just how important and how frequent these deviations are.

Part II. Balanced Economic Life

Any contention that a city—large or small— ought to be economically self-sufficient is an obvious absurdity. It is neither desirable nor, in the present era, possible. Nevertheless, it may justly be contended that a good city ought to have a balanced economic life. Specifically, this means that under present conditions a city should be: (a) one whose economic activities are sufficiently diversified to provide relatively steady employment, (b) one which provides in its retail establishments and other facilities most of the goods and services its people need, and (c) one in which there is a gradual and even increaese from the lowest to the highest personal incomes—rather than a sharp gap between

---

*The method of selection is described in the appendix.

TABLE 1. *Distribution of Employees in Trade and Industry, by Type of Work*

| CITIES | Percentage Employed in— | | |
	MANUFACTURING	WHOLESALE TRADE	RETAIL TRADE
A—Big business	77	5	18
B—Small business	60	10	30
C—Big business	78	3	19
D—Small business	59	9	32
E—Intermediate	78	2	20
F—Intermediate	82	2	16

SOURCE: U.S. Bureau of the Census.

a few very rich on top and a great many poor at the bottom. These characteristics of a balanced city economy are discussed below with reference to the six cities surveyed in this report.

These cities are identified throughout this study by letter;* cities A and C are the big-business cities, while B and D, respectively, are the small-business cities with which they are paired. The third pair of cities—E and F—are, respectively, big- and small-business, but in this case, it should be remembered, the distinction in industrial organization between the two is less pronounced. This third pair, therefore, is referred to in subsequent discussion as intermediate. A precise analysis of how all six cities fit the definitions provided for them may be found in appendix B.

Industrial Stability

In the big-business cities studied in this report a few absentee-owned corporations provide most of the industrial employment.† Moreover, manufacturing activity in these cities is concentrated in one or two industrial lines. On the other hand, in small-business cities manufacturing activity is conducted by numerous small, locally owned concerns operating in many industrial lines. This is, of course, in keeping with the definitions of big- and small-business cities adopted in this report.

The power of the great corporation in big-business cities, however, is further enhanced by the fact that specialization in manufacturing as such, as opposed to wholesale and retail distribution, is also greater in big-business cities. This means that in these cases the large absentee-owned corporations dominate not only the industrial pay roll but the pay roll of the entire city.

This is shown in the preceding table [table 1]. In big-business city A, 77 percent of all employees are engaged in manufacturing, as against only 60 percent in small-business city B. The corresponding figures for big-business city C and small-business city D are 78 and 59 percent, respectively. Clearly, in the small-business cities the proportion of workers is more evenly balanced as between manufacturing on the one hand and retail and wholesale distribution on the other. The data indicate—and further evidence is presented below—that the big-business cities are top-heavy industrially.

In cities E and F—the immediate pair—there is, however, no important difference in this respect; in fact, big-business city E is slightly less industrialized than the small-business city F.

Historical Background—Population

These differences in business structure among the cities studied are clearly a twentieth-century development, paralleling the rise of big business in these areas. In

---

*The names of the cities must be withheld because much of the data obtained from the U.S. Census Bureau, as well as other information, is regarded as confidential.
†Data on relative size of firm in the 6 cities are presented in appendix B.

TABLE 2. *Population Size and Rate of Growth,*[1] *1890–1940*

CITIES	POPULATION 1890	PERCENT INCREASE IN POPULATION					POPULATION 1940
		1890–1900	1900–10	1910–20	1920–30	1930–40	
A—Big business	10,000	35	190	240	60	−3	150,000
B—Small business	60,000	45	30	20	20	−3	150,000
C—Big business	5,000	60	50	135	90	3	60,000
D—Small business	20,000	35	60	20	10	−1	60,000
E—Intermediate	15,000	2	35	30	25	3	30,000
F—Intermediate	20,000	20	10	10	10	5	30,000

[1]Data in this table have been rounded in order to avoid disclosing the identity of the cities.
SOURCE: U.S. Census of Population.

1890 all six cities were trading centers, primarily servicing the agricultural areas around them. Small-business city B was then six times as large as big-business city A. Small-business city D was then four times as large as big-business city C. Cities E and F were around the same size. The population boom which subsequently occurred in the big-business cities is illustrated in table 2.

As big-business units were opened in cities A and C, workers were recruited at a rapid rate. Between 1890 and 1940, the population of A multiplied 15 times; in C there was an elevenfold increase in population. On the other hand, in the small-business cities B and D, as table 2 shows, the increase of population was neither so sporadic nor so swift. The rate of increase was due more to natural growth.

These changes in population were, of course, accompanied by changes in the degree of industrialization. In 1890 the small-business cities were more industrialized than the present big-business cities. This situation, however, was soon reversed as the giant corporations opened plants in the big-business cities.

Differences in population change were not as pronounced between the intermediate cities, although the increase was somewhat greater in the big-business city E.

Real-Estate History

The population booms in cities A and C were clearly the results of the rise of big business. As is frequently the case in such rapid developments, the sudden influx of workers was also accompanied by a real-estate boom, followed by the usual subsequent crash in real-estate values. As the result of real-estate speculation, the residential areas of the big-business cities are now widely scattered and capriciously situated, while the hearts of these cities are marred by slums. Thus, in one of the big-business cities, the number of residential lots increased more than fourfold within 7 years. At the present, only one-fourth of the various real-estate subdivisions within the city is occupied by homes. Obviously, under these conditions of scattered development, the operating costs of the city rose substantially above an economical level; homes which were rapidly and poorly built soon deteriorated into slums. The better residential areas are now found in the suburbs, while parts of the interior of the city resemble a ghost town.

These facts were of interest to note at this point because they are related so directly to historical population trends. Measures documenting the housing conditions in big- and small-business cities, however, are presented in the following [part].

Employment, Wages, and Number of Firms

Does big business perhaps lend stability to other aspects of city life? Is employment steadier; are wages more stable; is the turnover in business population less? A study of

CHART 1. *Fluctuations in Employment, Wages and Number of*
Establishments in Big- and Small-Business Cities,* 1925–1939

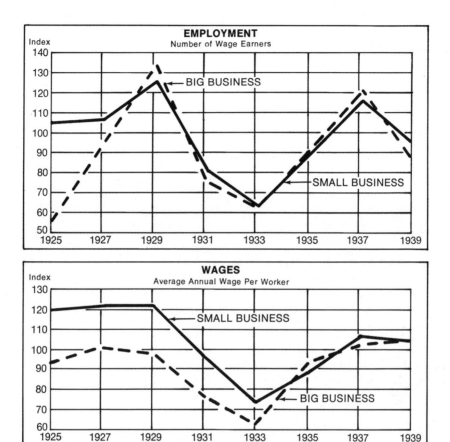

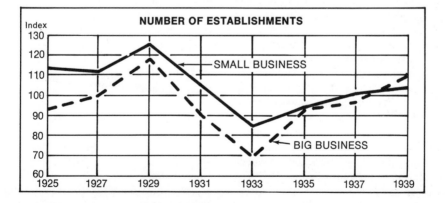

*Lines marked "small business" are based on simple averages of the index numbers for small-
business cities B and D. Lines marked "big business" are based on simple averages
of the index numbers for big-business cities A and C.
SOURCE: U.S. Bureau of the Census.

TABLE 3. *Indexes of Instability*[1]

	EMPLOYMENT	WAGES	ESTABLISHMENTS
A—Big business	29	16	16
B—Small business	20	15	13
C—Big business	64	16	19
D—Small business	27	12	10
E—Intermediate	19	14	13
F—Intermediate	8	8	12
Averages:			
Big business	37	15	16
Small business	18	12	12

[1]These indexes were obtained by computing chain index numbers showing percentage changes from one census year to the next for each of the series during the period 1925–39. The deviations between the chain index numbers and 100 were then added for each series, disregarding signs, and the sum was divided by the number of year-to-year changes. Thus, an index was obtained for each city showing the average percentage change from one census year to the next during the period 1925–39, disregarding the direction of change.

these factors in the cities under investigation shows that the contrary is true.

The fluctuations in industrial employment, industrial wages and number of establishments in the two distinctly big-business cities are compared in chart 1 with those in the two small-business cities. Although the swings of the business cycle were the dominating factor in all cases, the chart also shows that the drop from 1929 to 1933 in employment and in number of establishments—as well as the rise in subsequent years—was sharper for the big-business cities. In the case of wages, the cyclical downswing was somewhat sharper for the small-business cities while the rise was greater for the big-business cities.

The chart, however, fails to reveal the full extent of the difference in stability, as between the two types of cities. This difference is shown most clearly by the indexes of instability, as presented in table 3. These indexes show the average percentage change from one biennial census year to the next in the employment, wages, and number of establishments from 1925 to 1939. In every case instability is more pronounced in the big-business cities. Moreover, the difference is substantial, with the sole exception of wages in cities A and B, which had nearly the same percentage change.

Thus, the average percentage change in employment in big-business city C was 64 percent, as compared with 27 percent in small-business city D. The corresponding figures were 29 percent for big-business city A as against 20 percent for small-business city B. In wages the average change was 16 percent for C as against 12 for D; 16 percent for A as against 15 for B.

The average relative change in number of establishments was almost twice as great in big-business city C as in small-business city D, nearly 25 percent greater in A than in B. Likewise, as table 3 shows, instability in employment, wages, and number of establishments was considerably greater in big-business city E than in small-business city F.

If instability is a fault, economic and social—and few would contend otherwise—then it is certain that, when judged by this standard, the small-business cities are clearly the better communities.

Retail Sales

In small-business cities, as noted above, a large proportion of workers are engaged in retail trade. This suggests that a greater variety of goods and services are available at retail to residents of small-business cities

CHART 2. *Value of Retail Sales Per Capita*

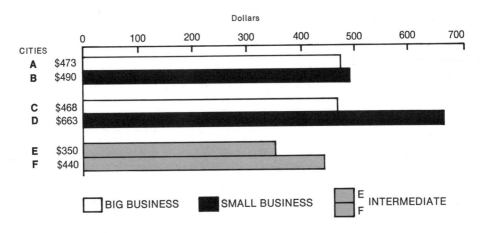

SOURCE: U.S. Census of Business, 1939.

—a fact which was corroborated by field investigation. As chart 2 shows, the value of retail sales per capita is greater in the small-business cities than in the big-business cities—$490 for B as against $473 for A, $663 for D as against $469 for C. Cities E and F also differ substantially in the same way. This is all the more striking in view of the fact that wages are higher in the big-business communities.*

These figures, of course, do not necessarily indicate that the average resident in small-business cities consumed more. Investigation reveals another reason for the difference in per capita retail sales. The residents of big-business cities in large measure go elsewhere to buy. In contrast, the small-business cities attract buyers from other areas. Generally speaking, stores in the small-business cities are better managed, more attractive, and offer greater variety.

There are several reasons for this difference in the quality of retail service, the principal one of which is the dominance of a few large absentee-owned industrial firms in the big-business cities. The result of this dominance, from a retailer's point of view, is continuous uncertainty. It has already been shown that fluctuations in employment

and wages are greater in big-business cities. However, of at least equal importance in this connection, is the fact that a decision on the part of a great corporation to close one of its plants might be sufficient to throw the majority of industrial workers in a big-business city out of jobs. For a retailer, dependent upon the town's ability to buy, this is a huge risk. The attitude of a typical retailer is illustrated by the following verbatim account of an interview between the sociologist and a big-business city merchant:

Question. "How much of the wage dollar earned here is spent elsewhere?"
Answer. "I would judge about 50 percent."
Question. "Why do you think that is so?"
Answer. "Well, there are better stores in X (a city about 30 miles distant, slightly larger)."
Question. "Why is that? Your store is as good as any store over there."
Answer. "Well, you don't see many as nice as mine around here. I'll tell you the reason, though. You see, when these big plants go bust everything in this whole place goes bust. When they're running like now, with the war, we do all right. But they have shut down in the past, and they might shut down again. Then what's to keep them from moving

* See appendix B on The Structure of Big- and Small-Business Cities.

somewhere else? People naturally hesitate to put money into nice retail stores always facing these possibilities, of a shut-down or a move-out. So when things do boom here, X gets a lot of our business."

Question. "Do the local banks reflect that situation? I mean is it hard to get money from them?"

Answer. "Say, even in good times you can't get money from them."

Question. "Well, what is needed to make retail trade flourish here?"

Answer. "What we need is diversified employment, so when one place isn't humming a man can go somewhere else in the town. A man can get a home, and then employment collapses, and then he has to sacrifice his home. Now it's the same way with retail trade and with investment generally. Nobody wants to set up retail shops here or anywhere else where one or two outfits own 50 percent of all the assets of the town. Their hazards are far too great."

Question. "May I ask how you manage to have such a nice place?"

Answer. "Sure; I own this whole outfit. As a matter of fact, my father did before me. It's all paid for. In addition, I have a little stock in (a major United States corporation) and a little farm my grandfather bought up. So when the plants slacken up or close down I can coast for awhile."

As indicated previously, there are several contributing reasons for the more abundant retail facilities in small-business towns. Small-business cities have greater recreational facilities and thus tend to attract more tourist trade. (As shown in the next [part], small-business cities spend nearly twice as much on recreation as do big-business cities.) Moreover, small-business cities attract more jobbers and wholesale buyers into the town. The many small, locally owned firms in these cities require the services of wholesalers in order to distribute their products. On the other hand, the big absentee-owned corporations usually manage their distribution problems from a central office located in a distant metropolitan center. It is interesting to note, in this connection, that there are twice as many hotel guest rooms in the small-business cities as there are in the big-business cities. Receipts from the hotel business in cities B and D are about four to five times as great as in cities A and C.

The Rich and the Poor

It appears likely on the basis of general consideration, that the distribution of income is more unequal in big-business cities than in small-business cities. Where big business dominates, one would expect to find at the top a few who are wealthy and at the bottom a great many who are poor. One would expect a substantial gap between the extremes. This follows from the fact that in big-business cities the independent middle class is squeezed and in some cases all but eliminated. It is in the small-business cities, on the other hand, that the independent middle class thrives.

Complete data on the distribution of income in the cities studied in this report are unavailable. Nevertheless, the evidence which is available tends to substantiate the generalization set forth above. In chart 3 is shown the number of income-tax returns made in each of the cities per 1,000 population. Clearly the relative number of people subject to the income tax was considerably greater in the small-business cities—38 out of every 1,000 in B as against 27 in A, 47 in D as against 24 in C. The difference was also substantial in cities E and F, indicating once more the resemblance they bear, respectively, to big-business cities and small-business cities.

In the lower section of chart 3 is shown the relative number of people whose incomes were $10,000 or over in each city. Again the contrast between big-business and small-business cities is very great. The number is 10 per 10,000 population in city B as against 5 per 10,000 in A, and 18 in D as against 2 in C. The difference in this respect between cities E and F is minor.

Taken as a whole, these data indicate clearly the strength of the independent middle class in small-business cities and its comparative weakness in big-business cities. They indicate as well that in big-business cities, dominated by large absentee-owned

CHART 3. *Medium and High Incomes*

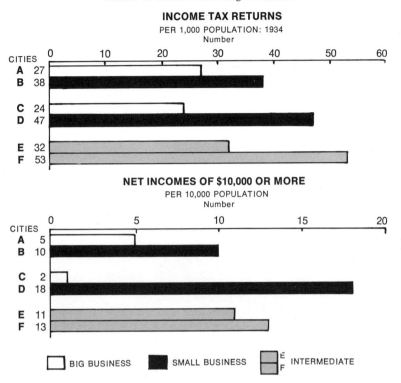

INCOME TAX RETURNS

PER 1,000 POPULATION: 1934
Number

NET INCOMES OF $10,000 OR MORE

PER 10,000 POPULATION
Number

☐ BIG BUSINESS   ■ SMALL BUSINESS   ▨ INTERMEDIATE

SOURCE: *Consumer Market Data Handbook*, U.S. Bureau of Foreign and Domestic Commerce.

firms, money in large quantities is siphoned out to other parts of the country.

Hence, it may be concluded that the ideal of a balanced city economy is much more closely approached by the small-business cities studied in this report than by the big-business cities. Employment in the small-business cities is more diversified, not only with respect to different lines of manufacture but with respect to the broad range of pursuits subsumed under "trade and industry." The range and quality of retail services are on a higher level in these cities. Fluctuations in employment, in wages, and in number of establishments are substantially smaller. A larger proportion of the people in small-business cities earn medium or high incomes and there is less of a gap between high and low incomes.

These factors all make for a higher level of civic welfare in the small-business cities. There are, however, other important factors

in civic welfare. In the following [part] the relative level of civic welfare—broadly defined—is measured for the six cities surveyed in this report.

Part III. Civic Welfare

The measurement of the relative level of welfare in cities is not as difficult as it may appear at first thought. It is true that a "good" city may mean different things to different people. Nevertheless, there are numerous standards of welfare on which virtually everyone will agree. Clearly a city is "better" if fewer of its children die during their first year after birth, if it has more parks for children to play in, and more recreation facilities for all age groups. Housing, health, utilities, cultural facilities, and per capita income, for example, are agreed upon as obvious elements in any measure of civic welfare.

TABLE 4. *Components of the G-Score or Index*

ITEMS	APPROXIMATE WEIGHT
Items of Health	
1. Infant death rate (reversed)	12
2. General death rate (reversed)	9½
3. Typhoid death rate (reversed)	5
4. Appendicitis death rate (reversed)	4
5. Puerperal diseases death rate (reversed)	4
Items of Education	
6. Per capita public expenditures for schools	8
7. Per capita public expenditures for teachers' salaries	6
8. Per capita public expenditures for textbooks and supplies	7
9. Per capita public expenditures for libraries and museums	6½
10. Percentage of persons 16 to 17 attending schools	4½
11. Percentage of persons 18 to 20 attending schools	7
12. Average salary high-school teacher	4½
13. Average salary elementary-school teacher	3½
Items of Recreation	
14. Per capita public expenditures for recreation	7
15. Per capita acreage of public parks	2½
Economic and "Social" Items	
16. Rarity of extreme poverty	6
17. Rarity of less extreme poverty	6
18. Infrequency of gainful employment for boys 10–14	5
19. Infrequency of gainful employment for girls 10–14	5½
20. Average wage of workers in factories	4
21. Frequency of home ownership (per capita number of homes owned)	6
22. Per capita support of the YMCA	6
23. Excess of physicians, nurses, and teachers over male domestic servants	6
Utilities and Durable Goods	
24. Per capita domestic installations of electricity	5
25. Per capita domestic installations of gas	7
26. Per capita number of automobiles	4
27. Per capita domestic installations of telephones	11
28. Per capita domestic installations of radios	6½
Other Items	
29. Percent of literacy in the total population (reversed)	3½
30. Per capita circulation of *Better Homes and Gardens, Good Housekeeping*, and the *National Geographic Magazine*	6
31. Per capita circulation of the *Literary Digest*	6
32. Death rate from syphilis (reversed)	4
33. Death rate from homicide (reversed)	3
34. Death rate from automobile accidents (reversed)	4½
35. Per capita value of asylums, schools, libraries, museums, and parks owned by the public	6½
36. Ratio of value of schools, etc., to value of jails, etc.	10
37. Per capita public property minus public debt	5

Leading sociologists have given considerable time and study to this problem of measurement. One of the Nation's best known social scientists, Dr. E. L. Thorndike,* has developed a measure of civic welfare including 300 different measurable items. These 300 items were examined from various statistical points of view in an effort to determine to what extent they were correlated with one another. By this procedure it was possible to eliminate all but 37 items and thus establish a measure of civic welfare fully as accurate as the larger one but more economical.

It is this measure of civic welfare—called by Thorndike a G-score—which is used in this report. The 37 items included in this index are listed in table 4.

In the following table [table 5] are shown the indexes† of civic welfare (G-score) computed for the six cities studied in this report. These measures show that in each case the level of civic welfare is substantially higher in the small-business cities. Thus the score in city B is 120 points higher or 17 percent above that of city A. In city D the score is 130 points higher or 19 percent above that of city C. In the two intermediate cases, E and F, the difference is much smaller. Nevertheless, the score in city F, which more closely resembles a small-business city, is 20 points higher or about 4 percent above that of city E, which more closely resembles a big-business city. The fact that both E and F have lower scores than the other four cities is due partly to regional differences, although both, of course, are in the same region.

Are the differences between the big-business and small-business cities large or small compared with the variation among all industrial cities in the United States? The original studies of Thorndike indicate that G-scores for industrial cities in the United States range from a low of about 400 to a high of about 850. Moreover, much of the difference found in these scores is accounted for by regional variations, thus, most of the low-score cities are in the South. The cities compared in this report, however, are in each case in the same region. It may be concluded, therefore, that the differences between big-business and small-business cities studied in this report are substantial, amounting to approximately one-fifth of the total difference between the lowest ranking industrial city found anywhere in the United States by Thorndike, and the highest ranking industrial city.‡

In charts 4 to 8 are shown measures of some of the individual standards employed for judging civic welfare; most of these individual measures are the same as those included in the over-all measures of civic welfare (Thorndike's G-score) described above. Three of the charts bear on health and sanitation, four on culture, recreation, and religion, two on education, two on housing, and two on utilities. In the great majority of these cases, the rating of small-business cities is clearly superior.

Thus, as shown in chart 4, housing conditions are clearly superior in the small-business cities. The top of this chart illustrates the relative prevalence of overcrowded housing conditions when judged by a standard commonly used for this purpose; namely, the number of dwellings with an average of more than 1.5 persons per room. For example, in big-business city A, more than 3.5 percent of all dwellings are overcrowded, when judged by this standard, as against only 1.4 percent of all dwelling units in small-business city B. In big-business city

TABLE 5. *Thorndike's Index of Civic Welfare*

	G-SCORE
A—Big business	690
B—Small business	810
C—Big business	680
D—Small business	810
E—Intermediate	560
F—Intermediate	580

---

* [E. L. Thorndike], *Your City*, 1939. Thorndike calls his measure an index of civic goodness.
† For the method of computing these indexes, see Thorndike, *op. cit.*, ch. X.
‡ In all, Thorndike's measurements covered 310 American cities.

CHART 4. *Housing*

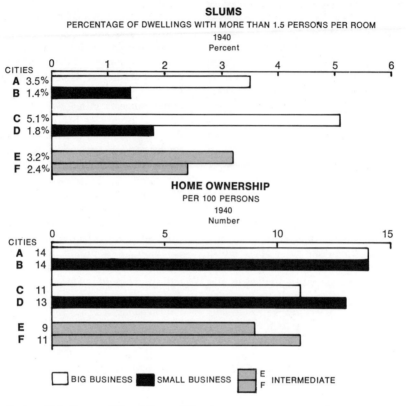

SLUMS

PERCENTAGE OF DWELLINGS WITH MORE THAN 1.5 PERSONS PER ROOM

1940

Percent

CITIES	
A	3.5%
B	1.4%
C	5.1%
D	1.8%
E	3.2%
F	2.4%

HOME OWNERSHIP

PER 100 PERSONS

1940

Number

CITIES	
A	14
B	14
C	11
D	13
E	9
F	11

☐ BIG BUSINESS   ■ SMALL BUSINESS   ▨ E F INTERMEDIATE

SOURCE: U.S. Census of Population and Housing.

C, 5.1 percent of all dwelling units are over-crowded as against only 1.8 percent in D. Similarly, big-business city E is more over-crowded than small-business city F.

The bottom of this chart shows that the proportion of homes owned by the occupants is slightly greater in small-business cities D and F than in the corresponding big-business cities, but is the same in cities A and B.

Similarly, from the top of chart 5 it is apparent that the chance that a baby will die within a year after birth is appreciably greater in the big- than in the small-business cities. The death rate of infants within a year after birth was 40.4 per 1,000 live births in big-business city A as against only 33.9 per 1,000 in small-business city B. The death rate was 45.7 in big-business city C as against only 24.9 in small-business city D.

For the intermediate pair, city F had a somewhat higher death rate than city E.

In the center of the chart, it is seen that small-business cities also show to advantage with respect to public expenditures on health. Although public expenditures on health per capita are the same in cities A and B, they are substantially greater in the other two small-business cities than in the corresponding big-business cities. On the other hand, public expenditures on sanitation per capita are in every case greater in the big-business city.

Chart 6 shows certain measures bearing on culture, recreation, and religion. Thus, public expenditures on recreation, per capita, are substantially greater in small-business cities B and D than in big-business cities A and C—$1.31 as against 87 cents, and $1.63 as against 59 cents. In cities E and F ex-

CHART 5. *Health and Sanitation*

INFANT DEATH RATE

PER 1000 LIVE BIRTHS
1940
Rate

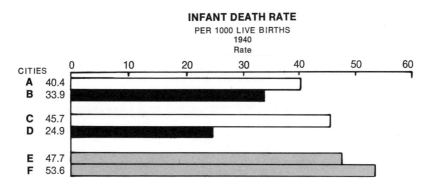

CITIES
A   40.4
B   33.9

C   45.7
D   24.9

E   47.7
F   53.6

PUBLIC EXPENDITURES ON HEALTH

PER CAPITA
1940
Cents

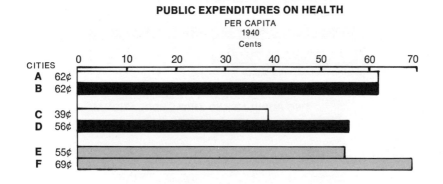

CITIES
A   62¢
B   62¢

C   39¢
D   56¢

E   55¢
F   69¢

PUBLIC EXPENDITURES ON SANITATION

PER CAPITA
1940
Dollars

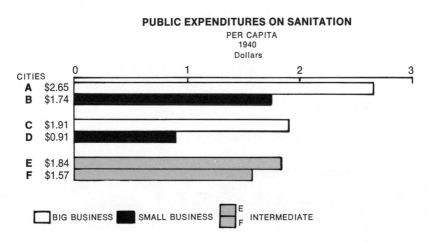

CITIES
A $2.65
B $1.74

C $1.91
D $0.91

E $1.84
F $1.57

☐ BIG BUSINESS   ■ SMALL BUSINESS   ▨ E / F INTERMEDIATE

SOURCE: U.S. Bureau of the Census.

CHART 6. *Culture, Recreation, and Religion*

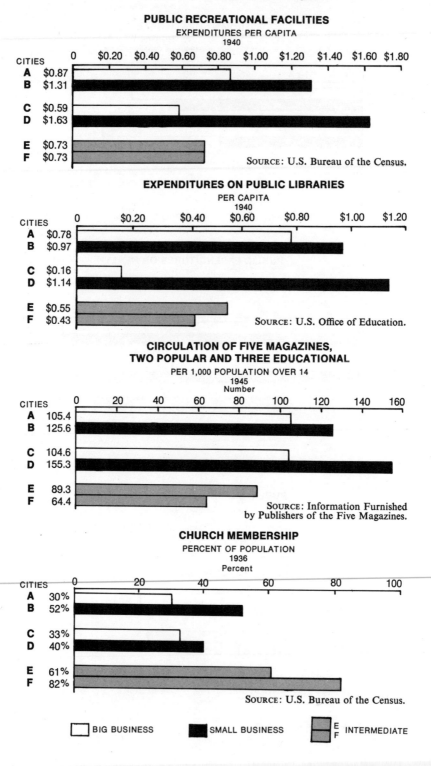

PUBLIC RECREATIONAL FACILITIES
EXPENDITURES PER CAPITA
1940

SOURCE: U.S. Bureau of the Census.

EXPENDITURES ON PUBLIC LIBRARIES
PER CAPITA
1940

SOURCE: U.S. Office of Education.

CIRCULATION OF FIVE MAGAZINES,
TWO POPULAR AND THREE EDUCATIONAL
PER 1,000 POPULATION OVER 14
1945
Number

SOURCE: Information Furnished
by Publishers of the Five Magazines.

CHURCH MEMBERSHIP
PERCENT OF POPULATION
1936
Percent

SOURCE: U.S. Bureau of the Census.

BIG BUSINESS   SMALL BUSINESS   E F INTERMEDIATE penditures are the same. Public expenditures on libraries (shown in the same chart) are also greater in small-business cities B and D than in the corresponding big-business cities. In this case city E, however, ranks somewhat higher than F.

Moreover, judged by magazine circulation, the interest of residents in literature and educational subjects is greater in small-business cities B and D than in the big-business cities. In this respect again, however, city E rates better than city F. The proportion of residents who are church members (shown in the bottom of chart 6) is in every case greater in the small-business city.

The record on two measures bearing on education (chart 7) is on the whole better in the small-business cities. Expenditures on

public schools per student are greater in small-business cities D and F than in the corresponding big-business cities, while in cities A and B they are the same. Again, it appears from the bottom of this chart that children are maintained in school for a longer period of time in small-business cities D and F. In this respect, however, big-business city A ranks somewhat higher than small-business city B.

Finally, in chart 8, it is shown that residents in small-business cities are in every case more adequately provided with the common utilities—telephones and electricity—than are the residents of the big-business cities.

Of course, the 13 items displayed in charts 4 to 8 do not represent fully the broad level of civic welfare in the six cities

CHART 7. *Education*

PUBLIC SCHOOL EXPENDITURES

PER STUDENT, 1937-38

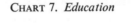

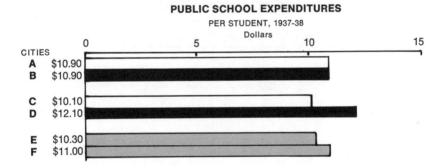

CITIES	
A	$10.90
B	$10.90
C	$10.10
D	$12.10
E	$10.30
F	$11.00

SOURCE: U.S. Office of Education.

PERCENTAGE ATTENDING SCHOOL

PERSONS 16 OR 17 YEARS OLD, 1940

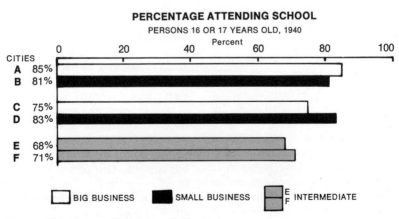

CITIES	
A	85%
B	81%
C	75%
D	83%
E	68%
F	71%

□ BIG BUSINESS   ■ SMALL BUSINESS   ▨ E F INTERMEDIATE

SOURCE: U.S. Census of Population, 1940.

CHART 8. *Utilities*

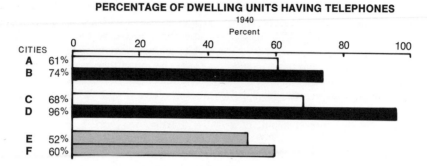

PERCENTAGE OF DWELLING UNITS HAVING TELEPHONES
1940
Percent

CITIES		0	20	40	60	80	100
A	61%						
B	74%						
C	68%						
D	96%						
E	52%						
F	60%						

SOURCE: American Telephone and Telegraph.

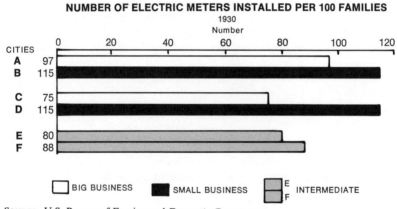

NUMBER OF ELECTRIC METERS INSTALLED PER 100 FAMILIES
1930
Number

CITIES		0	20	40	60	80	100	120
A	97							
B	115							
C	75							
D	115							
E	80							
F	88							

☐ BIG BUSINESS   ■ SMALL BUSINESS   ▨ E/F INTERMEDIATE

SOURCE: U.S. Bureau of Foreign and Domestic Commerce.

surveyed. These items were discussed for illustrative purposes only. A truly representative list of items, however, was employed in the 37-item G-score previously discussed. And this index shows clearly the substantially higher level of civic welfare in the small-business cities.

Part IV. Big Business, Civic Spirit, and the Middle Classes

Wages paid for work in manufacturing, wholesale distribution, and retail trade are greater in the big-business cities—and have been so for at least two decades. This is shown in appendix B. Nonetheless, small-business cities appear to have higher civic levels, a more balanced economy, and a greater degree of industrial stability. That their civic levels are higher has been shown

by the composite index, known as the G-score, and by a series of individual standards, presented in the preceding [part].

What is the answer to this paradox? Why are civic levels higher in the lower wage-scale, small-business cities? Is ·this situation merely the result of a historical accident or can it be traced to differences in industrial organization? That is the question with which this [part] is concerned.

It is believed, as a result of field investigation, that the lower levels of civic welfare in the big-business cities can be traced largely to their industrial structure—specifically to big business. One of the keys to this relationship may be found in an examination of "civic spirit" in big- and small-business cities, discussed below.

The Meaning of Civic Spirit

What is meant by civic spirit? This is an important question because the existence of an active spirit contributes to higher civic levels. Civic spirit may be said to exist in a city where there is widespread participation in civic affairs on the part of those able to benefit a community by voluntary management of civic enterprises. These enterprises may consist of attempts to improve the parks, obtain better schools, make the streets broader, etc.

Enterprises of this kind are carried on extensively only if there exists an active civic spirit. In the communities studied, it was found that civic spirit did not have firm roots in the big-business cities, and insofar as it existed it was of a different, and less active type than that which prevailed in the small-business cities. Essentially, it was found that big business tends to dry up civic spirit. There are at least six definite reasons why civic spirit—and thus civic welfare—tends to be higher in the small-business cities. These reasons are discussed below.

Civic Spirit and the Independent Middle Class

The independent middle class—particularly the small businessman—has traditionally been the chief participant in the management of civic enterprises.* For one thing, he usually has some time and money available with which to interest himself in these matters. He is, on the average, fairly well educated. His work in conducting a small business trains him for initiative and responsibility. He is thrown into constant contact with the administrative and political figures of the city.

Furthermore, the small businessman often stands to benefit personally as a result of civic improvement; for example, better highways and streets lead to greater sales for the retail merchant. Mere self-interest dictates that the businessman in the small-business city should be someone civically.

By participating actively in civic affairs, he widens his circle of contacts. This is of economic importance since businessmen are likely to buy and sell from each other extensively in small-business cities, while for retailers the good will of the community obviously has definite value in dollars and cents.

In the big-business cities, however, there is no particular reason for the officials of the giant corporations to be personally well-known among the small businessmen in the community. The economic condition of the giant corporation is in no way dependent upon contacts with local people. This fact that there is no economic incentive for officials of absentee-owned corporations "to be someone civically" is among the most important causes of the lower levels of civic welfare in the big-business cities.

The Size and Composition of the Middle Class

In big-business cities the independent middle class is characteristically much smaller than in the small-business cities. Thus, there are four times as many manufacturers in the small-business cities, and this is true despite the fact that the small-business cities are not quite so industrialized as measured by the proportion of employees who work in manufacturing. Furthermore, in small-business cities there are approximately three times as many business proprietors in all fields—retail, wholesale, services, manufacturing, etc.—as in big-business cities.

Moreover, the middle class is not only larger in the small-business cities; it is of a different kind. In the big-business cities the middle class tends to be the salaried employees of the absentee-owned corporations. In the small-business cities, it tends to consist more of the predominantly independent proprietors, firm members, and officials of local corporations.

This is evident from the following table which shows the composition of all persons

---

*It is shown later that the usual pattern of civic spirit in small-business cities involves the leadership of the independent middle class in civic affairs along with the cooperative participation of labor. Thus, where this pattern prevails, it is necessary that (1) the independent middle class assume civic leadership; (2) there be an actual—or at least a mutual belief in the—identity of interests of small businessmen and labor, and (3) there be a further identification of these interests with the welfare of the city as a whole.

CHART 9. *Percentage Distribution of Gainfully Occupied Workers, 1880–1939*

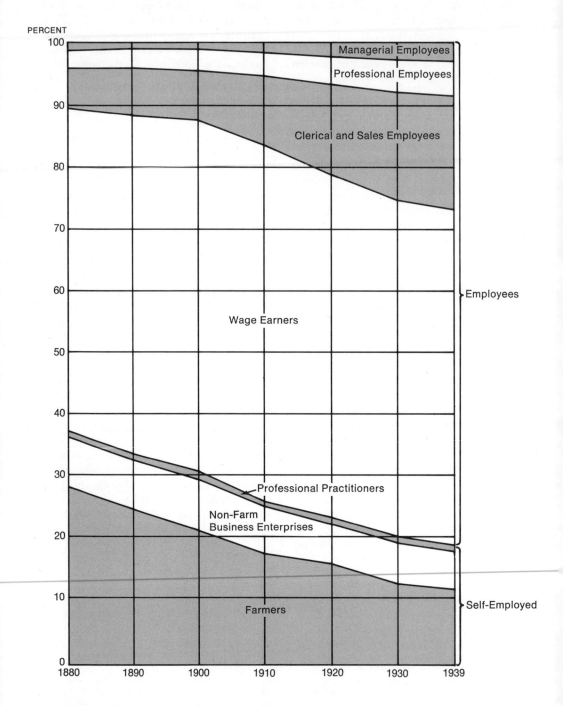

U.S. Department of Labor, Bureau of Labor Statistics.
SOURCE: "Productivity, Wages and National Income," The Brookings Institution, 1940.

	BIG-BUSINESS CITY	SMALL-BUSINESS CITY
	Percent	Percent
Proprietors and firm members	2	9
Officials of corporations	1	14
Salaried employees	97	77
Total	100	100

gainfully employed in manufacturing establishments other than wage earners in one of the pairs of cities studied. Although this information was available for only one of the three pairs of cities, the results may be expected to be similar for all cities having the same type of industrial composition.

The small-business city, relatively, has more than 4 times as many firm proprietors and 14 times as many officials of corporations. These differences in the composition of the middle class are actually wider than is indicated in the above figures, since they relate to manufacturing, and there are far fewer leaders in wholesale and retail establishments in big- than in small-business cities.

This difference in the composition of the middle class in the big- as against the small-business cities, as shown in the preceding table, is merely the local manifestation of a national trend—the trend of independent small businessmen being displaced by clerical and sales employees. Indeed, this trend has been powerfully reflected in the occupational distribution of gainful workers for the United States as a whole. Thus, as shown in chart 9 and in the summary tabulation below [table 6], in 1900 nearly 31 percent of all gainful workers in the United States were self-employed enterprises. By 1939 this figure had been reduced to 18.8 percent. The relative decline in the importance of agriculture was the most important cause of this decline. In addition, however, in 1900 a total of 8.2 percent of all gainful workers were nonfarm business proprietors. By 1939 this figure had been reduced to 6.1 percent. On the other hand the number of employees rose from 69.2 percent of all gainful workers in 1900 to 81.2 percent in 1939. And, what is more important to this report, clerical and sales employees showed a startling increase of from 8.0 percent of all gainful workers in 1900 to 18.3 percent in 1939.

In big-business cities the independent

TABLE 6. *Occupational Distribution of Gainful Workers, 1900–39, as a Percentage of All Gainful Workers*

	1900	1920	1939
All gainful workers	100.0	100.0	100.0
All employees	69.2	76.5	81.2
Wage earners	56.5	55.0	54.3
Clerical and sales employees	8.0	14.7	18.3
Professional employees	3.4	4.2	5.6
Managerial employees	1.3	2.6	3.0
All self-employed enterprisers	30.8	23.5	18.8
Farmers	21.4	16.0	11.8
Nonfarm business enterprisers	8.2	6.5	6.1
Professional practitioners	1.2	1.0	.9

SOURCE: Bell, Spurgeon, *Productivity, Wages, and National Income,* The Brookings Institution, 1940.

middle class is thus being displaced by a middle class consisting largely of the salaried employees of the giant corporations. From the point of view of civic spirit and civic welfare, this is of great importance. For there is apparently less incentive and less chance for these salaried people to take the lead in civic enterprises. They lack the economic independence and civic organization of an active small-business class. If they try to carry forward civic improvements, they can usually do so only with the permission—explicit or otherwise—of the corporation upon which they depend for their economic existence.

The Patterns of Success

The traditional pattern of success for the independent businessman consists of: (a) Founding a business enterprise and (b) conducting and expanding that enterprise. But in the big-business city the pattern is quite different; it involves (a) getting a "forward looking" job in one of the existing big corporations and (b) working one's way up the line within this corporation. This first type of success pattern may be called that of the business enterpriser; the second, that of the business careerist. Rising within a city's business and civic hierarchy is a far different affair from climbing within the corporate hierarchy. Obviously, as the economy becomes increasingly concentrated, the latter avenue to success becomes increasingly important and the former correspondingly declines.

It is in part a reflection of this situation that a far larger proportion of the "bright young men" in the big-business cities studied, failed to return from college to their own community. Rather, they typically sought distant, greener pastures for their business or professional life.

Although complete figures were not available, enough information was obtained from field investigation to corroborate this point that, proportionately, fewer college students return to their home towns in the big- than in the small-business cities. Thus, a school-board member of one of the big-business cities declared:

I have been a school-board member for some 10 years, and I know that as many as 10 percent of the high-school graduates from one of our high schools go to college, mainly the sons of lawyers, doctors, dentists, teachers, and the better real-estate people. But not more than 2 out of the 10 come back to this city. The girls go away and teach some place else. Rarely do our high-school graduates who have gone on to the normal schools come back to teach here. The boys go on into the large industrial plants elsewhere to be engineers. There are practically no father-son combinations; that is very rare in this town.

Not only do fewer of the "bright young men" return to the big- than to the small-business cities; those who do return to the big-business city are frequently drawn into the corporate hierarchy. Thus they adopt a form of economic life which offers little incentive or reward for civic activities.

The business careerist, of course, looks for his advancement, not to local individuals or institutions, but rather to the officials of the corporation. A good corporation man obviously represents the corporation, not simply the branch of it which happens to be located in his old home town. There is no reason for corporate officials to include among the standards used for promoting subordinates any contributions made to local civic welfare. Such contributions benefit the business careerist only if, by chance or design, they happen to benefit the profit position of the corporation. And, as is brought out later, civic activity which is of such a nature that it benefits the corporation often damages rather than benefits the city.

Not only does it appear that civic activity is conspicuously absent from the standards used in promoting him; the truly successful business careerist is one who moves, physically, out of the city. For real success in a great absentee-owned firm involves rising in the corporation. This in turn means getting out of town and into the central office.

In sharp contrast, the business enterpriser, the young man who returns to the small city and founds a local business, or carries on the business of his father remains locally rooted and locally orientated. His own business success is linked to his participation in civic affairs. The processes which encourage civic participation among businessmen in the small-business cities, as described above, apply to him.

In short, fewer of the "bright young men" return to the big- than to the small-business city, and a large proportion of those who do return are drawn into the big corporations. In either case their contribution to the community's welfare is ordinarily negligible. Thus, do the wellsprings of civic activity dry up as the American economy becomes increasingly concentrated.

The Distribution of Prestige

In small-business cities, as has been pointed out, the local businessmen compete in civic activity, thereby improving their own economic position and gaining in social prestige. In big-business cities, however, there is much less of such activity, even among independent small businessmen. Social prestige is gained by an entirely different route. It is achieved by "getting in with" and imitating those who hold the real power and prestige in the city, namely, the executives of the big corporations and their wives. Beside them, the standing of small businessmen in the community is dwarfed.

Field investigation has revealed that such social standing as the local middle class in the big-business cities may secure is obtained through association with the leading officials of the great absentee-owned firms, through following their style of living, through moving to their suburbs, attending their social functions, duplicating in miniature, so to speak, their behavior. Since the chief interests of the corporation group do not characteristically include civic affairs, the local middle class correspondingly tends to drift away from civic enterprises.

Interviews in the field with well-informed residents of a big-business city—school-board members, local businessmen, librarians—revealed the following facts:

1. The chief executives of the corporation—the plant managers and officials

having over $10,000 or $15,000 a year income—are without question at the top of the city's social structure. They do not typically have any material interests in civic affairs and, indeed, often look with condescension on "local stuff." During the 1930's this group, in some of the cities surveyed, moved out of the city's limits into an exclusive suburb of their own. "They have their own schools and parks, and their own social clubs and other activities."

2. The old local social leaders of the city, as well as the middle class in general, have been displaced as social leaders by the corporation group. The prestige of these former leaders was based upon long residence in the city, and in some cases, upon ownership of real estate. Their incomes range from $5,000 to $20,000 a year.

3. The old upper middle class now frequently acknowledges the social leadership of the corporation group. They struggle to be invited to the affairs of the new leaders. They attempt—usually without success—to marry into their circle. One of the most obvious symptoms of the drift of things is the definite movement of these old families into the exclusive suburbs built largely by the corporation managers.

4. The tendency of the old upper middle class to imitate and try to "get in with" the corporation group, coupled with the tendency of the "bright young men" to leave the city or become business careerists is creating a civic vacuum in the big-business city. Civic-minded leadership in the city's affairs is seriously lacking.

This matter of social prestige is possibly even more important to women than to men. Certainly, middle-class women are frequently more active than men in civic matters —particularly in those relating to education, health, and charities—if for no other reason than that they have more time available.

Although women will participate in civic affairs for a variety of reasons—including, of course, the simple desire to be of help and service to the community—they will generally participate to a greater extent if (*a*) "it is the thing to do," that is, if it increases their social prestige, or (*b*) it helps their husband's business. These motivating desires behind civic activity are much stronger in the small- than in the big-business cities; in fact, they are often practically nonexistent in the big-business cities.

In the big-business cities, women gain little social prestige by participating in civic affairs. This is because the women at the top of the city's social structure—the wives of the corporation's executives—are not concerned with local civic matters. They are usually concerned, rather, with trips to metropolitan centers, parties and other functions, journeys to the country, the very latest fashions, celebrities, etc. They are not even concerned with such an apparently important civic matter to them as education. This is because they send their own children to exclusive schools or because they have their own schools in their own suburbs, distinct and separate from the city's schools. A typical middle-class woman in a big-business city could work herself to the bone on civic matters and never be noticed or accepted by the executives' wives. But, if it became known that, by some chance, she happened to be well acquainted with a metropolitan celebrity, she might well be "in."

In the small-business cities, there is generally widespread participation in civic matters by wives of local businessmen. This means that civic activity is "the thing to do" and social prestige is gained from it. Rivalry develops for leadership in civic enterprises. And although this rivalry leads to many minor tempests, civic welfare usually gains from it.

A second underlying motive for women to participate in civic affairs—to help their husband's business—hardly exists at all in the big-business cities, but is very important in the small-business cities. The corporate officials in the big-business cities have very few business dealings with other businessmen in the city. Their dealings are largely with distant individuals, such as buyers of the plant's products, sellers of materials and parts, etc. Even when the official undertakes some deal with a local businessman, no social contact is required, no friendly relationship is necessitated; the name of the corporation is enough. This means, in effect, that it is completely unnecessary for the corporate official's wife to participate in civic activities in order to help her husband's business. The power of the corporation's name will readily provide him with all of the contacts in the city that he will ever require.

The situation is just the reverse in the small-business towns. There, the local businessmen usually have extensive dealings with each other. They often buy and sell from each other and to the same customers. Widespread contacts and friendly relationships with other businessmen in the town are a requisite to a successful business enterprise. Obviously, these contacts will be widened if the wife actively interests herself in civic matters.

There seems to be little doubt but that the active role played by women in civic affairs in the small-business cities definitely contributes to their higher levels of civic welfare.

Real and Apparent Power

Although the officials of the large absentee-owned firms have little interest in civic affairs, they, nonetheless, actually run the big-business cities studied in this report. The answer to this apparent paradox is that corporation men, in fact, take action in civic affairs only when these civic affairs impinge upon corporation interests. In such cases, the influence of corporation men is often exerted surreptitiously, behind the concealing facade of local puppets and official figureheads. It is in this sense that officials of the great absentee-owned firms in big-business cities possess the real power in civic affairs, although the apparent power may reside elsewhere.

The basis of power for the great absentee-owned firms is obvious—for one or a very few such corporations dominate the entire economy of a big-business city. As one retailer in a big-business city said, "If you live in this town, you just know that you're working for them, whether you're working in their plants or not." Their direct economic controls—which may spread, for example, to the control over local banks, etc.—are, therefore, taken for granted. Their indirect controls over virtually every facet of urban life are less obvious. The way in which these controls are promulgated and enforced is described, below, the information being based in all cases upon interviews with residents of big-business cities.

1. The most powerful weapon absentee-owned corporations possess is the threat to leave town. This threat is employed as a veto power, that is, as a measure of last resort to be employed against any city project which the corporation may seriously oppose. The projects opposed may involve any of a wide range of subjects, such as the level of real-estate taxes, the construction of a highway, or the demands of organized labor. In any event the powerful veto in the hands of large, absentee-owned corporations is in effect the power of life or death over the economic life of the town as a whole. It affects the town's bank, the chamber of commerce, small businessmen—especially retailers—labor and city officials alike. The history of its use in the big-business cities studied shows that it is effective.

Thus, in one of the big-business cities, an issue was up for decision. The word was passed down the line—through the town's largest banker and the secretary of the chamber of commerce—that the largest corporation was seriously considering moving its plants to another city. According to small businessmen in the town, as well as labor and city officials, there was near panic. The measure in question was dropped.

2. As evidence of disapproval of a city project, big-corporation officials may simply refrain from participating in activities of the sponsoring organization. Thus, they may absent themselves from meetings, or withhold financial support. These methods, investigations disclose, are also effective. In one big-business city, for example, the chief officer of the local chamber of commerce opposed measures supported by the big-corporation officials. The officials simply withdrew from the organization and did not return until shortly thereafter a new officer was appointed. Local residents said of the officer that, "He seemed a rather competent fellow. A lot of people around here liked him all right. It was just that he didn't fit in with the plants. That's why they pushed him out."

3. Officials of absentee-owned plants may exercise control, indirectly through one or more local small businessmen. "They don't want it to appear that they control things," a chamber of commerce official said. Nevertheless, behind the scenes—in this and in the other ways described—they do "control things." Of course, the use of small businessmen for this purpose is accomplished through devious means. Thus, in one case brought to the attention of a field investigator, a local businessman was accepted in the social circle of the big corporation officials. He was, figuratively, taken under the wing of one of the top families. He received membership in the best clubs, attended the proper functions, was given social stature out of proportion to that which he ordinarily might have expected. Finally, pressure was exerted to elect the local man to official positions in the leading civic organizations. Since big corporations usually control an undivided bloc of votes, this was easily accomplished. The result was to place the local man in a highly strategic position. Whether or not he was maintained there, however, depended entirely upon his behavior—specifically, on whether or not he followed orders promptly and expeditiously. In this case the local businessman was at one point induced to visit Washington to protest against a Federal decision involving his town. This decision, local residents agreed, would have benefited the small businessman's own economic interests, but would have interfered with the operations of the plant of the big absentee-owned corporation.

One local small businessman, a retail merchant who had once served as mayor of a big-business city, confided in a field investigator as follows:

> Question. How is it that you dropped out of politics?
> Answer. I had to—it was ruining my business. I'm really glad I'm not mayor any more.
> Question. How is that?
> Answer. Well, for example, a customer would come in here and say: "How about fixing my sidewalk? It's so badly cracked it's a menace to the family as well as passersby." I would say: "I'll see what I can do. I agree it sure does need fixing." So I would go to the boss (the man who ran the largest plant). He would just say no. So I would have to tell the customer no. It goes without saying that I would lose the customer and his friends, too.

This use of small businessmen in big business towns as the camouflaged shock troops of the corporate officials paralyzes the civic will of the middle classes and confuses their efforts. They see that civic activities which they believe ought to be pushed are opposed by members of their own class. This practice has the further effect of making the small businessmen the target for many of the grievances and complaints of the working men which are really caused by the corporate officials.

Labor and Civic Leadership

During recent years labor has played an increasingly active role in civic affairs. This is due to a wide variety of different causes including the organization of labor, the increased education and knowledge of the working man, the tendency of labor unions to take a more active role in political and governmental matters, etc.

Although this study was not directly concerned with the above factors, an examination was made of the difference in participation by labor in civic affairs between the small- and the big-business cities. It was found that, in the cities studied, labor was more likely to participate cooperatively in civic matters, along with other social groups, in the small-business cities. In the big-business cities, on the other hand, if labor participated in civic activities, it was more likely to do so independently and often in conflict with business groups.

Apparently this was due to a number of reasons. In the first place, the mere fact of smaller plants tends to informalize relations between owners and workers. Not only do the small-business cities have smaller industrial plants; they contain higher proportions of retail and wholesale employees. Working conditions in retail and service fields are especially conducive to close employer-employee relationships.

Also, in a small-business city it is much easier for a wage earner to visualize himself as a potential businessman. Moreover, the economic, as well as the social, distinction in a small-business city between the less prosperous businessmen and the more prosperous wage earners is often hazy at most.

All of these factors add up to closer and more informal relationship between workers and businessmen in the small- than in the big-business cities. Moreover, as shown above, the civic activities of business groups in a small-business city are typically of a kind more likely to elicit the cooperation of labor. Thus, there is a more cooperative—and in many cases—a more active, participation by labor in the civic enterprises of the small-business cities.

It may well be that in the future the reverse will be true—that labor will be more active in the big-business cities. Some portent of this was found in one of the big-business cities examined. There, traditional civic leadership had practically vanished. Corporate officials had built their own suburbs and took no interest in civic affairs. The former leaders in the city—the old upper middle class—were trying to follow them and "get in" with the corporation group. The small businessmen had lost their civic spirit and drive. Some of them had become "fronts" for the corporation officials. Others had seen too many worth-while projects blocked by the corporation and had become convinced of the futility of trying to do anything for the city.

Into this civic vacuum labor entered. At the time the field investigation was made, labor was undertaking civic responsibilities and pushing a number of different civic projects. It was actively interesting itself in the conduct of the city government. Civic leadership was passing into the hands of labor.

It should be realized, however, that while civic vacuums may develop in big-business cities, it does not follow that labor can readily step into such vacuums and assume civic leadership. While the executives of the big corporations may not be interested, themselves, in civic enterprises, they may, nonetheless, exercise their power to prevent anyone else from taking such leadership. The obvious result in this event is inactivity and stagnation in civic affairs.

Appendix A. The Selection of Cities

The selection of the six cities surveyed in this report was based in part on statistical considerations and in part on the informed opinions of individuals in Government and business.

The first step in selection was to compile a list of all cities in the United States within each of three population size groups and each of the four major regions of the country. The regions were the standard regions employed by the United States Bureau of the Census: Northeastern States, North Central States, the South, and the West. The population size groups were 25,000–50,000, 50,000–100,000, and 100,000–175,000. These particular population classes were selected for three reasons: (a) the interest of this report is in the more numerous smaller and medium-size cities; (b) in any event, surveys of larger cities would have been considerably more expensive and time-consuming; (c) there is relatively little statistical information available for cities under 25,000 population. In 1940 there were about 350 cities of 25,000–175,000 population in the United States.

From this list of cities were eliminated: (a) all those cities whose civic life was obviously dominated by nearby metro-politan centers; (b) all State capitals; (c) several cities which were built around various public institutions.

For each of the remaining cities the percentage of industrial workers of the total employed population was computed. "Industrial workers" were defined as all employees in manufacturing, construction, and extractive industries, according to the census classification of these industrial groups. The average percentage industrialization for all cities within the size range considered was 37 percent in 1940. All cities with less than 40 percent industrialization were then eliminated from the list. The remaining cities were then distinctly industrial cities, since each was industrialized more than the average of the original sample. As already shown, State capitals and other public institutional cities had been eliminated as well as suburbs and other communities dependent upon nearby metropolitan centers.

The next step was to compute for each of these cities the percentage of industrial workers in each of seven broad industrial groups:

Extractive industries
Construction
Textile and apparel
Chemicals, petroleum, and coal products
Iron, steel, non-ferrous metals, and their products
Machinery and transportation equipment
Other manufacturing industries

This measure of industrial concentration was taken as the first tentative indication of which cities were dominated by big business and which by small business. Accordingly, the cities within each region and population group were ranked according to the concentration of industrial workers in any one industrial group. So far as possible, then, cities at the top of the list were paired off with those at the bottom. Each of the pairs obtained in this way consisted of two cities with approximately the same population and the same geographic locality. However, one member of each pair was characterized by a relatively high degree of industrial concentration, the other by industrial diversity.

One further statistical test was applied to these cities. For each city the percentage of nonwhite population was computed. Pairs of cities were then eliminated from the list if the members differed appreciably with respect to the proportion of nonwhite population.

The cities now remaining, however, were suitable for study only if the degree of industrial concentration was in fact a true indication of industrial organization along big- or small-business lines. While used here as a rough indicator, it was recognized that this one criterion alone was not sufficient. It was still necessary to select from the pairs of cities remaining those which differed with respect to (1) concentration of industrial workers in a few big firms, (2) the prevalence of absentee-ownership of industrial firms. Since no comprehensive statistical information on industrial ownership and size of firms in cities is available, another avenue of approach had to be determined.

The method chosen was to communicate with Government officials and businessmen in or near the various cities remaining in the master sample list. This was done through the field offices of the Smaller War Plants Corporation, and in a few cases through the field offices of certain other Government agencies. Through these field offices businessmen and Government officials were questioned concerning their impressions of the relative importance of big firms

and absentee-ownership in the relevant cities. On the basis of these interviews the six cities studied in this report were finally selected, two pairs of which provided big-business—small-business contrasts, while the third provided an intermediate case.

Appendix B. The Structure of Big- and Small-Business Cities

Application of Definitions

How do the six cities studied fit the definitions of big- and small-business cities set forth in [part] I? In this appendix, the cities are examined in the light of those definitions. Table 1 presents the location and population size of each of the six cities.

The first pair of cities, as table 1 indicates, consists of a big-business city (A) and a small-business city (B), both located in the Middle West, with populations in 1940 of about 150,000. The second pair consists of a big-business city (C) and a small-business city (D), both located in the Middle West, with populations of about 60,000. The third pair consists of a big-business city (E) and a small-business city (F), though here the differentiation is not as sharp as in the case of the other cities. Both are located in the East, and have populations of about 30,000.

The data relevant to the three criteria of small-business and big-business cities are summarized for all six cities in the following three tables. Thus table 2 shows the concentration of employment in the big-business cities. In the small-business cities the number

TABLE 1. *Business Structure, Location, and Population of 6 Cities*

City Symbol	Business Structure	Location	Population[1] (1940)
A	Big business	Middle West	150,000
B	Small business	Middle West	150,000
C	Big business	Middle West	60,000
D	Small business	Middle West	60,000
E	Intermediate	Northeast	30,000
F	Intermediate	Northeast	30,000

[1]Source: U.S. Bureau of the Census. Figures are rounded in order to avoid disclosing identity of the cities.

TABLE 2. *Number of Industrial Firms and Average Number of Employees Per Firm*

CITIES	NUMBER OF FIRMS	AVERAGE NUMBER OF EMPLOYEES PER FIRM
A—Big business	42	1,270
B—Small business	409	83
C—Big business	38	614
D—Small business	159	92
E—Intermediate	18	437
F—Intermediate	32	325

SOURCE: Chambers of commerce and manufacturers' associations in each city.

of industrial firms was much greater—409 as against 42, and 159 as against 38. Moreover, the average size of industrial firms in the small-business cities was much smaller—83 employees as against 1,270 and 92 as against 614. Cities E and F, in accord with their definition, represent intermediate cases, although city E is more of a big-business community than city F, having only half as many firms and having a quarter more employees per firm.*

The relative importance of absentee ownership is shown in table 3. No less than 96 percent of all industrial workers in A were employed by absentee-owned firms, as against only 15 percent in B. In C, 93 percent of all industrial workers were employed by absentee-owned firms as against 13 percent in D. E and F again represent cases between the two extremes, with absentee ownership being higher in the former than the latter city. This table also shows that in all six cities the average size of absentee firms is much greater than the average size of all firms in each city, as shown in table 2, and that in the distinctly big-business cities, A and C, the absentee firms are especially large.

The third criterion, the extent of industrial diversification, is shown in table 4. It is obviously much greater in the small-business cities. In city A, 87 percent of all industrial workers are employed in one industrial group, as against 49 percent for B. In city C, 84 percent of all workers are employed in one

TABLE 3. *Percentage of Industrial Workers Employed by, and Average Size of, Absentee-Owned Firms*

CITIES	PERCENTAGE OF INDUSTRIAL WORKERS EMPLOYED BY ABSENTEE-OWNED FIRMS	AVERAGE NUMBER OF EMPLOYEES PER ABSENTEE-OWNED FIRM
A—Big business	96	6,431
B—Small business	15	155
C—Big business	93	4,338
D—Small business	13	197
E—Intermediate	84	2,206
F—Intermediate	61	2,120

SOURCE: Chambers of commerce and manufacturers' associations in each city.

* Of course, the relatively smaller number of firms E and F as compared with the other pairs does not indicate greater concentration. Cities E and F are of much smaller size than the other four cities.

industrial group as against 56 percent in D. In cities E and F the differences are also substantial, but, again, not as great as in the other two cases.

TABLE 4. *Percentage of Industrial Workers Employed in City's Main Industry*

CITIES	PERCENTAGE
A—Big business	87
B—Small business	49
C—Big business	84
D—Small business	56
E—Intermediate	73
F—Intermediate	47

SOURCE: U.S. Bureau of the Census. Percentage given for each city is for number employed in largest of 7 major industrial groups classified especially for this purpose by the Bureau of the Census.

Thus, cities A and C are clearly big-business cities—with the bulk of their industrial workers employed in one industry, by a few large firms which are absentee owned. Cities B and D are clearly small-business cities with the bulk of their industrial workers employed in many small, locally owned firms operating in several different industries. In the case of E and F the differences are narrower, with E more closely resembling a big-business city and F a small-business city.

The Problem of Control

Clearly, the big- and the small-business cities included in this report represent different types of industrial structures. Do these differences in industrial structures result in differences in civic levels? That is the principal question with which this report is concerned.

Before it can be answered, however, an examination must be made of certain factors other than industrial structures which may affect civic levels—factors such as geographic location, climate, and the character of the population.

If both cities in each pair prove to be approximately the same with respect to these "other factors"—if, in other words, the "other factors" are held constant, then differences in the levels of civic life can be attributed in large part to differences in the business structure—that is, to the influences of "big" versus "small" business.

Actually, in selecting the six cities, this was done. While the problem of comparing as complex a matter as entire cities cannot be solved mechanically, an effort was made to keep these "other factors" the same as between the two members of each pair of cities studied. Some of the more important of these "other factors" are as follows:

Geographical Location and Climate

Each of the members of every pair of cities is located in the same geographical and industrial region. Indeed, with one exception, the members of each pair are in the same State. All of them are within what is commonly known as the manufacturing belt of the country. Cities A and B as well as E and F are quite comparable distances from larger cities; city D of the C–D pair is closer to a larger metropolitan area than is C, but it is quite autonomous in its civic and social life. Cities A–B are both rather important urban areas in their own right.

This similarity of geographical location, of course, results in a similarity of terrain and climate. For instance, the maximum temperature over a year's period does not vary between the big- and the small-business city with which it is compared by more than 5 points; the minimum temperature, by 4 points. Variation in inches of rainfall is negligible. Thus no substantial differences in civic life between the big-business and the small-business cities can be attributed to differences in geography, terrain, or climate.

Type of Population

As already noted in table 1 the population size of the members of each pair of cities is approximately the same. However, another factor which might result in differences in civic levels is the difference in type of population. Higher proportions of nonwhite and foreign born are generally associated with lower wages and thus poorer living conditions. This would obviously affect civic levels. Although no complete control was possible over all the differences in type of population, these two factors—the percentage of nonwhite population, and the percentage of foreign born—were maintained on a nearly equal plane between the members of each pair of cities. These figures are presented in table 5.

Thus, in the first pair of cities, there is a difference of only one percentage point in the proportion of native white population. In the second pair, the difference is three percentage points; in the third pair, only six. The proportion of Negroes is negligible in all the cities. The proportion of foreign-born in the population is about the same in the first [two] pairs; in the third pair, the difference is more pronounced, with a slightly higher percentage in F.

Average Annual Wages

A further factor which might affect the civic level of a city is the average wages earned per year by manufacturing and other workers. In tables 6 and 7 it is shown that wages are almost uniformly higher in the big-business cities in manufacturing, wholesale distribution, and in retail trade. There are a few minor exceptions; wages were temporarily lower in big-business cities in 1933 in wholesale distribution, and in one

TABLE 5. *Composition of Population, 1940*

CITIES	NATIVE WHITE	FOREIGN-BORN	NEGRO
	PERCENTAGE		
A—Big business	85	11	4
B—Small business	86	12	2
C—Big business	86	10	4
D—Small business	89	9	2
E—Intermediate	86	13	1
F—Intermediate	80	20	0

SOURCE: U.S. Census of Population.

TABLE 6. *Average Annual Wage Per Worker in Manufacturing*

CITIES	1925	1927	1929	1931	1933	1935	1937	1939
A—Big business	$1,712	$1,769	$1,640	$1,291	$1,073	$1,614	$1,778	$1,796
B—Small business	1,424	1,449	1,441	1,118	791	951	1,155	1,172
C—Big business	1,424	1,615	1,649	1,275	1,047	1,509	1,657	1,713
D—Small business	1,346	1,373	1,391	1,133	920	1,119	1,318	1,261
E—Intermediate	1,264	1,219	1,254	907	803	985	1,248	1,288
F—Intermediate	1,136	1,206	1,198	1,091	900	1,004	1,076	1,010

SOURCE: U.S. Census of Manufactures.

TABLE 7. *Average Annual Wage Per Worker in Trade*

CITIES	WHOLESALE TRADE				RETAIL TRADE			
	1929	1933	1935	1939	1929	1933	1935	1939
A—Big business	$1,968	$1,369	$1,735	$1,758	$1,379	$1,078	$967	$1,100
B—Small business	1,951	1,441	1,403	1,582	1,266	1,009	891	985
C—Big business	2,350	1,344	1,715	1,864	1,415	996	963	1,080
D—Small business	1,778	1,432	1,547	1,577	1,328	1,054	965	1,036
E—Intermediate	1,660	[1]	1,296	1,496	1,067	1,129	866	948
F—Intermediate	1,539	1,337	1,469	1,429	964	1,072	941	969

[1]Not available.
SOURCE: U.S. Census of Business.

pair of cities in 1933 and 1935 in retail distribution. However, the succeeding rise in wages in big-business cities, in these cases especially, was greater. Hence, it can be concluded that this factor would tend to cause the levels of civic life to be higher in the big-business cities. This obviously would have the effect of making even more striking any finding to the effect that the civic levels are actually higher in the small-business cities.

Type of Industry

One factor which might affect the civic level of a city but which cannot be held constant consists of the differences in the specific lines of industry prevailing in each of the cities. Obviously, it is impossible to match the line of industry which is predominant in a concentrated industrial city with the lines of

industry which characterize a diversified industrial city. Yet, civic and social differences between two cities might be due in part to differences in the specific lines of industry prevailing in each of the cities. But these differences in lines of industry have their primary effect upon civic levels in differences in types of workers and in differences in wages. In other words, differences in lines of industry most directly affect the civic level first, by the different types of labor which are attracted to a city and second by different wage levels. Since, as has been shown, the types of populations are approximately the same, and wages are higher in the big-business cities, it may be concluded that any finding of higher civic levels in the small-business cities cannot be significantly ascribed to differences in lines of industry.

Local Industrial Structures, Economic Power, and Community Welfare*

Irving A. Fowler

An old ideological conflict over who should control economic activity and to what ends reappeared in postwar America. Most conservatives were alarmed by the growth of economic and political power of farmers, organized workers, and centralized federal agencies. Most liberals, on the other hand, were equally alarmed by the persistent presence of vast concentrations of private economic power, despite fifty years of vigorous anti-trust agitation. Both political camps were apprehensive over the American economy's stability. The continuous inflationary

spiral and its generation of acrimonious strife between labor and management inflamed the ideological clash further.

The deepest root of this ideological conflict rests in the cultural ideology of liberal capitalism, a system of beliefs about what the structure, control, and performance of the economy should be like. Shorn of considerable detail, the ideology prescribes an economic structure composed of many small, locally-centered economic units, controlled primarily by open and freely competitive market forces. The presumed result

Reprinted from Social Problems, 6 (*Summer 1958*), 41–51 by permission of the author and The Society for the Study of Social Problems. Copyright 1958 by the Society for the Study of Social Problems.
*A major portion of this paper was presented at the Eastern Sociological Society meetings in New York City, April 14, 1957. Acknowledgements are gratefully made to Robert Hardt for his critical review of an earlier draft of this paper.

is a maximum of economic welfare and a social environment responsive to the "needs of the people." The opposite structure, composed of a few large, absentee-centered economic units, administering prices in monopolistic markets, is proscribed, because it is presumed to result in a minimum of welfare and in a social environment exploitative of the people. The ideology also contends, implicity or explicitly, that social and political pluralism will result, that this pluralism is a valuable corollary of economic competition, and that the competition of men for political power will somehow serve the society in the same way as competition does in the economic sphere. More detailed examinations of the ideology are available in Galbraith (9, pp. 11–34), Moore (16, pp. 417–454), Williams (26, pp. 138–140), and Sutton (24, entire volume).

Ten years ago, Mills and Ulmer published a study of small-business versus big-business cities (15) confirming the ideological "theory." Their study tentatively concluded that big business tends to depress while small business tends to raise the level of local "civic" welfare, as measured by the Thorndike G score. Their more detailed findings were that small business cities had more "balanced" economies with larger proportions of independent entrepreneurs who showed greater concern for local civic affairs.

Publication of this and another study by the Senate Small Business Committee (10) created a furor over the respective contributions of small—versus big-business to societal and to local community well-being. The furor was another indication that the ideological issues were still very much alive in the behavior of many Americans.

Some social scientists are still as much victims of the ideology as other Americans. The ideology's prescriptions are implicit in the work of some community organization people. A few sociology texts still quote the Mills-Ulmer findings uncritically. (3, 5) Some economists continue to exhort public policymakers to legislate the ideology's prescriptions into law. (11, 17, 21) With so many Americans, lay and scientific, still basing their behavior on the cultural biases of the ideology of liberal capitalism, it is little wonder that empirical analysis of all types of social power have been impeded for so long.

The fact that the current American economy differs widely from that prescribed by the ideological "theory" needs little documentation here. Many studies show conclusively that oligopolistic markets are typical. (2, 9, 23) Big business managers share much economic control over these markets with leaders of large farm, labor, retail, and governmental organizations. Yet there is no evidence that the ubiquitous private "concentration of economic power" has had adverse effects on the *entire society's* social welfare. (4, 13, 25) A review of evidence on small- versus big-business dominance *in industrial cities* discloses, upon careful examination, highly variable effects. (8) The question of the differential effects of diverse kinds of local industrial structures and local well-being remained problematical enough to suggest that continuous study is required.

Purpose of paper. This paper presents the results of a recent empirical test of three hypotheses involving the relationship between the characteristics of local economies, local power structures, and community welfare. (8) The first hypothesis, derived from the ideology's implications and from one of the Mills–Ulmer study conclusions, asserts that:

> small-business industrial structures will produce higher levels of welfare than big-business structures, other relevant factors remaining relatively constant.

The second hypothesis, again derived from the ideology and from Mills and Ulmer's interpretation of their other findings, asserts that:

> local pluralistic power structures will produce higher levels of welfare than local monolithic power structures.

The third hypothesis asserts that:

> the "type of industry" variable has an equal, if not greater, effect on welfare as do other industrial structure variables, other relevant factors remaining constant.

Although Mills and Ulmer were unable to include "type of industry" in their classification of structures, a review of the evidence suggested that such an inclusion would be essential for more adequate classifications of local industrial structures. The factors to be held constant in the tests of the first and third hypotheses were geographical location, similarity of terrain, climate, size, and character of population. No factors were held constant in the test of the second hypothesis.

Method. The hypothetical tests were accomplished through partial* replication and extension of the Mills-Ulmer design: the *ex post facto* experiment. Thirty small New York State cities (10,000 to 80,000 in size in 1946) were selected in a fashion following the Mills-Ulmer procedure. Their general economic and demographic structures were analyzed prior to classifying their industrial and power structures for hypothesis tests. Small-versus big-business industrial structures were operationally defined in terms of the following two criteria and data:

a. *the degree of concentration of employment,* based on per cent of total industrial employment employed by large establishments, defined as those with 500 or more wage earners, arbitrarily defined at the 30 city median of 62.2 per cent, 1950; and

b. *the degree of local versus absentee-ownership,* based on per cent of total industrial employment employed by absentee-owned establishments, arbitrarily dichotomized at the 30 city median of 65.1 per cent, 1950.

Since institutionalized power relations inevitably involve the evaluation of the worth and distribution of goods and services (economic values), the prestige of others (stratification values), and the control of others' behavior in a territorial area (political power values), pluralistic versus monolithic local power structures were operationally defined in terms of the following five criteria and data:

a. *the degree of concentration of employment,* described above;

b. *the degree of industrial unionism,* based on the estimated per cent of all industrial workers organized in all types of legitimate industrial unions, arbitrarily dichotomized at the 30 city median of 80 per cent, 1947–1949;

c. *the degree of presence of the "old" middle class,* based on the per cent of total employed civilian labor force "self-employed," arbitrarily dichotomized at the 30 city median of 10.0 per cent, 1947;

d. *the degree of conformity to the social characteristics (nativity, ethnicity, and religion) of the American society's majority,* based on the estimated per cent of the total population native-born, white, Protestant, arbitrarily dichotomized at the 30 city estimated median, 1940; and

e. *the degree of political conservatism,* based on the per cent of total party enrollment registered in the Republican party, abitrarily dichotomized at the 30 city median of 59.6 per cent, 1947.

The hypothesis assumes that a "pluralistic" power structure exists when (a) there are diverse sources of social power, (b) exercised by numerous persons over smaller numbers of others, (c) in many separated spheres of social life. Contrariwise, a "monolithic" power structure exists when a small group of persons, deriving power from a few sources, hold power over numerous others in many spheres of their social life.

The light-dispersed versus heavy-concentrated industrial structures were operationally defined in terms of the following two criteria and data:

a. *the degree of concentration of employment,* described above; and

b. *the degree of light- versus heavy-industry,* based on annual average value added by manufacturing per

---

*Partially replicatory for two reasons: (a) limited research resources confined city selection to one state and to smaller size cities; and (b) the latter necessitated the creation of a new index of welfare, since the Thorndike G score was available for cities of 25,000 or over only.

industrial wage earner, arbitrarily dichotomized at the 30 city median of 52.24 per cent, 1947.

Local welfare was also operationally defined and measured in terms of a new composite index called the General Social Welfare (GSW) score, replacing the Thorndike G score used by Mills and Ulmer.* The GSW score was derived from a total of 48 individual variables,† ranked in terms of whether more or less of the item would be regarded as indicative of "high" welfare and the rank "one" always designated the "highest" value. These 48 ranking were combined into the following eleven major welfare subcomposites:

1. Income
2. Income security
3. Consumer purchasing power
4. Home ownershig
5. Housing adequacy
6. Health needs
7. Health facilities
8. Literacy
9. Adequacy of educational provision
10. Political expression
11. Municipal wealth and service

Mean ranks of these subcomposites were re-ranked and then totalled to derive the GSW scores. Lower values of the GSW scores denoted higher welfare levels. Arithmetically, the thirty cities' GSW scores would range from 11 to 330; the actual scores ranged from 89 to 277.

Controlled comparisons of cities were made with relevant variables held constant except the presumed independent variable: the prescribed and proscribed types of industrial structures.

A combination of two methods was used to equate the sample pairs of cities; *frequency distribution control* and *precision control*. The presumed dependent variables, the various levels of local welfare, were then compared to see if they confirmed or denied the predictions of the specific hypotheses.

Results. Table 1 presents seven pairs of cities for evidence to test the first hypothesis. The first five pairs compare well on five control variables (metropolitan status, population size, per cent foreign-born white, per cent non-white, and degree of dependence on manufacturing); the last two pairs compare well on three or four of these control variables. In each case of pairs, the top city is small-business with the least concentration of employment and the least absentee-ownership; the bottom city is big-business with the greatest concentration of employment and the most absentee-ownership.

The table shows that in only three out of seven pairs of cities are the results consistent with ideological predictions, that is, small-business structures having higher levels of general social welfare than big-business structures. In a series of less rigorous hypotheses tests, the same inconclusive results were found.

Table 2 presents a typology of local power structures based on dichotomized values of five of the listed criteria: degree of concentration of employment, industrial unionism, "old" middle-class, social heterogeneity, and political conservatism. On the assumption that each indexed criterion is of equal weight, there are six possible combinations of highs and lows, ranging from five highs and no lows (the most pluralistic end of the continuum) to five lows and no highs (the monolithic, or least pluralistic end of the continuum).

The findings from Table 2 are sharply opposite to the ideological expectations. Local pluralistic power structures in greatest conformity with the five attributes prescribed by the ideology were negatively associated with high levels of welfare. The monolithic (or least pluralistic) power structures, in which there existed the greatest likelihood of coalesced social, economic, and political elites, and the least likelihood of social

---

* Thorndike G scores were available for only 17 of the 30 selected cities. Despite dissimilarity in data, time period, and weighting, a rank order correlation of the 17 G scores with their corresponding GSW scores produced a coefficient of .69, significant at the .01 level. This finding supported the assumption that local welfare levels were fairly stable functions of underlying socio-economic structures.

† A complete list of these 48 items will be provided upon request.

TABLE 1. *Small- Versus Big-Business City Industrial Structures Contrasted in Ownership and Employment, by GSW Scores; 1930*
(*The Top City in Each Pair Is Small-Business*)

| Paired Cities | CONTROL VARIABLES[1] | | INDEPENDENT VARIABLES[3] | | DEPENDENT VARIABLE |
	Popul. 1940	Mfg. Ratio[2] 1940	Per cent Absentee Establ. 1950	Employed by Large Establ. 1950	GSW Scores[4] 1930–48
SB	28,589	48	47.2	14.7	203.5
BB	21,506	46	72.9	65.9	124.5
SB	18,836	47	38.4	41.1	94.5
BB	15,555	54	65.1	62.4	110.5
SB	23,329	71	15.5	0.0	167.5
BB	24,379	68	75.0	65.4	94.5
SB	12,572	74	48.8	21.9	173.5
BB	17,713	71	85.0	87.4	228.0
SB	10,666	78	3.5	0.0	204.0
BB	11,328	58	95.6	95.6	198.7
SB	42,638	62	13.2	47.0	150.5
BB	34,214	68	78.1	81.0	209.0
SB	10,291	42	29.4	0.0	139.5
BB	45,106	48	66.0	79.6	136.5

[1] All cities have independent metropolitan status. Two control variables, per cent foreign born white and non-white, have been excluded for lack of table space.
[2] The higher the ratio, the higher the degree of dependence on manufacturing. This ratio is based on the per cent of employees employed in industry, computed as a per cent of "aggregate employment" in four types of economic activity: industry, retail trade, wholesale trade, and service trade.
[3] The data for these indices was gathered in personal surveys of the selected cities. "Large" establishments were defined as those with 500 or more industrial employees.
[4] The lower the GSW score, the higher the local community welfare.

challenge to these cities from diverse socio-economic groups with their own socio-economic interests to pursue, were positively associated with higher levels of welfare. Equally interesting is the apparent linearity of the negative association in this sample of thirty cities—the higher the degree of local pluralism (socially, economically, and politically), the lower the local welfare score.

The third hypothesis asserted that the exclusion of the "type of industry" variable or criterion from any classification of industrial structures makes the latter inadequate. To make this test, structures with light industry and dispersed employment were compared with structures having heavy-industry and concentrated employment. Table 3 presents five pairs of contrasted cities with appropriate data on the control, independent, and dependent variables.

Analysis shows that in five out of five cases one type of structure is consistently and positively associated with higher welfare

levels. The hypothesis that "type of industry" has an important determinant effect on welfare can thus be accepted as tenable. In the paired cases studied, a specific general "type of industry" (heavy, producer goods industry, coupled with concentration of employment) had a consistently positive association with higher welfare levels.

The major findings of the study this paper reports were therefore as follows:

a. local "concentrations of economic power" *do not* have invariant "adverse" effects on local welfare levels;
b. the *type of industry* found in a local industrial structure has an important determinant effect on local welfare levels;
c. in the 30 cities studied, the industrial structures in *least* conformity with the ideological model (those with higher absentee-ownership, higher concentrations of employment, more heavy

TABLE 2. *Thirty Local Power Structures, by Degree of Pluralism and by Mean GSW Scores (Each Criterion Dichotomized into High and Low Values and Equally Weighted)*

	EACH TYPE		COMBINED TYPES	
No. OF CRITERIA ON WHICH CITIES ARE HIGH[1]	No. Cities	Mean GSW Scores[2]	No. Cities	Mean GSW Scores
Pluralistic Pole:				
A. Five Highs*	1	237.0	8	212.2[3]
B. Four Highs	7	208.7		
C. Three Highs	7	158.2	15	164.2
D. Two Highs	8	169.4		
E. One High	5	130.6	7	119.5
F. No Highs†	2	91.9		
Monolithic Pole:				
No. of cities	30		30	

*Low concentration of employment, high industrial unionism, large "old" middle-class, high social heterogeneity of population, and high political liberalism.
†High concentration of employment, low industrial unionism, small "old" middle-class, high social homogeneity of population, and high political conservatism.
[1]The following cities fall into the listed types: A) Hudson: B) Cohoes, Gloversville, Little Falls, Middletown, Oswego, Rome, Troy; C) Amsterdam, Auburn, Geneva, Glens Falls, Johnstown, Massena, Poughkeepsie; D) Beacon, Cortland, Dunkirk, Kingston, Olean, Oneida, Watertown, Watervliet; E) Binghamton, Corning, Elmira, Endicott, Jamestown, and F) Johnson City and Lockport.
[2]The lower the GSW scores, the higher the local community welfare.
[3]The differences between these mean scores are statistically significant. An H equal to 12.84 was computed with a probability of .01 being due to chance.

TABLE 3. *Light-Dispersed Employment Versus Heavy-Concentrated City Industrial Structures by GSW Scores: 1930–48 (The Top City Is Light-Industry with Dispersed Employment)*

	CONTROL[1]		INDEPENDENT		DEPENDENT
PAIRED CITIES	Popul. 1940	Mfg. Ratio 1940	An Av. Value added by Mfg. per Wage Earner: 1946	Per Cent Empl. by Large Est. 1950	GSW Scores 1930–48[2]
A.	10,666	78	$3,858	0.0	204.0[3]
B.	11,328	58	9,512	95.6	198.7
C.	23,329	71	4,037	0.0	167.5
D.	24,379	68	6,612	65.4	94.5
E.	22,062	55	4,944	32.2	223.0
F.	21,506	46	7,249	65.9	124.5
G.	12,572	74	4,624	21.9	173.5
H.	15,881	66	6,009	62.5	145.5
I.	28,589	48	3,745	14.7	203.5
J.	45,106	48	5,530	79.6	136.5

[1]See footnotes in Table 1.
[2]The lower the GSW score, the higher the local community welfare.
[3]Applying the H. test, and H = 260.8 results with a P less than .001.

industry) tended to have slightly higher welfare levels than structures with the opposite characteristics; and

d. in the 30 cities studied, the local power structures in *least* conformity with the ideological model (those with higher concentrations of employment, low degrees of industrial unionism, low proportion of the "old" middle-class, low degrees of political liberalism, and low degree of social heterogeneity) tended to have substantially higher welfare levels than the structures with the opposite characteristics.

Interpretation. The findings were obviously at sharp variance with the Mills-Ulmer study and ideological implications. The discordance of this study's finding with past evidence, which partially confirmed the ideology, requires a complex interpretation of related levels of socio-economic phenomena. But because the evidence is confined to just one level (local), this paper's interpretation can only suggest connections between the empirical findings and the conditions and processes in the larger economy.

The sample cities with big-business structures tended to have higher welfare levels for four reasons related to the technically advanced nature of modern industry. First, their more advanced technical mode of production demands larger numbers of more highly skilled and higher paid personnel. Being part of large national industrial organizations, with a greater degree of control over particular markets, such local establishments can more readily absorb such higher personnel costs. Second, their local establishment, usually the result of careful site selection and a long-range capital commitment, increases the local assessed valuation of industrial, and, indirectly, personal property, thus making more tax revenue potentially available for public services for longer periods of time.

Third, this relatively long-range commitment to site, this attraction of higher skilled personnel, plus the demand for specific supply relations, stimulates the growth of ancillary industries with similar characteristics. Finally, local consumers, like all consumers, benefit from the big-business establishment's contribution to the firm's and industry's constant increments to technically advanced productive methods and products. Thus, these and numerous other factors intimately related to the nature of the industry,* whether intensely competitive or monopolistically competitive, have as determinant an effect on community welfare as the nature of industrial organization of either.

All the above local benefits were contingent, however, on the specific industry's stage of development in the locality or region, and on deeper market forces in the entire economy. If the industrial units were newly located or in earlier developmental stages, these welfare benefits would be observable locally for some time, precluding of course, severe deflationary conditions. If, on the other hand, the local units were obsolescent and the entire industry's geographical center was shifting, such benefits could be subject to dramatic reversals. Thus, the expansion of new industries and the contraction of old has entailed highly dynamic geographical shifts of local centers of production. And, while the entire economy may benefit from locational as well as technological competition, these benefits will not and cannot fall evenly on the local populations involved. (14)

With the implication that local economic and political elites were coalesced, why did not the more monolithic local power structures depress local welfare in the manner that Mills and Ulmer described? (15, pp. 22–31) The answer is simply that in both studies the coalesced power of big-business structures was more apparent than real. Mills and Ulmer abstracted from their data only that which permitted the construction of the malevolent picture that adherents of the ideology would be expected to present.

Such a picture could not take into consideration the following types of socio-

---

*A large number of diverse variables were found associated with city welfare levels, the most important of which were: (a) the extent and availability of raw resources, (b) costs of assembling materials, and (c) costs of marketing finished products.

economic phenomena: (a) the immensely complex, historical growth pattern of modern industries and how their periodic "abuse" of economic power has provoked defensive-protective reactions of specific buyers and sellers; and (b) how these developing bargaining relations intersected in different structural locations. (9) All of which shows how historically in Western democracies the exercise of coalesced economic and political power and its consequences have been highly limited *to specific issues, groups or organizations, or areas.* Nor does their picture indicate how frequently big-business executives are disinclined to "exploit" local social elements. Angell, for instance, reports that big-business executives were either disinterested in local affairs, or, if involved, had a baneful influence on local affairs, not because of any abuse of power, but because they were inept and unrepresentative leaders. (1, p. 105)

Most evidence presented here would suggest that the actions of local economic and political elites were determined by larger forces over which neither they nor those exposed to their power have much control. Furthermore, little sociological attention is given to the local community dependence on extra-community organization and to the frequent relinquishing of local authority to the broader social structure as Sjoberg points out. (22)

Important factors in the modern situation would thus seem to have made it increasingly difficult to "abuse" economic power in the local community. Among such factors, the following appear to be highly significant: (a) the growth pattern of modern industry and defensive-protective adjustments of related economic groups and organizations; (b) the growth of public power to protect "public welfare"; (c) the growth of personal resistance to unlimited exercise of all types of social power; (d) the changing occupational structure, with its "professionalization" of labor (7); and (e) the solvent of increasing wealth. In short, the paradoxical finding that *local monolithic power was not abusive economically* can only be explained by the growing restraints upon it coming from the increasingly

pluralistic power in the general social structure.

Social Problem Implications. It appears obvious that these findings provide no calm harbor for those who hope ideological conflict over the respective contributions of small- versus big-business to local welfare will evaporate. So long as the "insecurity of illusion" (9) of the cultural ideology of liberal capitalism persists, tensions between important economic and political actors in the American scene will continue.

The tensions will provide fertile soil for the continuance of still other types of social problems, only a few of which can be mentioned here. There is some evidence, for instance, that irresponsible scape-goating of big-business executives had turned modern management's attentions to the labyrinths of "human relations" to such an extent that it has lost sight of its primary economic role: production. (6, 26) A frequent problem is the mass manipulation of ideological symbols to obscure issues in the political struggle for control of governments (State and Federal) and their power to intervene in private economic affairs in the name of "public welfare." Less frequently cited, but widespread, is the following type of abuse by *inaction of locally centered* private economic and political power holders: powerful local proponents of the ideology blaming extra-local forces or persons for their own inability to act constructively on the local scene, despite the availability of numerous "enabling" resources provided by extra-local organizations in the health, welfare, civil rights problem areas. Both of the latter are so frequently observable that they require no documentation here.

Social scientists have only recently begun to contribute solutions to those problems by systematic conceptual clarification and empirical analysis of significant power problem areas. Galbraith's differentiation between "original" and "countervailing" economic power and their dynamic development (9), Parson's clarification of economic and political power (18, p. 121), William's analysis of the interpenetration of American economic and political institutions (26), Rosenburg's application of Reisman's concept of "veto" groups to the desegregation issue (20, 19), and Sutton's detailed examination of the social functions of the American Business Creed (24) herald a significant "break-through" [in] the cultural biases against investigating power problems. A sociology of knowledge inquiry into the sources, supports, and consequences of these cultural biases would be a worthy additional contribution, and provide, at the same time, a greater historical understanding of past and future power struggles in democratic societies. At any rate, sociologists and economists appear ready to produce something like Lasswell's and Kaplan's treatise on power (12) in the field of the sociology of economic organizations and institutions.

Summary. This paper presented the results of an empirical test of three hypotheses derived from ideology of liberal capitalism and from a previous study of the presumed effects of small- versus big-business on local "welfare."

Small-business cities were found to have no higher levels of welfare than big-business cities; to the contrary, small-business cities tended to have lower levels of welfare. The "type of industry" was found to be an important criterion for more adequate classification of industrial structures. In the cases studied, heavier durable-goods industry and concentrated employment were associated with higher welfare levels. The major conclusion was, therefore, that "concentrations of economic power" *do not have invariably adverse* effects on community welfare.

In a less rigorous test of the local power structure hypothesis, similar results were found. The least pluralistic power structures (concentrated employment, low industrial unionism, small "old" middle-class, low political "liberalism," and low population heterogeneity) were associated with higher welfare levels.

These findings were obviously at sharp variance with the Mills-Ulmer study and with ideological expectations. A complex interpretation of related levels of socio-economic phenomena, tying the empirical findings of this paper to other observations on conditions and processes in the larger political economy, was required.

In the cases studied, big-business cities had higher welfare for reasons related to [their] monopolistically competitive and technically advanced nature. They paid higher wages, enhanced local property and tax revenues, stimulated the growth of ancillary industries, and, being forced to bargain with massive retail organizations, contributed indirectly to greater consumer satisfaction. All of these benefits, however, were dependent on whether the general economy was stable or deflationary.

Interpretation of the findings is facilitated, if conceptual distinctions are made between "original" and "countervailing" economic power, between "economic" and "political" power, and between intra-local and extra-local levels of organization. It is furthermore suggested that certain social problems will persist unless these distinctions are broadly disseminated among the people.

American social scientists have only recently broken through these biases. It would not be remiss to say that the American people and their democratic values would benefit immensely, if this "break-through" is consolidated by further intensive study.

References

1. Angell, Robert C., "The Moral Integration of American Cities," Supplement to the *American Journal of Sociology*, 57 (July, 1951).
2. Blair, John M., *et al.*, *Economic Concentration and World War II*, Report of the Smaller War Plant Corporation to the Special Committee to Study Problems of American Small Business, U.S. Senate, 79th Cong., 2nd Sess., Doc. No. 206 (Wash: USGOP, 1946).
3. Broom, Leonard, and Philip Selznick, *Sociology* (Evanston, Ill.: Row, Peterson and Co., 1955), pp. 420–424.
4. Clark, Colin, *The Conditions of Economic Progress* (London: Macmillan Co., 1940), pp. 148–149.

5. Cuber, John F., *Sociology: A Synopsis of Principles* (N.Y.: Appleton-Century-Crofts, Inc., 1955 edit.), pp. 413–418.

6. Drucker, Peter F., *The New Society* (New York: Harper and Bros., 1950).

7. Foote, Nelson N., and Paul K. Hatt, "Social Mobility and Economic Advancement," *American Economic Review*, 43 (May, 1953), 364–378.

8. Fowler, Irving A., *Local Industrial Structures, Economic Power, and Community Welfare: Thirty Small New York State Cities 1930–1950* (unpublished Ph.D. dissertation, Cornell University, September, 1954).

9. Galbraith, John K., *American Capitalism: The Concept of Countervailing Power* (New York: Houghton, Mifflin Co., 1952).

10. Goldschmid, Walter R., *Small Business and the Community: A Study in Central Valley of California on Effects of Scale of Farm Operations*, Report of the Special Committee to Study Problems of American Small Business, U.S. Senate, 79th Cong., 2nd Sess., No. 13 (Wash.: USGOP, 1946).

11. Hayek, Frederick A., *The Road to Serfdom* (Chicago: The University of Chicago Press, 1944).

12. Lasswell, Harold D., and A. D. H. Kaplan, *Power and Society: A Framework for Political Inquiry* (New Haven: Yale Univ. Press, 1950).

13. Leven, Maurice, Harold G. Moulton, and Clark Warburton, *America's Capacity to Consume* (Washington: Brookings Institution, 1934).

14. McLaughlin, Glenn E., *Growth of American Manufacturing Areas* (Pittsburgh: Bureau of Business Research, University of Pittsburgh, 1938).

15. Mills, C. Wright, and Melville J. Ulmer, *Small Business and Civic Welfare*, Report of the Special Committee to Study Problems of American Small Business, U.S. Senate, 79th Cong., 2nd Sess., No. 135 (Wash: USGOP, 1946).

16. Moore, Wilbert E., *Industrial Relations and the Social Order* (New York: Macmillan Co., revised edit., 1951), pp. 417–454.

17. Mund, Vernon A., *Government and Business* (New York: Harper and Bros., 1956).

18. Parsons, Talcott, *The Social System* (Glencoe: The Free Press, 1951).

19. Riesman, David, *The Lonely Crowd* (New Haven: Yale Univ. Press, 1950).

20. Rosenburg, Morris, "Power and Desegregation," *Social Problems*, 3 (April, 1956), 215–223.

21. Simons, Henry, *Economic Policy for a Free Society* (Chicago: University of Chicago Press, 1948).

22. Sjoberg, Gideon, "Urban Community Theory and Research: A Partial Evaluation," *American Journal of Economics and Sociology*, 14 (Jan., 1955), 199–206.

23. Stocking, George W., and Myron W. Watkins, *Monopoly and Free Enterprise* (New York: The Twentieth Century Fund, 1951).

24. Sutton, Francis X., *et al.*, *The American Business Creed* (Cambridge: Harvard University Press, 1956).

25. Woytinsky, [W. S.], *et al.*, *Employment and Wages in the United States* (New York: Twentieth Century Fund, 1953), pp. 49–53.

26. Williams, Robin M., Jr., *American Society: A Sociological Interpretation* (New York: Alfred A. Knopf. Inc., 1951).

Absentee-Owned Corporations and Community Power Structure

Roland J. Pellegrin and Charles H. Coates

The stratification system of a given community attains stability and remains basically unaltered over relatively long periods of time because, as shown in recent studies, the control of community affairs and policies resides in dominant interest groups which feel little incentive to disrupt the existing pattern of superordination and subordina-

Reprinted from The American Journal of Sociology, *61 (March 1956), 413–419, by permission of the authors and The University of Chicago Press. Copyright 1956 by The University of Chicago.*

tion. These groups exercise power[1] which is infinitely out of proportion to their number.

The mechanics of control by minority are clearly revealed in Floyd Hunter's work *Community Power Structure*.[2] Hunter examined the roles in community affairs and policy-making played by various cliques or "crowds" of leaders from the realms of business, finance, and industry. The power of these individuals and groups, he states, is effectively channeled through organizations, committees, and agencies which are concerned with community affairs—plans, projects, and policies.[3] Following his argument, this paper deals with the role played by executives of absentee-owned corporations in organized groups, such as associations, clubs, councils, and committees. Data were gathered between June, 1954, and May, 1955, through intensive interviews with fifty leading executives of the community and other persons who have worked with and observed corporation executives.

The Community Setting

Bigtown, the nucleus of a southern metropolitan area of approximately 200,000 inhabitants, is a fictitious name for a rapidly growing city whose rise to economic prominence in the region and nation has been meteoric. Above all, its growth is a consequence of new industrial plants. The residents of Bigtown derive their livelihoods from a variety of sources, but the most vital elements in the economic structure of the city are a number of absentee-owned corporations which manufacture and process industria! products mainly for non-local consumption The plants not only employ a large proportion of Bigtown's citizens and set the local wage pattern but make possible the existence of a multitude of smaller industrial and business concerns. The development of community facilities and services is in part dependent upon their financial contributions[4] and their co-operation in programs designed to improve the city. In short, they play a pre-eminent role in the dynamics of Bigtown life.

The Power Structure, Civic Affairs, and the Corporation

American cities apparently vary considerably in the extent to which dominant interest groups are united effectively for coordinated control of community affairs. As Hunter describes the situation in Regional City, groups are drawn together through mutual interests and common values and are held together by strong leadership, which integrates their efforts.[5] The cliques or crowds "go along" with one another's projects in anticipation of future reciprocity.

The leaders of Bigtown, many of whom are of cosmopolitan backgrounds, tend to view this pattern of control as ideal. They dwell at great length upon the power structure of other cities in which they have resided, where an informal "Committee of 50," "Citizens' Council," or like group controls civic affairs with a firm hand. These glowing accounts are typically accompanied by a pessimistic description of the situation in Bigtown. This community, as analyzed by some of its outstanding men, has a number of powerful interest groups but lacks effective liaison among them and leadership to unite them. Under these circumstances, a given "crowd" is unlikely to participate in a proposed project unless it foresees tangible gain.

This situation lends itself neither to effective community planning nor to adequate facilities and services for the citizenry. Many plans and projects are initiated by individuals and groups, but few indeed are carried through to fruition, either because of a lack of co-operation among powerful groups or negative reactions by one or more "crowds." The shortcomings of the city are popularly ascribed, however, not to power conflicts or apathy but to the rapid growth of the city and to the failings of its governmental officials.[6]

In the relative power vacuum which exists in Bigtown, community projects are usually doomed if they lack the approval of the industrial, absentee-owned corporations. There is no single crowd or clique of representatives of them, but their top executives communicate with one another informally and arrive at agreement on matters of policy. The executives of each corporation are then informed of the decision, making it possible for given community projects to be supported or vetoed through united action. Corporation support probably assures the success of a proposed project, while disapproval spells doom for it. Thus absentee-owned corporations are a decisive force in the power structure of Bigtown, since they constitute a balance of power among the competing interest groups of the community. On the other hand, as initiators of projects or policies, the corporations can ordinarily get support from a sufficient number of other enterprises to put across their goals.

Corporate participation in Bigtown's civic affairs has followed an intriguing pattern. While the interests of a corporation extend far beyond the local community and it is primarily concerned with furthering its own goals rather than those of cities in which its branches are located, there has been a tendency for absentee-owned corporations in the South to adopt local customs and practices, including a paternalistic attitude toward both their employees and the community.[7] The corporations of Bigtown have exhibited considerable interest in civic affairs, justifying their participation publicly in terms of "making this a better place for all of us to live." In past decades, of course, additional motivation for becoming community-conscious has been found in the corporation's concern for favorable taxation rates and good labor relations and for securing needed local facilities and services for its expanding enterprises. Thus a need for a favorable public conception of the corporation has been felt for a considerable period.

Recent changes in the region and nation, however, have also promoted the corporate concern with public sentiment. The threat posed by the gains of organized labor in the South has greatly stimulated the desire to develop and maintain a favorable public image as a weapon for use in labor-management controversy. There exists in Bigtown, as elsewhere in the nation, an almost incredible preoccupation with "public relations"—i.e.,

a constant and vociferous campaign designed to apprise the populace of the magnanimity and generosity of the corporations. Local media of communication constantly provide tangible evidence of corporate altruism in the form of statements concerning substantial financial contributions to civic projects and the heavy burdens of civic duties carried by top executives.

David Riesman has called attention to the emerging pattern of "conspicuous production" or "conspicuous corporate consumption," by means of which a corporation seeks prestige and plaudits for providing new employee benefits and services, luxurious buildings, machinery designed with aesthetic values in mind, and the like—much of which can hardly be justified economically.[8] In the same way, the corporations are contributing money and time to community projects as a favored means of creating and reinforcing a favorable public image of the corporation.

It must be strongly emphasized, however, that this active participation in civic affairs is motivated primarily by a desire to present the corporation to the citizenry in as favorable a light as possible and to maintain zealous guard over the corporation's interest and prerogatives. Not only does the corporation dictate the terms, but it decides what *social values* are to be implemented by its choice of projects and the policies followed by its agents. This is indeed participation with a purpose, the purpose being a double one: to further corporate interests and to exercise control over civic affairs in order to preserve the values of a conservative, business-oriented ideology. This is clearly revealed by an analysis of the role of the corporation executive in civic affairs.

The Executive's Civic Participation

Extent and types of participation. The executives of Bigtown's absentee-owned corporations are discriminating in their choice of civic associations. The modal number of affiliations with local organizations per person is but two, as contrasted with a modal number of four organizational memberships for executives in all other types of industrial, business, and financial enterprises.[9] Citing the number of memberships, however, is likely to give a misleading impression of the influence of corporation executives in civic affairs. When the types of organizations to which they belong are analyzed, it is discovered that in 60 per cent of the cases they belong to *both* of the two most powerful organizations in the community.[10] These two are policy- and decision-making bodies that play a vital role in charting the course of Bigtown's plans and projects.

Conversely, the executives of the absentee-owned corporations are heavily underrepresented in the less powerful organizations of the community. The restriction of their memberships primarily to the "elite" organizations not only shows a personal lack of interest in the lesser ones but means that the numerous youth, welfare, "uplift," fraternal, and other agencies are dependent upon others for support, direction, and sponsorship. A few of the top corporation executives participate in the work of these groups, primarily as members of boards of directors. They are especially likely to be found in organizations charged with the responsibility of disbursing large sums of money, since they are interested in the uses to which the money will be put. In general, however, the least influential organizations of Bigtown are forced to content themselves with membership from middle management and junior executive levels.[11]

The assignment of civic and committee memberships. Typically, the absentee-owned corporation in Bigtown has a list of executives eligible for membership in power-wielding civic organizations and for service on various "citizens'" committees and commissions created to plan for and supervise important special community projects. Community leaders generally expect the corporation to provide civic leadership commensurate with its size and influence; similarly, the corporation anticipates adequate representation in groups which chart the course of community affairs.

Almost without exception, the men chosen to represent the corporation are high-level executives with lengthy service. They have demonstrated time and again that they are familiar with corporation policies and that they can be relied upon to do a good job of representing the company and its interests. They will express opinions on any subject which indicates that they cherish the "proper" social values.

Executives are expected to belong to civic organizations and serve on committees as part of their jobs. The process by which an individual receives a committee assignment was described by an interviewee as follows:

> Let's suppose that Mr. X, a community leader or government official, is lining up men to serve on an important new committee or commission. He will contact the top executive in a corporation, Mr. Y, and explain the situation to him. Mr. X will then ask Mr. Y to provide him with a certain number of men. Sometimes the two disagree concerning the number to be assigned. Mr. Y will demand more representation if he evaluates the matter as important to the corporation's interests or if it involves basic community policy. If he feels the matter relatively unimportant, he will try to cut down the number of men he has to assign. If Mr. X especially wants a specific executive, say Mr. Z, to serve on his committee, he might ask Mr. Y for him. Mr. Y may agree to this choice, or he may not. In any case, his decisions are the final ones. He can always justify denying the request by stating that Mr. Z is too busy.
>
> Sometimes, if Mr. Z is widely known to have clearance for such activities from his superiors, Mr. X will contact him directly. In such a case, Mr. Z would O.K. the matter "upstairs" before committing himself.

If an executive is not on the "approved list," he is unlikely either to be given permission to serve or to absent himself from his job during workings hours, even if he should volunteer. Interviewees emphasized that only if there were a great deal of "public pressure," would a man not on the list obtain clearance to serve.[12] Another interviewee, who is in a position to be well acquainted with the practices of his own corporation, put the matter this way:

> Only a man who is naïve would accept invitations to participate in important community

affairs without the blessings of Mr. A, the top executive in our company. For a man to ignore the usual procedures for getting clearance, he'd either have to be unconcerned about his career or else be a complete ass. In fact, in my company, *executives at any level have to clear all their organizational memberships with top management.*

Policy and tactics. As an agent of his corporation, the executive is cautious in his public pronouncements. His superiors expect him to keep in mind company policies and interests, and he knows that he should emphasize at opportune moments a firm conviction that what is good for the corporation is good for the community. These expectations are not difficult to adhere to when he participates in organized groups, such as associations and clubs. The individual is informed ahead of time what the position of his company will be, and no decisions on his part are required. He merely has to proceed in accordance with predetermined policies and tactics.

It is through an examination of the executive's role in committees and councils created for specific projects that we gain insight into the extent to which his behavior is conditioned by the expectations of his superiors. Prior to the first meeting of a given committee or other similar group, the executive usually receives a briefing from his superiors on the company's position in the matter involved. In committee meetings he listens carefully for sentiments expressed by others and then reports the proceedings to his company. Thus his superiors are kept informed of what transpires, and he receives instructions as the project proceeds. If a committee unexpectedly seeks a vote on an issue which is not on the prepared agenda, the executive may plead for a recess in order to telephone for instructions. If the word must come from the national office, he may seek a longer delay by suggesting "Let's sleep on it!"

In civic matters, as reworked, the corporation seeks not only to protect and foster its own interests but to promote a conservative, business-oriented ideology. The general procedure is for Bigtown's executives to state their opinions in such a manner as to imply that anyone holding different ones is stupid, uninformed, or possibly subversive. The implication is that all "right-thinkers" must believe as the executives do. Thus a dissenter would be forced into a defense not only of his social values but of his intelligence and his patriotism.

Executives are constantly on guard lest fellow committee members divert funds to new projects suggestive of the "welfare state." Advocates of such measures are speedily labeled "controversial" and, if they persist, are referred to as "cranks" or "subversives"—a term once used only for political traitors. Deviants of this nature are, in the long run, however, weeded out; they are not able to obtain appointments to other committees. An old-timer, involved in such measures scores of times during the previous thirty years, observed:

> We freeze out these New Dealers and other Reds. When we appoint people to important committee posts, we look at their record. If an individual has gone all out on some crazy idea, his goose is cooked. If I am chairman of a group that is making appointments, I go stone deaf whenever someone suggests the name of one of these radicals. My hearing improves when a good, reliable person is mentioned as a possibility.

Said another informant:

> It frequently happens in the course of a meeting that someone will call attention to the heavy burden of civic responsibilities that is being carried by a small proportion of the population. Someone will say, "My God, it's a shame that just a few of us have to do all the work. Why, this community is just full of talented people who could help a lot, if only they wouldn't shirk their civic duties."
>
> At this point heads will nod vigorous assent, and comments along the same lines will be made by several persons. Then someone else will say, "Yes, all of this is true, but we have to select people we can depend on." Everybody agrees emphatically with this too, so the idea of enlarging the circle of policy-makers is dropped.

Thus a bow is made in the direction of what might be termed more democratic participation of the citizenry in policy-making.

As Hunter has pointed out in the case of Regional City, however, community projects can be carried out successfully only if the small group of policy-makers can marshal the co-operation of large numbers of lower-level workers who will perform the labor required to transform the policies and decisions into reality.[13] When Bigtown's leaders speak of the desirability of increasing participation in community affairs, they are referring to their wish for more followers, not leaders.

The individual's motivation for civic participation. C. Wright Mills and Melville J. Ulmer have pointed out that the executive depends for his career advancement upon his superiors rather than upon local individuals or institutions, and hence he is much more concerned with the affairs of the corporation than he is with those of the community.[14] This correctly implies that his civic participation tends to be a by-product of his job and his desire for career advancement. In the modern corporation the executive role requires a considerable capacity for organizing and manipulating ideas, men, and materials. A demonstration of ability in civic matters may well lead a man's superiors to exploit his talents in the administration of the corporation's internal affairs. Moreover, in his work with influential people in civic organizations and committees, the individual acquires experience and contacts which contribute to his personal development. Hence the executive may, through his outside activities, gain promotion for himself within his own organization.

Top executives of Bigtown are afforded many opportunities for gaining publicity for themselves and their corporations. Not only are these men granted clearance for civic participation by their superiors, but they are invited to join many civic organizations. It is even possible for an executive to migrate to Bigtown from outside the South and in a short time become known as an outstanding civic leader.

The junior executive, through his participation in the lower levels of civic organizations of less prestige and power, can likewise build a reputation in a hurry. This attention-getting activity is especially important for young men employed in corporations in which the individual tends to be just one of a large and "anonymous" mass of junior executives.

Thus the desire for advancement in his career motivates a man to play a part in civic affairs. It would be a mistake, however, to assume that executives are active in community affairs solely to promote their own careers or the interests of the corporation. Not only are there many reasons why men become concerned with the affairs of the community, but a given individual may have several reasons for his activities. Some executives, for example, seem quite concerned with the "sorry state" of community services in Bigtown and cherish an altruistic hope of contributing toward improvement.

It should be added that another motive for civic participation is emerging from the peculiar role which the corporation executive plays in modern society. As contrasted with the earlier elite of the capitalistic world, the business owner, the modern executive is not an entrepreneur. He manages his corporation, but he does not own it. He is usually not wealthy and cannot indulge in flagrant conspicuous consumption. Subject to control by his own superiors, he is not free and independent. This situation led several interviewees, both corporation and non-corporation men, to speculate on civic participation as a means of compensation for the executive's lack of real power. One of Bigtown's entrepreneurs, quite conscious of his own powerful position, made the following remarks:

> I've been observing these corporation executives in action for about thirty years. Two things about them have really impressed me. One is their frustrated desire to be free and independent—that is, to be able to make independent decisions and exercise personal power. The other thing is the lengths to which they will go to conceal from their subordinates and the public at large their subservience to their masters up above, either locally or in the corporation's national headquarters.

The fact is that these fellows nurse a tremendous desire to be big-shot capitalists. But they are not, and they know it. Some of them try to hide this fact by holding a tight rein on their subordinates, using this means to demonstrate their power. Others try to further the impression that they are big shots by being hyperactive in community affairs.

Thus, lacking many of the satisfactions and powers of the entrepreneur, the corporation executive seeks means of displaying authority and independence which he knows to be functions of his position rather than his personal prerogatives. He may conceal his frustrations by playing to the hilt the role of entrepreneur, so long as his own superiors do not see fit to curtail his activities and restrict his powers.

This research report has focused upon the influence of absentee-owned corporations and their executives in the civic affairs of a single community; hence the extent to which the phenomena described and analyzed are typical of American cities must be deter-mined by further comparative research. Future investigations may identify circumstances making for variation in the patterns of informal control in various types of urban environment.

It should be observed that this analysis of Bigtown's power structure has centered attention solely upon one interest group—the absentee-owned corporations. A broader investigation would examine the structures and functions of the multitude of other competing—co-operating factions which actively seek to influence policy-making in civic affairs.

Attention has also been concentrated in this study upon the role of executives in civic matters deemed important to those in control of the corporation and which are potentially controversial—i.e., matters involving decisions to be made in terms of goals and values. Happily, perhaps, not all community affairs are decided in an arena in which the combatants are hostile and competing interest groups. Some matters are resolved through quick consensus, since all agree on the desirability of certain goals.

Notes

1. "Power" is defined herein as the ability to direct and control the activities of others in the pursuit of goals which are established in accordance with a given set of social values.
2. Floyd Hunter, *Community Power Structure: A Study of Decision-Makers* (Chapel Hill: University of North Carolina Press, 1953).
3. Floyd Hunter, *Host Community and Air Force Base* (Air Force Base Project Technical Rept. No. 8 [Maxwell A.F.B., Ala.: Research Institute, Human Resources, 1952]), p. 5.
4. Corporations not only pay taxes (directly and indirectly) but make outright gifts to community projects and collect contributions from their employees during various fund-raising "drives."
5. [Hunter], *Community Power Structure*, [*op. cit.*], chap. iv.
6. The typical interviewee in this study described local governmental officials as relatively powerless figures who do not have the backing of influential groups but secured their positions through the support of working-class voters. Indeed, these officials were more often than not targets of ridicule for those who evaluated their positions in the power structure. Note the differences in roles between these officials and those of Regional City, where governmental figures are subservient to the dominant interest groups (see *ibid.*, p. 102). The relative lack of integration of Bigtown's interest groups makes it possible for governmental officials to sponsor civic projects which are sometimes successful, in spite of opposition from one or another of the "crowds." Interest groups find it difficult to express publicly opposition to projects which attract widespread public support. To do so would be "bad public relations," perhaps unprofitable in the long run.
7. Cf. Harriet L. Herring, "The Outside Employer in the Southern Industrial Pattern," *Social Forces*, 18 (October, 1939), 115-26.
8. [David Riesman], "New Standards for Old: From Conspicuous Consumption to Conspicuous Production," in his *Individualism Reconsidered and Other Essays* (Glencoe, Ill.: Free Press, 1954), pp. 228-29.

9. In contrast, executives in absentee-owned corporations had twice as many memberships in state and national organizations as did the other executives (modal numbers, 2 and 1, respectively). These comparisons of local and non-local affiliations of the two groups may indicate the relative lack of dependence of the former upon the community for a livelihood, prestige, etc. The personal futures of the former group are much less tied in with the fortunes of Bigtown than are those of the latter.

10. In 90 percent of the cases, membership was held in at least one of these two top organizations. Executives from other types of enterprises were also well represented in the two organizations—42 percent belonged to both, and 77 percent to one or the other. Being from many enterprises, these persons outnumber the executives from absentee-owned corporations in these two organizations. It should be noted, however, that, because of the size and influence of the large absentee-owned corporations, each is allotted more memberships in these organizations than are given to smaller enterprises. Since there is agreement within the absentee-owned corporation as to policies and procedures to be followed by its executives and since the interests of these corporations are generally not conflicting, their executives constitute an effective minority in dealing with the executives from other enterprises, which frequently represent conflicting interests.

11. To his superiors, "excellent service" in these civic groups identifies the junior executive as responsible and clear-thinking. The young executive, in turn, may regard his civic duties as a means of demonstrating an ability to serve his employers in a higher capacity.

The assignment of junior executives to civic projects is discussed in Aileen D. Ross, "The Social Control of Philanthropy," *American Journal of Sociology*, 58 (March, 1953), 451–60. This article provides keen insight into corporate participation in civic "drives" or "canvasses."

12. This "public pressure," the authors concluded, consists of demands for an individual's services after he had demonstrated at a lower level that he is either an unusually competent "idea man" or a workhorse.

13. [Hunter], *Community Power Structure*, [*op. cit.*], p. 65.

14. C. Wright Mills and Melville J. Ulmer, *Small Business and Civic Welfare: Report of the Smaller War Plants Corporation to the Special Committee To Study Problems of American Small Business* (Senate Doc. No. 135 [79th Cong., 2d sess.]) (Washington: Government Printing Office, 1946), p. 26.

The Role of the Absentee-Owned Corporation in the Changing Community

Paul E. Mott

To be effective, the members of an organization must organize their centers of power to carry on day-to-day routine production and to change those routines when relevant environmental and internal problems impinge on them. Since communities are organizations, these imperatives apply to them just as they do to any category of organization. Much of what is referred to as classical, or even modern, democratic theory and practice consists primarily of statements about how best to organize communities and societies to meet the second of these criteria of effectiveness. Such practices as free speech, the free competition of ideas, voting, and majority rule are intended to maximize the probability that the population will be aware of the problems they must face, have access to the broadest possible range of solutions, and have mechanisms for select-

An original article written for this volume.

ing peacefully from among those solutions the one(s) that will become the new routines or norms.

Against these yardsticks of democratic prescriptions, many social scientists have measured existing community and societal practices. The proportion of the population that participates in elections or voluntary associations, the extent to which various points of view are available to the public, and the extent to which the public pays them any attention are but a few of the better known questions investigated. But perhaps the most fundamental of these concerns centers on the organization of power itself. Many of the studies of community elites are parallel to those mentioned above in their intent on measuring community practices against some standard of democratic theory. It is assumed that prolonged domination of public decision-making by a single elite, particularly an elite without authority, reduces the effectiveness of the community and is not democratic. Dominance by a single elite limits the ranges of solutions more nearly to those of that elite. But if there are viable, competing elites drawn from different social bases, the processes of problem identification, solution, and action are more eclectic and the range of problems attacked and solutions proposed is broadened. A succession of studies by the Lynds,[1] Hunter[2] and many others record the dominance of community affairs by an elite of economic notables. Again, this condition was decried because of the negative effects that dominance by any culturally homogeneous elite would have on the ability of the community to change, to be more effective.

More recently, this last concern has broadened to include the actions of managers of units in absentee-owned corporations. If absentee-owned corporations are found to be dominating the decision-making of local communities, then all of the familiar problems from an earlier era of economic dominance are also present. On the other hand, corporate withdrawal from community involvement can have the same effect via a different route. Corporate inaction can act like a veto, resulting in the defeat of many solutions to community problems. Also, the community can lose the political and associational services of a highly talented segment of its population: the executives of the absentee-owned corporations.

When research attention was focused on the community actions of local managers of absentee-owned corporations, a set of findings emerged that showed no clear pattern of corporate-community relations. In their study of Baton Rouge, Pellegrin and Coates found the community rather pervasively dominated by the local representatives of decentralized industrial organizations.[3] Robert O. Schulze found the opposite pattern in his study of Ypsilanti, Michigan: of the three automobile manufacturing companies with factories located in the area, only one attempted to participate in community decision-making.[4] In another study Clelland found that the economic dominants generally were withdrawing from associational involvements and commitments, but their withdrawal from political affairs was more gradual.[5] We can infer from Jennings' study of Atlanta that participation in community decision-making was higher for local economic elites than it was for the representatives of absentee-owned corporations.[6] No inference is possible from Dahl's study of New Haven because the leaders of the absentee-owned corporations were included in a larger category of economic notables which also included local businessmen.[7]

Some social scientists have attempted to resolve these seemingly conflicting findings by constructing propositions which distinguish among types of companies or subcultures and relate the use or nonuse of influence to these differences.[8] Others cast their lot with the finding that the executives of absentee-owned corporations are withdrawing from participating in instrumental community activities.[9] These penchants to generalize must be questioned because the number of cases is small and because there are important differences in conceptualization and techniques of measurement among these studies. The first order of business is to reexamine the studies themselves to see if the apparent conflicts are real.

The purpose of this paper is to take a first step in examining these conflicting findings. The position is taken that it is *ordinarily* to the best interests of a corporation to participate in community affairs if for no other reason than self-protection. Further, there are at least two reasons and probably more why researchers who should have found corporate involvement did not find it. First, the classes of acts of influencing that were looked for represented but a small part of the spectrum of methods of influencing. Each of these assertions is discussed in detail below and then applied to a restudy of Ypsilanti.

Power and Power Roles

Schulze portrayed the local management of Ford and General Motors as being inactive in Ypsilanti's political affairs. But this conclusion was partially a consequence of a traditional and somewhat narrow operational definition of the concept of power. This operational definition of power involves the direct, interpersonal manipulation of others through the use of economic resources and associational positions. Such interactions as suggesting, persuading, and coercing were central to this approach to the study of power. Finding that the corporate elite was not involved in the associational life of Ypsilanti and not interacting with the political leaders over matters of public policy, Schulze concluded that they had withdrawn from the elite structure or never had joined it. But aren't there other forms of power just as pervasive and effective that are not quite so obvious in their exercise?

Corporations, like any organization, contain resource or ecological power. This form of power derives from the fact that the company controls valued and scarce resources, mobilizes large numbers of people, and provides them with income. As the ratio of company resources to community resources increases, the ecological power of the company in the community also increases. A prerequisite of effective organizational functioning requires that ecological power be utilized to a fairly high degree.

Corporate leaders are constantly making internal decisions in an effort to maintain desired levels of corporate effectiveness; by making these decisions, the company dominates the rhythms of related activities in the community. In other words, harmonious responses can be elicited from the other subgroups in the community without the exercise of direct, interpersonal influence.

This discussion of the corporation-community resource ratio suggests the fundamental reason for a reexamination of the Ypsilanti situation. If a company has a large installation in a community, it has to be involved in the affairs of the community at least to the extent of protecting its investment. But as the ratio shifts increasingly in favor of the corporation, the range of problems relevant to the corporation increases also. Educational problems, poor hospitals, roads and traffic control affect their labor force, which constitutes a significant share of the population of the community. And if the ratio favors the corporation, it may be more likely to act on these problems because it has a correspondingly greater chance of success due to its ecological power. In Ypsilanti and Ypsilanti Township this ratio definitely favors the two largest corporations —Ford and General Motors—therefore, we must expect that they affect community affairs, unwittingly or otherwise.

Power also derives from the fact that our society is still dominated by a set of values that is very compatible with the interests of businessmen. Values are a basis of power as long as they are adhered to by people in positions of power, because they may guide the actions of these people. We are suggesting here the important distinction between decision-making and decision-shaping. Policy decisions may be *made* by political leaders without any direct interpersonal influencing from economic dominants, but these decisions may be *shaped* in the minds of the political leaders by the social values they share with businessmen. Value compatibility is a form of power far more subtle and effective than persuasion, coercion, and the other traditional techniques of interpersonal influence. A cobweb or sociometric study of the decision-making process is unlikely to reveal this relationship between the political and economic elites. We must look then for techniques that a corporation might use to reinforce its social value-power in the community.

The appearance of noninvolvement may be created by the use of yet a third source of power: that derived from informal contractual agreements. Using its potential ecological and social value-power, the corporation may cause the community leaders to rearrange parts of the social structure as a condition for locating a factory there. It may demand a specific tax arrangement that will not be violated without corporate concurrence. It may demand certain water, fire, and police services and paved access routes or require certain improvements in the hospital and educational facilities. The researcher who studies the community *after* the company has located a plant there may find people busy improving the school system, the hospitals, the roads, etc., but not see that these activities are a consequence of the exercise of corporate power. The situation in Ypsilanti must be reexamined to see if informal contractual arrangements have resulted from an earlier exercise of power.

The above discussion suggests some additional types of power that might be exercised and still create the impression that power was not being exercised by the corporation at all.

If these forms of power are being utilized, then the next question is: Who is using them? It is apparent from Schulze's discussion that it is not the managers of the absentee-owned corporations. Theorems from organizational theory provide us with some guideposts to new roles. Social scientists have suggested that when the level of technology, the surplus wealth, and the population size of the organization increase, its division of labor increases also.[10] In an earlier era the owner or manager of a business enterprise had to be more of a generalist than he need be today. Community relations were among his many role requirements. But if we find today that the manager is not active in community affairs, does it follow that his company has ceased to be interested in

them? Most of our largest corporations now have high levels of technology, surplus wealth, and, by definition, large labor forces. The corporate division of labor may now contain specialists in the handling of community relations. By interviewing the manager about his community activities, we may simply be missing the mark. Since both Ford and General Motors meet the criteria of this hypothesis, we may expect both to contain specialized roles for handling community relations.

In sum, we anticipate that both of the major absentee-owned corporations in that community must be extensively involved in community affairs because the ratio of corporate-community resources necessitates and favors involvement. We anticipate that the exercise of corporate power in the community is lodged in roles other than that of the plant manager and that the occupants of these roles may be using a variety of subtle manipulative techniques in the exercise of corporate power. Finally, we look for informal contractual arrangements as an important means of community control by the corporations.

Ypsilanti Revisited

To determine the roles that Ford and General Motors are playing in Ypsilanti and Ypsilanti Township, initial contact was made with the corporations themselves. The national headquarters of both corporations are located less than a one-hour drive from Ypsilanti: a fact that is highly significant for understanding why the managers of the Ypsilanti plants are not active in community relations. As the Director of Community Relations at Ford Motors told me, "Of course he [the Ypsilanti plant manager] is not active in Ypsilanti, we can handle those problems from here. The company has a straight production man in that job." Thus, neither Ford nor General Motors are truly absentee corporations.

Community Relations at the Corporate Level
Both Ford and General Motors have departments specializing in community relations activities, but their basic policies, structures, and functioning differ in important ways.

Community relations at Ford Motors is located within a larger department which is concerned with political activity at the national, state, and local levels. It is a highly consolidated, complex, and well-financed operation. In each locality where the company has one or more factories, it has a community relations committee. The committee is composed of management personnel from all of the local Ford factories. These committees meet once every other month for five or six hours in the evening. The agendas for the meetings are determined by the community relations department in Ford's central headquarters, not by their local committees. One-half of the agenda is devoted to national issues and the other half to local issues. The chairman of the local committee has continuing responsibility for community affairs. This assignment is rotated annually among the local executives on the committee with the plant manager taking his turn about every six years, depending on the size of the committee. The structural value of this arrangement was described by the Director of Community Relations:

> The chairman of each local committee speaks for Ford Motor Company, but the plant manager can speak only for his division. If we worked through the plant manager solely, he would have to refer problems to his division chief and then from there they would come to us. That would be too cumbersome. This way, we have a direct corporate voice in the community.

Each local committee has an array of corporate specialists it can call on for advice on unusual community problems. For this purpose, the country is divided into twelve regions and each region has political activity and public relations advisors available to the local committees in that region. Tax and property lawyers are available on request from the legal division of the company. The local committee can, on appropriate occasions, hire local lawyers, newspaper men, or public relations firms to provide assistance in local activities. The Director of Community Relations said:

> When a committee first starts out in an area where we have just built a plant, they frequently use the services of our specialists. But as they get more knowledgeable about civic and governmental affairs, they call on them and on me less and less.

Community relations at General Motors is a less consolidated activity at the corporate level, but more centralized vis-à-vis the General Motors local community relations committees. These differences are best illustrated by tracing the route of a local community relations problem. If the problem is essentially legal in nature, it is referred by the local committee to the legal division of the company for solution. If the problem is of a political or public relations nature, it is referred to the relevant section of the public relations department. The local committee does not have the freedom of action that Ford Motors committees have. The failure of General Motors to coordinate activities between the legal and public relations departments was revealed when a key member of the legal department admitted that he was not aware of the community relations functions of the public relations department before talking with this investigator.

> They could have been helping us all these years! It's tough going into these communities sometimes. The community is riled about a smoke problem or a zoning proposal, or they are out to make a tax grab. I usually work with a local laywer. I wish the company would make the local plant manager live in the community. It would be a great help to me if I had one knowledgeable, friendly person to turn to in the community.

Like Ford Motors, General Motors divides the country into twelve regions with a community relations specialist located in each region. But unlike Ford Motors, this specialist handles the local political problems rather than advising the local committees on how to handle them. The illusion of corporate inactivity created by the inactivity of local plant managers masks genuine involvement of extra-local specialists.

Community Relations at the Local Level
The activities of the local committees evidence the actual policies of Ford and General

Motors on involvement in local affairs. In both corporations, the local committees are composed of key management personnel in the local plants. There is only one committee in an area regardless of the number of factories located there.[11] The Ford Motors committees are engaged in an extensive range of programs. There are programs of the good-will variety: used motors are given to automobile shops in the local schools, cars are provided for driver education programs, and, occasionally, land is given or loaned to the community for specific uses. Public relations activities are also extensive. Films are made available to local organizations, a speakers bureau is maintained, there are visitors days at the factories, and political leaders are invited to luncheons at the factories. The content of speeches given by executives is controlled by the corporation through its agenda-setting mechanism for the local committees. Ford Motors also encourages its employees to engage in civic activities, permitting leaves of absence to employees who are elected to public office and maintaining an elaborate system of recognition for community activity. Annual awards are given to employees who have made noteworthy contributions to the community. These awards are carefully allocated to make certain that the major social categories of people are represented. Since employee participation in community affairs is voluntary rather than obligatory, the corporation does not bear the onus for the errors of its employees in public office. The effectiveness and potential usefulness of this program is illustrated by the fact that at the time of this research in Ypsilanti, both the mayor and the mayor pro tem were employees of Ford Motors. The President of the Ypsilanti Township Board of Supervisors was also a Ford Motors employee.

Another of the activities of the local committees indicates how extensively Ford Motors is involved in local affairs. Each year the local committee does a "Climate Study," which is a review of the functioning of the local community. The criteria of the climate studies are primarily concerned with the interests of the company, but as the chairman

of the Ypsilanti committee pointed out to me:

> Where do our concerns leave off? We can't afford not to be concerned about street lights! Last year our Climate Study yielded about fourteen or fifteen things that we thought were wrong with the town. We started working on them right away, talking to people downtown. One of the things that we thought was poor was the quality of vocational education. We made some recommendations and offered to prepay our taxes to help them with it.

The local activities of the General Motors committee were more nearly those of a public-relations oriented veto group. They made contributions to local charities and had the usual quota of good-will activities. The committee encouraged employees to participate in community activities, but they did not reward the participants with award dinners, publicity, or leaves of absence. A member of the community relations staff said, "We do not subscribe to the N.A.M. [National Association of Manufacturers] program of employee participation in politics. We fight when it is important and not otherwise." In other words, only problems that affect the company seriously receive corporate attention.

Each General Motors committee is required to monitor local political activities carefully for signs of problems that could affect the company. Such problems are reported to the relevant department of the company for action. In the community relations department the issues received are given action priorities. A key member of that department explained, "There are some things that we don't want to get involved in; they are too minor. Other things we feel very strongly about and we really go after them." Handling the problems is the work of specialists, however, and not the local committee.

The Political Impact of Community Relations Activities

Examples of the effectiveness of these programs, particularly the Ford Motors program, were readily available. As was mentioned, the three top political offices in the city and township, at the time of this study, were held by Ford Motors employees. A member of the local committee was emphatic in his feeling that the involvement of their employees in community affairs helped the company:

Question: Does it ever hurt the company to have employees in public office? By that I mean do they sometimes bend over backwards so far to be fair to others that they actually hurt the company?
Answer: No, as long as I can remember that has never happened.
Question: Well then, do you think that having these people in public office helps the company?
Answer: Of course it helps us! I'll give you some examples of how it helps us. When we came into this area (the township plant), we found that our access routes to the plant passed through two townships. We wanted those roads paved. People (political leaders) from both townships worked here. You see it's easier to get them together (they can meet in the plant), easier to talk to them, and they know what that means and why we need smooth roads. We finally got our roads because our people were in elected offices. . . .
   It helps, but that doesn't mean that you can go down and tell them what to do. They listen to us and then they can do what they want anyway. But if a man has any sense, he will see things the right way, although I don't think it would affect his job if he didn't. . . .
   We discuss our climate studies with these people too.
   Another problem was over the access routes to our Ypsilanti plant. We had a lot of trouble getting the cars in and out at shift changes. We talked to [an employee who was an elected official] and we had a patrolman out there every day. Hell, he [the political leader] knew the problem, he was in the traffic himself!

One of the events that Schulze used as evidence of General Motors' apathy over community affairs was the annexation issue. Ypsilanti's political leaders had tried on previous occasions to annex the part of the township that contained the General Motors plant (then operated by Kaiser-Frazier

Motors). These efforts had failed. The unwillingness of General Motors to take a position on a renewal attempt at annexation killed the proposal. This unwillingness was not out of apathy, however, it was a calculated failure to exercise power to achieve precisely the objective that was achieved. A member of the community relations department of General Motors said:

   We don't have a single policy on annexations. Recently we had one of these issues come up in [mentions the name of a city of 100,000 population]. We had a very large plant in the township. In this case we were for annexation because the city had better fire and police protection and a lower tax base. We sided with the city and when the township sought an injunction after the referendum, we provided the city with legal advice to fight it.
   In Ypsilanti Township you have a different matter. The local committee told us about the visit from the downtown delegation. We decided not to go along with them. Our plant is sitting on top of an excellent supply of water from artesian wells, the township taxes are low, and we have our own fire protection system. If the people around the plant had wanted annexation, though, we would have gone along with them. But we checked with them, and they didn't.

It is obvious that General Motors is typical of most elements in the political arena; they are engaged in the politics of self-interest. They will fight or support the residents of the townships after determining where their own interests lie. But it is difficult to see how Schulze could have reasonably expected the management of General Motors to support annexation into Ypsilanti or to participate in its political and social affairs. The factory is not located in the town, but in the township. In this case the company's interests did happen to coincide with those of the political leaders of the township.

Schulze also cites the case of a Ford employee, who was also a political leader, and who "left" his Ford Motors job. The implication was raised that Ford Motors might have removed him because of his community activity and this possibility evidenced the company's lack of concern for community relations. A member of the Ypsilanti community relations committee said that this was not the case. The company encouraged employee participation in local affairs as a matter of policy. But this employee was so involved in local affairs that he was doing a very poor job in the plant. He was forced to choose between his roles and elected to leave the company.

By virtue of their good relations with the community and the township both of these companies have received valuable parcels of land for a nominal sum, fire lanes have been added or improved, and other small advantages have accrued. But the greatest value of their community relations programs rests in what does *not* happen. A member of the Ford community relations committee put it this way:

> We are forced to be concerned about community affairs. An irate community can cost you money in lots of hidden ways. You don't get the people you want in the labor market. You are more likely to get work slowdowns. People won't sell you the land you need for expansion. Tax assessors could increase your taxes and nobody would care. A rampant city council can cause you all kinds of trouble. No, we have to be in community relations.

Entering a Community

One of the reasons mentioned earlier as a partial explanation of the illusion of corporate noninvolvement was the exercise of power before the company will locate a factory in a community. The existence of informal agreements that operate as constraints on the decision-making processes of political leaders is a very powerful and subtle control device. Both Ford and General Motors utilize this type of power. In Ford Motors the process of influencing a community begins with the decision by a division of the company to construct a new factory. Careful studies are done using long lists of criteria for the selection of the site for the new facility. But before the decision to locate a plant in any community is finalized, the community relations department is informed of the tentative location and invited to begin its phase of the operation. The community

relations personnel set up informal meetings in the community with the mayor, members of the council, the president of the Chamber of Commerce, and the members of the school board. The willingness of the community leaders to have the factory located in their midst is assessed in these meetings and, if they are willing, the framework of an informal corporate-community agreement is shaped. Agreements are formed concerning school and hospital needs, fire and police protection, annexation status, roads, and water facilities. Company tax experts study the local tax structure and make working agreements with county and community officials on the company's tax rates. If these negotiations have proved favorable, then the decision is made to go ahead with the location of the plant in the selected community.

At this point the negotiations surface in the community. A company executive makes a major address to an audience composed of the members of several local voluntary associations. This address initiates a public relations campaign on what Ford Motors will do for the community.

General Motors follows a similar procedure: the major differences are that more departments are involved in the decision to locate in the community and the procedures for reaching informal agreements with the local elites are less thoroughly organized. General Motors did not follow its customary procedure in Ypsilanti Township because of the unusual circumstances that prompted the location of the plant there. One of its factories had burned down. Since this plant was the sole producer of essential parts, it had to be replaced immediately. The Ypsilanti plant was purchased from Kaiser-Frazier Motors and began producing the needed parts within six months of the fire. There was no time to negotiate any agreements with the township leaders. Corporate personnel were quick to point out that this was an unusual situation.

Summary and Conclusions

In his study of Ypsilanti, Schulze tested the proposition that community elites were bifurcating into two fairly distinct elites: the political and economic dominants.[12] He suggested further that the latter group may divide into two groups: the Main Street and absentee-corporate elites.

This study was not intended to question the soundness of the bifurcation or trifurcation hypotheses: on the contrary they fit the facts of Ypsilanti precisely. Ypsilanti has three distinct elites based on three sources of power, political, local economic, and absentee-corporate. These elites are not joined into a single monolithic structure. This study was intended to discount the conclusion that the absentee-owned corporations had withdrawn from involvement in the social and political affairs of Ypsilanti and Ypsilanti Township. A case has been made for the necessity of minimal corporate exercise of power in the corporate self-interest. The appearance of noninvolvement—based on the absence of executives living in the community and participating in its associational life—is illusory. The fact that the plant managers do not appear to be manipulating the political affairs of the community heightens this illusion of noninvolvement. Corporate power is being exercised; new roles using new methods are being developed. Community relations has become the work of specialists who combine the techniques of public relations, employee involvement in community affairs, and hard negotiation to maximize their social-value and resource power.

It is a mistake to discount public relations activities as a viable tool in community control activities. The tendency of sociologists to discount corporate good-neighbor programs attests more to their personal sophistication than it does to the ineptness of the programs. The corporation that has fostered good community relations avoids many hidden costs, heightens the effectiveness of its social-value power, and can improve its relations with its own employees whom it supports in community activities. We say "can improve" because the political leaders who worked for Ford Motors often found themselves in positions of role conflict and resented some of the pressures that the corporation put on them. But for most of the active employees the facilitation offered by the company apparently created good will.

It is clear that the General Motors program in community relations was not as well developed as the Ford Motors program: it emphasized reaction to issues involving corporate interests rather than the broadly conceived program of community involvement used by Ford Motors. In a later article, it will be shown that corporate philosophies differ greatly with regard to programs of community relations. Many are still relying on the local manager to handle their community relations. These corporations tend to be smaller and have less surplus wealth. Others are slowly evolving programs like that of Ford Motors, but they are often in a very embryonic state of development.

Since these programs are in such an early stage of development, it is too early to do trend analyses and to conclude the outcome of these trends. The nature of propositions about social phenomena is at issue here. For example, if we hypothesize that as the population of an organization increases, the number of subgroups will also increase, we are saying that some groups encounter the problem of increasing size and solve the problem by selecting from among a fairly limited set of alternative solutions: the dependent variable in any sociological hypothesis is no more than the most commonly selected solution or reaction to the problems posed by the independent variable. The sociologist may fashion such a hypothesis without empirical referents by utilizing social theory, but he cannot prove it true unless a number of events have occurred in several organizations: size must increase, some parts of the population must become aware of the increase, there must be a fairly limited range of alternatives, and one or more of them must be selected. We have suggested above that social theory is on the side of corporate involvement in the community, but this is not to say that corporations have become aware yet of the importance of community relations programs, or of the community problems they actually have, or of useful alternatives to their present activity or inactivity. The students of community power have photographed corporations in a milling stage in their evolution.

Neither Ford nor General Motors can be said to be engaged in a heavyhanded domination of local affairs. They restrain themselves from such complete engagement because they are aware that domination of local affairs can have serious, adverse effects on the corporate image and because they are wealthy corporations that can afford to pay a little more than they otherwise might in order to be an accepted part of the communities where their factories are located. Their politics are the politics of self-interest supplemented, particularly in the case of Ford Motors, with the politics of community interest. With their great resources it would be easy for both corporations to dominate community affairs completely. As will be shown in a subsequent article, some corporations do seek this complete domination of local affairs. However, a greater threat to community effectiveness is the development of an overconsensus of values in the community because the corporation has been successful in creating the image of the corporate good citizen. It is difficult to muster a sufficient coalition to push through some social change if that change is opposed by an obviously benevolent good citizen of tremendous size and power.

Notes

1. R. S. Lynd and H. M. Lynd, *Middletown* (New York: Harcourt, Brace, & World, 1929).
2. F. Hunter, *Community Power Structure: A Study of Decision Makers* (Chapel Hill: University of North Carolina Press, 1953).
3. R. J. Pellegrin and C. H. Coates, "Absentee-Owned Corporations and Community Power Structure," *American Journal of Sociology*, 61 (March, 1956), pp. 413–419. Also in this volume.
4. R. O. Schulze, "The Bifurcation of Power in a Satellite City," in Morris Janowitz (ed.), *Community Political Systems* (New York: Free Press, 1961), pp. 19–80.
5. D. A. Clelland, "Economic Dominance and Community Power in a Middle-sized City," Paper delivered at the Meetings of the Ohio Valley Sociological Society, May, 1962.
6. M. K. Jennings, *Community Influentials: The Elites of Atlanta* (New York: Free Press, 1964).
7. R. A. Dahl, *Who Governs? Democracy and Power in an American City* (New Haven: Yale University Press, 1961).
8. M. N. Goldstein, "Absentee Ownership and Monolithic Power Structures: Two Questions for Community Studies," in B. E. Swanson (ed.), *Current Trends in Comparative Community Studies* (Kansas City, Mo.: Community Studies, Inc., 1962), pp. 49–59.
9. T. N. Clark, "Power and Community Structure: Who Governs, Where, and When?," A paper read at the annual meeting of the American Sociological Association, 1965, p. 4, proposition 14.
10. See, for example, R. Naroll, "A Preliminary Index of Social Development," *American Anthropologist*, 58 (1956), 687–715; W. F. Whyte, "The Social Structure of the Restaurant," *American Journal of Sociology*, 54 (January, 1949), 302–310; R. M. Cynert and J. G. March, *A Behavioral Theory of the Firm* (Englewood Cliffs, N.J.: Prentice-Hall, 1963); R. F. Bales, "Some Uniformities in Behavior in Small Social Systems," in G. E. Swanson, T. M. Newcomb, and E. L. Hartley (eds.), *Readings in Social Psychology* (New York: Holt, Rinehart and Winston, 1952), pp. 146–159.
11. The exception to this rule occurs in Ford Motors where the Ford dealers in each area are organized into separate community relations committees. These committees complement the industrial committees very nicely in that they are members of the downtown economic elite. Working in tandem, the two groups can and do have important effects on community and state decision-making.
12. Schulze, *op. cit.*

Economic Change and Community Power Structure: Transition in Cornucopia

Robert Mills French

One theme which pervades much of the literature on community power is that factors in the larger world play an increasingly important role in shaping local community structure. Representatives of state and national governments, of widespread organizations, and especially of great corporations take much of the initiative for local community action out of the hands of the citizenry.

To better describe the process, Warren developed the concept of the horizontal and vertical dimensions of community.[1] The strictly local facets of community life extend over only those matters which do not directly concern external or higher levels of business or government; they are thus unidimensional or horizontal. Those elements that are linked to a higher government than the local political scene or those businesses that are dependent on a larger market or that are part of a widespread corporate network exist on several levels and thus can be conceptualized as vertical. The influence of these two dimensions in the affairs of local communities has shifted as they have become more dependent on vertically based institutions.

The most widely studied example of this shift is the transformation that occurs when control of a community's economic institutions passes from local to outside interests. Thus the key element in Yankee City's change and subsequent turmoil was the entrance of outsiders into the previously locally-owned and -managed shoe industry.[2] Cibola's bifurcation of power likewise occurred when economic control slipped out of the hands of locals into those of absentee-owned corporation managers.[3] Similar outside factors

changed Springdale, Dairyville, and Wheelsburg, to name several of the communities studied which have been so transformed.[4] The effect of vertical influences on the horizontal community is not random, but follows a definite pattern of increasing pluralism in local sociopolitical affairs while the community's economic determination passes into the hands of outsiders who remain aloof from local affairs.[5]

Why the managers of absentee-owned corporations should eschew participation in the affairs of the local community was suggested by Norton E. Long:

> For some of the members at least, the corporation represents a value-laden institution that outranks the local community as a focus of loyalty and a medium for self-realization. It would scarcely be saying too much and perhaps is tritely apparent that people may be more citizens of the corporations for whom they work than of the local communities in which they reside.[6]

A look at the career patterns of corporate executives would support Long's analysis. The executive may move many times within the corporate structure, going from one community to another with the only continuity in his life provided by the firm. To put this in the terms we have introduced, the corporate executive is more concerned with the vertical community of which the corporation is a part, than with the horizontal community where a particular office or factory of the corporation happens to be located. His interest is in how the corporate branch which he manages relates to the rest of the corporation, a vertical structure, rather

An original article written for this volume.

than how it relates to the surrounding horizontal community. His concern with local affairs extends only so far as the affairs of the corporation extend. Participation in local matters will not help the corporate manager to ascend in the corporate hierarchy and could even involve him in a conflict of interests which could be detrimental to his career. The safest course for him is to become involved in local affairs only when it is clearly in the interests of the corporation. This may make the corporate manager less than a good citizen, but as we have noted, he is primarily a citizen of the vertical corporate community and only incidentally a member of the local horizontal community.

The hypothesis that is suggested by this discussion is that *external or vertical influences on the local or horizontal community will bring about a bifurcation of horizontal leadership with economic control being assumed by outsiders, while sociopolitical control remains in the hands of locals. With the true economic dominants removed from local affairs, lower participants will feel less constrained so that the sociopolitical sphere will become more pluralistic as bifurcation is realized.*

Plan and Setting of the Study

In order to test our hypothesis it was necessary to find a community which had recently experienced economic transformation by outside factors, in order to make comparisons between the community's power structure before and after economic change. The city of Cornucopia, Illinois, provided the perfect opportunity for study. With a population of 11,000 in 1960, Cornucopia seemed somewhat small for our purpose, but the fact that it had been an industrial community from its early days in the nineteenth century, combined with the news that the Chromeboat Auto Company had just selected it for the location of a large assembly plant employing 5,000 workers, outweighed any anticipated disadvantages. Chromeboat had not gone beyond the planning stages when this study commenced so that we enjoyed the rare opportunity to do a

"before-after" study of vertical influences on the horizontal community.

A picture of Cornucopia's leadership and socioeconomic structure immediately before Chromeboat's impact was compared to the situation several years after the coming of Chromeboat. Very early in the research it became apparent that knowledge of Cornucopia's past was important to understand its current characteristics. The resulting study focuses on Cornucopia at three stages of development over a period of about seventy-five years.

The first stage extends from the town's early days in the 1890s through the late 1940s when a single, locally-owned firm dominated Cornucopia's social and economic affairs. This stage was reconstructed through the use of public records, old newspapers, and interviews with survivors of this early era. The second stage began with the collapse of the early dominant local industry in 1948 and continued to the coming of Chromeboat in 1964. Reconstruction of this era was done primarily through interviews with local leaders, but in addition the power structure was ascertained through the use of a variety of reputational and decisional indices.[7] The final stage is the three year period following the coming of Chromeboat during which Cornucopia experienced the immediate impact of economic transformation. The community was observed directly during this stage and a replication of the earlier power structure analysis was made in 1967.

Early Cornucopia: A Pyramidal Power Structure

From its founding in 1886 until it was sold to outside interests in 1948, the American Sewing Machine Company dominated the life and affairs of Cornucopia. Locally owned and managed, the American saw itself as a "community company," and indeed it was, for when it prospered so did Cornucopia, when it suffered setbacks the town's payroll reflected the fact. Although there were other firms operating in Cornucopia throughout this period, they were all small and relatively unimportant in the town's economic life, which was completely dependent on its mainstay—the American.

Throughout its long life in Cornucopia the American was owned and run by a single family. All of the directors of the firm were related, directly or by marriage, to the founder. Cornucopia's Bainbridge family enjoyed a status in the community similar to that of Middletown's Ball family.[8] Like the early leaders of Yankee City's shoe industry, Bainbridge, American's founder, and, to a lesser extent, those directors who followed him were held in awe by the community they dominated.[9] Theirs was more than simply economic dominance; what they did was perceived as "for the good of Cornucopia." Just how they accomplished this exalted role is not clear, for, unlike Cibola's early economic dominants who participated in public duties and often held the mayor's office,[10] no officer of the firm was ever elected to public office and, until the last president of the firm took office in 1928, the American avoided all overt involvement in community affairs.

Lack of formal involvement should not be viewed as a lack of influence or control, however. There is abundant evidence that what the firm wanted, it got, including low taxes and utilities rates, roads, lack of unionization, etc. On numerous occasions issues were resolved as the plant director desired as the result of informal pressure on a man-to-man basis. Perhaps the most important informal relationship was between the firm's director and the mayor, who was usually an American employee. Being employed by the factory was apparently important in the election of a mayor, for the factory manager would urge the men to vote for the "factory candidate."

Although the last president of the firm denied that the firm ever used its economic influence with the mayor to affect his actions, he did comment: "I thought possibly it was wise to have someone there [in the mayor's office] that might listen to any objections we had if something occurred that was going to be detrimental to us. . . . Having mayors in our employ made it easier to talk to them."

If these early economic dominants did not control the town to the point of holding important public office, it was because they found it advantageous not to become personally involved. Their power, based upon virtually complete economic control, enabled them to direct the affairs of Cornucopia from behind the scenes. The director of the American Sewing Machine Company enjoyed ultimate power; he was the apex of a pyramidal structure.

The Interim Period

When the American closed down and the last of the company directors left Cornucopia, a power vacuum and an economic crisis resulted. The shock to the town's economy was eased somewhat by the availability of jobs in a nearby city for those workers willing to commute and by small absentee-owned firms that were attracted to Cornucopia through the efforts of businessmen and city officials. The power vacuum did not remain for long as our study demonstrated.

In an attempt to ascertain what happened to Cornucopia's power structure after the demise of the American Sewing Machine Company, a variety of research techniques was employed. Positional leaders were identified, a reputational power structure was constructed by use of Schulze and Blumberg's battery of five questions,[11] and decisional leaders were sought along the lines suggested by Polsby.[12] In addition, Bonjean's refinement of the reputational technique was employed,[13] but regardless of the technique used, the same small group of influentials appeared. They had come into prominence concomitantly with the fall of the American Sewing Machine Company. Table 1 shows the ranking of these "new" leaders.

If one asked the townspeople of Cornucopia who ran the town before the coming of Chromeboat, the answer would have been Fred Husk with no other individual even in the running. Indeed, it would have been easy to conclude that the pyramidal power of the old American directors had simply been assumed by Fred Husk. He owned the

TABLE 1. *1964 Ranking of Cornucopia's Reputational Influentials by Thirty-Two Community Leaders*

INDIVIDUAL	RANK	%	BASIS OF POWER
Fred Husk	1	94	Economic Dominant, Newspaper Publisher, Political Boss, Activist
R. Fengler	2	75	Economic Dominant, Financial Baron
Jes Paisley	3	66	Positional Leader—Mayor
Bob Michaels	4	44	Positional Leader—Chamber of Commerce Secretary
Al Leonard	5	38	Activist, Head of Downtown Merchants
Tim Henry	6	31	Economic Dominant, Ascending in Banking and Business World
'Doc" Fox	7	28	Economic Dominant, Activist
Ed Brim	7	28	Economic Dominant, Activist
Norm Friend	7	28	Activist, Positional Leader—City Engineer
Bob Whalen	7	28	Activist, Spokesman for Downtown Merchants
Wil Keener	8	25	Economic Dominant, Retired Industrialist
M. Heater	8	25	Positional Leader—School Superintendent
Larry Kaske	8	25	Activist, President of Chamber of Commerce
Lev Jensen	8	25	Activist, Spokesman for Downtown Merchants
Henry Moon	8	25	Economic Dominant, Head of Local Industrialists
Art Downey	9	22	Economic Dominant, Retired Financier, represents "Old Cornucopia"
Floyd Bugle	10	19	Positional Leader—Road Commissioner, Chairman of Republican Party
J. Fox	11	9	Activist

local newspaper and thus shaped much of local opinion; he was involved in many issues and usually headed the committees on which he served. Even the community leaders who were much more knowledgeable about community affairs than the average Cornucopian rated Husk far above all other leaders on reputational indices. If one had simply tallied up the decisions in which the various leaders had been involved, Husk again would have been the clear choice for key decision-maker.

Closer examination of community issues revealed a curious fact, however. Although Husk participated in many issues and had an opinion on all events which he expressed via his newspaper, he completely avoided direct participation in youth welfare projects and could not control certain other issues. Indeed, the course of action taken in school matters, charity drives, the building of a new YMCA, etc., usually reflected the wishes of R. Fengler, the second ranking reputational leader. Although Fengler became personally involved in only one issue and remained virtually unknown to the average Cornucopian, he wielded behind-the-scenes-power in many sectors of the community. Far and away the most wealthy man in the community, Fengler owned large tracts of land in and around town, owned and directed the most important bank, and dominated the financial affairs of downtown Cornucopia. Several lower-ranking leaders were loyal to Fengler and could be expected to express his wishes in issues which he chose not to become involved in, and at least one decisional leader was in his employ and was provided time away from work for community affairs.

Fengler and Husk were in fact the heads of two dominant factions. Fengler described the situation well: "If it's a question of politics or public opinion, then he's [Husk] the one. If it's a question of money, it's me." Whether or not Fengler could have challenged Husk's dominance never came to the test because local politics did not interest Fengler and he avoided those issues most important to Husk.

The style of the two men was entirely different. Husk was very active and often resorted to heavy-handed tactics to get his way. Fengler, on the other hand, could be effective from behind the scenes and shunned direct participation, a fact which Husk much resented and criticized. Although Husk attacked Fengler whenever he could, his efforts were singularly unsuccessful and both men remained in firm control of their area of dominance. The pyramidal power structure of early Cornucopia had split into two "independent sovereignties each with its own sphere of influence."[14] Although each man had his loyal followers, most lower-ranking leaders attempted to avoid falling into one or the other faction, for depending on the issue at hand, they knew that it would be necessary to work with both leaders at times.

Unrealized Bifurcation

How these two men could wield the type of influence they did is puzzling when one considers Cornucopia's economy at that time. Following the demise of the American Sewing Machine Company, the community became dependent on a number of smaller firms ranging from an absentee-owned firm with 677 employees to local firms with under ten workers. In December of 1964 there were thirty-six firms in Cornucopia; nineteen, or 53 percent, were locally owned, the rest were absentee owned. The absentee firms were much larger than the local concerns, however, so that of Cornucopia's 2,362 employees, only 19 percent (454) worked in local firms, whereas 81 percent (1,908)

worked in absentee-owned firms. In effect, Cornucopia had already experienced social and economic bifurcation before Chromeboat had even arrived on the scene. There was no indication, however, that lower participants in the sociopolitical sphere felt less constrained than they had before, as was hypothesized.

Closer analysis of Cornucopia's economy suggests why the complete effects induced by bifurcation had not occurred. Although the town's economy was dependent on absentee-owned firms, no single industry dominated the town with its payroll or taxes as had the American Sewing Machine Company. The absentee managers were uninterested in community affairs and remained virtually unknown to the community and each other. The result of these factors was that the true situation of economic dependence on absentee-owned industry was unrealized and the local leaders had assumed power which was without an economic base. Husk and Fengler could dominate local affairs much as had the owner-presidents of the American Sewing Machine Company before them, even though neither man could wield the ultimate economic sanctions available to their predecessors.

Why the community accepted Husks', and to a lesser extent Fengler's, dominance is puzzling. Although Fengler had economic power over many of Cornucopia's merchants, there is little evidence that he used this influence in ways other than to urge recalcitrant merchants to support charity drives. Husk lacked even this support for the often tyrannical power he wielded. Whether it was simply indifferent, or had not yet realized that the situation had changed and Husk was not just another American Sewing Machine Company director, Cornucopia continued to be dominated by paternalistic leaders who lacked the basis for such power. Husk acted like the boss of a political machine, yet he had no list of patronage jobs to give; he successfully bullied men whose livelihood he could not readily endanger. With bifurcation Cornucopia was open to sweeping change, yet it continued to knuckle under to boss rule.

Cornucopia Under the Influence of Chromeboat

The most dramatic impact that Chromeboat had on Cornucopia in the three years studied while it was establishing itself in the community was its effect on the local economy. Labor was tight not only in Cornucopia but in the entire region from which workers could commute to the Chromeboat plant. Because its wages are determined by a national contract with the United Auto Workers, Chromeboat could not take advantage of the lower local wage scale so that its starting wages were often higher than the top wages of local firms. A crisis ensued for local firms whose best help often deserted them, forcing the adoption of higher wage scales in order to compete for new help and to retain the workers they already had. Every local manager was affected; typical comments were: "The only help left on the old $1.50 wages are illiterates or housewives"; or "We used to pay $1.35 for floor-sweepers, now they won't come in for less than $2.25. It's not Cornucopia anymore!" Estimates of just how drastic wage increases were ranged from 50 percent for help in special skilled areas, to more conservative figures of 15 to 30 percent overall.

Local industrialists faced other problems brought about by the coming of Chromeboat. Most often mentioned among the complaints was Chromeboat's monopolization of railroad facilities for shipment of new autos. It seemed probable that some of the low-overhead, limited expansion type of industry that had managed to subsist, if not thrive, in Cornucopia before Chromeboat would not survive the impact of increased competition for labor and services.

The problems of the downtown merchants were similar to those of the industrialists. Although they were enjoying increased sales, the merchants apprehensively watched the building of new shopping centers on the edge of town, which surely meant disaster to their own gloomy stores with unimaginative window displays and limited lines of merchandise.

Unlike the situation that existed before the coming of Chromeboat, in which community leaders and merchants failed to recognize the dominant economic role of absentee-owned industry in Cornucopia, everyone felt the influence of Chromeboat. The rapidity with which Chromeboat had dominated the town's economic affairs bewildered and embittered many Cornucopians. Like it or not, the town was denied a role in determining its financial fate; bifurcation was complete.

Increased Pluralism

Although not as dramatic as the changes in the economy, important changes were taking place in Cornucopia's leadership structure nonetheless. It became apparent very early in the power study replication that important shifts had occurred. A simple ranking as in Table 2 shows only part of the story. When the more knowledgeable[15] "key influentials" rankings are extrapolated from the total, the shift in power is startling. Not only had Fred Husk slipped to second place in the rankings behind R. Fengler as both Tables 2 and 3 show, but in the eyes of the most knowledgeable leaders, Husk shared his secondary rank with two other leaders. In addition, as Table 3 indicates, more individuals were perceived as having important roles in community affairs in 1967 than in 1964.

Comments made during interviews come directly to the point which the indices suggest: "Your questions are tougher to answer now than they were three years ago. There are more people involved, but it's hard to say who's really running things." The outgoing president of the Chamber of Commerce was even more blunt: "Leadership in town has diversified—Husk no longer can tell the town how to run things."

Analysis of community decisions illustrated the extent of Husk's decline in ability to force his point of view. Whereas Husk had been the dominant figure in most community issues in 1964, he was the key man in only one new issue. His support was not only not sought, but other leaders dared to openly oppose him. That community affairs were

TABLE 2. *1967 Ranking of Cornucopia's Reputational Influentials by Twenty Community Leaders, Change in Rank from 1964*

INDIVIDUAL	RANK	%	1964 RANK	BASIS OF POWER (IF NOT IN TABLE 1.)
R. Fengler	1	100	2	
Fred Husk	2	90	1	
"Doc" Fox	3	65	7	
Tim Henry	3	65	6	
Henry Moon	4	60	8	
Jes Paisley	5	50	3	Just elected as State Representative
J. Fox	6	45	11	
Art Downey	7	40	9	
Max Larch	7	40	Unranked	Activist, Directs Telephone Company
Wil Keener	8	35	8	
Ed Brim	8	35	7	
Jim Herder	9	30	Unranked	Economic Dominant, Manager of Chromeboat Factory
Kurt Betz	10	25	Unranked	Economic Dominant, New Owner of Bank
John Watt	10	25	Unranked	Economic Dominant, Activist
Larry Kaske	10	25	8	
Dr. R. Jeffers	10	25	Unranked	Activist, Local Chiropodist
Al Leonard	11	20	5	
Dick Matsen	11	20	Unranked	Positional Leader—Newspaper Editor, Son-in-Law of Husk
Wm. Brenner	12	15	Unranked	Activist
Lev Jensen	13	10	8	
Floyd Bugle	13	10	10	
John Storm	13	10	Unranked	Positional Leader—State's Attorney
Bob Whalen	14	5	7	
Bob Michaels	Unranked	—	4	Left town
M. Heater	Unranked	—	8	Left town
Norm Friend	Unranked	—	7	Left town

becoming more pluralistic is represented by the fact that although only half as many issues were observed in 1967 as in 1964, more individuals participated in some important capacity in 1967 than in 1964. Leadership in a given issue was more likely to be determined by the special interest and ability of a particular individual in 1967 than in 1964 when most issues were directed by Husk or those that would do his bidding.

Bifurcation limits the economic sanctions that local leaders can impose. Apparently, as lower-ranking leaders realize that they need not fear economic reprisal from key influentials, they are less inclined to take secondary roles. In effect, bifurcation encourages democratization of horizontal community decision-making. Ironically, the decisions of the more pluralistic horizontal community are less meaningful than they would have been in the past inasmuch as the crucial economic decisions are made in the vertical community beyond the influence of local leaders.

TABLE 3. *1967 Ranking of Cornucopia's Reputational Influentials by Eight Key Influentials**

INDIVIDUAL	RANK	%
R. Fengler	1	100
Fred Husk	2	88
"Doc" Fox	2	88
Henry Moon	2	88
Wil Keener	3	63
J. Fox	3	63
Jes Paisley	4	50
Tim Henry	4	50
Art Downey	4	50
John Watt	5	38
Dick Matsen	5	38
Al Leonard	6	25
Larry Kaske	6	25
Max Larch	6	25
Kurt Betz	6	25
Jim Herder	6	25
Wm. Brenner	6	25
John Storm	6	25
Ed Brim	7	13
Lev Jensen	7	13
Dr. R. Jeffers	7	13

*The highest ranked leaders in an earlier survey of community leaders.

Absentee Managers' Role

The bifurcation-pluralism hypothesis, which was only partially supported in the 1964 study, was strongly supported in the 1967 replication. Bifurcation of economic and sociopolitical power was clearly established with Chromeboat making all the crucial economic decisions but avoiding any sociopolitical role.

Chromeboat's executives avoided participation in Cornucopia's life or affairs, with only the plant manager, Jim Herder, residing in Cornucopia and holding token memberships in several organizations. Public relations protocol demanded representation of Chromeboat at Chamber of Commerce meetings, but this was merely a formality, for they avoided taking any meaningful role. During interviews these executives were contemptuous of local politics and culture and were chary of any involvement. Their fears were probably well founded, for as the following example illustrates, the absentee-manager who takes an active community role may face an irresolvable dilemma.

John Watt was the head of an absentee-owned foundry which in 1967 was the third largest employer in Cornucopia. Disgusted by the inefficiency of local organizations and bothered by feelings of guilt that he had done nothing to change matters, Watt became involved in Rotary, served as president of the Chamber of Commerce, and sat on the City Council. Shortly before we talked to him in 1967 he withdrew from Rotary and the City Council and refused to accept the renomination as Chamber president. He commented about his withdrawal from public life: "If something affects this company I can yell as a citizen; as a Councilman I was in a bind. As a plant manager I needed one thing, as a Councilman I knew another would be best." Watt was aware of the fact that community activities would not advance his career and might actually have harmed him because they took time that might have been used in corporate affairs.

The other absentee managers of Cornucopia recognized implicitly the hazards of community activism and, unlike Watt, felt no guilt that the focus of their loyalty was the corporation to the exclusion of the local community.

The relationship of the corporate manager to the local community is a curious one, for although he makes decisions which greatly affect the life of the community, he has no attachment to it and it is powerless to affect him.

Summary and Conclusions

We hypothesized that under the influence of the vertical community, power in the horizontal community bifurcates, with economic dominants remaining aloof from local affairs while the sociopolitical sphere becomes more pluralistic. To test this hypothesis, a study of Cornucopia was made. The study focused on the community at three stages in its life. The first stage, extending from the nineteenth century until the late 1940s, revealed a pyramidal power structure which was dominated by the heads of a locally-owned and managed industry. The second stage focused on Cornucopia from the demise of one economic giant, the local firm which had dominated the town in its early life, to the arrival of another, the Chromeboat Auto Company, which promised to dominate the community in the future. Although at this stage economic bifurcation had already occurred, because of the number of small absentee-owned firms dominating the town's economy and the absence of an obvious dominant, true pluralism and not taken place, for the power structure was dominated by two factional heads. The final stage, the three years immediately following Chromeboat's arrival in Cornucopia, saw economic affairs dominated by Chromeboat while the sociopolitical sphere experienced democratization as lower-ranking leaders challenged the dominance of the factional heads. As expected, the managers of absentee industry avoided partici-

pation in Cornucopia's sociopolitical affairs in both stage two and stage three. Even though they had great power to influence the life of Cornucopia, the absentee managers remained virtual strangers to the people whose fate they affected.

The hypothesis was strongly supported in stage three, but only partly valid for stage two. Apparently Cornucopia was in transition in stage two and could not completely make the transformation to a new sociopolitical structure until the full implications of economic bifurcation were realized. The effect of Chromeboat on the community was to force awareness of the fact that it was part of the larger economy. The Cornucopia of the past with its local economic giant, paternalism, and boss rule had died nearly twenty years before, but it took the shock of the coming of Chromeboat to finally lay "old Cornucopia" to rest.

Notes

1. Roland L. Warren, *The Community in America* (Chicago: Rand McNally, 1963), Chapters 3, 8, and 9.
2. W. Lloyd Warner and J. O. Low, "The Factory in the Community," in William Foote Whyte (ed.), *Industry and Society* (New York: McGraw-Hill, 1946), pp. 21–45.
3. Robert O. Schulze, "The Role of Economic Dominants in Community Power Structure," *American Sociological Review*, 23 (February, 1958), 3–9; also in this volume.
4. For the story of Springdale see Arthur J. Vidich and Joseph Bensman, *Small Town in Mass Society* (Princeton: Princeton University Press, 1958). Dairyville is the name given to the community studied by Roland L. Warren, "Toward a Typology of Extra-Community Controls Limiting Local Community Autonomy," *Social Forces*, 34 (May, 1956), 338–341. Wheelsburg is the community studied by Donald A. Clelland and William H. Form, "Economic Dominants and Community Power: A Comparative Analysis," *American Journal of Sociology*, 69 (March, 1964), 511–521; also in this volume.
5. See Oliver P. Williams and Charles R. Adrian, *Four Cities—A Study in Comparative Policy Making* (Philadelphia: University of Pennsylvania Press, 1963); Clelland and

Form, *op. cit.*; Ted C. Smith, "The Structuring of Power in a Suburban Community," *Pacific Sociological Review*, 3 (Fall, 1960), 83–88; Arnold M. Rose, "Communication and Participation in a Small City as Viewed by its Leaders," *International Journal of Opinions and Attitude Research*, 5 (Fall, 1951), 367–390; M. Kent Jennings, *Community Influentials: The Elites of Atlanta* (New York: Free Press, 1964); Jackson M. McClain and Robert B. Highsaw, *Dixie City Acts: A Study in Decision-Making* (Birmingham: Bureau of Public Administration, University of Alabama, 1962); Roland A. Pellegrin and Charles H. Coates, "Absentee-Owned Corporations and Community Power Structure," *American Journal of Sociology*, 61 (March, 1956), 413–419; also in this volume.
6. Norton E. Long, *The Polity* (Chicago: Rand McNally, 1962), p. 122.
7. Research techniques are discussed at greater length at a later stage of this paper. See notes 11, 12, and 13 for relevant references.
8. Robert S. Lynd and Helen M. Lynd, *Middletown in Transition* (New York: Harcourt, Brace & World, 1937).
9. W. Lloyd Warner (ed.), *Yankee City* (New Haven: Yale University Press, 1963), pp. 325–331.

10. Schulze, *op. cit.*
11. Robert O. Schulze and Leonard U. Blumberg, "The Determination of Local Power Elites," *American Journal of Sociology*, 63 (November, 1957), 290–296; also in this volume.
12. Nelson W. Polsby, "How to Study Community Power: The Pluralist Alternative," *Journal of Politics*, 22 (August, 1960), 474–484; also in this volume.
13. Charles M. Bonjean, in "Community Leadership: A Case Study and Conceptual Refinement," *American Journal of Sociology*, 47 (May, 1963), 672–681, also in this volume, successfully employed a method of studying community power which assumed that the more visible a community leader was, the more accurate would be his assessment of influence in the community of individuals. The technique was successfully replicated by Delbert C. Miller and James L. Dirksen, "The Identification of Visible, Concealed and Symbolic Leaders in a Small Indiana City: A Replication of the Bonjean-Noland Study of Burlington, North Carolina," *Social Forces*, 43 (May, 1965), 548–555. The technique was again replicated in Cornucopia by Robert Mills French and Michael Aiken, "Community Power in Cornucopia: A Replication in a Small Community of the Bonjean Technique of Identifying Community Leaders," *Sociological Quarterly*, 9 (Spring, 1968), 261–270. The technique proved effective in Cornucopia and in the present article the reputational rankings were obtained by asking community leaders, who themselves had been nominated by the heads of voluntary organizations, to rank top leadership.
14. This is the term used by Dahl to describe one type of community power structure. Robert A. Dahl, *Who Governs? Democracy and Power in an American City* (New Haven: Yale University Press, 1961), pp. 184–189.
15. For defense of this assumption see French and Aiken, *op. cit.*

Part IV.
Locating Centers of Power

Introduction

How can configurations of power, influence, and authority be measured? How can we find out who governs? In this part, we have included a number of articles that attempt to answer these questions.

In the first article, "Community Leadership: Directions of Research," Bonjean and Olson give a brief overview of the three methodological techniques that have been used either singly or in combination to identify community leaders: the positional, reputational, and decision-making approaches. The other selections in this part provide examples as well as criticism of each of these three methodological approaches.*

The Positional Approach

The assumption underlying the positional technique is that those who occupy key roles in the major social, economic, and political institutions of the community are indeed the community leaders. There seems to be a further implied assumption in this procedure that control over important community resources—economic (large manufacturing firms, banks, or retail stores, as well as wealth that is independent of such organizational bases), political (leadership roles in key ethnically, racially, or religiously based organizations, elected officials, etc.), and social (family social status) or other—is tantamount to leadership. There are difficulties with this assumption because some positional leaders do not choose to utilize their potential. There is the additional problem of deciding what roles in a community control important community resources; there is no detailed theory of power from which sorting criteria can be derived. This problem is compounded when comparative studies of a number of communities differing in size and economic base are made. A good illustration of this problem as well as of this procedure can be found in various attempts to define the "economic dominants" of several communities—two such attempts appear in this part. In the first, "The Determination of Local Power Elites," Schulze and Blumberg include the following roles in their category of economic dominants:

a. Heads of all industries employing seventy-five or more workers.
b. Heads of all banks with total assets in excess of $1,000,000.
c. Persons who were members of the boards of directors of two or more of these industries and/or banks, thus serving as "interlocking" directors of the dominant economic units.

In the second attempt, "Shadow and Substance: The Social and Economic Notables," which is concerned with determining the "economic notables" in New Haven, a city almost seven times the size of Cibola, Dahl utilizes the following criteria:

a. "The president or chairman of the board of a corporation with property in New Haven assessed in any of the five years 1953–1957 at a value placing it among the fifty highest assessments in the city.
b. Any individual or group of individuals with property in the city assessed in the years 1953–1957 at a value of $250,000 or more.

*Many of the studies included here utilize more than one type of methodological procedure. Therefore, their categorization was made primarily on the basis of the clarity with which they illustrate a given methodological proceedure, not in terms of uiqueness of approach.

c. President or chairman of the board of any bank or public utility in the city.

d. Any individual who was a director of three or more of the following: a firm with assessed valuation of $250,000 or more, a manufacturing firm with fifty employees or more, a retailing firm with twenty-five employees or more, a bank.

e. All directors of New Haven Banks."

In his restudy of Atlanta, a city more than twice the size of New Haven, Jennings uses still a different set of criteria:

a. The top executive of a local firm or branch office of 700 or more employees, or

b. Members of the boards of directors of three or more locally centered firms, or

c. The top executives of the five leading financial (banking) units in the area.[1]

Obviously, utilization of these different criteria in cities with varying sizes and economic structures is likely to yield different types and numbers of economic dominants. For example, Schulze found 17 economic dominants,[2] Dahl found 238 economic notables, and Jennings located 41 economic dominants.

There are, of course, types of positional leaders other than economic ones. For example, Schulze and Blumberg identify fourteen top political and civic statuses such as the mayor, Chairmen of the Republican and Democratic Parties, etc. And Dahl defines "social notables" as families invited to the Assemblies of the New Haven Lawn Club over a number of years. Jennings[3] as well as Freeman et al.[4] have devised still other criteria for determining positional leaders. In the selection of positional leaders Freeman and his colleagues selected such leaders from seven institutional areas by varying the proportions according to an earlier study by D'Antonio et al.[5]

The important point here is that the results of studies are likely to vary, depending on the criteria utilized. What is perhaps most useful is the positional procedure, and

at the same time most seductive, is the parsimony of effort necessary for locating leaders and the reliability of the findings. At the same time there is the very serious problem of whether the top leadership roles in various social, economic, and political institutions are actually those most vitally and importantly concerned with decision-making in the community and, hence, whether they provide a valid understanding of the distribution of community power.

The Reputational Approach: Method, Criticism, Defense, and Refinement

The reputational method of locating community elites is based on the assumption that those having a "reputation" for power are indeed the powerful. Power is measured by attribution in the eyes of knowledgeable people rather than by any more direct method of its determination.

There are numerous variations on the technique for selecting reputational leaders, but they can be broadly grouped into one-step and two-step procedures.[6] In the one-step procedure a set of informants is asked to provide lists of community leaders. The exact question posed varies. For example, Fanelli asked: "Now who would you say are the five people in [community name] whose opinions on community affairs you respect most."[7] Schulze and Blumberg had a series of five questions that included:

"Suppose a major project were before the community, one that required a decision by a group of leaders whom nearly everyone would accept. Which people would you choose to make up this group—regardless of whether or not you know them personally?"

Other questions asked about persons "behind the scenes," as well as those influential at the state as well as national political levels.[8]

The nature of the informants has varied widely in one-step reputational studies. They include the heads of voluntary organizations,[9] a random sample of adults,[10] persons active in community affairs,[11] persons allegedly knowledgeable about community affairs,[12] as well as mixtures of these.[13]

The two-step procedure differs in that lists of leaders in various categories or community sectors are first compiled and then a panel of judges or experts chooses from among the names on these lists. This technique was used by Hunter[14] and later in a modified form by researchers such as Belknap and Smuckler,[15] Form and D'Antonio,[16] and Booth and Adrian.[17] The method is described in this section in the selection "Methods of Study: Community Power Structure," taken from Hunter's book. Hunter compiled a list of names in four areas: civic and community affairs, government, business, and social status. He then had fourteen judges pick the forty reputational leaders. Miller used a similar technique, although he compiled lists of leaders from various institutional areas such as business and finance, education, religion, society and wealth, political and government organizations, labor, independent professions, cultural institutions, social service, and mass communications, and then had the panel of judges select the reputational leaders.[18]

The two-step procedure was undoubtedly intended to cast a wide net in the community and to aid the judges in their task, although this step seems less essential if the judges are selected from diverse sectors of the community. For example, Belknap and Steinle used approximately sixty judges from eight areas in each of their two communities.[19]

Once the set of nominations for leadership are obtained, the researcher must then decide on "cutting points," that is, he must decide how many votes are necessary in order to be included in the pool of community leaders. In some communities there seems to be a natural clustering of nominations, thus simplifying the task of deciding who is to be included among the reputational leaders. In other cases there is wide dispersion of nominations, and the "cutting point" on the number of nominations is extremely arbitrary. Naturally, the number of community leaders so identified varies widely from one study to another, which makes comparisons of results with regard to background of institutional roles of leaders arbitrary at best, if not invalid.

Once the pool of reputational leaders has been identified, most studies have then interviewed these leaders or a sample from among them. They often are asked questions about their backgrounds, their organizational affiliations, their activities in the community, their knowledge and/or associations with other community leaders, and their own evaluations of who governs. The latter procedure permits the researcher to distinguish the "more important" community leaders (often called the "Upper Limits Group"[20] or "Key Influentials"[21]) from the total pool of reputational leaders (sometimes called the "Top Influentials"[22]).

The reputational technique became the focus of controversy and heated debate, its detractors coming primarily from the ranks of political scientists. The first and one of the most quoted criticisms came from Kaufman and Jones in their review of Hunter's book. Their article, "The Mystery of Power," is included as one of the selections in the readings that follow.

The most sustained criticism came from a group of political scientists who might be called the "Yale pluralists," whose real criticism seems to be directed more at the underlying philosophical assumptions of the reputationalists than the research procedure itself.[23] In a series of articles that stretched over an eight-year period Dahl,[24] Wolfinger,[25] and Polsby[26] articulated very strong arguments against the "elitist" models of power as well as the "reputational" technique. We have included critiques by both Wolfinger and Polsby among the articles that follow. Other critics, some of whose criticisms overlapped those of the "Yale pluralists," include Bell,[27] Long,[28] Herson,[29] Fisher,[30] and Rose.[31]

Some of the more telling criticisms of this methodological procedure, as summarized by Danzger,[32] Rose[33] and others, are as follows:

    a. the reputational technique measures opinions about power, not power itself;

b. it receives erroneous assessments by informants as a result of erroneous perceptions of the power structure or misunderstandings of questions intended to reveal those with power;

c. the method is diffuse and fails to acknowledge "issue specialization" (i.e., power is implicitly assumed to be equal over all areas) and instability of power (i.e., power is assumed to be stable over time);

d. it assumes that there is a power structure, but does not demonstrate it. Thus, the questions predispose the answers by asking, who runs things? rather than, does anybody run things?;

e. it is insensitive to the role of both formal political power and political parties in the study of community decision-making;

f. it confuses status with power, e.g., labor leaders who have power but low status are less likely to be nominated; and

g. it is insensitive to the feedback mechanisms in community influence systems, with the result that power is portrayed as a one-way process.

Most of these criticisms are valid judgments against the reputational technique, and they point out the pitfalls of researchers relying on this technique alone in attempting to locate community leaders. But do these criticisms mean that this approach is totally invalid? Should a study of community influence systems avoid such a research technique? It is impossible to answer such questions as these without comparative studies of community power in a large number of communities using a battery of different techniques and then comparing the results to determine just what the reputational technique is measuring. Such a definitive empirical study is yet to be done. Until it is, we are confronted with a literature that is full of recrimination and strong opinions, but which does not present definitive findings.

Several adherents have attempted to defend this technique either directly or by suggesting new directions of research.[34] At the same time they have disavowed the "elitist" bias which is often made against Hunter. That is, they argue that the technique is valid, although it does not always identify a single, cohesive leadership group in communities. We have included the article by D'Antonio and Erickson entitled "The Reputational Technique as a Measure of Community Power: An Evaluation Based on Comparative and Longitudinal Studies" in which they have attempted to demonstrate empirically, both by comparing the results of the reputational technique with those of the decision-making approach and by doing a longitudinal study, that there is a set of community leaders perceived to be generally influential. They do not imply that these leaders are active on all or even most community issues, however.

A second empirical study is included here that attempts to show the utility and meaning of the reputational technique: "Reputation and Resources in Community Politics" by Gamson. Gamson suggests that reputation for power is not only an indicator of resources, but a resource itself, and he demonstrates its relevance and effect in the resolution of community issues.

We have also included two additional articles which attempt to make refinements on the reputational method. The first, by Bonjean, develops a technique of locating visible, symbolic, and concealed leaders, "Community Leadership: A Case Study and Conceptual Refinement." The technique represents an empirical attempt to separate class, social status, and power which was later successfully replicated by Miller and Dirksen[35] and French and Aiken.[36] We have also included an article by Danzger entitled "Community Power Structure: Problems and Continuities," which also attempts to refine the reputational technique. Danzger extends the reputational approach by suggesting that the salience of goals to the actors involved in a decision-making situation also has important implications.

While the critics of the reputational approach have identified some telling weaknesses of this approach if it alone is used to identify community leaders, it does appear to measure certain important aspects of a community power system.

The Decision-Making Approach: Method and Criticism

We have included Polsby's "How to Study Community Power: The Pluralist Alternative" as one example of the pluralist position as opposed to the "elitist" or the alleged "stratification" theory of community power.[37] In fact, the series of articles by the "Yale pluralists"—Dahl, Polsby, and Wolfinger—can be considered as the avant-garde for one of the most serious and widely heralded studies to emerge from this debate: Dahl's *Who Governs?*[38] In his book, Dahl not only developed a theory of pluralism, but attempted to demonstrate how New Haven moved historically from a system of cumulative inequalities, or oligarchy, with concentration of resources, rewards, and power, to one of noncumulative and dispersed inequalities, or pluralism, with dispersion of resources, rewards, and power. In attempting to demonstrate his thesis, Dahl examined decisions in three issue areas: urban redevelopment between 1950 and 1959 (which included eight different decisions); the public schools during the same period (which included eight different decisions); and nine nominations for mayor during the period 1941–1957. He concluded that decision-making was highly specialized in New Haven, with the social and economic notables having little part to play in these decisions.

What is important here from the methodological point of view is that Dahl used participation in decisions as his criterion for leadership. This approach makes the implicit assumption that active participation in decision-making is leadership and that all such active involvements are equal. The methodology of this approach requires the researcher to select a number of community decisions that are supposedly representative of all community decisions and then to trace the decision-making process—who was involved and what they did. In this way the researcher can document the actual decision-making process, getting at behavior rather than reputation, at the actual possession and use of resources, not at reputation for having them.

The decision-making or issue approach was used by a number of researchers, primarily political scientists, either singly or in combination with other techniques. Presthus studied five comparable decisions in two communities: a school bond, new industry, a hospital, flood control, and a municipal building.[39] Similarly, Wildavsky,[40] Jennings,[41] McClain and Highsaw,[42] Scoble,[43] Freeman, *et al.*,[44] and Martin, *et al.*,[45] also utilized this technique, sometimes in combination with other techniques, in studying community decision-making. The latter work is particularly noteworthy both for the wide range of issues studied in the Syracuse metropolitan area and for its concern with this larger communal unit. In all, twenty-two decision-points were studied, and a majority of these were at the county level.

The Freeman, *et al.* study which appears later in this part is an excellent illustration of the decision-making approach, and like Martin, *et al.*, it is also a study of Syracuse. Through a procedure that is noteworthy for its thoroughness, they identified 250 community issues and then narrowed these to thirty-nine decisions (resolved during the period 1955–1960) which influenced the development, utilization, or distribution of resources. Eventually they identified 550 participants in these thirty-nine issues.

One of the greatest problems with the decision-making approach is in the selection of issues. What issues are most essential to the community? From what time span should the issues be selected? What sampling procedure, if any, should be utilized? What criteria can be utilized in determining when issues become decisions? These are only a few of the questions that the researcher using this technique must confront—and answer. The answers to such questions can have critical effects on research outcomes. One attempt to provide a series of criteria for the selection of issues appears below in "Community Power and a Typology of Social Issues" by Barth and Johnson. Similarly, the study by Freeman, *et al.*, mentioned before, also offers a solution to one of these questions by rigorously defining the criteria for selecting issues.

The decision-making procedure inevitably raises questions about the process of decision-making as well as about the types of roles that are relevant to the decision-making process. Presthus distinguishes between the initiation and the implementation of decisions.[46] Jennings has a more complex model which includes initiation of action, fixing priorities, utilizing resources for gaining acceptance of chosen alternatives, legitimation, and, finally, implementation.[47] On the other hand Martin, et al. identify seven types of roles that are critical for the implementation of many community decisions: the initiators, experts, publicists, influentials (key public officials and heads of important economic units), brokers, transmitters, and the authority of government.[48] This technique sensitizes the researcher to both the process of decision-making and the roles relevant to each stage of the process, two important aspects of community decision-making activities.

The decision-making approach has not been without its critics, however. There have been three types of critiques: (1) criticisms of Dahl's operationalizations of this technique in the New Haven Study, (2) criticisms of the decision-making technique itself, and (3) criticism of the philosophical assumptions underlying this approach.

With regard to the first, Dahl based many of his conclusions on the fact that few of the social and economic notables in the community had participated in the issue areas he selected.[49] On the other hand, as Price points out, these three issues were germane only to the political boundaries of New Haven, and not to the larger metropolitan area.[50] One can assume that in New Haven, as in other metropolitan centers, a sizable part of the middle class (including the social and economic notables) probably does not live in New Haven proper, with the result that they have less personal stake in these issues than in some others that would affect the entire metropolitan area such as those about air pollution, metropolitan sewage,

water, or the like; the creation of a metropolitan government (with a consequent loss of autonomy by some suburbs); or political parties at the county level. Price also questions the typicality of New Haven. The economic, political, and historical traditions of Eastern cities, especially those in New England, are quite different from those of other regions. For example, the percentage of persons with identifiable ethnic origins is greater in the East than in other regions. Similarly, a number of studies have shown that the form of government also varies by region.[51] The typicality of New Haven is further questioned by the fact that New Haven had received $790.25 per citizen in urban renewal funds as of June 30, 1966. This was $190 greater than the second highest city, White Plains, New York. Among the 582 cities of size 25,000 or more that were also in existence in 1950 and that were located in states that had enabling legislation for urban renewal prior to 1960, New Haven was more than eight standard deviations above the mean, which would be a rather unusual event if this process were a completely random one. Some of the striking differences in regional patterns with respect to urban renewal programs are shown in Table 1.

In another area that represents a city's ability to obtain federal self-help funds, New Haven was second highest in the nation in the amount of Office of Economic Opportunity grants it was able to obtain during the first two years of that program. Is New Haven in the vanguard or unique, or both? In any event it is certainly *not* a typical American city, if there is any such entity.[52]

A second type of criticism of the decision-making approach has been leveled by Bachrach and Baratz who point out that the sampling of only the issues that are actually raised in a community precludes obtaining information about the dynamics involved when issues are suppressed; i.e., issues raised in a community may be limited to "safe" ones through the manipulation of community values, myths, and institutional procedures.[53] The fact that a given issue is suppressed, e.g., the problem of Negro equality in Southern

TABLE 1. *Number of Urban Renewal Dollars per Capita by Region for Eligible Cities of Size 25,000 or more in 1960*

REGION	NUMBER OF CITIES	MEAN PER CAPITA URBAN RENEWAL DOLLARS RESERVED PER CITY	STANDARD DEVIATION
Northeast	159	$98.26	$115.68
South	136	50.85	68.92
Midwest	193	29.99	50.29
Far West	94	30.00	59.37

cities prior to 1954, indicates that power is being exercised. Thus, they question whether the issues raised exhaust the phenomenon of community power. Their answer is clearly in the negative. Their article, "Decisions and Nondecisions: An Analytical Framework," appears below.

Finally, the third type of criticism has pointed out differences in the philosophies of the chief practitioners of research on community power (political scientists and sociologists). In his article, "Power, Pluralism, and Local Politics" (included in this section), Anton delves into the assumptions that underlie the disciplines of political science and sociology, and consequently, the proclivities of practitioners of these disciplines to have an affinity for the decision-making and reputational approaches, respectively. By pointing out that political scientists are more likely to conceive of social reality in terms of an actor-individual, while sociologists are more prone to study roles in social systems, Anton clarifies many of the issues and confusions upon which this debate rests.[54]

What seems fairly clear about the community power debate is that a large amount of heat was generated over a relatively narrow range of concerns. It is difficult to argue today that one method is better or more appropriate than another; rather, each technique should be considered as a method of determining different aspects of the community decision-making structure. For example, it seems fairly clear that the reputational technique measures the degree of perceived potential resources, not actual resources. Variations in such perceptions

can have an effect on community decisions, as Gamson has shown.[55] Similarly, the decision-making method casts a wide net and helps to chart out important aspects of community decision-making that might otherwise be missed, such as the role of formal political leaders and political parties. At the same time, the possibility of suppressed issues and "nondecisions" is an important qualification of this technique. Thus, any study of community power must use a combination of these techniques to measure how power is distributed.

Comparisons of Approaches

A number of studies have utilized all of these approaches in trying to understand the power matrix in communities. One of the most competent, methodologically sound, and sophisticated is the study of Syracuse by Freeman and his colleagues, "Locating Leaders in Local Communities: A Comparison of Some Alternative Approaches," which is included in this section. Using the three previously discussed methods as well as an additional one they call the "social activity" (which measures those most active in voluntary associations), they are able to compare the results of these four techniques. They find that there is a high degree of agreement between the reputational technique and the positional technique, but that few of the reputational and positional leaders participate in making community decisions. They conclude that there are probably three types of community leaders: the Institutional Leaders (who have both positions of power as well as reputations for power), Effectors (who are the active participants in community decisions), and the Activists (who are active and hold office in organizations, but who participate in less essential ways in the community decision-making). They speculate that in an earlier era the institutional leaders and effectors may have been the same, but that there has probably been a bifurcation of community leadership as the community has become more differentiated. The Freeman, *et al.* study cannot be recommended too highly— it should be used as a model in any comparative study of community leadership systems.

In another study of decision-making in two communities that we have included here, "Community Power and Decision-Making: A Comparative Evaluation of Measurement Techniques," Blankenship did not find as much discrepancy between the institutional leaders and effectors or activists in decision-making. This raises the question of the historical, political, social, and economic variations in communities that may affect the degree to which these methods produce comparable results. One could speculate that in newer communities there would be a greater discrepancy than in older, more established communities in which participants would better understand the system. Or similarly, one could speculate that in communities that have little industrialization or have not experienced a high degree of structural differentiation, these techniques are more likely to produce similar results.[56]

The point is that neither these studies nor others such as those by Schulze,[57] Clelland and Form,[58] Presthus,[59] Agger, *et al.*,[60]

or Jennings,[61] which have used multiple techniques, provide enough clues to do anything more than speculate. One caution is in order, however. How does one classify leaders who are identified by two or more of these techniques? Should they be classified as reputational leaders, although they are also positionally determined leaders, or vice-versa? For example, in Jennings' study eighteen of his prescribed influentials (positional leaders) and fourteen of his economic dominants (another set of positional leaders) were also attributed influentials (reputational leaders).[62] In his analysis these thirty-two doubly-identified leaders are classified with the reputational leaders. Some of his statements, especially about the role of the economic dominants, are open to reinterpretation because of this classification problem.

The discussion here, as well as the readings that follow, discuss techniques that the researcher may utilize to locate centers of power in communities. These readings also point out some of the pitfalls and problems of each approach. Clearly, no one approach is sufficient in any study of community power. Any such study must utilize all three techniques. Only a comparative study of a number of communities (perhaps thirty or forty, selected so as to provide critical contrasts of some of the important variables suggested in Part III) can provide a true understanding of the value, validity, and meaning of these techniques. Until such a study is done, knowledge about community power and decision-making will remain as incomplete as the conclusions to this debate are tentative and heuristic.

Notes

1. M. K. Jennings, *Community Influentials: The Elites of Atlanta* (New York: Free Press, 1964), p. 25.
2. R. O. Schulze, "The Role of Economic Dominants in Community Power Structure," in this volume.
3. Jennings, *op. cit.*
4. L. C. Freeman, T. J. Fararo, W. Bloomberg, and M. H. Sunshine, "A Comparison of Some Alternative Approaches," in this

volume. Also see L. C. Freeman, *Patterns of Local Leadership* (Indianapolis: Bobbs-Merrill, 1968).
5. W. V. D'Antonio, C. P. Loomis, W. H. Form, and E. C. Erickson, "Institutional and Occupational Representations in Eleven Community Influence Systems," *American Sociological Review*, 26 (June, 1961), 440–446.
6. J. Walton, "Substance and Artifact: The

Current Status of Research on Community Power Structure," *American Journal of Sociology*, 71 (January, 1966), 430–438; and "Discipline, Method, and Community Power: A Note on the Sociology of Knowledge," *American Sociological Review*, 31 (October, 1966), 684–689.

7. A. A. Fanelli, "A Typology of Community Leadership Based on Influence and Interaction within the Leader Sub-System," *Social Forces*, 34 (May, 1956), 332–338.
8. R. O. Schulze and L. U. Blumberg, "The Determination of Local Power Elites," in this volume.
9. *Ibid.*
10. Fanelli, *op. cit.*
11. W. H. Form and W. V. D'Antonio, "Integration and Cleavage Among Community Influentials in Two Border Cities," in this volume.
12. D. W. Olmsted, "Organizational Leadership and Social Structure in a Small City," *American Sociological Review*, 19 (June, 1954), 273–281; Jennings, *op. cit.*
13. T. C. Smith, "The Structuring of Power in a Suburban Community," *Pacific Sociological Review*, 3 (Fall, 1960), 83–86.
14. F. Hunter, *Community Power Structure: A Study of Decision Makers* (Chapel Hill: University of North Carolina Press, 1953).
15. G. M. Belknap and R. H. Smuckler, "Political Power Relations in a Mid-West City," *Public Opinion Quarterly*, 20 (Spring, 1956), 73–81.
16. Form and D'Antonio, *op. cit.*, in this volume.
17. D. A. Booth and C. R. Adrian, "Power Structure and Community Change," *Midwest Journal of Political Science*, 6 (August, 1962), 277–296.
18. D. C. Miller, "Decision-Making Cliques in Community Power Structures: A Comparative Study of an American and an English City," in this volume; and "Town and Gown: The Power Structure of a University Town," *American Journal of Sociology*, 68 (January, 1963), 432–443.
19. I. Belknap and J. G. Steinle, *The Community and Its Hospitals: A Comparative Analysis* (Syracuse: Syracuse University Press, 1963).
20. Hunter, *op. cit.*
21. D. C. Miller, "Industry and Community Power Structure: A Comparative Study of an American and an English City" and "Decision-Making Cliques in Community Power Structures: A Comparative Study of an American and an English City," both in this volume.
22. *Ibid.*
23. Compare, T. J. Anton, "Power, Pluralism, and Local Politics," in this volume.
24. R. A. Dahl, "Hierarchy, Democracy, and Bargaining in Politics and Economics," in

Research Frontiers in Politics and Government (Washington, D.C.: Brookings, 1955), pp. 45–69; "The Concept of Power," *Behavioral Science*, 2 (July, 1957), 201–214; "A Critique of Ruling Elite Model," *American Political Science Review*, 52 (June, 1958), 463–469; and "Equality and Power in American Society," in W. V. D'Antonio and H. J. Ehrlich (eds.), *Power and Democracy in America* (Notre Dame: University of Notre Dame Press, 1961).

25. R. E. Wolfinger, "Reputation and Reality in the Study of 'Community Power,'" in this volume; and "A Plea for a Decent Burial," *American Sociological Review*, 27 (December, 1962), 841–847.
26. N. W. Polsby, "The Sociology of Community Power: A Reassessment," *Social Forces*, 37 (March, 1959), 232–236; "Three Problems in the Analysis of Community Power," *American Sociological Review*, 24 (December, 1959), 796–803; "How to Study Community Power: The Pluralist Alternative," in this volume; "Power in Middletown: Fact and Value in Community Research," *Canadian Journal of Economics and Political Science*, 26 (November, 1960), 592–603; "Community Power: Some Reflections on the Recent Literature," *American Sociological Review*, 27 (December, 1962), 838–840; and *Community Power and Political Theory* (New Haven: Yale University Press, 1963).
27. D. Bell, "The Power Elite Reconsidered," *American Journal of Sociology*, 64 (November, 1958), 238–250.
28. N. Long, "The Local Community as an Ecology of Games," *American Journal of Sociology*, 64 (November, 1958), 251–261.
29. L. J. R. Herson, "In the Footsteps of Community Power," *American Political Science Review*, 55 (December, 1961), 817–830.
30. S. Fisher, "Community-Power Studies: A Critique," *Social Research*, 29 (Winter, 1962), 449–466.
31. A. M. Rose, *The Power Structure: Political Process in American Society* (New York: Oxford University Press, 1967).
32. M. H. Danzger, "Community Power Structure: Problems and Continuities," in this volume.
33. Rose *op. cit.*
34. H. J. Ehrlich, "The Reputational Approach to the Study of Community Power," *American Sociological Review*, 26 (December, 1961), 926–927; W. V. D'Antonio and E. C. Erickson, "The Reputational Technique as a Measure of Community Power: An Evaluation Based on Comparative and Longitudinal Studies," in this volume; W. V. D'Antonio, H. J. Ehrlich, and E. C. Erickson, "Further Notes on the

Study of Community Power," *American Sociological Review*, 27 (December, 1962), 848–853; B. Abu-Laban, "The Reputational Approach in the Study of Technique as a Measure of Community Power: A Critical Evaluation," *Pacific Sociological Review*, 8 (Spring, 1965), 35–42; and W. A. Gamson, "Reputation and Resources in Community Politics," in this volume.

35. D. C. Miller and J. L. Dirksen, "The Identification of Visible, Concealed, and Symbolic Leaders in a Small Indiana City: A Replication of the Bonjean-Noland Study of Burlington, North Carolina," *Social Forces*, 43 (May, 1965), 548–555.

36. R. M. French and M. Aiken, "Community Power in Cornucopia, A Replication in a Small Community of the Bonjean Technique of Identifying Community Leaders," *Sociological Quarterly*, 9 (Spring, 1968), 261–270.

37. See Polsby, *Community Power and Political Theory, op. cit.*, which includes many of his earlier published articles and ideas.

38. R. A. Dahl, *Who Governs? Democracy and Power in an American City* (New Haven: Yale University Press, 1961).

39. R. Presthus, *Men at the Top: A Study in Community Power* (New York: Oxford University Press, 1964).

40. A. Wildavsky, *Leadership in a Small Town* (Totowa, N.J.: Bedminster Press, 1964).

41. Jennings, *op. cit.*

42. J. M. McClain and R. B. Highsaw, *Dixie City Acts: A Study in Decision-Making* (Birmingham: Bureau of Public Administration, University of Alabama, 1962).

43. H. M. Scoble, "Leadership Hierarchies and Political Issues in a New England Town," in M. Janowitz (ed.), *Community Political Systems* (New York: Free Press, 1961), pp. 117–145.

44. Freeman, *et al., op. cit.*, in this volume. Compare L. C. Freeman, *Patterns of Local Community Leadership* (Indianapolis: Bobbs-Merrill, 1968).

45. R. C. Martin, F. J. Munger, J. Burkhead, and G. S. Birkhead, *Decisions in Syracuse: A Metropolitan Action Study* (Bloomington: Indiana University Press, 1961).

46. Presthus, *op. cit.*, pp. 54–55.

47. Jennings, *op. cit.*, pp. 107–109.

48. Martin, *et al., op. cit.*

49. Dahl, *Who Governs?, op. cit.*

50. H. D. Price, "Review of *Who Governs?,*" *Yale Law Journal*, 71 (July, 1962), 1589–1596.

51. J. H. Kessel, "Governmental Structure and Political Environment: A Statistical Note About American Cities," *American Political Science Review*, 56 (September, 1962), 615–620; R. R. Alford and H. M. Scoble, "Political and Socioeconomic Characteristics of American Cities," *1965 Municipal Year Book* (Washington, D.C.: International City Managers' Association, 1965), pp. 82–97; L. F. Schnore and R. R. Alford, "Forms of Government and Socioeconomic Characteristics of Suburbs," *Administrative Science Quarterly*, 8 (June, 1963), 1–17; R. E. Wolfinger and J. O. Field, "Political Ethos and the Structure of City Government," *American Political Science Review*, 60 (June, 1966), 306–326.

52. These statements comparing New Haven to other cities are based on findings from a study of decision-making outcomes in American cities by M. Aiken and R. R. Alford, University of Wisconsin.

53. P. Bachrach and M. S. Baratz, "Two Faces of Power," *American Political Science Review*, 56 (December, 1962), 947–952; and "Decisions and Nondecisions: An Analytical Framework," in this volume.

54. T. J. Anton, "Power, Pluralism, and Local Politics," in this volume. The interested reader should examine R. A. Dahl's rebuttal to these criticisms in "Letters to the Editor," *Administrative Science Quarterly*, 8 (September, 1963), 250–256, as well as Anton's rejoinder in the same issue, 257–268.

55. Gamson, *op. cit.*

56. Compare, Schulze, *op. cit.*, in this volume; D. A. Clelland and W. H. Form, "Economic Dominants and Community Power: A Comparative Analysis," in this volume; and Freeman, *et al., op. cit.*, in this volume.

57. Schulze, *op. cit.*, in this volume.

58. Clelland and Form, *op. cit.*, in this volume.

59. Presthus, *op. cit.*

60. R. E. Agger, D. Goldrich, and B. E. Swanson, *The Rulers and the Ruled: Political Power and Impotence in American Communities* (New York: Wiley, 1964).

61. Jennings, *op. cit.*

62. *Ibid.*

Community Leadership: Directions of Research[1]

Charles M. Bonjean and David M. Olson

Although social scientists have attempted for quite some time to answer the question, "Who governs at the community level?" methodological and theoretical progress in this area of investigation has moved rapidly only within the past decade.

Prior to 1953 and publication of Floyd Hunter's *Community Power Structure*, the question, "Who governs?" was answered in much the same manner by both social scientists and the lay public. Those persons occupying important offices—elected political officials, higher civil servants, business executives, officials of voluntary associations, heads of religious groups, leaders of labor unions and others—were assumed to be those making key decisions affecting directly or indirectly the lives of most other community residents.[2] Political scientists made this same assumption by focusing on interest groups in studies of state and national governments. Their studies of community governments tended to concentrate on the structure and manifest tasks of the governmental units, while largely ignoring the private organizational positions.

Although a little-known study of the Chicago Board of Education in 1928 seemed to indicate that organizational officers may not, in fact, make the key decision,[3] it was Hunter who first seriously challenged the assumed relationship between office holding and decision making at the community level. Hunter's study of Atlanta indicated that institutions and formal associations played a "vital role in the execution of determined policy, but the formulation of policy often takes place outside these formalized groupings."[4] In other words, Hunter concluded that Atlanta (and possibly other communities) was governed by a covert economic elite.

Hunter's conclusions stimulated interdisciplinary interest, in community leadership patterns resulting in a large number of uncoordinated case studies (and later a few comparative analyses), some supporting and some negating his answer to the question, "Who governs?"[5] Different investigators have used different research techniques, have focused on different features of community leadership structures, and have criticized one another's methods and conclusions.[6] This presentation re-examines many of these investigations and their criticisms in order to assess current theory, methods, problems, and the emergent trends over the last decade. Comparability, continuity, and direction will be sought by attempting to answer the following three questions: (1) How is community leadership studied, or how are leaders identified? (2) What are the salient characteristics of leadership structures in the various communities that have been investigated? (3) What, if anything, may be related to leadership structure characteristics?

Identifying Leaders

Most studies of community leadership have used one of three techniques (or a combination or modification of the three) to identify community leaders—the positional approach, the reputational approach, or the decisional approach.

The Positional Approach

As was indicated above, this was the most widely used technique prior to 1953. It consists of the use of extensive lists of formal positions or offices to help define leadership. Those individuals holding the greatest number and most important offices in the

Reprinted from Administrative Science Quarterly, *9 (December 1964), 278–300, by permission of the authors and the Graduate School of Business and Public Administration, Cornell University. Copyright 1964 by the Graduate School of Business and Public Administration, Cornell University.*

munity are considered to be the key decision makers in the community.[7] Sometimes indexes are computed in an attempt to make the procedure even more precise.[8] Each potential leader is given a total score consisting of a sum of scores for all offices he holds. Top leaders are those with the highest scores.[9]

One variation of the positional approach is by way of a general institutional description of a local government such as that used in the study of New York by Sayre and Kaufman in which they described the major positional actors, their characteristics, their goals, and their strategies. In that instance neither was a set of issues isolated for special study nor was a set of leaders located by reputation; rather, all actors were examined on all issues generally.[10] A similar method was used in a comparative study of ten cities of varying sizes in Florida.[11] Also similar was Adrian's examination of the leadership roles of city managers, elected mayors, and interest groups in a comparative study of three cities.[12]

The validity and utility of the positional approach has been criticized from numerous standpoints—for example, because of the variation in terminology characteristic of different associations in designating similar offices.[13] But, in fact, the success or failure of this approach to the identification of community decision makers depends upon the degree to which its basic assumption is valid: those holding positions of authority actually make key decisions while those who do not occupy such positions do not make key decisions.

This assumption may be tested if results of the positional approach are compared with those of the other two approaches discussed below. Considering the relationship between office holding and decision making as a hypothesis, rather than as an a priori assumption, some investigations yield data that support the relationship while others contradict it.[14] It has been suggested that the hypothesis is usually supported in small communities, and thus in such communities the formal technique of leader identification is the quickest, most efficient, and the most

reliable method.[15] Two recent investigations indicate that even this may not be the case. Laskin and Phillett, using both the positional and reputational techniques, studied leadership in four small Canadian communities (ranging in size from 500 to 4,000 inhabitants) and found that only 38 per cent to 77 per cent of the reputational leaders were also formal or positional leaders.[16] Bonjean studied four communities, ranging in size from 33,000 to 202,000 persons, and found fewer reputational leaders holding public or associational office in the two smaller communities (62 per cent and 65 per cent) than in the two larger communities (75 per cent and 77 per cent).[17]

In short, although the positional approach has been widely used, it cannot stand alone because the assumption upon which it is based may not be valid for all communities. The use of this approach precludes accepting the legitimacy of leadership structures as problematic.

The Reputational Approach

This approach was first used in a study of community power by Hunter but was, of course, used earlier by Warner, Hollingshead, and others to study another dimension of social stratification—status.[18] Although this technique has numerous variations, essentially it consists of asking informants to name and rank the leaders in their community.[19] The informants may be a predesignated panel of experts or a random sample of community members, or they may be selected by what is known as the "snowball" or "cobweb" technique. The final list of leaders usually consists either of those individuals who have received the greatest number of nominations by the informants or of all leaders whose average ranking is above a certain arbitrarily set limit.

Although the reputational approach has probably been the most widely used technique in the study of community leadership, it has been criticized from several standpoints:

1. It does not measure leadership per se, but rather the reputation for leadership. Critics do not feel that a reputation for power is a valid index of power.[20] They have sug-

gested, as an alternative way to determine who "runs things," studying a series of concrete decisions in order to find out who specifically dominates those decisions (this approach will be discussed in detail below). Just as there may or may not be agreement on positional and reputational leaders, these criticisms indicate that there may or may not be agreement on decision-making dominants and reputational leaders. The most salient rebuttals to this criticism focus on the relationship between perception and behavior: "If we can ascertain that the way in which people perceive the power structure of the local political system affects the way in which they behave towards and in that system, then surely we are dealing with very meaningful and very useful considerations."[21]

2. The reputational approach incorporates an a priori assumption of a monolithic power structure. Some critics believe that different groups of elites probably have different scopes of interest, and thus there may be several structures of influence rather than merely one as the reputational approach may imply.[22] Associated with this general criticism are the related criticisms that "no study considers the full range of issues which come before a particular decision maker" and that "those [issues] that have been studied have been on the more dramatic side."[23] To the degree that some reputational studies have considered decision areas and have built this consideration into their techniques of investigation (for example by asking informants not only to name and rank leaders but also to specify those issues or institutions in which the nominee is active), this criticism has been met by some reputational analyses.[24] Another way to meet this objection is to ask what the earlier reputational studies assumed: Is there a small group which runs things in this town?[25]

A related problem is that the examples of power roles in reputational studies are too general and vague. Not enough evidence of action is present to permit a validation of the reputed and self-confessed leadership roles. Both Hunter in Atlanta and Thometz in Dallas give examples of elite action, but both also stress the long and complex bargaining process through which the elite reached agreement within itself and with external elements in the community. If other elements than the reputed elite can force that elite to negotiate and modify positions, those elements possess at least some kind of power.

3. This approach sometimes incorporates an a priori assumption about group structure. The critics indicate that even though some individuals have been designated by the reputational approach as having more power than other members of the community, one cannot assume that these highest ranking individuals make up a ruling *group* rather than merely an aggregate of leaders.[26] This criticism has been met by some investigators by incorporating sociometric and interaction checks in the method.[27]

4. Even if the above criticisms are met and even if there is a high correlation between power reputation and power per se, the reputational approach may not accurately identify leaders because (1) of inaccuracies in respondent perceptions—that is, private citizens may be unreliable sources of information,[28] (2) interviewer and respondent may not agree on what is meant by power—that is, the questions may not be valid,[29] and (3) when nominations and rankings are tabulated, the arbitrary cut-off points may be too high (and thus not include all of the leaders) or too low (and thus include some of the followers, as well).[30] The first problem may be handled to some extent by using a panel of experts (themselves perhaps determined by the snowball variation of the reputational technique) rather than by a random sample of community members.

Other reputational studies have begun with a panel of nominators selected for their knowledge of different sectors of community life. Both Hunter and Miller began with a diversified panel and both found a predominantly business-based elite.[31] Booth and Adrian, using the same method, found a diversified reputational elite which included not only businessmen, but also unionists and government officials who were professed leaders of the working class.[32] The second problem is common to all forms of survey research and has been answered adequately elsewhere (validity checks may be incorporated in this form of survey research as readily as in any other form of it). The third problem can be handled to some degree by using conventional tests of statistical significance (for example, including in the leadership category those nominees whose total number of nominations is significantly greater than the mean number of nominations of all nominees), by noticing clusters or conversely gaps in the frequency distribution of leadership scores, or by comparing the nominations of leaders themselves with those of other informants, to determine whether a specific individual should be included as a leader or not.

In short, the reputational approach, which has been the most widely used technique over the last decade, has been criticized on the counts cited above, but it has survived the wave of criticism. Why it has survived, in spite of its shortcomings, will be more apparent after a discussion of the third major approach to the study of community leadership.

The Decisional Approach

Also known as the "Event Analysis" or the "Issue" approach, this alternative is preferred by most of the critics of the reputational approach. It involves tracing the actions of leaders in regard to decision making and policy formation within the context of specific issues.[33] The tracing may be done by gathering data from extensive interviews, from attendance at committee and organizational meetings, from reports, speeches, and newspaper accounts, and so on.[34] The approach has as its major advantage the possibility of identifying overt power rather than power potential; it also provides a more realistic viewpoint of power relations as processes rather than as fixed structures. On the other hand, this approach also has several inherent limitations:

1. Given certain issues, where does the investigator start? Observing committee and organizational meetings appears to involve accepting the same relationship between authority positions and decision making

assumed by the use of the positional approach. How does the investigator know whether or not the decisions have already been made informally some time before the meeting, and how does he know if the committee or organizational members who appear to wield influence are not themselves being influenced by others who may, in fact, be covert? Decisional studies usually involve interviews to ascertain prior informal acts, motives, and influences. In that an attempt is made to identify informal influences, these interviews come close to the reputational approach, and to some degree meet this criticism. Presthus, for example, concluded that the decisional approach identified several government officials as powerful who, he concluded by also using a reputational approach, were only exercising ministerial or purely formal roles rather than actually making decisions.[35] It appears, then, that the decisional approach should be supplemented to some degree by the reputational approach.

2. To establish the rapport and gain the confidence necessary to be permitted to attend informal meetings (if they are a part of the influence structure) is quite time-consuming. Burgess, for example, spent three years in and out of Crescent City while she was "interviewing, observing, listening and occasionally participating in subcommunity activities."[36] Similarly, Dahl relied upon a collaborator who spent a year's internship in the New Haven city hall in "highly strategic locations."[37] It thus appears that the use of this approach would also include the decision to conduct an intensive study and description of influence patterns in a single community or subcommunity rather than perhaps a less intensive description and comparison based on the reputational or positional approaches in several communities. In short, this method is less expedient than either of the others.

3. By what criteria are the decisions or issues selected for study? Some agree that focus should be upon the "most important" areas, however they may be defined. At times the decisions are arbitrarily selected by the investigator. An alternative method is to ask respondents which they consider the most important community decisions. In effect,

this alternative uses the reputational method to begin a study of issue resolution. A start toward sampling of issues has been made by the suggestion that issues vary along five important dimensions: unique or recurrent, salient or nonsalient to leadership, salient or nonsalient to community publics, effective action possible or effective action impossible, and local or cosmopolitan.[38] Decisions have also been categorized into five subject-matter fields which are said to "differ in personnel, style of operation, and significance for public policy": race relations and inter-faith activity, good-government activities, welfare and fund-raising activities, cultural and hospital work, and business promotion, construction, and planning activities.[39]

4. Another criticism is that the study of decision making ignores those actors who may be able to keep latent issues from emerging into open controversy. The most important issues in a community may be submerged. To focus on the actual events and controversies is to assume the importance of the decisions selected and does not provide a means of examining nondecisions and the people who can keep them latent.[40] To examine this aspect of community power, research must seek the origins and rationale of the status quo. Studies with a historical dimension are better designed to probe the origins of the status quo than studies concerned mainly with recent events or reputations.[41]

Certainly a combination of methods (any two or all three) appears to be the most satisfactory means for the study of community leadership at our present stage of development. Apparently, some consensus exists in regard to this in that most of the more recent investigations have, in fact, used a combination of techniques.[42] In fact, its has been suggested that perhaps the different methods locate different types of leaders.[43]

Leadership Structure Characteristics

The answers to the question, "Who governs?" show even more variation than the techniques used to seek the answers.

At one extreme are Hunter's conclusions.[44] He allegedly found a monolithic power structure consisting of about forty individuals, most of whom were wealthy and important in business. These forty leaders all knew one another and all belonged to one of five cliques which were coordinated by about twelve leaders who wielded even more influence than the other twenty-eight. These individuals, according to Hunter, informally determined policy, which in turn was carried out by lower level leaders (including public officials and associational officers).

Other investigators have asserted that the administrators and politicians are the decision makers and furthermore are influenced, more or less, by a sizeable proportion of the rest of the community (the electorate). At least one of these investigators has even indicated that "politicians innovated policy choices and had their acceptability certified by the visible support of top businessmen."[45]

Leadership structures vary in many ways. In some communities, for example, leaders were found to be active in all decision areas, while in other communities the leaders varied with the decision. In still others, leaders of both types were found. In some communities, the leaders were found to know one another and act in concert, while in others they know one another and are rivals. In still others, they do not even know one another. Apparently no single descriptive statement —not even a very general one—applies to community leadership in general in the United States today (unless the statement includes variability itself).

Early investigators often studied one community, described its patterns of leadership, and then generalized (usually with some caution) to other communities.[46] Their critics responded in a similar manner, implying that such a pattern of leadership could be found in no American community.[47] Both investigators and critics are more tentative today, and although numerous issues are still at stake, a more realistic perspective appears to be emerging. Today, no one would deny the existence of different patterns of leadership in different communities or in the same community over time. Therefore, the focus is shifting to a concern with the range of possibilities. In other words, the types of questions that appear to be most salient to the study of community leadership today are concerned with (1) the various types of power structures that could function in contemporary American communities, (2) the important dimensions that differentiate these types of structures, and (3) the manner in which these dimensions can be measured.

The types of power structures that could function in American communities (and, in fact, have been described by the investigators cited in this paper) are many, and, indeed, little would be gained here from a brief description of each of them. Rather, what is needed is a means by which their main characteristics can be summarized and compared. One approach that has been successful in describing and comparing other types of social structures is the use of sets of ideal-type constructs.[48] Entire societies, for example, have been described and compared by the degree to which they approximate folk societies or urban societies.[49] Complex organizations are said to approximate the Weberian model of bureaucracy or the human relations model.[50] There is no reason why this same approach could not be used in the study of community leadership.[51] For example, using Hunter's findings and exaggerating the main characteristics of the leadership structure he found, an ideal type may be constructed that would logically fall at one extreme on our hypothetical yardstick and therefore could be used as a rough measure that would enable comparison and thus give some meaning to data that have been and will, no doubt, be found by others. One possible leadership model, then, is the Covert Power Elite, identified by the following characteristics: (1) leaders do not hold political offices or offices in associations, (2) they are not recognized by the community at large as key decision makers, (3) they are active in a wide range of decision areas, and (4) they work together as a group, rather than independently or in opposition.

Most ideal-type constructs have logical

opposites, which, in this case, would be a leadership model where: (1) leaders hold political or associational office, (2) leaders are recognized by the community at large as key decision makers, (3) leaders are concerned only with those decisions related to official areas, and (4) group structure may not be present (certainly, at least, primary relations would be absent). These characteristics, of course, probably best describe that type of leadership structure most consistent with the political formula of our society—legitimate pluralism.[52] Between these two extremes one would find independent sovereignties (covert subgroupings concerned with one or a few decision areas), rival sovereignties (visible, though not legitimate, subgroupings competing on any number of decisions), and interest groups (leaders may hold associational, but not political, office; concern is with one or a few decisions; and leaders are recognized by the community).[53]

In short, the following four characteristics appear to be the most important in identifying the two ideal-type leadership structures and thus perhaps any structure falling between these two:

1. Legitimacy

Where leaders hold public or associational office, the leadership structure is, in fact, an authority structure. Legitimacy is easily measured by collecting information on each leader (identified by either the reputational or decisional approach) in regard to political or associational offices. One measure of the leadership structure's legitimacy, then, is simply the proportion of leaders who hold or have recently held such offices.[54] The use of a percentage score enables the comparison of different communities that may have different numbers of leaders.

2. Visibility

This is a dimension separate from legitimacy. If all community leaders held political or associational offices, perhaps the leadership structure would be clearly visible. But the reverse is not equally as true. Leaders who do not hold positions of authority may or may not be covert. Thus legitimacy tells us nothing about visibility unless all leaders *are* public or associational officers. To measure visibility necessitates the use of the reputational approach, at least to some degree. Visibility may be roughly measured if the nominations and rankings of a panel of judges (or better, the leaders themselves) are compared with the nominations and rankings of a sample of the general public or some other segment of the community. Comparing the rankings by sets of informants yields three possible types of leaders: *visible* (those recognized by both the judges and the general public), *concealed* (those recognized by the judges but not by the general public), and *symbolic* (those recognized by the general public, but not by the judges).[55] The differential visibility of community leadership structures could be assessed by comparing the proportions of visible leaders.

3. Scope of Influence

One leader or set of leaders may participate in decision making in a wide range of issues in a community, or different leaders or sets of leaders may be active in different areas. Both types of leaders, in fact, could be found within the same community. Scope of influence could be measured in at least two different ways:

a. A list of actual or possible decisions in the community could be presented to each leader (or each informant), and he, in turn, could be asked to specify those decisions in which he (or his nominee) had participated in policy formation. Each leader could then be assigned a percentage score based on the number of decision areas in which he participated compared to the total number of decision areas. Scores within and between communities are important here, in that a summary score for any given community may be misleading if leaders of both types have been identified. A problem arises from the fact that the number of salient decisions may vary from community to community. If *possible* rather than *actual* decisions are used as the denominator, the total score will be affected by the number of actual decisions.

The problem is minimized, of course, if the investigator limits his concern to actual decisions.

b. The second method of measuring scope of influence is possible only if the decisional approach is used to identify leaders. If several different types of decisions are analyzed, each leader's role in each type of decision may be carefully assessed. Indeed, participation in decision making in four different types of issues, for example, would be evidence of *general* leadership.[56] Perhaps one criterion for selection using the decisional approach (or for inclusion on an interview schedule using the reputational approach) to assess scope of influence should be variability along the dimensions suggested by Barth and Johnson or by Banfield and Wilson.[57]

4. Cohesiveness

Given legitimate or nonlegitimate, visible or concealed, and general or issue leaders, they may or may not interact as members of a group (or perhaps several groups). It is possible that cohesiveness, certainly one characteristic of a group, could be measured, at least roughly, by the degree to which leaders nominate one another. Indeed, one sociometric statistic, the ratio of interest, purports to measure this group characteristic in precisely such a manner.[58] Interaction patterns, themselves, may be investigated by asking respondents to indicate those with whom they have worked (and in regard to which decisions). Cohesiveness has been treated in a particularly precise manner by Scoble. After finding three major factions by sociometric techniques, he determined that each was internally divided on policy preferences by using Rice's index of cohesion to measure their answers to a set of public opinion questions. Nevertheless, the factions possessed sufficient agreement for at least some members of each to participate as identifiable cliques on most decisions.[59] Other similar techniques, for example an acquaintanceship scale, have also been used to attempt to assess the group structure of leadership elites.[60] Such techniques appear to identify unitary, bifactional, multifactional, and amorphous patterns. These patterns may be found within either a general- or issue-oriented elite. The analysis of clique or factional patterns is very similar to that used in discussion of political parties (one-, two-, or multiparty systems), intraparty factions (one-faction, two-faction, or multifactional parties), and industrial competition (monopoly, oligopoly, or competition).

In summary, legitimacy, visibility, scope of influence, and cohesiveness appear to be the most significant dimensions of community leadership structures in that (1) they have been the major sources of disagreement and criticism, (2) a review of leadership studies indicates that variation may, in fact, be found along all four dimensions, and (3) they are useful in the identification of different types or models of leadership structures.

Antecedents and Consequences of Leadership Structure Characteristics

Given the tentative conclusion that community leaders may be identified and that leadership structures vary along certain dimensions from community to community, what has been found to be related to leadership structure characteristics? The search for such relationships is a fairly recent trend. Most of the earlier investigations were simply case studies attempting to describe the leadership structure or processes in one community. Explanation, of course, usually requires the examination of two or more cases and an attempt to account for their differences or similarities. Only through a comparative approach—studies of large numbers of decisions on comparable issues within one community over time or in many different communities—is it possible to make generalizations in regard to those phenomena which might be related to leadership structure characteristics.[61] The few comparative analyses of community leadership structures that have been undertaken usually deal with possible antecedents of community leadership structures or possible consequences of the same, but seldom, if ever, both. Many of these investigations have not been concerned with visibility, legitimacy, cohesiveness, or

scope of influence as leadership structure characteristics per se; some, however, do offer insights into relationships between these characteristics and antecedents and consequences.

Antecedents

That the characteristics of influence structures may be dependent on the nature of the society or community of which they are a part has been the basic relationship investigated by those concerned with antecedents of community leadership structures.

A number of comparative analyses have been cross-cultural comparisons seeking to test the hypothesis that leaders represent those institutions that are the most powerful and influential in the society at large. Thus, as might be expected, Miller found that businessmen exerted a predominant influence in community decision making in two United States cities, but in a British city other institutions were better represented.[62] According to Miller, this is in part a consequence of the higher social status of industry and its captains in the United States, and in part a function of city government in the British city—specifically an active community council requiring much time and work of its 112 members.

D'Antonio and his colleagues compared institutional and occupational representations in eight United States cities, the British city studied by Miller, and two Mexican cities.[63] They found that business provided the largest number of top influentials in all the United States cities as well as in the two Mexican cities. The two Mexican cities, however, gave the strongest evidence of a challenge to business by another sector of the community—government. They explain this as a consequence of the dominance of the PRI (*Partido Revolucionario Institucional*) in Mexico. The role of economic dominants over time in one community was studied by Schulze.[64] He noted, for example, that as the economic structure of the community changed, so did its leadership structure. As the community economic system became absorbed into the larger industrial complex of a nearby large city, local economic dominants participated less in community decision making, leaving it almost wholly in the hands of a group of middle-class business and professional men. The same relationship was observed by Clelland and Form in a more recent investigation of another community.[65] One implication of those studies concerned with the relationship between the community's institutional structure and leadership structure is the greater probability of legitimate, visible structures with limited scopes of influence in communities with complex institutional structures, or at least in those where a single institution or organization is not dominant.

Not only may the relative importance of different institutions influence the nature of the leadership structure, but characteristics of a single institution may also be important. Perhaps the most obvious, as suggested by Miller above, is the political institution itself. The perceptions and values of public officials may, of course, vary between communities. While they may play merely formal ministerial roles,[66] and therefore be rated low in reputation for power, they may also actively exercise independent and real power. On at least those issues which require government decision, government officers occupy potentially strategic positions. Studies of state legislators show that they vary considerably in their role orientations toward their jobs and toward other participants in the legislative process, and that these variations are linked systematically with their behavior as public officials.[67] City officials, both elected and appointed, might also be expected to vary in these respects.[68] One would expect, then, a positive relationship between activist role perceptions of public officials and the legitimacy, visibility, and definite scope of decision making.

Another institutional factor affecting community power is the party system. The boss of a cohesive political party who is also mayor has considerable independent power, though he, of course, does not lack external constraints on his behavior.[69] Rossi has suggested that professionalization of political roles and electoral competition in a diverse electorate lead to an independence of government actors from economic influence.[70]

The locale and procedures of decision making may have an important impact on leadership patterns. Some issues are public and are resolved only through a referendum. The referendum is potentially the least capable of control by a small covert elite. To have power, the leaders must be able to control both voter turnout and their voting.[71] Power is not subjected to this test if the issue is resolvable through private means, such as fund raising for an auditorium or hospital.[72] Decisions resolvable through formal positions occupy an intermediate category. The holders of formal positions may actually exercise power, or they may be open to degrees of influence from either covert elites or segments of the public.

The institutional structure of the community includes but one set of variables that may influence the nature of a community's leadership structure. Eighty-eight different community variables, ranging from population density to socioeconomic status, have been factor analyzed by Jonassen and Peres.[73] Seven factors were identified that accounted for most of the variation: urbanism (population size, density, and heterogeneity), welfare (health, wealth, employment, and education), influx (population growth), poverty (low income, dependent population), magnicomplexity (social, economic, and governmental complexity), educational effort, and proletarianism (propertyless, relatively poor, low-skilled and poorly paid workers). Bonjean examined four communities to see if any of these community factors were associated with any of the leadership structure characteristics discussed above.[74] It was found that those characteristics most closely associated with the Covert Power Elite type of structure were population influx (for example, the greater the influx, the less visible the leadership structure), poverty (for example, the greater the community poverty, the less visible the leadership structure), and magnicomplexity (for example, the less complex the community, the less visible the leadership structure). Although the same factors per se were not used, Presthus studied similar relationships in two communities. His conclusions show a relationship between magnicomplexity and the presence of a Covert Power Elite (in the same direction as was found in the investigation cited above),[75] a relationship between poverty and Covert Power Elite characteristics (also consistent with the findings set forth above),[76] and a negative relationship between urbanism and Covert Power Elite characteristics.[77]

Consequences

Even fewer studies have been concerned with consequences of leadership structure characteristics than with antecedents. Sociologists' interest here seems to be relating leadership structure characteristics to the effectiveness, efficiency, or quality of community projects, organizations, or institutions. Belknap and Steinle, for example, studied relationships between hospital systems and community leadership in two communities and found that the quality of hospital facilities, services, and so forth was higher in the community where the hospital board-members were also community leaders.[78] Hunter, of course, was concerned with the same types of relationships, noting for example, that community agencies were extremely careful not to incur the displeasure of top leaders and thereby be excluded from their interest and beneficence.[79] The same general type of relationship was studied by Dakin who was concerned with the relationship between variations in leadership structure and differences in the effectiveness with which four areas were organized for action on some area problem.[80] He also found that group struc-

ture and legitimacy were positively related to effective organization.[81]

The major consequence studied by political scientists is the "public interest." Interest group studies, and now community power-structure studies, cause political scientists to ask if a given distribution of power is in the public interest. While most investigators in this field distrust a monolithic power structure, especially if it is composed of economic rather than political actors, political scientists are generally content to raise the issue of the public interest without pronouncing a definitive answer.[82]

Conclusions

Basic changes have taken place in the study of community leadership over the past decade. The changes seem to indicate that there have been perhaps more continuity and direction in this area of investigation than would appear to be the case at first glance. Briefly, the basic trends have been: (1) a shift in preference and use from the positional to the reputational to the decisional method, and finally to a combination of methods for the identification of leaders; (2) growing consensus in regard to the variability of leadership structure over time and place, and thus more concern with the salient dimensions along which the variation takes place—legitimacy, visibility, scope of influence, and cohesiveness; and finally, (3) less concern with descriptive case studies and greater interest in comparative analyses of explanatory utility—that is, more concern with those factors that may be related to variations in leadership structure.

Notes

1. The authors gratefully acknowledge the valuable suggestions made by S. Dale McLemore and Ivan Belknap who read an earlier draft of this paper.
2. See, for example, Robert S. Lynd and Helen Merrell Lynd, *Middletown in Transition* (New York, 1937); W. Lloyd Warner, *et al.*, *Democracy in Jonesville* (New York, 1949); August B. Hollingshead, *Elmtown's Youth* (New York, 1949); Christopher Smith, Social Selection in Community Leadership, *Social*

Forces, 15 (1937), 530–535; and James E. White, Theory and Method for Research in Community Leadership, *American Sociological Review*, 15 (1950), 50–60. Investigations incorporating this assumption at the national level may be found in Wendell Bell, Richard J. Hill, and Charles R. Wright, *Public Leadership* (San Francisco, 1961), pp. 6–13.
3. George S. Counts, *School and Society in Chicago* (New York, 1928).

4. Floyd Hunter, *Community Power Structure* (Chapel Hill, N.C., 1953), p. 82.

5. The studies have been too numerous to cite here in a single footnote. Most of those published in monograph or book form or reported in the major journals will be cited in footnotes below.

6. For example, Robert A. Dahl, A Critique of the Ruling Elite Model, *American Political Science Review*, 52 (1958), 463–469; Herbert Kaufman and Victor Jones, The Mystery of Power, *Public Administration Review*, 14 (1954), 205–212; Nelson Polsby, The Sociology of Community Power: A Reassessment, *Social Forces*, 37 (1959), 232–236; Raymond E. Wolfinger, Reputation and Reality in the Study of Community Power, *American Sociological Review*, 25 (1960), 636–644; Peter H. Rossi, Community Decision Making, *Administrative Science Quarterly*, 1 (1957), 415–443; Nelson Polsby, *Community Power and Political Theory* (New Haven, 1963); Lawrence J. R. Herson, In the Footsteps of Community Power, *American Political Science Review*, 55 (1961), 817–830; Peter Bachrach and Morton S. Baratz, Two Faces of Power, *American Political Science Review*, 56 (1962), 947–952; Peter Bachrach and Morton S. Baratz, Decisions and Nondecisions: An Analytical Framework, *American Political Science Review*, 57 (1963), 632–642; Thomas J. Anton, Power, Pluralism, and Local Politics, *Administrative Science Quarterly*, 7 (1963), 425–457; and Morris Janowitz, Community Power and "Policy Science" Research, *Public Opinion Quarterly*, 26 (1962), 398–410.

7. Bell, Hill, and Wright, *op. cit.*, pp. 21–23, look at the "social participation approach" as a method distinct from the positional approach. Since, in most cases, participation involves occupying positions such as those described above (as well as less important positions such as "member" in an association or organization), the social participation approach is regarded here as simply a variation of the positional approach.

8. White, *op. cit.*, 54.

9. Studies that have used this technique exclusively or in combination with other techniques include those listed in n. 2 above as well as Robert O. Schulze and Leonard U. Blumberg, The Determination of Local Power Elites, *American Journal of Sociology*, 63 (1957), 290–296; Charles Freeman and Selz C. Mayo, Decision Makers in Rural Community Action, *Social Forces*, 35 (1957), 319–322; Robert O. Schulze, The Role of Economic Dominants in Community Power Structure, *American Sociological Review*, 23 (1958), 3–9; and M. Kent Jennings, Public Administrators and Community Decision

Making, *Administrative Science Quarterly*, 8 (1963), 18–43.

10. Wallace S. Sayre and Herbert Kaufman, *Governing New York City* (New York, 1960).

11. Gladys M. Kammerer, Charles D. Farris, John M. DeGrove, and Alfred B. Clubok, *The Urban Political Community* (Boston, 1963).

12. Charles R. Adrian, A Study of Three Communities, *Public Administration Review*, 18 (1958), 208–213.

13. White, *op. cit.*

14. Studies lending at least some support to this hypothesis include White, *op. cit.*; Freeman and Mayo, *op. cit.*; Robert A. Dahl, *Who Governs?* (New Haven, 1961); Richard Laskin, *Leadership of Voluntary Organizations in a Saskatchewan Town* (Saskatoon, Saskatchewan, 1962); M. Elaine Burgess, *Negro Leadership in a Southern City* (Chapel Hill, N.C., 1960); Arthur J. Vidich and Joseph Bensman, *Small Town in Mass Society* (Garden City, N.Y., 1958); and Benjamin Walter, Political Decision Making in Arcadia, in F. Stuart Chapin, Jr., and Shirley F. Weiss, eds., *Urban Growth Dynamics* (New York, 1962), pp. 141–187. Data clearly contradicting this hypothesis may be found in Hunter, *op. cit.*; Schulze and Blumberg, *op. cit.*; Schulze, *op. cit.*; Robert Presthus, *Men at the Top: A Study in Community Power* (New York, 1964); and Charles M. Bonjean, Community Leadership: A Case Study and Conceptual Refinement, *American Journal of Sociology*, 68 (1963), 672–681.

15. Richard Laskin and Serena Phillett, Formal Versus Reputational Leadership (paper read at the annual meeting of the Pacific Sociological Association, Portland, Ore., April, 1963).

16. Richard Laskin and Serena Phillett, Formal Versus Reputational Leadership Identification: A Re-evaluation (paper read at the annual meeting of the Pacific Sociological Association, San Diego, Cal., March, 1964).

17. Charles M. Bonjean, "Community Leadership: A Conceptual Refinement and Comparative Analysis" (unpublished Ph.D. dissertation, University of North Carolina, 1963).

18. See, for example, August B. Hollingshead, *op. cit.*, and W. Lloyd Warner, *et al.*, *op. cit.*

19. Among those investigations that have used the reputational approach exclusively or in combination with another approach are Hunter, *op. cit.*; Schulze and Blumberg, *op. cit.*; Jennings, *op. cit.*; Laskin, *op. cit.*; Burgess, *op. cit.*; Presthus, *op. cit.*; Bonjean, *op. cit.*; Ernest A. T. Barth and Baha Abu-Laban, Power Structure and the Negro Sub-Community, *American Sociological Review*, 24 (1959), 69–76; William H. Form and

William V. D'Antonio, Integration and Cleavage Among Community Influentials in Two Border Cities, *American Sociological Review*, 24 (1959), 804–814; William V. D'Antonio, William H. Form, Charles P. Loomis, and Eugene C. Erickson, Institutional and Occupational Representations in Eleven Community Influence Systems, *American Sociological Review*, 26 (1961), 440–446; A. Alexander Fanelli, A Typology of Community Leadership Based on Influence and Interaction Within the Leader Subsystem, *Social Forces*, 34 (1956), 332–338; Orrin E. Klapp and L. Vincent Padgett, Power Structure and Decision Making in a Mexican Border City, *American Journal of Sociology*, 65 (1960), 400–406; Delbert C. Miller, Industry and Community Power Structure: A Comparative Study of an American and an English City, *American Sociological Review*, 23 (1958), 9–15; Roland J. Pellegrin and Charles H. Coates, Absentee-Owned Corporations and Community Power Structures, *American Journal of Sociology*, 61 (1956), 413–419; Ivan Belknap and John G. Steinle, *The Community and Its Hospitals* (Syracuse, N.Y., 1963); Robert E. Agger and Daniel Goldrich, Community Power Structures and Partisanship, *American Sociological Review*, 23 (1958), 383–392; David A. Booth and Charles R. Adrian, Power Structures and Community Change, *Midwest Journal of Political Science*, 6 (1962), 277–296; Carol Thometz, *The Decision-Makers* (Dallas, Tex., 1963); George Belknap and Ralph Smuckler, Political Power Relations in a Mid-West City, *Public Opinion Quarterly*, 20 (1956), 73–80; and Harry Scoble, Leadership Hierarchies and Political Issues in a New England Town, in Morris Janowitz, ed., *Community Political Systems* (Glencoe, Ill., 1961), pp. 117–145. Contrary to a common assumption, a number of political scientists are represented in this group of researchers using the reputational approach.

20. William V. D'Antonio and Howard J. Ehrlich, eds., *Power and Democracy in America* (Notre Dame, Ind., 1961), pp. 92 ff. and pp. 132 ff. See also, Wolfinger, *op. cit.*, and Raymond E. Wolfinger, A Plea for a Decent Burial, *American Sociological Review*, 27 (1962), 841–847.

21. Howard J. Ehrlich, The Reputational Approach to the Study of Community Power, *American Sociological Review*, 26 (1961), 926. See also William V. D'Antonio, Howard J. Ehrlich, and Eugene C. Erickson, Further Notes on the Study of Community Power, *American Sociological Review*, 27 (1962), 848–854.

22. See, for example, Polsby, *Community Power and Political Theory;* Wolfinger, Reputation; Dahl, Critique; and Rossi, *op. cit.*

23. Rossi, *op. cit.*

24. See, for example, Presthus, *op. cit.*, p. 443 and p. 451. One typology that could be incorporated in reputational analyses has been set forth by Ernest A. T. Barth and Stuart D. Johnson, Community Power and a Typology of Social Issues, *Social Forces*, 38 (1959), 29–32.

25. See, for example, Presthus, *op. cit.*; Scoble, *op. cit.*; and Thometz, *op. cit.*

26. See, for example, Nelson W. Polsby, Three Problems in the Analysis of Community Power, *American Sociological Review*, 24 (1959), 796–803; Dahl, Critique; and Wolfinger, Reputation.

27. See, for example, Bonjean, *op. cit.*, and Robert O. Schulze, The Bifurcation of Power in a Satellite City, in Janowitz, ed., *Community Political Systems*, pp. 50–53.

28. See, in particular, Wolfinger, Reputation; Charles M. Bonjean, in Class, Status and Power Reputation, *Sociology and Social Research*, 49 (1964), 69–75, has also noted that some informants may confuse power with class and status characteristics.

29. Wolfinger, Reputation.

30. *Ibid.*

31. Hunter, *op. cit.*, and Miller, *op. cit.*

32. Booth and Adrian, *op. cit.*

33. Investigations that have used this approach include Dahl, *Who Governs?*; Warner Bloomberg, Jr. and Morris Sunshine, *Suburban Power Structures and Public Education* (Syracuse, N.Y., 1963); Burgess, *op. cit.*; Walter, *op. cit.*; Presthus, *op. cit.*; and Roscoe C. Martin, *et al.*, *Decisions in Syracuse* (Bloomington, Ind., 1961).

34. Burgess, *op. cit.*, pp. 5–6 and Appendix B.

35. Presthus, *op. cit.*, pp. 59–60 and p. 231.

36. Burgess, *op. cit.*, p. 6.

37. Dahl, *Who Governs?*, p. vi.

38. Barth and Johnson, *op. cit.*

39. Edward C. Banfield and James Q. Wilson, *City Politics* (Cambridge, Mass., 1963), pp. 248–250.

40. Bachrach and Baratz, Two Faces, and Decisions; and Anton, *op. cit.*, 453–455.

41. Dahl, *Who Governs?*, chs. i–vii; Schulze, The Bifurcation; and Booth and Adrian, *op. cit.*

42. For example, Burgess, *op. cit.*, used all three techniques; Belknap and Steinle, *op. cit.*, used both the positional and the reputational; Presthus, *op. cit.*, used all three; Bloomberg and Sunshine, *op. cit.*, used all three; and Delbert C. Miller, Town and Gown: The Power Structure of a University Town, *American Journal of Sociology*, 68 (1963), 432–443, used both the reputational and event analysis approaches.

43. Linton C. Freeman, Thomas J. Fararo, Warner Bloomberg, Jr., and Morris Sunshine, Locating Leaders in Local Communities: A Comparison of Some Alternative Approaches, *American Sociological Review*, 28 (1963), 791–798.

44. Hunter, *op. cit.*

45. Walter, *op. cit.*, 186.

46. See, for example, Hunter, *op. cit.*, especially chs. i and ix.

47. Especially Dahl, Critique; and Kaufman and Jones, *op. cit.*

48. For a more complete discussion of constructive typology and its role in social research see John T. Doby, ed., *An Introduction to Social Research* (Harrisburg, Pa., 1954), pp. 139–198.

49. Robert Redfield, The Folk Society, *American Journal of Sociology*, 52 (1947), 293–308.

50. Eugene Litwak, Models of Bureaucracy Which Permit Conflict, *American Journal of Sociology*, 67 (1961), 177–184.

51. Good starts in this direction have been made by William H. Form and Delbert C. Miller, *Industry, Labor and Community* (New York, 1960), pp. 538–543; by Dahl, *Who Governs?*, pp. 184–189; and by Roscoe Martin, *et al.*, *op. cit.*, pp. 10–12.

52. "Political formula" includes the system of beliefs and values which legitimize the democratic (or any other) system and specify the institutions (such as political parties, a free press, etc.) which allow for the distribution of power. See Seymour Martin Lipset, *Political Man* (New York, 1960), chs. ii and iii.

53. The types are suggested by Dahl, *Who Governs?*

54. Laskin and Phillett, *op. cit.*, have noted that it may be meaningful to chart formal leadership not only at the time of the study but also for several preceding years as well, because there may be a time lag of a few years between one's emergence as an organizational officer and his earning a general reputation for influence in the community.

55. For further elaboration see Bonjean, *op. cit.*, and Serena Phillett, An Analysis of Community Influence: Some Conceptual and Methodological Considerations (unpublished M.A. thesis, University of Alberta, Edmonton, Canada, 1963).

56. William V. D'Antonio and Eugene C. Erickson, The Reputational Technique as a Measure of Community Power: An Evaluation Based on Comparative and Longitudinal Studies, *American Sociological Review*, 27 (1962), 373–374.

57. See ns. 38 and 39.

58. For a discussion of the ratio of interest and other statistics of social configuration, see J. L. Moreno, ed., *The Sociometry Reader* (Glencoe, Ill., 1960), pp. 19–51.

59. Scoble, *op. cit.*

60. Schulze, The Bifurcation, p. 51.

61. See Rossi, *op. cit.*, 436–437, and Herbert Kaufman, The Next Step in Case Studies, *Public Administration Review*, 18 (1958), 52–59.

62. Miller, *op. cit.*, 13–15.

63. D'Antonio, *et al.*, Institutional and Occupational Representations, 442.

64. Schulze, The Bifurcation.

65. Donald A. Clelland and William H. Form, Economic Dominants and Community Power: A Comparative Analysis, *American Journal of Sociology*, 69 (1964), 511–521.

66. Presthus, *op. cit.*, pp. 423–424.

67. John Wahlke, Heinz Eulau, William Buchanan and LeRoy C. Ferguson, *The Legislative System* (New York, 1962).

68. Adrian, *op. cit.*; Gladys M. Kammerer and J. M. DeGrove, Urban Leadership During Change, *The Annals*, 353 (1964), 95–106; Gladys M. Kammerer, Role Diversity of City Managers, *Administrative Science Quarterly*, 8 (1964), 421–442; Karl A. Bosworth, The Manager *Is* a Politician, *Public Administration Review*, 18 (1958), 216–222; and Jennings, *op. cit.*

69. Edward C. Banfield, *Political Influence* (Glencoe, Ill., 1961).

70. Rossi, *op. cit.*

71. James S. Coleman, *Community Conflict* (Glencoe, Ill., 1957), found that voter turnout and referendum defeats were positively correlated (p. 19).

72. Scoble, *op. cit.*, pp. 136–138.

73. Christen T. Jonassen and Sherwood H. Peres, *Inter-relationships of Dimensions of Community Systems: A Factor Analysis of Eighty-two Variables* (Columbus, Ohio, 1960).

74. Charles M. Bonjean, Legitimacy and Visibility: Influence Structure Characteristics Related to Four Community Systems (paper read at the annual meeting of the Society for the Study of Social Problems, Montreal, Canada, August, 1964).

75. Presthus, *op. cit.*, p. 413.

76. *Ibid.*, pp. 413–414.

77. *Ibid.*, p. 415.

78. Belknap and Steinle, *op. cit.*, ch. viii.

79. Hunter, *op. cit.*, p. 198.

80. Ralph E. Dakin, Variations in Power Structures and Organizing Efficiency: A Comparative Study of Four Areas, *Sociological Quarterly*, 3 (1962), 228–250.

81. Dakin's measure of organizing efficiency was based on the amount of time it takes to organize a given number of people.

82. Banfield, *op. cit.*, ch. xii, and Roscoe Martin, *et al.*, *op. cit.*, ch. xiv.

A. The Positional Approach

The Determination of Local Power Elites[1]

Robert O. Schulze and Leonard U. Blumberg

We have witnessed lately a significant re-awakening of interest in American sociologists and political scientists in the study of community power structures and decision-making. Although an earlier impetus was provided by the work of the Lynds[2] and Mills,[3] the fund of relevant research remained meager until the publication of Hunter's study of Regional City in 1953.[4] Since that date a growing number of empirical studies have appeared.[5] In fact, sufficient research has now been completed to warrant some initial stocktaking—as evidenced by the recent appearance of Peter Rossi's suggestive summing-up and critique of the relevant literature.[6] Utilizing findings from two recent studies of a midwestern community,[7] we propose, in this paper, to take a further second look at two of the central methodological problems which confront students of community power: the techniques for determining community power elites and some consequences of different operations in doing so.

Most students concerned with the structure and dynamics of community decision-making have initially assumed that a theoretically fruitful and empirically tenable distinction can be made between the most powerful persons and units in a community and those having lesser degrees of power. To make this assumption is not to deny that power relations in the modern urban community are "unneat," nor is it to argue that community power can necessarily be con-ceived in the form of either a single or a simple pyramid; neither is it inconsistent with Simmel's long-recognized thesis that dominance is always a two-way street. One can acknowledge that all persons and units in the community exercise certain measures of influence and control without rejecting the proposition that some can mobilize such considerable resources—organizational, economic, psychological—that they have relatively most power over crucial community decisions and actions. Even C. Wright Mills, who in 1951 asserted that in contemporary America the "engineering of consent to authority has moved into the realm of manipulation where the powerful are anonymous,"[8] has since been moved to write a detailed and stimulating volume which suggests that the powerful may not, in fact, have become so very anonymous and that power relations may not have grown so nebulous, ill-defined, mercurial, and diffuse that they cannot be charted at all.[9] So we begin by assuming that communities and societies contain power elites which are somehow delineable.

The next and crucial question is this: How do we proceed to determine "the most powerful and influential" in American communities?[10] In general, sociologists and political scientists have employed one or the other of two techniques: one based on position and the other on reputation.

The method based on position involves selecting certain persons as most powerful

Reprinted from The American Journal of Sociology, *63* (*November 1957*), *290–296, by permission of the authors and The University of Chicago Press. Copyright 1958 by The University of Chicago.*

and influential on the basis of their official status in the community's institutionalized economic, political, and/or civic structures. Thus both Lynd and Mills—following Marx—have contended that crucial power decisions are the province of individuals holding the top positions in the major industrial, credit, and business units in the community. And although Stouffer utilized top political and civic (rather than economic) status, he likewise employed this in identifying community elites.[11]

A more prevalent technique has been to allow certain members of the community under study to do the determining. Based on local reputation and derived from theoretical formulations of Weber and Lasswell, with a debt to Warner, this method has been used most notably by Hunter[12] and Angell.[13] However, most students who have relied on local nominations have made use of a technique based on position as an intervening step. Thus the persons whose perceptions of community influence were utilized by both Hunter and Angell did not consist of randomly selected cross-sections of the local populations; they were, rather, individuals presumed to be knowledgeable because of their formal local social positions.

In this paper we ask the following questions:

1. To what extent do the methods based on reputation and on position yield similar or compatible answers to the question Who are the most powerful and influential in the community?

2. Considering only the approach based on reputation, what is the effect of using different panels of presumably knowledgeable persons?

The subject community—which we shall call Cibola— is a midwestern industrial city of some 20,000 inhabitants, located approximately 30 miles from one of the largest metropolitan centers in the United States. Over the past several decades and especially since World War II, Cibola has become increasingly involved in the industrial and social complex of this giant neighbor, Metro City.[14]

In attempting to determine Cibola's power elite(s), we used both techniques. With regard to that centered on reputation, we initially designated as our "nominating panel" the formal heads of the local (white) voluntary associations.[15] They were selected on the assumption that they were most representative of the broad, "grass-roots" base of local organized power. Each was asked five questions.[16] Although a total of 271 persons was named by at least one association head in response to at least one of the "perception of influence" questions, the 18 persons most frequently named accounted for the majority of all nominations. Accordingly, these 18 persons were designated as the public leaders of Cibola.

How did the composition of the public leadership category, as thus defined by reputation, compare with that of community elites determined on the basis of their positions in the economic or the political and civic organizations in Cibola?

Persons occupying the top formal status in the major local industrial and credit units were designated as the "economic dominants." They included the heads of all industries employing 75 or more workers, the heads of all banks with total assets in excess of one million dollars, and, in addition, persons who were members of the boards of directors of two or more of these industries and/or banks and who thus served in the formal "interlocking" of the dominant economic units. By this definition, a total of 17 persons was named as the economic dominants of Cibola.

There was almost no overlap between the public leaders and the economic dominants; specifically, the 17 economic dominants included but 2 of the 18 public leaders in the community.

A second method of employing criteria of position involves selecting persons filling the top political and civic status in the community. In his study, Stouffer selected as civic leaders fourteen objectively defined public statuses: mayor, president of the chamber of commerce, chairman of the Community Chest, president of the largest labor union, county chairman of the Republican and Democratic parties, commander of the largest American Legion post, regent of the DAR, president of the women's club, chairmen of the library and the school boards, the parent-teachers' association, the bar association, and the publisher of the largest locally owned newspaper. Applying this definition of civic leaders in Cibola, *only 4* of the 18 public leaders were found to occupy any of the fourteen top civic statuses in Stouffer's list. Various other objective criteria for selecting the political-civic elite of Cibola were considered (e.g., selecting the members of the city council and the school board and the top lay officers in the largest churches and in the businessmen's luncheon clubs), and the

results were compared with the leaders as defined on the basis of reputation. In no instance did the persons categorized as top political-civic leaders by any of these definitions include more than 4 of the 18 public leaders.

We may say, therefore, that the heads of voluntary associations definitely make a distinction between those persons who occupied the top formal political and civic offices and those who, in their opinion, wielded the most influence and exerted the greatest public leadership in the community.[17] The fact that the association heads selected so few of the nominal leaders of Cibola as the "real" influential public leaders attests to a

TABLE 1. *Rank Orders of Public Leaders as Perceived by Association Heads, Public Leaders, and Economic Dominants*

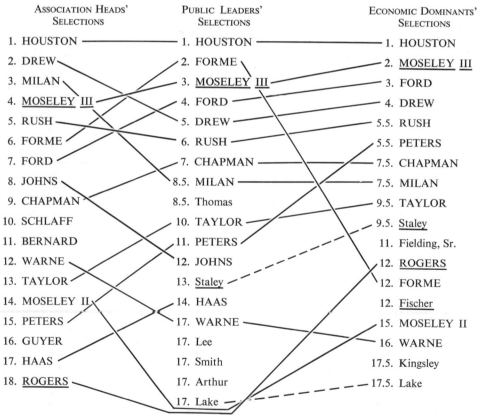

ASSOCIATION HEADS' SELECTIONS	PUBLIC LEADERS' SELECTIONS	ECONOMIC DOMINANTS' SELECTIONS
1. HOUSTON	1. HOUSTON	1. HOUSTON
2. DREW	2. FORME	2. MOSELEY III
3. MILAN	3. MOSELEY III	3. FORD
4. MOSELEY III	4. FORD	4. DREW
5. RUSH	5. DREW	5.5. RUSH
6. FORME	6. RUSH	5.5. PETERS
7. FORD	7. CHAPMAN	7.5. CHAPMAN
8. JOHNS	8.5. MILAN	7.5. MILAN
9. CHAPMAN	8.5. Thomas	9.5. TAYLOR
10. SCHLAFF	10. TAYLOR	9.5. Staley
11. BERNARD	11. PETERS	11. Fielding, Sr.
12. WARNE	12. JOHNS	12. ROGERS
13. TAYLOR	13. Staley	12. FORME
14. MOSELEY II	14. HAAS	12. Fischer
15. PETERS	17. WARNE	15. MOSELEY II
16. GUYER	17. Lee	16. WARNE
17. HAAS	17. Smith	17.5. Kingsley
18. ROGERS	17. Arthur	17.5. Lake
	17. Lake	

*These rank orderings are based on total frequency of "nominations" by the 143 association heads, the 18 public leaders, and the 17 economic dominants, respectively, in answer to the five "perception of influence" questions. Those defined as public leaders (the top 18 in the association heads' list) are indicated in CAPITALS; those defined as economic dominants are *underlined*. The public leaders' positions in the rank orders are connected by solid lines; the positions of others are connected by broken lines.

considerable degree of sophistication on their part.

On the other hand, that the heads of voluntary associations perceived so few of Cibola's economic dominants as community influentials may be due to the considerable social distance which perhaps separated most of them from the "real" centers of local power and influence. Our research design made it possible to test this possibility, for we asked the public leaders and the economic dominants the same "perception of influence" questions which we had previously addressed to the heads of associations and on the basis of which we had made our initial designation of public leaders. The over-all selections of the three panels— the heads of voluntary associations, the public leaders, and the economic dominants —are compared in Table 1.

While it is apparent that a nice similarity in rank orders did not obtain, Table 1 nonetheless reveals a high degree of consensus among all three categories interviewed as to the over-all composition of the local elite of power and influence. Thus the public leaders themselves specified 72 per cent (13 out of 18) of those defined as public leaders on the basis of nomination by the heads of associations. Likewise, the top group in influence as perceived by the economic dominants included 72 per cent of the men already categorized as public leaders. Only 3 of the 18 classified as public leaders failed to be included in the group selected by either the economic dominants or the public leaders.

Even more significant was the degree of agreement among the three panels with regard to the uppermost range of community power: of the 10 persons most frequently considered influential by the public leaders, 9 had, in fact, been operationally defined as public leaders; likewise, of the 10 most frequently regarded as influential by the economic dominants, 9 had been categorized as public leaders. Furthermore, 7 persons (Houston, Drew, Milan, Moseley III, Rush, Ford, and Chapman) are included among the top 9 in all three lists. And, finally, it is apparent that none of the panels discerned

those of dominant economic status as an appreciable segment of public leadership. Like the heads of associations, the public leaders themselves included but two economic dominants in the top group, while the economic dominants themselves regarded an only somewhat greater number of their fellow dominants as among Cibola's most influential—4 out of the top 18, or 22 per cent.[18]

These data show that, despite the fact that the heads of voluntary associations, the public leaders, and the economic dominants occupied different positions and played dissimilar roles in the local social structure, each category perceived substantially the same set of persons as most influential in the affairs of the community.

A question remains: If Cibola's most influential by reputation—its public leaders— were neither the community's economic dominants nor the current occupants of either its top political or civic offices, where did they fit into the local social structure? All were white males. Their median age was fifty-three; their median number of years' residence in Cibola was thirty.[19] In occupation they represented only the business and professional classes in the city, albeit a fairly wide range of positions within these broad categories.[20] In general, it may be said that the public leaders were drawn almost wholly from the old middle-class segment. Only one, to be sure, was an official in any of the "big-business" firms. (And he resigned and opened an insurance office in partnership with a local politician during the course of our research.)

It cannot be assumed, however, that the public leaders constituted a representative cross-section of Cibola's small-business and professional men. They were, rather, persons intimately involved in the community's voluntary associations who, in earlier years, had occupied responsible positions in local civic and political units. For example, the median number of memberships currently held by the public leaders in voluntary associations was 9 (compared with a median of 3 for the economic dominants); each public leader was a member of at least one of the three most prominent civic luncheon clubs (Rotary, Kiwanis, Lions), and 14 were members of the Chamber of Commerce. Furthermore, 89 per cent of the public leaders (16 out of 18) had, at one time, served as president of at least one local voluntary association, and 61 per cent (11 out of 18) as president of at least one of the five associations regarded by all three basic categories of power figures—the association heads, the economic dominants, and the public leaders themselves—as most influential in the community. Finally, while not more than one of the public leaders could have been regarded as a professional politician,[21] fully 89 per cent (all but 2) had occupied elective or appointive office in at least one of the local units of government: For example, 3 had served as mayor, 6 as city councilmen, 3 as school-board members, and 9 as appointive members of one or more of the several municipal boards and commissions.

We find, therefore, that, while a considerable majority of the local public leaders were businessmen, they were not the top businessmen, the economic dominants. Likewise, while almost all had held responsible civic and political positions in Cibola, they were not, with minor exceptions, among the community's formal civic and political leaders at the time of our study. Considering what we know about the power structures of other middle-sized American communities, it seems apparent that Cibola's public leaders were of the age, sex, race, length of residence, business and civic experience, and connections appropriate to community influence and leadership. And it became abundantly apparent, subsequently, that the public leaders did in fact constitute a closely knit friendship group which exercised substantial—if not always decisive—control over the community's decisions. Yet this important category of elites could not have been revealed had we relied solely on one of the usual methods based on position.

The two questions raised earlier in this paper may now be answered as follows:

The composition of the community's power elite, as defined by reputation, differs significantly from that defined on the basis of superordinate positions in *either* the local economic *or* the political-civic institutions.

However, the use of different panels of persons who may be assumed to be reasonably (although not similarly) knowledgeable does not produce significantly different results.

Generalizations based on the study of but a single community, as this is, are obviously provisional. Nevertheless, they strongly suggest the advisability of studying a community's power structures from at least two methodological perspectives—that based on position and that on reputation. It is not a question of whether one or the other is "right." Rather, by using both and by determining the nature and degree of similarity between the two resulting lists, valuable leads are found as to the structure and dynamics of local power. In Cibola, for example, the marked disparity between the categories of public leader and of economic dominant suggested—and further research confirmed[22]—a widespread and growing reluctance on the part of the economic dominants to become involved in the initiation and determination of local political decisions. And this, in turn, raised the larger question of the changing role of major economic units—especially absentee-owned corporations—in the local power structures of American communities.

Notes

1. Revision of a paper read at the annual meeting of the Eastern Sociological Society, April, 1956, in New York City. We wish to thank Morris Janowitz for helpful comments.
2. Robert S. Lynd and Helen M. Lynd, *Middletown in Transition* (New York: Harcourt, Brace & Co., 1937), esp. chap. iii.
3. C. Wright Mills, "The Middle Classes in Middle-sized Cities," *American Sociological Review*, 11 (October, 1946), 520–29.
4. Floyd Hunter, *Community Power Structure* (Chapel Hill: University of North Carolina Press, 1953). For a provocative review of Hunter's research by two unconvinced poli-

tical scientists see Herbert Kaufman and Victor Jones, "The Mystery of Power," *Public Administration Review*, 14 (Summer, 1954), 205–12.

5. See, e.g., Robert E. Agger, "Power Attributions in the Local Community," *Social Forces*, 34 (May, 1956), 322–31; Robert E. Agger and Vincent Ostrom, "The Political Structure of a Small Community," *Public Opinion Quarterly*, 20 (Spring, 1956), 81–89; George Belknap and Ralph Smuckler, "Political Power Relations in a Mid-west City," *Public Opinion Quarterly*, 20 (Spring, 1956), 73–81; A. Alexander Fanelli, "A Typology of Community Leadership Based on Influence within the Leader Subsystem," *Social Forces*, 34 (May, 1956), 332–38; John L. Haer, "Social Stratification in Relation to Attitude toward Sources of Power in a Community," *Social Forces*, 35 (December, 1956), 137–42; Martin Meyerson and Edward C. Banfield, *Politics, Planning, and the Public Interest* (Glencoe: Free Press, 1955); V. J. Parenton and Roland J. Pellegrin, "Social Structure and the Leadership Factor in a Negro Community," *Phylon*, 17 (1956), 74–78; Roland J. Pellegrin and Charles H. Coates, "Absentee-Owned Corporations and Community Power Structure," *American Journal of Sociology*, 61 (March, 1956), 413–19; Peter H. Rossi, "Historical Trends in the Politics of an Industrial Community," paper presented at the annual meeting of the American Sociological Society, September, 1956; Roland L. Warren, "Toward a Typology of Extracommunity Controls Limiting Local Community Autonomy," *Social Forces* 34 (May, 1956), 338–41.

6. Peter H. Rossi, "Community Decision-making," *Administrative Science Quarterly*, 1 (March, 1957), 415–43.

7. Leonard U. Blumberg, "Community Leaders: The Social Bases and Social-psychological Concomitants of Community Power" (microfilmed Ph.D. dissertation, University of Michigan, 1955); Robert O. Schulze, "Economic Dominance and Public Leadership: A Study of the Structure and Process of Power in an Urban Community" (microfilmed Ph.D. dissertation, University of Michigan, 1956).

8. C. Wright Mills, *White Collar* (New York: Oxford University Press, 1951), p. 110.

9. C. Wright Mills, *The Power Elite* (New York: Oxford University Press, 1956), esp. chaps. ii and iii.

10. There are certain possibly significant conceptual differences between the terms "power" and "influence," which, however, have been of much greater concern to theoreticians than to those doing actual field research. For present purposes, therefore,

we shall use the concepts as roughly synonymous (cf. Agger, *op. cit.*, p. 323).

11. Samuel A. Stouffer, *Communism, Conformity, and Civil Liberties* (Garden City: Doubleday, 1955).

12. Hunter, *op. cit.*

13. Robert Cooley Angell, "The Moral Integration of American Cities," *American Journal of Sociology*, 61 (July, 1951), Part 2.

14. Cibola is not encompassed, however, within the Standard Metropolitan Area of Metro City.

15. Eighty per cent of the heads of the 180 voluntary associations in the community were interviewed. None of the association heads whom we were unable to locate and interview was perceived as influential by any of the 143 interviewed, nor were their organizations regarded as influential.

16. These questions were:

1. "Suppose a major project were before the community, one that required decision by a group of leaders whom nearly everyone would accept. Which people would you choose to make up this group—regardless of whether or not you know them personally?"

2. "In most cities certain persons are said to be influential 'behind the scenes' and to have a lot to say about programs that are planned, projects, and issues that come up around town. What persons in [Cibola] are influential in this way?"

3. "If a decision were to be made in [the state capital] that affected [Cibola], who would be the best contact man to get in touch with state officials [besides local members of the legislature]?"

4. "Who [besides local members of Congress] would be the best people to get in touch with federal officials in [Metro City], Chicago, or Washington?"

5. "Are there any other people whom these leaders work with and who have not been named so far, but who should be included in a list of community leaders?" Since our object was to delineate a *general* category of community leadership, the individual responses to the five questions were combined in the final tabulation.

Previously, the association heads' responses had been totaled separately. It was found that all but 1 of the 18 persons subsequently defined as public leaders ranked among the top 19 in *both* the "major-project" and the "behind-the-scenes" questions. It was further noted that eliminating nominations in response to the remaining three questions changed somewhat the total scores and the rank order of the 18 most frequently named persons but had almost no effect on the over-all composition of the top 18.

17. Cf. F. A. Stewart, "A Sociometric Study of Influence in Southtown," *Sociometry*, 10 (1947), 11–31, 273–86. Although his research design was somewhat dissimilar, Stewart's findings were consonant with those reported here.
18. Of the few economic dominants regarded as top influentials by *any* of the three panels, *none* represented the five largest industries (all absentee-owned) or the two largest banks in the community.
19. Although they tended, thus, to be middle-aged men of fairly lengthy local residence, only 28 per cent of the public leaders (5 out of 18) were native-born Cibolans.
20. Specifically, they included 3 industrial executives (only 1 of whom, however, occupied a superordinate position in his firm and could therefore be called an economic dominant); 2 merchants (one of whom, also on the boards of directors of two local banks, was the second and final economic dominant

in the public leader ranks); 2 educators; 2 professional Chamber of Commerce officials; 1 (subordinate) bank official; 1 wholesaler; 1 realtor-insurance broker; 1 salesman; 1 attorney; 1 clergyman; and 1 retired person (formerly the owner of one of the relatively small, locally owned manufacturing plants).
21. One individual, although he had lately served as chairman of the state central committee of the Republican party and as an elective state official, indicated that his position as owner-president of a small local business college was his usual occupation and the one from which he derived most of his income. Occupationally, therefore, he was listed in n. 20 as an educator.
22. Robert O. Schulze, "The Role of Economic Dominants in the Community Power Structure," a paper read at the 1957. annual meeting of the American Sociological Society in Washington, D.C.

Shadow and Substance:
The Social and Economic Notables

Robert A. Dahl

The political leaders who practiced ethnic politics have by no means shuffled off the New Haven stage, but the newer problems of city life are likely to push them gradually into the wings. Meanwhile, what of the present-day patricians and entrepreneurs?

So far most of our evidence for changes in the characteristics of leadership in New Haven over the past century and a half has been drawn from information about *elected public* officials. It is altogether possible, however, that public officials do not represent the *real* decision-makers in a community; they may only be the spokesmen for influential leaders who may not hold

public office at all. It seems implausible in the extreme to suppose that covert leaders sat in obscurity behind the patricians, for in view of the social and economic structure of the time it is hard to imagine where the covert leaders might have come from, if not from among the patricians themselves—and evidently the patricians had neither the need nor the wish to rule covertly. Although a case might be made that the entrepreneurs had more liking for the prestige of leading elective offices than they had influence on the governmental decisions of the day, there seems to be no reason to suppose that the leading manufacturers of New Haven were

Reprinted from Who Governs? Democracy and Power in an American City *by Robert A. Dahl, Chapter 6, pp. 63–71, by permission of the author and Yale University Press. Copyright 1961 by Yale University Press.*

acting as front men for some other covert group in the community. But the suspicion that more recent politicians, who seem to lack some of the most important resources of the patricians and the entrepreneurs, may be political handmaidens of the well-to-do and the elect of New Haven is surely not ill-founded.

Two groups, the Social Notables and the Economic Notables, invite investigation, and in this chapter I shall try to describe the extent and limits of their influence on local governmental decisions.

The Social Notables

In the days of the patricians, when birth, wealth, education, and office were joined, it was a simple matter to determine a person's social standing. As these resources have separated from one another in recent years, it has become far from simple.

However, one symbol—perhaps the best —of membership in upper-class New Haven society today is an invitation to the annual Assemblies held in the New Haven Lawn Club. There are more exclusive criteria, and those who meet tighter criteria might look upon the Assemblies as a trifle undiscriminating. But the Assemblies are the closest approximation modern New Haven has to a list of families of highest social standing.

The Assemblies exist to provide that attenuated version of primitive puberty rites, the social debuts of the daughters of the elect. About 150 families from the greater New Haven area are invited. I shall take two recent years, 1958 and 1959, and arbitrarily select an earlier, 1951, so that members of a somewhat older but still active generation of Social Notables will be included. The continuity over the years is naturally very great; altogether 231 different families were invited to the Assemblies during these three years.

How influential are these Social Notables in public affairs? Do the Notables hold public offices bearing directly on public decisions? Whether or not they hold public offices, are they influential overtly or covertly in the making of government decisions? If they are influential, to what extent is their influence attributable to their social position?

To answer these questions, I have chosen to examine three different "issue-areas" in which important public decisions are made: nominations by the two political parties, urban redevelopment, and public education. Nominations determine which persons will hold public office. The New Haven redevelopment program measured by its cost— present and potential—is the largest in the country. Public education, aside from its intrinsic importance, is the costliest item in the city's budget. It is reasonable to expect, therefore, that the relative influence over public officials wielded by the Social Notables would be revealed by an examination of their participation in these three areas of activity.

What do we find? First, quite unlike the patricians a century and a half ago, very few Social Notables participate overtly in public affairs. Out of nearly 500 elective and party offices in New Haven, in 1957–58 the Notables held only two—both minor positions in the Republican party. Out of 131 higher offices in public education (including members of the Board of Education, superintendent, assistant superintendents, principals, and PTA heads) the Notables held only two. They appeared in larger numbers however, in urban redevelopment. Out of 435 persons who were members of the Redevelopment Agency in executive or policy positions or were on the Citizens Action Commission or any of its numerous committees, some 24 notables appeared. (Table 1) Yet even in urban redevelopment an inspection of the names of the Social Notables indicates that with few exceptions their membership was more a result of occupation or economic position than of social standing.

Thus in the two political parties and in public education, the *proportion* of higher offices held by Social Notables was infinitesimal. To be sure, it was considerably larger in urban redevelopment, but even there the Social Notables held less than 6 per cent of the offices in 1957 and 1958. It might be argued, of course, that the number of Social Notables in office was *relatively* large, since

TABLE 1. *Number of selected public offices held by Social Notables, 1957–1958*

	POLITICAL PARTIES* N	PUBLIC EDUCATION N	URBAN REDEVELOP- MENT N	DUPLICA- TIONS† N	TOTAL, LESS DUPLICATIONS N
Social Notables	2	2	24	1	27
Others	495	129	411	38	997
Total	497	131	435	39	1024

*Includes major local elective offices and all party offices in the Democratic and Republican parties.
†I.e., persons in more than one column.

TABLE 2. *Percentage of selected offices held by Social Notables, 1957–1958*

	(1) ACTUAL %	(2) EXPECTED* %	RATIO (1) ÷ (2)
Political parties	0.4	0.2	2.0
Public education	1.5	0.2	7.5
Urban redevelopment	5.5	0.2	27.5
Percentage in three combined, less duplications	2.7	0.2	13.5

*Expected: percentage of Social Notables in total New Haven population 21 years or over.

they were, after all, a very tiny group. If one followed the practices of ancient Athens and filled these offices by random selection, an even smaller proportion of the offices would be held by Social Notables. Indeed, in the case of urban redevelopment, they held about twenty-seven times more positions than one would expect on a purely chance basis. (Table 2)

Looking at the matter in another way, however, the proportion of Social Notables holding office was very small. Even in urban redevelopment, only one out of ten held office in 1957–58; less than one out of a hundred held office in the political parties and in public education. (Table 3) Probably not more than two out of ten Social Notables held any public office of any kind—local, state, or national.

One could, no doubt, magnify these tiny proportions into great significance by assuming that the few Social Notables in public life are of extraordinary influence. Alas for such a hypothesis; the evidence to the contrary is devastating. Not only do the Social Notables refrain from participating in public affairs, but when they do participate

TABLE 3. *Percentage of Social Notables holding selected public offices, 1957–1958*

	%
Political parties	0.9
Public education	0.9
Urban redevelopment	10.4
Percentage in three combined, less duplications	11.7

—overtly or covertly—their influence is evidently not very great.

A rough test of a person's overt or covert influence is the frequency with which he successfully initiates an important policy over the opposition of others, or vetoes policies initiated by others, or initiates a policy where no opposition appears. If we apply this test to the issue-areas of party nominations, public education, and urban redevelopment over the period 1950–59, out of fifty persons who met the test there were only eight Social Notables. What is perhaps most striking of all is that only two of the eight were among the top five men of influence in any of the three sectors, and their influence was strictly confined to public education. (Table 4)

TABLE 4. *Social Notables as leaders, 1950–1959*

	PARTY NOMINA-TIONS N	URBAN REDEVELOP-MENT N	PUBLIC EDUCATION N	MORE THAN ONE SECTOR N	TOTAL, LESS DUPLICATIONS N
TOP LEADERS*					
Social Notables	—	—	2	—	2
Others	9	7	7	2	21
Total					23
MINOR LEADERS†					
Social Notables	1	4	1	—	6
Others	3	15	6	3	21
Total					27
Totals	13	26	16	5	50

*Participants who were successful more than once in initiating or vetoing a policy proposal.
†Participants who were successful only once in initiating or vetoing a policy proposal.

The patricians seem therefore to have continued on the course marked out after they were displaced in politics by the entrepreneurs of industry. For the most part, they have eschewed public office. The last Trowbridge to run for office was a Republican candidate for mayor in 1886; he was defeated. A Townshend was elected to the Board of Aldermen from the First Ward in 1904 and subsequently was even elected president of the Board by his fellow aldermen. His wife was an active Republican and was the first woman ever elected to the Connecticut General Assembly. Their son Henry became an alderman and in 1961 the Republican nominee for mayor. A few patricians lingered on in public office by virtue of legal anomalies that permitted them to name their successors on certain boards. Thus five Proprietors of Common and Undivided Grounds were first elected in 1641 for laying out "allotments for inheritance"; today their ancient prerogative still gives them indisputable control over the use of the Central Green. When a proprietor dies, his replacement is elected for life by the surviving proprietors; all are descendants of the original settlers. (In 1959, the names of the proprietors were Hemingway, Trowbridge, Seymour, Daggett, and Hooker. By way of comparison, another honorific anachronism, the Board of Selectmen, an elected body, consisted of six members named Schlein, Calandrella, Shields, Brown, Kelleher, and Gianelli.)

Social Standing and Economic Leadership

Do the Social Notables furnish the economic leaders of New Haven? Let us cast a wide net by including as an Economic Notable in 1957–58 any person in one of the following categories:

The president or chairman of the board of a corporation with property in New Haven assessed in any of the five years 1953–57 at a value placing it among the fifty highest assessments in the city.

Any individual or group of individuals with property in the city assessed in the years 1953–57 at a value of $250,000 or more.

President or chairman of the board of any bank or public utility in the city.

Any individual who was a director of three or more of the following: a firm with an assessed valuation of $250,000 or more, a manufacturing firm with fifty employees or more, a retailing firm with twenty-five employees or more, a bank.

All directors of New Haven banks.

After eliminating duplications, the Economic Notables numbered some 238 persons in 1957–58. By a curious coincidence, this number is almost exactly equal to the number of Social Notables. One might easily leap to the conclusion, therefore, that the two groups were substantially identical. But nothing would be in more serious error, for only twenty-four persons, or about 5 per cent of the total number of names on both lists, were both Social and Economic Notables.

In view of the evolving pattern of economic leadership touched on in Chapter 3 [see p. 31, this volume], it is not altogether surprising that the two groups have become somewhat distinct. If entrepreneurs of the last half of the nineteenth century were distinct from the patricians, something like that difference has persisted down to the present da . Nowadays most of the leading executi es in the larger corporations have come to top positions in New Haven after careers elsewhere; or if they have grown up in New Haven they have generally started life in circumstances sharply different from those of the socially elect.

James W. Hook, who at the time of his death in 1957 was chairman of the board of the United Illuminating Company and one of the leading business figures in New Haven, was born in Iowa; his successor, then the president of the firm, was born in Texas. The president and later chairman of the board of the Southern New England Telephone Company was a native of New Haven who had started his career as a bookkeeper, supplementing his slender income by leading a jazz band. The chairman of the board of the Armstrong Rubber Company was born in New York, the son of Irish immigrants. Olin-Mathieson executives come to New Haven from a vast national empire of diverse companies. George Alpert, president of the New Haven Railroad, is a Boston lawyer; many of the other top officials in the New Haven offices of the railroad originally came from other parts of the country.

For their part the Social Notables have gone into the professions, particularly law, or play passive roles as corporate directors and owners of real estate. They are particularly prominent among the directors of the leading banks; yet the bank executives themselves, the presidents and vice-presidents, now frequently duplicate the pattern of industry and commerce. Of the twenty-four Social Notables among the Economic Nota-

bles, six are bankers, four are lawyers, two are at Yale, and five head their own family firms.

Between the Social and Economic Notables there is a slight discordance, often low but discernible to the carefully attuned ear. One of the Economic Notables put it more bluntly than most:

> Well, we noticed that we weren't readily accepted into the inner circle, you might say, the "sanctorum" of New Haven society, the way these old multi-generation families were. We've only been here for forty years. We're newcomers. We're nouveau riche. We're trying to crash. I mean, the old, long [time] society crowd looks upon us as trying to horn in.[1]

On the other side was the view of one of the twenty-four Social Notables who was an Economic Notable according to our broad criteria but insisted that, "I don't really think I rate being described as an Economic Notable." He expressed his feelings about corporate life:

> I think that there's a growing conviction among all the old families that it's better to be in a profession than [sic] the practices and tempo of business now, which is not according to their taste. . . . It's certainly true with me and I think it's true with a great many people. . . . Business is no more like what it was in '24 than Rome was like what Marco Polo found in China. . . . The tax picture makes for a regal type of living on the part of executives and an outlook on the money standards and the standards of business achievement which is utterly foreign to the Yankee. . . . If you work for General Motors, you're careful what kind of a General Motors car you drive around in, depending on your [place in the] hierarchy. . . . My friend in the Shell Oil Company in Venezuela—there's limousines meeting him everywhere and he flies here and there and everybody gets everything for him and everything's on the expense account. Well, we just haven't grown up with it, that's all—at least most of us haven't.

The Economic Notables in Public Life

The Economic Notables participate more in public affairs than do the Social Notables. In the 1950s, however, their participation

TABLE 5. *Number of selected public offices held by Economic Notables, 1957–1958*

	POLITICAL PARTIES N	PUBLIC EDUCATION N	URBAN REDEVELOP- MENT N	DUPLICA- TIONS N	TOTAL, LESS DUPLICATIONS N
Economic Notables	6	—	48	2	52
Others	491	131	387	37	972
Total	497	131	435	39	1024

TABLE 6. *Percentage of Economic Notables holding selected public offices, 1957–1958*

	%
Political parties	2.5
Public education	—
Urban redevelopment	20.0
Percentage in three combined, less duplication	21.8

was largely confined to only one of the three issue-areas investigated, and this, as might be expected, was urban redevelopment. Forty-eight Economic Notables held offices in urban redevelopment as compared with six in the political parties and none at all in public education. (Table 5) One out of every five Economic Notables held some office in urban redevelopment; altogether they held 11 per cent of the offices in that field. (Tables 6 and 7)

That the Economic Notables should neglect office in the political parties and in public education might seem surprising and will no doubt astonish anyone who expects to find the hand of an economic ruling elite in every major domain of public activity. But the explanation is not obscure. Most Social Notables and many Economic Notables living in New Haven send their children to private schools; as a consequence their interest in the public schools is ordinarily rather slight. It is true that expenditures on public schools have a very large bearing on the local tax rate, but—it might be argued— the best place to control taxes is through the mayor and the Board of Finance, about which I shall say something in a moment.

Moreover, to hold office in the parties or in public education one must, with a few exceptions, have a residence in New Haven, and many of the Economic Notables live in the suburbs. In urban redevelopment, the mayor felt it important to have the support of the Economic Notables, and appointed members to his Citizens Action Commission without regard to where they lived. In 1958, eleven of the twenty-four members of the Citizens Action Commission lived in the suburbs; of the thirteen Economic Notables

TABLE 7. *Percentage of selected offices held by Economic Notables, 1957–1958*

	(1) ACTUAL %	(2) EXPECTED* %	RATIO (1) ÷ (2)
Political parties	1.2	0.2	6
Public education	—	0.2	—
Urban redevelopment	11.0	0.2	55
Percentage in three combined, less duplication	5.1	0.2	26

Expected: percentage of Economic Notables in total New Haven population 21 years old or over.

on the CAC, nine lived in the suburbs. To a lesser degree the manifold special committees operating under CAC followed the same principle.

Then, too, urban redevelopment bore a comparatively direct and self-evident relationship to the personal or corporate prosperity of the Economic Notables. Business leaders might ignore the public schools or the political parties without any sharp awareness that their indifference would hurt their pocketbooks, but the prospect of profound changes in ownership, physical layout, and usage of property in the downtown area and the effects of these changes on the commercial and industrial prosperity of New Haven were all related in an obvious way to the daily concerns of businessmen. However much they might justify their apathy toward public schools and politics on the ground that they were not experts in these areas, redevelopment looked a good deal more like the kind of operation corporate executives, bankers,

and utilities heads understood; it was, in a sense, business.

Finally, Economic Notables are busy men who, with only a few exceptions, have full-time business careers. Of course only a handful of the thousand public offices in question are full-time offices, and the part-time, often unpaid, offices are held primarily by men and women who have full-time jobs that leave them with no more time than the businessmen have to spend on public duties. However, it is not surprising that among any group of busy people only a few are willing to add participation in public affairs to the other demands on their time—even if, as is usually the case, the demand is only for a few hours a week. In their reluctance to give time to public affairs, the Economic Notables are not unique, for the orientation of American life to hedonistic and family satisfactions is a powerful pull against the gentle tug of public duty.

Note

1. From an interview. Hereafter, direct quotations from interviews will be given without footnote reference.

B. The Reputational Approach

Methods of Study: Community Power Structure

Floyd Hunter

Poplar Village, a community of about 7,000 population, was used as a community to test field schedules before attempting the more complex study of Regional City. Since the Poplar Village "dry run" has bearing on the

final methods employed in the larger community, it will be referred to here.

The methods utilized in studying community power structure fall into three categories: (1) theoretical analysis prior to field

Reprinted from Community Power Structure *by Floyd Hunter, pp. 262–271, by permission of the author and The University of North Carolina Press. Copyright 1953 by The University of North Carolina Press.*

investigation; (2) field investigation; and (3) an integration of field findings and social theory.

For a theoretical examination of materials on power structure a search of library documents was made. The books and periodicals listed in the bibliography were gleaned of excerpts which seemed pertinent to the problem. These excerpted materials were classified roughly according to the areas or topics to be studied in the field. Statements on power which seemed beyond the scope of the study, but which appeared fundamental to defining power in broad terms, were set aside as residual categories. For example, much discussion of power has centered around national and international ideologies. These may have real though indirect bearing on community power structure, but they were ruled out of consideration in this analysis. There were other similar categories.

Over a period of eighteen months newspapers from Regional City and Poplar Village were clipped of items bearing on the subject of power. Notes were taken of random thoughts occurring to the writer which were considered as being hypothetical. Documents in his possession relating to political activities in Regional City were classified. Personal correspondence and other documents relating to working experiences which seemed to have a bearing on the problem were likewise edited and classified.

From this preliminary analysis of materials and through an ordering of thought related to the writer's personal observations of community power relations, the frame of reference embodied in the postulates and hypotheses set down earlier was developed. A plan for field analysis was then devised.

The first problem in analyzing power relations in the field was that of determining which community leaders should be interviewed. The second problem was to work out a schedule of questions that would yield data pertinent to power alignments and dynamics within a given community. As has been suggested, Poplar Village served as a laboratory for working out methods and techniques for dealing with both of these problems.

Lists of leaders occupying positions of prominence in civic organizations, business establishments, a University bureaucracy, office holders in Village politics, and lists of persons prominent socially and of wealth status were secured. It was taken as axiomatic that community life is organized life, and that persons occupying "offices" and public positions of trust would be involved in some manner in the power relations of the community. It was felt that some leaders might not work through formally organized groups, but getting leaders from organizations would be a good start toward turning up leaders who might operate behind the scenes.

It was felt that getting to leaders in organizations was a direct method of turning up leadership. A rather extensive unpublished study of leadership had been made three years earlier in Poplar Village by a class in community organization which had utilized the door-to-door method of finding leadership by scheduled interviews conducted in every eighth house. All the leaders found belonged to at least one of several major organized groups, and would therefore serve as some check on the proposed approach in this study. Lists of organizational leaders were secured from University officials, records of the Village government, and the secretary of the local Merchants Association. Wealth leaders and socially prominent persons were listed by a University student, a mature person, who had lived in Poplar Village for some years and who knew intimately many of these persons. This informant began with one well known leader and "worked out from her," i.e., she took the names provided by her first informant and by a series of interviews with the persons subsequently named got from these people a consensus of opinion about others listed. None of the informants were provided with lists of names previously mentioned, but as the investigation proceeded there was a growing uniformity of opinion on who were the wealth and social leaders.

Since the list of business leaders provided by the Merchants Association was some two hundred in length, a self-rating of top leaders was made by businessmen to cut the list down for later interviewing purposes. It was, incidentally, a surprising thing to members of a team from a community organization class working on the current study to find so many business establishments in so small a village. Each businessman in a top listing of fifty chosen by the secretary of the Merchants Association was asked to select ten men from the total list who were, in his opinion, leaders of major business establishments in the community. This provided a listing of fifty-four names receiving the highest rating.

The four lists of names—civic, governmental, business, and status leaders—were then typed separately. Six "judges," persons who had lived in the community for some years and who had a knowledge of community affairs, were provided with these lists and asked to select from each one, in rank order of importance, ten persons of influence. The instructions were:

> Place in rank order, one through ten, ten persons from each list of personnel—who in your opinion are the most influential persons in the field designated—influential from the point of view of ability to lead others.

> If there are persons . . . you feel should be included in the ranking order of ten rather than the ones given, please include them.

The judges were also asked to choose from a list of fifty organizations the top ten in influence. In all cases assurance was given that replies would be treated confidentially. It should be said here, that immunity from having data sources revealed was promised to all informants throughout the study in both communities. It was always stated that the researcher was interested in "process" of power or influence activities rather than in identifying persons. It was necessary to use actual names to get data, but all names are disguised in this exposition of the findings.

There was a high degree of agreement among the judges as to who the top leaders were in the four fields. Among business leaders there was unanimous opinion on six out of ten leaders. Other business leaders received four votes in two cases, and three votes in two cases. Among governmental personnel there was unanimous opinion on four out of ten persons, with four persons receiving five votes, and the remaining two tied with four votes each. There was more division of opinion concerning leaders in the University personnel; yet out of 77 choices, one person received six votes, four received five votes, and the remaining five persons garnered four votes each. None received a unanimous vote in the civic personnel list. One person received five votes, five received four votes, and the remainder tied with three votes each. Only five names were added to the lists by the judges, and each of these received but one vote, that of the person naming him.

Since the schedule of questions to be asked community leaders would allow for additional leaders to be named, and because of the high degree of correlation between the choices of the judges, it was decided to carry the judging process no further in Poplar Village. The decisions of the judges had given a basic list of forty persons to interview in the community. A schedule of questions was then prepared.

The design of the schedule was arranged as follows: Identifying information was asked concerning age, sex, birthplace, occupation, kinds of property owned, number of employees supervised or directed, education, place of residence, and length of residence in Poplar Village. Questions were also asked to ascertain whether the informant's interests were local, state, or national in scope. Each informant was asked to select five top leaders from the list of 40 names provided on the schedule, and to add names, if the ones provided were not top leaders in his opinion. Each was asked why he made the choices he did.

Three questions were designed to get the degree of interaction of each person with others on the list. These questions were: Do you belong to any organization of which the others are members? Have you worked with any of the others on committees and approximately how many? Specify other contacts with others on the list, e.g., intimate business relationship, might call for advice, etc.

A scale was constructed to determine how well each person knew the others. Each interviewee was asked to indicate about each of the others whether he knew him socially, knew him, knew him slightly, heard of him, or not known to him.

Each interviewee was asked to identify persons of wealth among the community leaders and to identify persons of "society" status. A question was also asked to ascertain whether or not individuals on the list of leaders tend to act in cliques in relation to community projects. Committee groupings were also examined in relation to local, state, and national problems.

Methods of clearing with others on projects were inquired about, and the way in which an individual cleared with others was ascertained, in some degree, by the question, "In your opinion how do the men on the list operate in relation to community projects: in the forefront of affairs, behind the scenes, or in other ways?"

A final set of questions was related to two decisions which recently had been made in the community in an effort to reveal each individual's relation to these decisions.

A graduate class in community organization aided the writer in carrying the schedules into the interviewing stage of the study in Poplar Village. (Field work in Regional City was carried out exclusively by the writer.) Each member of the class carried two or three schedules to the field with written instructions. A group of periphery leaders were also interviewed—nine in number—to see whether they as a group would compare in any way with the listed leaders. The periphery leaders were persons who had been on the lists scrutinized by the judges, and had received one or more votes by the judges but who had not received enough votes to make the master list of community leaders.

A total of thirty-three of the forty persons on the master list of leaders were interviewed on the schedules provided. Three refused to answer the questions. One claimed that she did not know enough about the subject to answer intelligently. One considered the subject impertinent. The third told the interviewer that he did not consider himself a local leader since his interests were in affairs beyond the bounds of the Village. Seven people were not seen by interviewers either because they were unavailable through being out of the city or for other reasons. Most interviewees were extremely cooperative. Of the nine periphery leaders, three refused to be interviewed.

The experience of running schedules in Poplar Village brought out several things concerning methodology. First of all, and negatively, the schedule was too lengthy. In some cases one and one-half hours were required in filling out the form. It was clear that the schedule would need revision for further use in Regional City. Secondly, the interviewers were not clear on certain aspects of administering the schedule. Some let the interviewee fill out his own schedule. Others filled out the schedule for the person interviewed. This lack of clarity in instructions had value in that it was thereby learned that having the field worker fill in the schedule was a more satisfactory process than having the interviewee do it. It was decided that the field worker should hold the schedule in his hands during interviews in Regional City.

Time-consuming questions such as, "Name the organizations of which you are member with other leaders on the list," and, "Approximately how many committees have you served on with other individual leaders within the past five years?" were eliminated from the schedule of interviewing in Regional City, following the test run in Poplar Village. The schedules were streamlined to "check mark" proportions wherever possible. It was recognized that some of the leaders in Regional City carried heavy responsibilities, greater in the majority than did leaders in Poplar Village. They could not have spent even a hour being interviewed in some cases.

The methods of getting basic lists of power personnel, and of using judges to cut the list to manageable interviewing proportions, were used in Regional City much as in Poplar Village. The details varied, of course, but the methods remained basically the same.

The Community Council in Regional City, a council of civic organizations, provided preliminary lists of leaders in community affairs. The Chamber of Commerce provided business leaders of establishments employing more than 500 employees and of financial houses doing the largest volume of clearances. The League of Women Voters provided lists of local political leaders who had at least major governmental committee chairmanship status. Newspaper editors and other civic leaders provided lists of society leaders and leaders of wealth.

In Regional City fourteen judges were used to give their opinions on who were top leaders on each of the lists thus provided. These judges revealed a high degree of correlation in their choices. The judges represented three religions, were male and female, young and mature people, business executives and professional people, and Negro and white. It was felt that the number of judges should be larger in Regional City than in Poplar Village because of the size of the community and because elements of bias were highly possible in so large and complex a community.

Of the leaders chosen in civic affairs, by the fourteen judges with fifty persons to choose from, the correlation was as follows: one received eleven votes, one received ten votes, one received eight votes, four received six votes, one received five votes, one received four votes, and the last received but three votes. Others receiving votes did not exceed two in any case, and the other votes were singles scattered among twenty-one persons on the list. Fourteen persons received no votes at all. The same clustering of votes held with selections from the lists of governmental officials and business leaders, with the clustering of votes more sharply defined among the latter. The widest range of opinion occurred when the judges were asked to name social prestige leaders. Some judges were unable to give replies to this question. There was apparently little consensus on "status-society" leaders among our judges. In a sense, therefore, names given in this area of possible leadership were arbitrarily included.

Negro names were included on the list of personnel submitted to the judges, but in only three instances did the judges vote for them, and they were Negro judges with one exception. The Negro community of Regional City has a population almost one-third of the total number of inhabitants. Consequently a separate and similar study was projected for this group. The same techniques of using status-rating judges was used by a panel of Negro judges, and the correlations in relation to Negro leadership were similar in pattern to the white community.

The structural pattern of the form used for studying leadership in the Negro community paralleled that used for the whites, except the names listed were Negro leaders chosen by Negro judges. The need to study the Negro community in Regional City grew out of field experience. This community was found to represent a sub-power grouping of considerable significance which could not be overlooked, particularly since many of the issues suggested to the field investigator by white power personnel revolved around Negro-white relations.

In order to ascertain whether or not there was the same degree of interaction between the top leaders in Regional City and some group with whom they might be compared, a group of fourteen professional persons were interviewed using the same interview schedule as that used with the top power leaders. All professional persons interviewed were earning more than $5,000 a year, with none earning more than $10,000 annually. The rates of interaction between these professionals fell far below those in the top leadership brackets and there were other basic differences which have been pointed out in an analysis of our field materials. As a method of checking to see how near center we were with the top leadership group, we found this method a useful tool.

The method of interviewing in Regional City consisted of going through the schedule of questions with each interviewee and noting any remarks that he made as each question was asked. If the interviewee wished to discuss any phase of a particular question more fully than the schedule allowed, the worker maintained an attentive role, asking such questions as would clarify the interviewee's statements. Early in the study in Regional City a question was added to the interview form: "Who is the top leader in the community?" This question was asked following the question related to the " ten" leaders. It usually elicited discussion. Certain information given by individual interviewees was sometimes verified with other informants, if such verification did not violate the confidential nature of the total interviewing situation.

C. The Reputational Approach Criticized

The Mystery of Power

Herbert Kaufman and Victor Jones

I

There is an elusiveness about power that endows it with an almost ghostly quality. It seems to be all around us, yet this is "sensed" with some sixth means of reception rather than with the five ordinary senses. We "know" what it is, yet we encounter endless difficulties in trying to define it. We can "tell" whether one person or group is more powerful than another, yet we cannot measure power. It is as abstract as time yet as real as a firing squad.

Countless analyses of this evasive phenomenon have been attempted; the list extends from the period of the earliest writings on politics to the present day, and the roster of authors includes many of the most distinguished names in the history of social and political thought. It is the triumph of Floyd Hunter's study that his approach possesses a freshness and boldness even in this company.[1]

Despite the abundance of the literature and the eminence of the writers on power, however, the subject is probably not much better understood today than it was when men first undertook to examine it systematically. And here lies the failure of Hunter's book: it adds little, if anything, to the arguments of his predecessors. Its merit lies not so much in what it achieves as in what is suggests for future studies of power.

Hunter's treatment of power is empirical. Power to him is "a structural description of social processes . . . , a word . . . used to describe the acts of men going about the business of moving other men to act in relation to themselves or in relation to organic or inorganic things." He is concerned with it in the context of the community "because of a strong conviction that the community is a primary power center and because it is a place in which power relations can be most easily observed" (pp. 2–3). These premises lead him to an investigation of power leadership patterns in a city of half a million population—a real city, not an imaginary one, disguised by the pseudonym Regional City.

In fact, Regional City is a metropolitan

Reprinted from the Public Administrative Review, 14, 3 (Summer 1954), 205–212, by permission of the authors and the American Society for Public Administration. Copyright 1954 by the American Society for Public Administration.

community and the power structure that Hunter describes controls the policy decisions of a population that spills out of the central city into twenty-three suburban municipalities and the unincorporated areas of three counties. Many political scientists will applaud the boldness of a sociologist in studying a metropolitan community instead of generalizing about the social structure of metropolitan areas from a study of small communities.

The leaders of the community were identified from four lists of names—civic, governmental, business, and status leaders—complied by the researchers; a total of 175 names was thus collected. These lists were submitted to a panel of six "judges," described as "persons who had lived in the community for some years and who had a knowledge of community affairs," who were asked to rank the names. These rankings were then tallied, and forty names were selected as the power leaders. Regional City is located in the South, and this method, it developed, excluded the Negro population almost entirely, so the same technique was separately applied to the Negro subcommunity to discover its place in the power picture. Are there other subcommunities in Regional City with a structured leadership? Do all of the 135 persons nominated for leadership but not selected as power leaders by the panel function solely as satellites of the top forty?

The book is essentially a study of the relationships of these selected individuals with each other and with the rest of the community. Using a variety of sociometric and charting devices and a great deal of interview material, Hunter comes to a number of conclusions about the power structure of Regional City that may here be stated in abbreviated—and doubtless oversimplified— form.

The leadership of Regional City is in the hands of the forty white power-wielders for all practical purposes. Twenty-three of these are in commerce, finance, and industry; five are "leisure personnel," that is, "persons who have social or civic organization leadership capacities and yet do not have business offices or similar places in which they conduct

their day-by-day affairs"; only six are professionals; government is represented by but four; two labor leaders, representing large unions, are on the list (pp. 11–13 and Appendix). The roster, in short, is predominantly middle class, and fairly heavily upper middle class; Dodsworth would have felt completely at home in the company of Regional City's elect.

These are the people who run Regional City, according to Hunter. The policy-making machinery of the community is concentrated largely in their hands (pp. 104, 230, 232). This handful of individuals in a city of half a million makes the key decisions affecting the lives and welfare of the entire populace.

The leadership group is integrated. Its members tend to cluster in the most desirable areas of town; there is a remarkable pattern of interlocking memberships in social, civic, charitable, religious, and fraternal organizations; there are considerable business contacts. They are conscious of their position in the community. Hunter has succeeded in capturing a good deal of the flavor of their lives and in conveying it rather vividly to the reader; he brings them to life.

The leadership group is more or less isolated from the community whose affairs it directs. The leaders' lives are not like the lives of most of the other Regional City dwellers. The leaders are more comfortable. They do not feel the same economic pressures. They operate as a more or less closed group, and they are self-selecting with regard to admission to the charmed circle. They mingle with each other rather than with outsiders. Hunter concedes that they are probably aware of the social problems of the rest of the population, but the pattern of their lives tends to set them apart all the same.

The leadership makes the policy decisions; it depends on a substructure to execute those decisions. The composition of the substructure is not analyzed in any detail, but it seems to comprise the professions, the governmental and business bureaucracies, the political organizations, the churches, and the lesser officers of the social and other organizations and institutions of Regional

City. These people are depicted as the executors rather than the initiators of policy; they function as the mechanism by which the policy decisions of the leadership group are translated into action, the machinery that turns the rudder whenever the steering is turned by the real leaders.

II

Whether or not there is a small ruling elite in Regional City is of importance principally to Regional City; whether a conceptual framework capable of handling the problem of power has been developed is of importance to social scientists everywhere, and perhaps to mankind as a whole. It is possible sometimes to arrive at the right answers by chance even when one adopts an invalid method of solving a problem;[2] the fortuitous selection of a correct solution is then of little consequence, for it affords little opportunity to attack similar problems—or even different versions of the same problem—with expectation of success. Hunter may thus be right or wrong about the social structure of Regional City, but that is beside the point if his methods are faulty. Unfortunately, they are, and these shortcomings are probably more important than any chance accuracy in his conclusions.

The major deficiency of Hunter's treatment of power in Regional City is his proneness to take for granted precisely what must be proved, and, by this practice, to predetermine his findings and conclusions. Specifically, his point of departure is the question: what persons in Regional City constitute the elite of the community, what are these persons like, and what regular contacts do they have with each other? This inquiry assumes the existence of the elite has been established, and, since Hunter's own method is empirical, presumably established by an empirical standard. Nothing could be further from the truth. That there is a small group running the city is not demonstrated but presupposed, and this presupposition relieves Hunter of the obligation to develop any objective measure of power. He begins his structure at the mezzanine without showing us a lobby or a foundation.

In point of fact, one of the most difficult things to demonstrate scientifically is the power of one individual or group over others. We all have strong intuitive reactions, to be sure, but to prove the relationship objectively is not the same thing at all. For one thing, it is rarely quite clear that the course of events would be different had the power-wielders failed to exert their influence; if the same events occur no matter what they do, their claim to power must be regarded as spurious, in much the same way as the claim of any group to have power over the sun because they will it to rise in the east and set in the west. It is conceivable that life in Regional City would continue in much the same direction and at much the same tempo as at present even if all forty of the leaders identified by Hunter disappeared one night, and this suggests that they may themselves be carried along by the continuing forces at work in the community as well as directing those forces.[3] Certainly this is the case in many primitive societies, where the force of custom is much greater than the power of any individual or group of individuals; however, if one were to approach these societies with Hunter's a priori premises, one would soon "discover" leaders.[4]

But even if the activities of a group clearly had some relationship to the course of events, that in itself would *still* not dispel the ambiguities that plague the analysis of power. Simon[5] has pointed out additional difficulties in the identification of power. If the tie between A and B is asymmetrical—i.e., A influences B but B does not influence A at all —he argues, the measurement of power is comparatively simple. In reality, however, such situations rarely exist. There is feedback, in which an individual attempting to influence the behavior of others is himself influenced by their reactions, adjusting his own behavior according to the fashion in which they respond to him. Moreover, there is, according to Simon, an even graver complication in what Friedrich has called "the rule of anticipated reactions"; what power personnel do is conditioned not only by how those they try to influence *actually* act, but by how the leaders *expect* them to act; again, the power personnel have themselves been influenced, though there is no tangible evidence of the fact except (as Simon points out) when they guess wrong.

It may have been the instinctive perception of these difficulties involved in trying to handle power operationally that persuaded Hunter to choose his group relatively arbitrarily from the membership in certain selected organizations of the community, and to entrust final choice of his subjects to the judgment of his "jury" or panel of informed local residents. But avoiding problems is not the same as solving them. And Hunter's substitute for a reliable index of the location and degree of power is certainly a dubious one; it is not the way one would try to decide who the wealthiest people in the community are or what the city's average temperature is. All the arguments against arriving at *these* determinations through the votes of a lay panel apply with equal force against using this method for the measurement of power. To be sure, we have more or less reliable yardsticks by which to assess wealth or temperature, and a yardstick is lacking in the realm of power. But this means that Hunter has tried to deal with a phenomenon before adequate tools are at hand to handle it, and his findings must therefore be regarded as intuitive—mature and rich in insight, but intuitive all the same—rather than scientific.[6]

In short, Hunter skirts or ignores the unanswered questions, treating them as though they had been resolved when in truth they have not been, in order to come to grips with the indisputably fascinating aspects of power. The result is certainly an intriguing description. But the study must be regarded as far from conclusive because it rests, in the last analysis, on a faulty base.

This may be the reason for the appearance of elements within Hunter's own data suggesting that the impression with which he leaves the reader is in some ways misleading. Admittedly, Hunter specifically disavows any claim that the group with which he is concerned is the sole power center in Regional City:

No pretense is made that the group to be discussed represents the totality of power leaders of the community, but it is felt that a representative case sample is presented, and that the men described come well within the range of the center of power in the community.[7]

Despite this qualified disclaimer, however, the total impact of the book gives the reader the sense of a supreme military headquarters in which forty top strategists arrive at a consensus on what is to be done, and of a series of lesser commands that spring into action only at the behest of the supreme commanders. Indeed, Hunter's primary source of anxiety is that these strategists reach their decisions in virtual isolation from the people who are most affected by them. His denial that they function as the single power core of Regional City is more than outweighed by the structure of his presentation and the depth of his concern.

But there is some evidence that the group he studied engages in bargaining of some sort to secure the kind of program it wants, and that the bureaucratic and professional substructure actually imposes limits on the discretion of the top leaders. When, for example, some of the Negro citizens of Regional City instituted suit to secure school facilities for Negro children equal to the facilities provided for white children, the power leaders identified by Hunter, instead of invoking all the sanctions at their disposal, decided to try "to make concessions to the Negro community in the matter. They feel that the Negroes are not serious in their suit but are bringing it forward to have a better bargaining position with the community leaders" (p. 222). In the light of the state of relations between whites and blacks in the Deep South, the willingness of the most powerful people in Regional City to negotiate with Negro leaders on this fundamental issue can doubtless be interpreted as strong evidence that the flow of influence is not quite so one-sided as the book indicates, and that the process of bargaining, especially where other white groups are involved, is probably much more widespread than one would conclude from Hunter's presentation.

To take another example, the influence of

the substructure personnel on the top leaders is indicated by the fact that "the power leaders have action initiated for them more often than they initiate action" (p. 226). "The under-structure personnel play around with the lesser issues in many cases, and, through their channels of communication with the power leaders, some of their issues may be picked up for top level policy consideration" (p. 225). In this event, presumably, they are no longer lesser issues, but become major ones.

Hunter here finds himself in the same dilemma as Weber, who saw the bureaucracy as both a controlling factor in society by virtue of its monopoly on certain types of expertise and as a passive mechanism to be operated by whatever group happens to be in a position to manipulate it. But whereas Weber observes *both* of these contradictory characteristics of bureaucracy (though without attempting to resolve the quandary), Hunter blithely ignores his substructure's influence (except for the brief passage cited) and stresses only its submissive qualities. Yet if the substructure personnel of Regional City can decide what issues the top leaders will take up, and if, in addition, the leaders are dependent upon them in many technical matters, then we cannot escape the conclusion that the substructure is not only actually making important social decisions but is also in a position to use its technical competence as a factor in bargaining for what it wants.

These examples are isolated instances that Hunter mentions only in passing. But they give the reader pause. It would seem from these fragments that power is somewhat more diffused in Regional City than one might infer from the way he presents his analysis. In this light, there is more than casual significance in his remark, "the personnel with which the current discussion is concerned represents but a minute fraction of the community in which it moves and functions" (p. 60). He has not given us a study of the power structure of Regional City at all! Rather, he has set forth a portrait of one of the groups having some power over some things at some times. The place of this group in the interplay of power groups in Regional City is never

made clear, and what from some indications may be a pluralist society emerges under Hunter's hands as a sternly monolithic organization. At best, the study is incomplete; at worst, it may be invalid.

That is not to say a set of pluralist preconceptions is to be preferred; this may lead to as many difficulties as beset those who attempt to impose a monistic interpretation of power on the facts. Rather, we need an approach that recognizes all the possibilities without prejudging the results of the research. Hunter does not escape this pitfall. Consequently, though he has produced an interesting and stimulating volume, it is striking more for showing us how far we still have to go than for the distance it carries us beyond where we were.

III

Students of metropolitics and people who wish to annex territory to the central city, or reorganize the county into a metropolitan government, or rewrite the city charter would be relieved if they had only to address themselves to a small group of easily identifiable decision makers. But their experience contradicts this theory. They would probably characterize the political process in which they have been caught time and again as exceedingly complex, "as much of a tangle and as full of movement as a canful of angleworms."

The principal issue that Hunter uses to illustrate the way the top decision makers work together and the way they manipulate the rest of the community is the annexation of territory to the central city and the realignment of functions between the city and the county.[8] The basic recommendations of the Local Government Commission, known as "The Plan of Development," were enacted during 1950 by the state legislature. This success, practically unknown in other metropolitan areas, Hunter attributes almost entirely to the development of interest in, and support for, the project on the part of the leadership group:

> There are, perhaps, a score of . . . factors which have entered into the present demand

for the extension of city boundaries beyond their present limits. The main fact is that there is now substantial agreement among the leaders that this improvement in governmental operation should be made. (p. 217)

Once they had achieved consensus on this issue, an official committee was established to carry out the program. Only five members of the committee, incidentally, were power leaders; the remainder were selected from the substructure. The policy having been arrived at, its implementation was assigned to the executive machinery, with only a small segment of the elite taking part in this phase, apparently to supervise the execution. That's all there was to it—or so its seems to Hunter.

Those who have ever been drawn into the efforts to change local government and administration, however, cannot but feel dissatisfied with Hunter's tantalizing description of the process by which this decision was reached in Regional City. "In recent years," he observes, ". . . there has been a growing awareness on the part of many leaders and of a substantial portion of the citizenry that the situation was one that needed to be remedied" (p. 216). How was that awareness born? Was it perhaps the result of the work of some "uninfluential" group in the community, working long and hard and carefully to produce the consensus that Hunter treats in such casual fashion? In other words, is there someone behind the power leaders on some issues? And how important was that "substantial part of the citizenry?" Could it be that Hunter's power leaders are in reality *following* a ground swell of public opinion? "There would seem to be no particular merit in attempting to analyze why each of the power leaders was vitally interested in the improvement plan" (p. 218), Hunter contends; in brushing aside this question and the "score of factors" involved in the making of this one decision (which actually turns out to be a whole network of decisions comprising property rights, bonded indebtedness, taxes, etc.), he evades the center of the problem of power in the improvement of government in metropolitan areas.

Equally deficient is the blithe assumption that announcement of a plan is the most important step in metropolitan improvement. Students of administration are well aware that policy decisions can be and frequently have been sabotaged by a bureaucracy opposed or sometimes only indifferent to them. That Regional City has come as far along the reform road as it has is indeed an impressive development, but it hardly constitutes sufficient grounds for concluding that only a few dozen people are responsible; if the plan succeeds, it will doubtless be because the consensus on it was a good deal wider than this book suggests. The power to execute policy is the power to alter or make policy; Hunter assumes this is not true in Regional City, but he nowhere demonstrates the validity of his assumption.

One of the greatest barriers to metropolitan integration is the tendency of people to identify themselves with the local corporate unit of government in which they live rather than with the larger metropolitan community of which they are a part. The carefully developed schemes of many a metropolitan planner have foundered on the rock of this sentiment, and many small communities persist in their local loyalties even when it is demonstrably uneconomic to do so. Yet this phenomenon, so familiar to planners, is not examined by Hunter at all in his account of Regional City's Plan of Development. At the very outset, he places "psychological motivation in power relations [in] another residual category" (p. 4) and therefore excludes it from his discussion (although economic motivation is constantly referred to as a determinant of behavior as if it were not psychological). All inquiry that omits such an important category of factors may have some positive values, but it is perfectly clear that it does not meet the needs of the student of metropolitan government and politics.

IV

Hunter is profoundly distressed by the power structure of Regional City. It upsets him that the leaders "are able to enforce their decisions by persuasion, intimidation, coercion, and, if necessary, force." "In some cases they have the machinery of government at their bidding. In many cases they control large industries in which they reign supreme in matters of decision affecting large numbers of the citizenry" (p. 24). He is disturbed that they use these elements of compulsion to secure compliance with their decisions and to suppress opposition if and when it occurs. For, he declares,

> This situation does not square with the concepts of democracy we have been taught to revere. The line of communication between the leaders and the people needs to be broadened and strengthened—and by more than a series of public-relations and propaganda campaigns—else our concept of democracy is in danger of losing vitality in dealing with problems that affect all in common. (p. 1)

He therefore closes his book with an entreaty that the "bottom structure" of the population be brought more fully into the deciding process than is now the case, and that this be done by building and strengthening "associational groupings"—the labor unions, the welfare agencies, the professional societies, the Negro organizations. In this way, he argues, the flow of communications upward from "the little man" can be increased, the participation of all elements of the population in the making of community decisions can be enlarged, and the "paralysis of action and the suppression of dissatisfaction" that now prevail can be eliminated and the functioning of our democracy thereby reinvigorated.

It is not so much with the nature of his proposal for diffusing power as with the weaknesses of his evidence that power is in fact as centralized as he contends that these reviewers have taken issue. But even if, for a moment, for the sake of argument, they were willing to accept his evidence as probative, they would still be concerned about a serious omission in his recommendations. That is the neglect of the political process as a means by which the excluded elements of the populace might impress themselves upon decision-making in Regional City.

Hunter gives little consideration to political parties, either as a factor affecting existent power structure or as a means of opening up the decision-making process. Yet many of the decisions of the power leaders take the form of official pronouncements or actions by the government of Regional City, and the government is responsive to the parties that help it win office. The parties, however, are not monolithic organizations completely under the thumb of a small group; V. O. Key, Jr., has shown that the Democratic party in the one-party areas of the South "is merely a holding company for a congeries of transient squabbling factions. . . ."[9] Against the strongly entrenched group alleged to be ruling Regional City, associations of the kind recommended by Hunter would have little direct leverage; in a test of power, the leaders would unquestionably win easily. But in the welter of coalitions and compromises among the fragments of the party system, with each faction seeking strength wherever it can find it, the associations of currently voiceless masses would have a bargaining position through their votes and their donations of time and energy and money that would enable them to exert some influence. Then, even the elite could not ignore them.

Nor is this merely theoretical speculation; Hunter himself provides the evidence that it is already the case in fact. The most disadvantaged citizens of Regional City, the Negroes, have already discovered the principle, and have pressed their claims not upon the people Hunter calls the leaders but upon the politicians of the city.[10] The politicians do listen to them and do respond to them; the community leaders, who ought not to be concerned about these interactions in the substructure if the leaders are actually as powerful as they are represented, do manifest some anxiety. The parties thus furnish a convenient avenue for the exercise of influence over the inner circle; this avenue is scarcely explored by Hunter when he seeks the means of transforming the power structure of the metropolis.

V

Students of administration—public and private, local, state, national, and international—will find a great deal of interest in *Com-*

munity Power Structure in spite of its short-comings. For one thing, it makes enjoyable reading. For another, the problem with which Hunter is concerned is as relevant to administrative organizations of every kind as to urban communities; we, too, are dealing with the business of moving men to act. We can learn from every study of the nature of power and influence.

We are also in a position to *contribute* a great deal to the study of these phenomena. The organizations on which administration, as a profession, focuses its attention are in many respects smaller, more manageable, and perhaps slightly less complex than the vast network of institutions Hunter sought to penetrate. In this respect, they seem particularly well suited to observation and experimentation for research. We have made some

progress in this direction since the administrative behavior approach came into its own less than a decade ago, but it is clear that we are still not far beyond the starting post. Hunter's study may well provide a challenge and stimulus that will help to move us farther and faster along the road.

It is easy for us, as political scientists, to be critical of a sociologist when he ventures so close to our pastures. But none of *us* has moved in with such a study of the structure and dynamics of power in a metropolitan community. If we do move in, we shall certainly benefit from working with sociologists. Clearly the time for such collaboration to begin is in the period of research design. This is more difficult, but also more responsible and useful, than reviewing a book after it is published.

Notes

1. Mr. Hunter's book [Floyd Hunter, *Community Power Structure* (Chapel Hill: University of North Carolina, 1953)] was discussed at a two-day conference of the New England Committee on Political Behavior at Wesleyan University on November 21–22, 1953. Besides Mr. Hunter and the authors of this review, the following were present: Paul H. Appleby, Stephen K. Bailey, Oliver Garceau, Stanley Gordon, Robert D. Leigh, Sigmund Neumann, John Owens, Lawrence Pelletier, Ira deA. Reid, E. E. Schattschneider, Martin Trow, and Coleman Woodbury. We are indebted to the members of the conference but absolve them from all responsibility for our statements.

2. This is not to say Hunter definitely *is* right, although many will find corroboration in their own intuitive assessments of familiar power situations and in eminent authorities —Pareto and Michels in their general theories, for example, and Brogan and Laski in their specific comments on local government. *If* he is right, the validity of his methodology is not thereby established; that is all that is here asserted.

3. In fact, there is some evidence of this in Hunter, at p. 246: "The situation, as observed in this study, is that the policy-makers have a fairly definite set of settled policies at their command [perhaps "commanding them" would be more accurate], which have been historically functional in the community. New problems which arise are measured

by the standards of older policy decisions. . . ." This seems to suggest a continuity that limits the discretion of the power leaders, although Hunter does point out that policy "adjustments are made to fit new conditions whenever the situation warrants. . . ." The full implications of the weight of tradition and custom and the expectations of the community are explored nowhere in the book.

4. Even without the inherent bias of Hunter's approach, it would not be surprising if random interviewers were to perceive a single leadership group in any situation. The assumption that there is always such a finite, often tangible, cause is deeply imbedded in the thought patterns of our culture, and there is no reason to doubt that it would be projected into a situation even if the queries did not themselves prejudice the replies. This is a fatal defect in Hunter's panel and interview technique.

5. Herbert A. Simon, "Notes on the Observation and Measurement of Political Power," 15 *The Journal of Politics*, 500–16 (1953). While it is true this article, which makes explicit many of the difficulties in observing and measuring power, did not appear until long after the publication of Hunter's book, most of the sources on which Simon relies preceded Hunter, notably, Harold D. Lasswell and Abraham Kaplan, *Power and Society* (Yale University Press, 1950).

6. See Ruth Rosner Kornhouser, "The Warner

Approach to Social Stratification," in Reinhard Bendix and S. M. Lipset (eds.), *Class,
Status and Power* (Glencoe, Ill.: The Free
Press, 1953), pp. 224–55.
7. P. 61. See also his statement at p. 62: ". . . I
doubt seriously that power forms a single
pyramid with any nicety in a community
the size of Regional City. There are *pyramids*
of power in this community which seem
more important to the present discussion
than *a* pyramid."
8. This was voted the principal issue in Regional
City by the top decision makers themselves;
see pp. 215, 223.

9. [V. O. Key, Jr.] *Southern Politics in State
and Nation* (Alfred A. Knopf, 1949), p. 16.
10. "The Negro citizenry is becoming increasingly organized . . . and the politicians are pay-
ing more attention to the demands of this
group" (p. 257). "Subcommunity [i.e.,
Negro] leaders never rate inclusion on the
white upper-policy-strategy committees but
are approached informally to get their
opinions. This process is a relatively fixed
pattern. The exception may lie, to some
extent, in the realm of partisan politics"
(p. 128).

Reputation and Reality in the Study of "Community Power"*

Raymond E. Wolfinger

Few books in recent years have had more
influence on the study of local politics than
Floyd Hunter's *Community Power Structure*.[1]
Based on a new research technique which
promised to make the study of political
influence easier and more systematic, this
volume reported that power in "Regional
City" (Atlanta) was concentrated in a small,
cohesive elite of businessmen. Following the
publication of *Community Power Structure* a
number of researchers used Hunter's method
in other cities and, for the most part, produced similar findings of business dominance.[2] The basic assumption underlying
this method is that reputations for influence
are an index of the distribution of influence.
The researcher asks respondents either to
rank names on a list or to name individuals

who would be most influential in securing the
adoption of a project, or both.[3] He assigns
power to the leader-nominees according to
the number of times they are named by
respondents; the highest-ranking nominees
are described as the community's "power
structure." This technique for describing a
local political system is referred to below as
the *reputational* or *power-attribution* method.

Several scholars have criticized Hunter's
work on various grounds,[4] but there has been
no detailed evaluation of the reputational
method. Judging by the flow of research
making use of this technique,[5] it continues
to be highly regarded.[6] The purpose of this
paper is to explore the utility of the reputational method for the study of local political
systems. This inquiry involves two questions:

Reprinted from the American Sociological Review, *25 (October 1960), 636–644, by permission of
the author and the American Sociological Association. Copyright 1960 by the American Sociological
Association.*

*My thinking on the topics covered in this paper has been greatly influenced by Robert A. Dahl
and Nelson W. Polsby. I am indebted to them and to Fred I. Greenstein, Charles E. Lindblom, and
Barbara Kaye for their many valuable comments on an earlier draft of this paper.

(1) Are reputations for power an adequate index of the distribution of power? (2) Even if the respondents' perceptions of power relations are accurate, is it useful to describe a political system by presenting rankings of the leading participants according to their power?

It can be argued that the reputational method should be regarded as merely a systematic first step in studying a city's political system rather than a comprehensive technique for discovering the distribution of power. Under this modest construction the researcher would not rely on the method to identify and rank all decision makers but would use it as a guide to knowledgeable persons who would in turn give him leads to other informants until he had a complete picture of the political system under study. Viewed in this unambitious light, the reputational technique is little more than a methodologically elaborate variant of the older procedure of asking insiders—city hall reporters, politicians, and so on—for a quick rundown on the local big shots in order to identify potentially useful interviewees.

The reputational researchers do not make such modest claims for their method,[7] nor do their critics take such a limited view. While I am not aware of any explicit published statement to this effect, the reputational studies give the impression that the technique is regarded as considerably more than a ritualized political introduction. The putative validation of findings yielded by this method,[8] the assumption that a "power structure" consists of those persons most often given high rankings by panels of judges,[9] and a tendency to limit descriptions of decision making to the activities of the top-ranked leaders[10] all point to a belief that this method is a sufficient tool to study the distribution of political power in a community.

The Problem of Ambiguity

Assuming for the moment that it is worthwhile to rank political actors with respect to their power, is the reputational method adequate for this purpose? There are two major causes of ambiguity inherent in asking respondents to name in rank order the most powerful members of their community: the variability of power from one type of issue to another; and the difficulty of making sure that researcher and respondent share the same definition of power. Each of these problems is examined in turn below, using the familiar concept of power: "A has power over B to the extent that he can get B to do something that B would not otherwise do."[11] The term *scope* is used to refer to those actions by B which are affected by A's exercise of power; for example, the major scope of a school superintendent's power is public education.[12]

In order to compare the power of two individuals one must either assume that power is distributed evenly for all scopes or present a different set of rankings for each scope.[13] Otherwise, if A is judged to be the most powerful man in town on school affairs and B is named the most powerful on urban renewal there is no way to compare their power except by asserting that power in one scope is more "important" than in another. Most of the reputational researchers, by their failure to specify scopes in soliciting reputations for influence, assume that the power of their leader-nominees is equal for all issues; some researchers specifically state that they are concerned with "a general category of community leadership."[14] This is an exceedingly dubious assumption. It is improbable, for instance, that the same people who decide which houses of prostitution are to be protected in return for graft payments also plan the public school curriculum. Moreover, recent research reveals specialized leadership, for example, in studies of Bennington, Vermont,[15] and New Haven.[16]

An individual's political power varies with different issues. Therefore "general power" rankings are misleading. Furthermore, the researcher cannot be sure that his respondent is not tacitly basing his rankings of community leaders on an implicit scope, with the result that an individual may be given a high general power rating because he is perceived to be very influential on a particular issue which is either currently important to the community or salient to the respondent.[17] Data presented in a paper by Robert Agger—the only case, I believe, in which respondents' rankings are presented both for specific issues and general power—suggest that this is more than an academic possibility.[18] Agger reports the number of nominations received by each of eight leader-nominees. Three of these reputed leaders received the bulk of the nominations for "most influential," but the distribution of nominations in the three specialized areas is quite different: "H," who was not named as generally influential by a single respondent, received 47 per cent of all nominations for most influential on "community welfare"; "G" received 4 per cent of the nominations for general influence and 29 per cent for influence on school affairs; the corresponding figures for "F" were 5 and 35 per cent. What scopes these respondents had in mind when they made their nominations of general leaders is anybody's guess.

The validity of the reputational method is weakened by the difficulty of determining whether the interviewer and his respondents have the same idea of what the former seeks. The problem of defining political power has vexed generations of social scientists, many of whom have suggested definitions which display considerable conceptual and logical ingenuity. A researcher asking questions based on this complicated concept can either inflict his definition of power on each respondent or use a simplified analogous question. It would require a "man in the street" to be cooperative to the point of masochism to stand still while an interviewer labored through the definitions and qualifications that are found in the literature on power. But the alternative embraced by many researchers has equally great disadvantages because of the ambiguity of their questions. Several researchers have used some variant of the following question: "If a project were before the community that required *decision* by a group of leaders—leaders that nearly everyone would accept—which *ten* on the list of forty would you choose?"[19] This question could ask for popularity, malleability, or willingness to serve on committees.[20] Hun-

ter's "Who is the 'biggest' man in town?" is also susceptible of numerous interpretations.[21]

The ambiguity of such questions is illustrated by a study in which the researchers asked 107 steel union members and officials to identify the "big shots" in town.[22] The respondents named the banker, the Chamber of Commerce, the mayor, other city officials, the gambling syndicate, and the steel company, which dominated the town economically. No respondent mentioned the union or its officers. Hunter and others might take this as evidence of the union's political impotence. But the union obviously was an influential force in local politics. All but three of the respondents said that the police were friendly and partial to them in collective bargaining, the most important issue for most union members; the three exceptions termed the police neutral. In fact, the union leaders had made a deal with the mayor, trading union political support for police favoritism. The police were so friendly that they cooperated in periodic drives in which all non-members were forcibly prevented from entering the steel plant. Most union members did not, however, view police favoritism as a *political* phenomenon. One might also explain their listing of "big shots" as attribution of status rather than power (with the exception, perhaps, of the gambling syndicate).

The reputational method appears to be particularly susceptible to ambiguity resulting from respondents' confusion of status and power. This difficulty is amplified by the low esteem in which labor leaders, local politicians, and municipal officials are often held, as well as by their usually lower socio-economic status compared to businessmen and leaders of charitable organizations. In many cities control of political parties and municipal offices has passed from "Anglo-Saxon" businessmen to people of recent immigrant stock and generally lower social status.[23] For example, scarcely any New Haven economic or social leaders participate in party politics, an activity in which the city's populous Irish, Jewish, and Italian groups predominate.[24] In another New England city where the outnumbered high-status

Yankees have shifted their attention and aspirations to activities in which money, leisure, and social status count more heavily, "the functions of status allocation and recognition, which were once performed by public office-holding, have been shifted in this period to ... the community service organization."[25]

These differences pose a problem for reputational researchers, who often rely on voluntary organizations for initial nominations of leaders. The nominees are then ranked by panels which usually are composed largely of business and professional people. One might expect that as the wealthy become less influential in politics they value political office less highly.[26] In these circumstances, questions which do not distinguish between status and power, and between public and private scopes, are likely to lead researchers to leader-nominees whose power may be exercised chiefly on a country club's admissions committee. Businessmen, when asked questions about "projects," are apt to base their answers on those types of private activity in which they are most active and influential, and which are most salient to them. This may be one reason why the reputational method tends to turn up ruling elites consisting largely of businessmen.

Ambiguity can be minimized by asking questions about specific scopes and eschewing the "Who's the local big shot?" approach. This would eliminate situations in which the interviewer assumes that he is getting reports on political power when respondents in fact are ascribing status or merely revealing who pulls the strings in the Rotary Club's program committee. Limiting the question to specific political issues still will not impose on respondents the same criteria that might lead a social scientist to define a certain event as reflecting a power relationship, but it is probably the best that can be done with this method.

Specifying scopes minimizes ambiguity and provides a more accurate description of politics by permitting comparisons of influence in different areas. This procedure also gives the respondent a cue to reality and weakens the force of local myths about poli-

tics. A man willing to assert that Yankee bankers run "everything" might make a more cautious reply when asked specifically about the municipal welfare department.

The Prevalence of Misperception

Assuming now that interviewer and respondent have in mind the same phenomenon, how accurate are the respondent's perceptions? There is some evidence that these are inaccurate, and to date none of the power attribution studies has been validated on this point by other means.[27]

One of the most striking examples of inaccurate perception appears in a footnote to a paper by Pellegrin and Coates on the influence of absentee-owned corporations in a southern city:

> The typical interviewee [a businessman in this study described local government officials as relatively powerless figures who do not have the backing of influential groups but secured their positions through the support of working-class voters. Indeed, these officials were more often than not targets of ridicule for those who evaluated their positions in the power structure. ... The relative lack of integration of Bigtown's interest groups makes it possible for governmental officials to sponsor civic projects which are sometimes successful, in spite of opposition from one or another of the "crowds" [of big business]. Interest groups find it difficult to express publicly opposition to projects which attract widespread support. To do so would be "bad public relations," perhaps unprofitable in the long run.[28]

In the text of this paper the authors emphasize the power of the absentee-owned corporations and report that they can veto any project which they oppose and secure the adoption of any measure they support.[29] Perhaps Pellegrin and Coates were unaware of the implications of the quoted passage, both for their thesis about the distribution of power in "Bigtown" and for the more general assumption that reputations are an adequate index of the actual distribution of power. Whether the passage reveals inaccurate perceptions or an eccentric definition of power, however, it is clear that these respondents' rankings of the community's most powerful men are open to serious question. So many alternate interpretations of such responses are possible that relying on them to define a "power structure" is unwarranted.

If private citizens are unreliable sources of information, people who are active in public life are not much better informants, either on general or specific questions. Key observes that "Such general conclusions [about the political efficacy of various groups] by politicians and other 'informed' citizens are wrong so much of the time that one becomes skeptical of all such remarks."[30] Rossi reports a striking example of misperception in "Bay City," where Republican politicans explained that their lack of success with various ethnic groups was due to the energetic activities of the local Catholic priests on behalf of the Democratic party. Actually most of the priests were Republicans.[31]

In New Haven a number of prominent citizens active in public affairs could not identify other decision makers in the same policy field. This was most notably revealed in interviews with members of the executive committee of the Citizens Action Commission, a group of about 20 men who direct the Commission's activities in various aspects of civic betterment. This group has been described as the "biggest muscles in town" and includes among others the President of Yale University and the Dean of the Yale Law School, the presidents of the local power and telephone companies, the President of the New York, New Haven and Hartford Railroad, leading bankers and attorneys, the heads of several nationally known industrial firms, the President and Secretary of the Connecticut Labor Council, AFL-CIO, and the Democratic National Committeeman from Connecticut. Although these men meet formally once a month and often get together at other CAC functions, many of them could not identify other committee members. For example, a regular and articulate participant spoke glowingly about the pleasures of his association with the other men on the committee and of his fond image

of them all sitting together around the conference table, but, except for friends he had known before the CAC was founded, he was unable to identify a single member. Another active participant, describing his fellow committee members, thought that the president of the Labor Council was a realtor employed by the New Haven Redevelopment Agency. Clearly, these respondents' replies to questions about the relative political influence of various New Haven leaders were not very informative.

New Haven politicians were not much better reporters of the distribution of power. Several of them, interviewed on a particular issue, told researchers that a local figure was the "real power" behind the scenes and always had his way; and then, discussing the same measure, added that another politician, opposed to the first, had "rammed it through the board—no one could stand up to him." An enduring item in the political folklore of New Haven is that one political figure or another is nothing but an errand boy for Yale University. As one would expect, this accusation is most credible to those individuals who are hostile either to Yale or to whichever politician is currently so attacked. Some experienced political figures so devoutly believe this charge that they are impervious to contrary evidence. If people who are professionally involved in community decision making cannot perceive accurately the distribution of political power, how can the rankings of less well-informed respondents be accepted as anything more than a report of public opinion on politics?

The Inutility of Influence Rankings

The reputational method, then, does not do what it is supposed to do: the ranking of leaders is not a valid representation of the distribution of political power in a given community. But assuming that reputations for power do in fact constitute an adequate index of power, nevertheless the resulting list of powerful individuals would not be useful without additional research which would make the method largely redundant, and even this utility would be very limited.

In compiling a list of leaders ranked according to the degree of power attributed to each of them, the researcher must have some means of limiting its size. Hunter, in selecting the arbitrary number of 40 for his leadership group, assumed what he set out to prove: that no more than 40 people were the rulers of Atlanta, possessed more power than the rest of population, and comprised its "power structure."[32] He assumed that political power was concentrated in a very small group and concerned himself with identifying its members. Hunter's key question might be paraphrased as follows: "What are the names and occupations of the tiny group of people who run this city?"

Any a *priori* definition of the size of a leadership group carries such an implicit assumption about the distribution of political power. The vital point is the establishment of a cut-off point, a criterion which determines the size of the group. If the criterion is placed too high, it may exclude so many significant actors that only a small part of the total amount of influence exercised in the community is included—the top 40 leaders may be outweighed by the next 200 power-wielders.[33] If too low, it may result in diluting the leadership group with many non-leaders. Clearly the important consideration here is the shape of the influence "pyramid": the more steeply its sides slope, the fewer people in the elite group and the higher the researcher's cut-off point can be. Yet if he knows enough about the community to envision such a pyramid, he already knows much of what the power-attribution method is supposed to tell him, and a great deal more.

There appears to be no way out of this dilemma without making an assumption crucial to the problem. If the researcher's questions do not specify the number of leaders the respondent can nominate and only a few actors are mentioned, he is in effect passing this problem along to his respondents. For while each of the respondents may believe that the person (or persons) he names is the most powerful single individual, nominations of the most influential man in town do not include information about how much power he has compared to other actors. If the researcher decides to establish the cut-off point by a "break" in number of nominations, or by including the nominees who account for a majority of nominations, he is passing the buck to a statistical artifact, for he still has no way of knowing that his criterion corresponds to political reality.

The identification of leaders which the reputational method is supposed to achieve has very limited utility for another reason. A demographic classification of such leaders is not a description of a city's political system because it does not indicate whether they are allies or enemies. To establish the existence of a ruling elite, one must show not only that influence is distributed unequally but also that those who have the most influence are united so as to act in concert rather than in opposition.[34] One cannot conclude that the highest-ranked individuals comprise a ruling group rather than merely an aggregate of leaders without establishing their cohesiveness as well as their power.

Most of the reputational researchers consider this point, but then go on to draw conclusions about the probable decisions of their putative elites by assuming that political preferences can be inferred from socioeconomic status. This inference is questionable on a number of grounds.[35] It assumes that the members of the body politic can be divided into two groups on the basis of a dichotomizing principle (such as relationship to the means of production) which determines all their policy preferences. Thus there will be a "class position" on every issue, with the same people on the same side on all issues. This in turn assumes that economic status is the only variable that determines political preferences. But associations between socioeconomic status and positions on various issues represent correlations, not categoric divisions; there are always sizeable numbers of people on the minority side. Furthermore, persons of different economic status may have similar attitudes on the basis of shared vocational or sectional interests: both the United Mine Workers and coal mine owners worry about competition from other fuels; New England workers and merchants alike are concerned about departing industries. For people in official positions the "norms of the office" represent role demands which often predict behavior more consistently than status. Finally, politicians want to win, to the point at times where they are ideologically indifferent. Even "issue-oriented" politicians accept the need to compromise.

While most political leaders in Bennington were business or professional men, they were split into several durable and bitterly opposed factions on the issues which Scoble studied.[36] In New Haven the six most prominent politicians have the following occupations (or occupational background, in the case of the mayor, a full-time official): attorney (two), undertaker, bond and insurance broker, realtor, and public relations director. The first three are Republicans, the others, Democrats. The two parties are quite differentiated; a change in regime seven years ago brought marked changes in municipal policies. The policies followed by these six men cannot be predicted by reference to their occupations. It should be noted that few of the power-attribution researchers even mention the party identifications of their leader-nominees.[37]

Another weakness of the reputational method is that it assumes and reports a static distribution of power.[38] The three New Haven Democrats mentioned in the preceding paragraph are currently much more powerful than the three Republicans, in large measure because the Democrats are in office. The outcome of elections may be relevant to the distribution of power, a consideration which apparently has escaped the power-attribution researchers and for which their method is ill-suited. Changes in the nature and distribution of the sources of power are assumed to occur very slowly, so that the only strategy for a group engaged in political action is to persuade the real elite to go along with it.[39] The model of the political process resulting from the reputational method assumes an equation of potential for power with the realization of that potential. (It may be a misnomer to refer to this as a "process";

actually the reputational researchers appear to assume a kind of equilibrium.) This in turn assumes that all resources will be used to an equal extent and thus that political skill is unimportant. Either elections are of no consequence or one side will win all of them.

It would be interesting to replicate some of the power attribution studies at five-year intervals to learn how persistently the same individuals are nominated as leaders. A study by Donald Olmsted suggests that quite different lists might result.[40] His panel of "knowledgeable citizens" named 30 community leaders in 1943 and again in 1949; the names of only nine people were on both lists. One would expect some attrition by death, moving, and so on, but the locale of Olmsted's study did not have an unusually unstable population.

Shifting distribution of power, whether the result of elections or of other factors, presents a problem in political analysis which appears to be unsolvable by the power-attribution method. While some individuals might maintain some or all of their power after a change in regime, others would not, and some relatively powerless persons would be placed high in the "power structure." The inclusion of all political actors within a supposed power elite would be neither surprising nor discriminating. The interesting questions about politics are concerned with the dynamics of policy making and are badly warped in static, reified rankings of individuals whose demographic classification is a poor substitute for analysis of goals, strategies, power bases, outcomes, recruitment patterns, and similar questions. When energetic political organization can affect elections and issue outcomes and thus "make new power,"[41] description of a dynamic process by a static concept appears to be a mismatch of method and subject matter. The gifts and energies of social scientists can be better used than in this pursuit.

Notes

1. [Floyd Hunter, *Community Power Structure*] Chapel Hill: University of North Carolina Press, 1953.
2. Robert E. Agger, "Power Attributions in the Local Community," *Social Forces*, 34 (May, 1956), pp. 322–331; Robert E. Agger and Vincent Ostrom, "The Political Structure of a Small Community," *Public Opinion Quarterly*, 20 (Spring, 1956), pp. 81–89; Robert E. Agger and Vincent Ostrom, "Political Participation in a Small Community," in Heinz Eulau, *et al.*, editors, *Political Behavior*, Chicago: Free Press, 1957, pp. 138–148; Robert E. Agger and Daniel Goldrich, "Community Power Structures and Partisanship," *American Sociological Review*, 23 (August, 1958), pp. 383–392; Ernest Barth and Baha Abu-Laban, "Power Structure and the Negro Sub-Community," *American Sociological Review*, 24 (February, 1959), pp. 69–76; Orrin E. Klapp and L. Vincent Padgett, "Power Structure and Decision-making in a Mexican Border City," *American Journal of Sociology*, 65 (January, 1960), pp. 400–406; Delbert C. Miller, "Industry and Community Power Structures: A Comparative Study of an American and an English City," *American Sociological Review*, 23 (February, 1958), pp. 9–15; Delbert C. Miller, "Decision-making Cliques in Community Power Structures: A Comparative Study of an American and an English City," *American Journal of Sociology* 64 (November, 1958), pp. 299–310; Robert O. Schulze and Leonard U. Blumberg, "The Determination of Local Power Elites," *American Journal of Sociology*, 63 (November, 1957), pp. 290–296. Hunter himself did similar research in Salem, Massachusetts; see Floyd Hunter, Ruth Connor Schaffer and Cecil G. Sheps, *Community Organization: Action and Inaction*, Chapel Hill: University of North Carolina Press, 1956. George Belknap and Ralph Smuckler, in using the reputational method, do not assert that their top leaders dominate decision making or comprise a unified group, and do not regard their findings as descriptive of a political system; see their "Political Power Relations in a Mid-West City," *Public Opinion Quarterly*, 20 (Spring, 1956), pp. 73–81.
3. Hunter asked several authoritative sources, e.g., the Chamber of Commerce and the League of Women Voters, for lists of leaders in their respective fields and then asked a panel of judges to rank the ten most powerful persons on each of the four lists of leaders. The top ten names on each list comprised the 40 persons whom Hunter termed the top leadership in Regional City. He interviewed most of these 40 and from these and other sources presented a description of the "community power structure," the pattern that explained policy making in Regional City. Succeeding studies did not always use this two-step nomination and ranking procedure; and in some cases the reputational researchers elaborated their description of the "power structure" by interviewing leader-nominees and other informants.
4. Robert A. Dahl, "The Concept of Power," *Behavioral Science*, 2 (July, 1957), pp. 201–215; Dahl, "Hierarchy, Democracy, and Bargaining in Politics and Economics," in Stephen Bailey, *et al.*, *Research Frontiers in Politics and Government*, Washington, D.C.: The Brookings Institution, 1955, pp. 45–69; Dahl, "A Critique of the Ruling Elite Model," *American Political Science Review*, 52 (June, 1958), pp. 463–469; Herbert Kaufman and Victor Jones, "The Mystery of Power," *Public Administration Review*, 14 (Summer, 1954), pp. 205–212; Nelson W. Polsby, "The Sociology of Community Power: A Reassessment," *Social Forces*, 37 (March, 1959), pp. 232–236, Polsby, "Three Problems in the Analysis of Community Power," *American Sociological Review*, 24 (December, 1959), pp. 796–803; Peter H. Rossi, "Community Decision-Making," in Roland Young, editor, *Approaches to the Study of Politics*, Evanston: Northwestern University Press, 1958, pp. 363–382.
5. One of the most ambitious of these projects is Edwin H. Rhyne's attempt to test the commonly accepted proposition that political systems with two-party competition are most conducive to popular participation in political decision making. He reports the opposite conclusion but emphasizes the tentative nature of his findings. See his "Political Parties and Decision Making in Three Southern Counties," *American Political Science Review*, 52 (December, 1958), pp. 1091–1107. See also William H. Form and William V. D'Antonio, "Integration and Cleavage among Community Influentials in Two Border Cities," *American Sociological Review*, 24 (December, 1959), pp. 804–814.
6. With the major exception of the review article by Kaufman and Jones, *op. cit.*, reviews of *Community Power Structure* were favorable and in some cases enthusiastic. See the following reviews: Jack London, *American Journal of Sociology*, 60 (March, 1955), pp. 522–523; C. Wright Mills, *Social Forces*, 32 (October, 1953), pp. 92–93; Louis Smith, *Journal of Politics*, 16 (February, 1954), pp. 146–150; Donald S. Strong, *American Polit-*

ical Science Review, 48 (March, 1954), pp. 235–237. London disagreed with Hunter's attribution of power to individuals rather than groups, but did not contest his finding that the business element in Regional City dominated policy making. For other endorsements of the reputational method see Gordon W. Blackwell, "Community Analysis," in Young, *op. cit.*, pp. 305–317; William J. Gore and Fred S. Silander, "A Bibliographical Essay on Decision Making," *Administrative Science Quarterly*, 4 (June, 1959), p. 106. Arthur Kornhauser, "Power Relationships and the Role of the Social Scientist," in Kornhauser, editor, *Problems of Power in American Democracy*, Detroit: Wayne State University Press, 1957, p. 196.

7. Blackwell, Gore and Silander, Rhyne, and Schulze and Blumberg are among those who see it as a more ambitious technique. Blackwell hails Hunter as a pioneer who has made a significant methodological contribution to the study of politics, *op. cit.*, p. 317.

8. Blackwell, *op. cit.*, p. 317; Miller, "Industry and Community . . .," *op. cit.*, p. 10n.

9. Miller, "Industry and Community . . .," *op. cit.*, p. 10, and "Decision-making Cliques . . .," *op. cit.*, pp. 300–301.

10. Hunter, *op. cit.*, *passim*. See Kaufman and Jones for a criticism of this limitation, *op. cit.*, pp. 209–211.

11. Dahl, "The Concept of Power," *op. cit.*, pp. 202–203. This is similar to Herbert Simon's definition of influence in *Models of Man*, New York: Wiley, 1957, pp. 65–66; and to Harold D. Lasswell and Abraham Kaplan's definition of power as participation in the making of decisions in *Power and Society*, New Haven: Yale University Press, 1950, p. 75.

12. For similar uses of this term see Dahl, "The Concept of Power," *op. cit.*, pp. 203, 205–206; and Lasswell and Kaplan, *op. cit.*, pp. 73, 77.

13. See Dahl, "A Critique of the Ruling Elite Model," *op. cit.*, pp. 463–464, and "The Concept of Power," *op. cit.*, p. 206.

14. Schulze and Blumberg, *op. cit.*, p. 292n. Miller and Hunter also express interest in a "general power structure." See Hunter, Schaffer and Sheps, *op. cit.*, pp. xi–xii; and Miller, "Industry and Community . . .," *op. cit.*, p. 10, and "Decision-making Cliques . . .," *op. cit.*, p. 300.

15. Harry M. Scoble, "Yankeetown: Leadership in Three Decision-Making Processes," presented at the annual meeting of the American Political Science Association, Washington, D.C., 1956.

16. See Robert A. Dahl, "Organization for Decisions in New Haven," paper presented at the annual meeting of the American Political Science Association, St. Louis, 1958; and Polsby, "Three Problems . . .," *op. cit.* References to New Haven are based on research on decision making in that city by Dahl, Polsby, and the writer, including a year of direct observation of the activities of the mayor and his chief officials.

17. Polsby has suggested several possible referents for responses made when issues are unspecified; see his "The Sociology . . .," *op. cit.*, p. 232n.

18. Agger, "Power Attributions . . .," *op. cit.* A study soliciting nominations in several specialized areas produced quite different rankings of individuals in each of three scopes, with the exception of one nominee, the local newspaper editor. See A. Alexander Fanelli, "A Typology of Community Leadership Based on Influence within the Leader Sub-System," *Social Forces*, 34 (May, 1956), pp. 332–338.

19. This question was first used by Hunter, *op. cit.*, p. 62. The same question or a variant was used by Miller, "Industry and Community . . .," *op. cit.*, p. 12, and "Decision-making Cliques . . .," *op. cit.*, p. 301; Barth and Abu-Laban, *op. cit.*, p. 72; and Schulze and Blumberg, *op. cit.*, p. 292n.

20. Hunter tacitly acknowledges this drawback in mentioning that one very powerful man in Regional City ranked comparatively low on responses to this question because of his reputation for refusing to serve on committees, *op. cit.*, p. 64. This question assumes that the nature of the "project" under consideration would make no difference in one's nominations.

21. Hunter, *op. cit.*, p. 62. Polsby has pointed out the ambiguity of such questions; see "The Sociology . . .," *op. cit.*, p. 232. The influence of the wording of questions on respondents' answers has long been a serious problem for public opinion researchers and others. Some of the reputational researchers seem not to have been too careful about the phrasing of their questions. It would be interesting to use split-pair techniques to learn how responses vary with changes in the wording of the basic "Who has the power?" question. See, e.g., Hadley Cantril, *Gauging Public Opinion*, Princeton: Princeton University Press, 1947, Chapters 1 and 2.

22. Joel Seidman, Jack London, and Bernard Karsh, "Political Consciousness in Local Unions," *Public Opinion Quarterly*, 15 (Winter, 1952), pp. 692–702.

23. James B. McKee has described this process in Lorain, Ohio in "Status and Power in the Industrial Community: A Comment on Drucker's Thesis," *American Journal of Sociology*, 58 (January, 1953), pp. 364–370. McKee reports that union leaders do not

participate very much in decision making in private civic welfare activities and that politically powerful members of minority ethnic groups still tend to have rather low social status. See also Peter H. Rossi and Alice S. Rossi, "An Historical Perspective on the Functions of Local Politics," revision of a paper presented at the annual meeting of the American Sociological Society, Detroit, 1956.

24. See Dahl, "Organization . . .," op. cit.; and Polsby, "Three Problems . . .," op. cit.

25. Rossi and Rossi, op. cit., p. 15.

26. "Far too frequently they [businessmen] also have a strong distaste for politics and politicians—a distaste that can be particularly strong when the politicians happen to be Democrats" (The Editors of Fortune, The Exploding Metropolis, New York: Doubleday, Anchor Edition, 1958, p. xvii). Scoble reports that his respondents tended to nominate as leaders those individuals who agreed with them, op. cit., p. 41, as do Agger and Goldrich, op. cit., p. 391.

27. Blackwell maintains that studies which Hunter has conducted in other communities have verified the findings of his inquiry in Regional City, op. cit., p. 317. But Hunter's description of the political system in City A is not evidence for the accuracy of his description of City B; and since he has not studied Regional City by means of an alternative procedure, his method has not been validated. Miller reports correlations between choice as a "key influential" and some forms of participation in civic groups, but none of these activities has been shown to be an index of political power. See his "Industry and Community . . .," op. cit., pp. 12, 13. He also asserts that "A valuable test of this technique" of power attribution was conducted by John M. Foskett and Raymond Hohle, ibid., p. 10n. See the latter's "The Measurement of Influence in Community Affairs," Research Studies of the State College of Washington, 25 (June, 1957), pp. 148–154. But Foskett and Hohle merely compared the lists of leaders chosen by a number of variants of the reputational method and found a high association between them, which did not test the method by comparing its results with findings produced by another method.

28. Roland J. Pellegrin and Charles S. Coates, "Absentee-Owned Corporations and Community Power Structure," American Journal of Sociology, 61 (March, 1956), p. 414n.

29. Ibid., p. 414.

30. V. O. Key, Southern Politics, New York: Knopf, 1950, p. 139n.

31. Peter H. Rossi, "The Study of Decision Making in the Local Community," University of Chicago, 1957 (mimeo.), p. 20.

32. Kaufman and Jones mention this limitation, op. cit., p. 207.

33. Cf. Robert K. Merton, "Patterns of Influence: A Study of Interpersonal Influence and of Communications Behavior in a Local Community," in P. F. Lazarsfeld and F. N. Stanton, editors, Communications Research, 1948–49, New York: Harper, 1949, pp. 180–219. Miller defines "power structure" so that it is composed of the most frequently nominated individuals, without knowing whether the "pyramid" of power is shaped so that his a priori criterion of nomination will coincide with an actual cut-off point in the distribution of power. Thus he reports that there are 12 "key influentials" and 44 "top influentials" in a city of half a million people, but presents no evidence of their ability to dominate Seattle's political system. See Miller, "Industry and Community . . .," op. cit., p. 10, and "Decision-making Cliques . . .," op. cit., pp. 302–303. Other reputational researchers are less explicit about this assumption. In his later article, Miller expresses some doubt about the extent of business dominance in Seattle. These uncertainties are based on interviews with a few participants, however, not on the reputational method; the latter technique turned up a business ruling elite.

34. Cf. Dahl, "A Critique of the Ruling Elite Model," op. cit., p. 465.

35. Several writers have noted this fallacy. See, e.g., Rossi, "Community Decision-Making," op. cit., pp. 366–369; Reinhard Bendix and Seymour M. Lipset, "Political Sociology," Current Sociology, 6 (1957), pp. 84–85; and Lipset, "Political Sociology," in R. K. Merton, et al., editors, Sociology Today, New York: Basic Books, 1959, pp. 106–107.

36. Scoble, op. cit., p. 41.

37. The major exception is the work of Agger and his associates; see note 2 above.

38. This has been pointed out by Polsby, "The Sociology . . .," op. cit., p. 232; and by Rossi, "Community Decision-Making," op. cit., pp. 366–369.

39. Blackwell makes this assertion explicitly, op. cit., p. 307.

40. "Organizational Leadership and Social Structure in a Small City," American Sociological Review, 19 (May, 1954), pp. 273–281.

41. See, e.g., Francis Carney, The Rise of the Democratic Clubs in California, New York: Holt, 1959.

D. The Reputational Approach Defended

The Reputational Technique as a Measure of Community Power: An Evaluation Based on Comparative and Longitudinal Studies*

William V. D'Antonio and Eugene C. Erickson

Introduction

Data gathered from continuing research along the United States-Mexico border provides a basis for evaluation of the several criticisms which have been leveled against the so-called reputational technique for the study of community power. The most persistent criticisms have come from Dahl, Polsby, and Wolfinger. They have questioned (a) the existence of such a social phenomenon as a "community power structure" and (b) the utility of the reputational approach even if such a power structure should exist. Furthermore, they argue that the concept of a community power structure as derived by the reputational technique necessarily implies the existence of a monolithic, solidary power elite.

Dahl[1] argues that a rigorous scientist who used the reputational technique should say nothing more than that he had a list of people who had the reputation for influence and power. Wolfinger is more adamant; he states that this currently popular research

design "is found to be seriously deficient as a technique for the study of a local political system."[2]

Despite these criticisms, many political sociologists continue to use this technique simply because the criticisms have not demonstrated that the reputational technique is inadequate.[3] These critics have studied community power by using the issues or the positional technique.[4] They examine in detail the way in which issues arise and are resolved and employ extensive lists of formal positions or offices to help define leadership.[5] In fact, these scientists have not tested the reputational technique, but have criticized it on the basis of the use of other techniques.

It is important to note that Dahl does not deny that there are such people as influentials. In discussing his findings from New Haven, he says, "On any single issue, there are only a few influentials; one usually finds that for any particular sector of policy only a small number of persons ever initiate alter-

Reprinted from the American Sociological Review, *27 (June 1962), 362–376, by permission of the authors and the American Sociological Association. Copyright 1962 by the American Sociological Association.*

*The paper was presented at the annual meeting of the American Sociological Association, September, 1961. We should like to express our appreciation for support from funds made available by the Division of Hospital and Medical Facilities of the United States Public Health Service for project W-108, "Anglo-Latino Relations in Hospitals and Communities," and the Carnegie Corporation for a project dealing with the United States-Mexican Border. Both projects are under the general direction of Charles P. Loomis, whose personal help is gratefully acknowledged. We wish to acknowledge the helpful criticisms of Professors Donald Barrett of the University of Notre Dame, Howard J. Ehrlich of the Ohio State University, Ralph Goldman, Robert G. Holloway, A. O. Haller of Michigan State University and Gerhard Lenski of the University of Michigan.

251

natives or veto the proposals of others."[6] Dahl and his co-workers question, rather, the hypothesis that there is a relatively small group of persons who are influential over a *number* of issue areas. And they wonder whether the reputational technique can discover this group if it should exist. Thus, Wolfinger argues that

> The researcher cannot be sure that his respondent [when answering the question on general influence] is not tacitly basing his rankings of community leaders on an implicit scope, with the result that an individual may be given a high general power rating because he is perceived to be very influential on a particular issue which is either currently important to the community or salient to the respondent.[7]

Polsby also argues that the reputational technique may be measuring such variables as a status elite, leaders with respect to some issue which has been of recent interest in the community or an issue which has been particularly salient to the respondent.[8]

These critics offer the alternative hypothesis that American communities are made up of a number of segmented "power structures," that people have limited scopes of influence, and that these scopes are narrowly restricted to the institutional sectors with which they (the influentials) most closely identify.[9] This is their "pluralist" interpretation of American politics.

If their contention is correct, then of course *general* community influentials do not exist in today's American community. It is the task of this paper to confront these criticisms and the hypothesis resulting therefrom. We will do so by addressing ourselves to the following questions:

1. Is the community power structure obtained by the reputational technique an aggregate of limited-scope influentials, of a simple status elite, or of persons who are perceived to be general influentials?
2. Is there longitudinal reliability to the lists of general influentials obtained by use of the reputational technique?

3. Is there evidence of a relationship between the reputation for general influence and the actual exercise of power in a broad range of community decisions?

Methodology

The data presented here were gathered between September, 1954 and September, 1959. In the original research project in 1954–55, the focus of interest was the kinds of self and national images held by people living in border communities. For a number of reasons which have been set forth elsewhere,[10] it was decided to study the images held by the political and business influentials of the border communities of El Paso, Texas, and Cd. Juarez, Chihuahua, Mexico. To find out who the influentials were, a modification of the Hunter technique was used. Informal discussions with knowledgeables were held.[11] Among other questions each was asked to nominate twelve persons whom he considered to be "most influential" in his community. These exploratory data revealed that the business and political sectors of the community might be "controlled by different groups of people. The formal interview shedule included separate sections for questions dealing with business and politics. The following questions were asked at the end of the sections on business and politics respectively:

1. Who are the most influential businessmen in this community, that is, men most influential in the business affairs of the community?
2. Who are the men who have been the most influential in the government and politics of this community in recent years?

In both questions twelve names were requested and the respondents were not given any prearranged lists to choose from.[12] Lists of business and political influentials were built up in both cities and formal interviews were obtained from these influentials.

In the course of the interviewing in 1954–55 it became obvious that the reasons why people were chosen as influentials should be determined. Therefore, data were gathered on issues in which the influentials were supposedly involved, particularly ongoing issues, which seemed to be affecting the way the questions about images were being answered. Crucial items seemed to include the extent to which lists of business and political influentials overlapped, and the extent to which the two groups seemed to work together or at cross-purposes on projects.

With the aid of a grant to study Anglo-Latino relations in community and hospital affairs, another study was designed in 1958. Enlisting the cooperation of social scientists at San Diego State College, University of Arizona, and New Mexico State University, and with a jointly-constructed interview schedule, the relationship between reputation and decision-making was examined in San Diego, Tijuana, Tucson, Las Cruces, El Paso, and Cd. Juarez.[13] This time the usual technique of getting knowledgeables from different institutional sectors was used to provide a list of 50 persons who were the "most influential" in community affairs in general. These were persons who could and did initiate, block, or significantly help resolve issues of broad community interest.

In each community the lists compiled by interviewing knowledgeables were combined into one grand list of top influentials, which shall hereafter be referred to as the general influence index. These indexes varied between 22 and 45 persons in the several communities. In the formal interviewing that followed, each respondent, whether or not he was an influential, was asked to select the ten most influential persons in the community. The respondents were free to add names to the list presented to them.

Since El Paso and Cd. Juarez had been intensively studied three years previously, the technique was modified in these two communities. The lists of business and political influentials obtained in 1955 were combined into one general influence index. This procedure yielded lists of some eighty names for each community. These lists were then presented to a small group of knowledgeables who were asked to evaluate the lists, to

eliminate, add to, or in any other relevant manner make the lists conform to their perception of the community's top influentials. The knowledgeables provided information which was used to reduce the lists to about forty-five persons in each community.[14] From that point on, the same techniques were used in all six communities.

At the same time the way in which issues were resolved in the six communities were compared. One issue (concerning health) was common to all communities. At least one other issue was also examined in each community. An attempt was made to interview all the so-called Key and Top Influentials and to ascertain what role, if any, they had played in these issues. Other persons significantly involved in the issues were interviewed and data were gathered through written records, newspapers, and other published reports.

To probe further this problem of scope of influence and reputation *vs.* reality, an additional question was asked prior to the questions dealing with specific issues, and before the respondent had seen the general influence index from which he would choose the ten most influential persons:

> Suppose that a major hospital project were before the community, one that required decision by a group of leaders whom nearly everyone would accept. If you were completely free to choose, which people would you choose to make up this group—regardless of whether or not you know them personally? (Seek eight names)

In answer to this question, the respondent could name anyone without benefit of list or suggestion.

To summarize briefly: in 1954–55 the names of the top business and political influentials in El Paso and Cd. Juarez were gathered. Separate lists were obtained for the most influential people in business and the most influential in government and politics. In 1958, names of those persons in six southwestern and Mexican communities who would be the best leaders to gain support for a hospital project in a community were gathered. The actual decision-making process with respect to health projects and at least one other project in each of these six communities were analyzed and the names of the reputed most influential persons in community decision-making were gathered.

The findings to be described and analyzed involve:

(1) comparison of the business and political influential lists of 1955 from El Paso and Cd. Juarez and addressed to the question of limited scope of influence. Brief comment on the extent of overlap in the lists will be made. According to the criticisms cited above, business and politics are two different scopes of influence. There should be little or no overlap of persons assigned influence in each.[15]

(2) comparison of the 1955 business-political influential lists with the 1958 list of persons who were selected for the ideal hospital project committee for El Paso. Again, if this ideal hospital project is perceived as a different scope there should be no overlap between the "scope" lists if the criticisms are correct. Expectation of overlap should also be minimized by the fact that three and a half years elapsed between interviews.

(3) comparison of the 1958 general influence indexes in the six communities with the nominations for the ideal hospital committee and addressed to both the questions of scope and "status." Since the hospital list was determined first in the interview, and the respondents were not presented with a prearranged list of names, only slight correlation between the specific area of a hospital project and general community influence is expected if influence is limited to a particular scope.[16] In addition, if "status" is the criterion of the inclusion of a name on a general influence index but is not a criterion on a limited influence index, but slight correlation between the lists would be expected.

(4) comparison of the 1955 business-political influential lists with the 1958 general influence index in El Paso. If there is no reliability to the reputational technique, no overlap between this 1958 index and the 1955 lists would be expected, because the time difference is almost four years.[17]

(5) analysis of the relationship between reputation for influence and actual decisions made in El Paso during the 1950's.

Findings

1. *El Paso and Cd. Juarez business and political influentials, 1955.* Eighty-nine persons were interviewed in El Paso; sixty-eight agreed to name the most influential businessmen, and their choices yielded 131 names. Of these, fifty-one persons received three or more votes as business influentials.[18]

Seventy-three of the respondents selected political influentials, nominating 101 persons. Of these, thirty persons received three or more votes as political influentials.[19] On this basis, seventy persons were selected as business or political influentials in 1955.

Among the top twenty-five business influentials in El Paso, nine received three or more votes as political influentials also. Among the lower twenty-six businessmen, only two received votes as political influentials also. The same pattern emerged among the political influentials; nine of the top fourteen received strong support as business influentials. In fact, only two of them, both businessmen primarily, were holding public office at the time. The others were either lawyers or businessmen who gave a great deal of time to local politics. Of the lower sixteen of the political group, only two received support as business influentials. Thus, there was a tendency for the sociometric leaders of one group to be chosen as influentials in the other group also. In fact, nine persons were sociometric leaders in both groups.

In Cd. Juarez there was much less overlap than occurred in El Paso. Eighty-two persons were interviewed; sixty-seven voted for business influentials and suggested 115 names. Of these, forty-seven received three or more votes. Sixty-nine respondents selected political influentials, a total of 78 names being suggested. Thirty-six received three or more votes.

Eight Mexican businessmen received three or more votes as both business and political influentials in Cd. Juarez. Five others received less than three votes on one of the lists. None of the top businessmen ranked in the top half among the political influentials. This lack of overlap in Cd. Juarez cannot be taken to mean that the businessmen in the Mexican community were not interested in political affairs, and restricted themselves to business activities. It reflects, rather, the fact that Mexico's revolutionary party (PRI) has maintained tight control over community affairs. The respondents apparently recognized this fact. But, in spite of this, some businessmen were trying to wrest power from the local government during 1955. A group of them did succeed in gaining control of the city from 1956 to 1959. The leaders of this group were the men receiving votes as political influentials. It should be added that the Mexican respondents tended to concentrate their voting more than the Americans. Leadership appeared to be more crystallized. It is our conclusion that the business-political lists from Cd. Juarez in 1955 reflect the bitter cleavage that existed between these two groups at this time.[20]

In summary, in El Paso, eleven of the seventy persons (16 per cent) named as in-influentials were on both the lists while in Cd. Juarez, eight of the seventy-five persons (11 per cent) were on both lists. However, among either business or political influentials the majority were "limited" in influence in both cities. But this generalization would not hold for a certain number who were perceived to have influence beyond the limits of a single sector. In El Paso, as contrasted with Cd. Juarez, the overlap tended to be among the "most influential" in a given sector. Thus, 9 out of 25 top business influentials were political influentials and, conversely, nine out of the fourteen top political influentials were business influentials.

2. *1958 El Paso hospital project committee compared with 1955 political and business influence lists.* Table 1 reveals that among the persons named to the ideal hospital committee in El Paso in 1958, sixteen out of the top twenty mentions had been called influentials in either business or politics in 1955.[21] Ten persons were named on all three lists. Again, the businessmen who were perceived as Key Influentials in both business and politics in 1955 received a majority of selections for the ideal hospital committee in 1958.

3. *The 1958 hospital project committees and the 1958 general influence indexes in six communities.* For San Diego, we correlated the number of votes given all persons listed as general influentials and the number of mentions these individuals or other persons received as a proposed member of the hospital committee. The number of votes one person received as a Key Influential varied from zero to twenty-three votes as "most influential." On the other extreme, seven persons, though they were among the influentials, received no votes as most influential while they received zero to four nominations for the hospital committee. The index

TABLE 1. *Position on 1955 Business and Political Index of Top 20 Ideal Hospital Committee Members as Selected by General Community Influentials in 1958, for El Paso*

1955 POLITICAL INFLUENTIALS SELECTED FOR HOSPITAL COMMITTEES	1955 BUSINESS INFLUENTIALS SELECTED FOR HOSPITAL COMMITTEE		
	Not Mentioned on Business Index (n)	Top Influential (n)	Key Influential (n)
Key Influential	1	1	3
Top Influential	0	2	4
Not mentioned on political index	4	5	0

of the number of mentions a given individual received varied from zero to eighteen. Five persons received no mentions on the hospital committee though they remained on the influential index. A product moment correlation on these scores yielded an r=.92, an extremely high correlation.[22]

Let us now take a closer look at the interrelations between cases which fall on the extreme axes of the two coordinates for all communities.

In pursuit of the Key Influentials, we divided the list of those mentioned for the hospital committee on the basis of the ten receiving the most mentions *vs.* the remainder. Table 2 presents the data for each community in this manner.

There are two reasons why an individual

may have received the extreme low score (viz., "0" votes) on the general influence axis: (1) that he was named as top influential but received no votes naming him as a Key Influential, or (2) that he was not named as an influential at all but was mentioned as a possible member of the hospital committee. Though there are from one to six cases in each of the six cells corresponding to the Low-High quadrant, in only two communities were *any* of these persons among those who received no votes as Key Influential. The two exceptions are El Paso in which three of the five persons in the Low-High quadrant received no votes on general influence and Las Cruces in which one of the four persons in this quadrant was not mentioned as most influential. Thus, the more

TABLE 2. *The Number of Persons with High and Low General or Limited Influence for Each of Six Communities, 1958*

COMMUNITY AND LIMITED INFLUENCE[a]	GENERAL INFLUENCE[a]		TOTALS	CHI-SQUARE x^2	P[b]
	Low (n)	High (n)			
San Diego	(11 or less—12 or more votes)				
High (8 or more mentions)	1	9	10		
Low (7 or less mentions)	26	2	28		
Totals	27	11	38	20.73	<.0005
El Paso	(10 or less—11 or more votes)				
High (4 or more mentions)	5	6	11		
Low (3 or less mentions)	79	5	84		
Totals	84	11	95	17.94	<.0005
Tucson	(13 or less—14 or more votes)				
High (8 or more mentions)	6	4	10		
Low (7 or less mentions)	90	6	96		
Totals	96	10	106	8.45	<.005
Las Cruces	(12 or less—13 or more votes)				
High (6 or more mentions)	4	6	10		
Low (5 or less mentions)	72	4	76		
Totals	76	10	86	20.76	<.0005
Ciudad Juarez	(8 or less—9 or more votes)				
High (5 or more mentions)	6	7	13		
Low (4 or less mentions)	72	5	77		
Totals	78	12	90	17.68	<.0005
Tijuana	(3 or less—4 or more votes)				
High (3 or more mentions)	5	8	13		
Low (2 or less mentions)	62	3	65		
Totals	67	11	78	24.47	<.0005

Note: The four quadrants giving the results for each community will be symbolized Hi-Hi—Hi General Influence, High Limited Influence; Hi-Low—High General Influence, Low Limited Influence; Lo-Hi—Low General Influence, High Limited Influence; and Lo-Lo—Low General Influence and Low Limited Influence. In the case of each community the Hi-Hi and Lo-Lo combinations are substantially greater in frequency than would have been expected by chance.
[a]Marginals for High are Fixed at Ten for Each of Six Communities.
[b]P is one-tailed.

votes a given individual received as a general influential, the more mentions he is likely to have received as a member of a specialized hospital committee.

The converse situation in which High general influentials received no mentions for the hospital committee is also revealing. In El Paso, two of the five persons in the High-Low quadrant received no mentions on the hospital committee while they received a large number of mentions on the general influence index, and in Cd. Juarez, one of the five High influentials received no mentions for the hospital committee. Again, the predominant tendency is for the Key Influentials to be among the persons mentioned for directive positions on specialized committees.

If influence is "parcelled out" to various substantive issue areas as Polsby, et al. suggest, a question calling for nominations to a hospital committee would have yielded only those persons within this limited sphere of influence. The general influence index would, on the other hand, yield individuals from many limited scope areas or, as has been contended, persons with genuine "multiple" scope—what Merton calls "polymorphic"[23] —influence.

If limited influence were unrelated to general community influence, a person who received a high number of mentions on the nomination as a hospital committee member could have received either a high or a low number of votes as a general community influential. Or conversely, if an individual had received a low number of mentions on the hospital committee, he likewise might receive many or few votes on the general influence dimension. Our findings, in all cases, indicate that if an individual receives few mentions on the specialized hospital committee, he will receive few votes for general community influence. Conversely, if he receives a high number of mentions on a hospital committee, he will receive a relatively higher number of votes as a general community influential.[24] The circumstances of the interview make it unlikely that any mental set developed whereby the answers to one question determined the answers to the

other. For example, almost everyone chose one medical doctor for the hospital project, but only one suggested that he was a general community influential.

A related point should be mentioned here. No respondent challenged the idea of being asked to select general influentials. It seems fair to assume that they believe that such persons exist. In fact, the word influential seemed to be well understood by them. W. I. Thomas long ago reminded us that if something is perceived to be real, it can have very real consequences. More recently, Seligman has reminded us that leaders are leaders because there are followers who consider them leaders.[25]

These data also permit certain observations on the argument that the general influence index determined by the reputational technique measures "status" and not "influence." Let us state the argument. Polsby and Wolfinger argue that the following statements may be true:

(a) A general influence index will be a measurement of "status."
(b) A limited scope index of influence will not be a measure of "status."

Therefore, from (b) it follows

(c) That a measurement of "status" will not be a measurement of limited scope influence.

By a simple syllogism from (a) and (c) the conclusion follows

(d) That a general influence index will not be a measure of limited influence.

As has been reported, our findings indicate that the contrary is true. Thus,

(e) A general influence index does imply a measure of limited influence (or possibly that the two are measurements of the same phenomena).

Again, however, by syllogism from (e) and (b) it follows

(f) That a general influence index is not a measure of "status."

This statement, of course, contradicts (a).

In other analyses of these data this argument has been explored in much more detail. In brief it can be shown that it is not surprising that a high evaluation of "status" will coincide with a high evaluation of influence, be it general or limited. Thus, the argument presented alone is misleading.[26]

4. *Findings on the longevity of influence.* The question of longevity of influence is directly relevant to the criticism that salience of high prominence of conspicuousness of issues owing to recency in time directs the responses of persons to questions in which reputed general influence is being assessed. Thus, given the reputational technique used at two different time periods, variations among those named as influentials would occur (if the salience hypothesis were true) on the basis of the issues with which each is associated and which are dominant at the time of the interviews. If, however, there is a similarity in the lists of names obtained over an extended time period, and if the notion is rejected that this occurs only because the same complex of issues has been pending for a long period, then the salience hypothesis may be rejected.

As described above, the lists of business and political influentials from 1955 were combined in El Paso in 1958. Data on changes appear in Table 3.[27] The names of potential influentials from other community sectors were added and presented to the knowledgeables. They culled the list of forty-nine persons, by indicating retirements, deaths, and power demise. When all the votes for Key Influential had been tabulated, nine new names that had not appeared on either list in 1955 had been added. None of these nine were sociometric leaders in 1958. There were forty holdovers from 1955 business and political influentials. Conversely, this means that thirty-two persons were dropped from the lists.

Actually, sixteen persons had withdrawn in one way or another from public life between 1955 and 1958. Withdrawal can mean death, retirement or near retirement, or loss of power for some other reason. Of the sixteen who had thus "retired" only one was a Key Influential on either list in 1955. Of the twenty-two still active, none was a general community influential. The respondents, both influentials and others, strongly supported the index prepared by the knowledgeables.

These data reveal that both the knowl-

TABLE 3. *Withdrawals from Public Life of Persons Named as General Influentials in 1958 and as Business or Political Influentials in 1955, for El Paso*

| ACTIVITY IN PUBLIC LIFE | PERSONS NOT NAMED IN 1958 BUT NAMED IN 1955 AS INFLUENTIAL IN | | | Totals |
	Business and Politics	Business Only	Politics Only	
Withdrew between '55 and '58*	1	5	4	10
Still active	0	6	16	22
Totals	1	11	20	32

| ACTIVITY IN PUBLIC LIFE | PERSONS NAMED IN 1958 AND NAMED IN 1955 AS INFLUENTIAL IN | | | Not named in 1955 | Totals |
	Business and Politics	Business Only	Politics Only		
Virtually withdrew between '55 and '58†	1	0	5	N/A	6
Active	9	10	15	9	43
Totals	10	10	20	9	49
Holdovers from 1955		40			

*Withdrawal from public life can be retirement, death, or loss of political office.
†These six persons had all virtually retired. None received more than one vote as a Key Influential in 1958.

edgeables and the respondents know the difference between limited scope influence and general influence. Furthermore, they are keenly aware of the dynamics of power and power change as measured in a three to four year period.

A multiple correlation of the general influence index of 1958 on the political and business indexes (n = thirty-four since withdrawals are eliminated) yields an $R_{x \cdot yz} = .683$. This informs us that 47 per cent of the variation in the general influence index can be ascribed to the variation in the political and business indexes. This would seem to be a substantial correlation considering the present state of knowledge concerning the components of influence. (A possible further inference is that if this general index of influence does tap multiple areas of specialized influence it is a parsimonious measure whose usefulness is great.)

These data indicate also that persons named as Key Influentials at one time tend to be named at a later time, regardless of the issues intervening. Therefore, it is concluded that influentials are influential for a reason (or in addition to a reason) other than mere salience of a problem facing a community at a given time. Aside from the perennial problems which confront community leaders,

such as traffic control, freeways, etc., the specific issues which were stated as dominant in this community had changed substantially over these four years.

An analysis of these data on the longevity of influentials bears out the above conclusion. To assert the existence of general community influentials is not to assert that all decisions are made by the same man, or that these influentials never change. It is merely to assert that change may be slow, and that a certain degree of continuity does exist. Human beings die, retire from public life, get elected to high public office, lose office, or become active for personal motives. All of these factors may affect the structure of influence in a community. A rough picture of continuity and change is presented in Table 4. The twenty-five individuals who were Key Influentials on at least one of the three influential lists are shown; all of them were present in 1958. Let us consider briefly the degree of mobility, change, stability, and independence of this "group" of leaders.

Three persons (S, X, and Y) who had held public office at the time of or just prior to the 1955 study, have since largely retired from political life. Two of them were not even selected as general influentials in 1958. Two other influentials were reputed to be

TABLE 4. *The Key Influentials on the Three Influence Indexes, 1955–1958*

| | | | | 1958 GENERAL INFLUENTIALS | | | | | |
| | Not Mentioned | | | Low | | | High | | |
1955 Business	NM[a]	Low	High	NM	Low	High	NM	Low	High
1955 political									
High	Y, X	W	—	—	S, T, U	L	J, K	F	A, B
Low	—	—	—	—	N	M, O	—	G, H, I	C, D, E
NM	—	—	V	—	—	P, Q, R	—	—	—

Key to occupations of individuals

A—Banker
B—Contractor
C—Newspaper Publisher
D—Contractor
E—Banker
F—Banker
G—Corporation Lawyer
H—Newspaper Editor
I—Newspaper Editor
J—Mayor in 1958, County Political Office in 1955
K—Federal District Judge
L—Construction, Former Mayor
M—Industry (near retirement in 1958)

N—Retail Merchant (Department Store)
O—Wholesale Business
P—Broker (near retirement in 1958)
Q—Industry
R—Retail Merchant (near retirement in 1958)
S—Miscellaneous Enterprises (Mayor 1955)
T—Insurance
U—Wholesale Business (near retirement in 1958)
V—Retired in 1958 (Business)
W—Retired in 1958 (Business)
X—Retired Politician
Y—Retired Politician

[a] Not mentioned

completely retired (V and W), while another four were said to be almost ready for retirement and were characterized as not very active anymore (M, R, P, and U). It was said that P was not participating very much, but that he still could if he wanted to. Q and N were said to be businessmen who did not care to get involved in general community affairs.

The remaining fourteen of the twenty-five persons listed in Table 4 were chosen as Key Influentials on at least one of the three influence indexes, and twelve had been chosen on all three lists. Two others (J and K), both career politicians, were Key Influentials on the 1955 political index and the 1958 general index. J had moved up from county clerk to become mayor in this interim. K was the city's elder statesman who had held every important local office and during this whole period was one of the highest ranking federal officials in the community. Almost every respondent admitted that K was not "actively" engaged in decision-making. Presumably he was named as influential because of all he had done and potentially *could* do for the city. One respondent put it well when he said: "If he should speak up on any issue, the whole city would sit up and listen." Another Key Influential, G, indicated that he consulted informally with K almost weekly to get his opinion on civic matters.[28]

There is no doubt that certain political positions are seats of potential power no matter which individual occupies them. For most of the individuals encompassed in this study, the loss of the political position has meant the loss of most of that power. While Stewart may be right in saying that "influentiality is nothing if not a highly individualized characteristic,"[29] the data suggest that holding public office may be important for some people, or may be one means by which the potential for influence can be brought to fruition. Whatever else this characteristic may be, it is clear from our knowledge of individuals A-K that a desire to be a community decision-maker is part of the picture. So also is the holding of some top executive post in either business or politics.

5. Reputation and reality: decision-making in El Paso. Four types of decisions in El Paso were analyzed[30]: (1) municipal elections; (2) the establishment of United Fund; (3) establishment of a new community hospital; and (4) establishment of new bridge facilities between El Paso and Cd. Juarez.

Data on the 1955, 1957, and 1959 elections have been analyzed. The process by which the United Fund came to El Paso was carefully reviewed. The establishment of a new community hospital in El Paso in 1958–1959, which was at least in part a political

TABLE 5. *Roles Played by Key Influentials in Six Key Issues in El Paso During 1950's*

	UNITED FUND	PRIVATE HOSPITAL	GENERAL HOSPITAL	ELECTIONS		BRIDGE
				1955	1957	
Issue resolved by	B, C, D, E, G, I	B, C, D, E, G, I	Voters, Med. Ass'n, County Judge, H, I	B, G, I, M, P, S, T, U, Voters	H, J, Voters	H, I, S, County Judge, Others
Involved but on losing side	N		X	H, J, Y	B, G, I, S, T	J, N, Others
Minor involvement	F, M, O, P, Q, S, T, U, Others	L, M, N, O, P, Q, R, S, T, U, V, F	J, K	A, F, N, X	A, K	F

event, was studied in detail. The taxpaying citizens had to approve the establishment of a separate hospital district and a bond to help pay for the new hospital. Our study was begun before the issue was resolved and the outcome was correctly predicted on the basis of the data available. The roles played by various individuals and groups were also assessed. (Data were gathered indicating the most influential persons in setting up a private hospital in El Paso in 1952. Since this action involved many of the same people who were involved in the other issues discussed above, it will be mentioned below.)

The first analysis concerns the establishment of new bridge facilities between El Paso and Cd. Juarez. This was a problem of long-standing duration. It came out into the open in 1955 and was not finally resolved until 1959.

Table 5 summarizes the issues that were resolved in El Paso in the 1950's and the roles played by the influentials in these issues.

The results of our analysis support Dahl's statement that in any single issue only a few influentials are directly or importantly involved in the decision. But, the thesis that leaders are limited to single scopes of influence is not supported. The newspaper editors, who often bitterly opposed each other (H, I) were involved in most of the issues. So also were the business group B through G, with whom individual I was allied. B through G did identify themselves as a group and they did engage in a variety of activities, from United Fund to local elections. They established the United Fund in El Paso in the early 1950's, and soon thereafter planned, built and, during the entire period of its history, have controlled the direction of a new private 240 bed hospital. They were decisively influential in the elections of 1955, but lost badly in 1957, when they opposed the election of J, the first Spanish-name person to be elected mayor of El Paso.

It is worth adding here that in 1959, this same group, B-G strongly supported J for re-election. In fact, J was re-elected without opposition.[31] These data support Rossi's con-

tention that businessmen are not averse to politics, but only to losing.[32]

The bridge issue deserves brief comment. Since two countries were involved, and state and federal government agencies had to give their approval to any new facilities, the issue became very complex. It was further complicated by the fact that one group of businessmen wanted no major changes, while another group wanted to see new bridges to the east of the two already existing. There appeared to be a stalemate in 1958, but the influential who had just been elected county judge had said that he thought he could resolve the issue as soon as he got settled in office, and he did. He also played a major role in the successful resolution of the community hospital issue.

It can be tentatively concluded from our analysis of the data on issue resolution that most businessmen tend to restrict their community activities to such programs as United Fund and building private hospitals and career politicians restrict themselves to governmental projects. Newspaper editors, especially where there are two with opposing interests, as in El Paso, seem to get involved in all issues, and take stands because they are in opposition. But it must also be asserted that some businessmen were Key Influentials on the general influence index, were Key Influentials on both lists in 1955, and were active in political elections in El Paso. These men were also the ones who had resolved the United Fund and private hospital issues.

Summary and Conclusions

As we noted at the outset, this paper has been limited to the presentation of data (and arguments) directed at certain criticisms of the reputational technique. However, the implications of the findings are broader than the limitations. Thus, we can conclude as follows:

(1) The reputational technique does seem to measure general community influence when the question is stated to get at this factor in decision-making. Respondents did not merely repeat the same names in response to questions about the most influential in

business, or in government or politics, or for a hospital project, or for general community decision-making. But there was a significant overlap; a group of about one dozen persons consistently reappeared on all lists. This group did not constitute one single solidary clique by any means.[33] No one ever suggested that they all acted in concert, but they were perceived to be persons who had more than a single scope of influence.

(2) The technique seems to be highly reliable. In six communities studied simultaneously, high correlations were found between those chosen as influentials in a specific area (ideal hospital project) and those chosen as general community influentials. Furthermore, in two of these communities, there was the opportunity to make a longitudinal comparison, over a four-year time span. There is considerable evidence for the existence of a perceived community power structure.

(3) The attribution of influence may be viewed as one by-product of the process of differential evaluation in a social relationship. It must be expected that this evaluation will be "related" to other elements of evaluation such as the attribution of status, of a specified value-orientation, etc. In addition, the linkage or carryover of evaluations from one social relationship to another would surely be an expectation. In short, it is not surprising that consistencies occur between evaluations of status and influence. A large number of other elements are probably involved in this evaluational system. The data presented in this paper have been addressed as arguments. (Other research has carried the analysis to greater detail.) It has been concluded that the *substitution* of the status concept for that of general influence would seem to be invalid.

(4) In actual decision-making, only a small group from the total number of influentials ever was actively involved in any particular issue. This small group was in fact made up largely of the Key Influentials discussed above. A variety of issues were selected, requiring legitimation and resolution by various means. It was concluded that businessmen do get involved in politics and other issues.

Our findings suggest that a group of general community influentials did in fact exist in El Paso and that its existence has had important consequences for the community during the 1950's.

Probably El Paso is no more typical of American communities than is New Haven, Connecticut, Schulze's Cibola or Miller's Pacific City. Nevertheless, at this time there appears to be a broad continuum of power alignments in American communities even without taking into account such variables as size, industrial complexity, political party strength, ethnic and labor union groups, existence of opposing newspapers, or broad cultural differences.[34] While in our judgment, based upon our data, it appears that business values still strongly influence community life, this influence does not mean complete control over all community issues. Political action counter to the dominant business interests is possible and did in fact occur in El Paso during the 1950's. It is also possible that a certain selectivity among the forms of influence relationships perceived is taking place in both the research techniques used in this study and those used by Dahl, Polsby, and Wolfinger.

Finally, the reputational technique, imperfect at best in its present form, did provide us with a picture of the dynamics of power during the 1950's. Whether in fact it reveals a community power structure or is merely a parsimonious way of getting the key "limited scope" influentials all together on one list which can be handled with relative ease cannot be conclusively stated, and may in fact be a problem involving the development of better operational definitions. Our evidence supports the generalization that at least in some American communities, some individuals have more than a limited scope of influence. The differences between the findings of Wolfinger, Polsby, Dahl, and those reported here and elsewhere by Miller and others, may be a matter of methodology, or of the structural variables mentioned above or of the differences in the theoretical assumptions concerning the phenomenon of influence itself. The question seems to us to be not whether to abandon this technique in favor of some alternative (or to abandon the alternatives), but rather as Rossi suggests, to find out under what conditions each technique provides the most fruitful approach to the study of community decision-making and eventually how to assimilate these techniques into a broader methodological scheme.[35]

Notes

1. Numerous articles and books present ideas relevant to the subject. See Raymond E. Wolfinger, "Reputation and Reality in the Study of Community Power," *American Sociological Review*, 25 (October, 1960), pp. 636–644. Also for special significance to this article are Nelson W. Polsby, "The Sociology of Community Power: A Reassessment," *Social Forces*, 37 (March, 1959), pp. 232–236; N. W. Polsby, "Three Problems in the Analysis of Community Power," *American Sociological Review*, 24 (December, 1959), pp. 796–803; and Robert Dahl, "Equality and Power in American Society," in Wm. V. D'Antonio and H. J. Ehrlich, editors, *Power and Democracy in America*, Notre Dame, Ind.: University of Notre Dame Press, 1961.

2. Wolfinger, *op. cit.*, p. 636 (abstract).

3. Foskett and Hohle have also presented a valuable test of this technique assessing its relation to other methods of determining influence. See John M. Foskett and Raymond Hohle, "The Measurement of Influence in Community Affairs," *Research Studies of the State College of Washington*, 25 (June, 1957), pp. 148–154.

4. See Linton C. Freeman, Warner Bloomberg, Jr., Stephen P. Koff, Morris H. Sunshine, and Thomas J. Fararo, "Local Community Leadership," *No. 15 of the Publications Committee of University College, Syracuse University*, p. 2.

5. For example, Polsby, "Three Problems . . .," *op. cit.*, p. 798.

6. Dahl, *op. cit.*, p. 7.

7. Wolfinger, *op. cit.*, p. 638. A brief but trenchant commentary on Wolfinger's criticisms was made by Howard J. Ehrlich, "The Reputational Approach to the Study of Community Power," *American Sociological Review*, 26 (December, 1961), pp. 926–927.

8. Polsby, "The Sociology . . .," *op. cit.*, p. 232, fn. 5.

9. The concept, scope, is used to imply a limitation in the substantive areas in which an ego has influence over an alter. For example, a medical doctor's influence might be limited to the substantive area of health.

10. See William H. Form and William V. D'Antonio, "Integration and Cleavage among Community Influentials in Two Border Cities," *American Sociological Review*, 24 (December, 1959), pp. 804–814.

11. Knowledgeables are persons in positions of some importance in community organizations, who may or may not turn out to be influentials, e.g., general manager of the Chamber of Commerce, City Clerk, newspaper reporter, etc.

12. One major difficulty was that the respondents had to sit back and think for quite a while about names. Occasionally a respondent became anxious because he could not think of the name of a person whose business or political connections he knew well. Some respondents found it easy to decline to answer because they felt that it would take too long, or they couldn't remember enough names to be fair to all the potential influentials.

13. See William V. D'Antonio, William H. Form, Charles P. Loomis, and Eugene C. Erickson, "Institutional and Occupational Representations in Eleven Community Influence Systems," *American Sociological Review*, 26 (June, 1961), pp. 440–446, for further descriptions of the communities studied.

14. We are aware of the possibility that we might be leading the knowledgeables by presenting them with lists selected in 1955. However, the nature of their response, and of our research activity lead us to believe that a bias did not occur. As will be brought out later, we found that when we brought together the two separate scopes, business and politics, into one general influence index, the knowledgeables and other respondents tended to eliminate those whose influence was limited to a single scope.

15. Polsby did in fact report finding some overlap in the lists of issue-area influentials in New Haven. He reported that 15 out of 435 persons were involved in urban redevelopment and political issues. But Polsby calls this an insignificant overlap. If all 435 were influentials of the same or near equal magnitude, this would probably be valid. Polsby further observes that even those who were active in more than one issue-area were limited by the energy and time which they could devote to more than one issue in the same period.

A number of questions are raised by these

findings and the way in which they are interpreted. How is the significance of overlap to be measured? Is it relevant to combine as part of a leadership pool (as Polsby has done) all persons who hold political office, in government as well as in political parties, regardless of the importance of the office, and the attitude of the incumbent? How is it possible to reconcile the large leadership pools which Polsby, *et al.* used to examine decision-making with Dahl's admission that on any single issue only a small number of persons are active and influential? Doesn't the use of such large pools merely distort the reality of the decision-making process? Is it valid to say that a community power structure does not exist unless the same group of persons are equally influential on all matters? For Polsby's position on some of these questions, see "Three Problems . . .," *op. cit.*

16. It is true that the single scope *which determines* general influence could be the one that has been chosen by chance. To have this occur in six communities, however, is indeed unlikely. It is even more important to consider that the respondent did not simply select an ideal hospital committee and then go on to look at a list of some fifty names from which he had to choose the ten most influential. Sandwiched between these responses were the two questions on key issues, and on these questions the respondents were asked to discuss their participation in these issues, and the roles of other individuals and groups. Thus, it would be difficult to argue that any single "mental set" or scope was in their minds as they examined the general influence index.

17. Data for sections three and four are taken from Eugene C. Erickson, "The Reputational Technique in a Cross-Community Perspective: Selected Problems of Theory and Measurement," unpublished Ph.D. Dissertation, 1961, Michigan State University.

18. The problem of deciding what degree of consensus is necessary for inclusion on the general influence index is still unresolved. Empirically, a small group of some 12–15 persons received a high number of votes. Between 20 and 30 received three or more votes. Beyond that, a long list of persons were nominated only once or twice. This extended list approaches the leadership pools used by Polsby in his research report. Our findings indicate that those who receive the most votes are the actual decision-makers in the community. It is open to question whether our findings are really at variance with those of Dahl, Polsby, and Wolfinger. It appears that Schulze found a pattern similar to ours in Cibola as did Belknap

and Smuckler in a Michigan community. See Robert O. Schulze, "The Bifurcation of Power in a Satellite City," in Morris Janowitz, editor, *Community Political Systems*, Glencoe, Ill.: The Free Press, 1961, esp. pp. 39–40, and George Belknap and Ralph Smuckler, "Political Power Relations in a Mid-West City," *Public Opinion Quarterly*, 20 (Spring, 1956), pp. 73–81.

19. Since these lists were obtained by completely open-ended questions, the minimum consensus level set was three votes on either list.

20. A full account of the cleavage and the struggle between business and government in Cd. Juarez will be found in William V. D'Antonio and William H. Form, *Business and Politics in Two Border Cities*, monograph, forthcoming.

21. It has been common for researchers to separate the very top vote-getters from the larger body of influentials for certain analyses. See, e.g., William H. Form and Delbert C. Miller, *Industry, Labor, and Community*, New York: Harper & Brothers, 1960, pp. 444 ff., and Floyd Hunter, *Community Power Structure*, Durham: North Carolina Press, 1953, p. 70. The terms used to distinguish these groups are "Key Influentials" and "Top Influential." (Hunter used the phrase "Upper-Limits Group," *ibid.*) Generally, the Key Influentials are the ten top ranks as selected by the influentials themselves. They are, in effect, sociometric leaders.

22. The correlations for the remaining communities were also high. These correlations were El Paso, $r = .65$, $N = 95$; Cd. Juarez, $r = .55$, $N = 90$; Las Cruces, $r = .76$, $N = 86$; Tucson, $r = .71$, $N = 106$; and Tijuana, $r = .71$, $N = 78$. These correlations are substantially beyond a point which might have been anticipated by chance. In each of these cases, many more persons have been mamed as general influentials without having been mentioned on the hospital committee and vice versa, than was true for San Diego. Nevertheless, the trend in all of these correlations is very similar.

23. Robert K. Merton, *Social Theory and Social Structure*, Glencoe: The Free Press, 1957, pp. 413–415.

24. As column four in Table 2 shows, the Chi-square for each community is significant beyond the .01 probability level, since any χ^2 6.64 is significant at this level. If those persons who received no mentions on the hospital committee or no mention on the general influence index are eliminated from the table, a new set of Chi-squares can be computed. This was done and the results were for San Diego, $\chi^2 = 18.37$; for El Paso, 9.98; Tucson, 1.45; Las Cruces, 6.43; Cd.

Juarez, 6.71; and Tijuana, 5.58. A Chi-square equal to 5.41 has a probability of .02. Therefore, all except Tucson are significant at that level.

25. Lester Seligman, "The Study of Political Leadership," *American Political Science Review*, 44 (December, 1950), pp. 904–915; see also Ehrlich, "The Reputational Technique . . . .," *op. cit.*, p. 926.

26. See Erickson, *op. cit.*, for a detailed treatment of this issue.

27. The reader should be cautioned that these conclusions are subject to accepting the assumption that four years is a significantly long period of time to permit generalizations on longevity. Olmsted found substantial differences in evaluation of influence over a six year time period. See Donald Olmsted, "Organizational Leadership and Social Structure in a Small City," *American Sociological Review*, 19 (May, 1954), pp. 273–281. From our continued contact with these communities, however, we are fairly sure that these assertions are valid.

28. As recently as June, 1961, however, K was called on by certain persons in the community to use his influence on an important community issue. The meeting was publicized and K's picture appeared in the newspapers. He was billed as an elder statesman on this occasion but he *was* active.

29. Frank A. Stewart, "A Study of Influence in Southtown," II, *Sociometry: A Journal of Inter-Personal Relations*, 10 (August, 1947), p. 273.

30. There is a general acceptance by all scientists studying community decision-making that a fundamental step is to study a broad variety of issues of community significance. An attempt has been made to do this in our research in these Southwestern communities. For a commentary on the importance of this point, see Peter H. Rossi, "Community Decision-Making," in Roland Young, editor, *Approaches to the Study of Politics*, Evanston, Ill.: Northwestern University Press, 1958, pp. 381–382. Also see discussion between D. C. Miller and Robert A. Dahl, in D'Antonio and Ehrlich, *op. cit.*, Chapter 4.

31. In 1955, most of the business and political influentials expressed themselves as opposed to the idea of having a Spanish-name person as mayor. By 1958, however, these same leaders had reconciled themselves to the fact. They had decided that J could indeed "do the job." In April, 1961, J was appointed ambassador to Costa Rica, an event which left the political picture in considerable confusion.

32. Peter H. Rossi, "Theory, Research and Practice in Community Organization," in Charles Adrian, editor, *Social Sciences and Community Action*, East Lansing, Mich.: Institute of Community Development and Services, 1960.

33. In this sense a solidary "power elite" was not found, though there seems to be the phenomenon described by Hunter, *op. cit.*, and suggested by C. Wright Mills, *The Power Elite*, New York: Oxford University Press, 1956. Thus, if Dahl, Wolfinger, and Polsby were arguing that there is no power elite there would be little to dispute. To suggest, however, that there is no small group of persons whose influence is "general" (or polymorphic) is not consistent with our findings.

34. For an analysis of the broad overlapping similarities of the personal characteristics of influentials regardless of the community in which they appear, see Erickson, *op. cit.* Also, see Delbert C. Miller, "Democracy and Decision-Making in the Community Power Structure," in D'Antonio and Ehrlich, *op. cit.*, Chapter 2, esp. pp. 58 ff.

35. Peter H. Rossi, "Community Decision-Making," in Roland Young, editor, *op. cit.*, p. 379.

Reputation and Resources in Community Politics

William A. Gamson

In the post mortem which accompanies any political defeat, the losing group will typically take itself to task for various failures. There is, in such analyses, a tendency to assume that the exercise of influence alone determines the outcome of a decision. The other side is seen as having been more effective—as having spent more resources or as having used its resources more efficiently. While this may be true, it is also possible in such cases that the losing side was quite effective, while the winning side did little or nothing to further their cause. The exercise of influence is only one element in the outcome of political issues.

It is helpful, in speaking of influence, to start with the notion of a decision to be made. Influence can then be handled very well, as Dahl has suggested,[1] using the notion of conditional probability. The amount of influence a social unit has had on a decision is represented by the difference between the probability of the desired outcome before and after the influence attempt. To say that one has influenced a decision means simply that he has changed the probability of the desired outcome in the intended direction.[2] By such a definition, the presence or absence of influence cannot be clearly inferred from whether or not the would-be influencer is on the winning side of a decision. A partisan group in a community may start with little chance of an alternative being accepted. By waging a vigorous fight they may reach a point where acceptance or rejection is touch and go. Ultimately, of course, the measure will either pass or fail, but we should not judge this group to have had influence only if it passes. The move from an almost certain failure to a near-miss is a mark of their

influence. Similarly, a victory cannot be taken as prima facie evidence of influence since a narrow victory by a partisan group in a situation in which they would have won doing nothing is no indication of influence.

This paper is concerned with understanding the outcome of community issues and, in particular, with the role that those with a general reputation for influence play in such outcomes. Factors other than influence may, in some cases, put severe limits on the possible effects which partisan groups or individuals may have. Accordingly, it seems useful to take as a working assumption the asymmetry of the influence task for different partisan groups. Those on one side of an issue are likely to have a natural advantage over those on the other side, an advantage which will enable them to win if they simply hold their own in an influence contest.

What is the nature of this "natural advantage"? Most broadly, it is the advantage that falls to those who do not carry the burden of proof. In relatively stable situations, this advantage is held by those who would maintain a present arrangement against those who would alter it. Many community issues arise from the presentation of a proposal to alter some existing facility or service or to add some new facility. The burden of proof in such cases generally rests with the side proposing the change. For example, if a new school is proposed, those who oppose it may raise any number of questions about need, cost, design, site, and so forth. It is not necessary to resolve such questions in order to block action on this proposal: if they remain unanswered, this is generally sufficient.

The communities studied here are not

Reprinted from The American Journal of Sociology, *72 (September 1966), 121–131, by permission of the author and The University of Chicago Press. Copyright 1966 by The University of Chicago.*

undergoing acute crises. They are, then, a special case in which the natural advantage falls to those who would maintain existing conditions. To admit the existence of such an advantage is not to argue that those who desire change will fail but only that they will fail in the absence of influence no greater than that exercised by the other side. In the discussion which follows, special attention is given to the role of "reputational leaders" in such an influence process.

Reputation and Resources

A number of investigators interested in the operation of power in the community have elicited lists of names of community "leaders." Typically, a panel composed of heads of civic associations or some other group actively involved in public affairs is asked to nominate individuals and the nominees are in turn interviewed.[3] This "reputational method" of studying community power has been sharply attacked both for the interpretations that are made of the list of names obtained and, in more basic ways, for the use of such questions at all. To quote Polsby, "asking about reputations is asking, at a remove, about behavior. It can be argued that the researcher should make it his business to study behavior directly rather than depend on the opinions of second hand sources."[4]

What does it mean, we may ask, when an individual or group of individuals is frequently named as "influential" by those involved in community political affairs? Are such reputations meaningless in themselves, telling us no more at best than we might more efficiently learn from studying actual influence over decisions? Reputation, I will argue, is a resource; as such, it refers to potential influence rather than influence in use. Reputation is not simply the manifestation of the possession of large amounts of resources but is, itself, a resource in the same sense that money, wealth, or authority might be. This argument requires some discussion of the concept of resources.

What is it that an influencer uses to exercise influence? In any decision, there exists some "thing" or "weight" such that if enough of this weight is applied to the decision-makers the probability of an alternative being accepted or rejected will be changed. This thing must satisfy two important conditions to be considered a resource. First, it must be possessed by or, more accurately, *controlled* by the influencer. He must be able to determine its use. Second, he must be able to bring it to bear on decision-makers in interaction with them.

Since in any society certain things are widely valued, certain resources are both of high applicability across a variety of decision-makers and of high stability of value over time within a particular set of decision-makers. It is the possession of such general resources rather than of more idiosyncratic ones that is of significance for understanding the stable potential to influence the outcome of decisions.

Many authors have distinguished among the ways that resources are used to produce influence.[5] The most relevant distinction for the present argument is implicit in a number of these discussions, but it is made most explicitly by Parsons. In the terms which will be used here, *sanctioning* influence is the addition of new advantages or disadvantages (conditional or not) to the situation of the decision-maker. *Persuasion* influence operates on the orientation of the decision-maker, changing the connection he sees between a decision outcome and his goals without the addition of any new advantages or disadvantages to the situation.

It is not difficult to conceive of sanctioning resources of high stability and generality. A person who holds a position of great potential influence in an elaborate network of institutional and interpersonal relationships possesses a powerful set of inducements. It is virtually certain that there will be some present or future alternative that he can influence that present decision-makers care about. Furthermore, it is a valuable political asset to have such a potentially influential person obligated to oneself.

It is possible to talk about a similarly general basis of persuasion? Clearly, we can conceive of persuasion resources which are highly limited in scope. Expertness, for example, is only a resource for those areas in which the influencer is considered knowledgeable. Are there more generalized and stable persuasion resources?

A generalized reputation for "wisdom" or "good sense" is just such a stable persuasion resource. There are individuals who are respected by particular groups in a community not because of any *specific* expertness they may have on the issue at hand but because they are believed to be generally "knowledgeable," "sound," "reliable," "unselfish," "intelligent," and so forth. In other words, they are believed to possess certain stable personal qualities that transcend any given issue and make their opinion more convincing. A highly successful lawyer, for example, who actively participates in community affairs may find that his success is regarded by public officials as a sign of grace. While his persuasion resources on issues involving legal matters may be particularly great, he will carry with him a generalized reputation which acts as a resource—even on issues for which he has no special qualifications.

He has no persuasion resources, of course, among those who do not accept his reputation. Resources are categorized here in terms of their applicability to decision-makers. A spokesman who enjoyed the complete confidence of members of some solidary group would have a persuasion resource with respect to decisions made by his followers. However, his influence over this group might in turn be used as an inducement for public officials who wish the group's votes in an election.

A theoretical justification for identifying reputational leaders is being offered here. One asks about reputation simply to identify those who have reputation; such reputation is significant because it is a stable and generalized persuasion resource. Of course, we may quarrel with the method used to identify such people. One technique is to ask community decision-makers a question such as: "In many communities, there are people who are generally listened to when they take a position on community issues because they are believed to have good judgment. Are there any such people in ———?" Those who are frequently named form an operational definition of "people with stable persuasion resources." The validity of such a question concerns how well it measures reputation, not its connection with influence behavior.

Those who are named as "reputational leaders" simply comprise a pool of individuals with resources. No claim is made that they form a ruling elite or even a cohesive group of any sort; such claims must rest on demonstration of a number of additional characteristics. Those with resources may or may not be friendly with each other socially. If they all belong to the same clubs and organizations, this is an important additional fact about the organization of resources in the community. The list by itself tells us nothing about this fact.

Similarly, agreement on policy among reputational leaders is an empirical question. The list might contain, for example, political rivals who are never found on the same side. Or, it might contain individuals with different spheres of interest who tacitly or explicitly agree to remain neutral on issues outside of their major province. The only thing we wish to maintain about the list of reputational leaders is that, because they possess significant amounts of resources, their social organization is significant for the understanding of stable power relations in the community. The relations among members and their actions is a variable which will be related to the outcome of decisions in a variety of important ways.[6]

The Study

The data to be presented here are drawn from a study of fifty-four issues in eighteen New England communities. The towns were generally small, ranging in population from 2,000 to 100,000 with the median size about 10,000. Seven of the communities were essentially suburbs of Boston, three were resort towns, and the remaining eight were more or less independent cities with some industrial base of their own. All but two of the communities were in Maine or Massachusetts.

Material on these communities was gathered through interviews with 426 informants, an average of twenty-four per town, supplemented by information from a variety of documents. Interviewing was done by teams of three or four individuals who stayed in each community for several days. Three issues were studied in each town, one of which—fluoridation—was common to all eighteen. The presence of a decision on fluoridation was, in fact, the basis of selection of these communities, and the eighteen include all those New England communities which made a fluoridation decision during an 18-month period of data collection.

Respondents were asked to name the most important issues that had arisen in their town in the previous 5 years. Of the fifty-four issues studied, twenty-six were mentioned by a majority of the respondents in the town.[7] In eleven of the eighteen towns, a majority mentioned a particular issue first or as most important and in all but one of these the issue was included in the fifty-four studied. Besides the eighteen fluoridation issues, eleven concerned schools, eleven were issues over the development of some new community facility or service, eight were zoning issues, and the final six were a miscellaneous assortment which included changes in the form of government and urban renewal.

The interviews themselves were with two categories of respondents—with active partisans on both sides of each of the three issues and with reputational leaders. The active partisans on the three issues studied were asked to name people in response to the following question: "In many communities, relatively few people are able to affect the outcome of issues sometimes because they are in a position to make key decisions or because they have the ability to persuade others to follow their leadership. Would you tell me the names of the most important and influential leaders in this community even if they do not hold public office?"[8] Those dozen individuals most frequently named

were also interviewed and, in the course of the interview, asked this same question.

The criteria for inclusion on the list of reputational leaders should control for certain irrelevant variables between towns. Interviewers differed in the amount of probing they did for names, the total number of respondents interviewed in a town varied from nineteen to thirty-one, and the average number of people mentioned by respondents varied from town to town depending on the degree of consensus that existed and the volubility of respondents. By using as a base the total number of mentions,[9] we can control for all of the above variables. In communities where (1) the interviewers probed vigorously, (2) a large number of interviews were taken, and (3) the respondents were prolific in their naming, a large number of total mentions will emerge. Requiring a fixed proportion of the total for eligibility means that an individual must be named more frequently in such a town than in one where few names are mentioned over all.[10]

Before we can assess the influence of reputational leaders on the outcome of the fifty-four issues, we must examine other aspects of these issues. Each is characterized by campaigns by one or both sides, but the intensity of these campaigns varies considerably. Furthermore, some of these efforts have as their object the adoption of some new proposal while others have the maintenance of existing arrangements as their goal. It is only against this backdrop that we can meaningfully connect winning efforts with influence. We must show that the active participation of reputational leaders on a side has some effect over and above the sheer amount of campaign activity and the natural advantage of defending the status quo.

Campaign Activity

All of those who were active on either side of an issue were asked a series of questions about the nature of campaign activities. These questions varied from such open-ended ones as "What did those in favor (opposed) actually do to promote their side, that is, what kinds of activities?" to a specific check list of sixteen activities. On several items respondents were asked to compare the campaigns of the two sides. From these descriptions of activities, we characterized each side's campaign on two dimensions—the magnitude of total activity and the degree of organization.

For the first of these dimensions, each respondent's description was culled for statements characterizing the extent of particular activities or characterizations of the campaign as a whole (e.g., "they spent a tremendous amount of money on advertising and literature," "we spent a whole year trying to convince people with a tremendous campaign in the last four weeks"). Independent coders were asked to classify the amount of activity for each partisan group as either "great," "some," or "little."[11]

For the degree of organization, heavier reliance was placed on the check list of activities. Many of the activities, such as holding meetings to decide and plan what to do, distribution of literature to the general public, circulating petitions, and raising money to support activities, require some degree of formal organization. They are typically carried on by groups that establish an ad hoc organization for the purpose with publicly identifiable leaders or else are carried on by some existing organization in the community. Other kinds of activities require less formal organization but do require interaction among those implementing them. These include telephone campaigns, selective distribution of literature, and participating at meetings or discussions. Finally, there are activities that require neither formal organization nor interaction—for example, writing and answering letters to newspapers, attending or testifying at council meetings or other official proceedings, or simply talking informally to people one encounters. Each campaign was characterized by the highest degree of organizational activity carried on. If the first category of activities occurred, than the campaign organization was characterized as formal regardless of what semiformal and informal activities

occurred as well. Thus, an informal campaign was one in which *only* informal activities occurred. Each of the 108 campaigns was coded as either formal, semiformal, or informal.

With each partisan group's campaign characterized in this way, it is possible to compare the two sides on each issue. Interestingly enough, the winning side has only a modest advantage in amount of activity and organization; it had either more activity or more organization on only 48 per cent of the issues while the losing side had more on 33 per cent.[12] For the remainder, the two sides were equal in activity and organization or, in one case, the winning side was higher on one criterion while the losing side had the advantage on the other.

On forty-eight of the issues it was possible to identify one side with an effort to change the status quo in some fashion while the other side favored postponement of action, further study of need, a counter alternative requiring less change, or simply the maintenance of existing arrangements. The side identified with change was victorious in 42 per cent of these cases against 58 per cent for those who opposed the immediate action proposed.

It was hypothesized above that it takes more effort[13] to change the status quo than to maintain it, and Table 1 supports this. In almost two-thirds of the cases in which the side supporting change won, they made a greater campaign effort than the other side. However, when the side supporting no change won, they made a greater effort only a third of the time; two-thirds of the time they were able to win with no more effort than the losing side.

Reputation and Success

There are two prior questions which we must ask about reputational leaders before we can examine their impact on issue outcome. First, to what extent are they actively involved as partisans on the issues studied? Second, to what extent do they act in unison when they are active; that is, how often are the predominantly on the same side? Having answered those questions, we can examine their impact when they are both active and relatively united.

Activity. Activity is measured in two ways. Respondents were asked, for each issue studied, if they were at all active. If they answered affirmatively, they were asked to describe such activity; only efforts to affect the outcome are included here or, in other words, non-partisan activities are excluded. Respondents were also asked for the names of the people "who have done most of the work in favor (against)." There were some individuals who, out of circumspection or modesty, did not rate themselves as active but were named as active by others. An individual will be considered active on an issue either if he rates himself as active and can describe some confirming partisan activity or if two or more other people rate him as active in favor or against.

A total of 161 reputational leaders were interviewed, 92 per cent of those identified as such. How frequently are they active? First, it is worth asking what a finding of inactivity might mean. Only three issues were studied in each town. These were salient and controversial issues, but many decisions which affect large numbers of individuals never become controversial or attract widespread interest. Thus, the absence of signs of activity by reputational leaders does not preclude their activity on many other issues which were not studied. As it turns out, however, these cautions are largely unnecessary because 82 per cent of the reputational leaders were active on at least one of the issues studied! Enlarging the number of issues studied per town could only have the effect of further cutting the already small pool of non-active reputational leaders. Furthermore, 41 per cent of the reputational leaders were active on a majority of the issues studied. All in all, there can be little doubt that reputation for influence is highly associated with activity on issues in these communities.

Unity. Do those reputational leaders who engage in partisan activities act as a cohesive force or do they compete to determine the outcome of the issue? There were thirty-four issues on which at least three reputational leaders were active; with less than three, it makes little sense to ask about the extent of agreement. The active reputational leaders are unanimous on only nine of the thirty-four issues. If we use a less stringent criterion than unanimity, we still find that there is two-thirds or less agreement on eleven of the thirty-four issues.

Caution is necessary in interpreting this evidence of disagreement among reputational leaders. Among the many decisions that arise in a community, it is those few which produce serious competition that are likely to become salient. A proposal on which reputational leaders were united in opposition might have difficulty reaching a stage where it would become salient enough to be cited as an "important" community issue. Similarly, a proposal on which reputational leaders were united in favor with no significant amounts of competing resources arrayed on the other side is also unlikely to have high

TABLE 1. *Campaign Effort and Success in Changing the Status Quo*

WINNING SIDE	SUPPORTED CHANGE		SUPPORTED STATUS QUO		CHANGE ISSUE IRRELEVANT
	Per Cent	(N)	Per Cent	(N)	(N)
Made greater campaign effort	65	(13)	32	(9)	(3)
Made same campaign effort*	10	(2)	29	(8)	(0)
Made smaller campaign effort	25	(5)	39	(11)	(1)
Total (N = 52)	100	(20)	100	(28)	(4)

*Includes one case in which the winning side was higher on amount of activity but lower on amount of organization.

salience or high ratings of community concern. Thus, our method of selecting issues
may contain a heavy bias toward those issues
in which there is a substantial amount of
disagreement among major resource-holders.

Nevertheless, the amount of disagreement revealed here tends to discourage any
view of the reputational leaders as a cohesive group united behind common objectives.
While there may be unstudied issues on
which unanimous agreement existed, there
are also likely to be others on which significant disagreement existed. There were only
two among the eighteen communities studied
in which active reputational leaders were
undivided on all three issues: in only five of
the eighteen towns was there as much as 80
per cent agreement on all three issues.

There is other evidence that the reputational leaders fail to comprise any sort of
cohesive political force. In twelve of the
eighteen towns, the list of reputational
leaders contains individuals who are known
to be political rivals or even political enemies. In some cases, there are individuals
with a long history of political combat; in
others, there are spokesmen for rival solidary
groups. In the remaining six communities
where the pool of reputational leaders did
not contain clear protagonists, there were
many instances of no more than casual acquaintance among members of the list. All
in all, with the exception of three towns with
both issue agreement and no evidence of
sustained political rivalry among members of
the pool, reputational leaders fail to form
anything resembling a cohesive united political clique.

Success. When the reputational leaders are
active and united, do they end up on the
winning side? They do about 75 per cent of
the time on the issues studied here (17 of
23 issues). But perhaps they are simply
fellow travelers, joining with the more active
and organized side. It turns out, in fact, that
they support the more active side only 56 per
cent of the time but are on the winning side
about three-fourths of the time. Furthermore, as Table 2 shows, when the side with
the smaller effort is victorious, it is just as
likely to have reputational leader support as

is the side with greater effort when it wins
(35 per cent versus 36 per cent).

It might be argued that reputational
leaders are associated with successful outcomes mainly because they support the status
quo and thus gain the natural advantage
of such support. This is decidedly not the
case; reputational leaders, when united and
active, support the side favoring change more
than twice as often as they support the
side favoring the status quo (15 versus 6
times). This means that, to achieve victories,
they must typically overcome the natural
advantages of the other side. As Table 3
indicates, they are able to do this with some
success. In fact, the side proposing change
has considerable difficulty without the active
support of the reputational leaders and their
opposition amounts to a virtual veto. In half
the cases where the winning side supported
change, they had the support of the reputational leaders and only one success occurred
against reputational leader opposition. When
the winning side supported the status quo,
they had the support of the reputational
leaders only 18 per cent of the time.

Is the support of reputational leaders or a
stronger campaign effort more likely to produce a victory for the side favoring change?
With so few cases, it is not easy to disentangle variables. However, Table 4 has some
suggestive evidence that reputational leader
support may be most critical. With such
support, the side favoring change is successful two-thirds of the time *regardless* of
relative campaign effort. However, such
campaign efforts clearly make an important
difference when reputational leaders are
divided or inactive. The side favoring change
wins almost half the time with a greater
campaign effort but only one-sixth of the
time when it fails to make a greater effort.

It is instructive to look at the six cases in
which the reputational leaders were united
and active on the losing side. Two of these
were efforts to have comprehensive zoning
plans adopted, one involved the approval of
a new high school, one a major change of
land use in the central business district, and
one an ambitious and expensive harbor-
development project. In four of these five

TABLE 2. *Reputational Leader Support and Campaign Effort*

WINNING SIDE	MADE GREATER CAMPAIGN EFFORT		MADE SAME CAMPAIGN EFFORT		MADE SMALLER CAMPAIGN EFFORT	
	Per Cent	(N)	Per Cent	(N)	Per Cent	(N)
Had reputational leader support	36	(9)	20	(2)	35	(6)
Had divided or inactive reputational leaders	56	(14)	80	(8)	41	(7)
Had reputational leader opposition	8	(2)	—	—	24	(4)
Total (N = 52)	100	(25)	100	(10)	100	(17)

TABLE 3. *Reputational Leader Support and Success in Changing the Status Quo*

WINNING SIDE	SUPPORTED CHANGE		SUPPORTED STATUS QUO		CHANGE ISSUE IRRELEVANT (N)
	Per Cent	(N)	PER Cent	(N)	
Had reputational leader support	50	(10)	18	(5)	(2)
Had divided or inactive reputational leaders	45	(9)	64	(18)	(2)
Had reputational leader opposition	5	(1)	18	(5)	—
Total (N = 52)	100	(20)	100	(28)	(4)

TABLE 4. *Reputational Leader Support and Campaign Effort by Success in Changing the Status Quo*

SIDE FAVORING CHANGE	HAD REPUTATIONAL LEADER SUPPORT				HAD NO REPUTATIONAL LEADER SUPPORT*			
	Had Greater Effort		Had No Greater Effort†		Had Greater Effort		Had No Greater Effort	
	Per Cent	(N)	Per Cent	(N)	Per Cent	(N)	Per Cent	(N)
Won	67	(6)	67	(4)	47	(7)	17	(3)
Lost	33	(3)	33	(2)	53	(8)	83	(15)
Total (N = 48‡)	100	(9)	100	(6)	100	(15)	100	(18)

*Cases where reputational leaders were opposed and where they were divided or inactive are combined here.
†Case of equal effort and of smaller effort are combined here.
‡Four cases in which change was not an issue are omitted here.

cases, the leaders of the defeated forces felt that they had lost a round but that the fight was not over. However, they spoke of modifying the alternative in important ways—of asking the town for half a loaf or of toning down the proposal in various ways.

None of the variables discussed here illuminate the sixth defeat. It involved the rezoning of a considerable area of land from residential use to business use. Reputational leaders were active and united against the proposal, participated in a campaign which was apparently *more* extensive in both organization and activity than the other side, and were beneficiaries of the natural advantage of defending the status quo. I can do no more with this case than present it as evidence that the arguments above are not tautological.

Conclusion

Reputational leaders are not presented here as a ruling elite. They are presented as an aggregate of individuals with resources. In particular, I have argued that their reputation is itself a resource and not simply an indicator of resources. If this argument is correct, then we ought to find that they have some success in influencing the outcome of issues when they are active and united. Unfortunately, we cannot simply look at whether they are on the winning or losing side because other factors besides their influence are affecting the outcome. The factors focused on here were the amount of campaign effort and whether the campaign aimed at changing or preserving the status quo. The data indicated that a more active or more organized campaign was necessary to change the status quo than to maintain it.

Reputational leaders are, with few exceptions, active on at least one of the three issues studied in their respective communities. However, they are frequently active on opposite sides, although this may merely reflect a method of issue selection which emphasized controversy. When they are both active and united, they are on the winning side about three-fourths of the time. This is not merely a function of their participation on the more active side, for they have as high a proportion of victories when they support the less active side. Furthermore, they may be making a contribution to the campaign effort and thus exercising additional influence through their contribution to this variable. Nor is their success an artifact of the natural advantage gained from supporting the status quo. On the contrary, they achieve their success *against* this advantage. They are united and successful in support of change two-thirds of the time.

In short there seems to be some reality to reputation. This reality is consistent with a theoretical interpretation of reputation as a resource. I have no desire to defend the past uses and abuses of the reputational method, but neither am I inclined to heed Wolfinger's "plea for a decent burial."[14] A decent convalescence seems more in order.

Notes

1. Robert Dahl, "The Concept of Power," *Behavioral Science*, 2 (July, 1957), 201–15. Herbert A. Simon and James G. March have suggested similar formulations.

2. One might wish to talk of changes in an unintended direction as "negative influence," but this issue is not relevant for the discussion here.

3. It is not my intention to review or even cite such studies here. Nelson Polsby's *Community Power and Political Theory* (New Haven, Conn.: Yale University Press, 1963) has a reasonably complete list of citations and a highly critical review of these studies. See esp. pp. 45–68.

4. *Ibid.*, p. 51.

5. These include John R. P. French, Jr., and Bertram Raven, "The Bases of Social Power," in Dorwin Cartwright (ed.), *Studies in Social Power* (Ann Arbor, Mich.: Institute for Social Research, 1959), pp. 150–67; Herbert Kelman, "Processes of Opinion Change," *Public Opinion Quarterly*, 25 (Spring, 1961), 57–78; Amitai Etzioni, *A Comparative Analysis of Complex Organizations* (Glencoe, Ill.: Free Press, 1961); Franz L. Neumann, "Approaches to the Study of Political Power," *Political Science Quarterly*, 65 (1950), 161–80; Morris Janowitz, *The Professional Soldier* (Glencoe,

Ill.: Free Press, 1960); Herbert Goldhamer and Edward A. Shils, "Types of Power and Status," *American Journal of Sociology*, 45 (September, 1939), 171–82; John Harsanyi, "Measurement of Social Power, Opportunity Costs, and the Theory of Two-Person Bargaining Games," *Behavioral Science*, 7 (January, 1962), 67–80; and Talcott Parsons, "On the Concept of Influence," *Public Opinion Quarterly*, 27 (Spring, 1963), 37–62.

6. The argument above focuses on persuasion resources. Most studies using the reputational method have not had such purposes in mind, and a variety of wordings have been used. What of asking for the names of people "who run the town," "who would be needed to get a new project across," or "who have a lot of influence on the outcome of decisions"? The responses to such questions may frequently include those who possess persuasion resources, but some individuals might be included for other reasons. It seems likely, although one would have to demonstrate this, that those frequently named individuals who do *not* possess persuasion resources do possess sanctioning resources. If this is true, then those who are named would still comprise a pool of individuals with resources and all of the above arguments for studying reputational leaders would apply.

7. Issues were selected for study through examination of community newspapers and some informal checking with newspaper editors and city clerks. It was possible to miss issues on whose importance there was considerable consensus since this could not be discovered until the interviews were completed. Thus, five issues named by a majority of respondents were not studied.

8. Unfortunately, this question is not the one called for by the theoretical argument above nor is it directed, as it should be, to a sample of decision-makers. Thus, to treat our reputational leaders as a pool of resource holders we must assume that those named have some kind of stable and general resources, though not necessarily persuasion resources.

9. That is, Σm_i, where m_i is the number of times the ith individual is mentioned.

10. To be included, an individual must be mentioned more than some fixed proportion of the total mentions. The setting of such a fixed proportion is rather arbitrary, and I have set it here at 3 per cent of the total because such a figure yields an average of about 10 people per community. The number per town ranges from 6 people at the low end to 13 at the other extreme. The number of mentions required for inclusion ranges from 3 to 8, with an average of about $4\frac{1}{2}$. Since the average number of respondents per town is about 24, this means that a reputational leader is named by a minimum of about 1/5 of the respondents in his town, a figure obtained by dividing the average number of mentions required for inclusion (4.6) by the average number of respondents (24). This figure of 1/5 of the respondents provides some interpretation for the, by itself, meaningless criterion of 3 per cent of the total mentions.

11. Initial coding plans were more ambitious, but difficulties in achieving satisfactory reliability forced resort to this crude classification. Intercoder agreement for these three categories was above 80 per cent for the 108 campaigns being coded.

12. The base for these figures and for the subsequent analysis is actually 52 rather than 54 issues. Two of the issues are excluded because of ambiguity over the outcome, which made it impossible to designate a winner.

13. The phrase "campaign effort" refers to the measure of amount of activity and degree of organization taken in combination. A side will be characterized as having greater effort if it is at least equal on one of these measures and greater on the other.

14. Raymond E. Wolfinger, "A Plea for a Decent Burial," *American Sociological Review*, 27 (December, 1962), 841–47.

E. The Reputational Approach Refined

Community Leadership: A Case Study and Conceptual Refinement[1]

Charles M. Bonjean

The phenomenon of power-leadership decision-making at the community level has received a great deal of attention from both sociologists and political scientists during the past decade.[2] Many of these investigations, especially those conducted by sociologists, have been criticized on the grounds that the method of investigation used—the reputational approach—is inadequate for several reasons.[3] (1) The approach enables the investigator to find a monolithic power structure when, in fact, such a structure may not exist in the community. (2) Assuming there is a monolithic structure, this approach may lead to premature closure (not including all the leaders) or may lead to the inclusion of non-leaders. The problem is the cutoff point in the final list of nominees. (3) If the reputational approach is used, we must take into consideration inaccuracies, in respondent perceptions. Private citizens, it is claimed, may be unreliable sources of information. (4) Interviewer and respondent may not agree on what is meant by "power." Certain questions used may not mean the same thing to both interviewer and respondent or there may be no consensus in regard to the meaning of the question among respondents.

The purpose of this investigation is to attempt to indicate how these shortcomings may be overcome through an extension of method and a refinement of concepts. The collection of additional data—sociometric and other—on a sample of community leaders so designated by the reputational approach makes it possible to probe group characteristics and internal differentiations of the sample. Analysis of the data indicates that reputational leaders are, in fact, meaningful groups and not artifacts of the operational measures in at least one community —Burlington, North Carolina. Because of the heuristic nature of this investigation no specific hypotheses will be tested, but one general hypothesis of an exploratory nature will be entertained: A conceptual refinement of the term "community leader" based on the method of investigation itself will lead to greater agreement among investigators, will satisfy to some degree the basic criticisms listed above, and may serve as a useful basis for comparative studies in the future.

The Community

Burlington, located in north-central North Carolina, has a population of approximately 33,000 (1960) and a suburban population of about 15,000 (1958 est.). Approximately 125,000 live in the city's trade area, which extends 8 miles to the west and 20 miles in all other directions. The population of the city increased slightly more than 33 per cent between 1950 and 1960, an increase due primarily to industrial expansion and new industries. Eighty-eight per cent of the population is native-born white, and 11.4 per cent is Negro (1960).

Primarily an industrial community, Burlington ranks sixth in the nation in hosiery production and leads the South in the number of hosiery plants. Of the city's seventy-eight industrial establishments, thirty are hosiery mills and fifteen other produce textile products. Among the 3,073 counties in the United States, Alamance, of which Burlington is the largest city, ranks 216th in the number of manufacturing plants and 203d in the number of industrial wage earners—well in the top 10 per cent on both items. A total of 19,000 persons are employed in Burlington's industries.[4]

The city operates under the mayor-council type of government.

Method of Investigation

The empirical objectives of the investigation have already been stated: to isolate a group of community leaders according to standard methodology and to further delimit this group on the basis of other measures. A two-step reputational analysis supplemented with sociometric and interaction data was used to attempt to fulfill these objectives.

The executive secretary of an established community association was asked: "Who are the community leaders who really get things done around here?"[5] He was asked to rank up to twenty leaders in order of over-all influence and to specify those leaders he had worked with as well as the areas of participation.[6] Using his list as a starting point, interviewers asked each individual named by him to do the same. This was continued until new lists yielded many more duplications than nominations. After forty-five interviews it was evident that there was relatively high agreement in regard to sixteen community leaders and little agreement on the remaining one hundred nominations. Additional interviews would probably have had the same results—more nominations for the sixteen top leaders and more names to add to the remaining list of one hundred. According to Moreno, this assumption has general

validity and may be termed the "socio-dynamic effect":

> It might be anticipated that increasing the chance probability of being chosen by allowing more choices within the same size population and thus lessening the chance probability to remain unchosen will gradually bring the number of unchosen to a vanishing point and likewise reduce more and more the number of comparatively little chosen.
>
> However, in actuality, this does not take place. . . . The further choices allowed go more frequently to the already highly chosen and not proportionately more to those who are unchosen or who have few choices. The quantity of isolates and little chosen comes finally to a standstill whereas the volume of choices continues to increase for those at the upper end of the range.
>
> The sociodynamic effect apparently has general validity. It is found in some degree in all social aggregates.[7]

Thirty-eight of the forty-five respondents became informants by naming individuals and ranking them. Their 116 nominations were tabulated and weighted—a weight of 20 assigned to each first-place choice, 19 to a second place choice and so on down to one for a twentieth-place choice. The total leadership score assigned to each of the 116 individuals mentioned consists merely of the sum of the weighted choices.

Leadership scores ranged from 350.5 for Neal Allen, the top leader, in the community, to one for Mrs. Robert Cain, who received one twentieth-place vote.[8] Fourteen of the 116 persons mentioned received scores of more than 100 and two received scores between 90 and 100. No other person received a total leadership score higher than 70 and most were far below this score.[9] Thus, because of the high agreement regarding the selection of the first sixteen as leaders and because of the lack of consensus in regard to the remainder of the sample, it was assumed that, *if* a power elite existed in Burlington, these sixteen individuals would be the basic element of its membership.

Most power structure studies stop here in regard to the reputational approach. (Two exceptions, studies conducted by Robert O.

Schulze and A. Alexander Fanelli, will be discussed briefly below.) But using the same data and analyzing them from a different standpoint may yield additional valuable information. Thus a second step in the data analysis is incorporated. In Burlington, of the forty-five informants, twelve were in the leader category (members of the top sixteen),[10] the other thirty-three were not. The second analysis utilizes only the choices and rankings of ten of the twelve "leaders."[11] When this is done a new picture emerges— the "power elite" has gained new members (because of high agreement among these twelve, but no or few nominations from the remainder of the informants) and assigns much less power to other nominees (because of no or few choices from the elite). This modification of the reputational approach does not incorporate an arbitrary cutoff point, and, at the same time, it reduces the likelihood of inaccuracies in respondent perception (in that the "judges" are determined by the first analysis). The wording of the question and the additional requirement for judges to list the nominees' spheres of influence seems to overcome the problem of ambiguity. The possibility of ambiguity and

the desirability of judges is indicated by comparing leader and non-leader rankings (Table 1). That there is little agreement between the two sets of rankings is supported statistically, as Spearman's rank correlation for the two groups is .012.

Two questions must be answered before further discussion. First, does this method imply an a priori assumption that a monolithic power structure does exist in the community? Second, have we really established a power elite?

In regard to the first question, it should be noted that this technique allows for disagreement as well as for agreement in regard to leadership choices. If there were no leadership elite in the community we would expect little or no agreement in leadership selection. There is no reason to reject the assumption that the technique is able to indicate the absence of a power structure, as well as its presence.

Obviously, all of Burlington's 48,000 residents (including suburbs) could not conceivably play leadership roles, strictly on the grounds of accepted role definition. When one starts cutting down a population of this size by factors of two for sex (excluding

TABLE 1. *Ranking of Sixteen Leaders by Themselves and by Non-Leaders*

LEADER	TOTAL SAMPLE (N = 38)	LEADERS (N = 10)	NON-LEADERS (N = 28)	DIFFERENCE	LEADER TYPE*
Neal Allen	1	1	2	−1	v
James Barton	2	2	3.5	−1.5	v
George Welles	3	10	1	9	s
Mike Reynolds	4	3	5	−2	v
Tom White	5	9	6	3	v
R. V. Daniels	6	4	11	−7	c
Terry Jones	7	13	7	0	s
Percy Roberts	8	17	3.5	13.5	s
Charles Martin	9	11	12	−1	v
Thomas Mintler	10	14	9.5	4.5	s
A. G. Curtis	11	7	13	−6	c
Richard Murphy	12	16	8	8	s
Harold Smith	13	5	14	−9	c
Harold B. Green	14	6	15	−9	c
LeRoy Barton	15	8	16	−8	c
Harvey Harris	16	15	9.5	5.5	s
Dan Morley	—	12	—	−5	c

*Leader types: *v*, visible; *s*, symbolic; *c*, concealed.

females), perhaps three for age bracket (excluding those too old and those too young), X_1 for income sufficient to insure some leisure, X_2 for education and so on, the result *is* a limited group. The size of this group is unknown in Burlington, but it is reasonable to assume that it is *at least* 116 (based on nominations alone). The 445 choices made by the 38 informants *could* have been distributed evenly, indicating a power vacuum. In fact, they were not. Of the 445 choices, 201 were directed to the top sixteen nominees ($\bar{X} = 12.6$); the other 224 were directed to the remaining 100 nominees ($\bar{X} = 2.24$). Had there been the least possible agreement in leadership selection in regard to the leadership pool of 116, each nominee would have received almost four (actually 3.86) votes. Adopting 3.86 as the mean and 4.6 as the standard deviation (an estimate based on the range, which in this case is 22), an upper confidence limit of 4.97 (at the 99 per cent level) may be computed. In other words, we may assume that choices are no longer random if we are able to isolate a number of individuals, each receiving five or more choices. As a matter of fact, the number of choices assigned to the judges selected by the first step of the method ranges from six to twenty-two. No one in the remainder of the "leadership pool" has more than four choices and most have only one. An informal analysis of rankings (as opposed to sheer number of choices) seems to indicate, even more convincingly, that a power vaccuum does *not* exist in Burlington.[12]

At least two validity checks may be employed to ascertain whether or not the technique actually has established a power elite.

First, if most top leaders also select one another as top leaders and, second, if, in fact, they actually indicate that they interact with one another, it seems reasonable to assume that a *group* has actually been discerned as opposed to a mere aggregate of individuals with similar characteristics.

By constructing a sociogram (Figure 1) showing the first three leadership choices of the top ten leaders completing this section of the interview schedule, an index of the degree to which these leaders form a group is available. Of the thirty possible choices (ten leaders times three choices each), twenty-four are within the elite designated by the entire sample. Thus, the *ratio of interest*, one aspect of group cohesiveness, is .80.[13] This statistic (the number of in-group choices divided by the total possible number of such choices) is meaningful only when compared with that of another group. The only group available for comparison at this point is the remainder of our sample of informants. Of their eighty-four possible choices, forty-five are directed to the top sixteen (ratio of interest = .53). Assuming the remainder of our informants do not form a group and are not a part of the elite group, we have a basis for comparison and consequently can test for statistical significance of differences between proportions. In this case, a *t*-test yields $P < .001$.

A second validity check, "interaction," also indicates that Burlington's power elite resembles a group more than it does an aggregate. As was indicated above, after listing and ranking leaders, each informant was provided with a check list of thirty community activities (although not all were found to be salient in Burlington) and was asked to indicate those individuals he "worked with" on each of the thirty activities. Significant here is the fact that a number of interaction patterns could be noted that *were not* connected with formal memberships.[14] For example, a cross-tabulation of responses indicates that five of the ten leaders say they have worked with one another regarding "who gets elected to municipal office," yet none hold offices themselves nor do they hold formal positions in a political party. Eight of the power elite name one another in the area of attempting to attract new industries to the community. All in all, interaction patterns *within* the leadership elite are discernible in twenty-one of the possible community activities. In each case the patterns involve between three and eight of the ten interviewed leaders.

Thus, because the data indicate mutual choices between members of the power elite as well as interaction within the elite, most

FIGURE 1. *Leadership Ranking by Ten Leaders. Uncircled are not Top Leaders.*

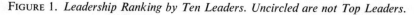
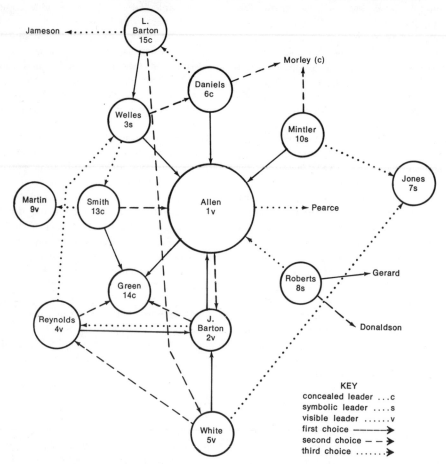

of the sixteen leaders uncovered by the reputational approach may be considered as a group rather than merely an aggregate, It should be noted, however, that four of the top sixteen leaders—ranks 8, 10, 11, and 12 (see Figure 1)—received no first, second, or third place choices within the power elite. It is apparent that their position in the leadership group is thus derived from one or both of two phenomena: their leadership score was a consequence of rankings beyond three by members of the elite *or* their leadership score was a consequence of high ranking by non-leaders. Also several other individuals, not originally identified as elite members, were given such choices. This brings us more directly to the second

step in data analysis—an attempt to determine differentiations *within* the power elite.

Types of Leaders

Assuming that the sixteen persons uncovered by the first step in data analysis are the most qualified to perceive others of their kind, the next step should be to compare the leaders as perceived by one another with how they are perceived by that proportion of the sample not designated as part of the power elite. Such a comparison would yield three possible leadership types: (1) The leader who is assigned approximately the same amount of power by both other leaders and non-leaders. (2) The leader who is assigned more prestige by leaders than by non-leaders. (3) The leader who is assigned more prestige by non-leaders than by leaders.

Leaders of the first type will be termed *visible leaders* because they are playing roles in the community that are perceived and known by the community at large. Leaders of the second type will be termed *concealed leaders* because they have more influence within the leadership circle or power elite, and consequently in the community in general, than the community at large realizes. Leaders of the third type will be termed *symbolic leaders* because they probably do not wield as much influence in the community as the community at large thinks they do.

Looking at the comparison of leaders shown in Table 1, all three types may be distinguished. Arbitrarily setting a rank variation of five (true limits of 4.5 or greater) as the point where leaders are classified as concealed or symbolic rather than as visible, there are five visible leaders, six concealed leaders and six symbolic leaders. Sixteen of the leaders, of course, were uncovered by the general reputational approach; but a seventeenth was located by the modification described here. Leader types are indicated on both the sociogram and Table 1 by the symbols "v" (visible), "c" (concealed), and "s" (symbolic).

For this differentiation to be meaningful, the next step is to determine whether or not there is a relationship between leader type and other variables. In attempting to locate differences between symbolic and concealed leaders, there are no patterns or trends in regard to age, type of business, number of employees, types of activities engaged in, memberships (including religion), or education.

There is, however, one basic difference between the two extreme types of leaders—symbolic and concealed. Four of the six symbolic leaders are members of prominent Burlington families—families that have lived in the city for several generations, that are wealthy, and that have passed the family business on to the person listed as a leader. Murphy (12), before his death, was the top officer in a hosiery mill that had been in his family for three generations; Roberts (8) is the second-generation administrator of his family's hosiery mill; Jones (7) inherited his father's automobile dealership, and Harris (16) is the member of a family possessing all of the characteristics except the last (inheritance of family business). Only Welles (3) and Mintler (10) differ in this respect from the other symbolic leaders. Welles's symbolic placement may be explained by the fact that he is paid by the city businessmen for work in community affairs. Thus he occupies a position highly visible to the community in general, but one of perhaps less importance in the sphere of policy formation and decision-making than in the actual execution of policy. Thus, this deviant case analysis seems to further validate the method proposed here. Only Mintler's placement as a symbolic leader is unexplainable. This may indicate a necessary change in method. The arbitrary rank variation set forth for classification as a concealed or symbolic leader was five (4.5 true limit). Mintler was a borderline case. The difference between leader and non-leader ranking was exactly 4.5. This may indicate that the arbitrary difference is set too low—perhaps, for example, the true limit should be raised to five.

The concealed leaders differ markedly from the symbolic leaders. Only one of the six concealed leaders *owns* a large business or industry and this leader, Congressman Green, founded his businesses himself, rather than inheriting them. In other words, his wealth is at least a generation newer than is the wealth of most of the symbolic leaders. His concealed status may also be due to the fact that he is the local power structure's link with a larger, more influential power structure at the state or national level.[15] As such, perhaps he would be more closely connected to the elite personnel and consequently more visible to them at the community level than to the remainder of the sample, who perhaps have a more macroscopic conception of his role. It is interesting to note that Allen, the leader receiving the greatest number of choices and highest ranks, ranked Green first. The other five concealed leaders do not own businesses—two are professionals and three are the local administrators of subsidiaries of state or national corporations. Five of the concealed leaders spent their childhood or longer outside of Burlington and thus, compared with the symbolic leader group, are relative newcomers. The outstanding observation is that none is from a traditionally prominent Burlington family. This suggests that non-leaders perhaps think more in terms of the status or class dimensions of stratification when asked to name community leaders, whereas leaders themselves are more apt to think in terms of the power dimension. It suggests further that non-leaders may not recognize changes in the leadership base or power elite but think instead that those that have always been powerful will probably continue to be so. In other words, individuals who have formerly ranked high on all three dimensions of social stratification—class, status, and power—may through time have lost, to some degree, one of these characteristics, but for several years a "halo effect" will operate to influence the general viewpoint. Schulze's Cibola findings lend some credulity to this hypothesis (economic dominants exerted sociopolitical power as well as economic power in the past, but currently have relinquished the former in that community).[16]

Critics of stratification studies continually remind us of the necessity to distinguish between class and status.[17] Studies of the third major aspect of stratification—power —face the same problem. High status or class position may lead to the assumption by informants of high power positions. Thus it becomes necessary to differentiate between three different types of community leaders—class (economic) leaders, status (reputational) leaders, and true power leaders. The *hypothesized* relationship between the methodological distinction of visible, concealed, and symbolic leaders to class, status, and power leaders, as suggested by this sensitizing exploratory investigation, is summarized in Table 2. Two important relationships should be noted: (1) the traditional reputational

approach uncovers symbolic leaders who are actually not members of the power elite. (2) It may *not* uncover actual members of the power elite if these members rank low in either class or status.[18]

TABLE 2. *Hypothesized Relationship between Methodological Types and Stratification Components*

	CLASS	STATUS	POWER
Symbolic	High	High	Low
Visible	High	High	High
Concealed	Low	Low*	High

*The concealed leader may rank high in either class or status position, but not in both.

Thus, a second step needs to be added to the reputational approach if its use is to be continued in this type of study. The second step, of course, is the one that has been outlined here—the comparison of rankings by leaders and non-leaders and the classification of leaders into three types based on rank differences. This method itself is a useful heuristic device at the single case-study level of investigation. When power studies reach the comparative level (examining two or more leadership structures simultaneously), it should be even more useful as it is one means of assessing one of the most controversial and central characteristics of such structures—their visibility. Are leaders and leadership behavior overt or covert? Furthermore, is this characteristic, the structure's visibility, related to community attributes?

The first question may be answered in regard to the case at hand. The second answer must be delayed until a uniform methodological approach is applied to the study of other communities. In Burlington, the leadership structure is partly visible and partly concealed. The structure's "star," Neal Allen, is visible. Although it is a subjective impression, it seems that one factor coinciding with Allen's number one rank in the community may be that he is a coordinator of community affairs. In other words, because so many of the other top leaders, each with his own specialized community interests, select Allen as the top leader, his function may be that of assigning priority to various projects (some visible and some concealed) and attempting to integrate and interrelate them. Supporting evidence is that he is a member of all important civic organizations but holds formal offices in none of them. Informants furthermore remarked, for example, "He really isn't active himself as far as *doing* things goes, but he certainly has more influence than anyone else in town." On the other hand, most of the other top leaders (both visible and concealed) direct their activities toward only one or two institutional spheres of the community—usually economic plus one other. Other than Allen, only two leaders, Welles (3) and Reynolds (4) are active in more than two institutional areas of participation. In summary, Burlington's leadership structure may be seen as a network of overlapping subgroups, some visible and some concealed, co-ordinated by one central visible figure. This structure is not too unlike the smaller and simpler power structure described by Arthur J. Vidich and Joseph Bensman in Springdale and is similar to the structure described by Schulze in Cibola—three groups of dominants linked by two individuals occupying "dual statuses."[19]

Conclusion

Adding a second step in data analysis, interaction checks, and statistics of social configuration to the traditional reputational approach used in the study of community power-leadership decision-making and distinguishing between three types of leaders (1) takes account of and, to varying degrees, answers the criticisms of the traditional reputational approach, (2) serves as a heuristic device leading to more penetrating modes of analysis in itself, (3) emphasizes that structural characteristic—visibility— that has been a major source of disagreement and discussion, and (4) suggests interrelationships between the concepts "class," "status," and "power" that may later contribute to a more general theory of stratification.

The fact that all generalizations discussed above are based on, and derived from, only one case study obviously requires cautious intepretation. They are offered here only as material for hypotheses—hypotheses to be tested by this investigator in the near future in other communities and to be modified, improved, or rejected by other interested investigators.

Notes

1. This investigation involves one facet of community affairs in the Piedmont Industrial Crescent being studied by the Institute for Research in Social Science of the University of North Carolina under a grant by the Ford Foundation. The leadership studies are under the direction of E. William Noland, who suggested a number of revisions and modifications of this investigation. Revisions and useful suggestions were also made by Richard L. Simpson and Ernest Q. Campbell of the University of North Carolina.

2. Including Floyd Hunter, *Community Power Structure: A Study of Decision Makers* (Chapel Hill: University of North Carolina Press, 1953); Roland J. Pellegrin and Charles H. Coates, "Absentee-owned Corporations and Community Power Structure," *American Journal of Sociology*, 61 (March, 1956), 413–19; Charles Freeman and Selz C. Mayo, "Decision Makers in Rural Community Action," *Social Forces*, 35 (May, 1957), 319–

22; Robert O. Schulze, "The Role of Economic Dominants in Community Power Structure," *American Sociological Review*, 23 (February, 1958), 3–9; Delbert C. Miller, "Industry and Community Power Structures: A Comparative Study of an American and an English City," *American Sociological Review*, 23 (February, 1958), 9–15; Ernest A. T. Barth and Stuart D. Johnson, "Community Power and a Typology of Social Issues," *Social Forces*, 38 (October, 1959), 29–32; Nelson W. Polsby, "Three Problems in the Analysis of Community Power," *American Sociological Review*, 25 (December, 1959), 796–803; Orrin E. Klapp and L. Vincent Padgett, "Power Structure and Decision-making in a Mexican Border City," *American Journal of Sociology*, 65 (January, 1960), 400–406; Arthur J. Vidich and Joseph Bensman, *Small Town in Mass Society* (Garden City, N.Y.: Doubleday & Co., 1960); Robert A. Dahl, *Who Governs? Democracy and Power in an American City* (New Haven, Conn.: Yale University Press, 1961), and Benjamin Walter, "Political Decision Making in Arcadia," in F. Stuart Chapin, Jr., and Shirley F. Weiss (eds.), *Urban Growth Dynamics* (New York: John Wiley & Sons, forthcoming).

3. By reputational approach, of course, is meant asking certain members of the community under investigation to list and rank the most powerful and influential leaders in the community. The approach has also been termed the "snowball technique" since one informant's nominees become the next informants. Critics of this technique include Robert A. Dahl, "A Critique of the Ruling Elite Model," *American Political Science Review*, 52 (June, 1958), 463–69; Herbert Kaufman and Victor Jones, "The Mystery of Power," *Public Administration Review*, 14 (Summer, 1954), 205–12; Nelson W. Polsby, "The Sociology of Community Power: A Reassessment," *Social Forces*, 37 (March, 1959), 232–36; Raymond E. Wolfinger, "Reputation and Reality in the Study of Community Power," *American Sociological Review*, 25 (October, 1960), 636–44, and a number of the investigations listed in n. 2.

4. *Hill's Burlington and Graham City Directory* (Richmond, Va.: Hill Directory, Inc., 1958), pp. i–xiii.

5. This was but one question included in a standardized interview schedule consisting of seventy-eight questions (both poll type and open end) and requiring from forty-five minutes to four hours to complete.

6. Thirty specific activities were listed. They could be grouped into seven general participation areas: economic, welfare, livability, educational, political, philanthropic, and desegregational.

7. J. L. Moreno, *et al.*, *The Sociometry Reader* (Glencoe, Ill.: Free Press, 1960), p. 36.

8. "Neal Allen" and "Mrs. Robert Cain" are pseudonyms as are the names and affiliations of the other leaders and non-leaders specifically referred to in this investigation.

9. It is impossible to include the full data here because of space limitations. The investigator will provide mimeographed copies of additional data or will answer more specific questions on request.

10. Of the sixteen top leaders in Burlington, only twelve were interviewed. One died shortly after the study had started, one was not in the city during the time of the study, and, although the other two were interviewed they asked to keep the schedule in order to complete some "difficult" questions and did not return it.

11. Of the twelve leaders interviewed, two refused to rank leaders and to indicate those they interact with. Thus, sociometric choices and actual information regarding interaction are available for ten of the sixteen leaders.

12. These data were not subjected to the same sort of statistical analysis as described above because of time and cost limitations and because the first test was thought to be convincing enough to support the argument in question. The informal analysis was used merely as a quick check.

13. For a discussion of the ratio of interest and other statistics of social configuration see Moreno, *et al.*, *op. cit.*, pp. 19–51.

14. This is not the first investigation conducted where interaction has been designated as a necessary "check." An "acquaintanceship scale" was used successfully by Schulze and described in a report published subsequent to the research described here (see Robert O. Schulze, "The Bifurcation of Power in a Satellite City," in Morris Janowitz [ed.], *Community Political Systems* [Glencoe, Ill.: Free Press, 1961], p. 51).

15. See Floyd Hunter, *Top Leadership U.S.A.* (Chapel Hill: University of North Carolina Press, 1959) for a discussion that supports this tentative hypothesis.

16. Schulze, in Janowitz (ed.), *op. cit.*, pp. 40–41.

17. Including Paul K. Hatt, "Stratification in the Mass Society," *American Sociological Review*, 15 (April, 1950), 216–22; Harold F. Kaufman, Otis Dudley Duncan, Neal Gross, and William H. Sewell, "Problems of Theory and Method in the Study of Social Stratification in Rural Society," *Rural Sociology*, 18 (March, 1953), 12–24; Kurt Mayer, "The Theory of Social Classes," *Harvard Educational Review*, 23 (Summer, 1953), 149–67; Gregory P. Stone and William H. Form, "Instabilities in Status: The Problem of Hierarchy in the Community Study of Status Arrangements," *American Sociological Review*, 18 (April, 1953), 149–62, and others.

18. A. Alexander Fanelli ("A Typology of Community Leadership Based on Influence within the Leader Subsystem," *Social Forces*, 34 [May, 1956], 332–38), sets forth a method that enables the investigator to distinguish between the symbolic and visible leaders (he calls them prestige influentials and active influentials), but that ignores the possibility of concealed leaders. Schulze's distinction between economic dominants and public leaders (in Janowitz [ed.], *op. cit.*, pp. 19–80) has the same shortcoming, but obviously the economic public leader distinction has other merits and is thus not as comparable to the method being discussed as is the Fanelli distinction.

19. Vidich and Bensman, *op. cit.*, pp. 110–230, and Schulze, in Janowitz (ed.), *op. cit.*, p. 52.

Community Power Structure: Problems and Continuities[*]

M. Herbert Danzger

This paper is concerned with locating theoretical and methodological difficulties in the study of community power. Interest will be directed to formulating these difficulties as researchable problems and in suggesting some new directions for research. This will be done through a careful re-examination of some of the major concepts utilized in the study of community power as well as through a methodological evaluation of this research. For the sake of simplicity, I shall use Hunter's pioneer study in the area, *Community Power Structure*,[1] to indicate the types of problems presently confronting researchers in this area. Discussion will not, however, be limited to Hunter's work.

Methodological Difficulties

The significance of Hunter's work has been said to lie in the introduction of sophisticated research techniques to an area formerly without them.[2] If so, it may also be said that it is precisely the use of these techniques that has raised the great storm of controversy still raging in the literature on power structure, more than a decade after Hunter first published his work.

The controversy centers on the logic of the research procedures employed rather than on the specific techniques and their execution. The major criticisms are as follows:[3]

1. Since Hunter's technique is "reputational," his data are not power acts, but opinions—albeit of "informed" people—on who has power.[4]
2. Assessments of the power structure by "informed" informants may actually be incorrect. This may be a result of (a) their unfamiliarity with the researcher's use and meaning of the word "power,"[5] or, (b) more important, their perception of the power structure may be inaccurate or distorted. A sizable body of data lends credence to this claim.[6]
3. The Hunter approach to power is far too general in its implication. (a) It fails to differentiate areas over which various members of the "elite" wield power, apparently assuming that power is wielded in all areas by the same elite;[7] (b) it tends to imply that the distribution of power is stable over time, neglecting the possibility that power may be redistributed, as under a change in political administration.

A Strategy for Solution of Methodological Difficulties

Each of these criticisms could be rephrased as questions open to empirical investigation, the results of which would then indicate the validity of the Hunter technique for research

Reprinted from the American Sociological Review, *29 (October 1964), 707–717, by permission of the author and the American Sociological Association. Copyright 1964 by the American Sociological Association.*

* I am indebted to my mentors at Columbia University; to Robert K. Merton who read an earlier draft of this paper; to Amitai Etzioni, for his encouragement and interest; and particularly to David Rogers (presently at New York University) for keeping my nose to the grindstone of empirical data. An earlier draft of this paper was also read by my colleagues at Queens College, Victor Gioscia, Norman Goodman, Walter Klink, Elizabeth K. Nottingham and Melvin Reichler. Their helpful comments are much appreciated.

on community power. The questions would be the following:

1. Does the informant's perception of power actually correspond to power structure as measured by some objective means?
2. If the informant's perception is "incorrect," or if objective "correctness" cannot be determined, then what is the relation between power structure as perceived through the reputational technique and as perceived through other techniques?
3. What do "informed" informants mean by the term power? Do they understand this term in the same sense as the researcher?
4. Do the leaders identified through use of the reputational technique lead in several "scopes of power" or is their leadership restricted to one or few scopes?
5. Is the power structure as described through the use of the reputational technique stable over time or is it merely a description of power based on the highly variable "popularity" of certain individuals at a particular moment?

The first three questions may be answered by comparing the power structure as perceived through use of the reputational approach with the power structure as perceived through another technique or techniques. If it is the same, then we can assume (a) that reputation for power corresponds to the realities of the power distribution; (b) that the respondents understand the term power or use it in a way similar to the usage intended by the researcher; (c) that one's research techniques have located informants whose perception of the power structure is indeed accurate.

The answers to the last two questions would require a study designed to assess power over specific scope of action. This inquiry may easily be built into the reputational method. Nothing inherent in the method necessitated the assumption that power is wielded across the board.

To answer the final question,[8] whether the perception reported is a stable one, a panel type technique, i.e., a reinvestigation of a particular community after a "suitable" lapse of time (to be determined), would indicate whether the technique describes the real distribution of power resources or momentary popularity. These descriptions should be highly stable, if the technique does describe the distribution of power resources, since these are unlikely to undergo rapid changes in distribution.

D'Antonio and Erickson take a significant step in the direction of answering some of the critics of this method [9]through a reexamination of the power structure of El Paso and C. Juarez some three years after their first study. But as Polsby points out, the "study has not proven the value of the reputational technique in a way which permits full confidence to be placed in conclusions expressing renewed faith in the reputational method."[10]

This same study by D'Antonio and Erickson also attempts to answer the criticism that the reputational method fails to specify the "scope of power" of the leaders. Identifying "general" leaders without attempting to gather data on the scope of power might have resulted in the "status" leaders (people of much celebrity but little power) being chosen as the "top powers" in the community. But critics of the reputational approach admit that "this problem [i.e., whether leaders are general or specific] does not affect the method's intrinsic validity . . . for there is no reason why reputations for influence cannot be solicited in specified issue areas."[11]

As I have already pointed out, the first three questions could be answered if the description of a power structure obtained through the reputational technique were compared to results obtained through use of some other technique. D'Antonio and Erickson cannot rightly claim to have done this because their data, including their data on the hypothetical hospital situation, is essentially also obtained through the reputational technique.

To the best of my knowledge only one

other attempt has been made to compare data obtained on community power structure by various methods. Freeman, et al.[12] compare four methods of obtaining data on community power: the reputational, positional, local activity and participation.[13] They found substantial agreement on leadership (a) when reputational and positional methods were utilized, *or* (b) when participation and social activity were the criteria. When the four procedures were compared with still another—determining leadership on the basis of organizational participation (i.e., the participation rate of organizations rather than individuals)—again, the same pattern emerged. But the results obtained with either of the first two methods differed considerably from those obtained by either of the latter two.[14]

When the four procedures were used to determine the proportion of leaders who were government officials or employees or professional participants, the results of the participation (decision-making) technique differed sharply from those of the other three, which were in substantial agreement.[15]

Freeman and associates go on to define three basic types of "leaders." "Institutional Leaders" are discovered by the reputational technique, or by position, or by organizational participation. These people are for the most part not personally active in community affairs.

> There is no evidence [in Syracuse] that they have any direct impact on most decisions which take place. Their role may easily be limited to that of lending prestige to or legitimizing the solutions provided by others. They might conceivably be secret decision-makers, but it is more likely that they serve to provide access to the decision-making structure for their underlings: the *Effectors*.[16]

The effectors are found by studying participation; they are the active workers in the actual process of community decision-making. "Many . . . are government personnel and professional participants, and others are the employees of the large private corporations directed by the Institutional Leaders. . . ."[17]

The third type of leaders are called the Activists "seemingly, by sheer commitment of time and effort to community affairs, these Activists do help to shape the future of Syracuse."[18]

Freeman and associates conclude that:

> The various approaches to the study of community leadership seem to uncover different types of leaders. The study of reputation, position or organizational participation seems to get at the Institutional Leaders. Studies of participation in decision-making, on the other hand tap the Effectors of community action. And studies of social activity seem to seek out the Activists who gain entry by dint of sheer commitment, time and energy.[19]

The evidence offered by Freeman, et al., indicates then, that although comparisons cannot be made between the decision-making and the reputational methods, nevertheless useful comparisons might be made between the reputational, positional, and organizational participation methods.[20] This would not "validate" the reputational method, as informants used in reputational procedures are likely to make their judgments about the power structure on the basis of "position" or "organizational participation," at least in part. But it would indicate the degree of agreement one could anticipate between the reputational, positional and organizational participation methods.

While full agreement between the reputational method and the other·two should not, in general, be anticipated (as informants are not likely to restrict themselves solely to these dimensions but may well include status considerations, popularity and the like) this comparison would indicate (a) the extent to which these "extraneous" considerations do enter informants' judgments, and (b) where, in the social structure of the community, they are likely to be granted more prominence. The latter point is particularly important as it might well indicate where one is likely to find individuals who are well informed with respect to whatever elements the researcher has chosen to investigate, thereby minimizing the chances of utilizing informants with misperceptions of these elements of the power structure. In addition, this would permit calculation of the effects on the power structure of perceptions (and misperceptions) of power.

One other criticism has been leveled at the Hunter study. Wolfinger points out that isolating and identifying the leaders does not describe a city's political system because "it does not indicate whether they are allies or enemies."

> To establish the existence of a ruling elite, one must show not only that influence is distributed unequally but also that those who have the most influence are united so as to act in concert rather than in opposition. One cannot conclude that the highest-ranked individuals comprise the ruling group rather than merely an aggregate of leaders without establishing their cohesiveness as well as their power.[21]

This criticism appears to have been dropped in recent discussions of power structure.[22] Apparently, all agree that no "power elite" exists. Researchers seem intent on identifying powerful individuals only. Yet to describe community power without considering this factor may be to distort political reality. Power may be cumulative, and numerous individuals, each with little power, may have great power when united. Apparently criticism of the ruling elite position has been so severe that the problem has simply been dropped.[23] The criticism does have some validity but it has been taken so far that at present it seems to suffocate any consideration of similarities of interest among the top leadership, to the point that no attempt is even made to find whether there are *areas* in which such a similarity of interest exists.

What is needed then, is a theoretical scheme that will permit the researcher to deal with rivalries and alliances at the same time. For example, one might distinguish different levels of analysis—organizational rivalries and institutional alliances. I shall later indicate one possibility for handling this problem in terms of institutional alliances.

Power: Theoretical Ambiguities[24]

For almost a decade now, students of power structure have been debating the validity and meaning of findings in this area. The debate has centered on methodology, as I have already indicated. But it seems to me that the major source of difficulty is not methodological weakness but rather lack of conceptual clarity of the key term—power.[25]

Researchers in this area have by and large been satisfied with rather peremptory definitions of power. With few exceptions, most researchers have neglected definitions of power in the literature, defining power in such a manner that they have focused on precisely those elements that theorists of power have held unimportant. It is my contention that failure to specify this concept is at present a prime source of difficulty in the study of community power, not only in the reputational approach, but also in the decision-making approach.[26]

Studies of community power have been concerned with "who wields power,"[27] focusing on the personalities involved in the power wielding process. But it is not clear what theoretical advantages are offered by this statement of the problem.[28] If power were defined as "potential," instead, the central query would be "who can wield power when he so desires?"

Had he used this formulation, Hunter would not have needed to weight the votes for top leadership. At a number of points Hunter is forced to interject that the votes of the "informed" informants do not accurately describe the ranking of power in the community because some of the most powerful people prefer not to participate directly in the processes of leadership.[29] As a result their rating in terms of votes is less than objective measures of power would demand. To put it another way, the leader has power but does not choose to exercise it, because less powerful individuals, who *are* involved in the decision-processes, will effect outcomes in line with his general interests.

The preferable research strategy then, is to define power as *potential capacity* for action. This definition is certainly not new.

Weber defined power as "the probability that one actor within a social relationship *will be in a position* to carry out his own will despite resistance."[30] Here the element of potential is clear. Bierstedt defined power as "latent force,"[31] and a more recent discussion of power states simply, "Power is considered in this paper to be potentiality for action."[32]

The different usage characteristic of studies of community power seems to have resulted in a distorted perception of power structure. A recent review of power structure studies by Schermerhorn points this up rather sharply.[33] He says that the apparent power vacuum at the top, in Schulze's study of a community with absentee-owned corporations,[34] may be a consequence of the fact that the local community is no longer in a position to make decisions significantly affecting corporate interests.

> This situation may represent a power potential rather than a power vacuum. Corporations with local branches may decide not to throw their weight around in small communities, but these firms hold in reserve a weapon of great effectiveness, namely the ability to move any local plant to a different location. In towns where employment is mainly dependent on one or two large companies, a decision to relocate manufacturing units can disrupt the entire economic base of the community. Although such decisions depend on national and international market supply conditions, they are related to local political factors also. Absentee-owned corporations pay a disproportionate share of taxes in small towns; as a result, the local government refrains from changing the tax structure drastically upward for this would kill the goose that lays the golden eggs. As long as this tax situation continues, corporations can afford to maintain the kind of hands-off policy noted by Schulze. But such abdication of power is conditional rather than fixed policy.[35]

Focusing on potential power would have made this clear. Schulze is no doubt aware of this for he points out that "the Cibola study appears to document the absence of any neat and direct relationship between *power as a potential for determinative*

action, and power as determinative action itself."[36]

Further Clarification of Power

A second difficulty for research on power is inherent in the definitions used by both Hunter and Weber. Both define power in terms that tend to force the investigator to focus on the most powerful, to overlook the power of the less powerful, to fail to differentiate the areas or scopes of power, to neglect the ongoing dynamics of power relations—the give and take involved. Instead the investigator is forced to focus on who has made what *successful* power decisions. Power is seen as a relationship in which the actor exercising power is either able to get his way, in which case he has power, or unable to get his way, in which case he has no power.[37]

I suggest that the word "dominance" be applied to describe the situation where an actor succeeds in effecting a favorable outcome (successfully carries out his will despite resistance), and that the term "power" be used to describe the potential available to any actor for obtaining a goal, whether or not this actor can successfully use his potential.[38]

The Abramson, *et al.*, definition of power is probably most suitable to handle this problem. They propose to measure power in terms of the "lines of action available to each actor in the situation."

> Lines of action are all those possible and suitable action sequences for translating an actor's aspirations into realizations. . . . The number of those open lines of action available to each actor is the measure of the power of the actor. Power so defined concerns potentiality for action and the existence of alternative causes for action.[39]

By this definition, the power of both the dominant and subordinate actor, or the power of any number of actors in a power relationship, may be considered. The situation where one actor has all the power (i.e., lines of action) and the other has none is conceived as a limiting case.

The Measurement of Power

Definitions of power used in the study of power structure run into difficulty when attempts are made to measure power. At first glance, a "lines of action" definition of power appears to provide a better measure of power, and one which is easily calculated.[40] But a close examination of this model brings another problem to light. Abramson, *et al.'s* definition of power requires a common specified objective. For it is only in terms of such defined objectives that the actors have sufficient knowledge to spell out the lines of action available to them. Community power, however, involves undefined long-term objectives. The authors raise the question of measuring long-term power but suggest no solution to the problem.[41]

Furthermore, this model of power faces a problem that plagues other models as well. If two actors are involved in a conflict, in which a goal highly important to one actor is less important to the second actor, then the actor for whom the goal is more important can be expected to feel that expenditure of more energy, money, etc., for that goal is worthwhile. The actor for whom the goals are less important will feel that using certain lines of action requires too great an expenditure for that goal, despite the fact that resources may be "objectively" available. He has less power, but not because he has fewer resources, or is unaware of other lines of action.

Clearly then, two elements determine which actor is dominant in a conflict: resources and desirability of the goal. If power is considered to be potential *ability* (rather than willingness) to effect a favorable outcome (in other words, possession of the requisite means or resources—which in turn provide lines of action), then to determine power we must be able to separate this potential ability from the importance of the goal.

Abramson, *et al.*, attempt to avoid this difficulty by stating that one of the prerequisites for calculating power is that there be a *common* specified object. The assumption here is that so long as both actors are concerned with the same goal, examining the lines of action will provide a full description of the resources available, since goals are identical. Yet this does not solve the problem, for the same goal may have a different priority for each of the actors in conflict.

Separating resources from desirability of goal is particularly important when comparing the power of elites in different institutional orders. Assuming that the goals of the economic, religious, and political elites are wealth, sacredness, and hegemony, respectively, how can one assess their relative power by comparing outcomes or counting lines of action? What is important to one may not be important to another.

The Abramson, *et al.*, scheme for measuring power, then, cannot be used without modification in studying community power, as no common specified goals exist. Instead, we must fall back on analyzing outcomes of power conflicts. But the lines of action model should be kept in mind to sensitize the researcher to the power of the nondominant actors. The difficulty of separating resources from desirability of goal may be handled by the rough but expedient measure of postulating certain key values for the elites of different institutional orders. For the sake of simplicity, assume that goals for each elite may be divided grossly into two categories, salient and non-salient, and assume further that an elite will exert itself to its full capacity, i.e., use all lines of action available, for salient goals but will not exert itself fully for non-salient goals.

Two types of goals may be thought of as salient: (1) the "pure" goals of an institutional order—e.g., wealth in economy, sacredness in religion, etc.; (2) the organizational imperatives of the different institutional elites, e.g., funds, members, physical plant. Unless these imperatives or "system needs"[42] are met, the entire organization may break down, with the result that the "pure" institutional goals are also lost. Thus, if the source of funds for a religious organization[43] is threatened, that organization can be expected to respond vigorously. Similarly, if the legitimacy of the employer's authority over his workers is challenged, the economic organization can be expected to counter sharply.

Salient goals[44] are therefore both the "pure" goals and the system needs of an organization in any institutional order. Thus defined, salience can be used to assess the relative power of elites in different institutional orders, despite the fact that a particular goal may have different salience for the contending elites.

Where a goal is salient to elite A but not salient to elite B, and elite A is able to attain the goal in the face of B's opposition, we do not have a strong indication that elite A is more powerful, for B may not have used available lines of action. If, on the other hand, elite B is successful even though the goal is not salient to it, then we know that B is a great deal more powerful than A. If the goal was equally salient or equally non-salient to both, then we may simply assume that the elite that attained the goal had more lines of action available, i.e., was more powerful.

This relationship is expressed by the paradigm below. This paradigm permits the researcher to give weight—though only in a rough way—to the importance attached to the goal by the actors in a conflict. A separate calculation of power—i.e., lines of action of resources—is then possible.

As a brief illustration of the utility of this paradigm, let us examine Hunter's findings[45] (aside from the issue of their validity), ings. There has been some confusion over the meaning of these findings[45] (aside from the issue of their validity), even among those who champion Hunter's work. But essentially only a single point is at issue—

whether the power structure is monolithic or polylithic. All the evidence seems to indicate (and this includes some positional and decision-making data parenthetically reported by Hunter)[46] that the economic elite is dominant. A number of other questions might be raised at this point.

1. What *degree* of dominance do they exercise (in terms of the proposed paradigm)?
2. How much power is available to the non-dominant elites?

For example, one might divide the community into four institutional orders—economy, polity, science and religion[47]—and ask how much power each elite has when compared to any of the others.

3. What resources are available to each elite that provides it with the power it has (no matter whether or not it is dominant)?
4. Under what conditions is the elite of a given institutional order dominant?
5. Which factors diminish and which increase an elite's power in the community?
6. Which factors tend to produce monolithic structures and which polylithic structures within each institutional order?

Some of the researchers in this area have begun to consider these questions. For example, Rossi has examined the effect of a diversified economic base on the community power structure[48] considered as a single entity. (It might, however, be useful to consider the factors affecting the "clustering of

GOAL	OUTCOME	INFERENCE
Salient for A, non-salient for B Salient for B, non-salient for A	A dominant } B dominant }	Unclear
Salient for A, Salient for B Salient for A, Salient for B	A dominant } B dominant }	Dominant actor somewhat more powerful
Salient for A, non-salient for B Salient for B, non-salient for A	B dominant } A dominant }	Dominant actor much more powerful

power" for each institutional order separately.)

Rogers attempts to isolate some variables affecting the *political* system, drawing on Hunter and numerous other studies of community power. His list is far more extensive than Rossi's. It includes the following variables: degree of industrialization; population size; degree of heterogeneity of population along ethnic, religious, and occupational lines; scope of local government; and political and economic organization of working-class groups.[49]

My own research has indicated that some other factors might be considered, particularly in assessing the power of the religious elite: the degree of organization of various elites; the stage of development of the community—whether undergoing growth, stagnation or decline along such dimensions as population, wealth, degree of industrialization, etc.; ties to extra-community power structures; and access to mass media and other communication channels.[50]

Some specific hypotheses on the place of the religious elite have been developed.[51] Reexamination of materials on community power indicates that, other conditions being equal, the power of the religious elite will be greater to the extent that it controls the channels of communication. Control of communication seems to be the base of the religious elite's power, as control of wealth is that of the economic elite. The evidence seems to show that it is this factor, rather than the secularization of modern society, which seems to affect the power of the religious elite in the community. In addition, the evidence indicates that where the distribution of wealth is sharply unequal, the religious elite will not be the most powerful elite in a community, no matter whether or not it controls communications. Many more applications of this approach are possible; I shall try to demonstrate its utility in a forthcoming paper on the power of the religious elite.

Notes

1. Floyd Hunter, *Community Power Structure*, Chapel Hill: University of North Carolina Press, 1953. Hunter's study is still utilized as a take-off point for much of the research in this area. Recent methodological discussions still refer to this classic.
2. Peter Rossi has said that Hunter's introduction of new research techniques to the study of community power sparked new interest in an area dormant for several years. "Social Structure and Power in Local Communities," a paper read at the annual convention of the American Sociological Association, New York, August, 1960. Gordon Blackwell also hails Hunter as a pioneer who has made significant methodological contributions to the study of politics. Cited in Raymond Wolfinger, "A Plea for a Decent Burial," *American Sociological Review*, 27 (December, 1962), pp. 841–848. Freeman, *et al.*, write "Since the publication [of Hunter's work in 1953] studies of community leadership have been in vogue. . . . In fact, a recent compendium of research in community leadership lists 559 studies, most of which have been published since 1953." Linton C. Freeman, *et al.*, *Local Community Leadership*, Syracuse, N.Y.: Publication #15, Publications Committee, Syracuse University, 1960, p. 2.

3. Raymond Wolfinger, "Reputation and Reality in the Study of 'Community Power,'" *American Sociological Review*, 25 (October, 1960), pp. 636–645. Attempts to answer these criticisms have in my opinion been unsuccessful thus far. In response to this set of criticisms, Ehrlich, a follower of the Hunter "reputational" approach, points out that reputation for power is an element that affects the political structure of a community. Essentially this is no defense of the methodology, since it concedes instead that the method may be getting at nothing more than reputation and merely indicates that reputation is a factor to be considered, a point which no one would argue, but which is irrelevant. Ehrlich also points out, by way of concession, that the "reputational approach" deals with potential power rather than power as it is actually exercised. I shall deal with this latter point in the next section. See Howard J. Ehrlich, "The Reputational Approach to the Study of Community Power," *American Sociological Review*, 26 (December, 1961), pp. 926–927.

4. The critics point out that there may be a vast difference between possession of power and reputation for the same. See for example, Herbert Kaufman, "The Mystery of Power," *Public Administration Review* (Summer

1954), or Nelson W. Polsby, "Three Problems in the Analysis of Community Power," *American Sociological Review*, 24 (December, 1959), pp. 796–804. This point is treated most extensively by Wolfinger, "Reputation and Reality . . .," *op. cit.*

5. *Ibid.*

6. Wolfinger cites two cases supporting this possibility, one in his own study of New Haven, where a life-long resident of the city, a prominent manufacturer who was a Republican and active in public affairs, failed to identify an individual who had been the leader of the Republican party in New Haven for 20 years; second and much more crucial, the fact that Hunter found it necessary to conduct a separate study of the power structure of the Negro sub-community because the "Negroes were so excluded from the lists of supposed leaders." "A Plea for a Decent Burial," *op. cit.* Hunter's study of Salem, Mass. seems to run into the same difficulty. Hunter himself points out that the "leadership" of Salem were incorrect in their perceptions of the leaders of the Polish sub-community. Floyd Hunter, Ruth C. Schaffer, and Cecil G. Sheps, *Community Organization*, Chapel Hill: University of North Carolina Press, 1956, p. 60. Wolfinger cites a number of other such instances in "Reputation and Reality . . .," *op. cit.*, pp. 641 ff.

7. "Most of the reputational researchers, by their failure to specify scopes in soliciting reputations for influence, assume that the power of their leader-nominees is equal for all issues; some researchers specifically state that they are concerned with 'a general category of leadership.' This is an exceedingly dubious assumption. It is improbable for instance, that the same people who decide which houses of prostitution are to be protected in return for graft payments also plan the public school curriculum. Moreover, recent research reveals specialized leadership, for example in Bennington, Vermont and New Haven." *Ibid.*, p. 638. See also Polsby, *op. cit.*, and Wolfinger, "A Plea for a Decent Burial," *op. cit.*

8. Once the method has been validated, the question of how long specific types of resource distribution endure could be empirically investigated.

9. Specifically, they answer the last two questions, although they address themselves to all five. Their answer to the first set of questions can be rejected on Wolfinger's grounds that it is simply another attempt to use the reputational method to validate itself. See [William V.] D'Antonio and [Eugene C.] Erickson, "The Reputational Technique as a Measure of Community Power," *American Sociological Review*, 27 (June, 1962), pp. 362–376, and Wolfinger's reply, "A Plea for a Decent Burial," *op. cit.*

10. Nelson W. Polsby, "Community Power: Some Reflections on the Recent Literature," *American Sociological Review*, 27 (December, 1962), pp. 838–841.

11. Wolfinger, "A Plea for a Decent Burial," *op. cit.*

12. [Freeman, *et al.*] *Metropolitan Decision-Making: Further Analyses from the Syracuse Study of Local Community Leadership*, Syracuse, N.Y.: University College of Syracuse University, 1962. A later version of the findings presented in this monograph appeared in an article by Freeman, *et al.*, "Locating Leaders in Local Communities," *American Sociological Review*, 28 (October, 1963), pp. 791–799. Where possible, reference will be to the later article.

13. The four criteria are defined as follows ([Freeman, *et al.*] *Metropolitan Decision-Making*, *op. cit.*, pp. 13–14.):
    Participation—participation in the decision-making process; ranked in terms of the number of decisions in which they were involved.
    Social activity—membership in various organizations—number of memberships in such groups as community service, business, professional, political, etc.
    Reputation—respondent asked to list the most influential leaders in the community.
    Position—leaders are the titular heads of the largest organizations in each of seven institutional areas.

14. Freeman, *et al.*, "Locating Leaders in Local Communities," *op. cit.*, pp. 796–797.

15. *Ibid.*, p. 797.

16. *Loc. cit.* In this statement "decision-making structure" apparently refers to the structure of relationships involving only decisions taken by legally constituted governmental organizations (or affiliated groups) and by formally organized voluntary associations. The "power structure" is also involved in "decision-making," as decision-making is inherent in all political or power acts, but power structure does not necessarily involve formally constituted organizations. In the Freeman, *et al.*, report, "access to the decision-making structure" means access to the decision-making positions in these formally constituted groups. In Syracuse, such access is controlled by "institutional leaders." The decision-making structure might also mean the configuration of those involved in the formal decision-making process ("Effectors"), as they relate to each other. In other words, in the first sense, and in the paper cited, the term designates organizational positions; in the

second sense, it applies to the actors making decisions.

17. *Ibid.*, p. 798.

18. *Loc. cit.*

19. *Loc. cit.* There is an interesting parallel between this threefold category of leaders and the three groups of leaders Hunter found, i.e., upper-limits power personnel, lower-limits personnel and under-structure personnel. (The first two are also referred to as "policy makers" and "activators," respectively.) The reputational method therefore appears not to be inherently limited to uncovering Institutional Leaders. Apparently, this is simply a result of the focus of study selected.

20. Such comparison opens the possibility of using the participation of the sum of all employees of an organization as an indicator of the power resources afforded by a position, along the lines suggested by Freeman, *et al.* This notion might be extended further by considering also the *location* of these employees as an indication of the *strategic distribution* of the power resources. Other power resources afforded by position might also be considered, as, for example, the power of loan associations over their borrowers. Investigating such factors might indicate more fully the specific powers of various "positions."

21. R. A. Brady, *Business as a System of Power*, cited in Hunter, *Community Power Structure*, *op. cit.*, p. 102.

22. There is no mention of it in Wolfinger, *op. cit.*, nor in Polsby, *op. cit.*, nor in numerous other articles by followers of the reputational school in the *American Sociological Review* from 1961 through 1963.

23. The disagreement is sharpest on the level of the national power structure. Among the critics one finds Robert Dahl, "A Critique of the Ruling Elite Model," *American Political Science Review*, 52 (June, 1958), pp. 463–469; David Riesman, "Who Has the Power?" in Reinhard Bendix and Seymour M. Lipset (eds.), *Class Status and Power*, Glencoe, Ill.: The Free Press, 1953, pp. 154–162; Talcott Parsons, "The Distribution of Power in American Society," in his *Structure and Process in Modern Societies*, Glencoe, Ill.: The Free Press, 1962; Daniel Bell, "The Power Elite Reconsidered," in his *The End of Ideology*, New York: Collier Books, 1961. On the other hand, the ruling elite model is supported by such theorists as Marx, Mosca, and Michels, and such empirical investigations as that undertaken by Brady, *op. cit.*; The National Resources Committee, "The Structure of Controls" in Bendix and Lipset (eds.), *op. cit.*, pp. 129–154; and C. Wright Mills, *The Power Elite*,

New York: Oxford University Press, 1956, among others.

24. Another source of ambiguity stems from the use of the concept "structure" in discussions of power. D'Antonio and Erickson, *op. cit.*, write ". . . the reputational technique . . . did provide us with a picture of power during the 1950's. *Whether in fact it reveals a community power structure* or is merely a parsimonious way of getting the key 'limited scope' influentials all together on one list which can be handled with relative ease cannot be conclusively stated. . . ." Clearly, in this statement, "structure" refers to a tightly knit power elite. When "structure" is used in this manner, the researcher studying community power relationships must formulate his hypothesis in terms of the existence or non-existence of a power structure. But surely more alternatives are available. Power can be more or less concentrated, it can be more or less stable over time, more or less power can be available to the elite, and so on. Viewing power in terms of this all-or-nothing model blurs these other distinctions, which may be of critical importance in the study of community power.

The term "structure," as generally used in sociology, refers simply to relatively stable social relationships or patterns of interaction. See for example Harry M. Johnson, *Sociology: A Systematic Introduction*, New York: Harcourt, Brace, 1960, p. 48. When used in this sense, a "power structure" simply means stable patterns of interaction with regard to power—whatever form these relationships take, whether they are tightly or loosely structured, etc.

Others have also noted the confusion surrounding this concept. Cf. Thomas J. Anton, "Power Pluralism and Local Politics," *Administrative Science Quarterly*, 7 (March, 1963), pp. 425–458, for an extended criticism of the concept "power structure" from a different viewpoint. Anton points out that the contention between sociologists and political scientists in this area seems to flow from the different elements with which each discipline is concerned in the study of community power.

25. The concept of power has received little critical evaluation by students of community power. Howard J. Ehrlich, *op. cit.*, has distinguished potential from actual power, arguing that the reputational approach pioneered by Hunter taps potential, not actual power, but Ehrlich's is not a thoroughgoing attempt to specify the concept, and furthermore Hunter does not use power in the sense of potential. What he really studies is reputation for power, which includes an

assessment of power potential (resources) as well as "actual" power in Dahl's sense, meaning acts of power. Respondents are highly likely to judge power in terms of an unspecified mixture of both.

26. Some of the problems facing those using the decision-making approach are the following: (1) Individuals who are actually powerful, i.e., who actually participate in the decision-making, may not have participated in the decision-making process on a particular issue, for either of two reasons: (a) the issues at stake may not be salient to certain powerful elites, or (b) the particular issue chosen by the researcher may have involved not the most important leaders but only those at the second level. (2) Researchers using this approach must differentiate scopes of power in which individuals may be said to be leaders. But why have they chosen to investigate leadership in scope "X" rather than scope "Y"? What criteria do they apply to determine which scopes are essential? If no such criteria exist, then no claim to generality of leadership can possibly be made, especially when only a few sets of decisions are examined at one specific point in time.

Robert Dahl is aware of the problem and attempts to deal with it. (*Who Governs: Democracy and Power in an American City*, New Haven: Yale University Press, 1961.) He selected three issue areas "because they promised to cut across a wide variety of interests and participants" (pp. 333 ff.). These were (1) redevelopment, (2) public schools, (3) nominations and a new city charter. But even such general interest problems do not present a full picture of the power structure. Examining these issues only, the religious elite appear to have no power at all, but if an issue like birth-control were examined, an entirely different picture might emerge. Cf. Kenneth Wilson Underwood's description of just this issue in his *Protestant and Catholic: Religious and Social Interaction in an Industrial Community*, Boston: The Beacon Press, 1957.

27. Hunter has defined power as "a word . . . used to describe the acts of men going about the business of moving other men to act in relation to themselves," *op. cit.*, pp. 2–3. In *Power and Society*, Harold D. Laswell and Abraham Kaplan define power as participation in the making of decisions (cited in Wolfinger's "Reputation and Reality . . .," *op. cit.*). In neither of these definitions is power a potential capacity. Wolfinger uses Dahl's definition: "A has power over B to the extent that he can get B to do something that he would not otherwise do." The potential aspect of power is included here

(he can get B to do something), but it is not central.

28. Description of the leaders' background characteristics may certainly be of value, provided that "crucial" characteristics are described. (One wonders what advantage there is in knowing the age of the "top leaders," or how their offices are decorated.) Hunter certainly indicates some "crucial" characteristics—wealth, control of others, economic life-chances, and so on. But if Hunter had defined power as "potential" he might have been more keenly concerned with describing the resources controlled by the leadership and perhaps with spelling out how these resources facilitate the exercise of power.

29. This same difficulty confronts the decision-making school. Individuals known to have power (i.e., control of resources) may not participate in the decision-making process on certain specific issues or may not personally participate, though it is widely known that other participants are actually their agents.

30. Max Weber, *The Theory of Social and Economic Organization*, translated by A. M. Henderson and Talcott Parsons, New York: Oxford University Press, 1957, p. 52 (emphasis added).

31. Robert Bierstedt, "An Analysis of Social Power," *American Sociological Review*, 15 (December, 1950), pp. 730–738.

32. E. Abramson, *et al.*, "Social Power and Commitment: A Theoretical Statement," *American Sociological Review*, 23 (February, 1958), pp. 15–23.

33. Richard A. Schermerhorn, *Society and Power*, New York: Random House, 1961.

34. Robert O. Schulze, "Economic Dominants in Community Power Structure," *American Sociological Review*, 23 (February, 1958), pp. 3–9.

35. Schermerhorn, *op. cit.*, pp. 95–96.

36. *Ibid.*, p. 9 (emphasis added).

37. According to Weber, the actor must be in a position to "carry out his will"; if he cannot, he has no power.

38. This is in line with widespread usage of this term. See for example, Wolfinger, "Reputation and Reality in the Study of 'Community Power,'" *op. cit.* For a different usage of the term see Herbert Goldhammer and Edward A. Shils, "Types of Power and Status," *American Journal of Sociology*, 45 (September, 1939), pp. 171–182. See also Schulze, *op. cit.*

39. Abramson, *et al.*, *op. cit.*, pp. 15–17.

40. The authors suggest that to measure power, lines of action contending actors need simply be counted. This could be done by asking each of the contenders how many lines of

action he has to reach a certain defined common goal. If an actor is unaware of lines of action objectively available to him then the line is not open, for a line of action exists only when recognized as such by the actor. This measurement has the distinct advantage of enabling the researcher to measure power before the action is resolved and is thus superior to *post hoc* measurement of success.

41. *Ibid.*

42. For a theoretical statement of system needs, see Talcott Parsons, Robert F. Bales and Edward A. Shils, *Working Papers in the Theory of Action*, Glencoe, Ill.: The Free Press, 1953, chs. 1–2. These are theoretical statements, and it is difficult to operationalize them. At the same time, one must bear in mind that people within an organization may be unaware of system needs (as Parsons states them) and treat them as though they were not important. For my purposes, the actor's perception of what his organization needs is critical. But one cannot simply take the actor's statement on this point at face value, for claims that certain goals are salient are often nothing more than attempts to legitimate action in a new sphere. Parsons' system needs might be considered as essentially a kind of objective check on the actors' claims.

43. Whether one or many organizations will respond will depend on the nature of the threat. If only a single organization is threatened, the elite of an entire institutional order will probably not respond unless the challenge also threatens the others, in the long run, or a particularly broad "roof organization" is involved.

44. [Robert] Merton has suggested in a personal communication that the notions of "salience" or "non-salience" may be sociological counterparts of the social-psychological concepts of "involvement" and "apathy" in certain social systems.

45. D'Antonio, Ehrlich, and Erickson, *op. cit.*

46. [Hunter] *Op. cit.*, pp. 62 ff., 162–189.

47. This breakdown of society into four institutional spheres follows Kingsley Davis. See his discussion of the conditions under which one or another of these elites is dominant in a society in *Human Society*, New York: Macmillan, 1949, ch. 14.

48. Peter H. Rossi, "Community Decision-Making," *Administrative Science Quarterly*, 1 (March, 1957), p. 440. In a later paper, Rossi extends this list. "Theory and Method in the Study of Power in the Local Community," unpublished paper presented at the 1960 annual meeting of the American Sociological Association.

49. David Rogers, "Community Political Systems: A Framework and Hypothesis for Comparative Studies," Columbia University, 1962, mimeo. There are numerous other comparative studies, but it is not possible to list them all. Form and Miller present some conceptions about types of community systems (*Industry, Labor and Community*, New York: Harper, 1960, pp. 538–543). In addition, their work contains a fairly extensive bibliography on power structure. Roger's paper contains a more recent bibliography on this literature and draws a bit more from the work of political scientists. See also Burt Swanson (ed.), *Current Trends in Comparative Community Studies*, Public Affairs Monograph Series #1, Kansas City, Mo., 1962.

50. I have examined these factors in greater detail in my unpublished Master's thesis, "The Place of the Religious Elite in the Community Power Structure," Columbia University, 1962.

51. The theoretical framework from which these hypotheses were drawn requires an extended presentation which is not possible at this point due to the limitations of space. It draws on the stratification theory of Hans Zetterberg (See Murray Gendel and Hans Zetterberg, *A Sociological Almanac for the United States*, New York: The Bedminster Press, 1961, p. 1; the bulk of Zetterberg's theory was presented in class lectures at Columbia University in 1958–1959) and the organizational theory of Amitai Etzioni (*A Comparative Analysis of Complex Organizations*, Glencoe, Ill.: The Free Press, 1961.) The theoretical model is presented in my thesis (*op. cit.*), pp. 33–60.

F. The Decision-Making Approach

How to Study Community Power: the Pluralist Alternative*

Nelson W. Polsby

Political scientists are beginning to view certain major contributions to the study of community politics less favorably than one would have expected after hearing the fanfare surrounding the original acceptance of these works.[1] Often billed as studies of "community power structure," these works have been produced mostly by sociologists, whose orientation has been to study the politics of American communities as a subsidiary aspect of social structure.[2] "The political organization of Jonesville," writes one such scholar, "fits the rest of the social structure ... curving or bulging with the class outlines of the body politic."[3]

The faults which critics have found with studies following this general conception of politics as an epiphenomenon of social stratification are many, varied and serious. They include the charges that this conception encourages research designs which generate self-fulfilling prophecies,[4] and that it leads to the systematic misreporting of facts[5] and to the formulation of ambiguous and unprovable assertions about community power.[6] It would be gratuitous for me to re-explore these criticisms here. It would be more profitable, instead, to describe some of the ways in which students have evaded— apparently with success—the various disabilities of the stratification approach to the study of community power. With judicious unoriginality, I shall call the alternative research strategy to be outlined here the "pluralist" approach. Old, familiar pluralistic presumptions[7] about the nature of American politics seem to have given researchers strategies for the study of community power which are both feasible to execute and comparatively faithful to conditions in the real world.[8] What follows is an attempt to explain why this seems to be the case for pluralist studies, but not for stratification studies.

The first, and perhaps most basic presupposition of the pluralist approach, is that nothing categorical can be assumed about power in any community. It rejects the stratification thesis that *some* group necessarily dominates a community.[9] If anything, there seems to be an unspoken notion among pluralist researchers that at bottom *nobody* dominates in a town so that their first question to a local informant is not likely to be, "Who runs this community?," but rather, "Does anyone at all run this community?" It is instructive to examine the range of possible answers to each of these questions. The first query is somewhat like, "Have you stopped beating your wife?," in that virtually any response short of total unwillingness to answer will supply the researchers

Reprinted from the Journal of Politics, *22 (August 1960), 474–484, by permission of the author and The Southern Political Science Association. Copyright 1960 by The Southern Political Science Association.*

*This article is a paper of the New Haven Community Leadership Study, and owes a great deal to Robert A. Dahl and Raymond E. Wolfinger. I am also grateful to George M. Belknap, Norton E. Long and Robert O. Schulze, but none of these gentlemen should be held responsible for the notions presented here.

with a "power elite" along the lines presupposed by the stratification theory.[10] On the other hand, the second question is capable of eliciting a response which *could* lead to the discovery of a power elite (*i.e.*, "Yes"), or any of an infinite number of stable, but non-elitist patterns of decision-making (*i.e.*, "No, but ..."; "Yes, but ..."), or total fragmentation, or disorganization (*i.e.*, "No").

What sort of question is likely to follow "Who runs the community?" in a questionnaire? Obviously, something like "*How* do the people named in the above response run the community?" This entirely probable pattern of investigation begs the question of whether or not those said to rule actually do rule. In the pluralist approach, on the other hand, an attempt is made to study specific outcomes, in order to determine who actually prevails in community decision-making. Consonant with the desire to study actual outcomes, which requires arduous and expensive field work, outcomes in a few (but, for reasons of expense, usually only a few) issue-areas are studied closely. More than a single issue-area is always chosen, however, because of the presumption among pluralist researchers that the same pattern of decision-making is highly unlikely to reproduce itself in more than one issue-area. In this expectation, pluralist researchers have seldom been disappointed.[11] They recognize, however, the possibility that the same pattern *could* reproduce itself in more than one issue-area. Since actual behavior is observed, or reconstructed from documents, witnesses, and so on, it is possible to determine empirically whether or not the same group rules two or more issue-areas. The presumption that the existence of a power elite is unlikely does not, in other words, prevent the finding of such an elite if the data so indicate.

A superficially persuasive objection to this approach might be phrased as follows: "Suppose research in a community discloses different patterns of decision-making in each of three issue-areas. This does not rule out the possibility that all other issue-areas in the community are dominated by a single power elite." How can pluralists meet this objection? First, it is necessary to acknowledge the *possibility* that this is the case. However, pluralists can (and do) protect themselves in part by studying significant issues. In the New Haven study, for example, of which this paper is an outgrowth, we studied (1) nominations by the two political parties, which determine which persons hold public offices; (2) the New Haven Redevelopment program, which is the largest in the country (measured by past and present outlay per capita); (3) public education, which is the most costly item in the city's budget; and (4) a campaign to revise the city charter.[12] In Bennington, Scoble studied political nominations and elections, the issue of consolidation of various municipal governments, the formation of a union high-school district, and the construction of a new high-school building.[13] A pilot study, by Long and Belknap, of a large eastern city embraced the problems of transportation, race relations, traffic, urban redevelopment and recreation,[14] while, in the San Francisco Bay area, Belknap studied the issues of urban redevelopment, transportation and race relations.[15] None of these issues was trivial; they probably were, in fact, the most important issues before these communities during the time these studies were being carried out. What sort of a power elite is it —it may appropriately be asked—which asserts itself in relatively trivial matters, but is inactive or ineffective in the most significant areas of community policy-making?

Stratification theory holds that power elites fail to prevail only on trivial issues.[16] By pre-selecting as issues for study those which are generally agreed to be significant, pluralist researchers can test stratification theory without searching endlessly in one issue-area after another, in order to discover some semblance of a power elite. After all, it cannot be reasonably required of researchers that they validate someone else's preconceived notions of community power distributions. If the researcher's design is such that any power distribution has an equal chance of appearing in his result, his result may not properly be criticized on the grounds that it did not conform to expectations. The burden of proof is clearly on the challenger in such a case to make good his assertion that power is actually distributed otherwise.[17]

Another presumption of the pluralist approach runs directly counter to stratification theory's presumption that power distributions are a more or less permanent aspect of social structure. Pluralists hold that power may be tied to issues, and issues can be fleeting or persistent, provoking coalitions among interested groups and citizens ranging in their duration from momentary to semipermanent. There is a clear gain in descriptive accuracy involved in formulating power distributions so as to take account of the dimension of time, as pluralists do,[18] since it is easily demonstrated that coalitions *do* vary in their permanency. To presume that the set of coalitions which exists in the community at any given time is a timelessly stable aspect of social structure is to introduce systematic inaccuracies into one's description of social reality.

Why do pluralists reject the idea that *some* group necessarily dominates every community? The presumption that communities are likely to be less rather than more permanent in their patterns of decision-making is no doubt part of the answer, but another part is an even more fundamental conception of human behavior as governed in large part by inertia. This view leads pluralists to put a high value on overt activity as indicative of involvement in issues and to look upon the collection of "reputations" for leadership as a much less desirable research procedure.[19]

Pluralists consider as arbitrary the inclusion of certain groups as being "implicated" in decisions when these groups themselves reject such involvement.[20] For pluralists, "false class consciousness" does not exist, because it implies that the values of analysts are imposed on groups in the community. They reject the idea that there is any particular issue or any particular point in the determination of an issue where a group must assert itself in order to follow its expressed values. Rather, the pluralist assumes that there are many issues and many points at which group values can be realized. Further, pluralists presume that there are certain costs in taking any action at all. This refers not simply to the possibility of losing, of making political enemies, and so on, but also to the costs in personal time and effort involved in political mobilization, in becoming informed, in lobbying or campaigning and in taking the trouble to vote.[21]

It is a demonstrated fact that public activity of all sorts is a habit more characteristic of the middle and upper classes than of the lower classes.[22] Vidich and Bensman, for the first time in a community study, depicted the life of the lowest-class groups in the community sufficiently well so that the personally functional aspects of withdrawal from the community were revealed.[23] The presumption of inertia permits the researcher to regard the public sector of activity as but one facet of behavior capable of giving people satisfaction, and discourages the inappropriate and arbitrary assignment of upper and middle class values to all actors in the community.

The presumption of inertia also helps put economic and social notables into perspective. If a man's major life work is banking, the pluralist presumes he will spend his time at the bank, and not in manipulating community decisions. This presumption holds until the banker's activities and participations indicate otherwise. Once again, it is very important to make the point that this assumption is not scientifically equivalent to its opposite. If we presume that the banker is "really" engaged in running the community, there is practically no way of disconfirming this notion, even if it is totally erroneous. On the other hand, it is easy to spot the banker who really *does* run the community affairs when we presume he does not, because his activities will make this fact apparent. In the absence of the requisite activities, we have no grounds for asserting that the banker, in fact, does run the community.[24]

The pluralist emphasis on the time-bounded nature of coalitions and on the voluntary aspect of political participation leads to a further contrast with stratification theory, since pluralists hold that the "interest group" and the "public" are the social collectives most relevant to the analysis of political processes. In the sociologist's patois, politically important groups would be called phenomena of "collective behavior" rather than of "social structure."[25] Social classes in stratification theory are populations differentially ranked according to economic or status criteria, which embrace the entire community. Everyone in a community is a member of at least one but no more than one class at any given moment, and no one in the community falls outside the system. This is a legitimate heuristic construction; however, it is a mistake to impute to the apparently inescapable fact of class membership any sort of class consciousness. This sociologists have long recognized.[26] But they seem less willing to grant that it is equally incorrect to presume that those sharing similar market or status positions are also equidistant to all the bases of political power, or in fact share class interests. American society has never been noted for its interclass warfare, a fact often reported with a great show of surprise in stratification studies of American communities.[27]

Pluralists, who see American society as fractured into a congeries of hundreds of small "special interest" groups, with incompletely overlapping memberships, widely differing power bases, and a multitude of techniques for exercising influence on decisions salient to them,[28] are not surprised at the low priority which Americans give to their class membership as bases of social action. In the decision-making of fragmented government—and American national, state, and local governments are nothing if not fragmented—the claims of small, intense minorities are usually attended to.[29] Hence it is not only inefficient but usually unnecessary for entire classes to mobilize when the preferences of class-members are pressed and often satisfied in a piecemeal fashion. The empirical evidence supporting this pluralist doctrine is overwhelming,[30] however much stratification theorists may have misssed its significance for them, namely, that the fragmentation of American governmental decision-making and of American society makes class consciousness inefficient, and, in most cases, makes the political interests of members of the same class different.

Pluralist research is not interested in ascertaining an actor's ranking in a system presumed to operate hierarchically. Rather, pluralists want to find out about leadership *roles*, which are presumed to be diverse and fluid, both within a single issue-area over time, and as between issue-areas. Long and Belknap, for example, identify the following leadership roles in community decision-making: Initiation, Staffing and Planning, Communication and Publicity, Intra-elite Organizing, Financing and Public Sanctioning. [31]

By describing and specifying leadership roles in concrete situations, pluralists are in a position to determine the extent to which power structure exists. If there exist high degrees of overlap among issue-areas in decision-making personnel, or of institutionalization in the bases of power in specified issue-areas, or of regularity in the procedures of decision-making, then the empirical conclusion is justified that some sort of a "power structure" exists. By specifying leadership roles and activities, the pluralist research strategy makes it possible for an empirical determination of the bounds and durability of a community "power structure"—if one exists—to be described, and the stratification theory presumption that community power is necessarily general and relatively immutable can be discarded as arbitrary.

The final contrast I want to make between the pluralist and stratification methods has to do with their differing conceptions of what is meant by "power." I have already noted that stratification theorists emphasize the cataloguing of power bases, meaning the resources available to actors for the exercise of power.[32] Pluralists, on the other hand, concentrate on power exercise itself. This leads to two subsidiary discoveries. First, there are a great many different kinds of resources which can be turned to use in the process of community decision-making—many more resources, in fact, than stratification theorists customarily take account of. One list, for example, includes: money and credit; control over jobs; control over the information of others; social standing; knowledge and expertness; popularity, esteem and charisma; legality, constitutionality and officiality; ethnic solidarity; and the right to vote.[33]

The second product of the pluralist emphasis on power exercise is the discovery that resources are employed only with variations in degree of skill. The elaboration of the ways in which resources are employed enables the pluralist researcher to pay attention to what practical politicians customarily see as the heart of their own craft: the processes of bargaining, negotiation, salesmanship and brokerage, and of leadership in mobilizing resources of all kinds. This approach also makes possible a more realistic evaluation of the actual disposable resources of actors. A corporation may be worth millions of dollars, but its policies and liquidity position may be such that it cannot possibly bring those monetary resources into play in order to influence the outcome of a community decision—even one in which the corporation is vitally interested. And interest itself, as noted above, is differentially distributed in a pattern which pluralists assume is rational for most actors, most of the time. For example, Long and Belknap observe:

> Just as business organizations may be disinterested in community affairs because of the national scope of its (sic) operations, individual businessmen who move or are shifted from city to city may have little opportunity or incentive to participate in community affairs. Some businesses have strong pressures on them to give attention to community and metropolitan problems. Large department stores are particularly tied up with the destiny of the city and must decide whether to keep to the central city or decentralize in suburban shopping centers. Businessmen with a "metropolitan view"

would thus be expected to be found here rather than in the branch office of a national corporation.[34]

What practical recommendations emerge from this comparison of stratification and pluralist approaches to the study of community power?[35] First, the researcher should pick issue-areas as the focus of his study of community power. Second, he should be able to defend these issue-areas as being very important in the life of the community. Third, he should study actual behavior, either at first hand, or by reconstructing behavior from documents, informants, newspapers and other appropriate sources. There is no harm in starting with a list of people whose behavior the researcher wishes to study *vis-à-vis* any issue-area. The harm comes, rather, in attributing some mystical significance to such a list, so that the examination of activity and of actual participation in decision-making becomes superfluous. This recommendation is not meant to discourage the researcher from collecting information about the reputation of actors, or their intentions with respect to community issues, or their evaluations about the "meanings" of community incidents. All of these kinds of data are of immeasurable value in tracing patterns of decision-making. However, these cultural data must be accompanied by information about behavior so that the researcher has some way of distinguishing between myths and facts.

The final recommendation is of the same order: researchers should study the outcomes of actual decisions within the community. It is important, but insufficient, to know what leaders want to do, what they intend to do, and what they think they can do. The researcher still has to decide on the basis of his own examination of the facts what actually emerges from these various intentions, and not conclude prematurely that the combination of intentions and resources inflexibly predetermines outcomes.

Notes

1. For indications that disenchantment is setting in among political scientists, see the following: Robert A. Dahl, "A Critique of the Ruling Elite Model," *American Political Science Review*, 52 (June, 1958), 463–469; Herbert Kaufman and Victor Jones, "The Mystery of Power," *Public Administration Review*, 14 (Summer, 1954), 205–212; Norton E. Long, "The Local Community as an Ecology of Games," *American Journal of Sociology*, 64 (November, 1958), 251–261; Nelson W. Polsby, "The Sociology of Community Power: A Reassessment," *Social Forces*, 37 (March, 1959), 232–236 and "Three Problems in the Analysis of Community Power," *American Sociological Review*, 24 (December, 1959), 796–803; Raymond E. Wolfinger, "Reputation and Reality in the Study of 'Community Power'," *American Sociological Review*, 25 (December, 1960), in press. Sociologists also seem to be re-examining studies of community power: Reinhard Bendix and Seymour M. Lipset, "Political Sociology," *Current Sociology*, 6 (1957), 79–99; Peter H. Rossi, "Community Decision-Making," *Administrative Science Quarterly*, 1 (March, 1957), 415–443. Writings praising community power studies are quite extensive, and include the following: Gordon Blackwell, "Community Analysis," Roland Young (ed.), *Approaches to the Study of Politics* (Evanston, 1958), 305–317; William J. Gore and Fred S. Silander, "A Bibliographical Essay on Decision-Making," *Administrative Science Quarterly*, 4 (June, 1959), 106–121; Lawrence J. R. Herson, "The Lost World of Municipal Government," *American Political Science Review* 51 (June, 1957), 330–345.

2. For example, Robert S. Lynd and Helen M. Lynd, *Middletown* (New York, 1929) and *Middletown in Transition* (New York, 1937); Floyd Hunter, *Community Power Structure* (Chapel Hill, 1953); August B. Hollingshead, *Elmtown's Youth* (New York, 1949); W. Lloyd Warner, *et al.*, *Democracy in Jonesville* (New York, 1949); C. Wright Mills, "The Middle Classes in the Middle-Sized Cities," *American Sociological Review*, 11 (October, 1946), 520–529; Robert O. Schulze, "Economic Dominants and Community Power Structure," *American Sociological Review*, 23 (February, 1958), 3–9; Roland Pellegrin and Charles H. Coates, "Absentee-Owned Corporations and Community Power Structure," *American Journal of Sociology*, 61 (March, 1956), 413–419; Delbert C. Miller, "Industry and Community Power Structure," *American Sociological Review*, 23

(February, 1958), 9–15 and "Decision-Making Cliques in Community Power Structure," *American Journal of Sociology*, 64 (November, 1958), 229–310.

3. Warner, *et al.*, *op. cit.*, p. xviii.

4. See, *e.g.*, Kaufman and Jones, *op. cit.*

5. See Polsby, *op. cit.*

6. See *ibid.*, Dahl, *op. cit.*, and Kaufman and Jones, *op. cit.*

7. I am well aware that for other purposes the "pluralist" approach can be divided into several schools of thought. However, all variations of pluralist theory contrast effectively with stratification theory. Pluralist presumptions can be found, for example, in the writings of de Tocqueville and Madison, and in Arthur Bentley, *The Process of Government* (Chicago, 1908); E. Pendleton Herring, *The Politics of Democracy* (New York, 1940); David B. Truman, *The Governmental Process* (New York, 1953); V. O. Key, Jr., *Politics, Parties and Pressure Groups* (New York, 4th ed., 1959).

8. Among the researchers who have found pluralist presumptions about the nature of the political system useful are Robert A. Dahl ("The New Haven Community Leadership Study," Working Paper Number 1, December, 1957, mimeo); Harry Scoble ("Yankeetown: Leadership in Three Decision-Making Processes," presented at the meeting of the American Political Science Association, 1956); and George Belknap and Norton E. Long. See Long, *op. cit.*; Long and Belknap, "A Research Program on Leadership and Decision-Making in Metropolitan Areas" (New York, Governmental Affairs Institute, 1956), mimeo; Belknap and John H. Bunzel, "The Trade Union in the Political Community," *PROD*, 2 (September, 1958), 3–6; Belknap, "A Plan for Research on the Socio-Political Dynamics of Metropolitan Areas" (presented before a seminar on urban leadership of the Social Science Research Council, New York, August, 1957). See also a paper presented to this same seminar by Peter H. Rossi, "The Study of Decision-Making in the Local Community."

9. I present some of the characteristics of a stratification theory of community power in other papers, e.g., "Power in Middletown: Fact and Value in Community Research" (March, 1960), mimeo.; "Power as a Variable of Social Stratification" (November, 1959), mimeo.

10. See Kaufman and Jones, *op. cit.*

11. Wolfinger, *op. cit.*, has summarized findings on this point, pp. 7 ff.

12. See Dahl, "The New Haven . . . ," *op. cit.*, Polsby, *op. cit.*, and Wolfinger, *op. cit.*, and forthcoming publications of the New Haven Community Leadership Study.

13. Scoble, *op. cit.*

14. Long and Belknap, *op. cit.*

15. Belknap, *op. cit.*

16. See, for example, Pellegrin and Coates, *op. cit.*, and Lynd and Lynd, *Middletown in Transition, op. cit.*, p. 89.

17. See Dahl, "Critique . . . ," *op. cit.*

18. See. for example, Belknap, *op. cit.*, for an explicit discussion of this point. One stratification writer who has attempted to take account of the time factor is Jerome K. Myers, "Assimilation in the Political Community," *Sociology and Social Research*, 35 (January-February, 1951), 175–182. Myers plots a secular trend which indicates slow increases in the number of Italians and Italian-descended persons employed by New Haven municipal government over a fifty year period ending in 1940. Myers claims to have discovered "discrimination" against Italians, because they did not participate in city government jobs to an extent proportional with their representation in the total population of the city. His conclusion was that "the early or quick assimilation of New Haven Italians in the political system does not seem very probable. . . . All indications are that political assimilation is inevitable, although it is at least several generations away."

   By taking account of shorter-term cyclical movements within the allegedly "basic" structure, we may be able to explain the delay in the political assimilation of Italians.

   First, New Haven Italo-Americans were and are predominantly Republican in local politics, because in New Haven the Republican organization early and energetically courted the Italo-American vote. From 1920 to 1940, years in which that ethnic group would "normally" have been expected to come into their own as a politically significant minority group, the city government was in Democratic hands two-thirds of the time. It might be expected, therefore, that Italo-Americans would be less well represented among officeholders than if these circumstances were reversed. Second, in 1945, a Republican of Italian descent was elected Mayor, whereupon Italian-Americans invaded the top echelons of city government to such an extent that the Mayor pleaded in vain with one who was a candidate for President of the City Council to withdraw in favor of a Yankee Republican, on the grounds that there were "too many Italians" in City Hall, and that the Yankee members

of the Republican coalition should have some recognition.

19. See, especially, Wolfinger, *op. cit.*

20. See C. Wright Mills, "The Middle Classes . . . ," *op. cit.*, and my "The Sociology of Community Power," *op. cit.*, on this point.

21. See Anthony Downs, *An Economic Theory of Democracy* (New York, 1957); Robert E. Lane, *Political Life: How People Get Involved in Politics* (Glencoe, 1959); Samuel Stouffer, *Communism, Conformity and Civil Liberties* (New York, 1955), pp. 58 ff.

22. Lane, *op. cit.*, pp. 220–234.

23. Arthur J. Vidich and Joseph Bensman, *Small Town in Mass Society* (Princeton, 1958), pp. 69–70, 290–291. Studies of social status have been hampered by a similar problem of upper-class-centeredness. See the criticism of Warner on this point by Seymour M. Lipset and Reinhard Bendix, "Social Status and Social Structure," *British Journal of Sociology*, 2 (June, 1951), esp. pp. 163 *ff.*

24. See Bentley, *op. cit.*, pp. 175–222. Note, at p. 202: "If we can get our social life stated in terms of activity, and of nothing else, we have not indeed succeeded in measuring it, but we have at least reached a foundation upon which a coherent system of measurements can be built up. . . . We shall cease to be blocked by the intervention of unmeasurable elements, which claim to be themselves the real causes of all that is happening, and which by their spook-like arbitrariness make impossible any progress toward dependable knowledge."

25. Only one sociologist seems to have realized what this implies for the methods and conclusions of political analysis. See Rudolf Heberle, *Social Movements* (New York, 1951). The relevant theory is compactly expounded by Herbert Blumer in "Collective Behavior," in Alfred M. Lee (ed.), *Principles of Sociology* (New York, 1953), pp. 167–220.

26. Indeed, Max Weber, the most important "founding father" of modern stratification analysis, makes just this point. See Weber's "Class, Status, Party," in H. H. Gerth and C. W. Mills (eds.), *From Max Weber: Essays in Sociology* (New York, 1946), pp. 180–195, esp. p. 184.

27. See. for example, Lynd and Lynd, *Middletown in Transition, op. cit.*, pp. 454–455, 509; Alfred W. Jones, *Life, Liberty and Property* (Philadelphia, 1941), pp. 336–354; Warner, *et al., op. cit.*, p. 27; C. Wright Mills, "The Middle Classes," *op. cit.* Compare also Richard Centers, *The Psychology of Social Classes* (Princeton, 1948), and note the extent to which his conclusions outrun his data.

28. See, for example, Truman, *op. cit., passim.*

Alexis de Tocqueville, *Democracy In America* (New York, 1954), esp. Vol. I, pp. 181–205, 281–342, Vol. II, pp. 114–135.

29. See Robert A. Dahl, *A Preface to Democratic Theory* (Chicago, 1956).

30. Truman, *op. cit.*, summarizes a tremendous amount of this material.

31. Long and Belknap, *op. cit.*, pp. 9–11. See Polsby, "The Sociology of Community Power," *op. cit.*, and Edward C. Banfield, "The Concept 'Leadership' in Community Research" (delivered at the meeting of the American Political Science Association, 1958), for similar lists.

32. In papers cited in note 9 above.

33. Robert A. Dahl, "The Analysis of Influence in Local Communities" (May, 1959), mimeo. p. 10.

34. Long and Belknap, *op. cit.*, pp. 13–14. This corresponds to the findings—but not the interpretations—of Schulze, *op. cit.*, and of Pellegrin and Coates, *op. cit.*

35. This presumes that the researcher wants to make some generalizations about the "normal" distributions of power in community decision-making.

Community Power and a Typology of Social Issues

Ernest A. T. Barth and Stuart D. Johnson

In a recent critical analysis of the research approaches to the study of community decision making, Peter Rossi identified three major research gaps.[1] The first of these pertained to the fact that "none of the studies reviewed have considered the full range of issues which come before a particular decision maker."[2] The second is concerned with the fact that, "the issues which have been subjected to study have been on the more dramatic side, perhaps more properly labeled 'controversies'." This constitutes a research gap in the thinking of Rossi because "by and large we can expect that most issues up for decision are settled without becoming controversies."[3] The third major gap in present research involves Rossi's belief that, "Research on decision making should be extensive rather than intensive and comparative rather than the case study technique." He amplifies this point by saying, "three levels of comparison would be made: decision makers of different types, operating within different community and institutional settings, should be compared as they come to the settlement of a *range of issues*. This approach implies a sampling of decision makers, of *issues*, and of communities."[4]

It is the purpose of this paper to point out the importance of concern with the *type of issue* under consideration by decision makers and to suggest the basis for a typology of issues.[5]

The primary focus of recent research on community decision making has been on the identification of decision makers and the description of their background characteristics and interpersonal relations within a given community context. Relatively little attention has been given to the systematic analysis of the *conditions under which* influencing behavior occurs.[6] As Rossi has indicated, one set of such conditions involves issue content, and, in the thinking of the present authors, this condition has been greatly neglected.

Reprinted from Social Forces, *38 (October 1959), 29–32, by permission of the authors and The University of North Carolina Press. Copyright 1959 by the Williams and Wilkins Company.*

Failure to consider the impact of issue content on the selection of influentials has led to problems in building models adequate to describe structures of community influence. For example, Hunter, in his study of power in "Regional City," allowed his sample of community leaders to designate the issues which they thought were of major concern to the community.[7] He then discovered that these leaders held a central place in the decision-making processes centering on issues which they had described. One might ask whether the almost monolithic structure of leadership which he found in that community was not, in fact, an artifact resulting from his methodology. Might it not be argued that, had he set out to discover the patterns of power organization operating around a *range* of issues, he might have found a somewhat different and less solidary power structure? It might be further argued that if different types of issues in a community tend to be selective of different types of leaders, then the task which Hunter set before his respondents (i.e., that of choosing "the biggest man in the community," or of selecting the "ten leaders who nearly everyone would accept"), is an almost impossible task. His respondents might legitimately have asked, "Biggest man with respect to what type of activities?"

A second problem which is central to the understanding of the influencing process relates to observations that not all issues come to the attention of the most influential decision makers. If one distinguishes between the "top level" leadership and the "understructure" leadership, as did Hunter,[8] it becomes evident that some issues never come before the former group, while other issues achieve major importance to them.

A third consideration in the study of influence systems derives from attempts to compare influence systems, along with the processes which characterize them, in different community settings. For example, in attempting to characterize the structure of relations among the top leaders of "Pacific City," Miller developed the concepts of "top influentials" and "key influentials" who were viewed as interacting in accordance

with what he termed a "fluid coalition" model.[9] This model is distinct from the "monolithic power structure" model which Hunter felt described the structure of power relations in "Regional City."

Since the present authors find little reason to question the major findings and conclusions of either Miller or Hunter, aside from the methodological perspective mentioned above, it seems reasonable to assume that the structure of the influence system and the kinds of participants in decision-making processes vary with the types of issues facing a community at any given time. For example, the range of issues will be very different for a metropolitan center as compared to an open-country community; for a southern, as compared with a northern or western community; and for a college town as compared to an industrial center. For the reasons cited above, it appears then, that there is a pressing need for research leading to the development of a typology of issues.

Basis for an Empirical Typology of Issues

In a pilot project the authors attempted to derive a typology of community issues based upon institutional categories. In analyzing questionnaire data from a sample of community residents, issues were classed together when they appeared to deal with subject matter falling into given institutional sectors of community life such as economic issues, political issues, and educational issues. It nquickly became apparent that classificatio was arbitrary, some issues falling under two or more headings, and similar patterns of influencing behavior appeared in different institutional settings. Therefore, on the basis of this experience, it was concluded that such a classification of issue content would not produce a fruitful typology.

The pilot study did provide us with the following conclusions. In developing a typology of issues it is of primary importance to view the dimensions along which community issues are to be typed in terms of two major requirements. First, to be of maximum value, the dimensions must be generic to all issues. Second, variations in each dimension must be theoretically relatable to variations in patterns of influencing behavior. Thus, they must not only meet the test of logical inclusiveness, but they must also meet the empirical test of being "tied" to observable leadership behavior. Our concern in the present analysis is with the following three aspects of influencing behavior:

(1) the types of community structures involved in the flow of influence with respect to a range of issues;

(2) the direction of the flow of influence on any issue;

(3) the direction of the flow of communications around a range of issues.

Reanalysis of the pilot study data led to the development of the following five dimensions. Each meets the specifications mentioned above in that each is generic to all community issues, and each is relatable to the structure of influencing behavior. For these reasons it is suggested that they will profitably serve as a basis for the development of a typology of community issues. It should be noted, however, that each dimension is treated from the point of view of the actors in the community—in this case from the point of view of community leaders. It is their perception of community issues that modifies the type of action which they attempt to undertake with respect to the different kinds of issues.

1. Unique—Recurrent Dimension

It may be predicted that differential social organizations tend to evolve out of a community's recurrent experiences with a given type of community issue. Thus, the problem of dealing with recurrent issues, when they arise in a community, would in all likelihood be handled by constituted community agencies having access to regularly allocated resources. On the other hand, in the case of a unique issue (one which community leaders feel has not been previously experienced), no such structure or procedure would necessarily be available to members of the community. Therefore, when decisions must be made on such issues, leadership tends to be emergent, and resources would have to be developed. Such leadership would probably be less subject to formal community social controls. In addition, such leaders would also be more likely to have less restricted access to the *means* of power, such as money and the control of jobs, than in the case of a regularly organized community agency dealing administratively with a recurrent issue.

2. Salient—Nonsalient to Leadership

Community issues vary along a continuum from some that are central to the interests of community leaders and the organizational structures in which they hold positions, to some that are peripheral to their interests and of little concern to them. When an issue is of great importance to community leaders, but [is] perceived to be of little importance to the general public of a community, action taken on that issue may be unpublicized and directed through informal influence structures. If, however, leaders feel that a "public relations program—" is required, communications regarding the issue will generally flow from leaders to community members, frequently through the mass media. On the other hand, community leaders may be "forced to act" on some issues that are of little relevance to their personal interests when public pressures are brought to bear upon them. Under such circumstances, they may be *reacting* to the upward flow of communications exercised through formal mechanisms of the community such as political parties or the hierarchies of public offices.

3. Salient—Nonsalient to Community Publics

This dimension refers to the degree of prominence, or importance, which leaders feel the various community publics attach to specific issues. Issues of low salience to community leaders, which are perceived as being of low salience to the general public, are likely to be handled by professional community organizers or lower echelon power figures. In such cases, the flow of influence and communications would be predominantly from decision makers to followers. When an issues is thought to be highly salient to the public, the potential decision makers are likely to be concerned with the "public relations" of any decision. Under such conditions one might expect that the flow of communications and influence would be generally upward, from public to "decision makers."[10]

4. Effective Action Possible—Effective Action Impossible

Some issues might be highly salient to the members of a community, or a segment thereof, and at the same time be perceived as necessitating impossible decisions or requiring inaccessible resources. For example, many southern communities have felt a strong need to improve the level of education offered to the local children. However, often they have had to face the fact that money was not available for new buildings, libraries, and other facilities. In addition, they realized that it was difficult to attract well qualified teachers with the low salaries which could be offered. For this type of issue, the only type of action which is undertaken involves the development of "tension-reducing mechanisms," or, perhaps, merely the manipulation of symbols.

5. Local—Cosmopolitan Dimension

When the leaders of a local community perceive an issue as concerning programs and problems dealt with by other organizations in the state or nation, they tend to look, in many cases, to higher levels of organization for guidance and direction in program development. If, however, an issue is perceived as purely local in its implications, then it is probable that the range of alternative courses of action will be seen as less limited, and the need for recourse to "experts" from outside the community will be lessened.

Directions for Future Research

If this five-dimensional basis for a typology of community issues is to be fruitfully applied to the study of community power and influence, then the following steps will seemingly have to be undertaken:

1. An instrument will have to be devel-

oped for the purpose of measuring and locating specific issues along these dimensions.

2. A set of issues, representative of the variety of issues facing a given community will have to be obtained from community leaders, and the leaders will have to describe each issue in terms of the instrument referred to in step 1. Information will also be required regarding the patterns of influence and communications associated with each issue.

3. An empirical typology of community issues will have to be developed from the data on community issues.

4. Finally, the resulting typology of issues will have to be related to the patterns of influence and communications behavior. At this point one would expect to find identifiable patterns of influence and communications flow associated with each type of issue. It would also be expected that specific types of community structures would be regularly involved in the decision-making process for the different types of issues.

At the present stage of our thinking, it has appeared meaningful to conceive of issues as flowing through a life cycle approximating the public opinion life cycle suggested by Foote and Hart.[11] Thus, an issue would be visualized as "living through" five phases: (a) the phase of emergence of the problem; (b) the proposal phase; (c) the policy-making phase; (d) the program phase; and finally, (e) the appraisal phase. It is expected that different types of issues will exhibit varying patterns of influence and communications flow for the several stages of issue life cycle. Therefore, this factor would have to be controlled in selecting a sample of issues for study.

A classification of community issues based on the dimensions proposed in this paper will make it possible to control one of the major variables in the study of influence systems. In this manner, it should be possible to clarify some of the problems characteristic of attempts to identify the structure of influence systems. In addition, it should clear the way for comparative research on influence systems in different community contexts.

Notes

1. The authors wish to thank the Research Fund of the Graduate School of the University of Washington for the financial support which has made it possible for them to carry on research in this area.
2. Peter H. Rossi, "Community Decision Making," *Administrative Science Quarterly* 1 (March, 1957), pp. 438–39.
3. *Ibid.*, p. 441.
4. *Ibid.*, pp. 438–39.
5. For a further discussion of this point see Nelson W. Polsby, "The Sociology of Community Power: A Reassessment," *Social Forces*, 37 (March, 1959), pp. 232–36.
6. Rossi, *op. cit.*, p. 438.
7. Floyd Hunter, *Community Power Structure: A Study of Decision Makers* (Chapel Hill: The University of North Carolina Press, 1953).
8. *Ibid.*, p. 57.
9. Delbert C. Miller, "The Prediction of Issue Outcome in Community Decision Making," *Research Studies of the State College of Washington*, 25, No. 2 (June, 1957).
10. There appear to be two polar views of the community leadership or influencing process. In one, the leader, or decision maker, is seen as making decisions in a rather arbitrary fashion and then implementing them by manipulating the means of power at his command. The other view sees the decision maker in the *process* of decision making. It views him from the time he discovers the need for action on any particular issue until he takes action on that issue. This latter view focuses on the communications behavior of leaders. It stresses the fact that leaders are in constant communication with relevant (or interested) publics for any issue. Such an approach makes it problematic as to whether the leader is exercising individual initiative in announcing a decision, or whether he is simply expressing an already formed, but latent (uncrystallized) community consensus on that issue. It appears to the authors that both types of processes operate. The problem at present is to discover the conditions under which one takes precedence over the other.
11. Nelson N. Foote and Clyde W. Hart, "Public Opinion and Collective Behavior," *Group Relations at the Crossroads*, Sherif and Wilson, eds. (New York: Harper and Brothers, 1953), pp. 308–331.

G. The Decision-Making Approach Criticized

Decisions and Nondecisions: An Analytical Framework

Peter Bachrach and Morton S. Baratz

In recent years a rich outpouring of case studies on community decision-making has been combined with a noticeable lack of generalizations based on them. One reason for this is a commonplace: we have no general theory, no broad-gauge model in terms of which widely different case studies can be systematically compared and contrasted.

Among the obstacles to the development of such a theory is a good deal of confusion about the nature of power and of the things that differentiate it from the equally impor-

Reprinted from the American Political Science Review, *57 (September 1963), 632–642, by permission of the authors and the American Political Science Association. Copyright 1964 by the American Political Science Association.*

tant concepts of force, influence, and authority. These terms have different meanings and are of varying relevance; yet in nearly all studies of community decision-making published to date, power and influence are used almost interchangeably, and force and authority are neglected.[1] The researchers thereby handicap themselves. For they utilize concepts which are at once too broadly, and too narrowly drawn: too broadly, because important distinctions between power and influence are brushed over; and too narrowly, because other concepts are disregarded—concepts which, had they been brought to bear, might have altered the findings radically.

Many investigators have also mistakenly assumed that power and its correlatives are activated and can be observed only in decision-making situations. They have overlooked the equally, if not more important area of what might be called "nondecision-making," i.e., the practice of limiting the scope of actual decision-making to "safe" issues by manipulating the dominant community values, myths, and political institutions and procedures. To pass over this is to neglect one whole "face" of power.[2]

Finally, the case studies are often based upon inarticulate, perhaps unsound, premises which predetermine the findings of "fact."[3] A variety of complex factors affect decision-making—the social, cultural, economic, and political backgrounds of the individual participants; the values of the decision-making body as an entity in itself; the pressures brought to bear on the decision-makers, individually and collectively, by groups at interest; and so on. To say, as some do, that these factors are equally important is as far from the mark as it is to assume, as others do, that only one is of overriding significance.[4]

What is required, then, is a model in terms of which the determinants both of decision- and nondecision-making can be appraised, taking full account of the distinct concepts of power, force, influence, and authority. In this paper we are not so ambitious. We attempt only to lay some of the groundwork for a model, seeking (1) to clarify the attributes of what we consider key concepts for any study of decision- and non-decision-making and the essential differences among them, and (2) to show how these concepts can be utilized more systematically and effectively in case studies.

I

It is customary to say that this of that person or group "has power," the implication being that power, like wealth, is a possession which enables its owner to secure some apparent future Good.[5] Another way of expressing the same point of view is to say that power is a "simple property . . . which can belong to a person or group considered in itself."[6]

For at least three reasons this usage is unacceptable. First, it fails to distinguish clearly between power over people and power over matter; and "power in the political [or economic or social] sense cannot be conceived as the ability to produce intended effects in general, but only such effects as involve other persons. . . ."[7] Second, the view that a person's power is measured by the total number of desires that he achieves is erroneous; one cannot have power in a vacuum, but only in relation to someone else. Third and most important, the common conception of the phenomenon mistakenly implies that possession of (what appear to be) the instruments of power is tantamount to possession of power itself. Such a notion is false because it ignores the fundamental relational attribute of power: that it cannot be possessed; that, to the contrary, the successful exercise of power is dependent upon the relative importance of conflicting values *in the mind of the recipient* in the power relationship.

A few illustrations should clarify and enlarge our position. Imagine, first, an armed military sentry who is approached by an unarmed man in uniform. The sentry levels his gun at the intruder and calls out, "Halt or I'll shoot!" The order is promptly obeyed. Did the sentry therefore have power and exercise it? So it would seem; but appearances could be deceiving. For suppose that the intruder obeyed, not because he felt compelled to do so in the face of the threatened sanction, but because he was himself a trained soldier for whom prompt obedience to a sentry's order was part of a system of values he fully accepted.[8] If that was the case, there was no conflict of goals or interests between the two principals; the sentry's threatened sanction was irrelevant, and the result would have been the same if he, and not the intruder, had been unarmed. Because the soldier put obedience to a sentry's order at the top of his schedule of values, the threat of severe deprivations had no bearing on his behavior. In such circumstances it cannot be said that the guard exerted power.

Let us now suppose that a second man approaches the sentry and, like the first, is ordered to stop or be shot. But the second stranger ignores the order, attempts to smash through the gate, and is forthwith fatally wounded. If we assume that the intruder's intention was to sabotage the military installation, we can have no doubt that his and the sentry's values were in direct conflict. Even so, the sentry's fatal shot did *not* constitute an exercise of power. For it did not bring about compliance to his order—and it did not because, apparently, the intruder valued entry to the base more highly than either obedience to the sentry's order or his own wellbeing.

Suppose, finally, that a third man approaches the sentry box, a man who wants to die but cannot bring himself to the act of self-destruction. He therefore deliberately ignores the sentry's command and is duly shot to death. Did someone in this situation have power and exercise it? As we see it the "victim" did—for it was he, cognizant of the conflict of values between himself and the guard, who utilized the latter's supposed sanction to achieve his own objective.[9]

We reiterate that power is relational, as opposed to possessive or substantive. Its relational characteristics are threefold. First, in order for a power relation to exist there must be a conflict of interests or values between two or more persons or groups. Such a divergence is a necessary condition of power because, as we have suggested, if A and B are in agreement as to ends, B will freely assent

to A's preferred course of action; in which case the situation will involve authority rather than power.[10] Second, a power relationship exists only if B actually bows to A's wishes. A conflict of interests is an insufficient condition, since A may not be able to prevail upon B to change his behavior. And if B does not comply, A's policy will either become a dead letter or will be effectuated through the exercise of force rather than through power.[11] Third, a power relation can eixst only if one of the parties can threaten to invoke sanctions: power is "the process of affecting policies of others with the help of (. . . threatened) severe deprivations for noncomformity with the policies intended."[12] It must be stressed, however, that while the availability of sanctions—that is, of any promised reward or penalty by which an actor can maintain effective control over policy—is a necessary condition of power, it is not sufficient. It is necessary simply because the threat of sanctions is what differentiates power from influence;[13] it is insufficient because the availability of a sanction endows A with power over B only if the following conditions are met:

(a) The person threatened is aware of what is expected of him. In a power situation there must be clear communication between the person who initiates policy and the person who must comply.[14] If our imaginary sentry challenges a man who understands no English or is perhaps deaf, the sentry has—at least at the moment he issues his order—no power. In other words, power has a rational attribute: for it to exist, the person threatened must comprehend the alternatives which face him in choosing between compliance and noncompliance.

(b) The threatened sanction is *actually* regarded as a deprivation by the person who is so threatened. A threat by the President to "purge" a Congressman for failure to support the Administration's legislative program would be to no avail if the Congressman reckoned that his chances for reelection would be increased rather than reduced by Presidential intervention.

(c) The person threatened has greater

esteem for the value which would be sacrificed should he disobey than for another value which would be foregone should he comply. Fear of physical injury did not deter those Southern Negro "sitters-in" who put greater store by the righteousness of their cause. It is worth noting at this stage that threatened deprivations are often ineffectual because the policy-initiator, in deciding what sanction to invoke, mistakenly projects his own values into the minds of his subjects.[15]

(d) The person threatened is persuaded that the threat against him is not idle, that his antagonist would not hesitate *in fine* actually to impose sanctions. To illustrate, if a famous general calculates that the Presidents lacks the will or the popular support to employ his Constitutional prerogatives, he may ignore—even defy—the President's policy instructions.[16] Or, again, the success of a resistance movement based on the principle of nonviolence rests in large measure upon the assumption that those who can invoke sanctions will refrain from doing so, that value conflicts within A will prevent him from carrying out his threat against B. In point are the Indians who sat on the railroad tracks in defiance of the British and got away with it because (as the Indians well knew) the British put a higher value on human life than on obedience to their orders.[17]

We can now draw together the several elements of our conception of power. A power relationship exists when (a) there is a conflict over values or course of action between A and B; (b) B complies with A's wishes; and (c) he does so because he is fearful that A will deprive him of a value or values which he, B, regards more highly than those which would have been achieved by noncompliance.[18]

Several points must be made in reference to this definition. First, in speaking of power relations, one must take care not to overstate the case by saying that A has power over B merely because B, anxious to avoid sanctions, complies with a given policy proclaimed by A. This could well be an inaccurate description of their relationship, since A's power with respect to B may be extremely limited in scope, i.e., in range of values affected.[19] Thus, the power of a traffic policeman over a citizen may be confined to the latter's activities as a motorist—and no more than that. Moreover, in appraising power relationships account must be taken of the weight of power, i.e., the degree to which values are affected, and of its domain, i.e., the number of persons affected.[20] For example, the power of the Chairman of the House Committee on Ways and Means is limited mainly to fiscal affairs; but within this scope he wields immense power in the determination of Federal tax and expenditure policies (weight), which affect a vast number of persons—up to and including at times the President himself (domain).

Finally, account must be taken of what Friedrich has dubbed the "rule of anticipated reactions."[21] The problem posed by this phenomenon is that an investigation might reveal that, though B regularly accedes to A's preferred courses of action, A in fact lacks power over B because A just as regularly tailors his demands upon B to dimensions he thinks B will accept. As an illustration, if the President submits to the Congress only those bills likely to be palatable to a majority of lawmakers, he can hardly be said to have power over the Congress simply because all his proposals are enacted into law.

II

In Robert Bierstedt's opinion, "force is manifest power ... Force ... means the reduction or limitation or closure or even total elimination of alternatives to the social action of one person or group by another person or group. 'Your money or your life' symbolizes a situation of naked force, the reduction of alternatives to two."[22] Force in short, is power exercised.

We reject this view. As we see it, the essential difference between power and force is simply that in a power relationship one party obtains another's compliance, while in a situation involving force one's objectives must be achieved, if at all, in the face of *non*-compliance.[23] Thus, if A's demand for B's money or his life prompts B to surrender his wallet, A has exercised power—he has won B's compliance by threat of even more severe deprivations. But if A must kill B to get the money, A has to resort to force—he must actually invoke the threatened sanction —and thereby perhaps expose himself to severer deprivations too. By the same token, if and when thermonuclear weapons are transformed from instruments of a policy of deterrence into activated missiles of death, power will have given way to force.

There is another difference between the two concepts. A person's scope of decision-making is radically curtailed under the duress of force; once the fist, the bullet, or the missile is in flight, the intended victim is stripped of choice between compliance and noncompliance. But where power is being exercised, the individual retains this choice. Put another way, in a power relationship it is B who chooses what to do, while in a force relationship it is A.[24]

It follows from the foregoing that *manipulation* is an aspect of force, not of power. For, once the subject is in the grip of the manipulator, he has no choice as to course of action. It can be said, therefore, that force and manipulation (as a sub-concept under it) are, in contrast to power, non-rational.

An additional distinguishing attribute of force is that in some circumstances it is non-relational. For instance, if B is shot in the back by an unknown robber, he and his assailant have only a minimal interrelationship—especially when compared to a power confrontation where B must decide whether to accede to A's demands. A similarly minimal relationship obtains in cases involving manipulation, where compliance is forthcoming in the absence of recognition on the complier's part either of the source or the exact nature of the demand upon him.

In short, force and manipulation, like power, involve a conflict of values; but unlike power, they are non-rational and tend to be non-relational.

A number of implications may be drawn from this reasoning. One is that the actual application of sanctions is an admission of defeat by the would-be wielder of power. And so it is, to the extent that the prior *threat* of sanctions failed to bring about the desired behavior. A good case in point is the action of President Harry S Truman in 1951 when he relieved General Douglas MacArthur of his command in the Pacific on grounds of insubordination. By continuing to air in public his policy differences with the Administration, MacArthur virtually compelled Truman to dismiss him. The President's decision to apply sanctions was, however, an admission of defeat, an implicit recognition that he could not, by power or authority, obtain MacArthur's compliance to the Administration's policy of a negotiated settlement of the Korean hostilities. To be sure, policy defeats of this kind may prove to be only partial. For if the resort to force against one party effectively deters noncompliance on the part of others, now or in future, the employment of sanctions becomes a fresh declaration of the existence of power. This is, of course, the rationale of all who undertake punitive actions against others: the *use* of force in one situation increases the credibility of *threats* to use it in others.

At the same time, it is important to recognize that resort to force can result in a loss of power. Two cases can be distinguished. First, the invocation of sanctions often causes a radical reordering of values within the coerced person (as well as in those persons who identify closely with him), thereby undermining the pre-existing power relationship. A good illustration is provided by the largely abortive attempt of the Nazis during World War II to pacify the populations of occupied countries by killing civilian hostages. Contrary to German expectations, this policy produced a marked stiffening of resistance; evidently, the number of "prisoners" who put a higher value on freedom than on life itself rose sharply. Second, the deprivation may prove in retrospect far less severe than it appeared in prospect, as a result of which future noncompliance is not discouraged and may even be encouraged. For example, a child whose punishment for misbehavior is the temporary loss of a prized toy may find, *ex post facto*, that the loss is entirely bearable, that the satisfactions he gained from acting up are greater at the margin than the alternative foregone. In such circumstances, obviously, future defiance of parental orders is more likely than not.

Just as power may be lessened when force is resorted to, so also may power be lessened when it is successfully exercised, i.e., when compliance is obtained by mere threat of sanctions. As an illustration, Presidents of the United States have traditionally sought to exercise power over recalcitrant Congressmen by withholding patronage. But as a President exchanges a job appointment for votes—that is, as he successfully utilizes this source of power—his reserves for effecting further compliance dry up. As a corollary, repeated threats to invoke sanctions—threats never carried out—will gradually lose credibility in the minds of those threatened, until at length the threats cannot produce the desired behavior. This, in the view of many, was the basic flaw in the implementation of the stated American policy during the late 1950s of "massive retaliation at times and in places of our own choosing."[25] The same phenomenon applies to interpersonal relationships: a threat to withdraw one's love for another may be highly potent the first time, yet prove totally ineffectual if used again.

III

One person has *influence* over another within a given scope to the extent that the first, without resorting to either a tacit or an overt threat of severe deprivations, causes the second to change his course of action. Thus, power and influence are alike in that each has both rational and relational attributes. But they are different in that the exercise of power depends upon potential sanctions, while the exercise of influence does not. And there is an important difference between influence and manipulation: in situations involving the latter, but not the former, A seeks to disguise the nature and source of his demands upon B and, if A is successful, B is totally unaware that something is being demanded of him.

Although power and influence can and must be distinguished, the line between them is usually difficult to draw. This is especially true where B's reasons for acting in accordance with A's wishes are confused or multiple; in such circumstances B himself will be unable honestly to say whether his behavior was prompted by a fear of sanctions or, rather, by his esteem for "higher" values (e.g., wealth, respect, power, wisdom) than the one immediately at stake. Does the ambitious young man who submits unhappily to the every dictate of his rich uncle do so because he admires wealthy men (influence) or because he feels that unquestioning obedience is the price of a generous inheritance in the future (power)? Does the Majority Leader who unwillingly manages an Administration bill in the Senate do so because he is in awe of the Presidency and hence of the man who occupies the office (influence), or because he fears the President will actually punish him for noncompliance (power)? To say that the decisive test in situations like these turns on whether compliance is "voluntary" or "involuntary" is, in our judgment, not particularly helpful.[26]

The difficulty in distinguishing sharply and clearly between power and influence is further complicated by the fact that the two are often mutually reinforcing, that is, power frequently generates influence and *vice versa*. On this score, the case of Senator Joseph R. McCarthy of Wisconsin is especially instructive.[27] Shrewdly posing as the principal defender of the national security at the very moment when that became the dominant social value *vice* the inviolability of civil liberties. McCarthy managed for a period to stifle virtually all opposition to himself and what he stood for (influence). And from this base he was able to gain power, that is, to affect the making of actual decisions (votes in the Senate, acts of the Executive, etc.) by threats of severe deprivations (intervention in State political campaigns, destruction by accusation of the careers of appointive officials, etc.). By the same token, however, as public fears about national security subsided and concern for civil liberties grew, McCarthy's capacity to influence others sharply waned—and so, too, did his power.

Just because the distinction between power and influence is often blurred does not, however, lessen the importance of making the distinction. Nikita Krushchev had little or no influence over Americans, yet it is obvious he exercises considerable power over us. On the other hand, the Supreme Court of the United States has widespread influence (and authority) over us both individually and collectively; its power is slight indeed.

IV

While authority is closely related to power, it is not a form thereof; it is, in fact, antithetical to it.[28] In saying this, we reject both the traditional definition of authority as "formal power"[29] and that which conceives it as "institutionalized power."[30]

To regard authority as a form of power is, in the first place, not operationally useful. If authority is "formal power," then one is at a loss to know who has authority at times when the agent who possesses "formal power" is actually powerless; to say that Captain Queeg continued to have authority on the USS *Caine* after he was deposed of his command by the mutineers is to create needless confusion. Furthermore, to define authority as "formal power" is to fail to delineate the bounds of authority, other perhaps than to say that it ends where "real power" begins. For those who believe in limited or constitutional government such a construction is unthinkable.

To argue that "formal power" is circumscribed by law is also no answer. For it assumes without warrant the legitimacy of law. A policeman who demands obedience in the name of a law that is considered basically unjust will possess little authority in the eyes of persons steeped in the Anglo-American legal tradition. Nor is the problem completely solved by conceiving of authority in terms of constitutional legitimacy. Such a conception presupposes that all members of the community give allegiance to the constitution and the courts which interpret it. Do Federal courts have the authority to issue desegregation orders to southern school districts? According to many Southerners, in-cluding some learned in the law, the answer is in the negative.

Friedrich's analysis of authority seems to us the most appropriate. He defines the concept as "a quality of communication" that possesses "the potentiality of reasoned elaboration."[31] Like power, authority is here regarded as a relational concept: it is not that A possesses authority, but that B regard A's communication as authoritative. Also like power, an authority relationship implies rationality—although of a different order. That is, in a situation involving power, B is rational in the sense that he chooses compliance instead of defiance because it seems the less of two evils.[32] But in a situation involving authority, B complies because he recognizes that the command is reasonable in terms of his own values; in other words, B defers to A, not because he fears severe deprivations, but because his decision can be rationalized.[33] It is not essential, however, that A's directive be supported by reasoning; it is sufficient that the potentiality of such reasoning be present and recognized.[34]

If B believes that A's communication allows for reasoned elaboration when in fact it does not, it is "false" authority.[35] When the source of obedience shifts from "genuine" to "false" authority and B realizes that the communication cannot be elaborated effectively, then a relationship initially involving authority has been transformed into one involving power. For example, if a policeman demanded entrance to your house, you would probably comply on the implicit assumption that his demand was potentially supportable by reason. However, should you discover, once he was in, that his demand was *not* justifiable, your further compliance would undoubtedly derive from his exercise of power, not authority. The point is that the policeman's badge, uniform and gun—his symbols of "formal power"—do not constitute his authority. Whether he actually has that depends upon the authoritativeness of his communication, and that depends to a considerable degree upon the reasonableness of his command.

If the officer's elaboration of his demand to enter was sound in terms of the law, did he not have authority? Within the frame of our example, the answer is both no and yes. No, as far as you were concerned, since the elaboration did not make sense in terms of your own values. Yes, as far as society and its courts are concerned—provided, of course, that they themselves considered the law to be authoritative. As can readily be seen, in this kind of situation—which occurs frequently—authority is both a source of and a restraint upon the exercise of power; it both justifies and limits the use of power. But to those who believe in democracy this affords small comfort, unless authority itself is grounded upon reasoning that is meaningful to a majority of the people.

As a final note, it is worth observing that just as authority can be transformed into power, so can the reverse obtain. "Brainwashing" after the manner of George Orwell's "Big Brother" (and his real-life counterpart in Communist China) is a gruesome case in point; to obey Big Brother is not enough; you must *love* him. A different kind of illustration of the same point is the parent who uses the threat of spanking (power) to produce filial discipline which is based on acceptance of certain rules of the game (authority). Authority, in short, can cut both ways. In a humane and healthy society, it can perform the valuable function of limiting the behavior of men, especially those in official positions, to legitimate acts; for their actions must be potentially justified by "reasoned elaboration" in terms of values of a sane society. However, if the value frame of the society is pathological, authority, even as we have regarded it, can become a tool in furthering the state of pathology.

V

Perhaps the best way to summarize our effort to draw careful distinction among power and related concepts is to apply them in a "real world" context—say, a Southern community where white citizens have decided to abide by a Federal court's desegregation order. As should be evident in the accompanying table, we assume that different persons in the community had different reasons for bowing before the law.

Local officials and local businessmen, for example, were fearful of severe deprivations —they responded to an exercise of power. Those whites we style as "moderates," on the other hand, fall into two distinct groups: (a) those (Group I) who accepted as legitimate and reasonable the *substantive logic* underlying the Court order, and (b) those (Group II) who rejected the substantive ground but accepted the *judicial procedure* as legitimate and reasonable. Both groups, that is, responded to authority, in the vital senses that both perceived the Court's decree rationally and both considered it (even though on different grounds) to be capable of "reasoned elaboration."

A third body of whites—whom, following David Riesman, we label the "other-directed"—complied not because they feared severe deprivation (power) nor because they thought the order was reasonable and legitimate (authority), but because they felt obliged to follow the lead of those in the community they most respect (influence). Stated differently, although the "other-directed" group regarded the Court's ruling as illegitimate and unreasonable both on substantive and procedural grounds, it "went along with its betters."

Like those who were other-directed, the "masses," too, deferred to the newly dominant viewpoint in the community. But, unlike the former, the latter did so with little or no awareness of the issues at stake or of the fact that they were reversing their previous stand on the general question. The "masses," in other words, did not make a conscious choice between compliance and noncompliance with the Court order; following the pattern of manipulation, they simply conformed.

Under the heading of groups not complying with the Court order are officials who are incarcerated and fined for criminal contempt (force) and segregationist groups that are beyond the reach of the Court. Suffice it to say that the behavior of these groups— geared as they are to a different set of values —also can be analyzed and categorized in terms of power and its related concepts.

TABLE 1. *Hypothetical Behavior of Southern Whites to a Desegregation Court Order*

CONCEPT	SUBJECT
Power (relational, demand rationally perceived, conflict of values, threat of severe sanctions)	Groups Which Choose Compliance State and local officials (threat of criminal contempt) Businessmen (threat of economic boycott and race strife, resulting in loss of profits)
Authority (relational, demand rationally perceived and considered reasonable, possible conflict of values, no severe sanctions)	Moderates I (substantive grounds for Court's ruling reasonable) Moderates II (substantive grounds unreasonable, but judicial process legitimate and reasonable)
Influence (relational, demand rationally perceived, conflict of values, no severe sanctions)	"Other-Directed" Persons (judicial ruling, substantively and procedurally unreasonable, but apprehensive of standing in community)
Manipulation (non-relational, non-rational, no conflict of values nor sanctions)	Groups Which Choose Neither Compliance Nor Non-compliance Mass (conform to dominant behavior in community, with little or no recognition of the problem nor awareness of complying)
Force (relational to non-relational, non-rational, application of severe sanctions)	Groups Which Choose Noncompliance Defiant official subject to contempt of Court (incarceration reflects that values underlying defiance overshadow values gained by compliance)
Power, Authority, etc.	Extreme segregationists

VI

For our purposes, a decision is "a set of actions related to and including the choice of one alternative rather than another . . .,"[36] or, more simply, "a choice among alternative modes of action. . . ."[37] Thus, we differ sharply from Lasswell and Kaplan, to whom a decision is "a policy involving severe sanctions (deprivations)."[38] The basis for the contrast between our definition and theirs is clearcut: they hold that decisions are brought about solely by the exercise of power, while we believe that power is neither the only nor even the major factor underlying the process of decision-making and reactions thereto. We believe, in fact, that in some situations power is not involved at all, that in such situations the behavior of decision-makers and their subjects alike can be explained partially or entirely in terms of force, influence, or authority.

Our position can be clarified by reference to the following diagram. Two important points may be drawn from it. First, every social decision involves interaction between the one or more persons seeking a given goal and the one or more persons whose compliance must be obtained. Thus, if A's attempt to exercise power or influence or whatever over B is ignored, there is no decision.

FIGURE 1. *Diagram of Impulse and Response*

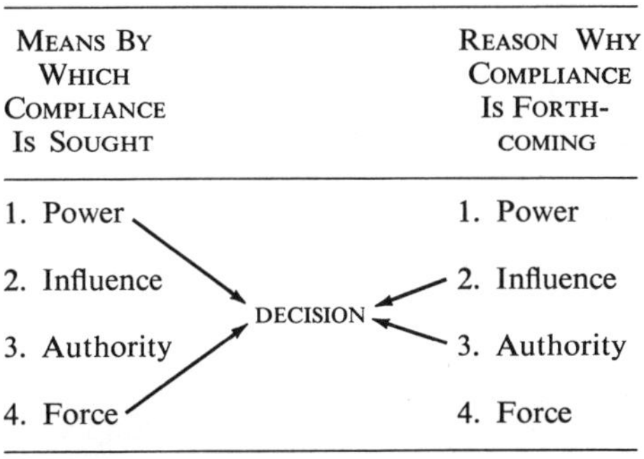

MEANS BY WHICH COMPLIANCE IS SOUGHT	REASON WHY COMPLIANCE IS FORTH-COMING
1. Power	1. Power
2. Influence	2. Influence
DECISION	
3. Authority	3. Authority
4. Force	4. Force

Second, compliance can be *sought* through the exercise of one or any combination of the four phenomena indicated on the diagram. However, if compliance is forthcoming, *it may or may not stem from the same source.* For instance, if B bows to A's wishes because A has threatened sanctions which B wishes to avoid, the resulting decision is one of "pure" power; both participants made their choices in the same frame of reference. On the other hand, if B's compliance is grounded, not on a fear of deprivations but on acceptance of A's values, the resulting decision is a hybrid case, in the important sense that A sought to exercise power but in fact exercised authority. Similarly, cases can be identified in which A has sought to exert authority while B's compliance was given because he was influenced (see diagram). The combinations are many—particularly if the analysis also takes into account situations where two or more of the phenomena come into play simultaneously.[39] The point is, in all events, that a decision cannot be said to be a result of power or influence or authority or force unless and until it is specified from whose point of view the decision is being examined, i.e., from that of the one who seeks compliance or the one who gives it.

It may be objected that this approach is unworkable for empirical analysis because it necessitates mind-reading. We think not. The courts of law do, and so can we, distinguish between "specific" intent and intent inferred from actual behavior. We believe, in other words, that it is both feasible and necessary to deduce from detailed observation of the situation why persons act as they do.[40] To put it still another way, there is no short-cut, no simple and mechanical method, for gaining a full understanding of the decision-making process.

We concede that our approach is less workable than that of Lasswell and Kaplan, Dahl, and others of that "school." On the other hand, because ours provides a broader conceptual frame within which to analyze decision-making, it makes easier the comparative study of the factors underlying different decisions in diverse circumstances. A road is thereby opened toward the development of a body of general theory with respect to the decision-making process. Moreover, because we distinguish carefully among the forces at work in any given situation, we minimize the risk of putting unwarranted emphasis upon one factor to the exclusion, wholly or partly, of others. Stated more bluntly, we put the phenomenon of power in proper perspective: we recognize that while decision making frequently does involve power relationships, it very often does not.

VII

The other side of the coin is *non*decision-making. When the dominant values, the accepted rules of the game, the existing power relations among groups, and the instruments of force, singly or in combination, effectively prevent certain grievances from developing into full-fledged issues which call for decisions, it can be said that a nondecision-making situation exists. This phenomenon is clearly distinguishable from the negative aspects of decision-making (deciding not to act or deciding not to decide), since the mere existence of the "mobilization of bias," to use Schattschneider's phrase, is sufficient to prevent a latent issue from becoming a question for decision.

It might be objected that since a nondecision, by definition, is a nonevent, it is not observable and therefore is not an operationally-useful concept. Although it is true that a nondecision is not visible to the naked eye, a latent issue is discernible and so is the mobilization of bias. Thus it can be said that the *nondecision-making process* (the impact of the mobilization of bias upon a latent issue), in distinction to a nondecision, is indeed subject to observation and analysis.

In their perceptive study, *Small Town in Mass Society* Vidich and Bensman, without calling it such, analyze the nondecision-making process in Springdale.[41] For example, they relate that the school administrators in the community had basic grievances but, cognizant of the dominant rural values prevailing in the community, the established tradition of deciding all town issues by unanimous vote, and the predominance of nonprofessionals in posts of leadership, the schoolmen prudently kept their grievances to themselves. In choosing this course of action, the school officials admittedly made a decision. But it was not one brought about by any decision or combination of decisions by others with respect to their grievances. Quite the contrary, it reflected the school-

men's realization that, by sustaining the mobilization of bias, the leaders of the community—even if indirectly and unconsciously—could, would, and often did exercise authority, power and influence against them.

In those instances when a latent issue of the type which is usually kept submerged is successfully pushed forward and emerges as a public issue (for example, the recent emergence of Negro demands in the South), it is likely that the mobilization of bias will be directly and consciously employed against those who demand a redress of grievances by the decision-making organ. In such instances, the decision-making process preempts the field previously occupied by the nondecision-making process. And in so doing, it necessarily jeopardizes the previously-established mobilization of bias.

If the concept of nondecision-making proves a useful tool of analysis, it appears to us at this juncture that it can be effectively studied in terms of the categories suggested in this paper for the examination of decision-making.

Notes

1. See, *e.g.*, Floyd Hunter, *Community Power Structure* (Chapel Hill, 1953); and Robert A. Dahl, *Who Governs?* (New Haven, 1961).
2. Peter Bachrach and Morton S. Baratz, "Two Faces of Power," *American Political Science Review*, Vol. 56 (December, 1962), pp. 947–52. A somewhat similar view, arrived at independently, may be found in Thomas J. Anton, "Power, Pluralism, and Local Politics," *Administrative Science Quarterly*, Vol. 7 (March 1963), p. 453.
3. See Bachrach and Baratz, *op. cit.*, pp. 947, 952.
4. *Cf.* Peter Rossi, "Community Decision-Making," in Roland Young (ed.), *Approaches to the Study of Politics* (Evanston, Ill., 1958), p. 359.
5. Thomas Hobbes, as paraphrased by C. J. Friedrich, *Constitutional Government and Politics* (New York, 1937), p. 12.
6. Harold D. Lasswell and Abraham Kaplan, *Power and Society* (New Haven, 1950), p. 75, draw this implication from the definition of power, i.e., "the production of intended effects," in Bertrand Russell, *Power: A New*

Social Analysis (New York, 1938), p. 35.
7. Lasswell and Kaplan, *loc cit.*
8. Agreement based upon reason represents another kind of interpersonal relationship —authority—which is discussed below.
9. It might be argued that the "victim" did not actually exercise power in this instance, because he had no sanctions with which to threaten the sentry. This objection misses the obvious point: the "victim" threatened the guard with severe deprivations (dishonor, imprisonment) if the guard did not perform his soldierly duty by complying with the "victim's" command that he (the "victim") be killed.
10. See part IV below.
11. See part II below.
12. Lasswell and Kaplan, *op. cit.*, p. 76. We have deleted "actual or" from the parenthetical expression because *actual* deprivation for nonconformity is a property of force, rather than power. This point is discussed further below.

The Lasswell-Kaplan definition is open to another criticism. They observe (p. 77) that "to have power is to be taken into account in others' acts (policies)." Strictly construed, this must mean that any and every person or group involved—in whatever degree—in decision-making must have power. For is not the farmer who markets .001 percent of the total supply of wheat "taken into account" by other buyers and sellers in just the same sense—though not, of course, in the same degree—as is the General Motors Corporation in the determination of automobile prices? Or, to change the illustration, is it not the case that, in the literal interpretation of the word, nonvoters as well as voters "participate," and therefore have power, in deciding close elections? We should think so. But if this is what is meant by power, how can we avoid concluding that no matter where we look, we shall always find that power is broadly diffused? To rephrase, if (a) we analyze the distribution of power solely in terms of decision-making and (b) we ascribe power to all who participate in whatever measure or with whatever "weight" ("The weight of power is the degree of participation in the making of decisions . . ." [ibid.], then (c) do we not necessarily prejudge that power in real-world situations will be widely dispersed? For further discussion of this general question, see Bacharach and Baratz, op. cit.

13. See part III below.
14. See Richard E. Neustadt, *Presidential Power* (New York, 1960), p. 21. Compare Thomas C. Schelling, *The Strategy of Conflict* (Cambridge, Mass., 1960), pp. 38–9.
15. This error, compounded by that of regarding power as something which is possessed, may well have underlain the policy of the United States toward Chiang Kai-Shek during the period (1944–49) of the Chinese civil war. It is entirely possible, that is to say, that in providing substantial amounts of armament to the Kuomintang regime, we mistook the instruments of power for power itself; and, in addition, by interpreting the Kuomintang-Communist struggle in terms of our own values, we utterly misread the temper of the great majority of the Chinese people.

The abortive invasion of Cuba in April 1961 is perhaps another example of the inherent dangers in projecting our values onto a populace holding a different collection of interests. Looking at the great body of Cuban nationals who were apparently bereft both of individual freedom and personal dignity, we concluded that we need only provide the opportunity, the spark, which would ignite nationwide uprisings against the Castro regime. But hindsight has indicated how badly we misread popular feeling in Cuba. See Stewart Alsop, "Lessons of the Cuban Disaster," *Saturday Evening Post*, 24 June 1961, pp. 26–27.

16. Neustadt, *op. cit.*, pp. 12–13. On the general point, see also Schelling, *op. cit.*, p. 6.
17. The point is also well illustrated by Franco-American policy differences in the early 1960s. Committed both to the defense of Western Europe and to strict limitation on the number of nations with independent nuclear forces, the United States was caught in a dilemma in its dealings with General de Gaulle. In the words of a contemporary observer, "De Gaulle . . . has played a judo trick on the United States . . . [He] means to fashion his 'European construction,' based on the *force de frappe* and the Franco-German axis and excluding the British and Americans. And he means to do this *under the umbrella of the American nuclear deterrent* . . . there is precious little the Kennedy Administration can do about de Gaulle's judo trick—short of removing its nuclear protection. And this has not been seriously considered. . . .'We're a bit like that little Dutch boy with his finger in the dike,' says one Kennedy adviser. Remove the American commitment to defend Europe, and the result is unmitigated disaster, not only to Europe but to the United States. Thus the United States, like the little Dutch boy, is immobilized. The strongest power in the Western alliance has amazingly little bargaining power in the alliance." Stuart Alsop, "Should We Pull Out of Europe?" *Saturday Evening Post*, 13 April 1963, p. 80. Emphasis in original.

The main point is made more pithily by "President Hudson" in Allen Drury's novel, *A Shade of Difference* (New York, 1962), p. 82: "The more real power you have, the less you can afford to exercise it, and the less real power you have, the more you can throw it around."

For further discussion of the relationship between power and commitment, see E. Abramson, *et al.*, "Social Power and Commitment Theory," *American Sociological Review*, Vol. 23 (February, 1958), pp. 15–22.

18. With Lasswell and Kaplan, *op. cit.*, p. 16, we define a value as "a desired event—a goal event. That X values Y means that X acts so as to bring about the consummation of Y."
19. *Ibid.*, p. 76.
20. *Ibid.*, p. 77.
21. [Friedrich] *Op. cit.*, pp. 17–18. A corollary proposition could be called the "rule of *mis*anticipated reactions." We refer to a situation in which one person grudgingly conforms to what he *thinks* another wants, but finds after the fact either that he misread the other's preferences or that the latter

never intended to invoke sanctions for behavior contrary to his preferences.

22. [R. Bierstedt] "An Analysis of Social Power," *American Sociological Review*, Vol. 15 (December, 1950), p. 733.

23. A major defect of Lord Russell's conception of power (see above, note 6) is that it utterly ignores this distinction. One can produce an "intended effect" through the exercise of either power or force.

24. It is often true, when force is operative, that A gives B the option to comply with his demands *between* blows. But in such circumstances, should B bend to A's wishes, he does so out of fear of further sanctions, in which case force is transformed into power.

25. One of the more penetrating critiques along these lines may be found in General Maxwell D. Taylor, *The Uncertain Trumpet* (New York, 1959).

26. According to Bierstedt, *op. cit.*, p. 731, ". . . influence is persuasive while power is coercive. We submit voluntarily to influence while power requires submission." In our view, if B submits voluntarily, power is operative; but if he submits under duress, force is operative.

   It is worth noting that under our definition it would be incorrect to say that Marx "influenced" Lenin, or that Haydn "influenced" Mozart, or that Jesus Christ "influenced" the Conquistadores. In each of these cases the second *shared* the values of the first, i.e., the relationship involved neither power nor influence, but *authority*. See part IV below.

27. See Richard H. Rovere, *Senator Joe McCarthy* (New York, 1959).

28. C. J. Friedrich, "Authority, Reason and Discretion," in C. J. Friedrich (ed.), *Authority* (Cambridge, Mass., 1958), p. 37.

29. Lasswell and Kaplan, *op. cit.*, p. 133.

30. Bierstedt, *op. cit.*, p. 733.

31. [Friedrich] *Authority*, pp. 36, 35.

32. As is perhaps obvious, if B chooses to defy A, the relationship no longer will involve power. This notion of rationality of choice is analogous to Thomas Hobbes's treatment of the relationship between fear and liberty. "Feare, and Liberty," he wrote, "are consistent; as when a man throweth his goods into the Sea for *feare* the ship should sink, he doth it neverthelesse very willingly, and may refuse to doe it if he will: It is therefore the action, of one that was free." *Leviathan*, Everyman Edition, p. 110.

33. Friedrich, *Authority*, p. 36. Reasoning also underlies the difference between authority and influence. Thus, if B complies with A's demand neither because he fears deprivations nor because his compliance is based upon reasoning, B has been influenced. This distinction will be further elaborated below.

34. *Ibid.*, p. 38.

35. *Ibid.*, p. 47.

36. Robert A. Dahl, "The Analysis of Influence in Local Communities," in Charles Adrian (ed.), *Social Science and Community Action* (East Lansing, Mich., 1960), p. 26.

37. Peter Rossi, "Community Decision-Making," in Roland Young (ed.), *Approaches to the Study of Politics* (Evanston, Ill., 1958), p. 364.

38. [Lasswell and Kaplan] *Op. cit.*, p. 74.

39. For example, A may employ both authority *and* power to gain B's agreement, and B's response may have a similarly dual basis. An apparent case in point is the relationship between Adolf Hitler and some of his military chiefs during World War II. On this, consult William L. Shirer, *The Rise and Fall of the Third Reich* (New York, 1960), pp. 366 ff. and *passim*.

40. The approach we have in mind is exemplified by the untutored, but nonetheless penetrating, study of "Springdale" by Joseph Vidich and Arthur Bensman, *Small Town in Mass Society* (Princeton, N.J., 1958). For further discussion of this point, see following section.

41. *Ibid.*

Power, Pluralism, and Local Politics

Thomas J. Anton

Much of the recent literature on the problem of community power has been influenced by the lively and continuing dispute over the merits of Floyd Hunter's *Community Power Structure*, published in 1953. Hunter, a sociologist, there described Regional City (a pseudonym for Atlanta, Georgia) as a pyramid of power, in which a small and homogeneous group of men worked their will upon the rest of the population. While Hunter's conclusions were essentially the same as conclusions reached by a number of sociologists and anthropologists in other studies of American communities,[2] this book brought a sharp reaction from two political scientists.

Criticism of Hunter

"Shocked disbelief" would perhaps be too strong a phrase to describe this reaction; nevertheless it conveys something of the tone expressed by Herbert Kaufman and Victor Jones in the first important critical review of Hunter's work.[3] The sources of this disbelief are difficult to locate, inasmuch as both reviewers admit that "none of *us* [political scientists] has moved in with such a study of the structure and dynamics of power in a metropolitan community."[4] On the other hand, Kaufman and Jones were among "those who have ... been drawn into ... local government and administration" and who therefore "cannot but feel dissatisfied with Hunter's tantalizing description of the process by which ... decision[s] ... [are] reached in Regional City."[5] In other words, the reviewers thought of themselves as men with practical experience in a field that Hunter had attempted to describe from an academic vantage point. Presumably, this experience provided the basis for the charge that Hunter ignored or understated the influence of such groups as the party organizations,[6] the professionals,[7] or the Negroes.[8] Hunter, asserted the reviewers, had not been faithful to the facts of the case:

> He has not given us a study of the power structure of Regional City at all! Rather, he has set forth a portrait of one of the groups having some power over some things at some times. The place of this group in the interplay of power groups in Regional City is never made clear, and what from some indications may be a pluralist society emerges under Hunter's hands as a sternly monolithic organization. At best, the study is incomplete; at worst, it may be invalid.[9]

Now it is one thing to charge error when the facts are known and can be demonstrated with evidence; it is quite another thing to charge error on the basis of vaguely defined personal experiences in other places, at other times, by other men. Kaufman and Jones were aware of this weakness in their case and accordingly saved their heaviest criticism for Hunter's methods. Whether Hunter's picture of Regional City is true or false, they wrote, "is beside the point if his methods are faulty.' "Unfortunately," the reviewers continued, "they are, and these shortcomings are probably more important than any chance accuracy in his conclusions."[10]

Hunter's major difficulty, wrote Kaufman and Jones, was that instead of asking, "Is there any structure of power here, and if so what does it look like?" he had asked, "Who are the power elite of this community, what are they like, and how do they operate?" For the reviewers,

Reprinted from the Administrative Science Quarterly, 7 (*March 1963*), 425–457, *by permission of the author and the Graduate School of Business and Public Administration, Cornell University. Copyright 1962 by the Graduate School of Business and Public Administration, Cornell University.*

This inquiry assumes the existence of the elite has been established, and since Hunter's own method is empirical, presumably established by an empirical standard. Nothing could be further from the truth. That there is a small group running the city is not demonstrated but presupposed, and this presupposition relieves Hunter of the obligation to develop any objective measure of power. He begins his structure at the mezzanine without showing us a lobby or a foundation.[11]

But, the reviewers suggested, such a foundation may well be impossible to construct. "There is an elusiveness about power," they wrote, "that endows it with an almost ghostly quality."[12] We seem to know what it is, we think we can tell when it is being exercised, but somehow it seems to be impossible to measure it scientifically. Hunter, for example, was not able to demonstrate that the course of events in Regional City would be any different in the absence of power exertion by his elite. It was quite conceivable to Kaufman and Jones that "continuing forces at work in the community" shaped the activities of the elite just as much as the activities shaped the elite.[13] Moreover, even if Hunter had been able to demonstrate that his elite did in fact exert decisive power over events, argued Kaufman and Jones, "that in itself would *still* not dispel the ambiguities that plague the analysis of power."[14] All power is not asymmetrical; there are feedbacks which help to shape the use of power, and all this is complicated by anticipation of feedbacks by the powerful.[15] Hunter's use of a panel to select the powerful was similarly plagued with difficulties; responses identifying the powerful may reflect nothing but a culturally defined predisposition to believe that there is, after all, someone in control. There may not be, and the panelists may not be sufficiently well-informed to know it. This, argued the reviewers,

> is not the way one would try to decide who the wealthiest people in the community are or what the city's average temperature is. All the arguments against arriving at *these* determinations through the votes of a lay panel apply with equal force against using this method for the measurement of

power. . . . Hunter has tried to deal with a phenomenon before adequate tools are at hand to handle it, and his findings must therefore be regarded as intuitive . . . rather than scientific.[16]

The review of Hunter's book by Kaufman and Jones was in some ways an important milestone for political science. Although the book was challenged on both substantive and methodological grounds, the devotion of so much space to a sociologist's work in the *Public Administration Review* constituted a recognition of the relevance of this kind of inquiry for those who labored in the twin vineyards of political science and public administration. Indeed, lurking between every line of the review was an implicit exhortation to political scientists to start working on this problem, if only to substantiate the belief that Hunter was wrong about Regional City. Secondly, this essay—unintentionally, perhaps—expressed a radically different substantive conception of local politics which apparently developed out of the experience of the reviewers. The concept of the academic sociologist was of a pyramidal structure of local power; Kaufman and Jones, men experienced in the operations of local government, conceived of local power as having many centers rather than a single center. Their view later came to be dubbed, "the pluralist alternative."[17] Finally, a methodological alternative to Hunter was offered. In place of Hunter's "intuitive" approach, they called for efforts that were more "scientific." Exactly what the two reviewers understood this term to embrace was not made entirely clear, but at the very least it called for increased efforts to measure power with precision, with a view toward giving scientific meaning to Hunter's intuitions.[18]

The significance of these contributions can be appreciated by reviewing the efforts of political scientists in the field of community studies in the eight years since the Kaufman-Jones review was published in the summer of 1954. The call for documentation has been met by a number of field studies completed or in process under the auspices of various political science faculties. Significantly, nearly all of the published results of these studies have substantiated the bold assertion of Kaufman and Jones, i.e., that local power systems are pluralistic rather than monolithic.[19] And studies of community power have increasingly turned away from Hunter's panel interview technique and toward what has been called "decision sociometry," a technique which attempts to isolate the specific roles of specific actors with regard to specific community decisions.[20] It would not be exaggerating, then, to assert that Kaufman and Jones did more in their book review than summarize a reaction of political scientists and point the way to further research; their review actually presented, in advance, a summary of the *results* of later research![7]

It should be emphasized that this rejection of Hunter's sociological work was not based on the nature of the empirical world. Hunter's report was dismissed primarily because what he wrote was inconsistent with the pluralist interpretation of that world. Similarly, the subsequent unanimity among political scientists working on community politics implies that whatever might be the nature of the empirical data, it will be presented within the boundaries of a standard framework. In short, there appear to be clearcut *disciplinary* differences of interpretation between sociologists on the one hand and "pluralist" political scientists on the other.[21] Nowhere are these differences more sharply drawn than in the meanings attached to the notion of power. If we are to understand and evaluate the contrasting interpretations, we must begin here.

Review of Hunter's Assumptions

Hypotheses about Power

It may be instructive to examine some of the preliminary remarks made by Hunter in the introduction to his study of Regional City. There he defined power in relatively simple terms, as "the ability of men to command the services of other men" either in relation to themselves or in relation to other men and things.[22] This definition was thought to be empirically useful, in that it conceived of power in terms of men and their actions in relation to one another, such actions being

easily observed. Equally important, Hunter made clear that "the term 'power' is no reified concept, but an abstract term denoting a structural description of social processes."[23]

Hunter's concept of power was spelled out further in a series of postulates and hypotheses regarding power structure. First among these was the idea that "power involves relationships between individuals and groups, both controlled and controlling," and because of this, "it can be described structurally."[24] Closely allied to this notion was another: "Power of the individual must be structured into associational, clique, or institutional patterns to be effective."[25] Further, "power is a relatively constant factor in social relationships with policies as variables."[26] From this third proposition Hunter deduced two corollaries: (a) "Wealth, social status, and prestige are factors in the 'power constant' "; and (b) "Variation in the strength between power units, or a shift in policy within one of these units, affects the whole power structure."[27] These propositions, or postulates, were taken by Hunter to be self-evident and formed what he called the "mental backdrop" to his research. Three other propositions were put forward by Hunter as hypotheses: (1) "Power is exercised as a necessary function in social relationships." (2) "The exercise of power is limited and directed by the formulation and extension of social policy within a framework of socially sanctioned authority." (3) "In a given power unit (organization) a smaller number of individuals will be found formulating and extending policy than those exercising power."[28]

Even if one does not agree with these propositions, they do provide a useful insight into the sociological concept of power.[20] That concept can be summarized in two assertions: (1) power exists; and (2) power refers to social, rather than physical, aspects of action.

For all its apparent simplicity, the first assertion (that power exists) requires comment, since it reflects an underlying willingness to accept the reality of power in social life which is not shared by all students of community power. This acceptance of power appears to be based, first, upon a recognition of the importance attached to the study of power by many generations of political and social analysts—from Plato to Russell, Jouvenel, and other theorists.[30] Far more significant than this historical relevance of power, however, is the importance of power from the point of view of sociological theory. "Power," said Hunter, "is exercised as a necessary function in social relationships," from which it follows that "power is a relatively constant factor" in these relationships. It is not essential here to discuss the sociological theory of stratification, on which such propositions are grounded.[31] What is important is that as a sociologist, Hunter *began* his researches by relating the study of power to an accepted body of theory. The study of power was thus legitimized within the framework of a discipline, and the researcher working within that framework was able to proceed on the basis of that discipline's definition of reality, which delimited the data he would accept as reflective of power relations

Concept of Community Power

That the concept "power" refers to social phenomena follows directly from several of Hunter's preliminary propositions. Hunter's starting point was the notion, expressed pithily by C. Wright Mills, that "power is not of a man."[32] In order for an individual's power to be effective at the community level, argued Hunter, "it must be structured into associational, clique, or institutional patterns." Note that Hunter did *not* say that individuals have no power. Indeed, he implied that *all* individuals have power, but not *community* power. But community, for Hunter, meant a set of recurring relationships among people, which constitute a separately identifiable social system.[33] Power, as part of this social system, involved just one set of these "relationships between individuals and groups," specifically, that set which had to do with the making of community policies. Thus, although all individuals held and exercised power; unless they participated in the set of relationships which had to do with community policy, they

could not, in Hunter's terms, be said to exercise community power.[34]

Note that this conception of a community social system and of power as an aspect of that system emphasizes *relationships* between people; that is, it is the interaction between people which actually defines both "community" and "power." Thus, while men in action provide the empirical data about power, it is the interaction between them, rather than their individual behavior, that is of central importance. These interactions or relationships could be described structurally, said Hunter, so that power became "an abstract term denoting a structural description of social processes." Clearly, Hunter's concept is similar to that of other sociologists, who understand social systems as systems of action in which the basic unit of description is summed up by another abstract term, role.[35] In these terms, Hunter's examination of the Regional City power structure involved answering the question: "Through what roles is the function of making community policies performed?"

The concept of the community as a social system proved useful to Hunter in a number of ways. To assume that several different structures exist together as a system, of course, implies that there is some necessary interrelationship between structures. Some of these interrelationships were indicated by Hunter when he postulated that "wealth, social status, and prestige are factors in the 'power constant.' " Similarly, he viewed the power structure itself as a delicately balanced system of interaction: "Variation in the strength between power units, or a shift in policy within one of these units, affects the whole power structure." In addition, Hunter suggested that, coincident with the social system, there was a system of beliefs which created a community consensus on the use of power: "The exercise of power is limited and directed by the formulation and extension of social policy within a framework of socially sanctioned authority." The system, then, is not only interdependent in terms of structures of action, but there is an over-all structure of beliefs that binds the various structures together.

It is important to understand that all these ideas were developed by Hunter *before* he did any field work in Regional City.[36] Drawing upon his familiarity with a large body of political thought and sociological theory, Hunter determined in advance to look at Regional City as a system of inter-dependent structured roles, and to focus his attention on just one of those roles. Hunter simply assumed that such a view would prove useful. Whether the assumption was justified would depend on his ability to get an answer to his concrete research question (i.e., through what roles is the function of making community policies performed?). It is also important to understand exactly how much was assumed in Hunter's formulation of the question. Hunter's definition of power involved the notion that it was unequally distributed (certain roles are more powerful than others) and that it was structured (certain roles are repeatedly involved in the exercise of power). His problem was to discover which roles in fact exercised community power, and the solution might have involved any of the social roles which made up the community (although past studies had indicated that certain roles were more likely to be powerful than others). Thus, while it is true that Hunter assumed a "structured" way of making community decisions, it would not be fair to charge that the roles he named as most powerful (businessman and banker, primarily) were also "assumed" rather than "discovered."

Analysis of Criticism

From this point of view, of course, much of the Kaufman-Jones criticism of Hunter appears wide of the mark, since it made little or no attempt to come to grips with the intellectual underpinning of Hunter's study. The result was curious: instead of criticizing the work that Hunter had done, Kaufman and Jones criticized Hunter for doing the wrong kind of work![37]

Idea of Ruling Elite

Other political scientists, however, soon became interested in providing a more direct confrontation to the sociological frame-work. Robert A. Dahl set the tone for several other critical articles by attacking the scientific value of the idea of a ruling elite.[38] His objection to the notion that some "they" run things in a community or in the nation was that the concept, as it had been formulated (by Hunter and Mills, in particular), could be neither verified nor proved false. This kind of theory, argued Dahl, was clearly unsatisfactory: "Whatever else it may be, a theory that cannot even in principle be controverted by empirical evidence is not a scientific theory."[39]

Could the concept of ruling elites be formulated to allow scientific verification? Dahl implied that he was not certain that this was possible, but he suggested some requirements to effect such a transformation. First, the meaning of the concept of "elite" must be carefully defined. For Dahl, a ruling elite "is a controlling group less than a majority in size. ... It is a minority of individuals whose preferences regularly prevail in cases of differences in preference. ... If we are to avoid an infinite regress of explanations, the composition of the ruling elite must be more or less definitely specified."[40] This concept could be stated in a testable form: "The hypothesis ... would run along these lines: Such and such a political system (the U.S., the U.S.S.R., New Haven, or the like) is a ruling elite system in which the ruling elite has the following membership. Membership would then be specified by name, position, socio-economic class, socio-economic roles, or what not."[41]

In order to test this kind of proposition, argued Dahl, great care would have to be exercised. In the simplest possible situation, he wrote, we can:

> Assume that there have been some number . . . of cases where there has been disagreement within the political system on key political choices. Assume further that the hypothetical ruling elite prefers one alternative. Then unless it is true that in all or very nearly all of these cases the alternative preferred by the ruling elite is actually adopted, the hypothesis (that the system is dominated by the specified ruling elite is clearly false.[42]

Dahl did not pretend that the research required by his test would be easily accomplished. But, he wrote, "*I do not see how anyone can suppose that he has established the dominance of a specific group in a community . . . without basing his analysis on the careful examination of a series of concrete decisions*. And these decisions must either constitute the universe or a fair sample from the universe of key political decisions taken in the political system."[43] Dahl, of course, found it "remarkable and indeed astounding" that Hunter had not applied this test to what Dahl referred to as the "major hypothesis" of his study.[44] Hunter, implied Dahl, had in fact applied a number of "improper" tests. He had, in the first place, confused a ruling elite with a group that had merely a high *potential* for control. Potential control is not actual control, and Hunter's failure to deal with specific issues prevented him from making any valid statements about power.[45] Secondly, Hunter appeared to be impressed by the unequal distribution of power in Regional City and may well have allowed his conclusions to be colored by this impression. But, argued Dahl, "it is fallacious to assume that the absence of political equality proves the existence of a ruling elite."[46] Finally, Hunter seemed to be guilty of drawing generalizations from a single type of community decision:

> Neither logically nor empirically does it follow that a group with a high degree of influence over one scope will necessarily have a high degree of influence over another scope within the same system. This is a matter to be determined empirically. . . . [In New Haven] it appears to be the case . . . that the small group that runs urban redevelopment is not the same as the small group that runs public education, and neither is quite the same as the two small groups that run the two parties.[47]

Dahl's criticism was powerfully argued, but it did not develop the conceptual and methodological presuppositions upon which it was based. As Dahl's study of New Haven progressed,[48] however, some of his associates provided a more systematic elaboration of the theoretical bases for their empirical

work. In part, this elaboration grew out of a systematic attack on the assumptions common to the sociological literature; in part it consisted of an exposition of ideas shared by pluralist researchers.

Permanency of Power Distribution

One of the first sociological notions to come under attack was the "presumption that power distributions are a more or less permanent aspect of social structure." "By designating their studies as examinations of power 'structure,' " Polsby wrote, "sociologists have implied that they are studying a repetitive pattern of events. Thus, one of the basic premises of sociological research has been that decision makers are likely to remain the same from issue to issue."[49] This kind of proposition had never been adequately tested, argued Polsby, who then proceeded to provide such a "test." After constructing lists of persons thought to be connected with the decision-making processes in each of three "issue-areas" in the city of New Haven, Polsby examined each list against the other two for an indication of overlapping leadership. Of a total of 1,029 persons included in the three leadership lists, only thirty-two were found to be active in more than one issue-area, from which the conclusion was drawn "that leaders were largely specialized in each of these three issue-areas."[50] The apparent implication was that no stable or repetitive structure of power existed in New Haven.

This denial of the permanency of power automatically raises a number of questions about the relationship between power and other structural aspects of social life. As noted earlier, sociological theory holds that power is likely to be very closely associated with wealth, social class, and social status. From an individual point of view, a man of great power would probably also be a man of great wealth and prestige. And, from a structural point of view, those fulfilling the role of decision maker would probably also stand close to the top of the class and status structures. Conceiving of any particular social system in this way permits sociologists to gather data efficiently and to generate hypotheses concerning the nature of the particular social unit under investigation. Moreover, since these structures are so closely related in theory, understanding something about any one or two of them would theoretically help in understanding the remaining structures.

But, of course, if there is no such thing as a "power constant," and if instead power is "tied to issues" which "can be fleeting or persistent,"[51] it follows that investigations of social class, status, or prestige are of relatively little use in understanding power. Wealth and prestige may, in fact, be prerequisites of power, "but the circumstances under which this is so remain a question for investigation" and cannot, therefore, be assumed.[52] The idea "that economic value distributions determine other value distributions, hence economic elites determine decisions in other sectors of the community."[53] comes close to Marxism: "By focusing upon economic elites ... research in community power shows the influence of the older, Marxist positions more markedly than the influence of more contemporary theoretical statements."[54] Indeed, current social theory "makes it plain that there is no *necessary* relationship between social, economic, and power elites."[55]

Nor did the validity of "contemporary theoretical statements" have to rest on assertion; there was empirical evidence available to buttress the pluralist position. It was possible to construct the economic elite of New Haven by listing the names of individuals who appeared at the top of various banking, commercial, industrial, and utility hierarchies, as well as individuals whose personal wealth exceeded an arbitrarily selected minimum figure. Such a list included 239 names. A status elite could be compiled by listing the names of those persons subscribing to the New Haven Cotillion of 1951, 1958 and 1959. This list included 231 names. "The possible overlap between these lists, 231 names, contrasts with the fact that only 25 names appear on both lists."[56] Equally important, when these lists were compared with the leadership lists for the three issue-areas previously men-

tioned, almost no overlap was found. Given the lack of significant overlapping between economic and status elites, and given the relatively small proportion of these elites actively engaged in any of the three decision areas, pluralists could argue vigorously against sociological assumptions about the relation of power to wealth, prestige, and so on.[57]

Panel Technique

But if Hunter's sociological assumptions about power were questionable, asking panels of local citizens to verify them was even worse. This technique, which was at the heart of Hunter's work,[58] did not get at *real* power. Instead, pluralists argued it could only get at reputation, i.e., the reputation for being influential. Not all reputations are deserved, and only those with *both* reputation and power ought to be called real leaders. "In other words, asking about reputations is asking, at a remove, about behavior. It can be cogently argued that the researcher should therefore make it his business to study the requisite behavior directly, and not depend on second-hand opinions."[59]

Most of the "reputational" researchers (e.g., Hunter), however, had paid little attention to actual behavior, preferring instead to rely on rankings of individuals according to how much general power they possess. But if "an individual's political power varies with different issues," as the pluralists asserted, then general power rankings had to be misleading. Wolfinger wrote:

In order to compare the power of two individuals one must either assume that power is distributed evenly for all scopes or present a different set of rankings for each scope. Otherwise, if A is judged to be the most powerful man in town on school affairs and B is named the most powerful on urban renewal there is no way to compare their power except by asserting that power in one scope is more "important" than in another. Most of the reputational researchers, by their failure to specify scopes in soliciting reputations for influence, assume that the power of their leader-nominees is equal for

all issues. . . . This is an exceedingly dubious
assumption. It is improbable, for instance,
that the same people who decide which
houses of prostitution are to be protected . . .
also plan the public school curriculum.[60]

Impossibility of Gaining Reliable Information

The failure to examine actual influence
exerted by individuals on specified issues
places the reputational method in disrepute
because of the impossibility of gaining reliable information from panel interviews. According to the pluralists, several conditions
make it impossible to rely on panel interviews for knowledge of the power structure.
First, there must always be a discrepancy
—sometimes serious—between the question
the researcher thinks he is asking and
the question the respondent thinks is being
asked. Asked "Who runs this town?" a
respondent may give an answer based on a
considerably different idea of what is meant
by "runs" than that held by the investigator. Since this problem is unavoidable,
questions of reputation can never be certain
to give the information that the researcher
seeks.[61]

Confusion Between Power and Status

Second, questions of reputation often
produce answers which confuse power and
status, or which fail to distinguish between
public and private scopes of influence. Thus
respondents may offer names of persons who
have high status because they are well known
even though such persons may not actually
wield power.[62] In New Haven, for example,
high-status people had almost completely
withdrawn from party politics and municipal office. The attempt to avoid this difficulty
by using a carefully selected panel can end
only in failure, for evidence available to
pluralists suggests that there are no specially
knowledgeable groups within the community.
Furthermore, since most of these special
panels tend to be drawn from high-status
groups, their answers can reflect only the
interests of their particular social stratum:

> Businessmen, when asked questions about
> "projects," are apt to base their answers on
> those types of private activity in which they

are most active and influential, and which
are most salient to them. . . .

> In these circumstances, questions which
> do not distinguish between status and power,
> and between public and private scopes, are
> likely to lead researchers to leader-nominees
> whose power may be exercised chiefly on a
> country club's admissions committee.[63]

The only way to minimize ambiguity, argue
the pluralists, is to specify types of decisions:

> A man willing to assert that Yankee bankers
> run "everything" might make a more
> cautious reply when asked specifically about
> the municipal welfare department.[64]

Ignorance of Power Distribution

Yet even this specificity is not likely to be
of much use in the face of a third defect of
the reputational approach: respondents are
not likely to have an accurate perception of
the local distribution of power. Existing
literature on communities makes it clear that
private citizens know little about the actual
power system. More significantly, interviews
with persons in New Haven who were active
in community affairs suggested that these
people, too, knew relatively little about who
held power. Wolfinger's question follows
naturally:

> If people who are professionally involved in
> community decision-making cannot perceive
> accurately the distribution of political
> power, how can the rankings of less well-
> informed respondents be accepted as any-
> thing more than a report of public opinion
> on politics?[65]

Unity of Elite Group

The final major defect of the reputational
approach noted by pluralists is its failure to
distinguish friends and enemies in the elite.
It is not enough simply to demonstrate the
existence of an elite, assuming that such a
demonstration is possible. It must also be
shown, argued the pluralists, that members
of the elite groups are willing to act together
for control. "The actual political effectiveness of a group," wrote Dahl, "is a function
of its potential for control *and* its potential
for unity."[66] In other words, those identified
as members of the elite must be shown to

agree on key political alternatives and on some set of specific actions for implementing decisions. Sociologists have generally inferred this kind of unity from the similarity of the class or status position of their reputational elite. But, the pluralists argue, "it is a mistake to impute to the apparently inescapable fact of class membership any sort of class consciousness. . . . It is equally incorrect to presume that those sharing similar market or status positions are also equidistant to all the bases of political power, or in fact share class interests."[67] Individual decisions "affect people's interests differentially, and people participate in those areas they care about the most," not on the basis of vaguely defined class interests, but rather on the basis of individual interests.[68] And, "the public sector of activity . . . [is] but one facet of behavior capable of giving people satisfaction."[69]

> If a man's major life work is banking, the pluralist presumes he will spend his time at the bank, and not in manipulating community decisions. This presumption holds until the banker's activities and participation indicate otherwise. . . . In the absence of the requisite activities, we have no grounds for asserting that the banker, in fact, does run the community.[70]

Pluralist Approach

It became quite clear that, from the pluralist point of view, neither the theoretical assumptions nor the techniques of investigation used by such sociologists as Hunter were acceptable. In their place, pluralist scholars offered an alternative approach designed to bring scientific precision to the study of power. It is interesting—and probably significant—to note that pluralists seemed to believe that their "scientific" work was paving the way to new knowledge. Curiously enough, wrote Dahl, "the systematic study of power is very recent, precisely because it is only lately that serious attempts have been made to formulate the concept rigorously enough for systematic study."[71] These recent attempts at scientific rigor were attributed to Harold Lasswell, whose important theoretical contributions and insistence upon conceptual clarity in the study of politics provided a seminal influence for later pluralist research.[72] Despite the acknowledged stature of Lasswell, the specific point of departure for pluralists was Dahl's article on the concept of power.[73]

Dahl's Concept of Power

Dissatisfied with the ambiguities surrounding the notion of power, Dahl here made an attempt to set out a more precise explication of the power concept and to indicate how such a reformulation could be made operational. Dahl's starting point was the intuitive notion that "*A* has power over *B* to the extent that he can get *B* to do something that *B* would not otherwise do."[74] To make this intuitive notion more precise. Dahl suggested a fourfold conception of the power relationship between *A* and *B*. A complete statement, he argued, would have to include references to the *base*, source, or domain of one actor's power over another, the *means* or instruments used in the exertion of power, the *amount* or extent of the power, and the *scope* or range of power. Clarifying his meaning, Dahl continued:

> The base of an actor's power consists of all the resources . . . that he can exploit in order to affect the behavior of another. . . .
> In a sense, the base is inert, passive. It must be exploited in some fashion if the behavior of others is to be altered. The *means* or instruments of such exploitation are numerous; often they involve threats or promises to employ the base in some way and they may involve actual use of the base. . . .
> Thus the means is a mediating activity by *A* between *A*'s base and *B*'s response. The *scope* consists of *B*'s responses. . . .
> The *amount* of an actor's power can be represented by a probability statement: e.g., "the chances are 9 out of 10 that if the President promises a judgeship to five key Senators, the Senate will not override his veto," etc. Clearly the amount can only be specified in conjunction with the means and scope.[75]

Dahl demonstrated the utility of his concept by ranking a group of U. S. Senators in terms of the amount of power each of them had with respect to Senate approval of foreign policy and tax measures. With considerable statistical ingenuity, Dahl concluded that, in the Senate, in the period 1946–1954, Senator George had high influence over foreign policy decisions and that Senator Byrd had high influence over tax and economic policy decisions.[76]

Dahl's Approach to Concept of Power
Neither Dahl's techniques nor his conclusions are as interesting, however, as his approach to both. It is clear that in thinking of power, Dahl was thinking primarily in terms of the *individual*. His basic unit of study is the actor and, while the possibility of applying this term to larger social aggregates (such as corporations or nations) is envisioned, his suggestions for research work are specifically aimed at precise measurements of the power of individuals.[77] Only briefly did he suggest that the problem might concern a relationship among people, and this recognition was quickly disavowed as he demonstrated the utility of his approach to power.[78] Thus, in his power rankings of U. S. Senators, Dahl approached each Senator as an independent individual with no identity save the individuality of his name. That Senator George was long chairman of the Senate Foreign Relations Committee, for example, was not considered in Dahl's attempt to attribute a power rank to him. The obvious implication—which contrasts sharply with the sociological approach discussed earlier—is that Dahl was not interested in the U. S. Senate viewed as a form of *social system* in which certain roles are enacted by certain Senators. His concern is rather for individuals conceived to be free from any permanent or systematic relationship to any other persons or things.[79] One begins to see here the basis for the pluralist view of the community as nothing more than an aggregation of individuals.

But individuals are important only because they are the holders, or carriers, of power, and the ultimate purpose of Dahl's work was to be able to rank specific individuals in terms of the precise amounts of power they wielded.[80] This objective suggests that power is something which exists independently of individuals, and that powerful individuals are persons who possess great quantities of power. It follows that power is also external to the observer, separate externally from other entities, and therefore capable of precise measurement. With these assumptions, it becommes easier to understand the pluralist stress on the development of objective techniques for measuring power, the denial of any necessary relationship between power and class or status, and the desire to get at "real" power rather than illusions of power.[81] Pluralist reluctance to make any substantive assumptions about the distribution of power in advance of empirical work is also clarified; for if there *is* power in the community that is *not* necessarily permanently linked to anything else, then power can be found anywhere—distributed at random, so to speak. Any preliminary assumptions concerning the location of power would necessarily then, run the grave risk of overlooking real power.

Pluralist View of Human Behavior
However, if individuals have power, the major pluralist problem is that they do not seem to have it for very long. Issues arise and are resolved, and for each different issue a different group of individuals is active in bringing about a decision and can therefore be said to have power with respect to that decision. This coming and going of power-holders accords with a fundamental concept of pluralist thought, namely, that human behavior is "governed in large part by inertia."[82] As used by pluralists, the notion of inertia involves two subsidiary assumptions. The first is that most people are motivated by self-interest; the second is that they are rationally aware of their interests and know how to enhance them. Thus, most people, because their interests are satisfied, are content to continue to do what they have always done, unless their interests are sufficiently threatened. Since each individual has different interests, each issue-area will arouse a distinct group of individuals to action designed to protect or advance their interests. Those who do not become involved can

only be said to be not interested. Thus, power will be held by a great many people in any given community, depending upon the number and nature of the issues that arise.[83] And unless divisive issues arise, there will be no grounds for concluding anything about power, for without issues there will be no activity indicative of power; and without "the requisite activities, we have no grounds for asserting that the banker [or anyone else], in fact, does run the community."[84]

None of this should be taken to mean that pluralists will not be able to find a power structure if one exists; on the contrary,

> pluralists want to find out about leadership *roles*, which are presumed to be diverse and fluid, both within a single issue-area over time, and as between issue areas. . . .
>
> By describing and specifying leadership roles in concrete situations, pluralists are in a position to determine the extent to which power structure exists. If there exists a high degree of overlap among issue areas in decision-making personnel, or of institutionalization in the bases of power in specified issue areas, or of regularity in the procedures of decision-making, then the empirical conclusion is justified that some sort of a "power structure" exists. By specifying leadership roles and activities, the pluralist research strategy makes it possible for an empirical determination of the bounds and durability of a community "power structure" —if one exists—to be described.[85]

In summary, then, pluralist assumptions concerning power begin with a view of society (or community, or any other social unit' as an aggregation of different individuals motivated by self-interest, predominantly rational (in the sense that they are conscious of their interests and active in seeking their fulfillment), and free from any permanent relationships with anyone or anything else. In order to make any generalizations about community power, therefore, it becomes necessary to give the closest kind of examination to all—or at least the crucial —issues. Alternatively it is possible, though much more difficult, to examine each individual in the community with a view to identifying the extent or amount of his power. Thus, in this view,

> the community power structure . . . becomes an inventory of leaders classified according to the numbers and kinds of decisions they make, or an inventory of policy-areas classified according to the ways in which policy outcomes are achieved. Special and general, repetitive and random aspects of community power can be identified by using these inventories.[86]

All this represents a point of view which contrasts sharply with the sociological outlook described above. Sociologists are interested in analyzing communities as systems of action; pluralists see communities as nothing more than aggregations of individuals whose behavior, far from being systematic in any way, is more or less randomly determined. The sociologist understands power as one aspect of all human action and closely related to other aspects; the pluralist thinks of power as a substance, separate from other substances, and therefore, capable of being weighed and measured. The basic unit of analysis for the sociologist is the role, composed of repeated actions of persons in the system; the basic unit of analysis for the pluralist is the actor-individual, whose actions are seen as basically unique and nonrepetitive. On these bases alone it is possible to join in Polsby's doubt that sociologists and pluralists do, in fact, study the same phenomena.[87]

Evaluation of Pluralist Approach

In view of these striking differences in interpretation, and in view of pluralist criticisms of the sociological tools of investigation outlined here, it becomes pertinent to ask whether the claims that have been made on behalf of pluralism are justified. Exactly how useful is the pluralist approach in developing empirical generalizations concerning community power?

Pessimism
Pluralists themselves tend to be rather pessimistic about the usefulness of their approach for developing generalizations. The whole problem of power is terribly complex, and since systematic study of the

problem is very recent, generalizations are not likely to be produced until some time in the distant future, if at all. Dahl, for example, noting that operational definitions of power are likely to differ widely because of differences in problems attacked, concluded that

> we are not likely to produce—certainly not for some considerable time to come—anything like a single, consistent, coherent "Theory of Power." We are much more likely to produce a variety of theories of limited scope, each of which employs some definition of power that is useful in the context of the particular piece of research or theory but different in important respects from the definitions of other studies. Thus we may never get through the swamp. But it looks as if we might someday get around it.[88]

It must be admitted that this pessimism is well founded, primarily because the pluralist scheme of analysis is ill-suited to drawing significant conclusions about community power. Generalizations—or theories—are usually based upon concepts that define the data and thus determine the kind of generalizations which can be made. Since the link between concepts and theories is so close, it is always necessary to exercise great care in the use of both. If one wishes to derive generalizations about community power, one must be sure to use concepts which define community power, so that significant empirical data can be gathered. As Marion Levy has written, "conceptual work in empirical science cannot be carried out in a vacuum. One must always know to some degree for what purpose concepts are to be used."[89]

Now it is a curious thing that the pluralists, who are so anxious to give precise measurement to *community* power, attempt to do so with an analytic scheme that places all its emphasis on *individual* power. If the community is seen as simply a collection of individuals who have differing amounts of power depending on the issue, then to determine the power structure, all that is required—according to the pluralist literature —is the discovery of those individuals who were active in decision making on selected key decisions. If the same people are found to make all or most of these key decisions (a

finding that no pluralist has yet made), the conclusion is warranted that a power structure exists, and these individuals comprise it. Logically, of course, such a conclusion cannot follow from pluralist assumptions, for the simple reason that examination of selected issues can reveal only the power of selected individuals, not the power of every individual or group of individuals in the community; therefore there is no basis for concluding that the group named as the power structure does in fact have more power than any other possible group.

Definition of Community Power
While it would appear to be somewhat ridiculous to require investigation of every individual and combination of individuals in a community before coming to any conclusions about power, that is nevertheless the logical outcome of a viewpoint which disclaims the utility of assuming any relationship between power and social structure. "The first, and perhaps most basic presupposition of the pluralist approach," wrote Polsby,

> is that nothing categorical can be assumed about power in any community. It rejects the stratification thesis that *some* group necessarily dominates a community. If anything, there seems to be an unspoken notion among pluralist researchers that at bottom *nobody* dominates in a town so that their first question to a local informant is not likely to be, "Who runs this community?" but rather, "Does anyone at all run this community?"[90]

In a similar vein, Dahl argued that "there is no more *a priori* reason to assume that a ruling elite does exist than to assume that one does not exist."[91] Thus, in the New Haven study, the first decision made by Dahl and his associates was "that no *a priori* assumptions would be entertained about the location in the population of 'real' ... community decision-makers."[92] But if nothing is assumed about power and if the community is defined as simply a collection of individuals with no permanent relationships to other persons or things, the form of community power structure cannot be determined unless all individuals are examined. As Dahl himself admitted, "unless we use the test [his test for a ruling elite system, described above] on every possible combination of individuals in the community, we cannot be certain that there is not some combination that constitutes a ruling elite."[93]

Fortunately, pluralists have shown themselves willing to sacrifice precise measurement for a more manageable research strategy, which involves (as noted earlier) close examination of selected issues. By careful selection and analysis of a few key community issues, pluralists have argued, inferences can be drawn concerning the whole spectrum of community power, without examining *all* decisions and *all* individuals who could be involved. This is certainly a reasonable position to take, but its utility depends entirely upon the community characteristics of the issues selected for analysis. A community study requires the research worker to select from all the data available to him those data which represent something called the "community." He must, in effect, draw an imaginary circle which separates that which is community from that which is not community. In order to draw this circle, he must have some idea of what he means by community, for unless he has an idea, he will have no criteria for choosing to deal with one kind of data rather than another. And if he is not clear about the bases for his choice of data then he will not understand the meaning of his findings. He may present material which reflects national or regional patterns and refer to it as "community" material. Or, at the other extreme, he may present data reflecting patterns of subcommunity behavior as community behavior. Thus, the researcher may find himself talking not about community, but about something which is more or less than community. Only if the issues selected for examination reflect the community level of generality can any inferences be drawn about community power.[94]

From this point of view, all pluralist conclusions concerning community power must be held suspect, for the pluralist literature does not attempt to come to grips with the notion of community. Instead, such issues as the protection of bawdy houses, the development of an urban renewal program, the control of public education, and the control of individual municipal agencies are all lumped together as though they possessed the same level of significance for the same social group, namely, the community. The criteria which led pluralists to treat such issues as community issues are not readily apparent. In the absence of criteria of this kind to distinguish between "community power" and "power exercised in the community," examination of specific issue-areas will produce little more than information concerning which individuals were involved in making specific policy decisions. Only when such decisions become identified as community decisions will information about them become relevant to the problem of community power.

Concept of Inertia

Other aspects of pluralist methodology create similarly important problems. Consider again, for example, the fundamental pluralist notion of "inertia" and the corresponding willingness "to put a high value on overt activity as indicative of involvement in issues." Does the concept "inertia" refer to lack of public involvement and does it apply to all individuals in the community, except in the development of an issue? If so, then the effect is to deny any public involvement—really to deny power—except in issues which may arise. Surely this cannot be the pluralist intention, for every community has some formal government continually active in public affairs, and such an assumption would deny its existence. On the other hand, if the continuous public activity of the formal government is admitted and considered to show inertia, does not the inertia of an agency active in public affairs imply a structure of power, in the sense of a recurring and repeated pattern of power interaction? Inertia cannot easily be ascribed to some and denied to others, for it is a fundamental concept of human behavior and therefore must apply to all individuals. The notion of inertia, then, forces the pluralist either to deny the existence of government as a wielder of power, or to admit that power is, in fact, a structured and therefore a recurring phenomenon.

Public as Opposed to Private Power

But the dilemma is never squarely faced. The pluralist can avoid it by the simple expedient of drawing a distinction between public and private power and asserting that he is interested in public power. Yes, all human behavior is conditioned by inertia, but there are some people (government officials) who have a continuing interest and are continually active in public affairs. For these people, inertia simply means continuation of activity which has to do with power. This continuation, however, does not imply structure, because of differences in the scope of power exercised by these public officials. Some, for example, decide school affairs, while others run the water department or decide which houses of prostitution shall be protected. Note, too, that the power of all these people is public, in the sense of being connected with public agencies. Businessmen, farmers, manufacturers, or just plain citizens also have inertia, but their inertia does not involve public agencies and therefore does not involve power. Only when their interests are affected by issues do such people become publicly active as power wielders. Unless these issues somehow involve public officials, however, no power will be involved and therefore it is economical for the pluralist to concentrate on public agencies and officials as the primary focus of inquiry. Thus, Wolfinger chided Hunter for his failure to distinguish "between public and private scopes" of power, and suggested that there is little value in discovering leaders "whose power may be exercised chiefly on a country club's admission committee." Far from denying the power of government agencies, then, pluralists have apparently concluded by *defining* power—and their research interests—in terms of public agencies!

Ambiguity of Pluralist Position

And what a curious twist this is. Under the guise of science we have now been led back to a disciplinary outlook whose inadequacy was the chief *raison d'être* for the increased interest in scientific method in postwar political science. Surely the study of power must involve more than the actions of government agencies. The pluralist approach seems to raise the question of the nature of political science as "science." Perhaps the fact that this is still a question helps to explain some of the deficiencies in that approach. Unlike sociology, political science has not yet reached even a modicum of agreement as to what it is all about and how it should treat terms such as "power."

Ambiguity with regard to the concept of power is a central characteristic of the pluralism discussed here. What, for example, could the pluralist conclude about the community in which no issues ever became subject to public dispute, or in which there was little or no overt political activity? Such communities are hardly atypical. Indeed, one of the most penetrating community studies yet published, *Small Town in Mass Society*, analyzed just such a case.[95] Yet on the basis of what has been presented here the pluralist would be forced to conclude that no power was being exercised in communities of this kind, presumably because everyone was content with the existing state of affairs (or at least not discontented enough to protest). So stated, the pluralist conclusion reveals an interesting conception of power not only as something physical, but also as something usable only in situations of *open conflict*. Since power depends upon the existence of conflict (or issues), there can be no power unless there is recognizable competition between individuals or groups. Thus all that has been learned in the twentieth century about the psychology of mass manipulation or about the persuasive power of such devices as credit, jobs, or social ostracism is ignored by this curiously one-sided notion of power.[96]

It might be suggested, of course, that many of the difficulties which could be expected to arise from this narrow view would normally be avoided, provided that pluralist researchers dug deeply enough, and were intuitive enough, to recognize conflict that was not apparent on the surface of community life. The question is, however, whether pluralism provides any reason for digging below the surface. The answer would appear to be that it does not. Pluralists quite vigorously deny the permanency of power—or to put it differently, that power is structured in any way. Thus if superficial evidence suggests that no power exists in a particular community, pluralist presuppositions warrant the conclusion that any further examination might well turn out to be a waste of time. Such a conclusion would be supported, secondly, by the inertia postulate that the basic reason for lack of public conflict is agreement: If citizens are satisfied enough to be inactive, there must be some minimal agreement on the course of public events.

Beyond this, there is the question of whether persons using pluralist methodology could recognize issues. Issues can be defined either by the observer's commitment to an ideological outlook that defines important problems or by his ability to comprehend fully the issue definitions of the people he studies. The pluralist literature, however, claims no ideology, other than commitment to empirical science—a commitment which emphasizes that which is rather than that which ought to be. And interestingly enough, pluralist ability to get "into the heads" of its subjects appears to be hampered by a similar acceptance of the existing political order.[97] The difference between the two questions that might be asked—"Why don't more people get involved in politics?" and "Why do people become involved in politics?"[98]— can be the difference between a critique and an apology.

None of the preceding criticism should be taken lightly, for pluralism claims greater scientific value than has previously been apparent in studies of community power. Yet this claim rests upon a method of analyzing power that has very limited utility. In studying the legislatures of certain (perhaps most) American states, for example, it would be difficult to avoid coming to ridiculous conclusions if one began with the assumption that only the observable activi-

ties of legislators and lobbyists were important.[99] Nor would it be any less difficult to make sense out of totalitarian systems of government if it were initially assumed that lack of protest signified satisfaction. Surely the historic passivity of the Southern Negro, for example, was due to something other than satisfaction with his position in Southern communities.[100] Considerations of this kind suggest that one of the major problems of the pluralist method is that it assumes too much and thereby begs a number of significant questions. Instead of relying on an independently derived formulation of the problem of power to reach empirical conclusions, pluralist assumptions of "inertia" and "satisfaction" are bootlegged into the analysis to explain phenomena (such as nonparticipation) which cannot be explained adequately by the original analytic scheme. The extent to which "inertia" or "satisfaction" may be important in a given community, of course, should be determined empirically. To assume them is to avoid the important question of what specific conditions produce inertia in a given community and the equally important question of how these conditions are brought about. The failure of pluralists to give empirical data for such significant problems suggests an ideological rather than a scientific orientation.[101]

Conclusion

Enough has been said here to provide some basis for the proposition that the so-called "pluralist alternative" is not as scientifically sound as some of its proponents would have us believe. Political scientists would do well to exercise some caution before rushing to follow this lead in analyzing community power. Yet, for all its defects, this approach is extremely important, precisely because it states a reasoned approach to the study of power and applies it to a level of government that offers many thousands of laboratories in which the approach can be modified, rejected, or confirmed. In the long run, differences of interpretation between sociological and pluralist schools of thought will have to be resolved in these laboratories.

In order for any such resolution to come about, however, it will be necessary to deal with the unsolved problem of defining "community." Neither sociologists nor pluralists have applied themselves very vigorously to this problem; as a result, much of their public dispute has been at cross-purposes.[102] Two further lines of inquiry may prove useful. One would attempt to come to grips with the problem posed by C. Wright Mills by asking the questions: "To what extent is power in American society organized at the local level? What kind of power is in fact exercised by American communities? What kind of power seems to be exercised predominantly by larger social units of one kind or another?"[103] Political scientists will recognize in these questions a problem familiar to them, that of federalism. What is suggested here is a re-examination of this concept using detailed empirical investigations to the fullest extent possible as a supplement to institutional analysis.[104] The second profitable line of inquiry would attempt a classification of communities according to those characteristics that define them as communities and according to the kinds of power characteristically located at the community level. Some work has begun already in this area, with impressive and potentially fruitful results.[105]

One final word: while it is important to recognize differences in interpretation, it is equally important not to be overcome by them. The final object, after all, is understanding, and no interpretive scheme can properly claim a monopoly here. George Santayana put it:

> No language or logic is right in the sense of being identical with the facts it is used to express, but each may be right by being faithful to these facts, as a translation may be faithful. My endeavor is to think straight in such terms as are offered to me, to clear my mind of cant and free it from the cramp of artificial traditions; but I do not ask anyone to think in my terms if he prefers others. Let him clean better, if he can, the windows of his soul, that the variety and beauty of the prospect may spread more brightly before him.[106]

Notes

1. This is a revised version of an earlier paper prepared for the Metropolitan Studies Unit of the Fels Institute of Local and State Government, University of Pennsylvania. I am indebted to Professor James G. Coke, former supervisor of the Unit, and to Professor Stephen B. Sweeney, Director of the Fels Institute, for providing the opportunity to review the literature on which this paper is based. In addition, I owe a great debt to my friends Herbert V. Gamberg, Henry W. Bruck, Cyril B. Roseman, Richard L. Sklar, and Oliver P. Williams for their incisive and valuable criticisms of the ideas expressed in this paper.

2. Some representative studies include: Robert S. and Helen Merrell Lynd, *Middletown* (New York, 1929) and *Middletown in Transition* (New York, 1937); Allison Davis, Burleigh B. Gardner, and Mary R. Gardner, *Deep South* (Chicago, 1941); James West, *Plainville, U.S.A.* (New York, 1945); Granville Hicks, *Small Town* (New York, 1946); John Dollard, *Caste and Class in a Southern Town* (2nd ed.; New York, 1949); W. Lloyd Warner, *et al.*, *Democracy in Jonesville* (New York, 1949); and Arthur J. Vidich and Joseph Bensman, *Small Town in Mass Society* (Princeton, 1958). For an interesting recent interpretation of American community studies, see Maurice R. Stein, *The Eclipse of Community* (Princeton, 1960). Why political scientists failed to pay much attention to earlier sociological analyses of American communities is an interesting question. Perhaps governmental reform has been a more important objective for political scientists than understanding. For a critique of the traditional political science approach to the study of local government, see Lawrence J. R. Herson, The Lost World of Municipal Government, *American Political Science Review*, 15 (1957), 330–345.

3. Herbert Kaufman and Victor Jones, The Mystery of Power, *Public Administration Review*, 14 (Summer, 1954), 205–212.

4. *Ibid.*, p. 212.

5. *Ibid.*, p. 210.

6. *Ibid.*, p. 211.

7. *Ibid.*, p. 209.

8. *Ibid.*, p. 208.

9. *Ibid.*, p. 209.

10. *Ibid.*, p. 207.

11. *Ibid.*

12. *Ibid.*, p. 205.

13. *Ibid.*, p. 207.

14. *Ibid.*

15. *Ibid.*, pp. 207–208.

16. *Ibid.*, p. 208.

17. Nelson W. Polsby, How to Study Community Power: The Pluralist Alternative, *Journal of Politics*, 22 (1960), 474–484.

18. Kaufman and Jones, *op. cit.*, p. 208.

19. Examples include Edward C. Banfield, *Political Influence* (Glencoe, Ill., 1961); Robert A. Dahl, *Who Governs? Democracy and Power in an American City* (New Haven, 1961); Norton E. Long, The Local Community as an Ecology of Games, *American Journal of Sociology*, 64 (1958), 251–261; Roscoe C. Martin, *et al.*, *Decisions in Syracuse* (Bloomington, Ind., 1961).

20. David B. Truman, Theory and Research on Metropolitan Political Leadership: Report on a Conference, *Social Science Research Council Items*, 15 (March, 1961), 2.

21. Dahl has already suggested this. See his Business and Politics: A Critical Appraisal of Political Science, in Robert A. Dahl, Mason Haire, and Paul F. Lazarsfeld, *Social Science Research on Business: Product and Potential* (New York, 1959), p. 36.

22. Hunter, [*Community Power Structure* (Chapel Hill: University of North Carolina Press, 1953)], p. 4.

23. *Ibid.*, p. 2.

24. *Ibid.*, p. 6.

25. *Ibid.*

26. *Ibid.*

27. *Ibid.*

28. *Ibid.*, p. 7.

29. No claim is made here that all sociologists would agree with every detail of Hunter's formulation. Instead, what is suggested is that Hunter and most other sociologists share certain basic ideas which provide a rough framework for this kind of research. For typical statements of this framework, see Kingsley Davis, *Human Society* (New York, 1949), pp. 478–508; Robin W. Williams, *American Society* (New York, 1956), pp. 200–264; and Kimball Young, *Sociology* (New York, 1942), pp. 571–608. A useful symposium on the sociology of power may be found in Lewis A. Coser and Bernard Rosenberg, eds., *Sociological Theory: A Book of Readings* (New York, 1957), pp. 123–167.

30. Plato, *The Laws of Plato*, trans. R. G. Bury (Cambridge, Mass., 1952); Plato, *The Statesman*, trans. J. B. Skemp, ed. Martin Ostwald (New York, 1957); Bertrand de Jouvenel, *On Power, Its Nature and the History of Its Growth*, trans. J. F. Huntington (New York, 1948); Bertrand Russell, *Power: A New Social Analysis* (New York, 1938); [Bertrand Russell], *Authority and the Individual* (London, 1949). The literature on power is voluminous; a few examples might include Vilfredo Pareto, *The Mind and Society*, trans. Andrew Bogiorno and Arthur Livingston, ed. Arthur Livingston (New York, 1935); Gaetano Mosca, *The Ruling Class*, ed. Arthur Livingston (New York, 1939); and Lord Cyril Radcliffe, *The Problem of Power* (London, 1952).

31. A near classic in this field is Pitirim Sorokin's *Social Mobility* (New York, 1927). Much of the current sociological literature on stratification adopts some form of functionalist interpretation. The standard references here are Kingsley Davis, A Conceptual Analysis of Stratification, *American Sociological Review*, 7 (1942), 309–332; and Kingsley Davis and Wilbert E. Moore, Some Principles of Stratification, *American Sociological Review*, 10 (1945), 242–249. For a critique of this view see Melvin W. Tumin, Some Principles of Stratification: A Critical Analysis, *American Sociological Review*, 18 (1953), 387–394. Somewhat different functionalist viewpoints are represented by Talcott Parsons, A Revised Analytical Approach to the Theory of Social Stratification, in R. Bendix and S. M. Lipset, eds., *Class, Status and Power* (Glencoe, Ill., 1953), pp. 92–128. Dennis H. Wrong provides a perceptive review of functionalist literature in The Functional Theory of Stratification: Some Neglected Considerations, *American Sociological Review*, 24 (1959), 772–782. Those interested in delving further into this literature will find the following reports useful: Donald G. MacRae, Social Stratification: A Trend Report and Bibliography, *Current Sociology*, 2 (1953–1954), No. 1, entire issue; and Harold W. Pfautz, The Current Literature of Social Stratification: Critique and Bibliography, *American Journal of Sociology*, 58 (1953), 391–418.

32. C. Wright Mills, *The Power Elite* (New York, 1957), p. 11.

33. Hunter, *op. cit.*, pp. 2–3.

34. *Ibid.*, p. 7.

35. Clarification of the role concept is generally attributed to the American anthropologist Ralph Linton. See Linton's work, *The Study of Man* (New York, 1936), pp. 113–119.

36. Hunter describes his study methods in an appendix to his book; see *op. cit.*, pp. 262–271.

37. Kaufman and Jones repeatedly challenged Hunter for his failure to study what he *should* have studied; see notes 12–15.

38. Robert A. Dahl, A Critique of the Ruling Elite Model, *American Political Science Review*, 52 (1958), 463–469.
39. *Ibid.*, p. 463.
40. *Ibid.*, p. 464.
41. *Ibid.*, pp. 464–465.
42. *Ibid.*, p. 466.
43. *Ibid.*
44. *Ibid.*
45. *Ibid.*, p. 465.
46. *Ibid.*
47. *Ibid.*, pp. 465–466.
48. Dahl, *Who Governs?*
49. Nelson W. Polsby, The Sociology of Community Power: A Reassessment, *Social Forces*, 37 (March, 1959), 232.
50. The test is reported in full by Polsby in his Three Problems in the Analysis of Community Power, *American Sociological Review*, 24 (1959), 796–803.
51. Polsby, How to Study Community Power, p. 478.
52. Polsby, Sociology of Community Power, p. 233.
53. *Ibid.*
54. *Ibid.*
55. Polsby, Three Problems in the Analysis of Community Power, p. 800.
56. *Ibid.*
57. The pluralist argument summarized here suffered from a failure to provide an adequate discussion of the criteria which led to the selection of the various elites. The absence of such a discussion rendered it impossible to determine whether and to what extent persons named as members of the various elites actually exercised leadership. Thus the conclusions drawn from overlap or nonoverlap studies were relatively meaningless.
58. See Hunter, *op. cit.*, pp. 262–271.
59. Polsby, Three Problems in the Analysis of Community Power, p. 797.
60. Raymond E. Wolfinger, Reputation and Reality in the Study of Community Power, *American Sociological Review*, 25 (1960), 638.
61. *Ibid.*
62. *Ibid.*, p. 640.
63. *Ibid.*
64. *Ibid.*
65. *Ibid.*, p. 642.
66. Dahl, Critique of the Ruling Elite Model, p. 465.
67. Polsby, How to Study Community Power, p. 481.
68. Polsby, Sociology of Community Power, p. 235.
69. Polsby, How to Study Community Power, p. 480.
70. *Ibid.*, pp. 480–481.
71. Robert A. Dahl, The Concept of Power,

Behavioral Science, 2 (July 1957), p. 201.
72. See, for example, Harold D. Lasswell, *Politics: Who Gets What, When, How* (New York, 1936); also [his] *Power and Personality* (New York, 1948); Lasswell and Abraham Kaplan, *Power and Society: A Framework for Political Inquiry* (New Haven, 1950); Daniel Lerner and Lasswell, eds., *The Policy Sciences: Recent Developments in Scope and Method* (Stanford, Calif., 1951); and Lasswell, Lerner, and C. Easton Rothwell, *The Comparative Study of Elites: An Introduction and Bibliography* (Stanford, Calif., 1952).
73. Dahl, Concept of Power, pp. 201–215.
74. *Ibid.*, pp. 202–203.
75. *Ibid.*, p. 203.
76. *Ibid.*, p. 212.
77. *Ibid.*, pp. 207–208.
78. *Ibid.*, p. 203. Here Dahl writes: "let us agree that power is a relation among people." But then see pp. 209–212 for application of Dahl's methods to the U.S. Senate.
79. Dahl, of course, was primarily interested in the *amount* of power possessed by various Senators. It is conceivable that his notion of *base* would encompass elements of a systematic view of individual power.
80. Dahl, Concept of Power, *passim.*
81. The desire to discover "reality" is one of the strongest themes running through all of the pluralist literature cited here. See, for examples, notes 67, 73, and 74.
82. This "fundamental conception" is discussed by Polsby, How to Study Community Power, pp. 479–481.
83. *Ibid.*
84. *Ibid.*, pp. 480–481.
85. *Ibid.*, pp. 482–483.
86. Polsby, Three Problems in the Analysis of Community Power, p. 800.
87. *Ibid.*, p. 803.
88. Dahl, Concept of Power, p. 202.
89. Marion J. Levy, Jr., *The Structure of Society* (Princeton, 1952), p. 230.
90. Polsby, How to Study Community Power, p. 476.
91. Dahl, Critique of the Ruling Elite Model, p. 467.
92. Polsby, Three Problems in the Analysis of Community Power, p. 797.
93. Dahl, Critique of the Ruling Elite Model, p. 476.
94. Attempts to define "community" have been summarized by George A. Hillery, Jr., Definitions of Community: Areas of Agreement, *Rural Sociology*, 20 (1955), 111–123; see especially his bibliography, pp. 120–123. A sampling of more recent attempts to define "community" might include Otis Dudley Duncan and Albert J.

Reiss, Jr., *Social Characteristics of Urban and Rural Communities, 1950* (New York, 1956); Fenton Keyes, The Correlation of Social Phenomena with Community Size, *Social Forces*, 36 (1958), 311–315; George A. Hillery, Jr., A Critique of Selected Community Concepts, *Social Forces*, 37 (1959), 237–242; and Harold F. Kaufman, Toward an Interactional Conception of Community, *Social Forces*, 38 (1959), 8–17.

95. Vidich and Bensman, [*op. cit.*].

96. Unlike political scientists, sociologists have paid a good deal of attention to techniques of social control other than physical violence. For a sampling of some of the best sociological thinking in this area, including contributions by Edward A. Ross, Emile Durkheim, George Herbert Mead, and Jean Piaget, see Coser and Rosenberg, eds., *op. cit.*, pp. 97–122. William H. Whyte, Jr., documents some of the informal pressures used to control the modern middle-class American at work and at play in *The Organization Man* (New York, 1956). For an interesting and important account of the use of the social sciences to control industrial workers, see Loren Baritz, *The Servants of Power* (Middletown, Conn., 1960).

97. Thus Polsby, for example, commends a recent discussion of an outcast lower-class group in a small town because the authors, "for the first time in a community study, depicted the life of the lowest class groups in the community sufficiently well so that the personally functional aspects of withdrawal from the community were revealed" (How to Study Community Power, p. 484).

98. Dahl has suggested that "it would clear the air of a good deal of nonsense if, instead of assuming that politics is a normal and natural concern of human beings, one were to make the contrary assumption that, whatever lip service citizens may pay to conventional attitudes, politics is a remote, alien, and unrewarding activity. Instead of seeking to explain why citizens are not interested, concerned, and active, the task is to explain why a few citizens are." See Dahl's article, Who Participates in Local Politics and Why, *Science*, 134 (1961), 1342.

99. For example, the well-known tendency of many state legislatures to pass legislation by unanimous or near-unanimous votes could, in these terms, be interpreted to mean that all or most legislators in a given state were agreed on all or most issues. The specific conditions which produce such voting patterns could then be ignored. For a recent work that does not ignore such conditions, see Gilbert Y. Steiner and Samuel K. Gove, *Legislative Politics in Illinois* (Urbana, Ill., 1960).

100. Both Dollard (*op. cit.*, pp. 314–362) and Davis, Gardner, and Gardner (*op. cit.*, pp. 483–538) provide extensive discussions of the sociopolitical techniques used to keep Southern Negroes under control.

101. In a slightly different context, C. Wright Mills attempts to sketch out the ideological underpinnings of the group approach to power (*op. cit.*, pp. 242–268).

102. A major difficulty with Hunter and those who follow him, for example, is the assumption that power is, in fact, organized locally for all purposes and for all things. This may or may not be true in some communities, at some times, and it is always incumbent upon the analyst to demonstrate the extent to which it is or is not true before proceeding to any statements about community power. While such assumptions concerning the location of general power at the community level may well be erroneous, pluralists have not been able to demonstrate it because of their failure to develop any explicit conception of what is meant by community. Thus, pluralists talk about issues, which may or may not be community issues, while the followers of Hunter talk about power, which may or may not be community power.

103. Mills (*op. cit.*, p. 39) writes: "Despite the loyal rhetoric practiced by many Congressional spokesmen, no local society is in truth a sovereign locality. During the past century, local society has become part of a national economy; its status and power hierarchies have come to be subordinate parts of the larger hierarchies of the nation. . . . Today, to remain merely local is to fail; it is to be overshadowed by the wealth, the power, and the status of nationally important men. To succeed is to leave local society behind."

104. The Federalism Workshop of the University of Chicago has been engaged in just this kind of analysis. See Morton Grodzins, "Federalism," in *Goals for Americans* (New York, 1961); and Daniel J. Elazar, "Local Government in Intergovernmental Perspective," in *Illinois Local Government* (Urbana, Ill., 1961).

105. Oliver P. Williams, A Typology for Comparative Local Government, *Midwest Journal of Political Science*, 5 (May 1961), 150–164.

106. George Santayana, *Scepticism and Animal Faith* (New York, 1923), pp. vi–vii.

H. Comparisons of Approaches

Locating Leaders in Local Communities: A Comparison of Some Alternative Approaches*

*Linton C. Freeman, Thomas J. Fararo, Warner Bloomberg, Jr.,†
and Morris H. Sunshine*

Most investigators would probably agree that leadership refers to a complex process whereby a relatively small number of individuals in a collectivity behave in such a way that they effect (or effectively prevent) a change in the lives of a relatively large number. But agreement on theoretical details of the leadership process or on how it is to be studied is another matter. Much of the recent literature on community leadership has been critical.[1] Gibb has suggested that there are a great many *kinds* of leadership—many different ways in which changes may be effected. He has proposed that leaders be assigned to various types including "the initiator, energizer, harmonizer, expediter, and the like."[2] Banfield has stressed the importance of the distinction between intended and unintended leadership.[3] And both Dahl and Polsby have called attention to the desirability of considering the *extent* of the effect a given leader has in expediting a particular change and the *range* of changes over which his effect holds.[4] It seems evident, then, that although these critics might agree with the minimum definition presented above, they would all like to see some additional factors included within its scope.

Polsby has translated the comments of the critics into a set of operational guides for research.[5] He has suggested that a satisfactory study of community leadership must involve a detailed examination of the whole decision-making process as it is exhibited over a range of issues. Here we should have to specify each issue, the persons involved, their intentions, and the extent and nature of their influence if any. Such a program represents an ideal that might be used to think about the process of community leadership. But as a research strategy, this plan raises many problems.

In the first place, both influence and intention are concepts presenting great difficulty in empirical application. Both require that elaborate observational and interviewing procedures be developed, and both raise reliability problems.[6] May we, for example, take a person's word concerning his intentions, or must they be inferred from his behavior? And even when two persons interact and one subsequently changes his stated position in the direction of the views of the other, it is difficult to *prove* that influence has taken place. But even if these questions were eliminated, a practical problem would still remain. To follow the prescriptions

Reprinted from the American Sociological Review, *28 (October 1963), 791–798, by permission of the authors and the American Sociological Association. Copyright 1963 by the American Sociological Association.*

*Support for this study was provided by a grant from the Fund for Adult Education to the University College of Syracuse University.
†In September, 1963, Warner Bloomberg, Jr., joined the faculty of the Department of Urban Affairs, University of Wisconsin at Milwaukee.

listed above would be prohibitively expensive, requiring detailed observation of hundreds (or thousands) of individuals over an extended period. To record all interaction relevant to the decisions under study, it would be necessary to observe each person in a large number of varied situations, many of them quite private. Even then it would be difficult to evaluate the impact of the process of observation itself. Given these considerations, Polsby's ideal has never been reached. All existing studies of community leadership represent some compromise.

Most authors of community leadership studies would probably agree that the critics are on the right track. But most have been willing (or perhaps forced by circumstances) to make one or more basic assumptions in order to achieve a workable research design. Four types of compromise have been common. They will be discussed below.

Perhaps the most realistic of the compromise studies are those based on the assumption that active participation in decision making *is* leadership. Typically, in such studies, one or a series of community decisions are either observed or reconstructed. In so doing, an attempt is made to identify the active participants in the decision-making process. These decision-making studies frequently are restricted to a small number of decisions, and they usually fail to present convincing evidence on the questions of intent and amount of impact. But they do provide a more or less direct index of participation. If they err it is by including individuals who, though present, had little or no impact on the decision. On the face of it this seems preferable to the likelihood of excluding important influentials.[7]

A second compromise approach is to assume that formal authority *is* leadership. Aside from arbitrarily defining which positions are "on top," these studies underestimate the impact of those not in official positions on the outcomes of the decision-making process.

The third approach assumes that leadership is a necessary consequence of social activity. This assumption leads to studies of social participation. Such studies have used everything from rough indexes of memberships in voluntary associations to carefully constructed scales of activity in such associations. In each case it is reasoned that community leadership results from a high degree of voluntary activity in community affairs. The social participation approach is thus the converse of the study of position. While the former stresses activity, the latter is concerned only with formal authority. But to the extent that activity in voluntary associations leads to having an impact upon community change, activists are leaders.

The final approach assumes that leadership is too complex to be indexed directly. Instead of examining leadership as such, proponents of this approach assess reputation for leadership. Their reasoning suggests that all of the more direct approaches neglect one or another key dimensions of the leadership process. They turn, therefore, to informants from the community itself. Often rather elaborate steps have been taken to insure that the informants are indeed informed. For example, positional leaders may be questioned in order to develop a list of reputed leaders or influentials; then the reported influentials are polled to determine the top influentials. In such cases it is reasonable to suppose that the grossly uninformed are ruled out.

Various critics have condemned the indeterminancy and subjectivity of this procedure.[8] But its defenders reason that the reputational approach is the only way to uncover the subtleties of intent, extent of impact, and the like in the leadership process. What, they ask, but a life-long involvement in the activities of a community could possibly yield sophisticated answers to the question "Who are the leaders?" The reputational approach, then, assumes the possibility of locating some individuals who unquestionably meet the criteria of community leadership, and who in turn will be able to name others not so visible to the outside observer.

Currently, the controversy continues. Proponents of one or another of these competing points of view argue for its inherent superiority and the obvious validity of its assumptions. Others take the view that all of these approaches get at leadership. But these are empirical questions; they can be answered only on the basis of comparison, not by faith or by rhetoric. A number of partial contrasts have been published, but so far no systematic overall comparison of these procedures has been reported. The present report represents such an attempt. An effort is made to determine the degree to which these several procedures agree or disagree in locating community leaders.

The data presented here represent a part of a larger study of leadership in the Syracuse, N.Y. metropolitan area. Two reports have been published,[9] and several additional papers are forthcoming.

Decision-Making

The study of participation in the decision-making process was of central concern in the Syracuse study. The first major task of the project team was to select a set of community problems or issues which would provide a point of entry into a pool (or pools) of participants in the decision-making process. Interviews were conducted with 20 local specialists in community study and with 50 informants representing diverse segments of the city's population. Care was taken to include representatives of each group along the total range of interest and institutional commitment. These 70 interviews provided a list of about 250 community issues. The list was reduced to a set of 30 issues according to the following criteria:

1. Each issue must have been at least temporarily resolved by a decision.
2. The decision must be perceived as important by informants representing diverse segments of the community.
3. The decision must pertain to the development, distribution, and utilization of resources and facilities which have an impact on a large segment of the metropolitan population.
4. The decision must involve alternative lines of action. It must entail a certain degree of choice on the part of parti-

cipants; and the outcome must not be predetermined.
5. The decision must be administered rather than made by individuals in "the market." For the purpose of this study, an administered decision was defined as one made by individuals holding top positions in organizational structures which empower them to make decisions affecting many people.
6. The decision must involve individuals and groups resident in the Syracuse Metropolitan Area. Decisions made outside the Metropolitan Area (e.g., by the state government), were excluded even though they might affect residents of the Metropolitan Area.
7. The decision must fall within the time period 1955–1960.
8. The set of decisions as a whole must affect the entire range of important institutional sectors, such as governmental, economic, political, educational, religious, ethnic, and the like.[10]

The next step in the research process required the determination of positional leaders or formal authorities for each of the set of 39 issues. The study began with those individuals who were formally responsible for the decisions. The element of arbitrary judgment usually involved in the positional approach was thus avoided. Here, the importance of a position was derived from its role in determining a choice among alternative lines of action rather than of being the consequence of an arbitrary assumption.

The responsible formal authorities were determined on the basis of documents pertinent to the 39 decisions. In addition, several attorneys were consulted to insure that correct determinations were made. The number of authorities responsible for making each of these decisions ranged from two to 57.

The interviews started with authoritative persons. Respondents were presented with a set of 39 cards, each of which identified a decision, They were asked to sort the cards into two piles: (1) "Those in which you participated; that is, where others involved in this decision would recognize you as being involved," and (2) "Those in which you were not a participant." For those issues in which they claimed participation, individuals were then asked to name all the others who were also involved. Here they were instructed to report on the basis of first-hand knowledge of participation rather than on hearsay. Respondents were also given a questionnaire covering their social backgrounds.

When the interviews with authorities were completed, their responses for those decisions on which they possessed authority were tabulated. Then, any person who had been nominated as a participant by two authorities for the same issue was designated as a first zone influential. Two nominations were deemed necessary in order to avoid bias due to accidental contacts, mistakes of memory, or a tendency to mention personal friends. In the final tabulations this same rule of two nominations was applied to authorities also. Therefore, no person is counted as a participant unless he has two nominations by qualified nominators.

As the next step, all first zone influentials were interviewed using exactly the same procedures as those used for authorities. Their responses were tabulated for the decisions in which they had been involved, and any person nominated by one authority and one first zone influential was also classified as a first zone influential and interviewed. Then any person nominated by two first zone influentials was designated a second zone influential —two steps removed from formal authority but still involved. We did not interview beyond these second zone influentials. We might have continued with third and fourth zones and so on; but on the basis of qualitative data gathered during the interviews, we suspected we were moving well into the periphery of impact on the outcome of decision making.

In all, 628 interviews were completed. Of these, 550 qualified as participants. These participants, then, are the leaders as determined by the decision-making phase of the Syracuse study. They were ranked in terms of the number of decisions in which they were involved. For the present analysis the 32 most active participants are considered.

Social Activity

Each of the 550 participants uncovered by the decision-making study was asked to complete a questionnaire covering his social background and current activities. These questionnaires were returned by 506 informants. The answers included responses to a set of questions designed to elicit as much information as possible about voluntary association memberships. Specific questions were included to determine memberships in the following areas:

1. Committees formed to deal with community problems.
2. Community service organizations.
3. Business organizations.
4. Professional organizations.
5. Union organizations.
6. Clubs and social organizations.
7. Cultural organizations.
8. Religious organizations.
9. Political parties, organizations and clubs.
10. Veterans' and patriotic organizations.
11. Other clubs and organizations.

Memberships in these organizations were tabulated, and a rough overall index to voluntary activity was calculated by simply summing the number of memberships for each person. The respondents were ranked in terms of number of memberships, and the 32 most active organizational members were included in the present analysis.

Reputation

Each questionnaire also invited the respondent to list the most influential leaders in the community. Eight spaces were provided for answers. Nominations were tabulated and, following traditional procedures, the top 41 reputed leaders were listed. The responses of those 41 respondents were then tabulated separately. The top 32 were derived from their rankings. This was done in order to maximize the chances that our nominators would be informed. As it turned out, however, the top 32 nominations of the whole group and the top 32 provided by the top 41 were exactly the same persons and in the same order. For Syracuse these nominations showed remarkable consistency all along the line.

Position

In determining the top positional leaders it seemed desirable to avoid as much as possible making the usual arbitrary assumptions. Traditional usage of the positional approach dictated the determination of the titular heads of the major organizations in business, government, the professions, and the like. Within each of these institutional areas choice could be made in terms of size, but it was difficult to determine how many organizations should be selected in each area.

An empirical resolution for this problem was provided in a recent report by D'Antonio, et al.,[11] These authors provided data on the proportions of reputed leaders representing each of the seven relevant institutional areas in 10 previous studies. Since agreement on these relative proportions was reasonably close for the six middle-sized American communities reported, they were used to assign proportions in each institutional area in the present study. The proportions derived from D'Antonio and those used in the present study are reported in Table 1. In this case positional leaders are the titular heads of the largest organizations in each of the institutional areas, and each area is represented according to the proportion listed in Table 1. Thirty-two organiza-

TABLE 1. *Percentage of Leaders in Each Institutional Area*

INSTITUTION	SIX CITIES	SYRACUSE
Business	57	59
Government	8	9
Professions	12	13
Education	5	6
Communications	8	6
Labor	4	3
Religion	5	3
Total	99	99

tions were chosen in all. As a check on its validity, the list of organizations was shown to several local experts in community affairs. They were in substantial agreement that the organizations listed seemed consistent with their perceptions of the "top" organizations in Syracuse. The heads of these organizations might be expected to have formal control over much of the institutional system of the community.

These, then, are the raw materials of the current study. An attempt was made to determine the degree to which these several procedures would allocate the same persons to the top leadership category.

Results

The several procedures for determining leaders did not converge on a single set of individuals. Top leaders according to one procedure were not necessarily the same as those indicated by another. An index of agreement for each pair was constructed by calculating the ratio of the actual number of agreements to their total possible number. Results are listed in Table 2.

It is possible that any of the methods used, if modified enough, would have yielded significantly different results.[12] The procedures we followed seem in their essentials to be like those followed in most of the studies so far published. (Those who believe they have altered the use of positions, nominations, memberships, or other indexes in such a way as to obtain a major difference in the output of the technique have only to demonstrate this by empirical comparisons.) Our impression is that most versions of each approach represent only vernier adjustments of the same device and thus can have only marginally differing results.

Table 2 suggests that there is far from perfect agreement in determining leaders by means of these four methods. In only one case do two of these methods concur in more than 50 per cent of their nominations. Reputation and position seem to be in substantial agreement in locating leaders. To a large degree, therefore, reputed leaders are the titular heads of major community organiza-

TABLE 2. *Percentage of Agreement in Determining Leaders by Four Traditional Procedures*

PARTICIPATION	SOCIAL ACTIVITY	REPUTATION	POSITION
25			
33	25		
39	22	74	

tions. They are not, however, themselves active as participants in decision making to any great extent.

Reputation for leadership seems to derive primarily from position, not from participation. But it appears unlikely that position itself constitutes a sufficient basis for reputation. The reputations, however, might belong to the organizations and not the individuals. In such a case, when an informant named John Smith as a leader what might have been intended was the fact that the Smith Snippel Company (of which John Smith was president) is influential in community decisions. Smith would thus have been named only because we had asked for a person's name. Our hypothesis, then, is that reputation should correspond with the participation rate of organizations rather than the participation rates of individuals.

On the basis of this hypothesis, the data on participation were retabulated. Each participant was classified according to his organization or place of employment. Then the head of each organization was credited not only with his own participation, but with the sum of the participation of his employees. In this manner an index of organizational participation was constructed and the top 30 organizational leaders were determined. Individuals so nominated were compared with those introduced by the earlier procedures. The results are shown in Table 3.

TABLE 3. *Percentage of Agreement Between Organizational Participation and Four Traditional Procedures*

TRADITIONAL PROCEDURE	PERCENTAGE OF AGREEMENT
Participation	33
Social activity	25
Reputation	67
Position	80

The proportions shown in Table 3 support our hypothesis. Organizational participation seems to uncover substantially the same leaders as reputation and position. The top reputed leaders, therefore, though not active participants themselves, head up the largest organizations, and the personnel of these organizations have the highest participation rates.

This result accounts for a great deal of participation in community decision making. Since organizational participation provides a workable index, many participants must be employees of large community organizations. But this does not explain the most active class of individual participants—those who were picked up by the individual participation index. These people seem to be virtually full-time participants in community affairs. We know that they are not organizational heads, but we have not determined who they are.

In view of the sheer amount of their participation, the top participants must be professional participants of some sort. And, as a class, professional participants in community affairs should be government officials and employees or full-time professional executives of non-governmental agencies formally and primarily committed to intervention in community affairs. With this as our hypothesis, the individuals nominated as leaders by the four traditional indexes were all classified into either government and professional or non-professional categories. Then percentages of government personnel and professional were calculated for all four indexes. The results are shown in Table 4.

Again the results support our hypothesis. The most active individual participants are typically government personnel.

The participation index thus gets at personnel quite different from those selected by reputational or positional indexes, or by

TABLE 4. *Percentage of Leaders According to Four Traditional Procedures Who Are Government Officials or Employees or Professional Participants*

TRADITIONAL PROCEDURE	PERCENTAGE OF GOVERNMENT PERSONNEL OR PROFESSIONAL PARTICIPANTS
Participation	66
Social activity	20
Reputation	20
Position	28

social activity. These differing cadres of people seem to represent *different kinds* of leadership behavior with respect to the local community.

Summary and Discussion of Results

These results indicate that at least in Syracuse "leadership" is not a homogeneous category. Which "leaders" are uncovered eems in large part to be a function of the-smode of study. The several traditional in dexes allow us to locate one or another of three basic types of "leaders."

First, there are those who enjoy the reputation for top leadership. These are very frequently the same individuals who are the heads of the largest and most actively participating business, industrial, governmental, political, professional, educational, labor and religious organizations in Syracuse. They are uncovered by studies of reputation, position, or organizational participation. In view of their formal command over the institutional structure and the symbolic value of their status as indexed by reputation, these individuals may be called the *Institutional Leaders* of Syracuse.

These Institutional Leaders, however, are for the most part not active participants in community affairs. There is no evidence that they have any direct impact on most decisions which take place. Their activity may be limited to that of lending prestige to or legitimizing the solutions provided by others. They might conceivably be participating decision makers in secret, but more likely they serve chiefly to provide access to the decision-making structure for their underlings: the *Effectors*.

The Effectors are located by studying participation. They are the active workers in the actual process of community decision making. Many of the most active Effectors are government personnel and professional participants, and the others are the employees of the large private corporations directed by the Institutional Leaders. In some cases, the Effectors are in touch with their employers, and it seems likely that their activities are frequently guided by what they view as company policy; but, judging from our data, they are often pretty much on their own. At any rate, these men carry most of the burden of effecting community change.

The third type of leader might be called the *Activists*. These are people active—and often hold office—in voluntary organizations, community service organizations, and clubs. Although they are not involved as often as the Effectors, the Activists do participate in decision making. For the most part they seem to lack the positional stature to be Institutional Leaders. Furthermore, they often work for or direct smaller organizations in the community. They lack the power base provided by association with government or one of the major industrial or business firms. Yet, seemingly by sheer commitment of time and effort to community affairs, these Activists do help shape the future of the community.

In conclusion, the various differing approaches to the study of community leadership seem to uncover different types of leaders. The study of reputation, position or organizational participation seems to get at the Institutional Leaders. Studies of participation in decision making, on the other hand, tap the Effectors of community action. And studies of social activity seem to seek out the Activists who gain entry by dint of sheer commitment, time, and energy.

In part, our results are dependent upon the Syracuse situation. It is likely that 25 years ago, when Syracuse was smaller and less diversified, the Institutional Leaders and the Effectors were the same people.[13] And

25 years from now this description will probably no longer hold. Other communities, in other stages of development and diversification will probably show different patterns. But until more comparative studies are done, conclusions of this kind are virtually guesses.

Notes

1. Cecil A. Gibb, "Leadership," in Gardner Lindzey (ed.), *Handbook of Social Psychology*, Vol. 2, Cambridge, Mass.: Addison-Wesley, 1954, pp. 877–920; Edward C. Banfield, "The Concept 'Leadership' in Community Research," paper read before the Annual Meeting of the American Political Science Association, St. Louis, Missouri, 1958; Robert A. Dahl, "A Critique of the Ruling Elite Model," *American Political Science Review*, 52 (June, 1958), pp. 463–469; Nelson W. Polsby, "The Sociology of Community Power: A Reassessment," *Social Forces*, 37 (March, 1959), pp. 232–236; Nelson W. Polsby, "Three Problems in the Analysis of Community Power," *American Sociological Review*, 24 (December, 1959), pp. 798–803; Raymond E. Wolfinger, "Reputation and Reality in the Study of 'Community Power'," *American Sociological Review*, 25 (October, 1960), pp. 636–644.
2. Cecil A. Gibb, *op. cit.*
3. Edward C. Banfield, *op. cit.*
4. Nelson W. Polsby, "The Sociology of Community Power: A Reassessment," *op. cit.* and Robert A. Dahl, *op. cit.*
5. Nelson W. Polsby, "The Sociology of Community Power," *op. cit.*
6. Herbert A. Simon, "Notes on the Observation and Measurement of Political Power," in his *Models of Man*, New York: John Wiley and Sons, 1957; James G. March, "An Introduction to the Theory and Measurement of Influence," *American Political Science Review*, 49 (June, 1955), pp. 431–451; James G. March, "Measurement Concepts in the Theory of Influence," *Journal of Politics*, 19 (May, 1957), pp. 202–226.
7. Numerous examples of this and other approaches to the study of leadership may be found in Wendell Bell, Richard J. Hill, and Charles R. Wright, *Public Leadership*, San Francisco: Chandler, 1961.
8. See the articles by Dahl, Polsby, and Wolfinger cited above.
9. Linton C. Freeman, Warner Bloomberg, Jr., Stephen P. Koff, Morris H. Sunshine, and Thomas J. Fararo, *Local Community Leadership*, Syracuse: University College of Syracuse University, 1960; Linton C. Freeman, Thomas J. Fararo, Warner Bloomberg, Jr., and Morris H. Sunshine, *Metropolitan Decision-Making*, Syracuse: University College of Syracuse University, 1962.
10. The entire set of 39 issues is described in the earlier publications of the study group, *op. cit.*
11. William D'Antonio, William Form, Charles Loomis, and Eugene Erickson, "Institutional and Occupational Representatives in Eleven Community Influence Systems," *American Sociological Review*, 26 (June, 1961), pp. 440–446.
12. The choice of the top 32 leaders in each category, is, for example, somewhat arbitrary. When another number is used, the *absolute* percentages of agreement vary, but their standings *relative* to one another remain stable.
13. For an interesting discussion of the development of a community leadership structure, see Robert O. Schulze, "The Bifurcation of Power in a Satellite City," in Morris Janowitz (ed.), *Community Political Systems*, Glencoe, Illinois: Free Press, 1961.

Community Power and Decision-Making: A Comparative Evaluation of Measurement Techniques[*]

L. Vaughn Blankenship

Two distinct, but related, points of disagreement may be discerned in the continuing debate over the study of community power and decision-making. One set of arguments is basically a methodological dispute with the self-styled "pluralists" challenging the validity and reliability of the 'reputational technique'—used by Floyd Hunter in his study of Regional City[1] and refined by those who have followed in his footsteps[2]— as a means for getting at the power structure of a community.[3] According to these critics, this approach at best measures only the reputation which different individuals have for power. What is needed is an objective indicator which measures *actual* power[4] and their recommendation for such honors is what has been characterized as "decision sociometry"[5]: the intensive study of a series of actual community decisions. Only through an analysis of the roles played by a number of actors in different decisions, the argument goes, can the true picture of community power be revealed.

The second basic point of disagreement centers around the interpretation and meaning of the results produced by the use of the different techniques. There is an impressively high correlation between the indicators used to reveal power and the findings reported. Those like Hunter who have used his approach find that power in the community is highly structured, unevenly distributed, with an overrepresentation of key economic roles —bankers, businessmen, corporation executives—and an underrepresentation of other roles, e.g., union leaders, politicians, in the power structure.[6]

Naturally this is what you have found, reply the pluralists since you started off by defining social power as being structured,[7] asked questions which severely limited the number of individuals who could be nominated as influentials and talked mostly to businessmen or only looked at those community activities—philanthropy, civic welfare, industrial development—which have traditionally been of great concern to the social and economic elite of the community. When we analyze what people *really* do through decisional analysis, we find that, while power is unevenly distributed, it is also fragmented, unstable, constantly shifting, and quite specific to each particular decision.[8] Furthermore, key economic roles are not nearly so powerful as the "elitists" make them appear.

Hardly surprising, respond those like Hunter, who have been characterized by their critics as "elitists." If you focus on *processes* instead of on *structures*, you are quite naturally going to find that a structure doesn't exist. In addition, you have selected community decisions which are relatively

*Collection of the data upon which this study is based was supported by grants from the Ford Foundation Committee on Public affairs; the Cornell University Social Science Research Center, and the National Institutes of Health, grant M5108(A). An additional grant from the Institute of Business and Economic Research, University of California, Berkeley, made possible some of the analysis presented here. The helpful comments and criticisms of George Strauss and Robert Holloway on an earlier draft of this manuscript are gratefully acknowledged.

minor in importance or have picked issues, e.g., political party nominations, education, slum clearance, in which, by definition, the formal organs of local government and professional politicians are most involved. You have equated *community* power with *public*, i.e., governmental, power.[9]

Missing from this debate to date are efforts to compare systematically the results achieved when these two approaches are used simultaneously to study leadership patterns in the same or several communities.[10] It may well be, as some seem to suggest by the direction of their arguments, that community leadership is a homogenous category and that "power structure" is a latent variable which can be indirectly measured in a number of ways. Thus using either the reputational technique or that of "decision sociometry" would produce basically the same result since both would be measuring the same underlying dimension of leadership. If Dahl had supplemented his work in New Haven with the reputational approach his results might have correlated highly with those produced by the methods he used. Furthermore, the study of "deviant cases"— those high on one measure and low on another—could have been a fascinating study in and of itself, suggesting much about the true dynamics of community power.

Conversely, it might be that community leaders are of different types. Thus the reputational approach turns up one type of leader, the decision sociometry technique another, with those who are picked up by both methods (or a third one) constituting still a third type. The power structure is not homogenous and this fact is reflected in the diverse images produced by the different measures of the phenomenon.[11]

In terms of what is known about leadership structures and processes in other social contexts, this latter hypothesis is certainly a plausible one. Furthermore, the work of Freeman and his associates in Syracuse, New York, gives credence to it. From their data they isolate (a) the *Institutional Leaders*, those with a reputation for influence who also often turn out to be the heads of the largest political, industrial, governmental

and religious organizations in the city; (b) the *Effectors*, those who don't enjoy the same widely spread reputation for leadership but who ". . . are the active workers in the actual process of community decision making";[12] and (c) the *Activists*, those who hold less important institutional positions than the *Effectors*, often in smaller community voluntary organizations, and who make being active in community affairs, almost a way of life. In the final analysis the relative merits of these and other approaches to the study of community power will be determined not by literary rhetoric and appeals to logic, but by empirical examination.

Using comparative data from two small communities in New York State, the present study examines the two contrary hypotheses outlined above. In a manner to be described below, decision participant information was collected on five key, generally comparable, community decisions in these towns. On top of this, data on reputed leaders was collected in both instances so that we are in a position to analyze the results produced by the two measurement techniques both *within* and *between* communities.

Research Setting and Design

The major purposes of the overall study of leadership in "Mapletown" and "West Valley" were to (a) look at the overall nature of power and decision-making in the two towns with a view to analyzing the impact of certain key community variables on the phenomena[13] and (b) to determine the consequences of certain aspects of the power structures for the functioning of the community-owned hospitals located in each.[14] Considerations associated with these intentions plus certain constraints of time, money and distance led to the selection of West Valley (pop. 8,480 in 1960) and Mapletown (pop. 5,967 in 1960) for study during the spring, summer and early fall of 1961.

As Table 1 shows, Mapletown and West Valley differ considerably in their degree of sociopolitical homogeneity. On only one item, family income in 1960, is West Valley

TABLE 1. *Sociopolitical Homogeneity in Mapletown and West Valley*

SELECTED CHARACTERISTICS	MAPLETOWN	WEST VALEY
Politics:		
Registered Republicans (1961)	71.0%	47.0%
Voted for Eisenhower (1956)	77.0%	57.0%
Nativity:		
Foreign Born or Foreign or Mixed Parentage (1960)	14.8%	22.0%
Northern European Descent (Age 20 and over		
in 1961)	82.6%	64.9%
Religion:		
Nominal Protestants (Age 20 and over in 1961)	75.2%	52.7%
Education and Family Income:		
Education (Age 25 and over in 1960)		
Average Years Schooling	10.4 yrs.	9.3 yrs.
Standard Deviation	2.8 yrs.	2.9 yrs.
Income:		
Average	$7.190	$6.681
Standard Deviation	5,462	5,029

a more homogenous community than Mapletown. The standard deviation for this item in Mapletown is $5,462 as compared with $5,029 in West Valley, a difference of $433. The overall picture of Mapletown which emerges from the data presented in the table is that of a homogenous, predominantly middle class,[15] Anglo-Saxon, Protestant community. The population of West Valley, by way of contrast, is divided almost equally between Catholics and Protestants, Republicans and Democrats; a small proportion of them come from the more favored parts of Europe and a higher percent are first or second generation Americans. Except for family income, it is clearly a less homogenous community in terms of these selected sociopolitical characteristics than Mapletown.

Both communities are located in the same predominantly rural part of New York state (50 miles apart) and serve as the "urban centers" for the surrounding countryside. Locally, neither is a "one-party" community, each has an elected council and mayor though West Valley is legally a city while Mapletown still had the status of a village at the time of the study. Both are industrial as opposed, say, to service or suburban communities though furniture manufacturing

and the railroad yards constitute the economic base of West Valley while heavy electrical equipment and small, independent oil producers make up that of Mapletown.[16]

Selection of the decisions to be studied in the two communities were based on several criteria. Since the type of decision has been postulated as a variable which affects the interplay of power,[17] the decisions in each community were matched where possible according to substantive content. The additional criteria which guided the choice of decisions for study were:

1. That they be of maximum importance in the sense that they involved substantial sums of money, basic changes in the community, affected a large number of the citizens of the community or some combination of these factors;
2. That they had been resolved sometime in the decade from 1950–60;[18]
3. That the decisions, or some of them involved, at least on the surface, the governmental institutions of the community while others, at least formally, were of a non-governmental nature;

4. That they be limited in number so that they could be analyzed in detail in the time available for the study.

On the basis of these considerations, the decisions selected in each community were:

Mapletown
1. Construction of the new Mapletown Memorial Hospital.
2. Bringing Simpkins Inc. (a new industry) to the community.
3. A school bond issue for a new elementary school.
4. Establishment of the Mapletown Flood Control Project.
5. Construction of the new Municipal Building-Fire Hall.

West Valley
1. Establishment of the West Valley District Hospital Authority in order to construct a new hospital.
2. Bringing the Dryden Components Co. (a new industry) to the community.
3. A school bond issue for a new junior-senior high school.
4. Establishment of the West Valley Flood Control Project.
5. Establishment of the West Valley (low cost) Housing Authority.

In addition to reconstructing each decision on the basis of available documents and reports, each participant in a decision was interviewed at least once and in some cases two or three times as to his role and the role of others in the decision. He was also asked to nominate anybody else he knew of "first hand" who had been actively involved in the decision, whether or not they had been in favor of it. Thus a snowball process was used to locate decision participants.

A person was interviewed as a participant if he met one or more of the following criteria:[19]

1. He had been an official member of a legal body, e.g., school board, city council, board of trustees, board of directors, etc., or an officer of a citizens committee, which was *formally* responsible for the issue involved;

2. He was (a) named as being an active participant (whether for or against) in the issue by individuals who were on bodies formally responsible for the decision and (b) nominated *himself* as having been actively involved;
3. He was nominated by at least three other individuals selected in terms of 1 and/or 2 above *whether or not* he also was willing to nominate himself as an active participant;
4. He was or had been a resident of the community at the time of his participation in the issue (thus excluding State and Federal officials).

The figures in Table 2 show the number of individuals who were active participants in each of the five issues in the two communities in terms of the above criteria. The total number of participants in Mapletown was 52 and in West Valley 47. Of these participants in both communities all but five were eventually located and interviewed.

TABLE 2. *The Number of Individuals Who Were Included in Each of the Community Decisions in Mapletown and West Valley*

DECISION	MAPLE-TOWN	WEST VALLEY
School Bond Issue	25	15
Bringing in New Industry	19	22
Community Hospital	16	14
Flood Control Project	6	8
Municipal Building-Fire Hall	7	X
Housing Authority	X	8

Our index of reputational power in each community was based on the nominations of two groups of "judges." The first of these groups consisted of all decision-participants who, when interviewed, were asked: "Suppose a major project were before the community, one that required decision by a group of leaders whom nearly everyone would accept. Which people would you choose to make up this group—regardless of whether or not you know them personally?"[20] An identical question was asked of a sample of the chief officers of some 20 organizations in the communities. In both instances no limit was placed on the number of names that could be mentioned though most respondents offered between six and ten.

The nominations of these judges were then pooled and those receiving three or more mentions were arbitrarily defined as community influentials. After these names were listed in order, those in approximately the top third of the list were categorized as Top Influentials. In Mapletown these individuals accounted for 59 percent of all nominations and in West Valley 52 percent. In both communities there was substantial consensus on half a dozen or so people and a second distinguishable group (in terms of the number of mentions received) stood just below them. From there agreement dropped sharply with about one-third receiving between three and five nominations.

Findings

We can ask the question about the relationship between reputation as a measure of power and decision participation as a measure of power in two ways: (a) Are those who are reputed Influentials also decision makers? and (b) Do those who have helped make these decisions also have a reputation for power? If the answer was an unqualified yes to both questions, then we could conclude that our two indices of community power measured

the same thing, that reputation and overt power were one and the same.

It is hardly surprising that the answer in both West Valley and Mapletown is only a qualified "yes": reputation and participation do join, but not always. Some have a wide reputation for power though there is no evidence that they participated in any of the five decisions except, perhaps, as onlookers. A handful of people were multiple decision participants yet received fewer than three mentions as community leaders.

Looking first at the data in Table 3, we see that in Mapletown 12 of the 14 Top Influentials (85.7%) and 17 of the Influentials (60.7%) were involved in one or more of the decisions. The participation of both Top Influentials and Influentials was, however, largely limited to one or two of the decisions studied. Only one of them participated in more than that.

In West Valley, however, the overall relationship between reputation for influence and participation is less strong. As the figures show, six of the Top Influentials (42.9%) and 20 of the Influentials (60.6%) did *not* participate in *any* of the decisions studies. In effect a majority of all of those constituting our reputed leadership "pool" in West Valley played no role whatsoever in these key issues. However, unlike Mapletown, those Top influentials in West Valley who *were* active, were active across the board, so

TABLE 3. *The Relationship Between Participation in Community Decisions and Reputed Influence*

| NUMBER OF ISSUES PARTICIPATED IN | TOP INFLUENTIALS | | INFLUENTIALS* | |
| | Mapletown | West Valley | Mapletown | West Valley |
	(N = 14) %	(N = 14) %	(N = 28) %	(N = 33) %
0	14.3	42.9	39.3	60.6
1	35.7	0.0	46.4	33.3
2	42.9	14.2	10.7	6.1
3–5	7.1	42.9	3.6	0.0
	100.0	100.0	100.0	100.0

*Individuals who received at least 3 nominations as Influentials. Does *not* include Top Influentials.

to speak. Just how true this is can be seen in Table 4.

TABLE 4. *Participation of Top Influentials in Mapletown and West Valley in Each Decision as a Proportion of the Maximum Overlap Possible Between Top Influentials and Participants on Each Issue*

	TOP INFLUENTIALS	
	Maple-town	West Valley
DECISIONS PARTICIPATED IN	% (N)	% (N)
Flood Control Project	20.0 (1)	62.5 (5)
New Hospital	42.9 (6)	50.0 (7)
New Industry	57.1 (8)	35.7 (5)
School Bond Issue	21.4 (3)	46.2 (6)
Municipal Building-Fire Hall	16.6 (1)	X
Housing Authority	X	42.9 (3)

Table 4 shows the degree of overlap which occurred (as a percent of the *overlap possible*) between high reputed power and actual participation in each of the five decisions studied. In only one issue in Mapletown, the decision to raise $100,000 to bring a new industry to the community, were a majority of Top Influentials involved. Only the hospital decision, involving Hill-Burton money and the raising locally of over half a million dollars through a fund drive, comes close to this. The ex-mayor was the only Top Influential participating in the flood control and municipal building projects.

Top Influentials in West Valley (largely the same ones as we saw earlier in Table 3) constituted a majority of the participants in the flood control project and half of them were involved in the new hospital issue. It is clear from Table 4 that those Top Influentials who *were* active in West Valley, were involved in all of the decisions studied.

If reputation for power does not guarantee that one will, in fact, be a decision-maker, particularly in West Valley, the opposite also holds true. Participation, especially multiple participation in these key community decisions, does not necessarily give one a reputation for power. This is least true in West Valley.

In that community, as Table 5 indicates, multiple participation in these decisions of the recent past and reputed influence went hand in hand. Of those active in only one of these issues, almost three-fourths (73%) were also non-Influentials, i.e., received no mention as power figures. None of those who played a part in only one decision were Top Influentials (though as we saw earlier above, some Top Influentials were completely inactive), and, conversely, 50 percent of those participating in two of these decisions and all of those involved in three of more of them were Top Influentials. In fact, everyone in West Valley who was a multiple participant received at least three nominations as general Influentials.

Multiple participants in Mapletown were less likely to have a reputation for power. There is some overlap between the two

TABLE 5. *Manifest Power, Measured by Participation, Compared with Reputational Power in Mapletown and West Valley*

MANIFEST POWER	REPUTATIONAL POWER					
	Non Influentials[1]		Influentials[2]		Top Influentials[3]	
No. of Issues Participated in	Mapletown %	West Valley %	Mapletown %	West Valley %	Mapletown %	West Valley %
1	51.4	73.0	32.4	27.0	16.2	0.0
2	27.3	0.0	27.3	50.0	45.4	50.0
3+	33.3	0.0	33.3	0.0	33.3	100.0

[1]Individuals who participated in one or more decisions but received 0–2 mentions as general Influentials.
[2]Individuals who received at least 3 nominations as Influentials. Does *not* include Top Influentials.
[3]Individuals in approximately the top third of those nominated as Influentials.

measures but it is less clear and consistent. While 51.4 percent of those in on only one decision were non-Influentials, 16.2 percent of them were also Top Influentials, and almost one-third of them received at least three nominations for general influence in community decision-making. Though there is a drop in the percent of multiple participants who are non-Influentials, it is not nearly as sharp as it is in West Valley. Only one of the three individuals who participated overtly in three or more of these decisions, the Mayor, was also among the Top Influentials. Likewise, one of these three received *no* mention as an Influential.

On the basis of their work in Syracuse, Freeman and his associates conclude that leaders with a high reputation for power are more likely to be the visible, economic captains of the community than are the activists, the actual makers of community decisions,[21] the "hewers of wood and drawers of water." Schulze's data on Cibola point in a similar direction[22] as do Hunter's findings in Regional City,[23] though Hunter maintains that, appearances to the contrary, Top Influentials *really* make the decisions. What evidence is there in Mapletown and West Valley that the two different approaches to the measure of power turn up different "kinds" of leaders?

The most active individuals in both communities, in terms of multi-participation as a measure of power, tended to be those whose positions were rooted in the politico-governmental structure of the community with inside access to resources and power available at the state and federal level. The Mayor of West Valley, poorly educated, inarticulate, a semi-skilled worker lacking middle class graces and virtues, was the closest thing to a professional politician in either town. He played a key role in all five of the decisions studied while his City Attorney, who displayed a phenomenal knowledge of the channels of access to higher governmental officials, was his working partner in four of them. Both were also widely recognized as Influentials and nominated as such.

Others who were almost as active in community decision-making in West Valley also received enough nominations to appear among the Top Influentials. However, all but one of these most likely owed their reputation for influence more to their *de facto* participation, made possible by some appointive tie to the local politico-governmental system, than to their commanding positions in key economic institutions. Among the five Top Influentials who were overtly *inactive* in the issues studied, two were clearly in visible, important economic positions in the community. The remainder were small, main-street businessmen whose primary, civic concerns centered around "city boosting" activities in the Chamber of Commerce.

Turning now to Mapletown, once again we find that the Mayor, a main-street businessman and realtor, and his City Attorney, County Chairman of the Democratic Party, were the most overtly active individuals in community decision-making. Qualitatively their participation was somewhat less central than that of their counterparts in West Valley but each participated in four of the decisions and, again, access to outside governmental officials and resources was an important ingredient for their involvement. The third multi-participant was the only individual in both communities who was active in as many as three of the decisions yet received *no* nominations as an Influential. His participation in at least two of these three, which was relatively marginal, can be explained solely on the basis of his specialized competence as a CPA and in the third instance he was a member of the school board during the bond issue decision. None of the three most active decision-makers, in terms of multi-participation, were economic dominants in Mapletown. Only one of them, the Mayor, enjoyed a wide enough reputation for influence to be considered a Top Influential. One received no nominations at all.

Both of the Top Influentials in Mapletown who were overtly *inactive* in all of our five decisions were in important economic positions. One was a corporate manager, an outsider to Mapletown, who purposefully did not become involved in any community affairs.[24] The other was a middle-aged, homegrown, rising bank executive who was just beginning to move into community affairs at the time of our study.

There is some evidence that "insiders" to the community decision-making process were more likely to nominate key economic dominants as Influentials than were "outsiders," especially in Mapletown.[25] In that community when we compare those mentioned most often as Influentials by decision participants with those ranked highest by organization officials, the differences are striking. Five of those individuals who were frequently nominated as Influentials by the "insiders," B, E, G, J, and H, do not even appear on the list of those most often mentioned by the "outsiders" as can be seen from Table 6.

Furthermore, there are some significant shifts in the rank order of the individuals appearing on both lists. The newly elected Mayor, for example, appears fourteenth on

one list, first on the other. The man ranked second in terms of influence by organization officials is ranked sixth by decision participants while the fourth ranking man on the decisions participant list appears in twelfth place on the second list. The "insiders" are more likely to nominate the top representatives of industry and finance in the community, the economic dominants, as Influentials and are a little less likely to select the chief governmental or political leaders favored by the organization officials.

When a similar comparison was made in West Valley it was found that, with one exception, the same individuals were mentioned most frequently by both the "insiders" and the "outsiders." Equally important, the rank ordering of those who were most often mentioned by these two groups was almost identical.

TABLE 6. *Individuals Nominated Most Often as Influentials by Decision Participants Compared with Those Nominated Most Often by Organization Officials in Mapletown*

DECISION PARTICIPANTS NOMINATIONS			ORGANIZATION OFFICIALS NOMINATIONS		
Rank Order	Name	Occupation	Rank Order	Name	Occupation
1	A	Corporation Executive*	1	N	(See opposite)
2	B	Corporation Executive	2	F	(See opposite)
3	C	Corporation Executive	3	I	(See opposite)
4	D	Corporation Executive	4	A	(See opposite)
5	E	Corporation Executive	5	C	(See opposite)
6	F	Bank Vice-President	6	OO	Lawyer-City Attorney-County Chmn., Demo. Party
7	G	Newspaper Owner-Editor	7	PP	Owner-Manager, Dept. Store
8	H	Bank President	8	K	(See opposite)
9	I	Small Businessman-Ex-Mayor	9	QQ	Engineer-Chmn., Town Republican Comm.
10	J	Corporation Executive	10	RR	Insurance Broker-Chmn. Young Republicans
11	K	Lawyer-Bank Counsel-Ex County Chmn., Rep. Party	11	L	(See opposite)
12	L	Small Businessman-Town Supervisor	12	D	(See opposite)
13	M	Bank Vice-President	13	SS	Lawyer-County Attorney
14	N	Bank Clerk-Mayor	14	M	(See opposite)
				TT	Housewife
				UU	Engineer

*Most of those classified as "corporation executives" are independent oil producers of considerable personal wealth who own and manage their own companies, though these companies have very few employees.

This certainly suggests that formal economic importance was either not equally visible or persuasive of general influence or both to all elements in Mapletown. Organization leaders appeared unaware of or quite willing to reject this criterion and to fasten more often on simple community activity or visibility in a politico-governmental position as an indicator of general influence. Those more privy to the realities of decision-making in Mapletown gave greater weight to economic position than did those standing on the periphery looking in.

Summary and Discussion

In small communities the size of West Valley and Mapletown one would expect to find a homogenous leadership structure with little divergence between those who govern, so to speak, and those who have a reputation for governing. This should be especially true for a politically and socially homogenous village like Mapletown.

A number of individuals in both communities played a role in one or another of the five decisions studied without gaining any widespread reputation for power as a result. Especially in West Valley this was the case where few who were involved in only one decision were nominated as Influentials.

In contrast to such one-shot contributors, who actually made up the majority of participants in both West Valley and Mapletown, those whose decision-making role spread over several issues generally enjoyed a fairly wide reputation for power, especially in West Valley. In that community everyone who was involved in three or more of the decisions was also a Top Influential.

It is significant that in both communities, despite other important differences in leadership and economic and social structure, it was the Mayor and City Attorney who were among the most widely active decision-makers. It is also clear in both that the reputation for influence which these people enjoyed was a function of the position itself. The young man elected Mayor during our study in Mapletown had previously played only a very minor role in one of the decisions

we studied yet received more mentions as an Influential from organizational leaders than any other person. On the other hand, ex-mayors and city attorneys received virtually no nominations as Influentials in spite of the fact that several of them had held office for six or seven years. As it turned out, most of the decisions we analyzed in Mapletown and West Valley involved some negotiations with federal or state officials at some point and these two positions, locally, are those with the most direct, formal ties to higher centers of government.[26] Thus those in these positions have a wide opportunity for participation in local decisions and are presumed, until experience, perhaps, proves otherwise, to be Influentials.

The participation of Top Influentials as a whole in actual decision-making differed substantially in the two communities. Economic dominants made up most of this group in Mapletown though, with two exceptions, they participated in some of the issues studied. Their participation, however, was much more specialized than in West Valley, being limited almost exclusively to the hospital and new industry decisions, decisions involving the raising of very large sums of local money.

Those of the Top Influentials in West Valley who were also decision-makers were generally active across the board. Indeed, it was this activity itself, rather than social class, economic position, or education, which distinguished them most markedly from those reputed influentials who were non-participants. Only two of them possessed the formal economic position found associated with reputed power in Mapletown and other communities which have been studied, and one of these two was very active, the other completely inactive.

In conclusion, there is considerable overlap in the results produced by our two measures of power in Mapletown and West Valley and in that sense leadership may be said to be homogenous: reputation and action join. We don't find the sharp distinction between them which some writers have predicted would exist and Freeman and his associates report in Syracuse.[27] However, the underlying dynamics of this homogeneity and the deviations from it are different in our two communities. In Mapletown we find overlap produced by broad but specialized participation whereas in West Valley it is the result of the hyper-activity of a few individuals.

These differences undoubtedly stem from the larger differences between the communities. A key variable here would appear to be the contrasting industrial bases of Mapletown and West Valley. Both the railroad and furniture industries, upon which West Valley is based, are depressed industries. Community leadership and a posture of responsi-

bility are not central to the role of an executive and thus are fringe activities which will often be dropped in times of internal economic crisis.[28] In addition, there are simply not the same number of formally important economic positions as there are in Mapletown with its numerous small, successful oil producers and two electrical equipment manufacturing plants. Economically and psychologically the latter community can afford the comparative luxury of decision specialization, a luxury which makes possible and, perhaps, compels the participation of more individuals in community decision-making.

Notes

1. *Community Power Structure* (Chapel Hill: The University of North Carolina Press, 1953).
2. William H. Form and Delbert C. Miller, *Industry, Labor and Community* (New York: Harper & Bros., 1960), esp. Part 3; Delbert C. Miller, "Industry and Community Power Structure," *American Sociological Review*, 23 (February 1958), pp. 9–15; Delbert C. Miller, "Decision-Making Cliques in Community Power Structure," *The American Journal of Sociology*, 64 (November 1958), pp. 299–310; William H. Form and William V. D'Antonio, "Integration and Cleavage Among Community Influentials in Two Border Cities," *American Sociological Review*, 24 (December 1959), pp. 804–814; Robert C. Hansen, "Predicting a Community Decision: A Test of the Miller-Form Theory," *American Sociological Review*, 24 (October 1959), pp. 662–671; and William V. D'Antonio and Eugene C. Erickson, "The Reputational Technique as a Measure of Community Power," *American Sociological Review*, 27 (June 1962), pp. 363–376. For a good summary of these developments see Lawrence J. Herson, "In the Footsteps of Community Power," *American Political Science Review*, 55 (December 1961), pp. 817–830.
3. Robert A. Dahl, "A Critique of the Ruling Elite Model," *American Political Science Review*, 52 (June 1958), pp. 463–468, and Raymond E. Wolfinger, "Reputation and Reality in the Study of 'Community Power'," *American Sociological Review*, 25 (October 1960), pp. 636–644.
4. Wolfinger, *ibid.*, and Nelson W. Polsby,

"How to Study Power: The Pluralist Alternative," *Journal of Politics*, 22 (August 1960), pp. 474–484.
5. David B. Truman, "Theory and Research on Metropolitan Political Leadership: Report on a Conference," *Social Science Research Council Items*, 15 (March 1961), p. 2. For a general review of these as well as other approaches to the study of community decision-making see Peter H. Rossi, "Community Decision Making," *Administrative Science Quarterly* (March 1957), pp. 415–443.
6. William V. D'Antonio, William H. Form, Charles P. Loomis, and Eugene C. Erickson, "Institutional and Occupational Representations in Eleven Community Influence Systems," *American Sociological Review*, 26 (June 1961), pp. 440–446.
7. Herbert Kaufman and Victor Jones, "The Mystery of Power," *Public Administration Review*, 14 (Summer, 1954), p. 207.
8. Robert A. Dahl, *Who Governs?* (New Haven: Yale University Press, 1961), chaps. 8–12, and Edward C. Banfield, *Political Influence* (New York: The Free Press of Glencoe, 1961).
9. See Hunter's review of Dahl's book, *op. cit.*, *Administrative Science Quarterly*, 6 (1962), pp. 517–519.
10. One exception, and a recent one, is the work done by Linton Freeman and his colleagues in Syracuse, New York and reported in Linton Freeman, *et al.*, "Locating Leaders in Local Communities: A Comparison of Some Alternative Approaches," *American Sociological Review*, 28 (October, 1963), pp. 791–798. Others have made partial com-

parisons of this sort, e.g., Harry Scoble, "Leadership Hierarchies and Political Issues in a New England Town," *Community Political Systems*, Morris Janowitz (ed.) (Glencoe, Illinois: The Free Press, 1961), esp. pp. 120–122.

11. Refinements of the reputational technique have also been used to develop a typology of community leadership. See Charles M. Bonjean, "Community Leadership: A Case Study and Conceptual Refinement," *The American Journal of Sociology*, 63 (May, 1963), pp. 672–681. Freeman, *et al.*, raise some questions about the utility of such refinements alone for constructing leader typologies on the basis of their data, *op. cit.*

12. Freeman, *et al.*, *op. cit.*, p. 797.

13. Robert V. Presthus, *Men At The Top* (New York: Oxford University Press, 1964), with a chapter by L. Vaughn Blankenship.

14. *Ibid.*, ch. 11 and L. Vaughn Blankenship, *Organizational Support and Community Leadership in Two New York State Communities*, unpublished Ph.D. dissertation, Cornell University, June, 1962.

15. For a more extensive discussion of the class structure of the two communities, see Blankenship, *op. cit.*, pp. 38–46.

16. Using the classification scheme developed by Chauncy D. Harris, Mapletown is a manufacturing city and West Valley a transportation city. "A Functional Classification of Cities in the United States," *Geographical Review*, 33 (January 1943). pp. 86–89. See also Blankenship, *op. cit.*, pp. 34–38.

17. Rossi, *op. cit.*; James E. White, "Research in Community Leadership," *American Sociological Review*, 15 (February 1950), pp. 59–60, and Ernest A. Barth and S. D. Johnson, "Community Power and a Typology of Social Issues," *Social Forces*, 38 (October 1959), pp. 29–32.

18. The one exception to this was the West Valley Flood Control Project. At the time of the study Congress had not yet appropriated money for the project. All of the preliminary work had been done, however, and consideration of the project by the Federal Government was in the final stages.

19. These are similar to those used by Freeman, *et al.*, *op. cit.*, p. 794.

20. This is identical with the question used by others to study community power structure. For example, see Form and Miller, *op. cit.*, p. 701 and D'Antonio and Erickson, *op. cit.*

21. Freeman, *et al.*, *op. cit.*

22. Robert O. Schulze, "The Bifurcation of Power in a Satellite City," *Community Political Systems*, *op. cit.*, pp. 19–79.

23. Hunter, *op. cit.*

24. See Schulze, *op. cit.*, for a more extended discussion of this type of withdrawal on the part of corporate officials.

25. "Insiders" being decision participants, "outsiders" organization officials. See above for a brief discussion on how these judges were chosen.

26. For a more detailed treatment of this type of relationship between the mass society and the small community see Arthur J. Vidich and Joseph Bensman, *Small Town in Mass Society* (New York: Anchor Books, Doubleday & Co., 1958), and Warren, Roland L., "Toward a Typology of Extra-Community Controls Limiting Local Community Autonomy," *Social Forces*, 34 (May 1956), pp. 338–41.

27. Freeman, *et al.*, *op. cit.*

28. George Katona, *Psychological Analysis of Economic Behavior* (New York: McGraw-Hill Book Co., 1951), esp. ch. 9.

Part V.

Interaction Among Centers of Power: Community and Subgroup Interactions

Introduction

The field of community power structure has matured considerably; it has lost its elite obsession. The older penchant to ferret out an elite composed of business leaders, who singlemindedly preserved in their own image the institutions of the community, has given way to a more complex and pluralistic view of communities. All manner and shapes of power structures are now known to exist. Therefore, the most generalized model of community views it as composed of a number of centers of power varying in the amount of power they possess and how they are related to one another. The factors that produce these variations were discussed in Part III: they serve as clues to the investigator as to what he should expect to find in any community that he chooses to study.

Now it is necessary to look more carefully at the dynamics of interaction among subgroups within communities. What does it mean in terms of human activity to say that centers of power are integrated or segmented, institutionalized or chaotic? It means that people in one group or category are interacting, attempting to interact, or avoiding interaction with people in other groups or categories and that their success or failure affects them and the entire community. This is the interface problem; its content and significance are examined in this section.

In "Politics and the Social Structure: The changing Nature of Political Organization," Whyte describes the role of the local political party as a broker between the ethnic poor and the city administration; in other words, the party fills the interface. The immigrant or untutored resident found the task of getting welfare or other assistance greatly simplified: he had only to tell his problem to his ubiquitous block leader. In exchange for his vote and other services the block leader was willing to send the message through the party apparatus to its members

in elected offices for appropriate action. Whyte shows that for the Irish the party was a highly integrated, institutionalized interface with the city administration, but for the Italian it was not. He also shows that the advent of federal welfare programs, which linked the poor directly to the giving agencies, effectively eliminated the party from the interface. The social worker became at least as familiar a figure on the block as the old block leader.

In "Analysis of the Social Power Position of a Real Estate Board," Bouma describes a different situation where no broker is needed. The real estate board he studied was able to marshall impressive power to influence community affairs directly through institutionalized channels. Prestige and knowledge of the administrative process were crucial assets that greatly simplified their efforts.

An interface with a far different set of characteristics is reflected in the third article, "Power Structure of a Sub-Community," which is taken from Hunter's book *Community Power Structure*. The Negro community is portrayed as having an elite of its own: one that has contacts with the Caucasian elite, but these contacts are informal, uninstitutionalized, sub rosa, and distant (the telephone was the usual means of interaction). Interaction usually occurred only when there was a crisis or other serious problem: otherwise segmentation was the rule.

In "Power and Structure the Negro Sub-Community," Barth and Abu-Laban replicated Hunter's technique in Pacific City, but there a different pattern of intergroup relations emerged. Negro leaders were less likely to know each other or to wish to maintain the segregation of the Negro sub-community. Contact with the White leaders was maintained primarily by the leaders of the larger Negro activist associations. The authors attributed these differences from Hunter's findings to the differences in the sizes of the Negro population, other macro-community characteristics, and the lack of class consciousness among Negroes.

In the last decade the type of participants and character of the Negro-Caucasian interface has changed in many communities. Killian and Smith illustrate these changes in "Negro Protest Leaders in a Southern Community." During a boycott the old Negro leadership, selected by Whites and noted for its accommodation, gave way to a new leadership, selected by Blacks and advocating new techniques. Direct action, the use of the mass media, and the use of collective economic power came into fashion. The older organization of the interface had failed to solve the problems of Negroes; the newer one was an experiment in successful manipulation. An interesting blend of strategies in interface confrontations is related by I. P. Bell in *CORE and the Strategy of Non-violence*.[1] In describing the lunch counter sit-ins organized by the youthful CORE leaders, she points out that because of divisive ideological viewpoints the CORE members did not have the participation or support for their desegregation attempts from the established Negro leadership. However, when the merchants wanted to talk to "whomever could stop these demonstrations," the CORE group brought the established Negro leaders into the negotiating sessions.

The mass society theorists, particularly Kornhauser, have proposed that when groups fail to achieve their objectives vis-à-vis other groups by legitimate means, they will withdraw or turn to illegitimate means. Regardless of legitimacy, the importance of this observation is that there is a search for effective means of interacting and thus the character of interfaces may change. Interfaces undoubtedly exhibit some interesting natural histories depending on the values, ethnic status, and so forth of the opposing groups. A currently fascinating pattern is the one discussed above between races in American communities. Accommodation has given way to direct action tinged with violence. There are signs that sporadic, hostile direct action sometimes evokes stable, institutionalized patterns of interaction. The selection, "Community Power and Strategies in Race Relations: Some Critical Observations," by McKee, reports on a strategy which has as its goal the development of the latter type of relationships. McKee evaluates the usefulness of the strategy from what has been learned about community power. He finds it inadequate in some respects, but interesting because it suggests how a particular type of interface might be created.

Clearly there is a paucity of research in this area, yet much is happening that will undoubtedly be documented and provide answers to the major questions in the area.[2] What factors determine the character of interfaces? What types of interfaces are associated with effective problem-solving? How do hostile, but interdependent groups relate to each other? Out of it should be developed a viable model of community which focuses on group interfaces as a key concept and develops explanations of dynamic phenomena in terms of the characteristics of the interfaces themselves.

Notes

1. I. P. Bell, *CORE and the Strategy of Non-Violence* (New York: Random House, 1968), pp. 82–104.
2. One additional study in the area of race relations is H. Pfautz, "The Power Structure of the Negro Sub-Community: A Case Study of a Comparative View," *Phylon*, 23 (Summer, 1962), 156–166.

Politics and the Social Structure:
The Changing Nature of Political Organization

William F. Whyte

When Boss Joseph Maloney lost his campaign for alderman in 1939, his Cleveland Club lost its last hold upon Cornerville, South Side, and Welport. The power of the organization had been wasting away for years, and, when the final collapse came, there was nothing that Maloney could do except look back upon the happier days from the 1890's through the 1920's, when the Cleveland Club, under its founder, Matt Kelliher, had dominated Ward 4. He told me the story of the club in this way:

> We had a captain in every precinct. He was a man who knew everybody in his precinct and could tell how just about all of them would vote. We had quite a variety of precincts. Over beyond ——— Street was a pretty high-class precinct. You had to have an educated man in charge there. Then we had another precinct where most of the freight handlers lived. That was a different kind of job.
>
> When people wanted help from the organization, they would come right up here to the office [of the club]. Matt would be in here every morning from nine to eleven, and if you couldn't see him then, you could find him in the ward almost any other time. If a man came in to ask Matt for a job, Matt would listen to him and then tell him he'd see what he could do; he should come back in a couple of days. That would give Matt time to get in touch with the precinct captain and find out all about the man. If he didn't vote in the last election, he was out. Matt wouldn't do anything for him—that is, unless he could show that he was so sick he couldn't get to the polls. When Matt heard what kind of a fellow the

man was, he could make up his mind about trying to do something for him.

> When a man got a job through our influence, he would keep on paying his dues, and around election time we would expect him to make some kind of contribution to support the campaign. We never accepted money to indorse any candidate. In that way we kept our independence. . . . When I first ran for representative—I didn't want to run; I was selected by the organization—I contributed $150 toward the expenses, and the organization paid the rest.
>
> In those days we held political office in order to be of service to the people. Of course, if Kelliher thought the city was going to buy a certain piece of property, and he had a chance to get it first, all well and good. He was in the real estate business and there was a lot of money in that business when the city was expanding. But, with him, service to the people always came first. He never took a cent for the favors he was able to do. Matt and I never sold our jobs or charged for a favor.
>
> In those days we really controlled. We could tell within fifty votes how the ward would go in any election. One time we changed the ward from Democratic to Republican overnight. That was in the mayoralty contest of 1905. There was a meeting in the club till three in the morning right before the election. We printed the slate we were backing and circulated it around as much as we had time for. When the people came to the polls, the captain would ask them, "Do you have the slate?" If they didn't, he would give it to them, and they would go in and vote it. When the votes were counted, we had carried the ward for the Republicans just like we carried it

Reprinted from Street Corner Society *by William F. Whyte, Chapter 6, pp. 194–199, by permission of the author and The University of Chicago Press. Copyright 1943 and 1955 by The University of Chicago.*

for the Democrats. One time a fellow says to Matt, "I'm not going to vote the ticket this time." There were thirteen votes against us in his precinct, and Matt would have given anything to know who the other twelve were.

Maloney explained the breakdown of the organization in terms of the shifting population, the New Deal, and the rise of "the racket element":

> Today everything has changed. We've got a floating population in the South Side now. People are moving out all the time. You can't expect a precinct captain to know everybody any more. It's only in Cornerville that people stay in the same place.
>
> Then the Italians will always vote for one of their own. We recognized them when we didn't need to. They didn't have many votes, and we could have licked them every time, but we gave them Italian representatives. We did it for the sake of the organization. But they wouldn't stick by us. The Italian people are very undependable. You can't trust them at all. They play a dirty game too. I estimate that now there are between eight hundred and a thousand repeaters in Cornerville every election. I've tried to stop that, but you can't do it. You can't tell one Italian from another.

In speaking of the disloyalty of the Italians, Maloney referred actually to a conflict of loyalties. From the time that the Italian immigrants got into street fights with their Irish predecessors, there was bitter feeling between the races. Since the Irish controlled the ward politically, the Italians, as long as they were in the minority had to follow the Cleveland Club in order to gain any political benefits. In recent years Italians who had the political support of the club were looked upon by Cornerville people as disloyal—traitors to the cause of Italian unity. As the proportion of Italian votes in the ward grew steadily, it was to be expected that the Italians would break away from the Cleveland Club.

To Maloney's charge about "repeating" in Cornerville, which is exaggerated but not otherwise untrue, Cornerville people reply with charges that the Cleveland Club would have fallen years earlier if it had permitted honest elections. My own observations and the unanimous testimony of Cornerville people indicate that the club used repeaters whenever needed. Maloney freely admitted that many of his voters lived outside the ward. "A man has a constitutional right to choose his own domicile. As long as he isn't registered in two places, it's all right." He continued his story:

> In the old days it was different. The New Deal has changed politics altogether. With home relief and the W.P.A., the politician isn't needed any more in a district like this. Years ago a man out of work would come to us to see what we could do for him. Now he goes on home relief and then he can get on the W.P.A. That's all he wants. This relief is a terrible racket.

I asked whether a man did not need political backing to get on the W.P.A., and Maloney said it could be accomplished without such aid. I took this question up with Carrie Ravello, the wife of the state senator, and she gave me this answer:

> That's right. If you're qualified, you can get on without going to a politician. But it will be four weeks before you get certified, and I can push things through so that you get on in a week. And I can see that you get a better job—if you're qualified. If you want to be a supervisor on a contracting job, I can't tell them, "Make Billy Whyte a supervisor," because you're not qualified for that job. You don't have the experience. I can only do something for you if you're qualified.

The corner boys corroborated some of these statements but added that many unqualified men with strong political backing had been able to get good W.P.A. jobs.

There were many politicians in Eastern City. The important question is: Whose political support was important in dealing with the W.P.A.? I asked Mrs. Ravello how she was able to help her constituents in this field. She explained:

> I know Dave Collins. He is the state administrator, head of all the projects in the state. I can go right into his office. He knows my connections with [United States] Senator Corcoran.

I asked how Collins had attained his position.

> He was appointed six months ago by the regional administrator. The regional administrator appointed him because he had the support of Senator Corcoran. Billy, I don't care what you say, these days it isn't what you know, it's who you know that counts.

She added that the most important connection one could have for the W.P.A. was the one with Senator Corcoran. Next in importance were connections with Representatives in Congress.

There were important changes in the federal administration of relief after the early days of the New Deal. In the beginning there was a tremendous demand for jobs, and there was no recognized means of distributing them except through the usual political channels. Paul Ferrante, the state senator's secretary, told me that the Ravellos obtained a number of work-assignment slips from a high state official so that, whenever they wished to place a man on a project they had simply to fill out a slip. As the federal relief setup developed and became established on a permanent basis, the powers of local politicians in dealing with relief were progressively curtailed.

This does not mean that relief was taken out of politics. It means that the pressure had to come from higher up in the political hierarchy. As Carrie Ravello pointed out, she was able to deal effectively with the W.P.A. administration because of her connection with United States Senator Corcoran. If she had not such connections, she could have accomplished very little. This was substantiated by the stories of many other Cornerville people. They did not speak of going to see Senator Corcoran. From the view of the corner boys, his position was so high as to be out of sight. They did speak of soliciting the aid of Congressman Branagan. The congressman had several secretaries, one of whom was a young Italian who lived in the ward. Through him many Cornerville people were able to get W.P.A. work assignments.

There was no state boss to whom Senator Corcoran was responsible. On a smaller scale, Branagan had a similar standing. He had his own organization, and, since he represented several wards in Congress, he was not subject to any one politican in any one of the wards. There was no longer a ward boss in the Matt Kelliher sense in any of these wards. This did not mean that Corcoran and Branagan were independent of all other politicians. They had to perform services for and make informal alliances with other politicians in order to perpetuate their power. The important point is that they dealt with other politicians in their own right and were not subject to dictation from anyone in the areas they represented. With the immense power of federal patronage in their hands, they had achieved such a commanding position that other politicians had to come to them in order to secure their constituents a share in the benefits of the New Deal. With only his own organization behind him, the ward politician had scant power, as the story of Joseph Maloney indicates. He had to subordinate himself to his congressman or United States senator in order to meet the demands of his constituents.

Thus it appears that the New Deal helped to bring about a political reorganization whereby the localized organizations of ward bosses were to a great extent supplanted by a more centralized political organization headed by the United States senator, with the congressman next in line, and the ward politicians assuming more subordinate positions.

Maloney concluded his story with a discussion of the racket element:

> Kelliher would never have anything to do with prostitution or with them fellows. . . . During prohibition, the bootleggers didn't mix in politics so much. Yes, they had to have protection, but they minded their own business more. Then, after repeal, the same people that had been bootlegging got the liquor licenses and when legalized horse and dog racing came along, they got into that. They've been spreading out all the time, and they've been trying to take over political control. It was in 1933 that I first realized how strong they really were. They got a lot of votes against me at that time. You see

men like Bob Madigan and Red O'Donnell can buy a lot of votes. Madigan runs that liquor place on —— Street, and O'Donnell controls a lot of horse rooms in this ward and has some liquor places too. They have a lot of fellows hanging around them, and they pass out a lot of free liquor, especially around election time. Then those number-pool fellows go right into people's houses, and they get quite a hold on the people. They've been spreading propaganda about me. Say an agent keeps his numbers and doesn't want to pay off on a hit. He tells the person, "I'm sorry, Joe Maloney had me pinched and the cops took all the slips off me, so I can't pay you." The people hold it against me, but it isn't true. I keep my hands off their business.

That crowd had been after me for a long time. They've been keeping their liquor places open after hours, and I didn't like that. And I don't think it's right to have them open on the Lord's Day either. And I knew that people were getting robbed in the —— Cafe, and I complained to the police about it. You see, the heart of the city is right in this ward. You'll find everything going on at night right down here.

They want to get me out of here. I've been threatened with a gun three times right in this office, and once a fellow pulled a knife on me. T. S. wanted to run me out of politics.

We might still be strong today if we hadn't picked up the wrong men. We elected Art Porcella representative, and he turned against us and went in with that racket crowd. Mike Kelly—he was my mistake. I really took him in against the majority of the organization. He had run for office three times, and he didn't get anywhere. Sometimes when a man ran against us, we recognized him and took him into the organization. Sometimes that policy worked out and sometimes it didn't. Mulrooney [a club member] was friendly with Kelly, and he says to me, "Why don't you give Kelly a chance?" So we talked to Kelly, and he promised he would be faithful to the organization. We indorsed him, but then when the campaign got under way, we began to hear disturbing reports that he was a weak candidate. We sent out our men to investigate, and we found that the reports were true. It looked like two Italian candidates were going to be elected. To prevent that, we had to do something we never did before, indorse just one candidate. That's the way we put Kelly across, and he just made it.

When he went to the legislature, Kelly didn't want to have anything to do with committees dealing especially with the affairs of the city. He wanted to get on the legal affairs committee, and through my influence I got him there. That was at a time when all this new legislation on liquor licences and horse and dog racing was coming through before that committee. Through that position he built up his law practice and got himself made counsel for the Liquor Dealers' Association. He caught me napping. While the racket element was fighting us from the outside, he was boring from within, and he did a lot of damage to the organization. . . .

Kelly fits right in with that element. That's why I had the police all against me in this last fight.

Analysis of the Social Power Position of a Real Estate Board

Donald H. Bouma

There are a number of ways of looking at the decision-making processes of a community. Historically, studies of this process have been primarily concerned with the formal authority structure, with legislatures, councils, commissions, and the like. This tendency to identify power and politics, setting decision-making in a political rather than a broader sociological context, obscures the larger area in which social power is manifest. The basic ingredients and the dynamics of the informal aspects of how a community goes about making a decision is a more recent concern.

The analysis of social power on the community level is the purpose of this study, with the focus on the impact of non-governmental forces on the making, legitimizing, and executing of community-wide decisions. The social power of these non-governmental forces is called "influence." The term "authority" is reserved for those having the legally recognized prerogatives for making community decisions.

In order to arrive at the basic factors influencing community decisions, the study was limited to an intensive analysis of one social organization, the real estate board, which had been particularly active and uniquely effective in determining decisions in a mid-western city of approximately 200,000 population which will be called Grand Valley. Authority groups and other influence groups were of concern only as they were encountered by the board in making community-wide decisions.

The term social power has been variously used in the past.[1] Following Max Weber, some have stressed the imposition of will; others have viewed it as an ethical problem, and some have identified social power with social status and wealth. Although at times power, status, and wealth do coincide, it is important to distinguish the three. For example, in some communities the old upper class, without loss of wealth or prestige, has lost its power to new elites of less wealth and prestige; in others, it has lost wealth without concomitant loss of power or prestige. It is important to determine what interrelationships and conversions are possible in any community, and using the terms interchangeably can only blur meaningful relationships.

Social power was used in this study in the sense developed by John Useem.[2] It is the concentration of influence and authority within a social system for making, legitimizing, and executing decisions which have consequences, intended or unintended, on the social chances of the members of that social system. By influence is meant the act of, or potential for, producing an effect in the determination of decisions without apparent force or authority. By authority is meant the prerogative, or precedence by virtue of holding an office, to engage in the decision process.

Authority depends on explicit rights and legally designated office. Influence is based on the social capital of individuals or groups. This, in turn, is produced by such things as resources, including money, time, and the like; skills in diplomacy, negotiation, and in handling the social factors met in the decision processes; technical competence in the area involved in the content matter of the decision; and various charismatic factors which may involve the assignment of unique attributes to the person or group concerned.

Legitimation denotes the formulation and presentation of socially acceptable reasons for justifying, explaining, and convincing those involved that the decisions are valid. Reasons are framed according to the sentiments and symbols in use in the social system. When adequate approval is secured the decision appears to be "right" and becomes "legitimate" to those concerned.

Two loci of decision-making are distinguished in this study and designated as arenas. The study was concerned with the real estate board's influencing of decisions in the arena of authority (legislative halls and city council chambers), and in the arena of public elections. Within this conceptual framework the study was concerned primarily with influence—the bases and prerequisites for a position of influence, the relationships to the value systems of the community, and the processes by which influence is legitimized.

There is a dearth of studies of the processes of influence in the full network of our social system. Our democratic ideologies have resulted in the minimization of the formal organization of the power structures. We have circumscribed and counter-balanced authority positions to restrict the symbols of power and to negatively evaluate power as an ethically sanctioned end. This circumscription of the scope of permissive formal organization of power has given rise to the growth of the informal arrangements in the influence processes. It is important for the adequate understanding of the structure and process of American community life to focus attention on these constellations of interacting informal power centers. It is highly necessary, not only from the standpoint of understanding the dynamics of a community, but also from the standpoint of contemplated social action, to ascertain the key influential structures in a community.

The nuclear centers of influence need

not be the same in each community. Given different aspects of social organization, varying strengths in the alignments of social groups, divergent value systems, and the like, this is not to be expected. While the Chamber of Commerce may occupy such a crucial influence position in one community, the AFL-CIO may occupy it in another community, and the local newspaper may be in the key position of influence in a third. In fact, in some communities there may be no power groups which are sufficiently potent to accomplish their ends alone. In such cases, one is likely to find loose and shifting alliances for the achievement of particular ends.

Whatever the specific alignments in a given community, whatever the group which occupies the key position of influence in a community, it is the process of influence in a community which needs careful study. The fact that the community itself, or the group which occupies the key position of influence, does not exhibit an awareness of the role of influence should not be a deterrent to such a study, although this may be one of the factors which has delayed giving this problem much attention in the past. Our early studies of social class had to overcome this same lack of awareness, this same lack of structuring of the phenomenon as a social creed.

Progress in the analysis of social power processes has been impeded by the fact that few of the theoretical frameworks designed have been tested in concrete situations. For example, the validity and workability of Lasswell's elaborate network of theorems and propositions concerning social power have never been tested in the crucible of community research. Progress has also been impeded by the almost complete preoccupation with empirical manipulations in many community studies with the concomitant disregard for the derivation of meaningful generalizations which can then be verified in subsequent research.

The real estate board was selected as the research focus because of several indications during the exploratory phase of the study that it was in a key position of influence in Grand Valley. Those in authority positions and heads of organizations in the city frequently mentioned the board as being an effective force in the making of community-wide decisions.

A study of the alignment of community groups on several controversial issues which went to the voters for decisions revealed that the real estate group had been victorious in each instance, while other groups also suggested as having influence, such as the Chamber of Commerce and the newspapers, had been defeated several times. The city's leading newspaper editorialized as follows: "We know from what has happened in the past that it is almost essential that any proposal to undertake a civic and school expansion program have the real estate board's support if it is to succeed."

The Grand Valley board had also been recognized by both state and national real estate associations for its effective community participation. It had been given the highest award granted by the National Association of Real Estate Boards for "civic activity." Mentioned specifically were the assistance of the local board in framing a new city zoning ordinance, the successful fight for rent decontrol, assistance to the city in its land value survey in preparing for scientific reassessment of the city, and its active support in helping to pass a two-mill twenty-year tax increase for a school building program.

The problem was approached in four ways. First, a study was made of the history of the board to determine its community relationships through the years and understand better the board as a social institution, its development as an organization, and the roots of its present structure.

Second, the dynamics of several community decisions, both in the arena of authority and that of public elections, were studied to determine the role played by the board in making, legitimizing and executing these decisions. Coming into purview here were the techniques employed, the extent of participation, the rationale employed, the approaches to various publics, the sensitivities to community value systems, symbol manipulation, the alignment of other power

groups, and the like. Newspaper accounts of these decisions were analyzed, including editorial stands, advertising campaigns, reports of alignments for and against the issue, arguments advanced, reports of public meetings concerned with the issue, the results, and group evaluations of the results. The official records of the board were studied in relation to these decisions to determine the kinds of techniques used, the money spent on shaping the decision, and the self-evaluation of the results. (After one of the decisions the board minutes concluded that it is "obvious from the results of the election that property owners in [Grand Valley] still follow the advice of the board.")

A third methodological technique employed in this phase of the study was that of participant observation. In one of the decisions studied, the writer actively participated in the decision-making process. He participated in a number of panel discussions and radio forums with realtors, watched their maneuverings for the support of other influentials, helped defeat them in a decision in the arena of authority (the city commission), noted their strategy in the fight for a referendum election in which they were ultimately successful, scrutinized their public utterances, and observed their manipulation of symbols in terms of the value systems of the various publics encountered.

Fourth, a study was made of the board and its individual members largely for the purpose of determining self images. This was done by attending meetings of the board of directors and of the entire membership, by studying the minutes of these meetings, and through interviews with individual realtors. Finally, interviews were held with community leaders to determine the community image of the board's power position.

The study revealed that the influence of the board on various community issues was long standing, deliberately designed, and marked by repeated success. The board was successful in influencing decisions in the arena of authority (the city commission and board of education). The fact that the board's stand on a given issue was sought after by those in authority indicated that they recognized the power position of the board. In some cases where the board was defeated in the arena of authority, it had carried its power struggle to the voting arena through referendum petitions. In this arena the board has never lost a decision, regardless of the alignment of opposing power groups.

In one of the referendum elections on public housing, after the ordinance has been passed by the city commission, the board found itself opposed by the Chamber of Commerce, the county council of churches and 32 affiliated organizations, social welfare organizations, union groups, and by the two daily newspapers. The realtors won by a 3–2 margin.

The board proved that it could take opposite sides of the same issue in different elections and win each time. One year it defeated a bond issue for new schools, although all other groups in the community were supporting it, with a carefully worked out propaganda campaign. Several years later it helped pass such a bond issue with a propaganda campaign based on an opposite set of rationalizations.

However, the concern of the study was not mainly to establish the fact that a real estate board in a certain city was actively engaged and traditionally successful in influencing community-wide decisions. Rather, the purpose was to move beyond the area of description to an analysis of the basic factors in the social power position of the real estate board. Why has the board been able to influence community decisions so effectively? How was the board able to take the negative side of an issue, develop a legitimation for it and win voter approbation, and several years later take the affirmative side of the same issue, develop an entirely different legitimation and again win voter approval? What generalizations can be derived concerning the social power position of an influential group which would provide understanding of other communities and other influential groups?

The factors found to be significantly operative in the social power position of the board in Grand Valley include the social cohesion of the group and its mechanisms of

social control, the financial structure of the organization, the cumulative character of social power, the social capital available to the group because of the technical information it possessed, the awareness of the value systems of various publics, direct participation of board members in authority positions, the handling of opposition groups, and the adequacy of the legitimation processes.

One of the basic factors in explaining the social power position of the board was the strong social cohesion of the group. Each member of the board was in competition with every other member as he sought listings of saleable property and sales to those seeking real estate. Yet the competitive orientation was submerged in the cooperative, and a united front was presented to the various publics involved in the decision-making process.

It is this social cohesion which, to a considerable extent, explains why the board has been able to exert a greater influence over decisions than other groups in the community. Although its membership is not large, comprising 425 representatives of 125 real estate firms, the board has been so effective in controlling its membership that the implementation of a decision was an "all hands" operation. After a decision was made by the board, or the directors, there was no room for internal opposition, and usually no room for neutrality. When a decision was made it was to be actively supported by the entire group, or various types of social control began to operate.

For example, the board decided to oppose a city commission proposal to the voters to repeal a tax limitation so that necessary city improvements could be made. The board spent close to $3,000 in a successful campaign to influence the voters to turn down the proposal. During the campaign, however, a prominent realtor ran a large ad in the newspapers advising home owners to "protect their interests" by removing the tax limit. The newspapers, which were backing the proposal, also published a news story quoting this realtor as being in favor of the repeal, indicating that realtors were not all agreed with the position their board had taken. The directors immediately ordered the offending realtor to desist from using the realtor emblem in any advertising on removal of the tax limit and to desist from using the term "realtor" when expressing his personal views. Informal controls were also used, and the realtor was silent through the remainder of the campaign.

Similarly, during the successful efforts of the board to influence voters against a public housing ordinance, several individual realtors admitted to those backing the proposal that they favored the housing ordinance, but could not come out publicly for it because of fear of retaliation from fellow realtors.

Neither was the board content with neutrality on the part of a member. In many cases the exercise of social power involved getting signatures on petitions which called for a referendum. In the case of one issue, the board needed 10,000 signatures on such petitions. Each real estate office was directed to obtain 100 signatures. A month later, noting that only 3,000 names had been obtained, the board decided to hire someone to complete the quota. The delinquent real estate offices were charged five cents per name for the needed signatures.

Other techniques for handling opposition points of view within the group had also been developed. One of the realtors was found to be particularly and vocally critical of the decisions of the directors, so the group decided to elect him to one of the nine positions on that policy-making group. In this way, the group felt, he would not only better understand the factors involved in decisions the directors made, but he would also be more hesitant to criticize policies he had a share in forming. The technique was very effective, and this realtor was later elected president of the board and became one of its most ardent supporters.

Social cohesion was also fostered by the practice of settling disputes within the group, rather than taking them to the courts. The board handled its own adjudication. The code of ethics of the board demanded that a realtor should so conduct his business as to avoid controversies with his fellow realtors but, in the event of controversy, to submit the dispute for arbitration to the directors and not to a court of law. The code also forbade a realtor to publicly criticize a fellow realtor.

The directors had the power to censure, suspend, fine, or expel members who were found to be at fault. A relatively small organization with a selected membership dependent for its business operations on the board-owned multiple-listing system, the board could easily enforce its discipline.

Hence the group provided strong pressures toward conformity. Members were accustomed to look to the directors for decision when differences arose and to abide by their findings. This carried over to those decisions of the directors which committed the board on community issues. As a result the solidarity of the group was assured and internal differences did not reach outside publics. Rather, these publics were impressed with the social cohesion and apparent uniformity and agreement in the real estate group. At times this united front image was fostered by the manipulation of solidarity symbols. On one issue the public was told through the newspapers that the directors voted unanimously to approve it. Actually, one of the nine directors voted against it according to the official minutes.

An additional factor in the social cohesiveness of the board was the work of the vigilance committee. This group watched the activities of the membership for violations of the code of ethics and breaches of the rules of the multiple-listing system. It was on the lookout for advertising violations, unsanctioned sales practices, questionable public utterances of the members, and other behavior considered violative of the codes of the group. Violations were reported to the directors who conducted a hearing and determined punishment.

The total effect of these factors was to provide the basis for a strongly knit organization, one which was prepared to play an effective part in the decision-making processes of the community.

A second factor in the analysis of the social power position of the board was the multiple-listing system. In brief, it provided that the property listings of each member realtor became the property of the board and every member had the right to sell from the listings. Thus every realtor was provided with a large "stock" of saleable properties with which he operated his business, and was not confined to attempting to sell only properties listed with his office.

The importance of the multiple-listing system lay in the following facts. It provided a major part of the income of the board, was an excellent public relations program, stimulated feelings of group pride in the organization, strengthened the position of the directors, gave an effective basis for discipline of members, developed a cooperative spirit among the members, and encouraged the growth of membership. All of these, in turn, are important in understanding the social power position of the board.

Annually over 80 per cent of the income of the board came from the operation of the listing system. Although chartered as a non-profit organization, the board admitted that the system was more than self-supporting and provided the board with a comfortable operating reserve. The income provided the board with a fund which could be used, and was used, to finance the participation of the group in the decision-making processes of the community, whether in the arena of authority or in the arena of public elections.

The directors had the authority to use this fund without consulting the membership. Therefore, the decision of the directors to take a given stand on a community issue did not have to be sold to the larger membership, but could be immediately implemented. Further, the availability of this fund meant that the directors did not have to assess the membership for finances to engage in the community decision-making processes, a technique used by many of the organizations which the board encountered in the social power struggles. The assessment technique always involves the dual hazard of stirring up protests and of not attaining the desired goal because of recalcitrants. (Such was the experience when the assessment system was first used by the American Medical Associa-

tion.) In either case, the group involved cannot with resoluteness and vigor begin a campaign on short notice.

The multiple-listing system also developed a feeling of in-group pride in the organization. The board had achieved national recognition because of its successful operation of the system and for its pioneering work in combining with it the system of photo-listing. Delegations from other cities came to observe the system in operation, and board personnel were in demand as speakers on this subject at regional and national meetings. This resulted in a strong we-feeling, a sense of satisfaction with the attainments of the organization, which strengthened social solidarity and acted as a buffer against criticism, both from within the group and from others in the community. The more successful a local group and the larger its national acclaim, the fewer the criticisms that will normally be levelled at it, and the better able the group is to shake off the critics. Further, the group appealed to this pride in the organization to get members to actively promote the ventures of the group, including those aimed at influencing community decisions.

The multiple-listing system resulted in a strengthening of the position of the directors. By placing the operation of the system in the hands of the directors and assigning to them all matters of arbitration when problems arose between members on business deals, a formerly loosely run and flimsily controlled organization of men with like interests became a tightly knit, closely supervised unit. The directors meet weekly to make decisions affecting the board as a whole, as well as the individual members. Because of the finality with which the directors spoke on the many details of the intricate multiple-listing system, the members were accustomed to looking in their direction for decisions. This socially conditioned the members to accept decisions of the directors concerning participation in the determination of community issues. The directors were aware of this, and the nine men, meeting frequently, could confidently and immediately take action when an issue arose. This is not to suggest that the directors had absolute power in the real estate group, nor that they never referred an issue to the membership for advice. It does, however, suggest that in a group which placed with the directors large responsibility for making final decisions on a large number of technical details, the members become conditioned to looking to the directors for other kinds of decisions and that the machinery for making decisions expeditiously is poised for utilization.

Since the machinery was there for making immediate and final decisions, no social issue calling for a community decision which arose caught the board unprepared to act. Those who sought board support or opposition for a community proposal usually needed to convince only the nine directors. This offered an explanation for the situation in which individual realtors have been asked why they had taken a certain stand on a community issue, and the reply was that they did not know, that they really were uninformed on the issue, but that the "directors have decided it." Given the internal power structure, the fact of an individual realtor supporting or opposing a community issue on which he is uninformed was no longer baffling. Further, the reply "the directors decided it" offered the realtor an effective defense when other groups in which he held membership, or his clients, friends or neighbors opposed a stand of the board and criticized him for it.

The multiple-listing system also provided an effective basis for control and discipline of the members. Since the individual realtor was dependent on property listing for carrying on his business, and since the board owned the listings, the board actually had control of the stock used by the member in making his living. Expulsion from board membership or even temporary suspension meant a blow to the member's business, since listings could only be bought or sold by members in good standing. Even though the expelled or suspended member had filed a listing himself, it became board property and could not be withdrawn.

Because of this strong disciplinary measure available to the group, a member could not afford to risk even temporary suspension. Thus his behavior conformed to the demands of the organization and social solidarity was preserved. No other organization in the community which concerned itself with the decision-making process had that kind of control available to it.

The multiple-listing system also served as a basis for social power by developing a cooperative spirit among the members. Today, Realtor A sells a house listed with the board by Realtor B and both profit by it on a split-fee basis. Tomorrow, Realtor B sells a house listed by Realtor C, both again profiting by the sale. Thus each realtor was continually aware of his dependence on the other members. Records revealed that over half of the sales were of this inter-office variety. This situation of interdependence may be contrasted with the strictly competitive nature of real estate transactions when a multiple-listing system is not used. Under such conditions a realtor benefits at the expense of others, as in the case of two similar businesses on the same street, and conditions are more conducive to the rise of suspicions, internal rivalries, jealousies, and animosities which often vitiate the strengths of the organization, which might have been used in influencing community decisions.

The multiple-listing system also stimulated membership growth and eliminated the problem of membership turnover. No membership drive has ever been held and members do not have to be persuaded to remain. The strengths of the board, in terms of time or finances, were not dissipated on maintaining the internal structure, but could be used in implementing decisions in the community. There was no fear that a stand taken would offend a member and that he might leave the organization. The assured loyalty of the members was an important social asset of the board.

A third basic factor in the analysis of the position of influence of the real estate board in determining community-wide decisions was the cumulative nature of social power. The board had been at the business of attempting to determine community decisions for a long time. It had developed the techniques, the "know-how," necessary for the establishment and maintenance of a social power position. It has accumulated skills in influencing decisions to be made in the arenas of authority and public elections. Its power position had developed a charismatic aspect in that there was a tendency on the part of some to look to the board for advice on a controversial issue, since it had been "right" so many times previously. It had over the years built up a network of relationships with those in authority positions and with other groups in the community which served as social capital to be used when needed in a decision-making process.

For example, the board had learned not to place great hopes on newspaper support in certain issues and had developed other techniques for reaching the public, such as direct mail. In several cases the board set up machinery to call every phone number listed to present its case. Faced with an adverse newspaper editorial policy on a particular issue, the board used large cartoon-type newspaper ads. So effective had this technique been that several people interviewed thought newspaper policy was reflected in the ads, rather than in the editorial pages. As one advocate of an issue indicated, "Although we had the newspapers behind us, people thought the paper were against it because all that they remembered was the full-page cartoons the real estate board ran."

The point here is not that people tended to be influenced more by clever ads than by editorials, but that they deduced newspaper policy from the ads. The board had learned that it had little to fear from newspaper opposition since circumvention techniques were tested and available.

The minutes of the board often mentioned luncheon meetings with those in authority "concerning real estate matters," often with the notation that "the officials now better understand the position of the board." This continuous contact established a pattern of relationships and channels of communication which could be effectively utilized by the board when necessary in the decision-making process. The board had accumulated skills in knowing the key person

or group in authority to contact, and also in sensing the degree of pressure or coerciveness which would be most fruitful on a given issue at a given time.

The cumulative aspect of social power is also indicated by the fact that those who are concerned with getting a decision made tend to consult the group known to have been effective in shaping past decisions. These consulting and conferring processes open up new areas in which the power group can influence community decisions, and the process is carried on in its own back yard. Instead of having to go to the voters or having to assert itself in the arena of authority on given issues, the board finds issues being brought to it and can involve itself in decision-making in its very early stages. Further, the influence is exerted in a nonpublic manner so that the risk of arousing negative community reaction, which so often is the response to a position of social power, is minimized. Thus a pattern of success in the decision process provided for the board the basis for maintaining and extending the social power position.

A fourth factor in the analysis of the social power position of the real estate board was its possession of knowledge and technical information in certain strategic areas in the decision-making process. Realtors were uniquely knowledgeable concerning taxation, assessments, city planning, zoning, housing, residential segregation, industrial and commercial relocations, and the like.

Since the property tax was the primary source of income for the support of municipal functions, and since any enrichment or extension of city and school services involved, generally, a shift in the property tax rate, the board's knowledge in the area of taxation placed it in a crucial position for influencing a whole array of allied community decisions. When the city devised a new city-wide zoning code the real estate board was asked to appoint a committee of its members to work with the planning department. The new ordinance was drawn in relation to the overall master plan to direct the outward growth of the city and to redevelop and rehabilitate certain areas in the city. The opportunity and ability to influence the construction of a zoning ordinance with such far-reaching consequences for the future growth, development, and rehabilitation of the community indicated another facet of the social power position of the board.

A fifth factor which explained the competency of the board in influencing community decisions was its awareness of, sensitivity to, and identification with the value systems of the community.

The real estate business is of such a nature as to develop in the realtors a keen awareness of the value systems of the community, primarily because of its intimate contact with people from all classes and segments of the community. Buying a home is in a real sense different than buying a spool of thread, a fur coat, a piece of furniture, or subscribing to a daily newspaper. Buying property usually involves frequent contacts with the realtor, the exchange of considerable information, and the discussion of preferences and social values.

Further, this close contact covers all segments of the community, cutting across racial, ethnic, economic, religious and other groupings. Through the contacts of individual realtors, the board developed an awareness of the value systems of the community, as well as those of the constituent publics. Of the opponents of the board in the influence processes of the community, none was so strategically situated for the development of awareness of value systems. For example, few members of the Chamber of Commerce came into close contact with the customer. This was especially true of those chosen to the board of directors, generally the most prominent businessmen in the city. What contact there was with customers was on a momentary basis or, in the case of many businesses, on a selective basis, so that no general awareness of values resulted.

The realtor must also be sensitive to community values. He does not depend on volumes of sales, but rather places great emphasis on each individual transaction and works hard at it. It is important that obstacles in the realtor-customer relationship be kept at a minimum. When the stand of the board on a controversial issue does not harmonize with the value system of the customer, it becomes a barrier to the transaction. Several realtors said that they favored the second school bond issue because they had lost too many sales when the board previously had actively opposed a millage increase for schools. "My customers blamed me because their children were attending school in antiquated buildings or on a half-day schedule," one of them said, "and I know it hurt my business."

This awareness of and sensitivity to community values enabled the board to determine the kinds of positions the public would support and partially explains the success pattern of the board. However, this also acted as a check on its social power position. Points were reached beyond which the board dared not go because of a fear that public reaction would interfere with the business possibilities of the individual realtor. This was one of the few limits to the social power position.

Not only was the board aware of and sensitive to value systems, but it also identified itself with these value patterns. One of the esteemed values in the community was home ownership, and each year Grand Valley is listed as a leading city in the country in percentage of home owners. Throughout its history the board had strongly identified itself with the interests of property owners, and fought battles in their name. A prominent citizen pleaded with the board to oppose a tax increase as it had done before, contending that "it is to your group that the home owners of the city will look for leadership." As Everett Hughes found in Chicago, "both the taxpayer and tax eater were forced to recognize the real estate board."[3]

Because of its identification with the interests of home owners the board could successfully legitimize its decisions on community issues in terms of home owner values. One member put it this way: "We were opposed to public housing because we felt that it would hurt our pocketbooks, but we talked tax threat to home ownership to the people." If the board was opposed to a suggested change it told the public that the proposal would involve a tax increase which was a "threat to home ownership."

When the board shifted its stand and favored a tax increase for schools, the legitimation was still in terms of home ownership and property values. In public statements the board told people that the suggested increase was best "for the home owner and tax-payer since antiquated and crowded school buildings hold back a community and affect property values."

The board's repeated stands against higher taxes, of course, easily identifies it with general community values. Everybody is presumably opposed to higher taxes. Although inadequacy of city and school services could conceivably backfire on the group responsible for the low taxes, diversion channels for the negative affect were opened up by charging city and school officials with unwise use of the "adequate" funds available.

Finally, the community took pride in being a conservative city, and it was characterized by a very slow growth pattern which necessitated few changes. The conservative stands of the board, generally urging a negative vote on issues, harmonized with this value.

A sixth factor in the power position of the real estate board was the direct participation of realtors in the arena of authority through the elective and appointive positions held by individual members. In such cases there was a confluence of the two aspects of social power—influence and authority—which were distinguished earlier. The realtor-councilman is as a realtor a member of a group having influence and, as a councilman, a member of a group having authority. In such situations the interaction between the two facets of social power becomes extremely close, and at times it is difficult to discern to what extent the influence structure is acting in the arena of authority, or to what extent the authority structure is used to advance or retard the cause of the influence structure.

The holding of authority positions by realtors opened up additional possibilities and unique channels for the exercise of influence. Realtors had extensive membership in the state legislature. After farmers and lawyers, the third largest group was made up of real estate and insurance men. For years two of the three state representatives from Grand Valley were members of the real estate board. This not only provided the board with direct access to the legislature for the implementation of decisions in that arena of authority, but also provided the board with observation posts so that impending decisions which affected its interests could immediately be brought to its attention.

Realtors were found in a wide range of other authority positions in Grand Valley, both in elective and appointive roles. They were widely used as consultants to various public groups. This identification in the public mind of realtors with authority positions having the legal prerogative of making community decisions conceivably carries over to decisions made by the board affecting the community so that there was a state of readiness on the part of at least some people to accept such influence decisions just as they accepted the authority decisions.

These were some of the important ingredients of the social power position of the real estate board in Grand Valley. It had successfully influenced many community decisions, both in the arena of authority and in the arena of public elections. Although social power is generally evaluated negatively in our society, and the image of the "man of power" or the "power group" is largely a negative one, the board exercised its power with a minimum of negative public reaction. For one thing, the board did not involve itself in every community decision—only those it considered major ones—and never endorsed candidates in elections. Further, it handled well the legitimation function and was able to make its position seem valid and right.

In our studies of the dynamics of community life it is important to identify those groups occupying positions of social power as well as the power figures, and it is vital that we see power and influence as something which can be quite distinct from prestige and winning a popularity panel contest. We also need to know the ingredients of the power position and social factors which sustain it.

Notes

1. Robert Bierstedt, "An Analysis of Social Power," *American Sociological Review*, 15 (December, 1950), pp. 730–738; H. H. Gerth and C. Wright Mills, *From Max Weber: Essays in Sociology*, New York: Oxford, 1946, p. 180; Herbert Goldhamer and Edward A. Shils, "Types of Power and Status," *American Journal of Sociology*, 45 (September, 1939), p. 171; Harold D. Lasswell and Abraham Kaplan, *Power and Society*, New Haven: Yale, 1950; Robert MacIver, *The Web of Government*, New York: Macmillan 1947, p. 87.

2. John Useem, "The Sociology of Power," unpublished paper read at annual meeting of the American Sociological Association, September, 1950.

3. Everett C. Hughes, "A Study of a Secular Institution: The Chicago Real Estate Board," unpublished doctoral dissertation, The University of Chicago, 1928.

Power Structure of a Sub-Community

Floyd Hunter

Regional City's Negro community hugs the heart of its business and commercial districts. As in many cities, it is characterized by poor housing, sub-standard community facilities, unpaved streets—all of which are used by a highly concentrated population. It is a segregated community—a fact of which most of its citizens are acutely aware. It is a functional community within the whole metropolis, furnishing the manpower which keeps much of the commerce of the town moving and which provides through its laboring force a sizeable proportion of the services demanded by all classes in the larger community. It is also an organized community. Its organization is of particular interest—especially its structure along lines of power.

As a preview to the materials to be presented in this chapter, it may be said that the pattern of power leadership within the Negro community follows rather closely the pattern of the larger community. The method of turning up policy-determinating leadership was the same as used in the larger community, but in this sub-community, Negro judges were used, seven of them, to give a basic list of leaders who might be questioned on leadership patterns.[1] The questionnaire to leaders was mailed, but a series of interviews was conducted to augment the data collected by correspondence.

As in the larger community, the Negro leaders tended to pick the same persons within their own community on policy matters, and there was a high rate of committee inter-

Reprinted from Community Power Structure *by Floyd Hunter, pp. 114–118 and 126–129, by permission of the author and The University of North Carolina Press. Copyright 1953 by The University of North Carolina Press.*

action among the top leaders. There was a clear differentiation between top organizations and lower ones on a scale of choices. A total of twenty-two organizations of top influence were selected by Negro leaders from a listing of more than 350. This figure alone represents the high degree of social organization within the Negro community.

The twenty-two organizations are structures through which policy decisions may be channeled. Many of them may be characterized as religious, fraternal, and welfare in nature. Two are economic organizations paralleling the Merchants' Association and the Chamber of Commerce in the city proper. Both of these groups are considered "weak and struggling" by leaders of influence. The Organized Voter's Association has much more influence, generally, than the business associations. The union organizations, with the exception of the Pullman Car Porters Union, are also considered weak.

While I do not wish to go into too much detail in describing individual leaders in the sub-community, I do wish to present a structural picture of leadership patterns and relate this pattern to the larger community power structure. Let us turn, therefore, to such an analysis, picking up more detailed data on organizational patterns as we proceed.

In a poll of the top leaders of the sub-community, twenty-three schedules give comparable answers in identifying persons of power and influence. The ranking of leaders in Table 1 gives a leadership array which may be compared with that found in the larger community as illustrated [above].[2] In examining the occupations of the Negro leaders one finds them falling into the following categories: nineteen professionals, eight commercial enterprisers; three banking and insurance operators; two leisure persons (social leaders); one civic worker (a retired postal employee); and one politician. This occupational listing differs markedly from that for top personnel in the larger community, where leadership is recruited largely from commerce and industry. Among the Negro professional workers are included a lawyer, a doctor, four educators, six minis-

ters, and seven social workers. These professionals all work on top policy-making committees and boards with the community business leaders. Their advice on policy matters is sought and taken by the leadership group as a whole. This pattern does not hold true in the larger community where the majority of the professional personnel are found only in the under-structure supporting the power elements.

The fact that six ministers were included on the list of leaders differs from the situation in the larger community where no ministers were chosen. It is interesting to note, however, that although the ministers were included on the list they were not considered top leaders in a policy-making sense by those within the leadership group itself who voted on them. Only one minister was voted into the upper-limits group of top leaders in the poll. This is interesting, because there is a belief abroad in the large community that if anything is to be done through leadership in the Negro community, the ministers, the educators, and possibly the undertakers should be contacted in about that order. The top policy leaders turned up in the study were found to hold, in order of rank, the following positions: publisher, banker, minister, educator, politician, social worker (2), insurance executive, civic worker, and lawyer. The other ministers (including two bishops), the educators, and the undertaker were subordinate to the persons holding the above positions.

Inquiry was made about this matter in the interviews. The answers may be summed up in the words of Morris Elam, civic worker, who said, "The ministers and the undertakers are mostly selfish in their approach to most community situations. They either want to get more for themselves or to increase the size of their own organizations. People catch on to that sort of thing and when they are asked to choose leaders, they think of people that are not so much out for their own benefit. The doctors here are in the same category. They are interested in making money, but they are withdrawn from community life. They could not lead anyone."

It was asked if the ministers would be

TABLE 1. *Sub-Community Leaders Ranked According to Number of Votes Received from Other Negro Leaders in Leadership Poll**

LEADERS	NUMBER OF VOTES
Calvert Smith	19
Courtney Jackson, Hedley Ryan	18
Myron Lake, Fortney Todd	17
Georgia Cravens	15
George Green	13
Cecil Bardon	12
Morris Elam, Claude Jones, Sidell Rumley	11
John Last	9
Gideon McKay, S. T. Story	8
Samuel Judson, Maude Lynde	7
Foster Ledder	6
Paisley Brown, Eva Trulowe	5
Elbert Johnson	4
Roy Clayton	3
Hyram Jasper, Maimie Stanton	2
Harvey Aberdeen, Nelson Hanson, Dolphan Greer, Blanche Keys, Mrs. John Last, Edmond Whitney	1
Myron Crookshank, Grant Missler, N. L. Norris, Gertrude Tylor, T. C. Whitlock	0

*Code numbers used in analyzing data and corresponding to names of leaders are as follows:

1. Trulowe	12. Missler	24. Keys
2. Mrs. J. Last	13. Aberdeen	25. Whitney
3. Last	14. Cravens	26. Rumley
4. Bardon	15. Elam	27. Tylor
5. Ryan	16. Lynde	28. Jasper
6. Whitlock	17. Hanson	29. Greer
7. Johnson	18. Crookshank	30. Smith
8. Brown	19. Ledder	31. McKay
9. Green	20. Story	32. Norris
10. Todd	21. Judson	33. Clayton
11. Stanton	22. Lake	34. Jones
	23. Jackson	

drawn in on projects to help secure agreement of opinion in the community—that is, after policy had been determined by the top leaders. One reply to this question was as follows: "Yes, the ministers have a part in getting projects under way and they can be helpful. You certainly would not leave them out, but I would not go to them *first* on a community-wide matter, because I would know that they would see a lot of reasons why they should not try to move the people. They would be thinking that any money-raising scheme, for example, would hurt their own contributions. They will go along on most things, if they think a lot of powerful people are behind a project."

From interviews with sub-community leaders the conclusion is clear that the process of decision on matters of policy rests with the top leaders, as it does in the larger community. The individual ministers representing church associations are utilized as channels of communication to apprise large numbers of people of these decisions. The civic associations stand in the same relationship to the leadership group. The process of decision within the upper group is called "getting it straight," that is, policy is informally cleared between top leaders, and the line is set, before it goes to the underlying mass of people.

The preconceived notion was carried into the study that the social fraternities were powerful organizations. There are a great number of Greek letter societies in the sub-community. Only one of them, however, was considered influential in civic affairs, and it comes almost at the bottom of our listing of top organizations. Some of the social fraternities on the list in the questionnaire received no votes at all as top influence organizations. The role of the fraternities seems to be in the area of social rather than power relations.

In general it may be said that the top associational groupings identified in the sub-community have a political content not found in the larger community. This is true even in the welfare and recreational associations. It may also be said that the leadership within the associations, while entertaining discussion on political matters, tends to a conservative approach to issues. For example, during the formation of a Progressive party in Regional City there was considerable discussion on what part Negroes should play in its activities. There was much open discussion of the matter in the associational meetings but the leadership was dedicated to remaining loyal to the traditional local parties of a more conservative nature. The Progressive party was stressing equal rights for Negroes in its platform in direct opposition to the older parties. This plank had considerable appeal to many of the citizens and the leaders did not openly oppose discussions of the issues presented by Progressive party candidates. They quietly worked against the movement, however. The process was described by one leader in these words:

"Many of us [the leaders] were in sympathy with the aims of the Progressive party, but we felt that more could be gained ultimately by sticking to the older parties. We discussed the matter of alignment very carefully among ourselves [the top leader group], and decided to play a waiting game. We knew that the Progressive party was scaring the leaders uptown and we thought the fright was good for them. If the party gained strength we could always threaten to go along with it, but we would wait and see.

"All of the leaders [in the sub-community] have one or two white men they can go to and discuss various matters that concern us. Whenever there is a threat of trouble or when the police get too brutal, we can get help from some of the men we know person-

ally. At the time of the Progressive party activity the white men got in touch with us. They wanted to know how our people were reacting to the propaganda being put out by this party. They said they were very much against the party and hoped we were. They said they had helped us in the past and they wanted our help now.

"We discussed this among ourselves and agreed to let the uptown boys dangle a little. We finally told them, however, that we were not for the Progressive party ourselves and we would do what we could to discourage it in the community here. We said we could not act openly, but we would do what we could. We figured that we would really gain more by such a move on our part. As things turned out the Progressive party was a flop. I definitely think we gained something by not going too radical. Our strategy is to get places for ourselves in the older parties."[3]

The sub-community leadership is here taking a position characterized by Oliver C. Cox as that of "protest within the *status quo* (desire to be 'counted in')."[4] This position, so succinctly summarized by Cox, would seem to describe the general tenor of the demands for recognition made upon members of the larger community by the top leaders in the sub-community.

The relationships between sub-community and larger community leadership are well illustrated in the description of actions taken relative to the Progressive party. The conversations between white and Negro leaders reported above were informal in nature. The telephone was utilized in most instances. The leader quoted met a leader of the larger community in a meeting of the Community Council and had an informal discussion with him afterwards. Sub community leaders never rate inclusion on the white upper-policy-strategy committees but are approached informally to get their opinions. This process is a relatively fixed pattern. The exception may lie, to some extent, in the realm of partisan politics.

Some of the top leaders in the sub-community do have access to the elected officials of the city, and on one or two occasions within the past five years some of the more progressive candidates for public office have visited the sub-community leaders in their offices. These visits are described as stealthy. None of the other top policy leaders of the larger community have ever made personal visits to the private offices of the sub-community leaders, but some of the top leaders have entertained visits from delegations of Negro citizens in their own offices—sometimes at the request of the sub-community leaders and again upon invitation by the white leader. Such interchange of visits keeps the top leadership informed concerning sub-community opinion on selected issues, but the practice is considerably restricted and formal. There cannot be said to be a free flow of information in most situations affecting the sub-community and requiring policy decision. Usually crisis situations are involved when the two groups meet. For example, the sub-community may have reached a point where they are *demanding* better school facilities or recreation facilities or housing. At such a point there is much withholding of information on both sides in order to maintain bargaining advantage.

Notes

1. Sub-community, as the term is used here, does not necessarily mean inferior, although many features of the sub-community could be so classified. It means rather that this is a community operating within a larger community.
2. See p. 63 [Table 2, in *Community Power Structure*]. All names as well as organizations with whom leaders are identified are disguised as in the discussion of the larger community.
3. The Progressive party will be referred to again as it relates to the dynamics of politics in the state and in the Regional City community. We are not concerned with describing the total program of this party, but only such parts of its activities as may illustrate specific points in our discussion, e.g., the dynamics herein illustrated.
4. See "Leadership Among Negroes," from *Studies in Leadership*, edited by Alvin W. Gouldner (New York: Harper and Brothers, 1950), p. 270.

Power Structure and the Negro Sub-Community

Ernest A. T. Barth and Baha Abu-Laban

Recently Bernard Barber noted that "a hard look at contemporary social science will show that there is very little consensus on a theory of influence and that there is also very little sound empirical research on which such a theory might be based."[1] Also, Roucek has commented that "there has been a definite disinclination to view the field of minority-majority relations as another aspect of human power relations."[2]

This paper reports findings from a study of influence and power as these phenomena operate within the context of the Negro sub-community of a large Northwestern city. The project was designed to replicate Floyd Hunter's work in the sub-community of

Reprinted from the American Sociological Review, *24 (February 1959), 69–76, by permission of the authors and the American Sociological Association. Copyright 1959 by the American Sociological Society.*

"Regional City."[3] Hunter presents one of the few exceptions to Roucek's criticism noted above. Such studies represent a major step in the direction of bringing the field of minority relations out of the special value context within which it has long been encompassed and placing it within the framework of general sociology.

A comparison of the findings reported in this paper with Hunter's permits the study of functional relationships between the structure of the influence system and other dimensions of community structure. Such case studies offer a valuable, if partial, approach to the comparative study of communities. For example, Pellegrin and Coates have investigated the relationship between absentee ownership of the major industries of a middle-sized Southern city and the structure of power relations within that community.[4] In a study of the structures of power in an American and a British community, Miller reports differences in the occupational distribution of power leaders in the two contexts, which are related to the differences in the value systems of the two nations reflected in different prestige rankings associated with similar occupations.[5] These researches demonstrate the fruitfulness of attempts to develop a typology of power structures within the framework of comparative community theory. In addition, they further the understanding of community process and structure.

The Negro Community in Pacific City

As Hunter's "Regional City" dominates the economic and political organization of the Southeast, so the "Pacific City" of this study dominates in the Northwest. The two communities are quite similar in total population and economic structure.[6] Stimulated mainly by the expansion of job opportunities during and following World War II, the Negro community of Pacific City has greatly increased in population within the past seventeen years. Federal Census data show that from a total of 3,789 in 1940, the Negro population of Pacific City expanded to 15,666 in 1950, an increase of 313.5 per cent for the

decade. It is estimated that at present the population is in excess of 25,000. The pattern of residential location is similar to that of most major American cities: Negroes are generally centrally located and highly concentrated in "black belt" areas. Although the city prides itself on its "liberal policies concerning race relations, the index of residential segregation is high in relation to other comparable cities.[7] Early in the 1940s Negro migrants to the city were characteristically young, male, unskilled workers. Available evidence indicates, however, that since 1950 the stream of migration has included an increasing proportion of more highly educated, married men engaging in professional activities.

There are some important differences between the Negro communities of Pacific City and Regional City. The 1950 Census data show that Pacific City's Negro population comprised a relatively small proportion of the total population (approximately 3.4 per cent), whereas in Regional City approximately a third of the population was Negro. As noted above, the Negro population in Pacific City more than tripled in the decade 1940 to 1950. The corresponding rate for Regional City during that period was about 16 per cent. The former dramatic increase has had a disturbing influence on the relatively stable pre-war Negro community of Pacific City. The incoming stream of migration has brought with it a large number of professionally trained Negroes of high occupational status; their leadership now appears to overshadow most of the "old time" community leaders. At the same time, many of the in-migrants came from Southern states, carrying the cultural characteristics of Negroes in that region, which, in many ways, were inconsistent with those of the Pacific City sub-community, resulting in some social disorganization.

The Negroes of Pacific City occupy somewhat more prestigeful and better paid jobs than those of Regional City. In 1950, a larger proportion of them were concentrated in service occupations, especially government jobs, as compared with the concentration of workers in the unskilled labor category in

Regional City. These occupational differences are reflected in the income figures for the two communities. The Federal Census data show that in 1949 the median income for whites in Pacific City was 2,356 dollars as compared with 2,218 dollars in Regional City, while Pacific City's Negroes earned an average of 1,709 dollars in that year as compared with 1,045 dollars for Negroes in Regional City.

One index of the differences in the overall patterns of interracial relations characteristic of the two cities may be seen in the legal structure of the two states. In Regional City the official policy of segregation in schools and other public facilities has long been supported by the law, while in Pacific City a state F.E.P. law has been in effect since 1949 as well as a longstanding "public accommodations" law. The state legislature recently passed an "Omnibus Civil Rights Bill" almost unanimously, with provisions for the protection of minority rights in housing as well as in public accommodations and employment. The schools of the community are officially non-segregated although the pattern of residential concentration has had its usual results: a high proportion of Negro children in relatively few schools.

Study Design and Methodology

Since this study was intended to replicate Hunter's work in Regional City, his research design was followed in so far as possible.[8] Therefore, during the initial stage of the project, in order to locate individuals characterized as influential within the Negro sub-community, lists of names of people who had held office in the major organizations of the sub-community, plus additional names gotten from interviews with Negro informants known to the authors, were obtained. The names of sub-community organizations through which influence might be channeled were taken from a list prepared by the Chamber of Commerce, supplemented by other organizations mentioned by Negro informants. Also, a list of "important issues for the sub-community" suggested by the informants was compiled. In addition, the

local Negro newspaper provided other names of leaders, organizations, and issues. From these sources, 154 potential influentials, 84 organizations, and about 12 issues were obtained.

Two questionnaires were constructed, one containing the names of the potential leaders and the other the organizations. A panel of ten Negro respondents, representative of the various institutional areas of the sub-community, was selected. In a personal interview each respondent reported how well he knew each potential influential and added names of others whom he believed to have been omitted. He then selected from the list the names of ten people he would choose "to help in a major project requiring a decision by a group of sub-community leaders." The interviewee also rated each of the organizations as "most influential," "influential," or "less influential" in initiating or supporting actions of importance to the Negroes in the city.

With information from the first ten interviews, the list of leaders was reduced to 33 names, each of which had received three or more choices from the ten previous respondents. The list of organizations was similarly reduced to a total of 27. These modified lists were submitted to six other Negro informants who, in turn, were asked to rate the leaders and organizations and to add the names which they believed to have been omitted. The resulting final lists consisted of 36 probable influentials and 27 organizations.[9]

A second phase of the field work involved interviewing the 36 probable influentials.[10] Each respondent was asked to fill out a questionnaire seeking information about his background and activities in the community.[11] The respondent was asked to indicate how well he knew each of the other influentials and to estimate his average monthly number of social and committee contacts with each; and, again, the respondents were invited to add the names of any leaders they felt had been omitted from the list. Each was asked: "If you were responsible for a *major* project which was before the community that required *decision* by a group of leaders—leaders that nearly everyone would accept—which ten on this list would you choose, regardless of whether they are known personally to you or not?"

Each influential also was asked to rate the 27 organizations on the three-point scale of influence, adding such other groups that he believed had been omitted. Finally, each was asked to name two issues or projects which he considered to be "most crucial" to the sub-community. The respondent indicated whether or not anyone had contacted him about each issue, whether he had contacted others, and what media

of communications were used in these contacts.

The Findings

Sub-Community Leaders. This study is primarily concerned with the 36 probable leaders whose names received three or more mentions by the panel of 16 judges. The names of these leaders, their occupations, the number of votes each received as a "top leader," and the number of mutual choices each received, are listed in Table 1.

TABLE 1. *Sub-Community Leaders Ranked by Number of Votes Received from Other Leaders in Leadership Poll*

LEADER	NUMBER OF VOTES	NUMBER OF MUTUAL CHOICES	OCCUPATION
1. Walters	31	9	Social Worker
2. Taylor	27	7	Lawyer
3. Bassett	25	6	Small business (druggist)
4. Troy	25	8	Minister
5. Barner	24	9	Architect
6. Baldwin	22	6	Lawyer
7. Smith*	20	10	Housewife
8. Treat*	17	4	Social Worker
9. Moster	16	6	Minister
10. Willard	15	4	Retired
11. Williams	13	4	Small business (bail bond)
12. Stephens	12	2	Social Worker
13. Worth	12	2	Small business (real estate)
14. Hardy*	10	3	Social Worker
15. Fallsworth	9	1	Small business (photographer)
16. Dunham	9	2	Physician
17. Young*	9	3	Office Secretary
18. Parks*	7	4	School Teacher
19. Main*	6	4	Personnel Clerk
20. Barrier*	6	1	Housewife
21. Olaf*	6	2	Sales (Insurance)
22. Ford	5	3	Small business (insurance)
23. Stone*	5	3	Unknown
24. Homer	4	1	Lawyer
25. Planter	4	2	Small business (nursing home)
26. McNeil	3	0	Dentist
27. Spear*	3	2	Small business (beauty school)
28. Masters*	3	1	School Teacher
29. Horne*	3	2	Unknown
30. Roberts	3	1	Physician
31. Moore*	2	0	Social Worker
32. Miller*	2	1	Sales (real estate)
33. Stewart	2	0	Lawyer (Pros. Office)
34. Taylor*	2	1	School Teacher
35. Sullivan	1	0	Small business (dry cleaning)
36. Gold*	1	1	Service Worker

*Denotes female leader.

Sixteen (or 44 per cent) of the leaders are women. This tends to confirm the popular belief, expressed by several of the leaders themselves, that women hold high positions in the leadership structure of the sub-community. Although two of the individuals high on the list in terms of number of votes are women, for the total group of 36 leaders women received an average of 6.1 votes compared with an average of 13.9 for men. This generally lower position of women in the leadership structure is probably due to the nature of their participation in the organizational activities of the community. Although, on the average, female leaders belong to about as many organizations as do men (8.42 memberships for men and 8.25 for women), women far exceed the men in fraternal and "social" activities. In this respect, we find many more women participating in the leadership activities of the sub-community than did Hunter. Male leaders concentrate their organizational activities in civic and professional organizations.

The findings concerning the age distribution of the leaders differ from those of Hunter. The mean age of the 36 Negro leaders was 44.8 years; Hunter's comparable figure is 54.3 years.

About 52 per cent of the leaders in the Pacific City sub-community were self-employed, averaging about three employees under their supervision. Two leaders supervised more than ten employees; a nursing home operator supervised 18 employees, and an insurance executive supervised 16 workers. (No non-leaders employed a sizeable number of workers.) Again these findings differ markedly from those of Regional City, where Hunter found that the "top leader" supervised 1800 workers and that eleven others supervised 25 or more workers. The much smaller figures for Pacific City reflect the positions held by the top leaders in the occupational structure of the community. Eight of the 36 leaders were engaged in small business activities, including insurance and real estate brokerages, a drug store owner, a beauty school, and a photography shop, while most of the leaders were professionals: five social workers, four lawyers,

three physicians, three public school teachers, two ministers, and one architect. If power within the community derives in part from high positions in its economic or political structure, it is clear that none of these leaders in Pacific City's Negro sub-community possessed such power.

Only four of the 36 leaders were locally born (within the state). On the other hand, 60 per cent of them came originally from the South. These figures reflect the impact of migration on the leadership structure of the community. Although the leaders had been in Pacific City for 16.5 years on the average, only 80 per cent of them owned their homes. The leaders had also achieved a fairly high educational status, having completed about 16 years of school on the average.

The "Top Seven Leaders." In an attempt to determine whether or not there was any "leadership clique" among the Negroes of Pacific City a special analysis was made of the seven persons who had been mentioned as "top leaders" by one half or more of the 36 people interviewed. These seven "elitists" were distinguished from the other leaders by superior educational attainment, *shorter* length of residence in the community, and by their sex, all but one being men. All of the top seven owned their homes and four of them were self-employed.

Hunter demonstrates that the "top leadership group in the Negro sub-community tends toward closure" in two ways. First, almost all of the leaders were known to each other ("Ninety per cent of the leaders know each other 'well' or 'socially'") and, second, his sociometric data show a correlation between the number of votes received as a top leader and the number of mutual choices.[12]

Acquaintanceship among the 36 leaders in this study was also very high, with 93 per cent of the leaders reporting knowing each other "well" or "slightly." Among the seven top leaders, all reported that they knew each of the others well. In addition, with the exception of "Smith-Baldwin," all of the top seven reported having both "committee and social contacts with each other regularly."

These findings tend to confirm those of Hunter on this point.

Table 1 lists the names of the leaders, the number of votes they received, and the number of mutual choices they achieved. The well known correlation between sociometric leadership standing and the number of reciprocated choices achieved as a leader holds for our top seven, for they received an average of 7.9 such choices whereas the remaining leaders averaged 2.0. A further indication of the formation of a "closed" top leadership group is the relationship between the actual number of mutual choices and the total possible number of mutual choices. Within the top seven, of the 21 possible mutual choices,[13] 13 (or 62 per cent) were actually made, and in only one case was there a reciprocal nonchoice.

These top seven were only slightly better known to the wider leadership group than were the others. Use of an "acquaintanceship score," with a range from zero (not known to any of the other leaders in the group of 36) to 105 (known well by all other members of the leadership group),[14] gave these seven an average score of 95.6 as compared with 90.9 for the remainder of the group.

One major differentiating characteristic of the top seven leaders is the degree to which they participated with others in organizational committee activities. Their participation average with the other leaders was 16.7 as compared with 10.6 such contacts for the remaining 29. This supports the contention of several of the respondents that "the top leaders in this community got there because they were very active in organizational work." The belief was expressed that if such activity ceased the top leadership position would quickly be lost.

The top seven shared one other characteristic: each had taken part, at one time or another, in interracial activities in an "equal status" context in which he (or she) acted as a spokesman for the Negro community. Here, perhaps, is a case of "prestige drainage," with Negro leaders draining prestige from the white leaders with whom they were in contact.

Issues Confronting the Sub-Community. If the nature of the power process in the local community is to be fully understood the types of issues that are most crucial to those who exercise this power must be analyzed. Each of the 36 leaders was asked: "What, in your opinion, are two of the major issues before the Negro community—either immediately past or current?" Table 2 lists the issues mentioned and the frequency of their mention.

From Table 2 it is apparent that the issues of concern to the leaders identified in this study were those associated with problems of interracial relations and the effects of minority group status, and more specifically, with attempts to change the existing social structure of the community. In spite of the

TABLE 2. *Issues Before the Negro Sub-Community Listed by Frequency of Mention by 36 Sub-Community Leaders*

TYPE OF ISSUE	NUMBER OF TIMES MENTIONED
Minority Housing	33
Civil Rights Legislation	17
Concentration of Minority Children in the Schools	11
Parks and Recreational Facilities in Minority Residential Areas	4
Discrimination in Employment and Career Counseling for Children	4
Police Brutality	1
Unity in Action within the Sub-Community	1
No issues mentioned	1

presence of at least one organization of Negro business men and the fact that several of the leaders were themselves business men, their major concerns did not directly involve business problems (or most political programs). In their position as *leaders in the Negro sub-community*, they were preoccupied with problems of the "Negro protest." In some measure, perhaps, this interest reflects the attitude that, lacking the needed power, their influence on major decisions concerning general economic and political policy in the community is minimal.

Community Organizations and the Structure of Power. The formal organizations and administrative agencies, as well as the less formal but relatively stable cliques, offer mechanisms through which community decision-making activities may be channeled. In Regional City, Hunter reports that, although the "top" and six other leaders in the sub-community did not generally work through formal policy committees, the majority did so.[15]

In an attempt to identify the organizations in Pacific City through which policy decisions flow, a list of the major organizations in the sub-community was drawn up.[16] Each of the 36 leaders was asked to rate each organization on a three-point scale as (1) most influential, (2) influential, and (3) less influential. These organizations are listed in Table 3 in order of the numbers of "most influential" votes.

In two respects this list is comparable to that reported in Hunter's study.[17] Although eight of the 27 organizations listed are of the Greek letter variety, none of these received more than two mentions as "most influential," indicating that at best they play a relatively minor role in the decision-making activities of the sub-community. And, again as in the case of Hunter's list, the organizations considered "most influential" (including the local Urban League, although its major function is community organization and case work) have a pronounced political content in their programs. With one minor exception, the churches, perhaps the most fully segregated of all sub-community organizations, were not mentioned—an interesting finding, especially in view of the fact that two of the top ten leaders are ministers.

Three further observations concerning these organizations are in point here. First, six of the top seven groups are directly concerned with interracial relations and "race betterment." Second, only one of the organizations on the entire list (ranking seventh) has as its principal interest the business organization of the sub-community. Finally, although union membership among Pacific City's Negroes is fairly widespread, only one union was mentioned, one that rated

TABLE 3. *Sub-Community Organizations Rated by 36 Sub-Community Leaders, Ranked According to Number of "Most Influential" Ratings Received*

ORGANIZATION	NUMBER OF "MOST INFLUENTIAL" RATINGS
Urban League	33
N.A.A.C.P.	29
Jackson Street Community Council	17
Christian Friends for Racial Equality	17
Association of Colored Women	16
Eastside Y.W.C.A.	16
East Madison Street Commercial Club	16
Cosmopolitan Century Club	9
Eastside Y.M.C.A.	8
Prince Hall Masons	6
The People's Institutional Baptist Church	4
The Brotherhood of Sleeping Car Porters	4
Philorati Club	4
Mary Mahoney Registered Nurses	3
Fraternal Organization	2
Veteran's Organization	2
Fraternal Organization	2
Fraternal Organization	2
Fraternal Organization	1
Sorority	1
Fraternal Organization	1
Fir State Golf Club	1
Fraternal Organization	1
Church Club	1
The Elks	1

low in influence. This finding is consistent with the fact that, although there are several professional Negro union leaders in the community, none of them was cited as a "top leader." It appears that the major concern of the Negro sub-community, as well as of its leaders, lies with issues centering around minority status and group protest.

It may be noted that no "luncheon clubs," "supper clubs," or other informally organized groups appear on the list of the influential organizations. Early in the field work, an attempt was made to discover any such groups, but only one, the "Sunday Night Supper Club," was mentioned. One informant, a recent migrant to the community and a highly trained educator, in citing this club, noted that several top leaders whose names appear in Table 1 were active members. However, the club was only recently organized and appears to be primarily a recreational group.

Summary and Conclusions

According to Mills, Hunter, Miller and others, the structure of power in American society and in American communities is derived in large part from the institutional structure of the society. The majority of the leaders identified by Hunter and Miller in their field studies were occupants of high positions in the economic organization of their communities. Mills argues that power resides principally in the realms of economic, political, and military organization, and suggests further, that the structure of the "power elite" is related to the rate and nature of social change in a society at any given time. The fruitfulness of a comparative approach to the study of power is suggested by these views. Such an approach would aim at specifying the conditions relevant to the type of power structure and processes in a community or society and would require a typology of community power structures.

Although the findings of this study do not, of course, make it possible to develop a systematic theory of power, the following conclusions are relevant to this purpose. First, it is evident that, although there is an identifiable structure of leadership in the sub-community of Pacific City at the present time, the leaders themselves are not "power wielders" or "decision makers" in the sense in which the terms are used by Hunter and Mills: they hold positions of little importance to the community's institutional structures; their decisions have no serious ramifications for the larger community.

In Pacific City there is an ecologically identifiable "Negro community"—why is there is no genuine power structure of the type found in Regional City? This lack can be attributed in part to the relatively small Negro population, insufficient to support large-scale separate institutions; in part to the rapid expansion of the population in the sub-community (evidence from interviews indicates that the old-leadership structure [prior to 1940] was disrupted and almost wholly destroyed by the impact of the incoming migrants); and in part to the attitudes of the leading figures in the minority community, who have worked hard for liberal legislation, better education for Negroes, and better housing on an open market. In this work they have been remarkably successful, and prefer not to risk these gains by supporting segregated institutions.

Several of the respondents insisted that it is incorrect to speak of a "Negro community" in Pacific City, maintaining that most Negroes are not conscious of being members of a racial community as they are in many other cities. Perhaps this helps to explain why the Negro leaders are those who are active in "protest" organizations—for these may be about all that remain of a Negro sub-community.

In any event, the sub-communities of Regional City and Pacific City represent quite different types. The well organized, stable structure of power in Regional City is missing in Pacific City. Although leadership groups have certain similar characteristics, those in Regional City wield power *within* the sub-community and those in Pacific City do not. Leaders in Regional City are motivated, at least in some measure, to maintain their segregated sub-community, while in Pacific City the leaders seek opposite goals. These findings emphasize the importance of the general community context in the study of power relations.

Notes

1. Bernard Barber, *Social Stratification: A Comparative Analysis of Structure and Process*, New York: Harcourt, Brace, 1957, p. 234.

2. Joseph S. Roucek, "Minority-Majority Relations in Their Power Aspects," *Phylon*, 17 (First Quarter, 1956), pp. 25–26.

3. Floyd Hunter, *Community Power Structure:*

A Study of Decision Makers, Chapel Hill: The University of North Carolina Press, 1954.

4. Roland J. Pellegrin and Charles H. Coates, "Absentee Owned Corporations and Community Power Structure," *American Journal of Sociology*, 61 (March, 1956), pp. 413–419.

5. Delbert C. Miller, "Industry and Community Power Structure: A Comparative Study of an American and an English City," *American Sociological Review*, 23 (February, 1958), pp. 9–15.

6. *Ibid.*

7. Donald O. Cowgill and Mary S. Cowgill, "An Index of Segregation Based on Block Statistics," *American Sociological Review*, 16 (December, 1951), p. 825.

8. Hunter, *op. cit.*, "Appendix: Methods of Study," pp. 262–271.

9. Cf. Robert O. Schulze and Leonard U. Blumberg, "The Determination of Local Power Elites," *American Journal of Sociology* 63 (November, 1957), pp. 290–296.

10. All of the interviews were conducted by Baha Abu-Laban, a former resident of the Middle East, whose swarthy appearance stimulated short friendly chats with the respondents and comments concerning his ethnic identity. The interviews were characterized by a high level of rapport in our judgment.

11. Twenty-nine of the 36 respondents returned these questionnaires.

12. Hunter, *op. cit.*, pp. 119 ff.

13. A "mutual choice" was defined as the instance in which there was a reciprocal selection as a top leader.

14. Each respondent was asked to indicate "how well he felt he knew" each of the other members of the leadership group on a four-point scale ("Don't know," "Heard of," "Know slightly," "Know well"), with each response assigned a weight from 0 to 3.

15. Hunter, *op. cit.*, p. 125.

16. The technique of obtaining this list of organizations is discussed above.

17. Hunter, *op. cit.*, pp. 125–126.

Negro Protest Leaders in a Southern Community*

Lewis M. Killian and Charles U. Smith

One of the significant features of race relations in the past five years has been the emergence of new patterns of Negro leadership in southern communities. Prior to the various court decisions which withdrew legal support from the traditional framework of segregation, Negro leadership gave the appearance of conforming to the pattern of "accommodating" or "compromise" leadership. Analyses of leadership in southern Negro communities, such as the treatment found in Myrdal's *American Dilemma*,[1] suggest that the compromise leaders held their positions primarily because they were acceptable to white leaders. They were also accepted by Negroes because accommodation was regarded as the most practical and effective mode of adjustment in the existing power situation.

The desegregation decisions of the U.S.

Reprinted from Social Forces, 38 (*March 1960*), 253–257, *by permission of the authors and The University of North Carolina Press. Copyright 1958 by the Williams and Wilkins Company.*

*The authors are indebted to the Society for the Psychological Study of Social Issues for a Grant-in-Aid which helped make this study possible. This is a revised version of a paper read at the twenty-second annual meeting of the Southern Sociological Society, Gatlinburg, Tennessee, April 17, 1959.

Supreme Court, even without extensive implementation, redefined this power situation. In the years following 1954 militant leaders, reflecting the protest motive instead of the theme of patience and accommodation, have moved into the focus of attention of both whites and Negroes. Whereas the accommodating leaders had not been widely known to the white public, largely because they operated in a noncontroversial and often clandestine manner, the new leaders quickly rocketed to fame or notoriety, depending upon the observer's point of view. Martin Luther King, defying the white power structure of his community and being featured on the cover of *Time* magazine, symbolizes this new leadership. Many white leaders have reacted by bewailing the "breakdown of communication" between the races, denouncing the militant Negro leaders as reckless, radical parvenues, and attempting to isolate them by parleys with hand-picked, "responsible" leaders. Both practical and theoretical considerations dictate the need for a new appraisal of Negro leadership in the South.

The north Florida community of Tallahassee is one of the southern communities in which a change in the pattern of Negro leadership seemed to accompany a crisis in race relations. The critical situation arose from a challenge to segregation on city buses, culminating in a boycott. Here, too, news media featured daily the names of militant Negroes who previously had been anonymous ciphers in the Negro community as far as most whites were concerned. There were allegations to the effect that "newcomers" had come into the community and stirred up the erstwhile contented population, and that the Negro leadership had "split" with the result that white leaders did not know with whom to deal. Hence this community was well suited for a case study of Negro leadership in crisis.

The situation proved an opportunity to get the answers, for this community, to certain questions. Was the leadership in this Protest Movement actually new to the Negro community, or were the new leaders merely people who had suddenly become known to the white community because of a change of strategy? If they were new to the higher levels of the power structure in the Negro community, had they actually displaced the old group of leaders or was the community split between two competing sets of leaders? A corollary is the question whether these "new leaders" drew their strength from popular support or simply from a tightly organized, activist minority.

Method of Study

The study, executed shortly after the end of the bus boycott, consisted of two related parts. The first was an assessment of the structure of Negro leadership through interviews with a panel of 21 Negroes tentatively designated as "leaders" by social scientists familiar with the community. This list subsequently proved to include what came to be defined as "old" and "new" leaders in almost equal proportions.

A panel of 21 white leaders was also selected. This panel included all of the white leaders who had dealt with the Negro community in connection with the bus protest, in either an official or unofficial capacity. It also included white functionaries who were known to have worked directly with the Negro community in connection with other matters, such as fund drives, civic projects, and community problems, both before and after the boycott. They are the white leaders who most often speak to the Negro community in behalf of the white community. Some of them are high in the power structure. That this group represents fairly the position of the white leadership in Tallahassee is indicated by the absence of opposition to their representations to the Negro community.

The names of the 21 Negroes tentatively listed as "leaders" were placed on a card which was handed to the subject during the interview. Then he was asked a series of questions about Negro leadership *before* and *after* the bus boycott, and told to respond by giving names from the list. The questions which are of interest here were:

1. As best you can recall, which would have identified as "leaders" among Tallahassee Negroes 2 years ago?
2. At that time, which do you feel were able to influence large numbers of Negroes on important public issues?
3. Which ones were able to express most accurately the feelings of most Negroes in Tallahassee on important public issues?
4. Which ones were able to deal most effectively with white leaders as representatives of the Negro group?
5. Now, at the present time, which do you feel are most able to influence large numbers of Negroes on important public issues?
6. Which are able to express most accurately the feelings of most Negroes, etc.?
7. Which are able to deal most effectively with white leaders, etc.?

Subjects were allowed to give as few or as many responses to each question as they wished, and Negro subjects were encouraged to include their own names if they felt they should.

After the data had been collected, the answers of white and Negro informants were tabulated separately. Each of the 21 potential Negro leaders was given a score and a rank on each question, according to the number of times his name was mentioned in response to the question. Hence each Negro had, for each question, a rank assigned him by the Negro informants and a rank assigned by the white leaders.

The second portion of the study was an attitude survey of a sample of the adult Negro population of Tallahassee. Every fifth address was taken from a list of all the households in blocks occupied only by Negroes. Any adult available at the address was interviewed. A total of 196 usable interviews were obtained. A Likert-type scale of questions concerning attitudes toward segregation in general, the bus boycott, and the leadership of the Bus Protest Movement was used. Key questions for purposes of this study were:

1. The Negro should not boycott to achieve his goals. (Agreement with this statement would represent a repudiation of the militant leaders.)
2. The old, established leaders in Tallahassee were more effective than the ones leading the bus protest.
3. The leadership in the Tallahassee Bus Protest is very good.

Subjects were grouped into three categories on the basis of whether their answers to these three questions reflected approval or disapproval of the leaders who had called for the bus boycott. Those who answered all three of the questions favorably were classified as "Highly favorable," those who answered two favorably were classified as "Favorable," and those who answered only one or none in this manner were placed in the "Unfavorable" category.

Findings

The interviews with the panel of potential Negro leaders revealed that a real change in leadership had indeed taken place between the "Pre-Boycott" and "Post-Boycott" periods. On the basis of high rankings on the answers to the questions "Who were the leaders?" "Who were influential?" and "Who were representative?" two years previously, six individuals were classified as "Pre-Boycott Leaders." Of these six, not one was found in the first five ranked on "influence" and "representativeness" in the Post-Boycott period. None of them were ranked even in the first ten on "influence," although two did remain in the first ten on "representativeness." An indication of how complete the turnover of leadership personnel was is the fact that of the first five ranked as both "influential" and "representative" in the Post-Boycott period, not one was among the first ten named as "leaders" in the Pre-Boycott period.

This change of leadership was also found to involve, as had been postulated, a replacement of Accommodating Leaders by Protest Leaders. Of the six Pre-Boycott leaders, five were ranked by Negroes as being most able to deal effectively with white leaders during this period. Five of the six were also ranked by whites as most able to deal effectively with white leaders. Four, including the three ranked highest by Negroes as "leaders," were ranked in the first five as "emissaries" by both Negroes and whites. This finding bears out the theory that, in the era of accommodation in race relations, leadership in the Negro community was based primarily on acceptability to white leaders and ability to gain concessions from them.

In contrast, none of the five "new leaders" were ranked by either Negroes or whites as among the five Negroes able to deal most effectively with white leaders in the Post-Boycott Period. In fact, none of them ranked in the first ten on acceptability to white leaders as it was perceived by Negroes. Clearly these new leaders were not seen by other prominent Negroes as "Compromise Leaders."

The panel of Negroes interviewed included both the "old leaders" and the "new leaders," plus some individuals who did not receive high rankings for either period. The Negro panel was divided, for purposes of further analysis, into an "old group" of subjects who had ranked in the first ten on the question concerning Pre-Boycott leadership, and a new group. The new group identified as the five most influential leaders in the Post-Boycott period the same five men who had been ranked as "new leaders" by the entire panel. The "old group" ranked four of these five men as the five most influential leaders in this same period, indicating that their perception of the change in leadership was almost the same as that of the "new group." Moreover, none of the "old group," including the "old leaders," gave their own names in response to the question on ability to influence large numbers of Negroes. Although during the course of the boycott some of the old leaders had openly challenged the influence of the new leaders, by the time of this study they seemed to have accepted the fact that they had been displaced. It is accurate, therefore, to say that a change, not a split, in leadership had occurred.

Although no intensive study of the individual characteristics of the old and new leaders was made, certain ones were evident. Even though at the time of the study, the boycott had ended and had obviously failed of its purpose to force desegregation of city buses, all of the New Leaders were strongly identified with it. All were officers of the organization which had led the boycott and all had been arrested and fined for "operating an illegal transportation system" (a car pool). In contrast, not one of the Old Leaders had been active in promoting the boycott, and at least two of them had opposed it as a tactic. Of the six Old Leaders, three were employed in the state-supported school system; none of the five New Leaders were state employees. There were three ministers among the New Leaders, none among the old. Although the Old Leaders had, as a group, indeed lived in the community a longer time than their successors, the shortest time that any of the New Leaders had lived in Tallahassee was three years. One of them had lived there over thirty years. It was only in a limited and relative sense that they could be described as "newcomers."

Since the New Leaders had been identified as synonymous with the leaders of the Bus Boycott, the questions asked in the opinion poll were suited to serve as a measure of their popular support. Were they leaders not only in the eyes of the small panel of prominent Negroes but also in the eyes of the Negro community? The results of the survey indicate that they were. When asked if the leadership in the Bus Protest was very good, 84 percent of the sample agreed that it was. Some inconsistency was found between the answers to this question and the question, "The old established leaders in Tallahassee were more effective than the ones leading the Bus Protest," since only 62 percent of the sample disagreed with this statement. But, to the extent that this sample can be taken as representative, it appears that the New Leaders did have majority support in the Negro community. Subjects were also asked to agree or disagree with the statement, "Should the Negro population of Tallahassee need to develop united action to obtain rights or services not connected with the Bus Protest, the people leading the Protest would probably be selected to lead such action." Again, strong majority support of the New Leaders was indicated, 82 percent of the sample agreeing with this statement.

Using the categories "Highly Favorable," "Favorable," and "Unfavorable," established earlier, an analysis was made of certain differences between Negroes showing greater or lesser support for the boycott and its leaders. The chi-square test of independence was used. Differences significant beyond the .01 level were found in age and education, the more favorably disposed subjects being younger and better educated. Those who were favorably disposed toward the boycott were more likely to own automobiles than those who were not, this difference also being significant beyond the .01 level. This difference may have reflected the fact that the boycott caused less personal inconvenience for car owners than it did for others, or it may have been that car ownership was an indirect measure of socio-economic status. No significant difference in ownership of real property was found between supporters and non-supporters, however, so the former explanation seems the more likely. This is also suggested by the fact that differences in occupation were not significant at the .05 level.

Summary and Conclusions

In the community studied, the impression that there has been a change in the quality of race relations is borne out. The clearest indication of this change is the replacement of the Old Leaders by New Leaders who clearly reflect the protest motive rather than any spirit of accommodation. These New Leaders have widespread popular support, and the extent of their influence is conceded by the Old Leaders whom they displaced.

Additional findings led [sic] added significance to this shift in Negro leadership. The panel of white leaders were found to perceive Negro leadership in the Post-Boycott period in almost the same way that the Negro leaders did. Of the six men ranked highest by

whites as "most influential" in the Post-Boycott period, four were among the Negroes' New Leaders. At the same time, most of these white leaders indicated that they were unwilling to deal with these New Leaders because the militant spokesmen were uncompromising in their opposition to segregation. It is only in this sense that communication has broken down between the races. The New Leaders are unwilling to communicate and negotiate with whites in the circumscribed, accommodating fashion of yesterday. The Old Leaders can no longer claim the support of the Negro population, no matter how acceptable they might be to the whites. As long as this situation prevails, the structure of the situation seems to permit only one kind of communication between the Negro community and the white power structure: formal, peremptory demands, backed by the threat of legal action, political reprisal, or economic boycott. So long as the New Leaders are not accepted as bona fide, albeit antagonistic, emissaries of the Negro community in the same way that the Old Leaders were, this would seem to be the only way in which they can get the attention of the white leaders.

While the present study was principally concerned with a description of the changes in Negro leadership in Tallahassee during the Bus Protest, there is evidence which indicates that the new leaders and new leadership are permanent in this community. Although they may have been "issue leaders" at first, they have continued to maintain their position of leadership as the sample of the Negro population predicted they would.

In the first place some of the "old" leaders were called upon by the Tallahassee City Commission to get the Negroes to agree to a compromise settlement in the early days of the bus protest. The efforts of the "old" leaders to do this failed completely and ever since they have made no overt efforts to regain the following they had prior to the bus protest. This is apparently due to their belief that neither the Negro population nor the city officials have confidence in them. The Negroes do not trust them because of what they regard as underhanded dealing with the City Commission. The city officials apparently feel that these erstwhile leaders cannot be trusted to gauge Negro sentiment accurately or to deliver results when called upon, because they lack following.

Secondly, the "new" leaders have continued to enjoy reasonable support for their undertakings. Some of them have moved into other areas of leadership, such as the NAACP, the Southern Christian Leadership Conference, and the Florida Council of Human Relations. One of them is president of the Tallahassee Chapter of the NAACP. Another is on the State NAACP Board and on the Board of Directors of the Southern Christian Leadership Conference.

Finally these "new" leaders have sought to keep the Negro community of Tallahassee militant and dynamic by continuing weekly meetings of the ICC, the organization formed to promote the bus protest, conducting institutes on nonviolence, taking preliminary steps toward school integration, working to get more Negroes registered and voting, and making many local and non-local public appearances in connection with the uplift of Negroes. Furthermore, the press has done much to contribute to their status as permanent leaders by seeking their opinions and comments on various matters affecting the Negro community in Tallahassee (e.g., the recent rape case).

The writers feel that the "new" leaders are becoming permanent leaders not because of the attractiveness of their personalities or their skill at organizing, but rather because they adhere rigorously to the *form* of militant leadership which is becoming the trend for Negroes throughout the United States. This new leadership is not of the accommodating type. It seeks gains for the Negro community through formal demands and requests, boycotts, lawsuits, and voting. The protest leaders are not concerned with whether or not the whites high in the power structure know, like, or want to deal with them. Until the "old" leaders are willing or able to translate their mode of leadership into a form similar to this, it appears that they will not again rise to prominence as leaders in Tallahassee.

Note

1. Gunnar Myrdal, *An American Dilemma* (New York: Harper and Bros., 1944), pp. 768–780.

Community Power and Strategies in Race Relations: Some Critical Observations*

James B. McKee

When Floyd Hunter published *Community Power Structure* (2) in 1953, it was the first of a recent series of sociological researches into social power in the community, and it remains the best known. Whatever its significance to sociology, however, Hunter's study gave theoretical perspective to one of several emerging strands of theory and action among intergroup relations practitioners and provided a new and fruitful basis for theorization between social scientists and this still developing profession. Intergroup relations practitioners have been sensitive to community power as one of several diverse elements relevant to community practice, at least since the work of Lohman, Bradbury, and others in Washington, D. C., in the 1940's. A scrutiny of more recent professional literature reveals frequent references to the importance of community power for community action.

This interest in community power gives considerable significance to the publication in 1955 of *A Manual of Intergroup Relations*, by John Dean and Alex Rosen (1), the second half of which is concerned with developing an intergroup relations strategy organized around the concept of community power structure. The book culminates six years of both research and action by a Cornell University study group under the leadership of John Dean. On the research side, the Cornell group studied on-going intergroup practice, and in the *Manual* report "accumulated intergroup experience"

for the benefit of less experienced professionals. On the action side, the Cornell group participated actively in professional development; Dean has been a member of the National Association of Intergroup Relations Officials (NAIRO) and, with Rosen, has conducted training workshops for group workers. The more than six years of persistent activity by the Cornell group constitutes the as yet most sustained and continuous association between social scientists and the social practitioners of this burgeoning profession. In addition, the publication of the book by a university long identified with support for intergroup relations, and support of the Cornell group by such foundations as Rockefeller and Russell Sage, gives to the *Manual* an intellectual influence little else in the scant literature can claim.

The field of intergroup relations lacks as yet any substantial literature about its professional practice, and its professional practice has not yet congealed into an orthodoxy. Thus, any discussion of community power is relevant to its concern for effective community practice. But the *Manual* goes much further: it elaborates a strategy for community action based upon "accumulated experience" that seeks to reshape a flexible perspective into an ideological commitment, and it asserts a set or principles for practice that, despite the tentativeness claimed for it, constitutes the most ambitious attempt thus far to develop a teachable orthodoxy of method and perspective. Its explicit rationale

Reprinted from Social Problems, 6 (*Winter, 1958–59*), *195–202, by permission of the author and the Society for the Study of Social Problems. Copyright 1958 by the Society for the Study of Social Problems.*

*A revised version of a paper read at the 8th Annual Meeting of SSSP at the University of Washington, Seattle, August 25, 1958.

is to provide some tentative codification of the hitherto unsystematized dicta of this new profession and thus to bring social science and social practice into closer collaboration. Such an influential effort warrants as close a reading by the social scientists for whom it purports to speak as by the social practitioners whom it seeks to teach.

A Model of Community Power

Dean and Rosen provide little explicit description of community power, and their conceptualization of it must be inferred from the context of discussion. They state that the interacting and overlapping "subcultures and organizational networks" of the community "are drawn together at the top by interlocking leaderships that represent what we might call the 'power structure'" of the community" (2, p. 124). They further specify that in a community of 50,000 to 100,000 there is an "inner core" of about a dozen leaders, with another fifty to one hundred around them, who either make the community's decisions or at least "clear" decisions made by others (2, p. 124). The social composition of this elite of "key leaders" is indicated by two criteria: status level and ideological orientation. They are drawn from the upper economic and social levels of the community and are ideologically "conservative." Dean and Rosen do not define "conservative" but assert that "intergroup relations has become a good 'cause' for conservatives to be liberal about. It is not basically threatening to their own economic and social status in the community and meets all the requirements of moral rectitude" (2, p. 125).

Although Dean and Rosen make no explicit reference to Hunter's study, or to any other, a careful reading of the two suggests that Dean and Rosen's model of social power in the community correlates closely with the description of community power structure to be found in Hunter. Since the relevant sociological literature is not yet extensive, it is readily understandable that Hunter's pioneering work might serve as a model of community power and thus be applied to communities quite different from the southern city that Hunter studied.

In his summary of this still relatively scant literature, Peter Rossi (5) compares some accumulated research findings, including his own, which present quite varied images of social power in the community. He specifically suggests that Hunter's Regional City, as a southern one-party community, may represent more highly concentrated power than is to be found in a more politically competitive community and that control over economic resources, as a basis for power, may be matched by leadership of significant solidary organizations. Rossi also points out that Hunter's study implies that the power elite controls *all* major areas of decision-making in the community, though in fact this is not empirically demonstrated in his study or in others. More recently, Delbert Miller (4), provides supporting evidence in his careful study of community power in two large cities, one American and one English, and suggests a continuum of community power structure, with Hunter's model placed near one end of the possible range. Our own research on Steelport (3) revealed that the CIO, the Democratic Party, the Catholics, and the major ethnic groups coalesced into a power bloc which wielded predominant *political* influence in the community.

Thus, what Hunter says about power in Regional City does not necessarily apply to all American communities. The major critical point is that the organization of social power in the community is frequently more varied and much less unified and monolithic than Dean and Rosen assume.

A Strategy for Race Relations

It is, however, a concentrated and monolithic conception of social power in the community, as Dean and Rosen derive it from Hunter, that is used in the *Manual* to develop a strategy for the improvement of race relations. Their specifics of strategy are based upon the assumption that the climate of opinion in America is favorable to desirable changes in intergroup relations. In several places in the *Manual* the authors assert that "fair practices" is an accepted goal in American society, and consequently the only major issue is effective strategy or means. At one point they remark that in America today there is "an established and growing tradition of civil rights . . . a not-so-well established but growing belief in 'fair practices' in employment, housing and welfare . . . an increasing acceptance of equality and fair play as a goal." They add that "individuals and groups striving to perpetuate discrimination and segregation find it difficult morally to justify their position . . . (2, p. 113).

The assumption made here is that the issue of intergroup relations is strategic, the moral problem having been resolved. For example, Dean and Rosen assert that "being 'for' good intergroup relations is like being against sin," and thus, "the main controversies, whatever the region, revolve around how much, how fast, and how far we should proceed" (2, p. 125). We have quoted these statements not to imply that they are incorrect but to emphasize the ideological and strategic importance of this assumption underlying the *Manual's* propositions on community action.

The strategy for community action as set forth in the *Manual* is made up of four elements: (1) the involvement of influentials; (2) the use of organized groups; (3) the role of the professional; and (4) the technique of negotiation.

1. It is a cardinal principle of Dean and Rosen that no strategy can be effective unless it involves representatives of the power structure, since "in most communities, the people really dedicated to better intergroup relations are not influential leaders in the community," and "community-wide action can go no further than local leaders are willing to move" (2, pp. 125, 128). And it is an explicit assumption of theirs that the involvement of such influentials is always possible, since, as previously noted, intergroup relations is an acceptable cause for conservatives.

2. Once one or more key influentials of the community are involved, effective strat-egy requires the development of further organization toward specific objectives, including all the familiar organizational paraphernalia of urban middle-class life: committees (both *ad hoc* and permanent), workshops, commissions, and boards.

3. The role of the functioning professional, according to Dean and Rosen, is largely that of strategist in the development of programs and policy in intergroup relations. The professional is rarely if ever the public leader but is preferably the "behind-the-scenes" operator. Dean and Rosen stress this last element, asserting that the overtly active professional incurs antagonism, and thus it is preferable for him to work through committees, letting others initiate the contacts, direct the negotiations, invoke the sanctions, etc. (2, p. 140).

4. Negotiations with "gatekeepers" constitute the basic approach to improving intergroup relations in the community, once a more permanent organizational structure has been set up. "The basic strategy of negotiation has two facets: (1) interpreting the consequences of change as *less* threatening than the reluctant gatekeepers suppose, and (2) interpreting the consequences of not changing the practices as *more* threatening by bringing negative sanctions to bear" (2, pp. 157–58).

A Comment on the Strategy

It is not within the scope of this paper to raise questions about the adequacy or effectiveness of this strategy. However, we do regard it as relevant to make three observations:

1. If intergroup relations professionals are to be advised to develop a strategy oriented to the realities of community power, they must also be advised that an adequate, workable image of a particular community's power structure is to be determined empirically.

2. The *Manual's* discussion of strategy seems to assume that only the proponents of improved race relations are strategically oriented, and therefore their planning need not provide for the possibility of organized

opposition or planned resistance on the part of others. Nevertheless, there is abundant evidence that the opponents of desegregation and antidiscrimination measures can and do organize to resist measures of change.

This failure to anticipate counter-strategy may be a consequence of Dean and Rosen's assumption that the climate of opinion is favorable to change. Although this may be true, one can easily underestimate the extent of genuine resistance to changes in established patterns of segregation and discrimination, especially where lip-service to equal rights is the public norm. The fact that overt verbal expressions of opposition are not easily possible is not, *ipso facto*, evidence of widespread community support or even of the absence of organized opposition.

The failure to anticipate counter-strategy may also be a consequence of the assumption that community power structure is monolithic. Certainly Dean and Rosen seem not to recognize the possibilities of social cleavage in the business community. They assume that because some of the power elite support the improvement of race relations, all will. But not this much unity of power and ideology necessarily exists. To talk of business and industry is to cover a wide variety of social functions and status levels, with quite varying orientations to specific issues. What Dean and Rosen have clearly noticed is that the better educated segments of the upper status levels are likely to be liberal on race, and this includes a considerable number of corporate executives. But it also excludes many, including the less well educated, the less cosmopolitan, the more locally rooted. And it does not necessarily follow that the former group controls all major loci of decision-making in every community.

3. The basic proposition in Dean and Rosen's strategy is that the major support for changing race relations is to come from the conservative power elite. If the established power structure can be induced to support new policies, they will be attained; if not, they will not.

To attempt to bring about policy changes by inducing the established power elite to make the decisions is one possible type of strategy. Dean and Rosen seem to assume it is the only one. They ignore the question of creating support for new policies by building a constituency in the community who have a genuine stake, personal or ideological, in effecting changes in the community's policies. Such a program has its own difficulties, of course, and calls for a different type of professional than that envisaged by Dean and Rosen. An organized Negro community, politically active and sensitive to every event that bears on race relations; an active middle-class liberal group; a Jewish community; church groups; women's organizations: these are some of the potentialities for building a constituency. Such a constituency, of course, can very well include segments of the community's upper status levels. For such a public as this, a professional practitioner would provide overt, recognized public leadership and not be only or always a behind-the-scenes operator.

Building organized public support for new policies in intergroup relations has significant implications for power structure. For one thing, such a process clearly threatens to challenge established power patterns and introduces a new force in the making of community decisions. Its effective pressure may induce cleavage in the existing power elite. And it may develop new sources of leadership in the community. Furthermore, such an alternative approach has ideological implications about problems of strategy that are of major significance.

Ideology and Strategy

The idea that a seemingly rational strategy may have ideological implications might occur to a perceptive reader of the *Manual* who noted the importance attributed to the climate of opinion and to the strategic use of community power. Dean and Rosen's approach stresses first as a basic postulate a favorable climate of opinion, and secondly a strategy of operating through local power structures. But nowhere does it relate the one to the other. By asserting that the climate of opinion has accepted fair practices as an

American goal, it seems to imply that success in intergroup relations is inevitable in time. If so, only a skillful execution of this agreed-upon goal, to narrow the gap between outmoded practice and accepted policy, needs to be made. In such a case, the emphasis upon community power structure merely asserts the responsibility of the established leadership of the community to realize in practice what it has agreed upon in policy.

But if, in turn, one infers from a reading of Dean and Rosen that the issue is still problematic but that the climate of opinion creates an opportunity, then problems of strategy and power are more relevant. But what, then, is the relationship between the climate of opinion and the community power structure? Is it effective strategy to involve the conservative leadership of the community because this leadership has *yielded to* the climate of opinion, or has the leadership in fact been primarily *responsible* in defining the climate of opinion? Dean and Rosen seem to imply that the climate of opinion pervades equally the entire community. But numerous opinion studies suggest that the better educated and those of higher social status are less prejudiced and more favorable toward intergroup relations programs than are the less educated and those of lower social status. This, in turn, suggests that a favorable climate of opinion exists because there is greater acceptance of improved race relations at the higher status levels of the community, and according to Dean and Rosen's model of community power structure, it is at these higher status levels that the influentials who make policy in the community are located. If this is the link between the favorable climate of opinion and community power structure, then Dean and Rosen's strategic reasoning is not difficult to follow. They interpret the developing climate of opinion as an opportunity to involve the community's decision-making leadership in the process of extending fair practices, since such a leadership is more willing to make such a change and possesses the power to do so.

Viewed from the perspective of a simple means-end schema, this may be a highly rational strategy. But if one notes the social values that are ignored, as well as the ramifying social consequences of any behavior-as-means, then one can hardly avoid suspecting that an ideological commitment lurks behind the seemingly rational and technical criteria for developing strategy.

Our attempt to focus on the unacknowledged ideological elements contained in the *Manual* produces a critique which asserts that: (1) the strategy offered in the *Manual* is conservative, in that, among available alternatives, it chooses those strategies which support the status quo; (2) in its techniques for effective action, it chooses and encourages manipulative behavior; and (3) it reduces the cause of intergroup relations from a moral to a technical issue, thus detaching it from a democratic and liberal frame of reference.

A careful reading of the *Manual* suggests that it has one basic ideological orientation: to operate within, and not outside of, independent of, or as a challenge to, the existing power structure. As a guide to action, this constitutes a definite value choice, not merely a technical one. If one considers each strategic choice as only one among a set of alternatives, then it is clear that the patterns of recommended choices is conservative—that is, is oriented to preserving the status quo in social power.

There are several crucial points in the *Manual* in which the conservative status quo preserving character of its action program becomes quite clear. For instance, the insistence on the behind-the-scenes character of the role of the practicing professional is one case in point. Dean and Rosen's model for the professional makes him not only a covert operator, and thus not a public leader, but a professional whose only initiative lies in his capacity to manipulate conservative community leaders. It may be that, in large part, this is what the social worker who specializes in community organization has become; but to use this as a standard for professional practice in race relations is to make an ideological choice of considerable significance. And it is not a decision derived objectively from sociological research.

The conservative nature of Dean and Rosen's action program is further suggested by the strategic avoidance of conflict with the power structure. For example, Dean and Rosen discuss the hypothetical possibility of a small committee examining real estate practices in the community. Since such an investigation would bring to light facts which would unite the real estate people in opposition, the authors suggest that key real estate people be made a part of the study, and then *may* "become motivated to take a greater amount of responsibility for the intergroup injustices . . ." (2, pp. 128–29). The action group, Dean and Rosen assert, *must* rely on the "sense of deepened responsibility" which such participation may provide. Evidently, no action would be planned which would be opposed by the power structure. If conflict developed, it would be only because pressure for action is generated by groups outside the power structure. But Dean and Rosen suggest no such possibility and offer such groups neither leadership nor strategy. This means that, for all practical purposes, action will go ahead at no more rapid pace and in no other direction than key people who are themselves violators of fair practices are willing to go.

Lastly, the conservative ideology is implicit in another element: the failure to develop an independent constituency for intergroup relations. Such a constituency might not only risk conflict with the status quo in community power; it might make the decision-making process more democratic and representative.

It follows logically that an approach to a program for action on race relations at the community level which is conservative in its choice of techniques and strategies, in the manner suggested above, would also be manipulative in its social action. (We here use the concept of manipulation to mean one individual's behavior in trying to induce or influence other individuals to act in accordance with his own goals, without their being aware of or understanding the purpose of the influence or inducement.) A manipulative orientation is always a possible consequence when the emphasis in social action is on technique, and when the end is either taken for granted, and hence unexamined, or when it is postulated by others (employers, etc.).

When a professional practitioner is asked to act in a situation in which his values and goals are not fully accepted (Dean and Rosen refer frequently to conservative boards), and in which he must operate within the framework of the community's power structure, with no independent constituency to support his program, and thus with no power base, the temptation to use manipulative techniques is strong. What alternative has he to inducing people to act in ways that will promote some specific goal, even though those so induced to act are not fully aware of the consequences of their own behavior, or of why the professional advises in the way he does?

The manipulative character of social action in race relations becomes logical, also, because the cause of race relations has been effectively detached by this strategy from the context of related social issues from which it originally received its moral support and significant meaning. Race relations has been one of several causes that have constituted the major issues for those liberals and radicals committed to images of a more democratic way of life: civil liberties, social welfare, the needs of the underprivileged, etc. Taken together, these issues have provided a body of values that has motivated challenge to the status quo and has provided opposition to local and national power structures. To detach the cause of race relations from such a frame of reference, to treat it as a separate issue, and to maximize the potentiality of conservative acceptance, is not merely a technical procedure: it is a choice defined by a conservative ideology. (And equally so, to refuse to separate the cause of race relations from its liberal frame of reference would signify a commitment to liberal values; in either case, the choice is moral, not technical.)

This detachment from its former context attempts to deny implicitly that race relations is related to other social causes, which, taken together, constitute an affirmation and evaluation of the historic liberal values. That Dean and Rosen are not entirely unaware of this historic linkage of causes is evident in their assertion that "intergroup relations is a good cause for conservatives to be liberal about." But they also point out that intergroup relations does not threaten conservative status and "meets all the requirements of moral rectitude." Are we, in any semantic sense, any longer speaking of either liberalism or a social cause?

Whether we are or not, Dean and Rosen posulate the manipulability of the conservative leadership because of its acceptance of a liberal issue. The widespread development of community agencies headed by professional practitioners, with their moderate programs for community action, might seem to stand as testimony to the success of this strategy.

But Dean and Rosen seem not to recognize that their appeal to the community's conservative power elite sets in motion a series of less naïve motives of its own for taking leadership and in effect co-opting the race relations situation in the community. The motives are several: the acceptance of leadership gives effective control over the scope and direction of the program, keeps the issue out of the hands of a more militant leadership, offsets the chance of the rise of new leadership, and thus lessens the threat to the status quo in power, and offers a fresh and important situation to be exploited for validation of its moral and civic leadership. The manipulated may indeed be actively counter-manipulating.

Conclusion

The use of the concept of community power structure in Dean and Rosen's *A Manual of Intergroup Relations* provides an object lesson in the problems of applied social science. Our evaluation stresses two points.

First, the ideology implicit in a social technique raises questions about the relation of means to ends that warrant careful examination by sociologists interested in the development of an applied sociology. The *Manual* by Dean and Rosen offers one possible approach to this relation, which, we suggest, is fraught with ideological problems and value choices. When Dean and Rosen choose those means that they believe will maximize attainment of their specific objective, they ignore the ramifying social consequences—for power structure, for social leadership, for historic social values. It is just such social consequences, however unintended, that suggest that for applied social science the selection of means is never merely a technical problem.

Secondly, the relationship of the research sociologist to the social practitioner has long been a matter of legitimate concern to both parties. The practitioner seeks valid generalizations which he can incorporate into social strategy and social policy. However, this legitimate request need not limit the sociologist's own image of his social role. In addition to serving as consultant, expert, and "resource person," he can also function, more independently and yet more responsibly, as social critic and analyst. This more intellectualized orientation might perform such functions as these:

1. Criticism of the use made of sociological concepts by social practitioners, to ensure that they are not applied without due regard for their tentative character, or that social practitioners do not assume their applicability in social contexts other than those from which they were derived by research.

2. Explication of ideological elements in social policy and social action programs, thus indicating what in a program is social science and what is not, and also what ideological use is made of sociological concepts and sociological research.

3. Exploration of the relationship of sociological concepts to social ideology. Do concepts have any necessary ideological mplications? Do some concepts fit more easily into a particular ideological context than do others? Do social practitioners select some conceptual tools, less for "practical" reasons than for reasons of value or ideology?

The now frequent involvement of sociologists in social problems and social policy makes imperative a thorough consideration of their relation to policy-making contexts and to the professional practitioners who help both to make and to execute policy.

References

1. Dean, John, and Alex Rosen, *A Manual of Intergroup Relations* (Chicago: University of Chicago Press, 1955).
2. Hunter, Floyd, *Community Power Structure: A Study of Decision Makers* (Chapel Hill: University of North Carolina Press, 1953).
3. McKee, James B., *Organized Labor and Community Decision-Making: A Study in the Sociology of Power* (Unpublished Ph.D. Dissertation, University of Wisconsin, 1953).
4. Miller, Delbert, "Decision-making Cliques in Community Power Structures: A Comparative Study of an American and an English City," *American Journal of Sociology*, LXIV (November, 1958), pp. 299–310.
5. Rossi, Peter H., "Community Decision Making," *Administrative Science Quarterly*, I (March, 1957), pp. 415–443.

Part VI.

Comparative Studies of Community Power

Introduction

If someone were to make even a cursory reading of every piece of literature that has ever been written about community power—actual studies as well as commentaries and summaries—the overriding conclusion that he would reach is that in spite of the endless attempts to develop a cogent and consistent understanding of community power and decision-making dynamics, no such understanding currently exists. If Hunter is taken as the thesis and Dahl the antithesis, then the field still awaits a synthesis.

For several years now various scholars have called for comparative studies of community power in order to unravel the meaning of the diverse and often contradictory findings of different studies of community decision-making dynamics. A number of comparative studies do exist, but no inquiry using any of the traditional methods has studied more than a handful of communities. The problem here is that it would take an enormous amount of resources—in terms of both staff and finances—in order to study systematically a large number of communities, especially if an attempt were also made to utilize all three methodological procedures discussed in Part IV. Thus far it does not appear that anyone has been able to gather together such resources, although the community data bank currently being developed at the National Opinion Research Center of the University of Chicago is clearly a major step in that direction.

Short of having available such a definitive study, there are three types of studies that can logically be included under the rubric of comparative studies of community power: (1) the comparative studies mentioned earlier that include only a small number of cases; (2) comparative studies that utilize the conclusions of previous studies of community power as data: and (3) comparative studies that examine the relationships between various community attributes and community "outputs" (such as urban renewal success, city expenditures, etc.). Some of the studies of the third type utilize the configuration of community power as an intervening, but unmeasured variable (a procedure which might be refered to as the "black box" approach). There appears to be growing enthusiasm, as well as an increasingly lengthy bibliography, in the last mentioned approach; the Hawley and Pinard studies and to some extent the Aiken study, all of which appear in this part, are illustrative of this approach.

Illustrative Comparative Studies

The articles included here by Miller and Form and D'Antonio are examples of the first type mentioned above. In the first article "Industry and Community Power Structure: A Comparative Study of an American and an English City," Miller tests Hunter's finding that businessmen dominate the community power structure. He finds support for Hunter's thesis in Pacific City, but notes that businessmen by no means predominate among key influentials in English City. Miller suggests that variations in cultural values between England and the United States and in the formal political structures of these cities partially account for these cross-national differences.

In the second of his two articles included here, "Decision-Making Cliques in Community Power Structures: A Comparative Study of an American and an English City," Miller tests the hypothesis that "... key influential leaders in a community influence policy-making by acting in concert through cliques." While there is some evidence to support the hypothesis, the most important evidence runs counter to it, leading him to conclude that there is little support for the hypothesis that a tightly organized clique runs English City, while Pacific City is intermediate between English City and Regional City (Atlanta) on this perspective. Miller concludes the article by suggesting that community power structures should be conceived as ranging on a continuum from highly stratified pyramidal structures (Hunter's report of Atlanta) to a ring (or decentralized) structure, such as he found in English City.

Form and D'Antonio studied two additional cities that were located in different national settings, El Paso, Texas, and C. Juarez, Mexico. Their conclusions are included in the article "Integration and Cleavage Among Community Influentials in Two Border Cities," although a more detailed report of these findings can be found in their book *Influentials in Two Border Cities*. Examining questions similar to those of Miller, they find first that economic elites dominated the decision-making structure of El Paso to a much greater extent than that of C. Juarez, but they conclude that there is no support for Hunter's hypothesis of a single, cohesive ruling elite.

In 1961 Barth published a very brief, poorly documented, but nevertheless intriguing study of the power structure of six communities that happen to be adjacent to military installations.[1]

In the next few years a spate of multi-community studies was published. For example, in 1963 Kammerer and her colleagues published a study of eight Florida communities in which they focus particularly on the formal political structure.[2] That same year Belknap and Steinle's study of the adequacy of medical services and its relationship to community power in two Texas communities also appeared.[3] In 1964 appeared Presthus's study of decision-making in two New York communities,[4] Kimbrough's study of community power and educational policy in four Southern

counties,[5] Blankenship's description of power distribution in two communities,[6] and Agger, Goldrich, and Swanson's study of four communities[7]—two in the Pacific Northwest and two on the Atlantic Seaboard. These researchers often found variations in the configurations of power in their communities, although this was by no means the main issue that these authors addressed. The Agger, Goldrich, and Swanson book is particularly noteworthy for attempting to go far beyond the previous concerns of the literature by developing typologies that include not only the nature of elites, but also mass participation as well as the political ethos of the given communities.

Community Structure and Configuration of Power

The findings of studies such as the above leave one wondering just what are the structural characteristics of communities—political, economic, and social as well as other factors such as age of city, region, size or rate of growth—that could possibly account for such variations in community elite configurations. While each of these is a comparative study of two or more communities, no one of these has a sufficient number of cases or adequate variations in population size or regional location to allow any definitive conclusions.

Faced with the prospect of having to obtain enormous personnel and financial resources (with few prospects in sight) in order to answer questions such as these, but having a large number of case studies or limited multi-community studies available, one logical procedure is to use these case studies as data in attempting to find some answers to these questions.

Using data obtained from a content analysis of thirty-three studies, which dealt with fifty-five communities, Walton finds that a number of factors, such as region, degree of industrialization, predominance of absentee-ownership, and degree of social cleavage, are related to variations in the configuration of community power. He also notes that the type of methodology utilized as well as the discipline of the researcher are related to the findings.[8] That is, there is a decided bias for sociologists to use only reputational techniques, and the use of these techniques alone is more likely to yield an image of concentrated power in a community. In his article included here entitled "A Systematic Survey of Community Power Research," Walton enlarges and extends his previous analysis.

Gilbert has done a study similar to Walton's. She was able to amass information on 166 communities, although for many of these the information is not from studies directly concerned with community decision-making. And she examines a number of dimensions of the political structure other than those studied by Walton—such as degree of community conflict and type of leaders involved. She also attempts to control statistically for the quality of her data.[9] Clark and his colleagues, using Gilbert's data, have also examined the relationships between a number of community attributes and two measures of the community decision-making structure; they also argue that their results are not a function of the method or discipline of the researcher.[10]

Attention is also called to a recent article by Clark in which he measures the degree of decentralization of community power by the average number of major actors participating in each of four decision-areas: urban renewal, the election of the mayor, air pollution, and the anti-poverty program.[11] While the article is primarily concerned with relating decentralization and various structural attributes of communities to two community "outputs," urban renewal and municipal expenditures, it also provides findings of the relationship between several community attributes—socioeconomic status, political structure, economic base, religious heterogeneity, etc.—and his measure of decentralization.

Aiken's article, "The Distribution of Community Power: Structural Bases and Social Consequences," which is included as the last article in this part, uses Walton's techniques, but, unlike Walton and Gilbert, it also utilizes more primary data sources for community characteristics. Aiken examines two questions: (1) What community characteristics are related to variations in the dispersion of community power? and (2) What are the consequences of decentralized power configurations for a limited range of community outputs, i.e., urban renewal, poverty programs, low-rent housing, and model cities? A large number of community characteristics—location in the North, a high degree of absentee ownership, non-reform political structures, heterogeneous population, lower socioeconomic status of the population—are found to be consistently, although not strongly, related to the dispersion of community power.

The discussion of how variations in community leadership configurations affect community outputs is a natural bridge to the third type of comparative community studies mentioned at the outset of this introduction: namely, the relationship between community structure, leadership configuration, and mobilization outputs.

Comparative Studies of Mobilization for Community Action

The effectiveness of a community and the quality of life of its citizens depends considerably on its ability to mobilize sufficient power to solve community problems. This is no easy feat. First, awareness of problems by community leaders is itself problematic. The problems of the poor remained invisible despite their seriousness for a great many years. Disbelief was a common reaction among Americans to assertions that there were thirty million people below the poverty line. Harrington details many reasons for the ignorance of affluent Americans.[12] Hunter shows that the habits and pathways used by his reputational elite minimized encounters with the problems of poverty.[13] The adequacy of interface relations for exchanging information and creating awareness of problems becomes essential for the maintenance of community effectiveness. In the absence of viable interfaces the media play a vital role in informing elites. Second, awareness of problems is no guarantee that they will be solved successfully or that the solutions will be accepted by the necessary elements in the population.

Against this backdrop the major question for students of community power becomes: What configurations of power and what power dynamics are associated with effective community performance? Very few studies have addressed themselves to this question, but the question itself is so important that this section of this reader has been set aside for studies addressed to it in the hope that there will be more to report in later years. There are increasing numbers of federal programs that require community action—model cities, poverty programs, urban renewal, public housing, neighborhood centers—and studies are being made of the conditions under which effective acceptance of these programs is most likely to occur. One example of such a study is Aiken's "The Distribution of Community Power: Structural Bases and Social Consequences," the concluding article of this part.

A pioneering effort to collect comparative data on configurations of power and community action is Hawley's article, "Community Power and Urban Renewal Success," which is included in this section. Hawley hypothesized that it was in communities with more centralized power configurations that effective action could be mobilized most readily, and he uses consideration and adoption of urban renewal programs as a measure of mobilization in examining his idea. There are important questions about the success of Hawley's effort centering around the meaning of his MPO Ratio (i.e., the proportion of managers, proprietors, and officials in the community labor force). Hawley assumes that low MPO cities (a low proportion of the labor force in these occupational categories) are associated with a high concentration of power, yet a case can very easily be made that the opposite is true. Hawley's own data show that low MPO communities are more likely to have a large manufacturing industrial base, less well-educated populations, older housing, and lower income and they are disproportionately located in the Northeastern states,[14] a close

copy of the profile of communities likely to have decentralized power configurations.[15] In communities with low MPO Ratios, centers of power based on labor unions and other blue-collar associations are more likely to be present.[16]

Despite these problems, Hawley's article is valuable because it suggests a strategy of research that deserves greater utilization. He brings to his research questions the proclivities and skills of demographers for doing secondary analyses on data collected for other purposes. When appropriate data can be located, the major barrier to ambitious comparative studies of communities, namely, large amounts of financial and staff resources, can be overcome. Further refinements in this strategy are made in the Walton and Aiken articles in this section, although in each of these two cases the measure of community power configurations involves a considerable number of compromises.

The Pinard article included in this section, "Structural Attachments and Political Support in Urban Politics: The Case of Fluoridation Referendums," also illustrates this strategy. The author selected as his community action variable the ability of communities to mobilize to accept or reject fluoridation of their water, measures of which are available in public records. To measure his independent variable—types and degrees of community integration—he uses a repertoire of indicator measures taken primarily from census data to substantiate his hypotheses. He finds support for the notion that higher community integration is associated with the issue mobilizability of the community.

In the last essay, Aiken, like Hawley, seeks to relate configurations of power to a range of mobilization outputs. He selects a larger number of community issues, however, and unlike Hawley, he finds that successful mobilization is most likely to occur in communities in which power is decentralized. The issues in this approach all involve the mobilization of some local resources in order to obtain external resources for the community. He qualifies his findings by suggesting that issues that involve the reallocation of existing community resources may not necessarily follow the same pattern.

The articles in this section are samples of some of the literature on various types of community issues—mobilization outputs—that have appeared recently in both sociological and political science literature. Some of the types of community "outputs" which have been studied are: the general social welfare, the quality of community services, formal political structures, voting turnout, municipal expenditures, urban renewal, fluoridation, and poverty programs.

As examples of these studies, there is the Williams and Adrian study of four Michigan communities in which they focus primarily on aspects of the political structure as they relate to the quality of municipal services.[17] The studies by Mills and Ulmer[18] and Fowler,[19] both of which are included in this reader, are examples of studies that primarily relate economic characteristics of the community to some "output" measures of general welfare.

Kessel has suggested that such community characteristics as community size, growth rate, heterogeneity, and economic base are related to the form of government: commission, mayor-council, or city manager.[20] And Cutwright has demonstrated that other structural features of communities are related to the incidence of nonpartisan electoral systems.[21] Alford and Scoble,[22] Schnore and Alford,[23] and Wolfinger and Field[24] have done still other studies in which the formal political structure is or can be conceived of as a community "output."

There are a number of studies of fluoridation outcomes besides those of Pinard such as Gamson,[25] Crain,[26] Crain and Rosenthal.[27] Crain, Katz, and Rosenthal[28] and others, Wolfinger and Field[29] and Clark[30] have examined urban renewal decisions as a type of community output. And Lineberry and Fowler[31] as well as Clark[32] and others have looked at municipal expenditures as a type of community output.

One of the problems with this body of literature is that no conceptual framework has yet been developed to account for such a wide range of issues. While there has been no shortage of explanatory independent variables—such factors as the economic structure,[33] political structure,[34] characteristics of the labor force,[35] educational attainment[36]—none of these has developed a conceptual framework comprehensive enough to account for such diverse findings. There are still other variables which seem to be of critical importance for understanding some community outcomes. In one ongoing research project the age and size of the city have been found to be consistently strong predictors of urban renewal, public housing, and poverty program outputs.[37] While neither of these is a particularly interesting variable, it could be argued that they are simply gross indicators of the degree to which given community power configurations have accumulated the actuarial knowledge and experience necessary for successful collective action. Undoubtedly, there are still other interpretations of these data and other community factors that will increase understanding of the issues raised here.

Another problem is that some of the issues involve mainly the reallocation of local community resources—fluoridation, municipal expenditures—while others involve a modest mobilization of some local community resources to obtain still greater resources from outside the community—urban renewal, poverty programs, public housing, model cities. Further, some decisions involve the formal participation of the local government—urban renewal, fluoridation, municipal expenditures, public housing, model cities—while another range of community issues does not necessarily require action by the formal governmental structure—community chest, neighborhood centers. It may well be that different types of conceptual models will be necessary in order to account for these different types of issue outcomes.

What seems fairly certain at this point is the need for the development of new concepts to understand the states of coordination within community systems. That is, concepts that reflect the number of interfaces in such systems, the quality of communication among them, the efficiency of resource utilization at each of these interfaces, and the probability of their successful activation, to name but a few of those which seem relevant at this time.

Finally, there is another body of literature that will prove useful to the student interested in community mobilizations—the literature on interorganizational relationships. There is a growing number of articles concerned with cooperation among organizations and the nature and characteristics of the

environments in which organizations function.[38] There seems to be a convergence of interests between the students of organizational behavior who are concerned with such issues as how the community environment influences, perhaps constrains, organizations as well as how organizations affect their environments.[39] Many of these problems are identical to those listed earlier concerning the interfaces among various community power centers.

Notes

1. E. A. T. Barth, "Community Influence Systems: Structure and Change," *Social Forces*, 40 (October, 1961), 58–63.
2. G. M. Kammerer, *et al.*, *The Urban Political Community: Profiles in Town Politics* (Boston: Houghton Mifflin, 1963).
3. I. Belknap and J. Steinle, *The Community and Its Hospitals: A Comparative Analysis* (Syracuse: Syracuse University Press, 1963).
4. R. Presthus, *Men at the Top: A Study in Community Power* (New York: Oxford University Press, 1964).
5. R. B. Kimbrough, *Political Power and Educational Decision Making* (Chicago: Rand McNally, 1964).
6. L. V. Blankenship, "Community Power and Decision-Making: A Comparative Evaluation of Measurement Techniques," in this volume.
7. R. E. Agger, D. Goldrich, and B. E. Swanson, *The Rulers and the Ruled: Political Power and Impotence in American Communities* (New York: Wiley, 1964).
8. J. Walton, "Substance and Artifact: The Current Status of Research on Community Power Structure," *American Journal of Sociology*, 71 (January, 1966), 430–438; and "Discipline, Method and Community Power: A Note on the Sociology of Knowledge," *American Sociological Review*, 31 (October, 1966), 684–689.
9. C. W. Gilbert, "Some Trends in Community Politics: A Secondary Analysis of Power Structure Data from 166 Communities," *Southwestern Social Science Quarterly*, 48 (December, 1967), 373–381; and "Community Power and Decision-Making: A Quantitative Examination of Previous Research," in *Community Structure and Decision-Making: Comparative Analyses* (San Francisco: Chandler, 1968); and "The Study of Community Power: A Summary and a Test," in Scott Greer, *et al.* (eds.), *The New Urbanization*

(New York: St. Martin's Press, 1968), 222–245.
10. T. N. Clark, W. Kornblum, H. Bloom, and S. Tobias, "Discipline, Method, Community Structure, and Decision-Making: The Role and Limitations of the Sociology of Knowledge," *American Sociologist*, 3 (August, 1968), 214–217.
11. T. N. Clark, "Community Structure, Decision-Making, Budget Expenditures, and Urban Renewal in 51 American Communities," *American Sociological Review*, 33 (August, 1968), 576–593.
12. M. Harrington, *The Other America: Poverty in the United States* (New York: MacMillan, 1962).
13. F. Hunter, *Community Power Structure: A Study of Decision Makers* (Chapel Hill: University of North Carolina Press, 1953).
14. A. H. Hawley, "Community Power and Urban Renewal Success," in this volume; see Table 3.
15. Compare P. E. Mott, "Configurations of Power," in this volume.
16. For a further discussion of the meaning of the MOP Ratio, see M. Aiken, "The Distribution of Community Power: Structural Bases and Social Consequences," in this volume. There have been other criticisms of Hawley's article; C. Straits, "Community Adoption and Implementation of Urban Renewal," *American Journal of Sociology*, 71 (July, 1965), 77–84.
17. O. P. Williams and C. R. Adrian, *Four Cities—A Study in Comparative Policy Making* (Philadelphia: University of Pennsylvania Press, 1963).
18. C. W. Mills and M. J. Ulmer, "Small Business and Civic Welfare," in this volume.
19. I. A. Fowler, *Local Industrial Structures, Economic Power, and Community Welfare* (Totowa, N.J.: The Bedminster Press, 1964).
20. J. H. Kessel, "Governmental Structure and

Political Environment: A Statistical Note about American Cities," *American Political Science Review*, 56 (September, 1962), 615–620.

21. P. Cutwright, "Nonpartisan Electoral Systems in American Cities," *Comparative Studies in Society and History*, 5 (January, 1963), 212–226.

22. R. R. Alford and H. M. Scoble, "Political and Socioeconomic Characteristics of American Cities," *1965 Municipal Year Book* (Washington, D.C.: International City Managers' Association, 1965), pp. 82–97.

23. L. F. Schnore and R. R. Alford, "Forms of Government and Socioeconomic Characteristics of Suburbs," *Administrative Science Quarterly*, 8 (June, 1963), 1–17.

24. R. E. Wolfinger and J. S. Field, "Political Ethos and the Structure of City Government," *American Political Science Review*, 60 (June, 1966), 306–326.

25. W. A. Gamson, "Reputation and Resources in Community Politics," in this volume; "Rancorous Conflict in Community Politics," *American Sociological Review*, 31 (February, 1966), 71–81.

26. R. L. Crain, "Fluoridation: The Diffusion of an Innovation among Cities," *Social Forces*, 44 (June, 1966), 467–476.

27. R. L. Crain and D. B. Rosenthal, "Structure and Values in Local Political Systems: The Case of Fluoridation Decisions," *Journal of Politics*, 28 (February, 1966), 169–195; and Rosenthal and Crain, "Executive Leadership and Community Innovation: The Fluoridation Experience," *Urban Affairs Quarterly*, 1 (March, 1966), 39–57.

28. R. L. Crain, E. Katz, and D. B. Rosenthal, *The Politics of Community Conflict* (Indianapolis: Bobbs-Merrill, 1968).

29. Wolfinger and Field, *op. cit.*

30. T. N. Clark, "Community Structure, Decision-Making, Budget Expenditures, and Urban Renewal in 51 American Communities," *op. cit.*

31. R. L. Lineberry and E. P. Fowler, "Reformism and Public Politics in American Cities,"

American Political Science Review, 61 (September, 1967), 701–716.

32. Clark, *op. cit.*

33. Mills and Ulmer, *op. cit.*; and Fowler, *op. cit.*; both in this volume.

34. Williams and Adrian, *op. cit.*

35. Hawley, *op. cit.*, in this volume.

36. R. L. Crain and D. B. Rosenthal, "Community Status as a Dimension of Local Decision-Making," *American Sociological Review*, 32 (December, 1967), 970–984.

37. This is a study of community decisions outcomes currently being conducted by M. Aiken and R. R. Alford of the University of Wisconsin.

38. See, for example, E. Litwak and L. Hylton, "Interorganizational Analysis: A Hypothesis on Coordinating Agencies," *Administrative Science Quarterly*, 6 (March, 1962), 395–420; S. Levine and P. E. White, "Exchange as a Conceptual Framework for the Study of Interorganizational Relationships," *Administrative Science Quarterly*, 5 (March, 1961), 583–601; S. Levine, P. E. White, and B. D. Paul, "Community Interorganizational Problems in Providing Medical Care and Social Services," *American Journal of Public Health*, 53 (August, 1963), 1183–1195; H. Guetzkow, "Relations Among Organizations," in R. V. Bowers (ed.), *Studies on Behavior In Organizations* (Athens: University of Georgia Press, 1966), pp. 13–44. F. E. Emery and E. L. Trist, "The Causal Texture of Organizational Environments," *Human Relations*, 18 (February, 1965), 21–32; S. Terreberry, "The Evolution of Organizational Environments," *Administrative Science Quarterly*, 12 (March, 1968), 590–613; M. Aiken and J. Hage, "Organizational Interdependence and Intra-Organizational Structure," *American Sociological Review*, 33 (December, 1968), pp. 912–930.

39. R. L. Warren, "The Interorganizational Field as a Focus for Investigation," *Administrative Science Quarterly*, 12 (December, 1967), 396–419.

A. Illustrative Comparative Studies

Industry and Community Power Structure:
A Comparative Study of an American
and an English City*

Delbert C. Miller

The role of business leaders[1] within a local community poses some challenging questions about the on-going processes of community decision making. Why do business leaders take an active interest in community affairs? What is the extent of their influence in the community? How do they exercise this influence?

These questions have been asked by sociologists who have sought answers by conducting research on both the community[2] and the national level.[3] However, community power structure as a field of knowledge still has wide areas in which research data are lacking.[4]

The purpose of this paper is to describe and analyze the characteristics of decision makers in an American and an English city. It has been repeatedly asserted that business men (manufacturers, bankers, merchants, investment brokers, and large real estate holders) exert predominant influence in community decision making. This is the central hypothesis under test. Hunter has recently demonstrated this hypothesis in his study of a large regional city of southern United

States.[5] This paper applies Hunter's basic methods to two cities of similar size and economic structure. The research design has been altered only to refine the conceptual framework and provide for more extensive data to test the hypothesis.

Research Design

Two cities with similar economic, demographic, and educational characteristics were selected. "Pacific City" is located in the Pacific Northwest, U.S.A., "English City" in Southwestern England. Both are comparable in many features with Hunter's Southern City. All of the cities qualify under the Harris classification as "diversified types."[6] The following summary shows the close similarity of the three cities.

> *Southern Regional City* in 1950 had a population of 331,000. It serves as the commercial, financial, and distributive center for the Southeastern section of the United States. It manufactures aircraft, textiles, and cotton waste products; is a transportation center of rail, air, bus, and truck lines; and

Reprinted from the American Sociological Review, *23 (February 1958), 9–15, by permission of the author and the American Sociological Association. Copyright 1958 by the American Sociological Society.*

*I am indebted for research assistance to Stuart D. Johnson, William Wilkinson, Esther Hirabayashi, and Anthony Baker, all of the University of Washington. Financial support by the Graduate School of the University of Washington is gratefully acknowledged. This report is one of a series describing tests of twelve hypotheses of community power structure in Pacific City (studied 1952–54; 1956–57) and English City (studied 1954–55). Other published work includes Delbert C. Miller, "The Seattle Business Leader," *Pacific North West Business*, 15 (February, 1956), pp. 5–12; and "The Prediction of Issue Outcome in Community Decision Making," Proceedings of the Pacific Sociological Society, *Research Studies of the State College of Washington*, 25 (June, 1957), pp. 137–147.

412

is a center of education possessing a large university and many small colleges.

Pacific City had a population of 468,000 in 1950. It is the commercial, financial, and distribution center for the Pacific Northwest. Major transportation lines are centered in the city and it has a fine port. The city is the largest educational center of the region with a state university and many small colleges.

English City, also a regional city, serves as the commercial, financial, and distributive center of the West of England. Its population in 1950 was 444,000. The major manufactures are airplanes, ships, beer, cigarettes, chocolate, machinery, and paper. It possesses an ocean port. The city houses a provincial (state) university and many private grammar schools.

The Community Power Structure[7] is composed of key influentials, top influentials, the community power complex, and those parts of the institutionalized power structure of the community that have come into play when activated by a community issue. When not active, the community power structure remains in a latent state. In this paper attention is centered upon the role of the top influentials and the key influentials as representative of a significant part of the community power structure.

The Top Influentials (T.I.) are persons from whom particular members are drawn into various systems of power relations according to the issue at stake.

The Key Influentials (K.I.) are the sociometric leaders among the top influentials.

Lists of leaders were secured from organizations and informants in nine institutional sectors: business and finance, education, religion, society and wealth, political and governmental organization, labor, independent professions, cultural (aesthetic) institutions, and social service. The initial lists included a total of 312 names in Pacific City and 278 in English City.

Ten expert panel raters were selected on the basis of the following qualifications: (1) knowledge of the leaders in one institutional sector with special thoroughness, (2) broad knowledge of the community, (3) many contacts with T.I. but not themselves K.I. Raters meeting these qualifications are com-

monly found among public relations officials, newspaper reporters, and some government officials. Raters were asked to designate each person as *most influential, influential,* or *less influential* on the specific criterion: "Person participates actively either in supporting or initiating policy decisions which have the most effect on the community." Those nominated most frequently as most influential were selected for interviewing.[8]

Personal interviews were held with a 50 per cent stratified random sample of 44 T.I. in Pacific City and 32 T.I. in English City. The sample had been stratified according to the nine institutional sectors enumerated above, and corresponding proportions of leaders from each sector were interviewed. During the interview each top influential was asked the following question: "If you were responsible for a major project which was before the community that required decision by a group of leaders—leaders that nearly everyone would accept—which ten on this list would you choose, regardless of whether they are known personally to you or not? Add other names if you wish."

Each respondent was asked to check a social acquaintance scale for each T.I. by don't know, heard of, know slightly, know well, know socially (exchange home visits). He was also asked to check each T.I. with whom he had worked on committees during the past two years.

The interview included questions on current issues, role played by respondent, persons and organizations that worked for and against issues. Ratings were also secured of influential organizations and associations in the community. The interview concluded with the question: "There are several crowds in (Pacific City) that work together and pretty much make the big decisions. Is this true or false?" The responses were probed.

A questionnaire was left with each respondent at the time of interview. The questionnaire called for background data, career history, business participation (other than own business), social, civic, and professional participation. These questionnaires were later collected through the mail or by a personal visit.

Newspaper accounts during the period of the study were used to record activities of T.I., committee appointments of T.I., activities of their wives, community issues, and interactions between institutions of the community.

Informants were interviewed to validate findings on clique behavior, and to describe activities of top influentials and the community power complex in the resolution of current issues.

Test of the Hypothesis

Evidence for a test of the hypothesis that business men exert a predominant influence in community decision making was secured from three major sources: from *interviews*: (1) Degree of sector representation based on panel selection of T.I., (2) Sociometric rank of each T.I., (3) Committee participation score of T.I.; from *questionnaires*: (1) Participation scores in business, social, civic, and professional organizations of T.I.; from *newspapers*: (1) Participation mentions (acts and opinions) of T.I., (2) Current committee appointments of T.I. for community activities.

In each of the three cities a panel of representative judges from various institutional sectors designated the most influential leaders in the community. Table 1 shows the institutional affiliation of the T.I. selected by the panels in the three cities. Business has the largest representation among the T.I. but there is a considerable spread over the other institutional sectors. A chi-square test applied to the frequency distribution in the three cities failed to reveal any significant variation in the panel selections. However, a different pattern emerged when the K.I. were selected by the T.I. themselves.

The K.I. are a significant feature of any community power structure for they are the sociometric leaders. The initiation and sanction of policy tends to be centered about them so that they may greatly influence the values which dominate in decision making. The K.I. are those persons who were most often chosen by th T.I. as the ten leaders they would want if they were responsible for a major project before the community and they were seeking leaders nearly everyone would accept.

The twelve influentials with the highest sociometric choice status are shown in Table

TABLE 1. *Top Influentials by Institutional Affiliation as Selected by Expert Citizen Panels*

Institutional Affiliation	Pacific City (N = 44)	English City (N = 32)	Southern City (N = 40)
	Per cent	Per cent	Per cent
Business	33	34	58
Labor	14	19	5
Education	10	9	5
Government	17	9	5
Independent professions*	12	13	15
Religion	7	9	0
Society and wealth	0	7	12
Social welfare and cultural leaders (combined)	7	0	0
Total	100	100	100

*Hunter says that both of the lawyers in Southern City are corporation lawyers. I have been inclined to classify them as part of the business representation, but I have not because they are lawyers of independent law firms. Lawyers are classified under independent professions unless they were reported as salaried employees in a business firm.

TABLE 2. *Key Influentials as Selected by Top Influentials and Ranked by Status as Influential Policy Makers*

Pacific City	English City	Southern City
1. Manufacturing executive	1. Labor party leader	1. Utilities executive
2. Wholesale owner and investor	2. University president	2. Transport executive
3. Mercantile executive	3. Manufacturing executive	3. Lawyer
4. Real estate owner—executive	4. Bishop, Church of England	4. Mayor
5. Business executive (woman)	5. Manufacturing executive	5. Manufacturing executive
6. College president	6. Citizen party leader	6. Utilities executive
7. Investment executive	7. University official	7. Manufacturer owner
8. Investment executive	8. Manufacturer owner	8. Mercantile executive
9. Bank executive—investor	9. Labor leader	9. Investment executive
10. Episcopalian bishop	10. Civic leader (woman)	10. Lawyer
11. Mayor (lawyer)	11. Lawyer	11. Mercantile executive
12. Lawyer	12. Society leader	12. Mercantile owner
Business Representation: 67 per cent	Business Representation: 25 per cent	Business Representation: 75 per cent

2 for the three cities. In Pacific City and Southern City of the United States business representation predominates among the K.I. A comparison of the proportions of business representation within the T.I. (Table 1) and the business representation within the K.I. (Table 2) reveals that the T.I. chose business men more frequently as K.I., in the two American cities.[9] In contrast, English City retains a representation of business among its K.I. (25 per cent) that corresponds closely to the business representation among its T.I. (34 per cent). Moreover, English City reveals a more even representation from the various institutional sectors of the community among its K.I.

This marked difference between the American cities and English City raises questions about community organization. Why should two labor leaders be among the outstanding leaders in English City while not one labor leader appears among the key influentials of the two American cities? These and other questions will be explored later when the findings of further analysis have been presented.

Evidence for the influence of the K.I. was sought by establishing measures of actual behavior for all the T.I. These measures included the activity of T.I. in committee work as reported in the newspapers over a two year period, and by their own statements

of committee participation. Likewise, we sought evidence of their activity as spokesmen in community life as reported by the newspapers. Participation scores were derived from adapted Chapin Social Participation scales for social, civic, professional, and other business affiliations.

Table 3 shows the Spearman rank-order correlations of the top influentials for these various forms of community behavior in Pacific City and English City. These correlations indicate that there is a definite correspondence between the policy committee choices designating K.I. and actual behavior patterns in both Pacific City and English City. The highest correlation is shown to be that between policy committee choice rank and the committee participation for a two year period as designated by the T.I. on the interview schedule. K.I. are very active in community affairs. However, this activity may not be reflected in newspaper accounts. There is no significant correlation in Pacific City between committee choice status and newspaper mentions of community activities; in English City there is a low negative correlation indicating that K.I. have received less newspaper publicity than T.I. This lack of publicity is in keeping with two features of civic activity as engaged in by K.I.: (1) much of their activity is policy making and is carried on quietly, and (2) there is a social

TABLE 3. *Spearman Rank Order Correlations Derived from Policy Committee Choice Rankings of Top Influentials and Ranking on Various Measures of Community Behavior*

POLICY COMMITTEE CHOICE RANK COMPARED WITH:	PACIFIC CITY (N=44)	ENGLISH CITY (N=32)
Committee appointments accepted during past two years, as shown by newspaper reports	.51	.43
Committee participation for two year period, as designated by T.I. on the interview schedule	.84	.67
Newspaper mentions of community activities and statements	.15	—.31
Participation in other businesses as owner or director	.53	.33
Participation in social clubs	.51	.47
Participation in civic organizations	.58	.43
Participation in professional organizations	.45	.34
Total social participation in business, social, civic, and professional organizations	.59	.48

convention that "key" leaders do not seek publicity. In England, a deliberate effort is made by some K.I. to keep their names from the newspaper as a role requirement of their social class. The similarities exhibited by K.I. in the two cities suggest that there are many common role patterns. The influentials participate widely in social, civic and professional organizations. Based on his research contacts, the writer believes that key community leaders develop skills and influence that enable them to originate action for others. It would appear that such leaders could exchange positions with comparable influentials in other American or English cities and soon come to function effectively as K.I. in another community. However, marked differences may be discerned between Pacific City and English City. In general, there is more participation of all kinds by Pacific City K.I., and especially in other businesses. This is because the K.I. in Pacific

City have a much higher business composition and because they rely more heavily on voluntary organizations for influence in community decision making.

Conclusion

Validity of the K.I. as identified is now assumed to be demonstrated with sufficient confidence to validate the hypothesis for Pacific City. Business men do exert a predominant influence in community decision making in Pacific City and Southern City. However, in English City, the hypothesis is rejected. The K.I. come from a broad representation of the institutional sectors of community life. Why should this difference exist between the two American cities and the English city? Two major factors seem to explain much of this difference. The first is the difference in occupational prestige values between the United States and England. In contrast to the United States "the social status of industry in England, and so of its captains is low by comparison with the law, medicine, and the universities."[10] Top business managers are recruited from the universities (and upper-class families) where the tradition of a liberal education predominates, and this kind of education emphasizes humanistic values and minimizes the business orientation that characterizes the social climate of the typical American university campus. Many top business leaders, educated at Oxford and Cambridge, reported during interviews that they regarded business life as a very useful activity but did not view it as occupying the whole man. They expressed a respect for scholarly pursuits. Indeed, specialized courses in business administration in the University are very few, and the tradition continues that business management is learned by experience within the firm. This value system plays a role in the selection of community leaders in English City just as the larger emphasis and prestige of business leadership influences the selection of community leaders in the two American cities.

A second major factor is the structure of city government. In Pacific City the city council is composed of nine members elected at large on a non-partisan ballot. These nine members have the following occupational affiliations:

Newspaper owner-editor	Business
Merchant	Business
Merchant	Business
Newspaper owner-editor	Business
Merchant	Business
Merchant	Business
Housewife (formerly teacher)	Professional
Jeweler (and labor officer)	Skilled worker
Bus operator	Semi-skilled worker

A background of small business predominates. None of the council members was chosen as a top influential by our panel raters or by top influentials. There is every indication that the top community leaders do not regard the council as a strong center of community power. The council tends to make decisions on community issues after a relatively long period of debate and after power mobilization has taken place in the community. During this period such groups as the Chamber of Commerce, the Labor Council, Municipal League, Parent-Teachers Association, and Council of Churches take stands. Council members may be approached and appeals made to them. Newspaper editors write articles. K.I. may make open declarations for or against the current issues and use their influence with the "right persons or groups." The mayor as administrative head and an elective official is both relatively powerful as patronage dispenser, and, at the same time, exposed to pressure from citizens to whom he may be indebted for his position either in the past or in the future.

In contrast to this pattern, English City has a city council composed of 112 members drawn from 28 wards. Each ward elects four members. When the council is organized, members are appointed to committees that meet once or twice a week. Issues that arise in any part of the community are quickly brought to the Council's attention. The city clerk is the administrative head of the city government. He is a civil servant appointed by the council on the basis of his administrative ability and serves under a requirement of impartiality as elections come and political parties change in power. The members of the Council are released by their employers from work at the time of meetings. They are paid a stipend by the local government for time lost from work and for any personal expenses incurred in attending meetings within or outside the city. Table 4 shows the occupational composition of 110 members

TABLE 4. *Occupational Composition of English City Council in 1955*

32 PER CENT TRADE UNION MEMBERS N = 37	30 PER CENT BUSINESS GROUP MEMBERS N = 33	37 PER CENT OTHER COMMUNITY SECTORS N = 40
2 Foremen	4 Manufacturers	2 Solicitors
16 Skilled workers	7 Wholesale and retail owners	1 Doctor
5 Semi-skilled workers	1 Cinema owner	1 Dentist
8 Clerical workers	4 Contractors	1 Engineer
4 Trade union officials	8 Company directors and secretaries	1 Accountant
2 Unskilled workers	1 Bank official	1 Auctioneer
	8 Insurance officials	1 Teacher
		2 Ministers
		3 Political party organizing secretaries
		3 National government officials
		12 Housewives
		12 Retired workers

(2 vacant seats) of English City Council in 1955.

The council is composed of three major groups, trade union members (32 per cent), business members (30 per cent), and other community members (37 per cent). Five of the twelve K.I. of the community are members and play major roles in their respective parties. The council is the major arena of community decision. Issues reach it directly, are investigated by Council committees, and are decided upon by a vote taken in the full council. Community organizations play important roles in debating the issues, but these are definitely secondary or supplementary activities. The community value system condemns any pressure tactics on the Council as "bad taste." However, in the council a caucus of elected party leaders is held before any important vote and a position is taken by the leaders for the party. The "whip" is applied and members are expected to vote as instructed. Such action is rationalized as necessary for responsible party government.

Two factors, a different occupational prestige system and a different council-community power complex, seem to explain the variation in the composition of key influentials who come to power in Pacific City and English City.

Notes

1. Cf. Howard R. Bowen, *Social Responsibilities of the Businessman*, New York: Harper and Bros., 1953, esp. Chapters 8 and 9; William H. Whyte, Jr., *Is Anybody Listening?* New York: Simon and Schuster, 1952, Chapter 1.
2. Robert S. Lynd and Helen M. Lynd, *Middletown in Transition*, New York: Harcourt Brace, 1937; Floyd Hunter, *Community Power Structure*, Chapel Hill: University of North Carolina, 1954; James B. McKee, "Status and Power in the Industrial Community: A Comment on Drucker's Thesis," *American Journal of Sociology*, 58 (January, 1953), pp. 364–370; Roland J. Pellegrin and Charles H. Coates, "Absentee-owned Corporations and Community Power Structure," *American Journal of Sociology*, 61 (March, 1956), pp. 413–417; Donald W. Olmsted, "Organizational Leadership and Social Structure in a Small City," *American Sociological Review*, 19 (June, 1954), pp. 273–281; Peter R. Rossi, J. L. Freeman, and James M. Shiften, *Politics and Education in Bay City* (forthcoming); Floyd Hunter, Ruth C. Schaffer, and Cecil G. Sheps, *Community Organization*, Chapel Hill: University of North Carolina Press, 1956.
3. Robert S. Brady, *Business as a System of Power*, New York: Columbia University Press, 1939; C. Wright Mills, *White Collar, The American Middle Classes*, New York: Oxford University Press, 1951; C. W. Mills, *The Power Elite*, New York: Oxford University Press, 1956; Karl Mannheim, *Freedom, Power, and Democratic Planning*, New York: Oxford University Press, 1950.
4. Ralph B. Spence, "Some Needed Research on Industry Within the Community," *The Journal of Educational Sociology*, 27 (December, 1953), p. 147.
5. Hunter, *op. cit.*, p. 113.
6. Employment in manufacturing, wholesaling, and retailing is less than 60 per cent, 20 per cent, and 50 per cent respectively, of total employment in these activities. See Chauncey D. Harris, "A Functional Classification of Cities of the United States," *Geographical Review*, 22 (January, 1943), pp. 86–89.
7. Cf. Albert J. Reiss, Jr., "Some Logical and Methodological Problems in Community Research," *Social Forces*, 33 (October, 1954), pp. 51–57; Gordon W. Blackwell,"A Theoretical Framework for Sociological Research in Community Organization," *Social Forces*, 33 (October, 1954), pp. 57–64; Conrad W. Arensberg, "The Community Study Method," *American Journal of Sociology*, 60 (September, 1959), pp. 109–124. The theory and concept used in this paper were developed jointly with William H. Form of Michigan State University.
8. A valuable test of this technique has been conducted by Foskett and Hohle. See John M. Foskett and Raymond Hohle, "The Measurement of Influence in Community Affairs," *Research Studies of the State College of Washington*, 25 (June, 1957), pp. 148–154.
9. A test of the significance of the difference between the proportions of business representation in Pacific City showed that the difference was significant at the .02 level. No statistically significant difference was found for Southern City, although the

direction toward increased business representation among its key influentials is indicated. If the two corporation lawyers were classified as business, the business representation would be 92 per cent, and a significant upward difference.

10. Bosworth Monck, "How to Make a Captain of Industry," *The Listener* (January 13, 1955), p. 57. Cf. C. J. Adcock and L. B. Brown, "Social Class and the Ranking of Occupations," *British Journal of Sociology*, 8 (March, 1957), pp. 26–32.

Decision-Making Cliques in Community Power Structures: A Comparative Study of an American and an English City

Delbert C. Miller

Research in community power structure has centered about two major tasks: (1) the identification of influential policy-makers and (2) the group relationships through which policy-makers wield their influence. A considerable body of research has accumulated to establish the identity of the influential persons in the community.[1] However, much less is known about decision-making cliques. Techniques for measuring the degree of clique solidarity are especially meager.[2]

This study was designed to test the following working hypothesis: *Key influential leaders in a community influence policy-making by acting in concert through cliques.* This hypothesis was examined within a comparative research design utilizing an American and an English city covering a period of study from 1952 to 1957.

In a southern regional city, Floyd Hunter describes a top group of policy-makers drawn largely from the businessmen's class. A pattern of twenty-one clique relationships were shown to exist between the forty top influentials. The most recognized groupings were known as "crowds" and were called the First State Bank Crowd, the Regional Gas Crowd, the Mercantile Crowd, the Homer Chemical Crowd, the Grower Bank Crowd, and the like. Each crowd had a leader. "Several of the top leaders within the crowds would clear with each other informally on many matters. Each man at the top of a crowd pyramid depended upon those close to him in business to carry out decisions when made."[3]

This finding strongly suggests the need for comparative studies of community decision-making. Behind Hunter's research lies the persistent question: To what extent do the findings from this particular southern city permit wider generalization to other cities. Pellegrin and Coates report that the generalization fits (with some variation) another large southern city called "Bigtown" which they studied between 1954 and 1955.[4] And Hunter, Schaffer, and Sheps claim that Salem, Massachusetts, presents a pyramid of power dominated by the business and industrial group organized into power cliques with clique leaders.[5] However, less solidary power structures have been reported by Rossi for New England's "Bay City," and by Schulze for midwestern "Cibola."[6] McKee, reporting on his study of Lorain, Ohio, has said that no one group can be labeled as a ruling group. A number of groups have varying effects upon decision-making in a given locus. "The pyramidical model is . . . inaccurate and misleading."[7]

This paper utilizes Hunter's basic methods on two cities of similar size and economic structure to examine the hypothesis of policy-making through cliques acting in concert.

Research Design

Two cities were carefully selected with similar economic, demographic, and educational characteristics. One was located in the Pacific Northwest, U.S.A., the other in southwestern England. Both are comparable in many features with Hunter's "Regional City." All the cities qualify under the Harris classification as "diversified types." The following summary shows the close similarity of the three cities:

Southern Regional City, as studied by Hunter in 1950–51, had a population of 331,000. The city serves as the commercial, financial, and distributive center for the southeastern section of the United States. It manufactures aircraft, textiles, and cotton waste products. It is a transportation center of rail, air, bus, and truck lines and is a center of education, possessing a large university and many small colleges.

Pacific City had a population of 468,000 in 1950. It is the commercial, financial, and distribution center for the Pacific Northwest. Major transportation lines are centered in the city, and it has a fine port. The city is the largest educational center of the region, with a state university and many small colleges.

English City, also a regional city, serves as the commercial, financial, and distributive center of the west of England. Its population in 1950 was 444,000. The major manufactures are airplanes, ships, beer, cigarettes, chocolate, machinery, and paper. It possesses an ocean port. The city houses a provincial (state) university and many private grammar schools.

The *community power structure* is composed of key influentials, top influentials, the community power complex, and those parts of the institutionalized power structure of the community that have come into play when activated by a community issue. In this paper attention is centered upon the role of top influentials and the key influentials as representative of a significant part of the community power structure.[8]

The *top influentials* (T.I.) are persons from whom particular members are drawn into various systems of power relations according to the issue at stake.

The *key influentials* (K.I.) are the sociometric leaders among the top influentials.

Lists of leaders were secured from organizations and informants in nine institutional sectors: business and finance, education, religion, society and wealth, political and governmental organization, labor, independent professions, cultural (aesthetic) institutions, and social service. The initial lists included a total of 312 names in Pacific City and 278 in English City. Ten expert panel raters were selected and asked to nominate those persons who were most influential in "actively supporting or initiating policy decisions which have the most effect on the community."[9] Forty-four T.I. were identified in Pacific City and 32 T.I. in English City.

The Method

The test of the hypothesis in Pacific City relied upon the following kinds of evidence:

A. Data from interviews with T.I.
1. Measures of group cohesiveness based on committee member selections of KI.
2. Acquaintance pattern of T.I. and K.I.
3. Committee participation as re-reported by T.I. and K.I.
4. Personal estimates of clique behavior among T.I.

B. Data from questionnaires received from T.I.
  5. Activity of K.I. in community organizations
  6. Patterns of overlapping membership of K.I. in business, social, civic, and professional organizations
C. Data from informant interviews
  7. Clique behavior and the dynamics of community decision-making processes

The identification of clique structures is an extremely difficult undertaking. Many respondents will claim cliques exist simply because they have seen persons together many times or have heard that certain people were good friends. Hunter relied upon the mapping of certain sociometric relationships based on committee choices, on participation patterns of influentials in issues as described by them, and on specific statements of informants. The researcher would like to make direct observations of K.I. when they are acting in relation to community issues and perhaps in other dealings with each other. Since this is almost impossible to obtain, cumulative indirect evidence is sought.

Results

In-group preference. The T.I. may range from a large group of independent persons to a small, autonomous group which is well organized and is actively organizing support of the community power complex. Along the continuum between these two poles, various degrees of solidarity may exist. In testing the hypothesis, the research task is to assemble the best measures to appraise the degree of solidarity. Important evidence gathered in this study (and in Hunter's) is the choice pattern of ten leaders made by each T.I. in the sample to the question: "If you were responsible for a major project which was before the community that required decision by a group of leaders—leaders that nearly everyone would accept—which ten on this list would you choose,

regardless of whether they are known to you personally or not? Add other names if you wish."

Personal interviews were held with a 50 per cent stratified random sample of 44 T.I. in Pacific City and 32 T.I. in English City. The sample had been stratified according to the nine institutional sectors enumerated above, and corresponding proportions of leaders from each sector were interviewed. Figure 1 is a sociogram showing the choices made by the K.I. in Pacific City who had been identified as the sociometric leaders of the T.I.

The Criswell Ingroup Preference Index was applied to all three test cities to ascertain the extent to which the key influentials chose within themselves in contrast to their outgroup choices to all remaining top influentials.[10] In order of intensity of in-group preference, the three cities exhibited the following index numbers: Southern City, I.P. $= 11.2$; Pacific City, I.P. $= 5.3$; English City, I.P. $= 3.0$. When the in-group preference is greater than 1.00, we know that the ratio of the K.I. in-group choices to their T.I. choices is greater than the ratio of K.I. membership to T.I. membership. The index scores shown indicate a high degree of K.I. in-group preference in all cities, but Southern City leads with an extraordinarily high score. These cross-group comparisons suggest that these in-group K.I. preferences may reflect a solidarity of the K.I. in their civic behavior within the three cities. However, the index scores are based only on sociometric choices; the actual influence and working relationships are not demonstrated by such data. Acceptance of the hypothesis of clique behavior in community decision-making awaits further evidence.

Acquaintanceship pattern. The acquaintanceship scores for K.I. and T.I. were derived from the interview schedules, which sought a response from each person as to his acquaintanceship with all other top influentials listed. This schedule asked each respondent to check one of five responses: Don't Know, Heard of, Know Slightly, Know Well, Know Socially (exchange of home visits). Scores of 1, 2, 3, 4, 5 were

FIGURE 1. *All choices of Six Key Influentials in the Interview sample of Pacific City to Other Key and Top Influentials.*

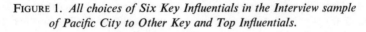

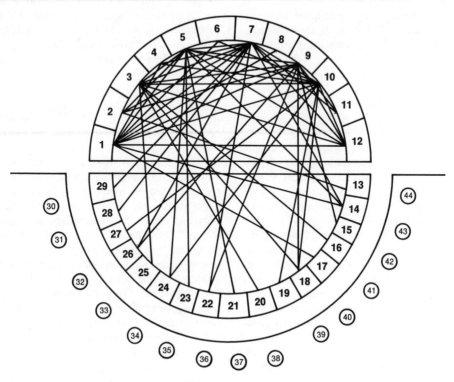

TOP INFLUENTIALS

TABLE 1. *Mean Acquaintanceship Scores for K.I. and T.I. in Pacific City and English City with t-Tests of Significance for Differences Between K.I. and T.I. Means*

TEST CITIES	K.I. MEAN SCORE	T.I. MEAN SCORE	t	d.f.	P
Pacific City	129.7	106.8	2.10	20	$\leq .05$
English City	131.0	107.1	2.21	14	$\leq .05$

allocated to each response category, and a total acquaintance score was derived from each interview respondent. Table 1 shows the mean acquaintanceship scores for Pacific City and English City for the K.I. and the T.I. and values of *t* for the differences between means. These scores show that the K.I. are better acquainted among the total population of influentials than are the T.I. in both Pacific City and English City. This evidence suggests an intensive pattern of social contact among the K.I.

Committee participation. Each interview respondent indicated whether he had participated on committees with each of the top influentials during the preceding two years. One point was given each respondent for each committee contact he reported. The mean score for the K.I. in Pacific City was 18.8, and 11.6 for the T.I. This difference was found statistically significant at the 5 per cent level. In English City the mean score for the K.I. was 17.5, and 12.3 for the T.I., and the difference was also statistically significant at the 5 per cent level. Again, the evidence points to a high degree of contact and possible K.I. dominance of committees.

The questionnaire which each respondent answered and mailed to us asked for participation in other businesses as a director or owner and in social, civic, and professional organizations. Scores were derived from participation in each type of organization[11] and also for total participation. The K.I. were consistently more active in both Pacific City and English City. In Pacific City the mean total participation score for K.I. was 69.9, and 46.4 for the T.I. In English City the mean total participation score for K.I. was 65.3, and 48.1 for the T.I. In both cities the differences were statistically significant at the .01 level.

Community participation was further analyzed to seek evidence of overlapping memberships, on the assumption that persons participating together in community organizations may use these organizations as communication centers for community decision-making or at least as places to reinforce friendships. We gathered ratings of social and civic organizations from all T.I.

as to their influence in the community. Selecting the most important organizations, we analyzed the K.I. membership to see whether any pattern of common participation could be discerned. Table 2 is a matrix pattern of the overlapping membership of the K.I. in the business, civic, and social organizations of Pacific City. Table 2 shows that mutual contact is established between the K.I. in business, social, and civic organizations, but the common participation established by the small group who interact in the business sector may be the most significant. Three of the K.I. whom informants have designated as meeting together when there is a serious financial crisis or money-raising need are among those most active in the business sector.

There is a grand total of ninety-four overlapping business, social, and civic memberships among the twelve key influentials. The rank-order correlation between the policy committee choice rank and rank position based on the overlapping membership is .42. This indicates that a moderate correlation exists and suggests that group interaction may build common ties and leadership reputations.

Direct testimony. All this indirect evidence points to an underlying pattern of common participation and friendships. It does not tell us whether the K.I. actually form crowds and make decisions about community affairs in concert. We decided to ask all T.I. in our sample and certain selected informants of Pacific City about community decision-making by putting this point-blank statement in front of them: "There are several crowds in Pacific City that work together and pretty much make the big decisions. True_____ False_____. Comments

_____

_____

_____." The top influentials interviewed in Pacific [City] answered according to Table 3.

Table 3 shows that (7) seven out of each (10) ten respondents believe that "crowds" exist in Pacific City. The Fisher Exact Probability Test was applied to Table 3 (ignoring the "Don't know" response) to find out

TABLE 2. Matrix of Overlapping Memberships of the 12 Key Influentials in Pacific City for Business, Social, and Civic Organizations

Key Influentials of Pacific City	Investment E	Investment U	Insurance W	Insurance P	Real Estate Y	Bank F	Bank P	Bank W	Social Club	Business Club	Golf Club	Masonic Lodge	University Club	College Club	Golf Club	Tennis Club	Chamber of Commerce	United Good Neighbours	Rotary	Municipal League	Community Chest	World Affairs Council	Orthopedic Hospital	Total No. Overlapping Memberships in Business, Social, and Civic Organizations
D. D.	×	×	×		×	×						×			×	×	×	×	×	×	×	×	×	15
H. E.	×	×	×	×					×	×		×					×		×	×	×	×		12
O. R.	×	×		×					×	×		×	×				×	×	×				×	11
T. S.	×	×							×	×	×	×		×	×	×	×							10
L. A.						×		×	×			×		×			×		×		×			8
R. F.							×		×	×	×	×	×				×	×						8
B. B.					×		×	×									×	×	×		×			7
A. Y.							×			×							×	×			×	×		6
C. S.									×	×	×						×	×		×				6
E. L.									×	×							×			×	×			5
L. C.									×	×	×													3
W. O.									×	×	×													3
	Total No. overlapping membership in business organizations = 21								Total No. overlapping memberships in social organizations = 37								Total No. overlapping memberships in civic organizations = 36							Grand total all overlapping memberships = 94

whether the K.I. and T.I. showed any significant differences in their replies. No statistically significant differences were shown.[12] Both groups of influentials believe that crowds exist and work together. However, these replies must be interpreted with great caution. The term "crowds" does not evoke a common meaning for all respondents.[13]

TABLE 3. *Answers by 22 T.I. to Statement "There Are Several Crowds in Pacific City that Work Together and Pretty Much Make the Big Decisions"*

	K.I.	T.I.	TOTAL
True	4	11	15
False	2	4	6
Don't know	—	1	1

What is pertinent is the basis of evidence for such opinions. Focused interviews of approximately 1 hour were conducted with each T.I. and K.I. and some carefully selected informants to probe for the basis of their opinions. Two patterned groupings emerge as the principal referents: (1) a general pattern of fluid coalition among influentials is discerned about most issues; (2) clique relations are observed around a set of specific situations. It is this second pattern which evokes the belief that crowds exist and make the big decisions in Pacific City. A few interview comments are quoted to show these two patterns.

Interview Evidence for a General Pattern of Fluid Coalition

There are no crowds as such. There are perhaps (10) ten main leaders and the majority of them must be behind any major controversial issue in Pacific City to make it successful. There are probably (30) thirty more persons, less active and less influential, who contribute their time and energy. I am not aware of any subgroups within this group of forty that cling together on issues generally. —A College President (K.I.).

There are no crowds as such, just fluid coalitions. I want to judge a case on its merits, and I refuse to bind myself into any reciprocal quid pro quo agreements.—Utility Executive and Former President of Chamber of Commerce (T.I.).

There are no "cliques" or "crowds." However, every group has their leaders; there are probably five from industry, five from labor, and five from lay groups who lead in their respective groups. If they can be "sold," the others will generally follow.— A Labor Leader (T.I.).

There are a group of about thirty men who are primarily responsible for the major decisions in Pacific City. Quite frequently they are the "second men" in important organizations who have both the approval of the top men and the youth and time to spend a large amount of time and energy on civic work. Many of the decisions are formulated informally in groups of two or three at social functions.—A Doctor (T.I.).

Pacific City has no rigid structure of leadership. No one person or one group runs the city. As issues appear, various persons take sides and push for their view. Different coalitions appear on the issues. However, there is a small core of four leaders, all of them are good fund raisers and people and groups turn to them.—Veteran Newspaper Writer (Informant).

Interview Evidence for Clique Relations Around a Set of Specific Situations

There are probably four groups in Pacific City who are stable and act as a group. The most influential one is the businessmen's group, who are largely Republicans, active in both city and state affairs, members of the Chamber of Commerce, Municipal League, and active in school-board elections. The second is the labor groups, who act together on some issues. There is a third group which is composed mainly of Democrats. They have their own money. There is also a fourth group which unofficially stems from the Council of Churches but influences mainly through individual Protestant ministers. They are interested in the character of various political candidates and boosted the last Governor.—A Republican Party Leader (T.I.).

There is no one crowd, but a key leader works through friends whom he respects and with whom he can get things done. Take yesterday afternoon. The President of the Symphony Board wanted help on the symphony drive. I met with E. B. and S. B. and L. B. [all K.I.] in L. B.'s office. We sat around and talked about who should head up the drive. B. G.'s name was suggested. I was tagged to go with E. B. and hang the job on him. That's the way things get done—informal meetings.

Now in politics, there are ten of us who have gotten together and tried to see that a good man was selected for mayor. We picked T. N., and you could have gotten 100 to 1 that he would have been licked, but he won. Now I haven't been in the mayor's office since. We don't dictate.—A Business Leader (K.I.).

There are several recognizable blocs that usually present the same front. The Chamber of Commerce is probably the most important bloc both in initiating and in influencing. Labor is generally well organized. Educational groups are usually united on issues such as passage of school bond levies but are too divided to present any solid influential body. Welfare agencies shy away from expressions of opinion and are not opinion molders. Newspapers and radio are not influential in local issues.—A Religious Leader (K.I.).

There are ten or twelve in the elite that make the big decisions. They are primarily in the business field, and they work in cliques, the cliques being formed with a member of this ten or twelve, and they delegate authority down to lesser influentials in their areas.—A Social Work Leader (T.I.).

There are five or six "big men" who make most of the decisions; they are important through private and corporate wealth and property. They are socially cohesive, stable, and mostly Republicans, but that is not an important factor. They vote consistently together on issues and are mainly interested in only the important decisions . . . "top-level" operators. There is a second-level group of about twenty-five who are mainly from business. Both the small and large groups are Chamber of Commerce members in part.—Lawyer and Former Mayor (T.I.).

These opinions do not lend themselves to any simple consensus, but a scrutiny of all the behavior and attitudinal evidence leads us to rejection of the working hypothesis in the following respects:

1. Key influentials do not repeatedly act in concert, utilizing subordinate groups. There is no "crowd" pattern in Pacific City

and English City such as Hunter reports for Southern City. Southern City represents a more structured organization of the top influentials with ties to subordinate groups.

2. There are key leaders who bring various other influentials around them when they are responsible for getting a civic project carried out. These groupings do have a pattern and tend to be repeated because key leaders find they can work best with certain leaders and can get the job done. However, there is a significant degree of fluidity. Various leaders may be called upon for the responsible direction of policy-making and different key influentials and top influentials may be drawn in. Both Pacific City and English City show a fluid core of 12–15 key influentials, with up to 150 top influentials. Different combinations appear with different issues. No one person or group dominates.

However, an acceptance and the working hypothesis is accorded in the following respects:

1. Relatively stable groups of leaders are identified with certain institutional sectors of the community through which they express common interest, i.e., business, labor, political party, education, and religion.

2. Solidarity of the key influentials is revealed in the group of ten K.I. who in Pacific City came together when the selection of a (conservative) mayoralty candidate for the primary was a community issue.

3. Certain key influentials come together when a very important fund-raising project is before the community or when a very serious financial or civic crisis arises. A similar pattern existed in English City.

4. Key Influentials tend to restrict their activity to policy-making. Sometimes they are sought out as advisers, as spokesmen, as fund-raisers or givers, and as nominal administrative heads. In this connection the city turns to a core group of 12–15 persons repeatedly. The activity in which they engage is pursued quietly and generally without publicity. In English City it is definitely in bad taste for any key influentials to seek newspaper mention. The importance and extent of their activity are disguised because

both qualities loom larger than is in evidence within the newspaper.

Summary and Interpretation

The three cities that have been studied are alike in many ways. There is a vigorous business leadership to be found in all three cities. There is a hierarchy of civic leadership in which various key influentials and top influentials have a "place." There are friendship groupings and patterns of common social and civic participation which bring people together. There are a large number of top influentials in all three cities (up to 100–150) who have a standing in the eyes of the total community and may be called upon for leadership services when a project is before the entire community.

The three cities that have been studied are different in many ways. English City does not look to its business leaders so much for civic leadership as do the two American cities. The business representation among the K.I. in Pacific City is 67 per cent; in Southern City, 75 per cent; in English City, 25 per cent. The solution of civic problems is carried on more directly by the city council in English City, while voluntary organizations are more fluid and the solidarity of the key influentials is less in both English City and Pacific City than in Southern City.[14]

These phenomena of community power raise the question of what models might be appropriate to describe the various behaviors which can be observed as a community is faced with various issues. Hunter has described a stratified pyramid with a broad base of leadership centering in a top group of policy makers drawn largely from the business class. Figure 2 shows this stratified model.

The writer believes that this model emerges sharply in Southern City because this city is an older, established community where the social system has been congenial to the growth of a social aristocracy and where business control has a history of hereditary growth. Indeed, Hunter points out that only 15 of the 40 top policy leaders gained a position of prominence on their own. All the others inherited their father's business or were helped by the wealth and connections of their fathers. Pellegrin and Coates have reported a verification of this model in "Bigtown," a rapidly growing southern city of 200,000, where the economy

FIGURE 2.

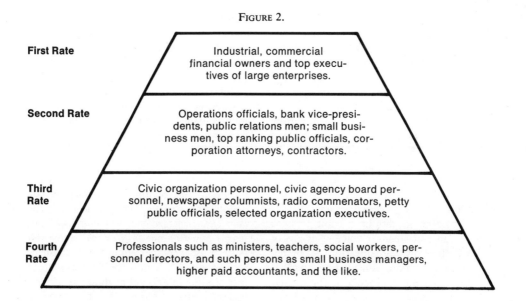

First Rate — Industrial, commercial financial owners and top executives of large enterprises.

Second Rate — Operations officials, bank vice-presidents, public relations men; small business men, top ranking public officials, corporation attorneys, contractors.

Third Rate — Civic organization personnel, civic agency board personnel, newspaper columnists, radio commenators, petty public officials, selected organization executives.

Fourth Rate — Professionals such as ministers, teachers, social workers, personnel directors, and such persons as small business managers, higher paid accountants, and the like.

is built upon a number of absentee-owned corporations. The managers and absentee owners of these corporations constitute a new elite which dominate policy-making in civic affairs.[15]

This model is not appropriate for English City and only partially so for Pacific City. It applies to Pacific City for a wide range of issues and projects, but it does not apply during many political campaigns when coalitions form and often defeat the leaders who are ranked according to the stratified model. It did not explain the defeat of the right-of-work issue in Pacific City in 1956.[16]

An institutional ring or cone model is proposed as a logical alternate construct to fit the pattern of community power as observed in political contests and as seen in certain issues. It reflects a number of current social forces in large industrial cities as shown by three major characteristics: (1) increasing heterogeneity of interests within the business sector; (2) the rise of new power structures; and (3) a growing autonomy and heterogeneity of interests in all institutional sectors accompanied by specialization and professionalization.

1. Increasing heterogeneity of interests within the business sector is manifested by the following characteristics:
    a) Certain manufacturers and merchants view expansion as a threat to labor supply and wage level.
    b) Rise of managers brings a new caution and results in many leaders playing a neutral role.[17]
    c) Financial and property ties grow more complex as outside interests enter. Branch businesses increase, community improvements seem to some as assets, to others as tax liabilities.
2. Rise of new power structures:
    a) Labor leaders have come to have an ever stronger voice as agents of their own organization; labor becomes more educated and participates more broadly in community organizations, especially in political

parties, government, and welfare organizations. A share in decision-making in the community is more easily attained by citizens of low status.
    b) Political and government leaders are exercising greater influence over more activities of community life. Military leadership has been given ever greater responsibility.
    c) Educational leaders command greater attention as the need for specialized personnel increases.
    d) Major business leaders are being recruited for managerial talent rather than from hereditary and exclusively educated classes.
3. Growing autonomy in all institutionalized sectors:
    a) Large-scale organization is growing in all sectors.
    b) Power of administration and policy-making is increasingly concentrated within the specialized personnel of the organization.

Figure 3 is a graphic illustration of those persons in English City who were ranked as having the highest personal influence over policy-making affecting the community. The ring structure shows the range of institutional representatives. The area of each segment is an approximation of the relative power of each segment as judged by the choice rank of the top influentials and by panel raters who were asked to review the strength of each institutional area in securing desired outcomes on a number of community issues. Those persons whose influence is greatest are shown toward the center of the circle. Note the representatives from the Labor party, the trade union and consumer cooperatives, the Citizens party, business, civic organizations, religion, education, and society. There is *no single solidary elite structure and no hierarchical dominance based on one institutional sector*. The pattern of personal influence is best described as a kaleidoscope of recognizable face shifting in and out of fluid coalitions as issues change. Leaders play a number of

FIGURE 3. *An Institutional ring or cone structure of influential persons in English City (1955)*

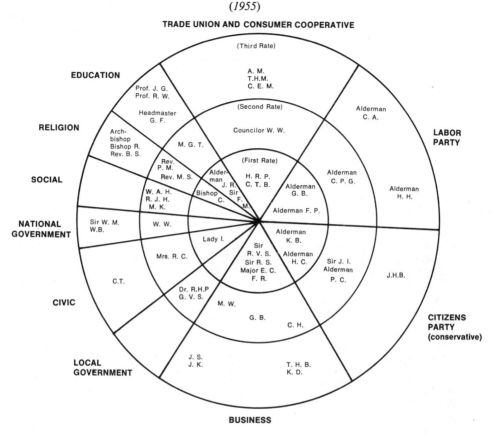

different roles, sometimes taking positive action, sometimes negative, often remaining neutral, and even withdrawing completely from various issues.

While the cone or ring model is most appropriate for English City, the stratified pyramid, with its solidary top business elite such as Hunter describes for Southern Regional City, is also a useful guide to the power potential in Pacific City. However, Pacific City shows markedly more fluidity among both the key and the top influentials as issues change. Religion and education

have a more influential role, numbering a college president and an Episcopalian bishop among its key influentials.

A continuum of community power structures is suggested for large cities ranging from the highly stratified pyramid dominated by a small but powerful business group functioning through cliques of high solidarity to a ring of institutional representatives functioning in relatively independent roles. We have said that Southern City, Pacific City, and English City range in the order named along such a continuum.

Notes

1. Floyd Hunter, *Community Power Structure* (Chapel Hill: University of North Carolina Press, 1953); John M. Foskett and Raymond

Hohle, "The Measurement of Influence in Community Affairs," *Research Studies of the State College of Washington*, 25 (June

1957), 148–54; Robert O. Schulze and Leonard U. Blumberg, "The Determination of Local Power Elites," *American Journal of Sociology*, 63 (November, 1957), 290–96; Peter H. Rossi, "Community Decision-making," *Administrative Science Quarterly*, 1 (March, 1957), 415–43; Delbert C. Miller, "The Seattle Business Leader," *Pacific Northwest Business*, 15 (February, 1956), 5–12.

2. Sociometric analysis is most commonly employed. For a brief statement of various methods of analysis see Charles H. Proctor and Charles P. Loomis, "Analysis of Sociometric Data," in *Research Methods in Social Relations*, ed. Marie Jahoda, Morton Deutsch, and Stuart Cook (New York: Dryden Press, 1951), Part II, pp. 561–86.

3. Hunter, *op. cit.*, p. 79.

4. Roland J. Pellegrin and Charles H. Coates, "Absentee-owned Corporations and Community Power Structure," *American Journal of Sociology*, 61 (March, 1956), 413–19.

5. Floyd Hunter, Ruth G. Schaffer, and Cecil G. Sheps, *Community Organization: Action and Inaction* (Chapel Hill: University of North Carolina Press, 1956), pp. 27–37.

6. Rossi, *op. cit.*; Robert O. Schulze, "Economic Dominants in Community Power Structure," *American Sociological Review*, 23 (February, 1958), 3–9.

7. James B. McKee, "Status and Power in the Industrial Community: A Comment on Drucker's Thesis," *American Journal of Sociology*, 58 (January, 1953), 369.

8. The concepts used in this paper were developed jointly with William H. Form, of Michigan State University.

9. A fuller description of this technique may be found in Delbert C. Miller, "Industry and Community Power Structure: A Comparative Study of an American and an English City," *American Sociological Review*, 23 (February, 1958), 10–11.

10. J. H. Criswell, "Sociometric Methods of Measuring Group Preferences," *Sociometry*,

VI, 4 (1943), 398–408.

11. Scores were allocated as follows: Business: 1 point for each directorship of business other than own, with 2 points for each board chairmanship or ownership of another business. Social, civic, and professional areas were each marked for every organization listed according to the number of categories marked from Attend Regularly (1 point), Committee Member (2 points), Officer (3 points).

12. Sidney Siegal, *Nonparametric Statistics for the Behavioral Sciences* (New York: McGraw-Hill Book Co., 1956), pp. 96–104.

13. In a letter to the writer, August 2, 1956, Floyd Hunter says: "I think I may have quoted and used the term 'crowds or cliques' rather broadly in the Regional City study, but it still has meaning for me. In several cities I have been in recently, it appears, too, that some of the corporate groups may be reluctant to 'bind themselves into reciprocal quid pro quo agreement,' but many such groups have followers identified with them that make up a 'crowd' in the minds of others in the community. It is a term that might be tightened up, however, and your field findings cannot be dismissed lightly."

14. Delbert C. Miller, "Industry and Community Power Structure," *American Sociological Review*, 23 (February, 1958), 14.

15. Pellegrin and Coates, *op. cit.*, p. 413.

16. Delbert C. Miller, "The Prediction of Issue Outcome in Community Decision Making," *Proceedings of the Pacific Sociological Society* ("Research Studies of the State College of Washington," 25 [June, 1957]), pp. 137–47.

17. This is well documented in Robert O. Schulze, "Economic Dominants in Community Power Structure," *American Sociological Review*, 23 (February, 1958), 7–9. However, the withdrawal of "economic dominants" exhibited in Cibola was not demonstrated in Pacific City or English City.

Integration and Cleavage Among Community Influentials in Two Border Cities*

William H. Form and William V. D'Antonio

Earlier studies in community power were largely concerned with identifying community influentials and providing illustrations of their power.[1] Two parallel assumptions about top influentials have dominated much of this research: that they constitute a solidary social system; that they are integrated in their values and perspectives. It is theoretically possible for neither of these conditions to hold.[2] Keller has emphasized the need to examine carefully the "degree of integration existing at the highest levels of the social system" to find out if there is, in fact, a sharing of values and perspectives which may be expected to "result in some coherent direction for the [community] as a whole."[3]

Therefore, two related research tasks appear to be urgent: delineating the degree of social integration among top influentials, and relating this to the social structure of the community. Miller's investigations of the degree of cohesion existing among the top influentials of three large cities are aimed largely at the first of these objectives.[4] But no one, to our knowledge, has systematically related such data on influentials to, first, their community participational patterns and, second, their degree of consensus on institutional values and perspectives. This is the major objective of this study.

A general positive correlation should be expected between the degree of social cohesion found among influentials and their degree of consensus on values, perspectives, and participational patterns. The research design commonly used to study community influentials, however, tends to hide evidence of social and valuational cleavages. In seeking consensual nominations for the most influential persons in the community, a list is obtained of businessmen who often appear to form a tightly knit social system.[5] Yet in cases of conflict and decision-making these persons often meet the resistance (sometimes successful) of others (often politicos) who may or may not be included in, say, the "top 40" list. Moreover, since subsequent interviewing avoids systematic probing of inter-institutional relations which are often the sources of conflict,[6] the range of potential cleavages is minimized. Studies using a community context design (within a given society) rather than a comparative design (using communities in different societies) further reduce the possibility of observing variable relations among influentials and differences in their perceptions of local inter-institutional relations.[7] The research design used here seeks to meet and overcome some of these shortcomings.

Research Design

Research Objectives. Two comparable communities representing different sociocultural

Reprinted from the American Sociological Review, 24 *(November 1959), 804–814, by permission of the authors and the American Sociological Association. Copyright 1959 by the American Sociological Association.*

*The research was sponsored by the Carnegie Corporation of New York and the United States Public Health Service under grants made to Charles P. Loomis to study "Anglo-Latino Relations" in the United States-Mexico border area. The authors are highly indebted to Dr. Loomis for his intellectual stimulation and material support. We are also indebted to Dr. Ann Olmsted for a critical reading of the manuscript.

systems (United States and Mexico) were studied simultaneously to investigate the relations among influentials representing political and economic institutions.[8] The following guiding hypotheses were derived from the proposition that the integration between economic and political institutions is greater in the United States than in Mexico:[9]

1. Significantly more influentials will be nominated as representing *both* the economic and political spheres in the "American" than in the Mexican community. Thus, the more integrated the institutions the more difficult it will be to differentiate economic from political influentials.

2. Differences in the social characteristics and participational profiles between the political and economic influentials will be smaller in the "American" than those in the Mexican community.

3. Perceptions which United States economic and political influentials have concerning extant institutional relations and practices in both countries will converge more than those of the Mexican influentials.

4. Political and economic influentials in the United States will agree more than the Mexican influentials on the identification of the main local community issues and the organizations which will line up in opposition to each other with respect to these issues.

Research sites. The border cities of El Paso, Texas, and C. Juarez, Chihuahua, were selected as research sites. They had certain features in common which enables us to test the above hypotheses. Yet their social, cultural, and historical differences provided the conditions necessary for demonstrating the impact of institutional relations on the social organization of influentials. The high degree of interaction between the cities allowed us to probe the perceptions of influentials in both communities of two types of sociocultural systems.

The two cities share a geographical setting along the Rio Grande River which ordinarily trickles through this semi-arid region. They have similar histories dating back to the late 17th century when the area was first occupied by the Spaniards. From the beginning the communities were primarily wholesale, retail, banking, and transportation centers for their large but thinly populated hinterlands. There, cattle raising and mining were the primary activities. Later, irrigation from the river, supplemented by underground waters supported the growing of cotton and other crops. As main points of entry for both countries for long segments of the border, both communities attracted tourist and related businesses. State and federal agencies concerned with international trade and immigration also located in the cities.

During and after World War II the communities boomed. At the time of the research (1955) they each contained about 140,000 people within the city limits, exclusive of the locally stationed military personnel. However, El Paso had become economically dominant, as a wholesale center, over an area which extended far into Mexico; it also had developed ore and oil refinement, cement, meat packing, clothing, and other industries. The demand for cheap labor became so great that ten to fifteen per cent of the labor force of C. Juarez was regularly employed in El Paso. An aggressive Chamber of Commerce, exploiting the climate, local scenic attractions, and the proximity of Mexico stimulated the growth of tourist business.

For many visitors from the United States, C. Juarez is a tawdry community living off tourist trade and vice. While tourism is a chief source of revenue, a "legitimate" Mexican community does exist. The city has four banks, large import-export houses, and small but important industries such as distilleries, breweries, textile mills, foundries, and meat packing, cotton-seed oil, and building products plants. In addition it has the usual urban facilities and the wide range of formal organizations found in the United States and other Mexican cities.

The two communities are highly interdependent. El Paso employs Juarenses and counts on them to patronize its retail stores. Both communities profit from "American" and Mexican trade, tourist and otherwise. Formal recognition of community interdependence is manifested by the regular joint meetings held by the Chambers of Commerce, service clubs, and fraternal, governmental, and many other organizations of the two cities. Moreover, majority of the residents of El Paso are Spanish-speaking, and many of them have family and other ties across the border. Yet notable contrasts are found in the physical and social organization of the two cities. C. Juarez is more densely populated, is poorer, and has less adequate institutional resources than El Paso.

Selecting the Influentials. During the exploratory phase of the study interviews were held with "knowledgeables" in business, labor, education, government, religion, mass communications, and "society" in both communities. They were asked to provide lists of people who had the most influence and power in the community. The nature of the responses to this question led us to view business and political influentials as two distinct groupings. Therefore, at two separate points in the formal interview, the influentials were asked to name the persons who were most influential in business and most influential in government and politics; if they asked whether or not the same names could appear on both lists they were told "yes."[10] Interviews were first held with those who had received the most consensual nominations from the knowledgeables. Further interviews were held with persons whom the influentials themselves named as influentials. Systematic attempts were made to escape possible "sociometric traps." Approximately 40 persons in the economic area and 20 in the political area were finally interviewed in each city.[11]

The Interview. An English and a Spanish interview schedule containing the same questions were prepared. The following data on the influentials were obtained: (a) social backgrounds, (b) nature and extent of cross-cultural contacts, (c) perceptions and evaluations of business and government practices, (d) perception and evaluation of business and government relations and the relations of these with each other and with other institutions, and (e) specification of local issues and of their protagonists and antagonists. It should be emphasized that in (c) and (d) the influentials were asked to evaluate the situation in their own community and in the community across the border. The cross-cultural slant of the questions was used to sharpen the respondents' observations concerning institutional relations in their own communities. The questions were developed and pretested during three months of exploratory research.

Findings

Hypothesis 1: Influentials in the United States will be nominated more often than Mexican influentials as representing *both* business and politics.

Influentials in both communities were asked to provide separate lists of people in the political and business realms. Table 1 shows that such institutional identification was easier for the C. Juarez influentials: only one-fifth of their nominees were identified as associated with *both* institutions, compared with over two-fifths of the El Paso nominees.[12] This difference is statistically

TABLE 1. *The Institutional Identification of Influentials in Two Border Communities*

INFLUENTIALS	EL PASO		C. JUAREZ	
	Number	Per Cent	Number	Per cent
Business only	23	38	29	48
Business and political	27	44	12	20
Political only	11	18	19	32
Total	61	100	60	100

$x^2 = 7.88$ d.f. $= 2$ p $= .05–.02$

significant and perhaps underestimates the differences since respondents made these overlapping choices without being asked to do so. Thus the hypothesis that institutional cleavage among business and political influentials in Mexico is greater than in the United States is strongly supported.

Despite differences in the size of businesses in the two communities, leading bankers, manufacturers, retailers, and wholesalers were chosen in almost equal proportions in both cities. The fact that seventeen business influentials in El Paso and nine in C. Juarez were also identified as political influentials points to the important place which economic dominants occupy in the total influence structure.[13]

Such parallels were not apparent among the political influentials of the two communities. Table 2 reveals that a higher proportion are found in the executive branch of government in C. Juarez while a higher proportion are found in the judiciary branch in El Paso. Legislative officials were seldom chosen as influentials, and none of them was selected as a "key" influential.[14] Non-government influentials in the Mexican City were all PRI party officials;[15] three of them were labor union officials. In El Paso all non-government influentials were lawyers and were either directly or indirectly allied with the business influentials. Moreover, four-fifths of the C. Juarez politicos were in office in contrast to only one-half in El Paso.

In the Mexican system, influence apparently is more an extension of executive authoritative positions than in the United States. Since the Mexican government is strongly centralized, power proceeds downward from the President to the Governors and thence to the municipalities. This institutionalized pattern places authority and influence at the same address within the political system, and the labor unions are more or less an appendage of that system. Businessmen seemingly must accommodate to the institutionalized party pattern in order to become political influentials.

For El Paso, the data suggest that holding political office is not a requisite for becoming a political influential, a role for which business success and political interest qualify the individual. If an office is held it tends to be in the judiciary branch of government, which is typically more stable and prestigious than the legislative or executive branches. This situation suggests the important role of lawyers in linking business and politics. In general, then, the data support the hypothesis of greater integration of economic and political institutions in El Paso than in C. Juarez.

TABLE 2. *Identification of Political Influentials**

IDENTIFICATION	EL PASO INFLUENTIALS		C. JUAREZ INFLUENTIALS	
	"Key"†	"Top"	"Key"	"Top"
Executive	4	2	13	1
Legislative		1		4
Judiciary	2	6		
Non-governmental	1	5	2	3
Total	7	14	15	8

*The chi-square test was computed for the association between communities and political identification. Key and top influentials were combined. Because of the small numbers in some of the cells a combination of chi-square and Fisher's exact probability test was used. Exact probability levels were converted into chi-squares and the individual chi-squares were totaled, giving a x^2 of 8.994, with 4 degrees of freedom and a probability between .10 and .05.

†Twice as many key influentials were chosen in C. Juarez as in El Paso. The differences are significant, the chi-square being 5.75 with one degree of freedom, yielding a probability between .02 and .01.

Hypothesis 2: Greater integration of business and political institutions in the "American," compared to the Mexican community, is associated with greater similarities in the social characteristics and community participation of institutional influentials.

Influentials in each city were compared for such social characteristics as age, place of birth, education, social origin, occupational mobility, social mobility, and organizational memberships. Data in Table 3 generally support the hypothesis. Almost no differences were found between the El Paso groups. The differences between the C. Juarez groups point to the weaker integration of the politicos with the wider community. The businessmen were more than five years older on the average than the politicos, and a relatively larger proportion of the former were born in the state of Chihuahua. Differences in educational achievement were greater between the C. Juarez than between the El Paso groups. In C. Juarez the businessmen were more highly educated, 70 per cent of whom had fathers in white-collar occupations as compared with 55 per cent of the politicos. Thus, it is not surprising to find that the political influentials were somewhat more upwardly mobile than the business influentials.

These differences were further emphasized in the amount of organizational participation. The business elite[16] in C. Juarez

showed relatively greater participation than the political elite, again pointing to the greater articulation of the former to other local structures. The cleavage between the groups is dramatized by the fact that nine-tenths of the C. Juarez business elites expressed no political party identification, compared with only five per cent of the politicos. In El Paso, the great majority of both elite groups identified themselves as "Democrats for Eisenhower."

Table 4 provides more precise data on organizational participation for the four groups. About the same proportion of business and political elites are represented in various El Paso organizations. A different pattern exists for C. Juarez. Vast differences were found in the Chamber of Commerce, Asociación Cívica,[17] service clubs, and in Catholic and welfare organizations, in which businessmen showed greater relative participation, while political elites were more strongly represented in the Masonic lodge.[18] Careful analysis of the data reveals that a group of about twelve businessmen dominated the Civic Association, the Chamber of Commerce, and several organizations sponsored by the Catholic Church, such as the Boys' Town; their main service club identification was with Rotary. None of the politicos was a member of Rotary, and only one, who was in opposition to the government, was a member of any of the associations dominated

TABLE 3. *Social Characteristics of Influentials in Two Border Cities*

	EL PASO INFLUENTIALS		C. JUAREZ INFLUENTIALS	
CHARACTERISTICS	Business	Political	Business	Political
Age: mean years	51.7	49.4	55.6	49.0
Education: median years	16.0	16.6	12.6	11.4
Born outside the state	50%	47%	50%	64%
Fathers in white-collar occupations	78%	80%	69%	55%
Mean number of organizational memberships	3.0	3.7	4.1	2.7
No political party identification	32%	20%	90%	5%
Number of cases*	38	19	37	22

*Varied slightly because of no answers to some questions.

TABLE 4. *Proportion of Business and Political Influentials Who are Members of Selected Local Organizations*

TYPES OF ORGANIZATIONS	EL PASO INFLUENTIALS		C. JUAREZ INFLUENTIALS	
	Business	Political	Business	Political
Chamber of Commerce	95%	70%	90%	9%
Service clubs	76	73	62	14
Church organizations	21	21	57	10
Masonic lodges	21	10	—	30
International committees	18	21	14	—
Community welfare associations	34	21	33	5
Asociación Cívica	—	—	30	—
Number of cases	38	19	37	22

by businessmen. In general, the data indicate that sharp differences exist between the C. Juarez influentials in their social characteristics, social backgrounds, and community participation.

Hypothesis 3: Perceptions of economic and political influentials in the United States concerning institutional relations and practices in *both* countries will converge more than those of Mexican influentials.

The interview was designed to probe the following areas: business practices, governmental practices, business-government relations, labor-management relations, educational relations, religious relations, and community problems.[19]

Business Practices. Mexican business is allegedly less competitive, more oriented to local markets, more custom bound, and more family controlled than business in the United States. The following questions were posed to compare the images of the four groups on the practices and social linkages of business:[20]

1. Is there more free competition in Mexico or in the United States?
2. Generally speaking, when compared to U.S. businessmen, do Mexican businessmen insist on higher profit rates or not?
3. Are Mexican businessmen inclined to reinvest more heavily in their business than businessmen in the United States?

4. Compared to U.S. businessmen, does the average Mexican businessman think more in terms of a mass market or is he satisfied with adequate profits from a limited market?
5. Is the Mexican more inclined to concentrate ownership in the family or does he prefer to have broader stock holdings?
6. Does the Mexican businessman tend to inherit his business position more or less than businessmen in the United States?
7. Are Mexican businessmen more or less inclined than U.S. businessmen to stress family and personal ties in the conduct of their business?

While these questions are biased in favor of "American" business ideology, their use seemed to be justified because exploratory research revealed that this ideology apparently had become the significant referent for C. Juarez businessmen. Since they enjoyed status-equal contacts with their counterparts in the United States they might not feel the need to defend themselves. This situation could actually obscure the cleavage between them and the local politicos. Thus a C. Juarez businessman might indicate that Mexican businessmen generally seek higher profits because they lack business experiences and must undertake greater risks. Politicos might also assert that Mexican businessmen seek higher profits but assert that they are greedy and selfish. Such probing as was possible tended to confirm this pattern.

As expected, there were no statistically significant differences in the responses of the El Paso business and political influentials on the seven questions. In all cases they asserted "American" superiority and endorsed the traditional image of the Mexican businessman.

Differences between the two Juarez groups were not as sharp as anticipated. In all seven questions, however, the differences were greater than between the El Paso groups. In two of the three questions concerning the role of the family in business, the pattern of high agreement between the two U.S. groups and disagreement between the two Mexican groups was maintained. This was most clearly apparent in question 6 which deals with amount of opportunity for mobility in U.S. business (see Table 5). While all the influentials in El Paso agreed that the Mexicans have less opportunity than "Americans," a reversal was shown by the Mexican groups. Almost half of the politicos insisted that the Mexican workers have equal or greater opportunity, while only one-fifth of the businessmen expressed this view. The C. Juarez politicos, perhaps, were responding in terms of their revolutionary ideology which emphasizes the equality of opportunity for all, while the Mexican businessmen expressed a perspective, characteristic of

businessmen in the United States, which stresses freedom from governmental control as a requisite for mobility.

Governmental Practices. Because political involvements may be more emotional than rational, the perceptions of political practices might be expected to differ more than perception of business practices. Such differences would be larger in Mexico where a greater cleavage was postulated between business and political institutions. Respondents were asked to compare the United States and Mexican society in three areas: the degree to which seven democratic ideals are more nearly realized, the degree of mobility possible within government, and the amount of graft and corruption in government.

The following question was asked in the first area: "On this card are listed a number of ideals commonly associated with a democratic society. Let us assume that both the United States and Mexico enjoy these ideals to some degree. In which country is each ideal more closely realized?"

Table 6 presents data on the degree of agreement between political and business influentials in each country. As might be expected, the majority of El Paso influentials of both types agreed that the United States had more nearly approximated all seven democratic ideals than Mexico. In the case of equal justice under law, however, the differences between the groups were statistically

TABLE 5. *Relative Opportunity of Workers in Mexico and the United States to Become Businessmen*

	EL PASO INFLUENTIALS		C. JUAREZ INFLUENTIALS*	
RELATIVE OPPORTUNITY	Business	Political	Business	Political
1. Mexican has greater opportunity	—	—	1	2
2. Same opportunities	1	—	7	8
3. United States has greater opportunity	36	16	26	9
Other responses	1	3	3	3
Total	38	19	37	22

*In the computation of the chi-square for C. Juarez influentials, categories 1 and 2 were collapsed and "other responses" were dropped.

$\chi^2 = 5.953$ d.f. = 1   p = .02–.01

TABLE 6. *Chi-Squares and Levels of Probability Between Business and Political Influentials for Their Perceptions of Relative National Attainment of Democratic Ideals*

	EL PASO INFLUENTIALS		C. JUAREZ INFLUENTIALS	
DEMOCRATIC IDEAL	Chi-Square*	Probability	Chi-Square*	Probability
Free speech	1.284	.30–.20	2.284	.20–.10
Free press	3.569	.10–.05	0.442	.90–.80
Freedom of religion	0.410†	.70–.50	5.790	.02–.01
Free, open and honest elections	N.T.P.	1.00	10.648	.01–.001
Equal justice before law	7.353	.01–.001	9.859	.01–.001
Protection of rights of property and				
management	0.542	.50–.30	5.549	.92–.01
Protection of rights of labor	1.044‡	.70–.50	1.071†	.70. 50

*Unless otherwise indicated all chi-squares have one degree of freedom.
†No test possible; both groups concurred unanimously.
‡Two degrees of freedom.

significant: while all of the businessmen admitted U.S. superiority, only two-thirds of the politicos so responded.

Table 6 shows that the political and business influentials of C. Juarez differed significantly in their evaluations of four of the seven ideals. A greater proportion of businessmen than of politicos felt that all of the ideals are more nearly realized in the United States. For only two ideals, however—free and honest elections, and equal justice under law—did a majority of the businessmen indicate U.S. superiority. Yet the majority of Mexican politicos (70 per cent) felt that the two countries had equally approximated all seven ideals.

Possible conflict between business and government may develop over the issues of corruption in government and collusion between businessmen and politicians. Seven questions sought general and specific views of graft in government. All four groups believed that corruption in the United States is largely a matter of politicians feathering their own nests, although larger proportions of the Mexican influentials pointed to other types of connivance. A similar pattern appeared for Mexico, but larger proportions of respondents refused to give their opinions. In the questions dealing with corruption in the two cities, the most frequent response was that politicians alone were responsible for local corruption, but C. Juarez businessmen

conceded that other groups (businessmen, union officials, and racketeers) entered into collusion.

On two questions comparing corruption in the two cities and nations, and on a question comparing the prevalence of bossism in the two countries, statistically significant differences appeared in the responses of the Mexican groups.[21] The businessmen maximized corruption and bossism in government, while the politicos minimized them. These differences suggest the difficulties of getting the two groups to function in an integrated way in community organizations (see Table 4) and in problem solving (see below).

This general pattern of similar responses for El Paso influentials and deviating responses for the two Mexican groups persisted in questions about the social origins of governmental officials in each country. Almost all political and business influentials in El Paso insisted that governmental recruitment in the United States was more representative of all social classes; most of the Mexican politicos attributed the same pattern to Mexico, but the Mexican businessmen were evenly divided on the question.

Business-Government Relations. An attempt was made to ascertain the degree of cleavage between business and government by asking the four groups directly to evaluate the degree of cooperation between business and government on both national and local levels, the degree of government regulation of business, and the amount of current government ownership of business in their countries.[22] The results of the chi-square tests of association on the images of business-government relations are presented in Table 7.

The El Pasoans were strongly in agreement that business and government enjoyed more amicable relations both locally and nationally in the United States than in Mexico, and also concurred that both government regulation and ownership of business were overdone in Mexico.

Since businessmen in the United States complain of any kind of regulation or control (except subsidies) by the government, it is not surprising to find them differing significantly from El Paso politicos on questions about this situation in their own country. As expected, the political influentials defended present government regulation and ownership as proper and necessary. In view of the fact that the businessmen insisted that business and government got along very well in the United States, their significant disagreement with politicos on these questions attests to the strength of the "conventional wisdom" of free and private enterprise.

The Juarenses tended to be more consistent. The businessmen saw business-government relations in the United States as much superior to the Mexican situation, both in general and with respect to regulation and ownership by government. The C. Juarez politicos thought business-government relations were about the same in both countries,

that Mexican government regulation and ownership was proper and just, and they agreed with the businessmen that the U.S. situation also was proper and just. That the chi-square on the question of government ownership in Mexico does not quite reach the significant level may be partially accounted for by the fact that the government owned PEMEX (Mexican Petroleum Industry) was at that time directed by a former citizen and businessman of C. Juarez who was without doubt the city's most illustrious "son."

Community Problems. Hypothesis 4: Political and business influentials in the United States will agree more than the Mexican influentials on the identification of the main community issues and the organizations which will be opposed with respect to these issues.

Both business and political influentials are concerned with the solution of community issues. They may be said to be integrated when they agree on the priority of problems facing the community, the groups which may be expected to support their positions, and the expected sources of opposition.

The four groups were asked to name the most pressing problems facing their respective cities. They all concurred that finding sufficient water for both farming and urban growth was the most pressing problem. El Paso influentials generally agreed that the remaining problems, in order of importance, were traffic control, new industry, educa-

TABLE 7. *Chi-Squares and Levels of Probability Between Business and Political Influentials for Their Perceptions of Business-Government Relationships*

	EL PASO INFLUENTIALS		C. JUAREZ INFLUENTIALS	
BUSINESS-GOVERNMENT RELATIONS	Chi-Square	Probability	Chi-Square	Probability
Bus.-govt. cooperation at local level	0.272	90 p 80	3.746	20 p 10
Bus.-govt. cooperation at national level	0.289	70 p 50	8.351	01 p 001
Govt. regulation of bus. in the United States	4.046	05 p 02	0.356	70 p 50
Govt. regulation of bus. in Mexico	0.029	90 p 80	5.562	02 p 01
Govt. ownership of bus. in United States	5.509	02 p 01	NTP*	1.00
Govt. ownership of bus. in Mexico	0.266	70 p 50	3.150	10 p 05

*No test possible; both groups agreed that it was "just right" in the United States.

tional expansion, stimulation of the economy, and delinquency control. They also agreed that local government and business associations were playing the most active roles in working together toward the solution of these problems. No organizations were singled out as derelict in their community responsibilities. The prevailing attitude was that the community agencies were concerned with the same problems and were cooperatively working toward their solution without opposition.

The need for expanded public utilities and educational services were the uppermost problems, next to water supply, in C. Juarez. With one major exception, C. Juarez influentials agreed in naming local problems; one-half of the businessmen felt that better local government was a major issue, while politicos gave this their lowest number of votes. These businessmen represented the most active opponents of the local government, and were strongly represented in the Civic Association mentioned above. They argued consistently that corruption in government was a long-standing problem in Mexico and one that prevented Mexico from having a better business climate. In fact, they insisted that such problems as education, traffic control, improved sanitation, and slum clearance would never be resolved until the whole structure of the Mexican government was changed. As might be expected, the politicos dismissed these charges as "mere politics."

Cleavages in C. Juarez were also apparent in the responses to questions seeking to identify the groups working to solve local problems. Four-fifths of the groups named by businessmen were under business dominance, namely, the Chamber of Commerce, service clubs, Asociación Cívica, and Catholic Church organizations. Government-dominated groups, including the government itself, were named by two-thirds of the businessmen as not doing their part to resolve these problems.

As occurred so often, the C. Juarez politicos tended to minimize the cleavage. They chose both their own groups and business-dominated groups in equal proportions as

helping to solve major community problems. Moreover, the political influentials generally did not claim that certain groups failed to carry out their community obligations. The politicos attributed no importance whatsoever to the political activities of the businessmen, dismissing them as the grumblings of a few self-seeking individuals. That such an evaluation missed the mark is demonstrated by the fact that the businessmen persuaded the President of Mexico to remove the Governor of Chihuahua, an act which had great repercussions in local government. The implications of this situation are beyond the scope of this paper, although it illustrates how cleavage may be temporarily resolved in Mexico.[23]

Conclusions

Studies of community power have suffered from the assumption that the top influentials represent a solidary or cohesive social system in communities which perforce have integrated institutional structures. The prior question of whether or not the elites are actually cohesive has been largely ignored. Bell and others point out that we cannot answer this question without knowing what interests and values are of importance to the elites.[24]

This study attempted to measure degrees of integration and cleavage between the business and political influentials in a cross-cultural setting. It was assumed that integration of political and business influentials might be measured by commonality of social backgrounds, common participation patterns, perceptual agreements on business and government practices, and by agreement on major problems facing the community and groups working for or against the solution of these problems.

In all four of these areas, integration between the influentials in El Paso was found to be greater than in the Mexican community. This difference may be explained in part by the fact that for C. Juarez businessmen, business-governmental relations in the United States serve as a major reference point for what they believe the Mexican situation ought to be. In contrast, the principal reference point for the C. Juarez politicos is turned inward toward Mexico City and focused on the national revolutionary ideology.

Even though the data suggest considerable integration between the economic and political influentials and institutions in El Paso, they do not support a simple model of community power structure in the decision-making process. The responses of the business and political influentials were by no means identical. While the reputational technique used to identify the influentials yielded data that support the hypothesis of business domination of local government, many questions are left unanswered. There is no clear-cut hierarchical arrangement in business which definitely places bankers above industrialists and industrialists above merchants. Nor are businessmen automatically ranked above government officials. Moreover, since local, county, state, and federal officials may be named as influentials in the local community, uni-dimensionality is not probable except in a party-dominated system, such as

that prevalent in Mexico. A simple model of community power structure also ignores the power potential of the citizens and other organized groups in the community. An adequate theory must relate the social structure of the influentials to that of the broader community.

Our data suggest that conflicts do not occur along institutional lines in the United States, but among different coalitions of business and political influentials. Conflict may concern means to reach given ends, rather than institutionalized goals. Thus a wide range of institutional facilities may be used to resolve local conflicts and to launch local projects. In contrast, institutional cleavages in Mexico call for the resolution of local problems by one institution or the other, limiting the number and range of organizational facilities which might be brought to bear on a community problem.

It would appear from the above considerations that comparative cross-cultural research is highly useful in the development of a more adequate theory of community power and decision making.

Notes

1. A brief bibliography of such studies appears in Robert O. Schulze and Leonard U. Blumberg, "The Determination of Local Power Elites," *The American Journal of Sociology*, 63 (November, 1957), pp. 290–296. A contrast in conception and identification of community influentials appears in Robert S. Lynd and Helen M. Lynd, *Middletown in Transition*, New York: Harcourt, Brace, 1937, and Floyd Hunter, *Community Power Structure*, Chapel Hill: University of North Carolina Press, 1954.
2. See Robert A. Dahl, "A Critique of the Ruling Elite Model," *The American Political Science Review*, 52 (June, 1958), pp. 463–469.
3. Suzanne Keller, "Sociology and Social, Stratification," edited by Hans Zetterberg *Sociology in the United States*, UNESCO, 1956. An excellent treatment of the problem is found in Robin N. Williams, Jr., *American Society* (Revised edition), New York: Knopf, 1956, Chapters 11 and 13.
4. Delbert C. Miller, "Industry and Community Power Structure: A Comparative Study of an American and an English City," *American Sociological Review*, 23 (February,

1958), pp. 9–15; Miller, "Decision-Making Cliques in Community Power Structure: A Comparative Study of an American and an English City," *American Journal of Sociology*, 64 (November, 1958), pp. 299–310.
5. See, e.g., Hunter, *op. cit.*; Robert Agger, "Power Attributions in the Local Community: Theoretical and Research Considerations," *Social Forces*, 34 (May, 1956), pp. 322–331.
6. See James S. Coleman, *Community Conflict*, Glencoe, Ill.: Free Press, 1957, pp. 21–25.
7. See Albert J. Reiss, Jr., "Some Logical and Methodological Problems in Community Research," *Social Forces*, 33 (October, 1954) pp. 51–57; Peter H. Rossi, "Community, Decision Making," *Administrative Science Quarterly*, 1 (March, 1957), pp. 440-441.
8. Influentials from other institutional sectors were not studied because they were perceived as having negligible influence on technological interchange, community issues, and international relations. This observation was supported by further interviewing done in 1958.
9. Cf. Williams, *op. cit.*; William P. Tucker

The Mexican Government Today, Minneapolis: University of Minnesota Press, 1957; Frank Tannenbaum, "Personal Government in Mexico," *Foreign Affairs*, 27 (October, 1948), pp. 44–57; Fernando de los Rios, "Remarks on Intellectual Life in South America," *Social Research*, 10 (February, 1943), pp. 100–117.

10. They were not asked to select names from a list. This technique departs somewhat from that used by Hunter and others. Although it still identifies influentials primarily by reputation, it adds a "check" on the nominations obtained from knowledgeables. Some 30 knowledgeables in El Paso and 25 in C. Juarez were also formally interviewed.

11. Tandem interviewing was used similar to that described in Harry V. Kincaid and Margaret Bright, "Interviewing the Business Elite," *The American Journal of Sociology*, 63 (November, 1957), pp. 304–311. Interviews with C. Juarez influentials were conducted in Spanish unless they insisted on using English.

12. Final institutional identification of the influentials for research purposes was determined by the frequency of the nominations.

13. This is somewhat contrary to the findings reported by Robert O. Schulze, "Economic Determinants in Community Power Structure," *American Sociological Review*, 23 (February, 1958), pp. 3–9.

14. "Key" influentials were the sociometric leaders among the influentials; the remaining are identified as "top" influentials. A common vocabulary has been worked out with Delbert C. Miller of Indiana University.

15. PRI means Partido Revolucionario Institucional, roughly the Institutional Revolutionary Party. The party has controlled Mexico since the Constitution of 1917. One PRI leader proudly stated that his party had the "best" organization of any in Latin America. It is divided into three major sectors: the small businessmen and property owners, the workers, and the peasants or small farmers. Although traditionally expressing an anti-private enterprise ideology and strongly favoring labor and the propertyless agricultural workers, the party has shown a markedly friendly attitude toward big business in recent years, at least on the national level. For an excellent analysis of the Mexican political system today, see L. Vincent Padgett, "Mexico's One-Party System: A Re-Evaluation," *The American Political Science Review*, 2 (December, 1957), pp. 995–1008. Padgett makes the point that organized public opinion is becoming of increasing importance to the PRI leaders in influencing their actions. Whether PRI will permit the growth of a second, contending political party, capable of winning at the polls, is problematic.

16. Used synonymously with influential. Political influential and politico are also synonyms.

17. A civic organization made up of business, professional, and other citizens interested in bringing about good government to C. Juarez. Because of the great overlap in membership of this organization and the Chamber of Commerce, local politicos claimed that the businessmen were "illegitimately" engaging in politics.

18. The Scottish and York Rites have vied for and held political power in Mexico since the earliest days of independence. Several of the business elite asserted, that one could not hope to get ahead in Mexican politics without joining one of the Masonic lodges.

19. Space limitations prevent detailed analysis of labor-management, educational, and religious relations in this paper. They will be analyzed in a forthcoming monograph.

20. These are somewhat abbreviated wordings of the questions.

21. The differences were significant at the .01 level by the chi-square test.

22. The point is often made that the border regions of the two countries are so untypical that local institutional relations depart from those commonly found in the interiors, a situation about which the respondents were asked to give their impressions. All of the El Pasoans stated that business-government relations in their community were typical of U.S. cities, and three-fourths of the Juarenses declared that parallel relations in C. Juarez were typical of other Mexican cities. The accuracy of their appraisals is supported by such works as Tucker, *op. cit.* and Hunter, *op. cit.*

23. Further research during the summer of 1958 revealed that the cleavage, wide as before, is now somewhat more structured. As an illustration of the growing influence of business within PRI, the President selected as candidate for Mayor of C. Juarez in the 1956 elections the businessman who had headed the opposition group in the study reported here. This caused a rift between the new group and the old PRI leaders. At the same time, other elites in the Civic Association became the formal leaders of the Party of National Action (PAN), thus splitting the original protesting group. Analysis of these data will appear in a forthcoming monograph.

24. Daniel Bell, "The Power Elite—Reconsidered," *American Journal of Sociology*, 64 (November, 1958), pp. 238–250.

B. Community Structure and Configurations of Power

A Systematic Survey of Community Power Research

John Walton

It has become convenient, if not conventional, to date the beginnings of scholarly concern with local leadership in 1953 when Floyd Hunter's *Community Power Structure* first appeared. While adherents to this convention hasten to add that several important studies of community decision-making appeared prior to 1953,[1] they properly credit Hunter with developing the first systematic technique for investigating the subject. As Bonjean and Olsen have remarked, "Prior to 1953 ... the question 'Who Governs?' was answered in much the same manner by both social scientists and the lay public."[2] In recent years, however, that situation has been altered.

The contents of this volume attest to the fact that, since Hunter's study, the field of community power has experienced vigorous growth and no small amount of controversy. While researchers seem to agree on the importance of studying leadership processes in order to explain community action or inaction, they have been sharply divided on the question of how power is distributed. Proponents of the "pluralist" view (who hold that power is widely distributed in American communities) have charged that "elitist" conceptions (or persuasions that power is narrowly distributed, chiefly among economic influentials) result from methodological biases.[3] The "pluralists" in turn have been criticized for failing to understand the community as an organized and structured system.[4] This state of affairs has been reviewed repeatedly and a number of different explanations offered for the disparate findings.[5] While methodological bias continues to be the most popular explanation, other observers have suggested that the differences may result from ideological biases,[6] failure to specify the meaning of "power,"[7] or from the fact that the communities do, in fact, differ.[8]

We are now confronted, on the one hand, with different interpretations of how community power is distributed, and, on the other hand, with different explanations of those differences. In view of this fact, a systematic examination of the research literature seems to be called for.

The purpose of this analysis is two-fold; first, the disentangle the sources of disparate findings in the studies and, second, to determine how far the existing literature takes us in the direction of identifying generalizations about community power structures.

The procedure employed here is unique in that it uses the results of other studies *as data* for testing a number of hypotheses concerning substantive and methodological correlates of community power structure. It should be noted that while such "tests" are indirect when dealing with propositions about power in communities, they are direct and entirely appropriate when dealing with propositions about previous research. Such "tests" are the subject of this paper.[9]

An original article written for this volume.

443

Procedure: Selection of Studies and Coding

The selection of studies was intended to be *exhaustive of the published literature in social science dealing specifically with community power structure.* Thus the thirty-nine studies dealing with sixty-one communities, listed in Appendix A, are to be regarded as a universe rather than a sample. The criteria given require some explanation. First, by dealing only with the published literature of a number of unpublished studies, especially dissertations, were excluded. Second, confining the analysis to the literature in social science excluded journalistic reports. Third, the criterion which requires that the study be specifically concerned with power structure excluded a number of community studies focusing on stratification, local government, and related aspects of social and political life. None of the criteria are absolute. Even in the case of deciding whether a study could be considered "published," a few difficulties arose. Decisions regarding the second criterion were facilitated by the existence of professional journals, although a few books required some judgment. By far the most difficult decisions surrounded the third criterion. The line between studies of local government and of power structure is often vague.[10] In such cases a decision was reached only after a careful scrutiny of the report for codeable findings on the subject of power structure. When such were found, it was conceded that the study dealt "specifically" with power. Once a tentative list of studies was compiled, it was compared with several assembled by other researchers.[11] Cases of omission were reviewed in the manner described, and several additions to the original list were made.[12]

Any claim to exhaustiveness is, of course, impossible to support empirically. An effort was made to accomplish this, but it is subject to the limitations of the writer's knowledge and the accuracy of a number of decisions made in connection with the three criteria. Whether another investigator employing these criteria would produce an identical list is open to question. However, several studi-ous reviews of the literature, which preceded this study, demonstrate considerable overlap, suggesting a high probability that any similar collection would not substantially differ. And, for present purposes, that appeared sufficient.

Because this is an analysis of research on community power, we shall be concerned with a single dependent variable, "type of power structure." The relationship between this and a wide variety of independent variables has been speculated upon in the literature. As a result, an attempt was made to cast the net as widely as possible, coding studies on the basis of as many independent variables as there was a certain minimum amount of information about. In the final organization of studies twenty-one independent variables were obtained. All of the coding was done by the writer and is therefore subject to certain limitations. Appendix B provides a code book and description for all the variables. Each study was held up to this outline; where no information, or insufficient information, was found on a particular variable, nothing was coded. On those variables where there was sufficient information the studies varied considerably in terms of clarity. This difficulty has been met by employing categories sufficiently general to provide reasonable comparability.[13] The results of this procedure are presented in Appendix C.

Hypotheses

The organization of studies provided in the comparative outline enables us to test a series of hypotheses which have been advanced in more limited contexts. The number of hypotheses which could be dealt with was, of course, limited by the range of codeable findings. A careful scrutiny of the literature yielded a unique hypothesis corresponding to each of the codeable independent variables. Thus, twenty-one hypotheses employing community power structure as a dependent variable were investigated. Because they are derived from a variety of sources, occasional modification has been necessary in order to keep the list to a manageable size and to provide conceptual equivalence with the data. The hypotheses fall into two categories: those dealing with methodological characteristics (the A group) and those dealing with substantive, community characteristics (the B group).

A. Methodological Characteristics

1. The reputational method tends to identify pyramidal power structures, while the decisional approach discovers factional and coalitional power structures.[14]
2. Studies focusing on public issues tend to find factional and coalitional structures, while a focus on private issues more frequently results in pyramidal descriptions.[15]
3. The definition of power as control or dominance leads to the discovery of pyramidal power structures, while a definition based on influence tends to lead to factional and coalitional findings.[16]
4. Political scientists tend to find factional and coalitional power structures more frequently than sociologists.[17]
5. Studies finding a high proportion of businessmen in the leadership group tend to identify pyramidal power structures more frequently than those with a lower proportion.[18]
6. Studies finding a high proportion of public officials in the leadership group tend to identify factional and coalitional power structures more frequently than those with a lower proportion.[19]
7. Studies finding a small number of community leaders tend to identify pyramidal power structures more frequently than those finding a larger number.[20]
8. Comparative studies tend to find factional and coalitional power structures more frequently than single case studies.[21]

B. Community Characteristics

1. Larger communities tend to have less concentrated power structures.[22]
2. Communities with increasing populations tend to have less concentrated power structures.[23]
3. Communities with heterogeneous populations tend to have less concentrated power structures.[24]
4. Socially integrated, heterogeneous populations tend to have less concentrated power structures.[25]
5. Regional differences obtain.[26]
6. The more industrialized the community, the less concentrated its power structure.[27]
7. The more diversified the economic base, the less concentrated the power structure.[28]
8. Communities with a high proportion of absentee ownership tend to have less concentrated power structures.[29]
9. Communities with adequate economic resources tend to have less concentrated power structures.[30]
10. Satellite communities tend to have less concentrated power structures.[31]
11. The city manager form of local government tends to be associated with a more concentrated power structure than the mayor-council or commission types.[32]
12. The greater the competition between political parties, the less concentrated the power structure.[33]
13. When changes in the distribution of power occur, they are in the direction of a greater dispersion of power, hence a less concentrated power structure.[34]

Results

It should be emphasized that the cell frequencies in all of the following tables represent communities, not studies. The community is taken as the appropriate unit of analysis here because a single study often deals with two or more communities, generally finding different types of power structure

TABLE 1. *Research Method and Community Power Structure*

	PYRAMIDAL	FACTIONAL, COALITIONAL[a] AND AMORPHOUS	TOTAL[b]
Research Method[c]			
Reputational	15	12	27
Decisional, Combined, Other	8	26	34
Total	23	38	61
	$Q = +.61$ $.02 > p > .01$		
Issues			
Public	0	11	11
Private	5	0	5
Both	11	17	28
Total	16	28	44
	$Q = -1.00$ Fisher exact $p = .0002$[d]		
Definition			
Control	10	11	21
Potential	1	7	8
Total	11	18	29
	$Q = +.73$ Fisher exact $p = .082$		
Discipline[e]			
Sociology	15	16	31
Political Science and Other	8	22	30
Total	23	38	61
	$Q = +.44$ $.10 > p > .05$		
Percent Businessmen			
Less than 49	4	5	9
50–74	4	15	19
75–100	9	6	15
Total	17	26	43
	Gamma $= -.30$ Not significant		

in contrasting cases. The chi-square test is employed here with the recognition that the assumption of independent cell frequencies is not fully met, since over half of the communities were investigated in conjunction with at least one other. This consideration did not seem important enough to dispense with an otherwise useful technique. The assumption does not apply to the Q measure.

Table 1 illustrates the associations between power structure and various aspects of research method.

As the data indicate, hypotheses A1, A2, A3, and A4 are all supported to varying degrees. Researchers using the decisional method, those studying public issues, those defining power as influence, and those with a background in political science, all tend to find less concentrated power structures more frequently than their opposite numbers.[35]

The proportion of businessmen found in the leadership group is high irrespective of the type of power structure found. The same result obtains for public officials, except that the proportion is lower. Hypotheses A5 and A6 are not supported.

If the cutoff point for large versus small leadership groups is set at twenty-five, the pyramidal finding is associated with smaller

TABLE 1 (*continued*). *Research Method and Community Power Structure*

	PYRAMIDAL	FACTIONAL, COALITIONAL[a] AND AMORPHOUS	TOTAL[b]
Percent Public Officials			
0–24	9	11	20
25–49	3	7	10
50	2	6	8
Total	14	24	38
	Gamma $= +.31$ Not significant		
Leadership Group N[f]			
Less than 24	9	4	13
25–49	5	10	15
50–74	3	4	7
75 or more	1	4	5
Total	18	22	40
	$Q = +.51$ $.05 > p > .02$		
Scope			
Single Community	12	21	33
Two or More Communities	11	17	28
Total	23	38	61
	$Q = -.06$ Not significant		

[a] The factional, coalitional, and amorphous categories are combined to avoid small N's and because each represents the absence of any concentration of power.
[b] The N's here and in the subtables that follow vary because the studies do not uniformly provide data on each variable.
[c] The decisional, combined, and case study methods are taken as one category here since the intention is to contrast the reputational approach with alternatives. The relationship between method and power structure is stronger when the "combined" cases are left out of the analysis.
[d] The computations here are based on public versus private, excluding the "both" category.
[e] No difficulty was encountered in classifying sociologists. In the case of political scientists, however, several researchers did not fit precisely into that category. These investigators belonged to the fields of government, public administration, and education. In the first two instances (McClain and Highsaw and Kammerer, *et al.*), I had no hesitancy in grouping them with the political scientists. In the third instance, the educator (Kimbrough) was also included with the political scientists in order to provide a contrast between sociologists and others. If the four communities studied by Kimbrough are dropped from the analysis, the patterns here and in Tables 3 and 4 are not changed.
[f] For purposes of computation, this variable is collapsed into two categories; <25 and >25. Although this finding is not especially surprising, it is worth noting since a small leadership group is not synonymous with a pyramidal power structure.

groups. This result is not dramatic at other levels, although A7 is moderately supported.

Hypothesis A8 is not supported, the results for comparative studies being similar to those of single case studies.

Turning now to community characteristics, the association of a given characteristic with the power structure is illustrated in Table 2. Population size is unrelated to power structure regardless of how the independent variable is collapsed. Hypothesis B1 is rejected.

In the case of population growth the significance is not striking, but interestingly, the direction of the relationship is different

from that predicted by the hypothesis, i.e., pyramidal power structures are found much more frequently in communities with increasing populations. Thus hypothesis B2 is rejected in favor of its converse.

No support is found for hypotheses B3 or B4.[36]

In the case of region some differences are apparent. Among communities with pyramidal power structures 60 percent were in the South and over 80 percent in the South and West. Less concentrated power structures are found more often in the Northeast and Northcentral regions.

Industrialization and economic base are

TABLE 2. *Community Characteristics and Community Power Structure*

	PYRAMIDAL	FACTIONAL, COALITIONAL AND AMORPHOUS	TOTAL
Population Size			
Less than 5,000	2	2	4
5,000–9,999	3	3	6
10,000–24,999	3	10	13
25,000–49,999	3	2	5
50,000–99,999	2	6	8
100,000+	9	15	24
Total	22	38	60
	Gamma = +.04 Not significant		
Population Growth[a]			
Increasing	14	18	32
Stable	3	9	12
Decreasing	0	3	3
Total	17	30	47
	$Q = .51$ $.20 > p > .10$		
Population Composition			
Homogeneous	7	8	15
Heterogeneous	10	14	24
Total	17	22	39
	$Q = +.10$ Not significant		
Population Integration			
Integrated	0	2	2
Cleavage	10	11	21
Total	10	13	23
	$Q = -1.00$ Not significant		
Region			
Northeast	2	7	9
Northcentral	2	8	10
South	14	16	30
West	5	4	9
Total	23	35	58
Industrialization			
Industrialized	13	22	35
Nonindustrialized	9	15	24
Total	22	37	59
	$Q = -.01$ Not significant		

TABLE 2 (*continued*). *Community Characteristics and Community Power Structure*

	PYRAMIDAL	FACTIONAL, COALITIONAL AND AMORPHOUS	TOTAL
Economic Base			
Diversified	12	19	31
Narrow	8	14	22
Total	20	33	53
	$Q = +.05$ Not significant		
Absentee Ownership			
Present	2	18	20
Absent	12	9	21
Total	14	27	41
	$Q = -.85$ $.01 > p > .001$		
Economic Resources			
Adequate	9	17	26
Inadequate	6	5	11
Total	15	22	37
	$Q = -.39$ $.30 > p > .20$		
Type of City			
Independent	14	22	36
Satellite	2	10	12
Total	16	32	48
	$Q = +.52$ $.20 > p > .10$		
Type of Government[b]			
Mayor-Council	9	10	19
City Manager	6	12	18
Commission	2	2	4
Total	17	24	41
	$Q = +.34$ Not significant		
Party Competition			
Competitive	0	10	10
Noncompetitive	10	12	22
Total	10	22	32
	$Q = -1.00$ $.02 > p > .01$		
Change in Power Structure			
Dispersion	2	17	19
Concentration	0	0	0
No Change	3	4	7
Oscillation	2	1	3
Decline Locally	1	2	3
Total	8	24	32

[a]The "stable" and "decreasing" categories are combined for computations.
[b]Following the hypothesis, "city manager" forms one category with "mayor-council" and "commission" combined for the other.

not associated with power structure types; hypotheses B6 and B7 are rejected.[37]

In the case of absentee ownership the relationship is unusually strong in the pre-directed direction, the presence of absentee-owned corrporations tending to be associated with less concentrated power. Both economic resources and type of city bear a moderate relationship to power structure; satellite cities and those with adequate economic resources tend to have less concentrated power structures. Hypothesis B8 is strongly supported while B9 and B10 are moderately supported.

The data indicate that hypothesis B11 must be rejected. Not only is the association between city manager government and power structure not significant, it is opposite the predicted direction.

The results on party competition are another case of an unusually strong relationship. No communities with competitive parties had pyramidal power structures. Hypothesis B12 is accepted.

As the right-hand marginal in the sub-table on change indicates, B13 is supported, most change being in the direction of a greater dispersion of power.

Before proceeding with any interpretation of these, zero-order level, findings, the question of their interrelationships must be evaluated.

From what has been said about the controversy surrounding this research literature, it is plausible to suspect that some of the reported findings may be artifacts of systematic disciplinary or methodological biases. Reference to Table 1 makes it clear that method and power structure are highly related as are discipline and power structure. From this, of course, it follows that method

and discipline will be highly related. Table 3 illustrates this fact.

The next questions is, how are these three related? Given the fact that the time-order is clear, discipline→method→results (power structure), one of three interpretations is possible: (a) the association between method and results is spurious and can be accounted for by the antecedent variable, discipline; (b) the association between all three represents a causal or developmental sequence;[38] (c) there is interaction among the three. Selection among these three alternatives requires only that we control for one of the two independent variables, i.e.;

> Within a system of three variables, all of which are related at the zero-order level, if the association between any two disappears with the third held constant, then the association between any other two will not change with the third constant and, in particular, cannot become zero.[39]

Holding constant the intervening variable, method, the result in Table 4 obtains:

Given the inference that "In general, the association between two variables in a developmental or causal sequence will tend to disappear when an intervening variable is held constant,"[40] we can conclude that a valid developmental sequence has been demonstrated; in this case the disciplinary background of the investigator tends to determine the research method he will adopt, and this in turn tends to determine the image of power structure that results from the investigation.

This demonstration is of interest beyond the context of community power, in that it documents the significance of the sociology of knowledge as a perspective for interpret-

TABLE 3. *Discipline and Research Method*

	SOCIOLOGY	POLITICAL SCIENCE, OTHER	TOTAL
Reputational	23	4	27
Decisional, Combined, Other	8	26	34
Total	31	30	61
	$Q = +.90 \quad p > .0005$		

TABLE 4. *Power Structure and Discipline by Research Method*

| | | REPUTATIONAL METHOD | | | DECISIONAL, COMBINED, OTHER METHODS | | |
| | | Discipline | | | Discipline | | |
		Sociology	Political Science, Other	Total	Sociology	Political Science, Other	Total
Power Structure	*Pyramidal*	13	2	15	2	6	8
	Factional, Coalitional, Amorphous	10	2	12	6	20	26
	Total	23	4	27	8	26	34
			$Q = +.013$			$Q = +.005$	

TABLE 5. *Data Summary*

VARIABLE	ASSOCIATION WITH POWER STRUCTURE	SIGNIFICANCE LEVEL	CONTROL FOR METHOD	VALID
1. Research Method	+.61	$.02 > p > .01$	———	X
2. Issues	−1.00	.0002	Replication	X
3. Definition	+.73	.082	Spurious	
4. Discipline	+.44	$.10 > p > .05$	Developmental sequence	X
5. Percent Businessmen	−.30	NS*	Specification	
6. Percent Public Officials	+.31	NS	Specification	
7. Leadership Group N	+.51	$.05 > p > .02$	Replication	X
8. Scope	−.06	NS	Specification	
9. Population Size	+.04	NS	Specification	
10. Population Growth	+.51	$.20 > p > .01$	Replication	X
11. Population Composition	+.10	NS	Replication	
12. Population Integration	−1.00	NS	Replication	
13. Region	———	———	Replication	
14. Industrialization	−.01	NS	Specification	
15. Economic Base	+.05	NS	Replication	
16. Absentee Ownership	−.85	$.01 > p > .001$	Replication	X
17. Economic Resources	−.39	$.30 > p > .20$	Specification	
18. Type of City	+.52	$.20 > p > .10$	Specification	
19. Type of Government	+.34	NS	Specification	
20. Party Competition	−1.00	$.02 > p > .01$	Replication	X
21. Change in Power Structure	———	———	Replication	X

*NS = Not significant.

ing social research. That aspect has been dealt with elsewhere and will not detain us here.[41]

For present purposes the foregoing demonstration requires that all the zero-order level findings in Tables 1 and 2 be reexamined controlling for the independent variables that are systematically biased in connection with the dependent variable, i.e., in order to eliminate the bias it is necessary to examine the partial associations of the dependent variable and each category of the systematically biased independent variables. Because the relationship between discipline, method, and results is a developmental sequence, as opposed to the case of spuriousness, controlling for either the antecedent or the intervening variable will produce the same effect. The procedure followed here involved control for the intervening variable, method, because it subsumes its own influence and that of the antecedent. The results of the partialing operations are, however, equally applicable to the case in which the antecedent, discipline, is controlled.

The multivariate technique, employed in this reexamination, enables certain conclusions to be drawn on the basis of the accumulated evidence, irrespective of methodological and disciplinary bias: That is, *if it can be shown that any of the relationships which were statistically significant at the zero-order level persist under conditions of control, then it can be inferred, on the basis of these data, that the relationship is a valid one.*[42]

Table 5 summarizes the original association of each variable with power structure and the nature of that association after controlling for method. The column labeled "valid" indicates those significant relationships that persist, are replicated, and can thus be judged as valid evidence regarding the current status of community power research.

Summary: Current Status and Directions of Research

The outcomes of this analysis can be summarized under the headings confirmed and negative results. Before listing these it

should be stressed once more that the low level of measurement employed, of necessity, in this study makes it more difficult for actual relationships to emerge. This principle, at once, gives us more confidence in the confirmed results and less in the disconfirmed.

Confirmed Results

1. The reputational method tends to identify pyramidal power structures more frequently than the decisional approach (Hypothesis A1).
2. Studies focusing on public issues tend to find factional and coalitional structures, while a focus on private issues results in a pyramidal description (Hypothesis A2). This appears to be a developmental sequence from method→type of issue→result.
3. Political scientists tend to find factional and coalitional structures more frequently than sociologists who find both types equally often (Hypothesis A4).
4. Discipline and method are linked in a developmental sequence with the type of power structure obtained.
5. A small number of community leaders is associated with a more concentrated power structure (Hypothesis A7).
6. Studies generally find a high proportion of businessmen (> 50 percent), a lower proportion of public officials (< 25 percent) in the leadership group. Relatively speaking the number of leaders is quite small (< 50).
7. Population growth is moderately associated with more concentrated power structures.
8. A large proportion of absentee ownership is highly associated with less concentrated power structures (Hypothesis B8).
9. Competitive party politics is highly associated with less concentrated power structures (Hypothesis B12).
10. Community power structures are changing in the direction of a greater dispersion of power (Hypothesis B13)

Negative Results

1. Definition of power seems to bear a spurious relationship to power structure and can be accounted for by method.

The following variables have not been shown to be related to power structure under conditions controlling for bias:

2. The proportion of businessmen in the leadership group (Hypothesis A5).
3. The proportion of public officials in the leadership group (Hypothesis A6).
4. The scope of the study (Hypothesis A8).
5. The size of the population (Hypothesis B1).
6. Population composition (Hypothesis B3).
7. Population integration Hypothesis B4).
8. Region (Hypothesis B5).
9. Industrialization (Hypothesis B6).
10. Economic base (Hypothesis B7).
11. Economic resources (Hypothesis B9).
12. Type of city (Hypothesis B10).
13. Type of government (Hypothesis B11).

In those cases where a finding, confirmed at the zero-order level, did not persist under conditions of control, we can conclude that the original association was produced by a systematic bias between discipline or method and the independent variable. The case of regional differences is illustrative; upon closer examination the relationship between region and power structure could be accounted for by the fact that Southern and Western cities were more frequently studied with the reputational method. Similar reasoning applies to other findings in this category.

Directions for Research

If the above findings were divided into the two categories of methodological bias and substantive results, it is clear that the former category would embrace most of the positive findings. In the substantive category most of the hypotheses are not supported. Among

those that are, several seem almost tautologous (e.g., those having to do with the number of leaders and party competition). We are left then, with a handful of propositions which do not seem to suggest any underlying generalizations. The findings relating to absentee ownership, party competition, and change, for example, might be construed as support for the familiar, commonsense conclusion that communities with a more complex social structure are more pluralistic. However, the finding on population growth (not to mention all the negative results) does not square with this interpretation. Similarly, the positive findings might suggest that the viability of local economic and political institutions is associated with a dispersion of power. Although several negative findings raise doubts about this, the statement may well be true. However, it is too broad to be of much explanatory use.

In short, the current status of research does not allow us to draw any firm generalizations regarding the distribution of power in local communities. The literature, however, is not without significance. Some guidelines for future research are suggested by our confirmed results as well as the negative ones. The following points summarize the key issues and tentative conclusions.

1. Since the type of power structure identified by studies which rely on a single method may well be an artifact of that method, future research should simultaneously employ several techniques and continue to compare the characteristics of each with the others.
2. Because disciplinary, if not ideological, biases appear to be operating, future investigators should be more cognizant of their own perspective.
3. The proportion of absentee-owned industry in the community appears to bear a close, although as yet unspecified, relationship to power structure.[43] Future research would be well advised to focus attention on this factor.[44]
4. Political party competition appears to be an important factor, although here

also the effects are not clear.[45] Again future research would do well to center attention on this relationship.[46]

5. In view of the large number of negative findings with demographic and certain economic variables, it may be reasonable to conclude that these are too gross and unrelated, in a direct way, to power structure to be of much use in any emerging generalization.

6. Because of the fact that nearly every study which concerned itself with change found some differences in the structure of power at different times, future studies should deal more systematically with this factor, especially with respect to the changing relationship between local institutions and larger governmental units.

7. While the debate between pluralism and elitism is by no means settled, certain "sub-issues" seem to be less conjectural than opponents realize. For example, we have found that studies generally agree on a high proportion of businessmen and a lower proportion of public officials in the leadership group. Similarly, the number of top leaders is small and overwhelmingly represented by upper-middle class, business, and professional interests (although this variable was not coded, the studies dealing with it are in considerable agreement). If some consensus is emerging here it would serve to free investigators from arguing "business dominance" and allow a closer look at the cohesiveness of leadership groups and the conditions under which they effectively exercise power.

8. By way of an interpretive conclusion, it seems that the future of community power structure research will depend upon progress in four areas:

   a. More attention to theoretically based propositions and "problem-induced" research rather than interdisciplinary polemics.[47]

   b. More longitudinal studies concerned with stability and change in the patterns of community power distribution vis-à-vis extracommunity centers of power.

   c. The development of more adequate conceptual schemes to specify the meanings of power, elitism, pluralism, etc., and allow reasonable and critical tests of the alternatives. Efforts in this direction may well conclude that the terms elitism and pluralism carry more ideological content and less discriminating power than are desirable for empirical and theoretical advances.

   d. The development of comparative methods which are reasonably economical and, at the same time, pertinent to the study of power.

Appendix A. Community Power Studies

The identifying names of each community in the comparative outline are those used in this study; frequently they are pseudonyms. The original studies, listed roughly in order of publication, are as follows:

1. Floyd Hunter, *Community Power Structure: A Study of Decision Makers* (Chapel Hill: University of North Carolina Press, 1953).
2. James B. McKee, "Status and Power in the Industrial Community: A Comment on Drucker's Thesis," *American Journal of Sociology*, 58 (January, 1953), 364–370.
3. Donald W. Olmsted, "Organizational Leadership and Social Structure in a Small City," *American Sociological Review*, 19 (June, 1954), 273–281.
4. Roland J. Pellegrin and Charles H. Coates, "Absentee-owned Corporations and Community Power Structure," *American Journal of Sociology*, 61 (March, 1956), 413–419.
5. George M. Belknap and Ralph H. Smuckler, "Political Power Relations in a Mid-West City," *Public Opinion Quarterly*, 20 (Spring, 1956), 73–81.
6. Alexander A. Fanelli, "A Typology of Community Leadership Based on Influence and Interaction within the Leader Sub-system," *Social Forces*, 34 (May, 1956), 332–338.
7. Floyd Hunter, Ruth C. Schaffer, and Cecil G. Sheps, *Community Organization: Action and Inaction* (Chapel Hill: University of North Carolina Press, 1956).

8. Harry N. Scoble, "Leadership Hierarchies and Political Issues in a New England Town," in Morris Janowitz (ed.), *Community Political Systems* (New York: Free Press, 1961), pp. 117–145.

9. Delbert C. Miller, "Decision-Making Cliques in Community Power Structures: A Comparative Study of an American and an English City," *American Journal of Sociology*, 64 (November, 1958), 299–310.

10. Robert O. Schulze, "The Bifurcation of Power in a Satellite City," in Janowitz (ed.), *op. cit.*, pp. 19–80.

11. William J. Gore and Robert L. Peabody, "The Functions of the Political Campaign," *Western Political Quarterly*, 11 (March, 1958), 55–70.

12. Arthur J. Vidich and Joseph Bensman, *Small Town in Mass Society* (Princeton: Princeton University Press, 1958).

13. Robert A. Dahl, *Who Governs? Power and Democracy in an American City* (New Haven: Yale University Press, 1961).

14. William H. Form and William V. D'Antonio, "Integration and Cleavage Among Community Influentials in Two Border Cities," *American Sociological Review*, 24 (November 1959), 804–814.

15. Orion Klapp and Vincent Padgett, "Power Structure and Decision-making in a Mexican Border City," *American Journal of Sociology*, 65 (January, 1960), 400–406.

16. Ted C. Smith, "The Structuring of Power in a Suburban Community," *Pacific Sociological Review*, 3 (Fall, 1960), 83–88.

17. Edward Sofen, "Problems of Metropolitan Leadership: The Miami Experience," *Midwest Journal of Political Science*, 5 (February, 1961), 18–38; Thomas J. Wood, "Dade County: Unbossed, Erratically Led," *Annals of the American Academy of Political and Social Science*, 353 (May, 1964), 64–71.

18. Edward C. Banfield, *Political Influence: A New Theory of Urban Politics* (New York: Free Press, 1961).

19. Ernest A. T. Barth, "Community Influence Systems: Structure and Change," *Social Forces*, 40 (October, 1961), 58–63.

20. Robert C. Stone, "Power and Values in Trans-Community Relations," in Bert E. Swanson (ed.), *Current Trends in Comparative Community Studies* (Kansas City, Mo.: Community Studies, Inc., 1962).

21. Linton C. Freeman, *et al.*, *Local Community Leadership* (Syracuse: University College, 1960).

22. Roscoe C. Martin, *et al.*, *Decisions in Syracuse* (Bloomington: Indiana University Press, 1961).

23. Jackson M. McClain and Robert B. Highsaw, *Dixie City Acts: A Study in Decision-Making* (Birmingham: Bureau of Public Administration, University of Alabama, 1962).

24. Benjamin Walter, "Political Decision-Making in Arcadia," in F. Stuart Chapin, Jr., and Shirley F. Weiss (eds.), *Urban Growth Dynamics* (New York: Wiley, 1962), pp. 141–186.

25. David A. Booth and Charles R. Adrian, "Power Structure and Community Change: A Replication Study of Community A," *Midwest Journal of Political Science*, 6 (August, 1962), 277–296.

26. Delbert C. Miller, "Town and Gown: The Power Structure of a University Town," *American Journal of Sociology*, 68 (January, 1963), 432–443.

27. Charles M. Bonjean, "Community Leadership: A Case Study and Conceptual Refinement," *American Journal of Sociology*, 68 (May, 1963), 672–681.

28. Ivan Belknap and John Steinle, *The Community and Its Hospital* (Syracuse: Syracuse University Press, 1963).

29. Gladys M. Kammerer, *et al.*, *The Urban Political Community: Profiles in Town Politics* (Boston: Houghton Mifflin, 1963).

30. Carol Estes Thometz, *The Decision-Makers: The Power Structure of Dallas* (Dallas: Southern Methodist University Press, 1963).

31. Floyd Hunter, *Housing Discrimination in Oakland, California*, A study prepared for the Mayor's Committee on Full Opportunity and the Council of Social Planning of Alameda County, 1964; and *The Big Rich and the Little Rich* (Garden City, N.Y.: Doubleday, 1965).

32. Donald A. Clelland and William H. Form, "Economic Dominants and Community Power: A Comparative Analysis," *American Journal of Sociology*, 69 (March, 1964), 511–521.

33. Francis M. Carney, "The Decentralized Politics of Los Angeles," *Annals of the American Academy of Political and Social Science*, 353 (May, 1964), 107–121.

34. Robert Presthus, *Men at the Top: A Study in Community Power* (New York: Oxford University Press, 1964).

35. Ralph B. Kimbrough, *Political Power and Educational Decision Making* (Chicago: Rand McNally, 1964).

36. M. Kent Jennings, *Community Influentials: The Elites of Atlanta* (New York: Free Press, 1964).

37. Robert E. Agger, Daniel Goldrich, and Bert E. Swanson, *The Rulers and the Ruled: Political Power and Impotence in American Communities* (New York: Wiley, 1964).

38. Aaron Wildavsky, *Leadership in a Small Town* (Totowa, N.J.: Bedminster Press, 1964).

39. Ritchie P. Lowry, *Who's Running This Town?* (New York: Harper & Row, 1965).

Appendix B. Code Book and Description of the Variables

VARIABLE	CODE NUMBER	DESCRIPTION
1. Type of Power Structure	1	Pyramidal—monolithic, monopolistic, or a single cohesive leadership group
	2	Factional—at least two durable factions
	3	Coalitional—fluid coalitions of interests usually varying with issues
	4	Amorphous—absence of any persistent pattern of leadership
2. Scope of Study	1	Single community
	2	Comparative—two or more communities
3. Region	1	Northeast
	2	Northcentral
	3	South
	4	West
	9	N.A.—not ascertained or inappropriate
4. Population Size	1	Less than 5,000
	2	5,000–9,999
	3	10,000–24,999
	4	25,000–49,999
	5	50,000–99,999
	6	100,000+
	9	N.A.
5. Population Growth	1	Increasing
	2	Stable
	3	Decreasing
	9	N.A.
6. Population Composition	1	Homogeneous—small proportion of racial or ethnic minorities
	2	Heterogeneous—large proportion of racial or ethnic minorities
	9	N.A.
7. Population Integration (only for heterogeneous populations)	1	Integrated—acceptance and inclusion of minorities into community life
	2	Cleavage—rejection and exclusion of minorities from community life
	9	N.A.
8. Type of City	1	Independent—relatively autonomous, central city
	2	Satellite—suburb or industrial satellite dominated by a larger nearby city
	9	N.A.
9. Industrialization	1	Industrialized—substantial amount of manufacturing and industry
	2	Nonindustrialized—residential or rural, sparse industrial development
	9	N.A.

VARIABLE	CODE NUMBER	DESCRIPTION
10. Economic Base	1	Diversified—variety of manufacturing, industrial or commercial establishments
	2	Narrow—single industry or specialized economy
	9	N.A.
11. Absentee Ownership	1	Present—large proportion of firms owned by interests outside the community
	2	Absent—principal firms locally owned
	9	N.A.
12. Economic Resources	1	Adequate—prosperous, low incidence of poverty and unemployment
	2	Inadequate—limited economic resources, high incidence of poverty and unemployment
	9	N.A.
13. Type of Local Government	1	Mayor-Council
	2	City manager
	3	Commission of town board
	9	N.A.
14. Political Party Competition	1	Competitive—an active two party system or an active political opposition
	2	Noncompetitive—one party dominance or lack of any political opposition
	9	N.A.
15. Issues Dealt With	1	Public—governmental, influence in matters of public jurisdiction, e.g., elections, schools
	2	Private—nongovernmental, influence in matters of private jurisdiction, e.g., attracting new industry
	3	Both
	9	N.A.
16. Definition of Power	1	Control—the ability to command or determine the outcome of a decision-making process
	2	Potential influence—the capacity for influence or possession of resources
	9	N.A.
17. Leadership Group N	1	Less than 10
	2	10–24
	3	25–49
	4	50–74
	5	75–99
	6	100+
	9	N.A.
18. Proportion of Businessmen in Leadership Group	1	0–24%
	2	25–49%
	3	50–74%
	4	75–100%
	9	N.A.

Appendix B. Code Book and Description of the Variables (*continued*)

VARIABLE	CODE NUMBER	DESCRIPTION
19. Proportion of Public Officials in Leadership Group	1	0–24%
	2	25–49%
	3	50–74%
	4	75–100%
	9	N.A.
20. Changes in Power Structure	1	Power has become more dispersed
	2	Power has become more concentrated
	3	No change over time
	4	Oscillation between concentrated and dispersed power
	5	Decline in the exercise of power locally
	9	N.A.
21. Discipline of Researcher(s)	1	Sociology
	2	Political science, public administration, government
	3	Other
22. Research Method	1	Reputational—informants are asked to identify the most influential people in the community when it comes to getting things done. Here leaders are nominated in a one-step procedure
	2	Reputational, two-step—informants are given lists of purported influentials and asked to evaluate them in terms of influence, usually by narrowing or ranking.
	3	Positional—leaders are taken to be those persons occupying important positions in formal and informal organizations
	4	Decisional—focuses on specific community issues and leaders are taken to be those persons active or instrumental in their resolution.
	5	Case study—less explicit methods based on observation
	6	Combined—simultaneous use of 1, 3 and 4 or 2, 3 and 4.

Appendix C. Comparative Outline Studies of Community Power Structure

Community and No. of Study	Type of Power Structure	Scope	Region	Population Size	Population Growth	Population Composition	Population Integration	Type of City	Industrialization	Economic Base	Absentee Ownership	Economic Resources	Type of Government	Party Competition	Issues	Definition	Leadership Group N	Percent Businessmen	Percent Public Officials	Change in Power Structure	Discipline	Research Method
1. Regional City	1	1	3	6	1	2	2	1	1	1	2	1	1	2	3	1	3	3	1	9	1	2
2. Lorain	2	1	2	5	9	2	2	1	1	2	1	9	9	1	3	2	9	9	9	1	1	5
3. Red Wing	2	1	2	3	9	9	9	9	1	1	9	1	9	9	9	2	3	4	9	3	1	1
4. Big Town	4	1	3	6	2	9	9	1	1	1	1	9	9	9	9	9	9	9	9	1	1	5
5. Community A	1	1	2	5	1	2	9	9	1	2	9	1	3	2	9	1	2	2	1	9	1	2
6. Bakerville	1	1	3	2	2	2	2	9	1	2	2	9	9	9	2	9	3	3	2	9	1	2
7. Salem	1	1	1	4	9	9	2	1	1	1	1	2	1	9	3	9	3	2	1	9	1	2
8. Bennington	2	1	1	3	2	9	9	1	2	1	1	1	9	1	1	1	4	2	3	1	1	6
9. Pacific City	1	2	4	6	9	9	9	1	1	1	9	1	1	9	9	1	3	2	1	9	2	2
English City	3	9	6	9	9	9	9	1	2	2	9	1	9	9	9	9	3	2	1	9	1	2
10. Cibola	2	1	2	3	1	9	9	1	1	1	1	9	2	9	1	2	3	3	1	1	1	6
11. Seattle	2	1	4	6	9	9	9	2	2	2	9	2	1	1	3	1	6	3	1	9	2	5
12. Springdale	1	1	1	1	9	2	9	1	1	1	2	1	3	2	1	9	1	4	2	5	1	5
13. New Haven	3	1	3	6	2	2	1	9	2	2	9	2	1	1	3	2	6	1	3	1	2	4
14. El Paso	3	2	3	6	1	1	2	2	2	2	1	2	9	2	2	1	4	3	2	9	1	2
C. Juarez	2	2	9	6	1	1	9	2	2	2	2	2	9	2	3	1	4	3	2	9	1	2
15. Tia Juana	4	1	4	3	1	9	9	2	2	2	1	9	9	2	9	1	3	3	1	3	1	2
16. Northville	1	1	3	6	1	1	9	9	1	9	2	9	2	9	9	9	2	4	9	9	1	2
17. Miami (Dade Co.)	4	1	2	6	9	9	2	1	2	9	9	9	1	2	9	9	2	3	3	9	2	5
18. Chicago	1	1	2	6	9	2	9	1	1	1	9	1	9	2	3	1	9	9	9	1	2	5

Appendix C—(continued)

Community and No. of Study	Type of Power Structure	Scope	Region	Population Size	Population Growth	Population Composition	Population Integration	Type of City	Industrialization	Economic Base	Absentee Ownership	Economic Resources	Type of Government	Party Competition	Issues	Definition	Leadership Group N	Percent Businessmen	Percent Public Officials	Change in Power Structure	Discipline	Research Method
19. Sanford	1	2	3	6	1	2	2	1	1	9	2	9	9	9	9	9	1	4	9	9	1	1
Amory	1	2	3	5	1	9	9	1	2	1	2	9	9	9	9	9	1	9	9	9	1	1
Algona	2	2	3	4	1	9	9	1	2	1	2	9	9	9	9	9	2	4	9	9	1	1
Gretna	2	2	3	5	1	9	9	2	1	1	2	9	9	9	9	9	9	9	9	9	1	1
Milton	4	2	2	3	2	9	9	2	2	9	1	9	9	9	9	9	9	9	9	5	1	1
Norwood	4	2	1	3	2	9	9	2	1	9	2	9	9	9	9	9	9	9	9	9	1	1
20. Service City	3	1	4	1	9	1	9	9	2	2	9	9	1	2	3	9	9	4	9	9	1	5
21. Syracuse	3	1	1	6	3	1	9	1	1	1	1	1	1	1	3	9	9	9	3	1	1	6
22. Syracuse (Oncndaga Co.)	3	1	1	6	1	1	2	1	1	1	1	1	1	1	3	2	9	9	9	1	2	4
23. Dixie City	3	1	3	5	9	2	2	1	1	1	1	9	3	9	1	1	2	4	1	9	2	6
24. Arcadia	3	1	3	6	2	2	9	1	1	9	9	9	1	9	9	9	9	9	9	9	2	5
25. Community A	2	1	2	5	9	2	9	9	1	2	9	2	2	1	1	9	2	2	2	1	2	2
26. Cerebrille	3	1	2	4	1	9	2	1	1	1	9	9	9	1	1	9	3	4	1	1	1	2
27. Burlington	1	1	3	4	1	2	9	1	1	1	9	1	1	9	3	9	2	9	9	9	1	2
28. Watertown	1	2	3	6	1	9	9	1	1	1	9	1	1	9	2	9	4	4	1	9	1	2
Centralia	1	2	3	6	2	9	9	1	1	1	9	1	1	9	2	9	4	4	1	9	1	2

	City																						
29.	Orange Point	5	2	4	9	9	9	9	3	9	2	2	2	2	2	9	2	2	1	2	3	2	1
	Floriana	5	2	1	1	4	9	9	3	9	2	2	1	2	2	2	2	2	2	3	3	2	2
	Center City	5	2	3	1	3	9	9	3	9	2	1	1	1	1	1	2	2	2	5	3	2	3
	Eastborne	5	2	1	4	9	9	9	3	9	2	2	2	2	2	9	9	1	1	4	3	2	1
	Westborne	5	2	3	9	9	9	9	2	9	2	9	2	2	2	2	2	1	1	1	3	2	1
	Dorado	5	2	1	9	9	9	9	1	9	2	1	2	2	2	1	2	2	1	1	3	2	3
	Hiberna	5	2	1	9	9	9	9	1	9	2	1	2	2	2	2	2	1	1	3	3	2	2
	Estiva	5	2	4	9	9	9	9	1	9	2	9	2	2	2	2	9	9	1	3	3	2	2
30.	Dallas	2	1	9	1	4	4	1	3	2	1	9	9	1	1	1	2	2	1	6	3	1	1
31.	Oakland	5	1	9	2	3	9	1	2	2	2	2	1	1	1	1	2	2	1	6	4	1	1
32.	Wheelsburg	6	1	5	3	3	5	9	3	2	9	9	1	1	1	1	9	1	1	6	2	1	2
33.	Los Angeles	5	2	1	9	9	9	9	9	2	1	1	9	1	1	1	1	2	1	6	4	1	3
34.	Edgewood	6	2	9	2	2	3	2	3	2	3	1	1	2	2	1	9	1	3	2	1	2	2
	Riverview	6	2	9	2	3	3	2	3	1	1	3	1	2	2	1	9	3	3	2	1	2	2
35.	Midway County	6	3	3	2	3	3	1	3	9	9	9	9	9	9	9	9	9	9	3	3	2	2
	River County	2	3	1	1	3	3	1	3	9	9	9	2	9	9	9	9	9	9	5	3	2	2
	Beach County	2	3	9	1	3	1	1	4	9	9	9	9	9	2	9	9	9	9	9	5	1	1
	Southern County	2	3	9	4	4	2	1	3	9	9	9	9	9	9	9	9	9	9	4	9	2	1
36.	Atlanta	6	2	3	1	3	6	2	1	2	1	2	9	1	1	1	2	2	2	6	3	1	3
37.	Farmdale	6	2	3	3	3	2	1	3	2	2	1	2	2	2	2	9	1	1	1	4	2	1
	Oretown	6	2	1	3	3	3	1	3	2	2	1	1	1	1	1	9	2	1	3	4	2	4
	Petropolis	6	2	1	2	3	4	1	3	2	2	1	1	1	1	1	2	2	2	6	3	2	4
	Metroville	6	2	1	2	3	3	1	3	2	2	1	2	1	1	1	2	2	1	6	3	2	1
38.	Oberlin	4	2	2	3	3	9	1	3	2	2	1	2	2	2	1	2	1	1	2	2	1	3
39.	Micro City	1	1	9	9	2	5	2	3	2	2	1	2	2	2	1	9	1	1	3	4	1	1

Notes

1. See for example, George S. Counts, *School and Society in Chicago* (New York: 1928); Robert S. Lynd and Helen M. Lynd, *Middletown in Transition* (New York: Harcourt, Brace & World, 1937); W. Lloyd Warner, *et al.*, *Democracy in Jonesville* (New York: Macmillan, 1946); August Hollingshead, *Elmtown's Youth* (New York: Wiley, 1949); Frank A. Stewart, "A Sociometric Study of Influence in Southtown," *Sociometry*, 10 (February and August, 1947), 11–31 and 273–286.

2. Charles M. Bonjean and David M. Olson, "Community Leadership: Directions of Research," *Administrative Science Quarterly*, 9 (December, 1964), 279.

3. Raymond E. Wolfinger, "Reputation and Reality in the Study of 'Community Power,'" *American Sociological Review*, 25 (October, 1960), 636–644; Nelson W. Polsby, "How to Study Community Power: The Pluralist Alternative," *Journal of Politics*, 22 (August, 1960), 474–484, and "Three Problems in the Analysis of Community Power," *American Sociological Review*, 24 (December, 1959), 796–804; Robert A. Dahl, "A Critique of the Ruling Elite Model," *American Political Science Review*, 52 (June, 1958), 463–469.

4. Thomas J. Anton, "Power, Pluralism and Local Politics," *Administrative Science Quarterly*, 7 (March, 1963), 425–457; Floyd Hunter, "Review of *Who Governs?*," *Administrative Science Quarterly*, 6 (March, 1962), 517–519.

5. Anton, *op. cit.*; Bonjean and Olson, *op. cit.*; M. Herbert Danzger, "Community Power Structure: Problems and Continuities," *American Sociological Review*, 29 (October, 1964), 707–717; Peter H. Rossi, "Community Decision-Making," *Administrative Science Quarterly*, 1 (March, 1957), 415–443; Morris Janowitz, "Community Power and 'Policy Science' Research," *Public Opinion Quarterly*, 26 (Fall, 1962), 398–410; William Spinrad, "Power in Local Communities," *Social Problems*, 12 (Winter, 1965), 335–356; Peter Bachrach and Morton S. Baratz, "Two Faces of Power," *American Political Science Review*, 56 (December, 1962), 947–952; Sethard Fisher, "Community-Power Studies: A Critique," *Social Research*, 29 (Winter, 1962), 449–466.

6. Robert Presthus, *Men at the Top: A Study in Community Power* (New York: Oxford University Press, 1964).

7. Danzger, *op. cit.*

8. Rossi, *op. cit.*; Edgar W. Butler and Hallowell Pope, "Community Power Structures, Industrialization and Public Welfare Programs," paper given at the sixty-first annual meeting of the American Sociological Association, Miami, Florida, August 1966. Community variation with respect to the distribution of power is, no doubt, a fact. The question under consideration, however, has to do with systematic differences in reported findings as these are associated with particular research methods, disciplinary orientations, etc. It seems highly unlikely that such systematic differences could be accounted for by community differences.

9. This paper represents an extension and elaboration of my article "Substance and Artifact: The Current Status of Research on Community Power Structure," *American Journal of Sociology*, 71 (January, 1966), 430–438. Here I have attempted a replication of the earlier piece using a larger collection of studies and the techniques of multivariate analysis. The result is a somewhat different set of findings, to which I have added a more extensive interpretation.

10. Several excellent studies were excluded from consideration because they dealt primarily with formal aspects of local government. See for example, Wallace Sayre and Herbert Kaufman, *Governing New York City* (New York: Russell Sage Foundation, 1960); Oliver P. Williams and Charles R. Adrian, *Four Cities—A Study in Comparative Policy Making* (Philadelphia: University of Pennsylvania Press, 1963).

11. For their assistance in providing bibliographies I am indebted to Michael Aiken, Terry N. Clark, and Claire W. Gilbert. Other sources employed included Wendell Bell, Richard J. Hill, and Charles R. Wright, *Public Leadership* (San Francisco: Chandler, 1961); and Charles Press, *Main Street Politics: Policy-Making at the Local Level* (East Lansing: Michigan State University Press, 1962).

12. These are the studies of Banfield, Carney, Walter and Hunter's studies of Oakland and Salem. See Appendix A.

13. This procedure sacrifices some precision in the interests of more extensive comparisons. Because the data are crude, certain reservations should be mentioned about their interpretation. Generally speaking, the lower the quality of the data, the more difficult it is to demonstrate statistically significant relationships and the more likely it is that such relationships may be obscured. For this reason we can have more confidence in positive findings and less in negative ones.

14. Dahl, *op. cit.*; Polsby, "Three Problems . . . ," *op. cit.*; David Rogers, "Community Political Systems: A Framework and Hypotheses

for Comparative Studies," in Bert E. Swanson (ed.), *Current Trends in Comparative Community Studies* (Kansas City, Mo.: Community Studies, Inc., 1962).

15. Anton, *op. cit.*
16. Suggestions in Danzger, *op. cit.*, and Anton, *op. cit.*
17. Presthus, *op. cit.*, and Anton, *op. cit.*
18. Spinrad, *op. cit.*
19. *Ibid.*
20. *Ibid.*
21. More frequently than being stated as a hypothesis, this is implied by critics calling for comparative studies.
22. Rogers, *op. cit.*
23. *Ibid.*
24. *Ibid.*
25. Delbert C. Miller and William H. Form, *Industry, Labor and Community* (New York: Harper & Row, 1960).
26. Suggestions in Paul A. Miller, *Community Health Action* (East Lansing: Michigan State University Press, 1953).
27. Rogers, *op. cit.*
28. Rogers, *op. cit.*; Miller and Form, *op. cit.*
29. Robert O. Schulze, "The Bifurcation of Power in a Satellite City," in Morris Janowitz (ed.), *Community Political Systems* (New York: Free Press, 1961), pp. 19–80; Roland J. Pellegrin and Charles H. Coates, "Absentee-Owned Corporations and Community Power Structure," *American Journal of Sociology*, 61 (March, 1956), 413–419; Robert E. Agger, *et al.*, *The Rulers and the Ruled: Political Power and Impotence in American Communities* (New York: Wiley, 1964); Ernest A. T. Barth, "Community Influence Systems: Structure and Change," *Social Forces*, 40 (October, 1961), 58–63.
30. Presthus, *op. cit.*
31. Schulze, *op. cit.*
32. Peter H. Rossi, "Power and Community Structure," *Midwest Journal of Political Science*, 4 (November, 1960), 390–401.
33. *Ibid.*; Agger, *et al.*, *op. cit.*
34. Maurice R. Stein, *The Eclipse of Community: An Interpretation of American Studies* (Princeton: Princeton University Press, 1960).
35. One possible interpretation of the finding on discipline is that sociologists and political scientists select different types of communities in which to do their research. That does not seem plausible, however, in view of frequent admissions by investigators that their research site was chosen on the basis of practical considerations such as proximity.
36. Here are two cases in which the present analysis disconfirms the findings of my earlier paper, see Walton, *op. cit.*
37. The finding on "industrialization" also dis-

confirms the earlier one, though "economic base" was not significantly associated with power structure in either study. It is in cases like this that the considerations raised in note 13 become pertinent. The crude nature of the data may be obscuring significant relationships in connection with these economic variables.
38. David Gold, "Independent Causation in Multivariate Analysis: The Case of Political Alienation Toward a School Bond Issue," *American Sociological Review*, 17 (February, 1962), 85–87.
39. *Ibid.*, p. 85.
40. *Ibid.*
41. John Walton, "Discipline, Method and Community Power: A Note on the Sociology of Knowledge," *American Sociological Review* (forthcoming).
42. This, of course, assumes that there are no other, uncontrolled factors influencing the relationship. The reasoning here is identical to the Lazarsfeld-Hyman procedure of multivariate analysis. The same strategy for overcoming possible biases in research reports has been separately developed by Raoul Naroll, *Data Quality Control: A New Research Technique* (New York: Free Press, 1961).
43. Researchers stressing the importance of this variable find differences in its effects. For example, one study found that a high proportion of absentee ownership resulted in a "power vacuum": see Pellegrin and Coates, *op. cit.* A second found a "bifurcation" of power: see Schulze, *op. cit.* A third reported less of a bifurcation than Schulze had found: see Donald A. Clelland and William H. Form, "Economic Dominants and Community Power: A Comparative Analysis," *American Journal of Sociology*, 69 (March, 1964), 511–521.
44. This question has been investigated in a comparative study of ninety-five cities. See Michael Aiken, "Economic Structure and Community Welfare," paper given at the sixty-first annual meeting of the American Sociological Association, Miami, Florida, August 1966.
45. An excellent comparative study which seems to support the findings of this review is Eugene C. Lee, *The Politics of Nonpartisanship: A Study of California City Elections* (Berkeley and Los Angeles: University of California Press, 1960). Another study, however, indicates that there is no relationship between a competitive electoral process and democratic decision-making in open power structures. See Edward Hoffman Rhyne, "Political Parties and Decision-Making in Three Southern Counties," *American Political Science Review*, 52 (December, 1958),

1091–1107. Similarly, inconclusive results appear in Agger, *et al.*, *op. cit.*

46. For suggestive treatments of this question on a comparative basis, see David Gold and John R. Schmidhauser, "Urbanization and Party Competition: The Case of Iowa," *Midwest Journal of Political Science*, 4 (February, 1960), 62–75; and Lee, *op. cit.*

47. A fact that seems to have been ignored by researchers and critics alike is the patently atheoretical character of the literature on community power. Explicit theoretical statements that will allow for the derivation and testing of propositions would seem to offer the most fruitful approach to resolving the continuing controversy over the distribution and exercise of power.

C. Comparative Studies of Mobilization for Community Action

Community Power and Urban Renewal Success[1]

Amos H. Hawley

Power, in most sociological studies, is conceived as the ability to exercise influence in a decision-making process. It is viewed as a personal attribute that distinguishes leaders from followers. Working with that conception investigators normally proceed by inquiring into the reputations of members of a community, establishing juries to winnow the great from the small, constructing sociograms to determine who interacts with whom, and so on. No matter what the methodological apparatus, investigators are uniformly led to the discovery that managerial and proprietary personnel, with occasional exceptions, constitute the power figures.[2] Some of the more sophisticated start with the assumption that managers and proprietors are the principal power figures and use their sociometric tools to discover how members of an elite are grouped about various kinds of issues to form power centers. Both procedures, as Wolfinger has recently pointed out, often rest on certain unspoken and unwarranted assumptions.[3] They appear to assume, for example, that

lines of influence are clearly perceptible to respondents. They also assume a static distribution of power among certain personalities. But the chief difficulty with the usual approach is that it is only applicable in a case study; it offers no facility for quantitative and comparative studies of the phenomenon. And that, it seems to me, is a disability inherent in a social-psychological approach to the study of community structure.

Before turning to an alternative way of treating the matter, a prefatory comment on the nature of that which is in question seems to be appropriate. It should be obvious that power in the social sphere, as with energy in the physical world, is ubiquitous. It is like energy, too, in that it appears in many forms. Every social act is an exercise of power, every social relationship is a power equation, and every social group or system is an organization of power. Accordingly, it is possible to transpose any system of social relationships into terms of potential or active power. Perhaps such a transposition is nothing more than the substitution of one terminology for another. At the very least, however, it focuses attention on the instruments of control and causes a social system to be viewed as a control mechanism.

The community, for example, may be conceived as an energy system. That is, as a system of relationships among functionally differentiated units the community constitutes a mobilization of power—the capacity to produce results—for dealing with the environment, whether physical or social. Each unit or subsystem—family, church, store, industry—is also an organization of power for the conduct of a function. Both the system and its subsystems tend to approximate a single organization model. Moreover, since the performance of its function by any one part affects in greater or lesser degree the conditions under which other parts carry out their functions, the parent system and each subsystem is an arena in which a more or less continuous interplay of influence occurs. Power, then, is expressed in two ways: (1) as functional power—that required to execute a function; and (2) as derivative power—that which spills over into external relationships and regulates the interaction between parts. The two modes of manifestation are necessarily connected. The type of function performed determines the kind of derivative influence transmitted to other parts or subsystems. There might also be a quantitative association, though the magnitude of the derivative influence is a consequence not only of the scale to which a function has developed but also of its position in the system. Those subsystems that are most instrumental in relating the system to the environment doubtlessly exert a greater derivative effect than do subsystems one or more steps removed from the key position. Space does not permit a full exposition of a system conception of power. Perhaps enough has been said to indicate that power is a product of a system having developed, that it is lodged only in a system, and that it is most appropriately treated, therefore, as a system property.[4] Whatever power an individual might appear to possess is in effect attached

to the office he occupies in a system. He acquires power by attaining to an office and he loses it when he is separated from the office. But the acquiring and losing of power is illusory; the property belongs rather with the office or, better still, to the system in which the office is a specialized function.[5]

In the conduct of its routine activities the system exercises its power through established and well-worn channels; the interplay of influence is institutionalized. But the structure of relationships through which power is communicated may leave various areas of interest or activity unattended, for example, private charity, religious digression and reform, the supervision of adolescents. When crises occur in such matters or when non-routine issues affecting the whole system arise, the existing structure is put to a test. It may or may not be effective in dealing with the exceptional circumstance. Whether it is effective would appear to be contingent on the way in which derivative power is distributed in the system. Where it is highly concentrated the community should be able to act as a unit in almost any emergency. On the other hand, where power is widely distributed a community may be able to act coherently only with great difficulty, if at all, when confronted with a novel problem.

This suggests a way of dealing with the variable quantitatively. A frustrating feature of studies of power has been the understandable failure to find a way to measure its amount. If, however, we can assume that an enduring system has sufficient force to regularly perform its normal functions, we can conclude that all systems of the same kind generate equivalent amounts of power. There remains a variable, namely, the way in which power is distributed. Any given amount may be in some instances concentrated in a small sector of the system or in other instances distributed more or less uniformly over all sectors or subsystems. The measurement of distribution appears to present fewer difficulties than does the measurement of the amount of power.

Now let me propose that the greater the concentration of power in a community the greater the probability of success in any collective action affecting the welfare of the whole. This follows, if it be granted that (1) success in a collective action requires the ability to mobilize the personnel and resources of the community and (2) that ability is greatest where power is most highly concentrated. The proposition does not say that a concentration of power assures success in any community venture. Various factors might intervene to defeat a collective project. Moreover, a concentration of power might be used to block a course of action. Power concentration, however, is not needed to defeat an action on the part of a community. That might occur as a result of power being so diffusely held that mobilization of the community cannot be accomplished.

Proceeding from the notion that system power resides in the subsystems or functional units of a community, we can infer that it must be exercised through the managerial functions of the subsystems. For it is those functions that co-ordinate the several other functions in their respective subsystems and articulate the latter with the larger system. In the absence of data on the number of managerial functions, I shall use the number of managerial personnel, that is, the number of people who reported occupations as manager, proprietor, or official in the Population Census, to measure concentration of power. Personnel, it should be stressed, is used only as a substitute for, and as an index of, functions.[6] Since the significance of the number of functions varies with the number of all other functions (i.e., the size of the employed labor force), it should be expressed as a ratio to the latter. Hence the lower the ratio of managers, proprietors, and officials[7] to the employed labor force the greater is the concentration of power. (This measure will hereafter be called the MPO ratio.)

As the dependent variable, that is, an example of collective action, I shall use success in urban renewal. Urban renewal, programed and administered by the Housing and Home Finance Agency, has the advantage of involving a standard procedure to which all participating communities must submit in like manner. Participation in the program by a municipality involves passage through a series of stages, differentiated by the extent to which the planning and other local arrangements required for federal financial support have been fulfilled. The stages are *planning, execution,* and *completion.* Arrival at the completion stage is unquestionably the best measure of success. Unfortunately only eighteen cities in the continental United States had by the end of 1959 advanced so far—hardly enough for statistical purposes. The next best indication of success in urban renewal is arrival at the execution stage. At that stage a city has completed its planning and has satisfied all administrative requirements for the receipt of a capital grant from the Housing and Home Finance Agency. The city is then either at the point of, or has embarked upon, the acquisition of land, the relocation of current occupants, and clearing and improving the land. At the end of 1959, ninety-five cities with population of 50,000 or more (in 1950) had advanced to the execution stage.[8]

For control purposes data on two other classes of cities of 50,000 or more population are employed. One class includes cities that entered the urban renewal program but for one reason or another abandoned their efforts sometime between 1950 and 1960. The thirty-eight cities that had that experience are called "dropouts." The second control class is made up of all cities, in states where urban renewal is legally permissible, that have not attempted urban renewal at any time. There are sixty-one such cities. All the members of this class, it is to be noted, are eligible for urban renewal assistance from the federal agency. There remains a sizable group of cities that are still in the planning stage. Eventually they will either pass into the execution stage or terminate their efforts; but at present their status is indeterminate. For that reason they are not included in the present study.

Whether urban renewal is a form of collective action that would call into operation the organization of the entire community may be debatable. The general scale of urban renewal projects is clearly relevant to the question. The average acreage involved in urban renewal projects in the 253 cities that were in the program in mid-1959 was 78.6 per city, or about one-eighth of a square mile. But one-fourth of all urban renewal acreage was contained in five cities; half the total was in nineteen cities. In the remaining cities the average acreage per city was 42.5, or a little over one-sixteenth of a square mile. That urban renewal, in the light of these magnitudes, represents a significant challenge to a community must be left as an unanswered question for the present. If it is regarded as a major undertaking in a community, it should certainly involve the local power structure. If it is considered to be a rather insignificant form of collective action, then as a dependent variable it provides a fairly severe test of the hypothesis.[9]

It seems advisable to restate the hypothesis in the operational terms set forth. The hypothesis is: MPO ratios are lowest in urban renewal cities that have reached the execution stage and highest in cities that have never attempted urban renewal. Dropout cities are expected to occupy an intermediate position between the polar classes.

The hypothesis is to be examined with reference to cities of 50,000 population or more. The abundance of data available for cities in that size range offers considerable latitude for refining the measure of power concentration and for the development of controls. In the following, however, the analysis of power concentration as an independent variable is confined primarily to ratios for the entire class of MPO's. Differentials within that class will be investigated in a later report.

As a preliminary test of the representativeness of cities of 50,000 population or more, their MPO ratios, for each urban renewal status class, are compared with those for all cities of 15,000–50,000 population, in Table 1. Observe that the two series of ratios are very similar. Thus it seems possible that findings for large cities might apply to all cities regardless of size. Further, though somewhat tangential, support of that conclusion is found in the fact that the number of years spent in the planning stage before reaching the execution stage is unrelated to size of city. No further attempt to ascertain the representativeness of large cities has been made.

It is also to be noted in Table 1 that the ratios conform to the hypothesis. Power is most highly concentrated in the execution-stage cities and most diffusely distributed in the never-in-program cities. That the concentration of power, as represented by the ratio of all MPO's to the employed labor force, is significantly greater in cities that have reached the execution stage in urban renewal than in the other classes of cities is apparent in Table 2. The probability that the association shown there is due to chance is less than 1 in a 100.

The quintile distribution of cities shown in Table 2 displays a considerable spread over the ratio range in each urban renewal status class. That raises a question of how some cities manage to get to the execution stage without a concentration of power. The complementary question of how other cities with marked concentrations of power escape urban renewal may be given a

TABLE 1. *Number and MPO Ratios, Cities by Size Class and by Urban Renewal Status*

URBAN RENEWAL STATUS	ALL CITIES OF 15,000 POPULATION AND OVER		CITIES OF 50,000 POPULATION AND OVER		CITIES OF 15,000–50,000 POPULATION	
	No.	MPO Ratio	No.	MPO Ratio	No.	MPO Ratio
Execution stage	136	9.0	95	9.0	41	9.1
Dropout	79	10.0	38	10.1	41	9.8
Never in program	402	11.0	61	10.8	341	11.1
Total	617	10.4	194	9.5	423	10.7

tentative a priori answer: that is, they are susceptible and may yet enter the program. In any event, it is doubtlessly true that factors other than the distribution of power operate on urban renewal experience or the lack of it.

For example, the probability that urban renewal might recommend itself to a community as a course of action should be somewhat contingent on the state of its physical equipment. If the equipment, in this instance its buildings, is fairly new and in good condition, urban renewal would make little sense. But where buildings are old or dilapidated a proposal to renew or rehabilitate would appear to be appropriate. Two measures of the condition of buildings are used here: (1) the percentage of all residential units constructed before 1920, and (2) the percentage of all residential units reported as dilapidated. Cities are classified relative to the median for each characteristic, providing two dichotomies. "Young" cities have less than 65 per cent of their houses built before 1920, and "old" cities 65 per cent or more of their houses built prior to that date. Cities with less than 4.7 per cent of their houses dilapidated are described as "low" on that variable while those with 4.7 per cent and over are classified as "high."

It is conceivable, too, that some cities might have anticipated the problems that invite urban renewal by having established a well-financed and strongly supported planning agency. Cities that have done so might not have to seek federal assistance for improvements. A contrary argument can also be advanced. Perhaps cities with substantial commitments to planning are more prepared to enter into a renewal project than are cities in which planning has not been developed to any appreciable extent. Notwithstanding my inability to resolve this question, the size of the planning budget might prove to be a factor of some consequence. For the purpose of control, planning expenditures are expressed as a ratio to total government operating costs in 1955. Ratios of less than .4 are below the median and thus identify their respective cities as "low" with respect to planning budgets, while ratios of .4 and over indicate cities with "high" planning budgets.

There is a strong likelihood, too, that central cities of metropolitan areas might be more favorably disposed toward urban renewal than suburban cities. That should follow from the fact that central cities are generally older than are suburbs. But it should also derive from the deconcentration trend through which central cities have been losing population and industry to outlying areas. Many large suburban cities have also begun to experience declining growth rates, though in only a few cases has the trend reached a critical stage. Where substantial losses, real or threatened, have been encountered urban renewal might appear to offer a means by which to reverse the trend. There is a second factor that calls attention to the central city-suburb distinction. That is the peculiar residential distribution of managers, proprietors, and officials. Since members of those groups tend to live in suburbs while working in central cities their numbers as reported in the Census fail to reflect accurately the number of such positions in each place. The only practicable solution to this difficulty is to control for

TABLE 2. *Quintile Distribution of Cities (MPO Ratios), by Urban Renewal Status**

URBAN RENEWAL STATUS	1ST (UNDER 7.7)	2ND (7.8–8.9)	3RD (9.0–9.9)	4TH (10.0–11.7)	5TH (11.8 AND OVER)
Execution stage	27	22	21	17	9
Dropout	3	9	8	8	7
Never in program	9	9	8	13	22

*$\chi^2 = 23.516$, $C = .330$, $P < .01$.

metropolitan status, that is, central city and suburb.

My operationalization of the concentration of power represents but one facet of a complex phenomenon. Other dimensions of that phenomenon should at least be admitted as control variables. For example, power may lie mainly in either the manufacturing or in the local service sector of a community's economy, whichever is most important. Relative importance is here measured by the ratio of manufacturing payroll to the combined payrolls in retailing, wholesaling, and service enterprises. Service cities have ratios of 1.5 or less and manufacturing cities have ratios of over 1.5.

The average size of manufacturing plant is another possible dimension of the distribution of power, especially if it may be construed as an indicator of the general scale of functional activities in the community. Size of plant is measured by the average number of employees per plant. Small-plant cities have averages of less than 70 employees; large-plant cities have over 70 employees per plant.

Still another expression of power distribution is found in the type of city government. In cities having a commission form of government, administrative responsibility is spread over a large number of nonelective officials. Such cities probably are unable to mobilize for action unless there is a fairly high concentration of power of the kind under study here. Administrative authority is more centralized where a mayor-council government exists. And in a city manager, government administrative authority reaches its highest degree of centralization and articulation. Hence, contrary to the findings of another study that type of city government is not important in determining urban renewal success,[10] I shall employ it as a control.

Two other controls having to do with the socioeconomic level of the resident population are used. Both assume that where the socioeconomic level is high the community may be prepared to act in a matter such as urban renewal independently of a concentration of power. The first, education, is represented by the proportion of the population with four or more years of college completed. The second, income, is measured by median income. Cities are dichotomized on the median for each variable. Cities with less than 6.0 per cent of their residents with four years or more of college education are "low," and those with over that proportion are "high." The median position for the median income array falls at $3,450; cities below and above that figure are "low" and "high," respectively.

Finally, region is included among the controls. To some extent regional differences combine differences in age of cities, dilapidation, income, education, and possibly other of the control variables discussed above. Thus it is reasonable to expect that the association of power distribution with urban renewal success might vary by region. Four regions are recognized for control purposes; northeast, north central, south, and west.[11]

MPO ratios for each urban renewal status class and with each of the ten controls applied successively are shown in Table 3. In no instance does the introduction of a control vitiate the association of power concentration with urban renewal success, though in a number of instances the dropout cities fail to hold an intermediate position between execution stage and never-in-program cities. Although the averages for dropout cities are affected by small numbers of cities in many cases, it is also possible that power concentration has been employed to defeat urban renewal in those cities. It is worth noting that even where the concentration of power is relatively great, as in old cities, mayor-council cities, manufacturing cities, large-plant cities, low-education cities, and cities in the northeast, the concentration varies with urban renewal success. There is no indication, in short, that the importance attached to the concentration of power is peculiar to any one type or class of city. Despite the fact that suburban cities are the preferred places of residence for a large proportion of the holders of administrative positions, urban renewal success seems

TABLE 3. *Mean MPO Ratios in Cities, by Urban Renewal Status, with Selected Variables Controlled*

| | URBAN RENEWAL STATUS | | |
CONTROL VARIABLE	Execution Stage	Dropout	Never in Program
Age of housing:			
Young	10.1	10.7	12.2
Old	8.2	9.5	9.5
Extent of dilapidation:			
Low	9.1	9.2	11.0
High	9.1	10.9	10.2
Planning budget:			
Small	8.8	9.3*	11.0
Large	9.6	11.3	11.6
Metropolitan status:			
Central city	9.0	10.8	10.1
Suburban city	8.9	8.5	11.9
Government:			
Manager	9.5	9.7	12.3
Mayor-council	8.8	9.4	9.7
Commission	8.7	12.1	10.2†
Industry:			
Service	10.0	10.9	12.6
Manufacturing	8.1	9.2	9.7
Size of manufacturing plant:			
Small	9.5	11.0	12.0
Large	8.1	8.8	9.5
Median income:			
Low	8.8	10.7	9.6
High	9.2	9.7	11.4
Education:			
Low	8.2	9.8	8.6
High	9.8	10.5	12.4
Region:			
Northeast	8.5	8.1	9.8
North central	8.5	10.6	10.4†
South	9.4	11.0	12.2†
West	11.9†	12.8*	12.6

*N is 5 or less.
†N is less than 10.

to require as great a concentration of power in suburbs as it does in central cities. Also of interest is the evidence that manager cities appear to be able to achieve urban renewal with less power concentration than do cities of other government classes.

To better assess the closeness of the association of power concentration with urban renewal success I have employed rank correlation analysis, using Kendall's tau–c. For this purpose the three urban renewal status classes are assumed to constitute a scale. Evidence that such an assumption is reasonable is present in Tables 1 and 3. The independent variable is treated in a quintile distribution of cities by MPO ratios, as in Table 2. The results are shown in Table 4, for which data a one-tailed test of significance was used.

It is clear from the findings in Table 4

TABLE 4. *Measures of Association of MPO Ratios with Urban Renewal Status, with Selected Variables Controlled*

CONTROL VARIABLE	TAU	x/σ	P
All cities	.267	4.112	.00003
Age of housing:			
Young	.239	2.568	.00510
Old	.236	2.689	.00360
Extent of dilapidation:			
Low	.258	2.801	.00260
High	.267	2.951	.00160
Planning budget			
Small	.243	2.159	.01540
Large	.305	2.430	.00750
Metropolitan status:			
Central city	.214	2.874	.00200
Suburban city	.402	3.337	.00048
Government:			
Manager	.429	3.711	.00011
Mayor-council	.134	1.387	.08230
Commission	.302	3.337	.00048
Industry:			
Service	.169	.998	.15870
Manufacturing	.220	3.175	.00068
Size of manufacturing plant:			
Small	.301	3.292	.00048
Large	.186	2.065	.01960
Median income:			
Low	.219	2.533	.00570
High	.266	2.833	.00230
Education:			
Low	.122	1.382	.08380
High	.363	3.995	.00003
Region:			
Northeast	.108	1.096	.13350
North central	.233	2.062	.01970
South	.388	2.805	.00260
West	.105	.649	.25780

that the concentration of power is positively and significantly associated with urban renewal success under virtually all conditions of control. Several exceptions occur, however. The relationship is not dependable for cities with mayor-council governments, with a predominance of service industry, with small proportions of college graduates among their residents, and with locations in the northeast and the west. Some of these exceptions appear to be contrary to the positive findings involving variables known to be closely associated with them (education and income, northeastern location, and manufacturing industry). Had it been possible to refine the controls, some of the inconsistencies doubtlessly would have disappeared.

The category of all managers, proprietors, and officials is quite heterogeneous; it embraces the full range of both size and type of unit in which such positions occur. Thus it is not unlikely that one or another subclass or industry group of managers, proprietors, and officials might be primarily responsible for the observed association. But the measures reported in Table 5 indicate that that is not the case. The correlation is statistically significant for every industrial class of managers, proprietors, and official but one. The one, public administration, not only falls short of significance, it is negative. Why the prospects for

urban renewal success should tend to increase with increases in the relative numbers of managers and officials in public administration poses an interesting problem. But that is not a question that can be pursued here. Nor is it possible to press the analysis of industry class of managers, proprietors, and officials further at present, though the fact that the relationship for each industry class taken separately responds differently to the application of controls clearly points to a need for a more intensive investigation.

While the findings reported in this paper should be regarded as exploratory, they clearly support the hypothesis that the lower the MPO ratio the greater the chance of success in an action program such as urban renewal. They also demonstrate the facility and the economy in research of a conception of power as a system property. Much remains to be done, however, to develop knowledge about that property. A factor of some importance is the composition of managerial positions in a city. The relative numbers in the key industry should prove decisive, if my initial argument is correct. What constitutes a key industry, of course, is contingent upon the function the city performs for the regional and national society. The pursuit of that question will doubtlessly suggest further lines of investigation.

TABLE 5. *Measures of Association of MPO Ratios with Urban Renewal Status, by Class of Industry, with Selected Variables Controlled*

Industry Class	TAU	x/σ	P
All industries	.267	4.112	.00003
Manufacturing:			
Salaried MPO's	.170	2.622	.00440
Self-employed MPO's	.209	3.229	.00137
Retail and wholesale trade	.214	3.300	.00097
Banking and finance	.209	3.229	.00137
Public administration	−.105	−1.162	.10740

Notes

1. I am indebted to Professors Albert J. Reiss, Jr., and Robert Somers for helpful advice in the preparation of this paper.
2. Representative studies include Floyd Hunter, *Community Power Structure* (Chapel Hill: University of North Carolina Press, 1953); Robert O. Schultz and Leonard U. Blumberg, "The [Determination] of Local Power Elites," *American Journal of Sociology*, 63 (1957), 290–96; Delbert C. Miller, "Decision-making Cliques in Community Power Structure," *American Journal of Sociology*, 64 (1958), 299–309; Paul Miller, "The Process of Decision-making within the Context of Community Organization," *Rural Sociology*, 17 (1952), 153–61.
3. Raymond E. Wolfinger, "The Study of Community Power," *American Sociological Review*, 25 (1960), 636–44.
4. This position has been stated recently by Richard M. Emerson, though he objects to the assumption of generalized power that is adopted, at least for present purposes, in this study ("Power-Dependence Relations," *American Sociological Review*, 27 (1962), 31–32.
5. The conception of power developed here is interchangeable with the ecological concept of dominance. Ecologists, however, have been content to treat dominance as an attribute of location or type of place, though the concept has always carried overtones of organizational properties. They have neglected to exploit the concept as an entree into the general problem of organization.

6. A similar notion appears in the introductory remarks of C. Wright Mills in his book on *The Power Elite* (New York: Oxford University Press, 1956). Nevertheless it soon becomes apparent that Mills is mainly concerned with the personal characteristics of the occupants of such positions.
7. For present purposes only managers, proprietors, and officials "not elsewhere classified" are used, [thus] eliminating technical positions that have no management or policy-determining functions. The category, it should be noted, is not limited to management positions in pecuniary establishments. It includes managers of art galleries, libraries, community funds, welfare agencies, and others.
8. Data on cities that have had urban renewal experience have been obtained from the *Annual Report of the Housing and Home Finance Agency*, 1951 through 1960 (Washington, D.C.).
9. *Urban Renewal Project Characteristics* (Washington, D.C.: Housing and Home Finance Agency, Urban Renewal Administration, June 30, 1959).
10. George S. Duggar, "The Relation of Local Government Structure to Urban Renewal," *Law and Contemporary Problems*, 26 (1961), 42–69.
11. Two other controls were used with similar results: population size and income as represented by the proportion of families with incomes of $10,000 or more per year

Structural Attachments and Political Support in Urban Politics: The Case of Fluoridation Referendums[1]

Maurice Pinard

In recent years, many communities throughout the United States have had to face the problem of whether or not they would add fluorine to their water supplies. In accordance with varying legal systems, this decision has been made either by the executive bodies of these communities, town meetings, or referendums.

In a slight majority of the cases examined here, where the decisions were made either by referendums or by town meetings, the proposal to install fluoridation equipment in the community was defeated (140 cases out of 262, i.e., 53.4 per cent). The identification of "structural" or "contextual" effects on community decisions is the focus of the analysis to be presented. It should be noted that the level of analysis adopted in this paper is not the individual behavior, but community behavior.[2]

It is first hypothesized that the various outcomes can be explained by the strength of the citizens' attachments to one another and to their community leaders. Communities can be seen as vast sociometric networks of individuals and subgroups more or less linked together and to their leaders. These networks may be such as to produce a closely knit, highly integrated community. On the other hand, the whole system may be only loosely interconnected, comprised of many independent subgroups, each one, though possibly integrated, being only loosely attached, if at all, to the others or to the community leadership. It is hypothesized that the community is more likely to support its leaders' policies in the former situation than in the latter.

Second, it is hypothesized that closely knit communities will also tend to take stronger stands either for or against the issue, since their high degree of integration makes them move, so to speak, as a unit, in one direction or the other. Whenever they make a favorable decision, which according to the first hypothesis, they are more likely to make, one should find that this approval is made with a greater unanimity than in less-integrated communities. By the same token, if the close-knit community should take a negative stand on the project (for whatever reasons, whether it be because the leaders disapprove of the project, because the whole community has become alienated from the leaders, or because some influential dissenting group alone leads public opinion), one should expect a greater consensus of opinion against the issue than in a community less well integrated.

In short, the first hypothesis states that stronger attachments to, and identification with, the community create conditions favorable to a positive outcome, while the second hypothesis asserts that the degree of integration is determinant of unanimity.[3]

The basic ideas of this research are derived from Coleman's model of community conflicts,[4] which postulates that the basic structure of a community, its group attachments, informal associations, and community organizations, is the major determinant of the course of controversies. Thus, he states that after some people and groups have been involved in a conflict through disagreement on a particular issue, other "people respond to the conflict according to their previous associations, attachments, and antagonism to other people and groups in the community; that is, one's existing relations with and feelings toward other persons already in the dispute become a means of being drawn into it."[5]

Consequently, "if one could lay out the networks of social relations, likes, dislikes and organizational attachments prior to a dispute, and then locate the initial nuclei of opposition, he would know better what preexisting attachments pull people to one side or another."[6]

Method of Community Decision

In order to test the above hypotheses,[7] let us first consider whether the community reached its decision at a town meeting or by a referendum.[8] The town-meeting method of decision should be more conducive to a positive outcome than the referendum procedure. In a town meeting the people gathered are more likely to be citizens who are interested in the community problems, who share the same values as the leaders, and who are more socially linked with them. Fewer unattached citizens would be likely to participate than in a referendum.[9] Consequently, fewer rejections of the project in such situations should be expected.[10]

The data reveal that 63 per cent of the communities that decided the issue at a town meeting approved the measure, while only 43 per cent of the communities deciding by referendum did the same.[11] This clearly supports the above expectation.

Turnout at the Polls

As Coleman points out, the strength of the turnout in popular elections is generally related to involvement and interest in political matters: A lower turnout tends to represent the votes of "those most *attached* to community affairs."[12] On the other hand, if the turnout is large, it means that less attached

people are more likely to participate in the referendum. Therefore, one would predict according to the first hypothesis that the lower the turnout, the more likely the measure is to be accepted. Furthermore, the second hypothesis leads one to predict that the lower the turnout, the more likely the referendum is to be approved or defeated by a strong majority (Table 1).

TABLE 1. *Voter Turnout for Referendum and Approval or Defeat of Measure*

	TURNOUT	
	Less than 25 Per Cent	25 Per Cent or More
Percentage of communities passing the measure*	46	36
No.	68	66
Of those passing the measure, percentage passing it with 60 per cent or more in favor†	68	42
No.	21	24
Of those defeating the measure, percentage defeating it with 60 per cent or more against†	84	67
No.	37	42

*a_1 (effect of turnout on outcome) $= .10$; $P(a_1{}^* \leq 0) = .12$.
†a_2 (effect of turnout on extreme outcomes, with approval or disapproval considered as a control) $= .21$; $P(a_2{}^* \leq 0) = .004$.

The reader can see that both expectations are corroborated by the data presented in Table 1.[13] Subsequent tables will show that the effect of turnout is maintained with the control of other factors.

Size of Population

It is well known that small communities are conducive to the formation of a closely knit social system. People in small towns are more likely to know each other and to have a greater amount of interaction among themselves through more diversified roles. They are more linked to each other in the pursuit of their interests, either economic, political, or social. These structural characteristics should lead to a more easy identification with the political elite of the community and create pressures to favour any action, even if only mildly backed, by this elite. Therefore, one would expect the smaller communities to be more receptive to a fluoridation project.[14]

The data do reveal such a relationship: 51 per cent of the communities with a population of less than 10,000 passed the measure, while only 40 per cent of the larger ones did so.[15] The relationship is not very strong, but will be shown to be partly strengthened by holding turnover constant.[16] This result is all the more striking since one could have predicted an opposite finding on two grounds: (1) small communities are usually depicted as much more conservative than larger ones, and (2) in general as well as in these data, small communities tend to have a larger turnout than large ones, a factor conducive to defeats.

The above result could be explained, not by a stronger-attachment thesis, but, as it may be suggested, by a process of self-selection: administrators in smaller communities know their citizenry better and therefore are in a position to present fluoridation projects only when they think that there is a high probability of approval.[17]

There is, however, another aspect of the result presented thus far that tends to confirm the prediction of this paper and that cannot be explained by a "self-selection" argument. If it is true that a positive outcome in small communities is a function of attachment to the administration, then one should

observe not only a positive response but also a stronger positive response to fluoridation projects in these communities. Similarly, within these communities, if any group commanding community identification, be it elite or not, wages strong opposition to the project, this opposition faction is less likely to face a strong pro-fluoridation group because a closely knit community is more likely to move as a unit. Therefore, in this event, a stronger negative response would be expected.[18] Note that this would be contrary to the self-selection hypothesis, according to which the results would be skewed only in the positive direction.

Table 2 is partly consistent with the above

TABLE 2 *Size of Community and Stand on Fluoridation*

	POPULATION		
	Less than 10,000	10,000– 25,000	More than 25,000
Of those passing the measure, percentage passing it with 60 per cent or more in favor	56	73	42
No.	32	11	12
Of those defeating the measure, percentage defeating it with 60 per cent or more against*	82	74	61
No.	38	23	18

*a_1 (effect of size on disapproval, comparing extremes) = .21; $P(a_1{}^* \leq 0) = .06$.

TABLE 3. *Relationship of Community Size and Stand of Fluoridation Holding Turnout Constant*

	LOW TURNOUT*		HIGH TURNOUT	
	Small Community†	Large Community	Small Community†	Large Community
Percentage of communities passing the measure‡	55	37	41	31
No.	33	35	37	29

* Less than 25%.
† Population less than 10,000.
‡ a_1 (effect of size) = .14; $P(a_1{}^* \leq 0) = .05$; a_2 (effect of turnout) = .10; $P(a_2{}^* \leq 0) = .12$.

argument. At least in the cases where the measure was defeated, the smaller the community, the stronger was the disapproval, clearly contradicting the self-selection hypothesis.[19]

Finally, since the turnout is generally lower in larger towns, thus favoring a positive outcome, the relationship observed above between size and outcome should be strengthened when the effects of turnout are controlled (Table 3).

This is partly true, although the relationship is not strengthened in the case of a high turnout, the percentage difference between small and large communities is increased when the turnout is low. Note also that both factors have an independent effect, with the size of the community having a somewhat larger influence.

The Unemployment Situation

The level of employment should also affect the degree and strength of attachments in a community. A high degree of unemployment is likely to produce at least two kinds of relaxation in the attachment network of the communities. First, it has been repeatedly found that the unemployed tend to isolate themselves socially as a result of their condition, even though they have more time for social participation.[20] It is easy to assume that this detachment from primary and secondary relations is also accompanied by attitudes of detachment and even alienation from the larger community.

Even more important is the finding that a high rate of unemployment in a community produces a widespread atmosphere of political apathy and detachment.[21] One can easily imagine how such feelings could be vented in an election. Latent economic and political attachments are relaxed; people feel more free to oppose their leaders in any opportunity presented them. (In a way, a referendum on any particular project always becomes a plebiscite for the incumbents.)

This expectation is supported by the data. While 48 per cent of the communities with a low rate of unemployment (4 per cent or less) adopted the flouridation project, 36 per cent of those with a higher rate of unemployment did the same.[22] Again this relationship will be shown to be strengthened with population growth constant in the case of in- and out-migration (see Table 5 below).[23]

Growth of Communities

Another impotant indicator of the degree of attachments in these communities, which can be obtained from census data, is their rate of growth between 1940 and 1950. Every increase in the population of a community by in-migration brings in new residents who can be assumed to have both weaker attachments within, and identification with, their new community. Such a community would then be, according to the present thesis, more prone to oppose a fluoridation project.[24] On the other hand, residents of communities that have undergone population decrease due to out-migration in the same period may feel disappointed with their leaders and be disaffected from them. They have probably lost the proximity of relatives, friends and acquaintances, and their community is no longer on the "road of progress."[25] One would thus expect such communities to reject fluoridation measures too.

Different from these two groups of communities are the ones subject to a natural increase, whose residents have been there for many years and are therefore closely identified with their community. In this instance one would expect a more favorable reaction to fluoridation projects.[26]

The findings are consistent with these predictions (Table 4). The communities that lost members by out-migration and those that gained new unattached persons by in-migration were both less favorable to fluoridation than the communities that experienced a natural increase.

However, there is some evidence in the research previously mentioned which runs counter to this finding. For instance, Green and Briggs found a relationship partly running in the opposite direction between the adoption of fluoridation and population growth.[27] Gamson and Irons also report a

TABLE 4. *Type of Community Growth and Stand on Fluoridation*

	OUT-MI-GRATION*	NATURAL INCREASE	IN-MI-GRATION
Percentage of communities passing the measure†	44	53	41
No.	50	92	109

*Out-migration, less than 5 per cent increase (including decrease); natural increase, increase between 5 per cent and 20 per cent; in-migration, larger increase.
†a_1 (effect of out-migration compared to natural increase) $= .09$, $P(a_1{}^* \leq 0) = .15$; a_2 (effect of in-migration compared to natural increase) $= .12$, $P(a_2{}^* \leq 0) = .06$.

similar finding in one other set of data and "no significant association" in a third set.[28] Though these samples are generally small,[29] it might lead one to think that the results remain inconclusive so far. In the present data the observed relationship is maintained or even strengthened[30] when the proportion of young people,[31] turnout, or unemployment are held constant (Table 5). In general, Table 5 reveals that when both the independent and the control variables have

a positive effect, the outcome tends to be favorable six times out of ten; when both factors exert a negative influence, the outcome is favorable only approximately three times out of ten.[32]

It is also interesting to note that the picture obtained for the cases of in-migration cannot apparently be attributed only to the negative votes of newcomers. Observe, for instance, that when the turnout is low (i.e., when newcomers are less likely to vote), the outcome is nevertheless negatively affected by in-migration. The presence of new migrants seems to produce a relaxation in the previous structure of attachments of older ones. If communities are viewed as huge sociometric networks in which newcomers are not all isolates, their presence can easily be conceived as disruptive of these networks, thus diminishing the previous social cohesion of the whole system.[33]

Ethnic and Racial Structure of the Communities

Ethnic and racial diversity in a community is a rather important and well-documented source of weak interconnectedness. An ethnic

TABLE 5. *Relationship of Type of Growth and Outcome, Holding Proportion of Young People, Turnout, or Unemployment Constant*

	OUT-MIGRATION		NATURAL INCREASE		IN-MIGRATION	
	No. of Communities	Per Cent Passing Measure	No. of Communities	Per Cent Passing Measure	No. of Communities	Per Cent Passing Measure
Proportion of young people:*						
Low†	19	26	29	38	36	31
High	17	47	37	60	53	42
Turnout:‡						
Low§	10	30	26	58	30	40
High	9	56	26	39	30	27
Unemployment:‖						
Low #	12	42	30	53	32	47
High	15	27	26	58	41	24

*a_1 (effect of out-migration compared to natural increase) $= .125$, $P(a_1{}^* \leq 0) = .10$; a_2 (effect of in-migration compared to natural increase) $= .125$, $P(a_2{}^* \leq 0) = .06$; a_3 (effect of youth) $= .18$, $P(a_3{}^* \leq 0) = .0001$.
†Of the total population 24 per cent or less is fourteen years old or younger.
‡a_1 (effect of out-migration compared to natural increase) $= .055$, $P(a_1{}^* \leq 0) = .34$; a_2 (effect of in-migration compared to natural increase) $= .15$, $P(a_2{}^* \leq 0) = .05$; a_3 (effect of turnout) $= .06 - P(a_3{}^* \leq 0) = .26$.
§Less than 25 percent turnout.
‖a_1 (effect of out-migration compared to natural increase) $= .21$, $P(a_1{}^* \leq 0) = .03$; a_2 (effect of in-migration compared to natural increase) $= .20$, $P(a_2{}^* \leq 0) = .01$; a_3 (effect of unemployment) $= .11$, $P(a_3{}^* \leq 0) = .10$.
#Unemployed consist of 4 per cent or less.

minority, even one of the upper class, is, for example, often likely to be unrepresented in community administration and to be resentful of their exclusion.[34] Accordingly, such minorities should be more likely to vote against a fluoridation project.

Two indicators of the ethnic and racial composition of the communities were obtained from census data. Surprisingly, the findings with both indicators seem at first sight contrary to the hypothesis (Table 6). Communities with a higher degree of ethnic heterogeneity are more likely to approve the fluoridation projects, and the South, despite its high proportion of Negroes, is the most favorable region. How is this to be accounted for?

TABLE 6. *Ethnic and Racial Composition and Stand on Fluoridation*

	COMMUNITIES PASSING MEASURE	
	No.	Per Cent
Proportion of population that is native white:		
80 per cent or more	163	39
79 per cent or less	31	55
Census regions:		
Northeast	72	57
South	37	60
North Central	92	44
West	61	31

Let us first consider the regional phenomenon. One reasonable interpretation is that in the South heterogeneity is of a different character than that of other regions; it is almost exclusively due to the presence of Negroes who are largely outside the social system, and even more outside the political system. The hypothesis that uses ethnic heterogeneity as a factor in accounting for the lack of support of an administration can only make sense in so far as the ethnic minorities *do* participate in elections. Since in the South a large reservoir of potential opposition is not likely to manifest its dissent, the likelihood of rejection of fluoridation projects is reduced accordingly.

TABLE 7. *Region, Turnout, and Stand on Fluoridation*

CENSUS REGION	LOW TURNOUT*		HIGH TURNOUT	
	No.	Per Cent Passing Measure	No.	Per Cent Passing Measure
Northeast	10	60	12	42
South	18	50	7	43
North Central	9	33	43	40
West	8	38	27	33

*Turnout of 19 per cent or less.

If this interpretation is correct, it should be apparent in the relationship between outcome and regions, with turnout held constant.[35] Table 7 shows that, at least when the turnout is relatively higher, communities in the South are not more favorable to fluoridation.

Moreover, a re-examination of the data in Table 6 pertaining to the association between outcome and ethnic composition reveals its spuriousness. As Table 8 shows,

TABLE 8. *Ethnic Composition and Stand on Fluoridation, Holding Regions Constant*

PROPORTION OF NATIVE WHITE	COMMUNITIES PASSING MEASURE*	
	No.	Per Cent
Northeast:		
High†	9	44
Low	11	36
South:		
High‡	10	70
Low	25	52
North Central:		
High†	64	39
Low	17	53
West:		
High‡	37	32
Low	21	29

*a_1 (effect of ethnic composition, Northeast and South only [see n. 36]) = .13, $P(a_1{}^* \leq 0)$ = .18.
†Native whites make up 90 per cent or more of population.
‡Native whites make up 80 per cent or more of population. Because of large differences in ethnic composition in the South, it was impossible to break this variable in a consistent way. Thus care should be taken in comparing the regions in this table, with ethnic composition constant.

when region is held constant, the hypothesized relationship reappears clearly in two regions and the inverse relationship disappears in a third one.[39] In the Northeast and the South, the larger the proportion of native white (i.e., the more homogeneous the community), the more likely the referendums are to be approved.[37]

Status Structure of the Communities

Finally, it was hypothesized that middle-class communities would be more favorable to a fluoridation project than lower-class ones,[38] since the former are likely to have a larger proportion of their residents closer to the assumed high status leaders than the latter; it was also hypothesized that communities with a relatively smaller variance in their occupational distribution might be more favorable to such a project, since such a small variance implies a greater integration of the community.

Again, the results of previous studies are not consistent with the foregoing proposition. Though they generally tend to indicate that middle-class *citizens* (where class is measured by occupation, income, or education) are more likely to be favorable to fluoridation than lower-class ones,[39] the relationship is often not linear.[40] A similar series of inconsistent results was found with respect to *communities*, where education and income were considered.[41]

What about the present results? The data in Table 9 show that, contrary to expectations, middle-class communities are *less* likely to favor fluoridation. Moreover, a series of controls revealed that this relationship is not a spurious one.[42] On the other hand, the zero-order relationship between variance in occupational distribution[43] and outcome is not clear. With a series of controls, however, this relationship ran, at least in part, contrary to expectations.[44]

How then can these findings be accounted for? The first one suggests that two closely related aspects of the social structure may be involved.

On the one hand, the above result may in part be due to a greater likelihood of

TABLE 9. *Occupational Distribution and Stand on Fluoridation*

	COMMUNITIES PASSING MEASURE*	
	No.	Per Cent
Proportion of gainfully employed males in professional and managerial occupational groups:†		
Low	52	48
Medium	47	40
High	59	37
Variance in occupational distribution:‡		
Low	58	41
Medium	64	45
High	36	36

*a_1 (effect of occupational structure, comparing extremes) $= .11$, $P(a_1^* \leq 0) = .12$.
†Low, 21 per cent or less; medium, 22–25 per cent; high, 26 per cent or more.
‡Low, 0.99 or less; medium, 1.00–1.14; high, 1.15 or more.

factions or divisions *within the social and power elites* of a community whenever these elites are relatively large.[45] In the same way that small communities cannot afford to become divided on such a project, to oppose their administration, and to thereby introduce strains into a closely knit social system, a relatively small upper-middle class within a community cannot afford to be divided politically because it is too closely tied socially. It is only when there is a relatively large upper-middle class that the possibility of having factions or an institutionalized opposition would arise.[46] Hence middle-class communities would be more likely to oppose fluoridation than lower-class ones.

On the other hand, this result could also be due to a different system of attachments *between the elites and the rest of the community*, depending on whether these elites are large or small. In the former case, they could easily be closed on themselves socially and self-sufficient for the fulfillment of the power roles in the community. This would tend to create a large gap between them and the other classes, and a referendum could then be more easily defeated.

Conversely, when the elites are small, their social contacts with the classes below them would tend to be more numerous and the latter would more easily occupy various power roles in the community,[47] thus creating a greater likelihood of adoption of a fluoridation project. (An analogous reasoning could be made when we consider the variance in the occupational distribution, rather than the size of the elites.)

Since these interpretations may appear as too easy a reconciliation with the data (one can always contrive a good interpretation ex post facto!), they will be submitted to a series of tests by inference.

First, if these interpretations are correct, that is, if the results of Table 9 reveal that it is difficult for a relatively small upper-middle class to stand internal divisions and to be isolated from other classes, communities with such a class distribution should take more extreme stands on the issue, whether for or against it. The data in Table 10 support this inference. Lower-class communities do exhibit a pattern of more extreme approval or disapproval.[48]

A second test by inference pertains to the simultaneous consideration of a third variable—the size of the communities. If the interpretations are correct, the first relationship observed in Table 9 should be par-

ticularly strong in small communities. Indeed, a relatively small upper-middle class in a large community may still consist of a large absolute number of people and consequently permit the existence of more than one political elite and a self-sufficient social and political life, whereas such a small elite in a small town is bound to be small both relatively and absolutely, precluding the maintenance of factions and the formation of a self-sufficient subgroup.

TABLE 11. *Size of Social Elite, Size of Community and Stand on Fluoridation*

	COMMUNITIES PASSING MEASURE*	
	No.	Per Cent
Communities of less than 10,000:		
23 per cent or less in upper-middle group	29	55
24 per cent or more in upper-middle group	40	38
Communities of 10,000 or more:		
23 per cent or less in upper-middle group	49	43
24 per cent or more in upper-middle group	40	35

*a_1 (difference of differences) $= (.55 - .38) - (.43 - .35) = .09$, $P(a_1* \leqslant 0) = .27$. The test applied here to see if the difference is significantly greater in small than in large communities follows Leo A. Goodman, "Modifications of the Dorn-Stouffer-Tibbitts Method for 'Testing the Significance of Comparisons in Sociological Data,'" *American Journal of Sociology*, 66 (1961), 355–63.

Again the data presented in Table 11 tend to support this inference. The difference between the two subgroups of small communities is 17 per cent, while for the two corresponding subgroups of large communities, the difference is only 8 per cent. As expected, within small communities, it seems to make more difference whether the elite is small or large than within large communities.

Thus far, the tests presented did not permit us to discriminate between the two suggested interpretations. A third test may be useful in this regard. The combination of the variance in occupational distribution

TABLE 10. *Size of Social Elite and Extreme Stand on Fluoridation*

	PROPORTION IN UPPER-MIDDLE CLASS*	
	Low	High
Of those passing the measure, percentage passing with 60 per cent or more in favor of it†	74	46
No.	19	22
Of those defeating the measure, percentage defeating with 60 per cent or more against it†	76	70
No.	29	33

*Low, 23 per cent or less; high, 24 per cent or more.
†a_1 (effect of occupational structure on extreme outcomes) $= .17$, $P(a_1* \leqslant 0) = .03$.

with the proportion of upper-middle-class residents gives a typology of community power structures in terms of small or large and of isolated or non-isolated elites.[49]

According to the first interpretation, communities with a small and isolated elite (Type I) should, because of their difficulty in sustaining internal divisions, be most favorable to fluoridation; those communities with a large and non-isolated elite (Type IV) should be the least favorable.

On the other hand, the second interpretation leads us to expect that a small and non-isolated elite (Type III), one that creates greater community integration, is the most favorable, and that a large and isolated elite (Type II) is the least favorable situation for adoption of the fluoridation measure.

Although the first interpretation is more clearly supported, by the data in Table 12, both can, however, be seen to be partly substantiated. Pending further tests, both would have to be retained.

Note that the original hypothesis predicted a relationship in the opposite direction (communities of Type I were expected to be the least likely to approve fluoridation, since they are primarily working-class communities, and communities of Type IV were expected to be the most likely to approve, since they are relatively higher-class communities).

TABLE 12. *Community Power Structure and Stand on Fluoridation*

	COMMUNITIES PASSING MEASURE*	
	No.	Per Cent
Isolated elite:†		
Small (Type I)‡	16	56
Large (Type II)	64	36
Non-isolated elite:		
Small (Type III)	62	45
Large (Type IV)	16	38

*a_1 (effect of power structures, comparing I and IV) = .18, $P(a_1^* \leqslant 0) = .15$; a_2 (effect of power structures, comparing III and II) = .09, $P(a_2^* \leqslant 0) = .15$.
†Isolated: variance of 1.05 or more; non-isolated: variance of less than 1.05.
‡Small, proportion in upper-middle occupational group of 23 per cent or less; large, 24 per cent or more.

Therefore, this section presents an unanticipated finding, revealing an interesting structural effect. While previous findings tend to show that middle-class *individuals* are more favorable to fluoridation than lower-class ones, middle-class *communities* seem to be less favorable than lower-class ones, the paradox being apparently explained by different structural arrangements within the elites and between the social classes. Further research would of course be needed to establish more firmly these findings, since the results of the last three tables are not all as conclusive as one might like them to be.[50]

Conclusion

The general hypothesis of this paper has been for the most part substantiated. Different degrees and patterns of attachments of a community to its leaders do in fact influence the political support the former is ready to grant to the latter. In turn, these degrees and patterns of attachments are largely influenced by structural factors very different from the sociopsychological ones often used in voting behavior studies. The size of communities, their rates of growth, their ethnic and racial composition, their occupational and power structures, and the conditions of their labor market are all important features of the social system that influence community decisions.[51]

These results confirm the importance of political processes that have often been discussed, but rarely empirically analyzed. To the extent that elites in a political system, either democratic or totalitarian, tend to be separated from the lower segments of the system by a series of horizontal and disjointed layers, the system is bound to produce a more-or-less large collectivity of politically unattached citizens that oscillate between apathy or systematic opposition to the leadership; this is true whatever actions the elites take, or whatever party may be in power. The middle class, on the other hand, seems less likely to exhibit such a pattern of behavior. As is suggested by these data, they are either attached as a whole to their leaders or are formed into two or more groups of equally attached citizens, each to its own political elite, opposing, and eventually replacing, each other in the leadership of a community.

The above comments suggest that the thesis and the findings of this paper are closely related to the theories of mass versus pluralist societies.[52] In both cases, the degree of interconnectedness between the members of a collectivity and the power centers is conceived as a major factor for the democratic process. But while the latter theories put a particular stress on the role of free intermediate groups as links between the many groups of a society.[53] the present research stressed, partly because of the data available, other aspects of the social structure producing a more-or-less integrated community. The results presented indicate that these different orientations could fruitfully be incorporated into a larger theoretical framework.

Notes

1. The author is particularly indebted to James S. Coleman of the Johns Hopkins University from whom he secured the referendum data and whose ideas and comments were most stimulating during the course of this research. Raymond Breton, Arthur L. Stinchcombe, and S. Stephen Kegeles are also thanked for their helpful comments on an earlier draft of this paper.
2. Such an orientation avoids the pitfalls of ecological analysis (see W. S. Robinson, "Ecological Correlations and the Behavior of Individuals," *American Sociological Review*, 15 [1950], 351–57; and H. Menzel's "Comment," in the same issue, p. 674).
3. Stated otherwise, the present hypothetical scheme implies an "asymmetrical" view of the political process instead of the two usual sides—one against the other—of the traditional "symmetrical" view. As will be seen later on, unexpected findings necessitate a reconsideration of the latter view.
4. James S. Coleman, *Community Conflict* (Glencoe, Ill.: Free Press, 1957).
5. *Ibid.*, p. 18.
6. *Ibid.* There are, of course, differences between a community controversy and a community referendum. While the latter is an institutionalized means of decision-making, the former is not. Furthermore, and related to this first difference, a controversy implies, by its very definition, group cleavages and antagonisms, while the outcome of a referendum can be the very manifestation of community integration or its simple absence. But it is contended that in both cases, the "social geography" of the communities can have very analogous effects.
7. There is a growing body of research on referendums that often supports the above hypotheses. Some of these findings will be discussed below. Space limitations, however, present an extensive examination of this research here. See, among others, W. A. Gamson, "The Fluoridation Dialogue: Is It an Ideological Conflict?" *Public Opinion Quarterly*, 25, 4 (1961), 526–37; W. E. Thompson and J. E. Horton, "Political Alienation as a Force in Political Action," *Social Forces* 38 (1958–60), 190–95; E. L. McDill and J. C. Ridley, "Status, Anomia, Political Alienation, and Political Participation," *American Journal of Sociology*, 68 (1962), 205–13; W. A. Gamson and Peter H. Irons, "Community Characteristics and Fluoridation Outcome," *Journal of Social Issues*, 17 (1961), 66–74; A. L. Green, "The Ideology of Anti-Fluoridation Leaders," *Journal of Social Issues*, 17 (1961), 18; Arnold Simmel, "A Signpost for Research on Fluoridation Conflicts: The Concept of Relative Deprivation," *Journal of Social Issues*, 17 (1961), 26–36; T. F. A. Plaut, "Analysis of Voting Behavior on a Fluoridation Referendum," *Public Opinion Quarterly*, 23 (1959), 213–22.
8. Most indicators of the independent variable have been taken or adapted from census data (U.S. Bureau of the Census, *U.S. Census of Population: 1950*, Vol. II, *Characteristics of the Population*, Part 2 ff [Washington, D.C.: Government Printing Office, 1952]). In addition, other indicators are employed, such as the strength of the turnout at the polls and the way in which the decision was reached, either by a town meeting or by a referendum (the town meetings and referendums considered in this paper were held between 1951 and 1955 in communities located throughout the United States).
9. The concept of attachment is here taken in a broad sense: it covers all kinds of social ties, from the primary relations to the secondary associations in larger groups, whether voluntary or not; it also covers the values, the interests, etc., through which one

identifies himself with particular persons and groups (see Coleman, *op. cit.*, pp. 25–26).

10. Since in the present data only a few cases are known to have been decided at a town meeting and since the cases in Massachusetts have been largely decided in that way, the two sets of data were pooled. The relationship holds, of course, in both sets of data:

	No. of Communities		
	Measure Passed	Measure Defeated	Total
Massachusetts data:			
Town meeting	30	15	35
Referendums	2	6	8
Present data:			
Town meeting	6	0	6
Referendums	92	120	212

The Massachusetts data are from A. L. Green and J. L. Briggs, "Fluoridation in Massachusetts: A Statistical Comparison of Communities" (Cambridge, Mass.: Social Science Program, Harvard School of Public Health, 1957), pp. 11–12. (Mimeographed.) One case which was in both sets of data has been eliminated from the present data. The method of decision is not known for some cases in the latter data.

11. $N = 41$ and 220, respectively. a_1 (effect of form of decision) $= .20$; $P (a_1{}^* \leq 0) = .008$. For this result as for the following ones, a_i represents the percentage difference (in the $n \times 2$ tables) or what amounts to the mean of the percentage differences in each pair of controlled comparisons (in the higher-order tables). The probability that $a_i{}^*$ could have occurred by chance, that is that $a_i{}^*$—the population effect parameter—is smaller than or equal to zero, is established as usual by finding the standardized normal deviate and by referring to tables of the standardized cumulative normal distribution. To this end, the variance of a_1 is estimated as the sum of the variance of each proportion, divided by the square of the number of paired comparisons. The justification for these procedures will be presented in James S. Coleman, *Introduction to Mathematical Sociology* (N.Y. Free Press of Glencoe, forthcoming).

12. Coleman, *op. cit.*, p. 19. To support his point, Coleman presents there a preliminary analysis of the same data.

13. Since the number of eligible voters in each community was unknown, the turnout was estimated as the proportion of voters among the total population.

14. Other researchers apparently found incon-

sistent results in this regard. Gamson and Irons report without details that in two other sets of data "no significant relationship between fluoridation action and population size" was found, and that in one other set, "the data show no correlation" (Gamson and Irons, *op. cit.*, p. 68). However, a re-analysis of one of the former sets of data by this writer (the other sets were not available) revealed that, while 60 per cent of the smaller communities of the sample have adopted fluoridation, only 18 per cent of the larger ones have done so, which strongly corroborates our hypothesis ($N = 42$ and 11 respectively; $P (a_1{}^* \leq 0) = .001$). This was recalculated from Green and Briggs, *op. cit.*, p. 3. The significant break on the independent variable in these data appears at a population size about 2,500 (the one adopted here).

15. $N = 158$ and 100, respectively, a_1 (effect of size) $= .11$; $P (a_1{}^* \leq 0) = .04$.

16. With the regions held constant, the corresponding percentage differences are for the Northeast, 33 per cent; the South, 24 per cent; the North Central, -4 per cent; the West, 0 per cent; α_1 (effect of size) $= .13$; $P (a_1{}^* \leq 0) = .10$.

17. The installation of fluoridation equipment is more common in large cities than in small communities. According to *Public Health Reports*, by 1956, the proportion of large cities (500,000 or more) fluoridating their water supplies was 55 per cent, while for communities with a population ranging from 10,000 to 500,000, from 2,500 to 10,000, and for communities smaller than 2,500, the figures were 28 per cent, 15 per cent, and 5 per cent, respectively. (Reported in Benjamin D. Paul, "Fluoridation of Community Water Supplies" [Cambridge, Mass.: Social Science Program, Harvard School of Public Health, 1958], p. 5. Mimeographed.)

18. Similar findings were reported in quite a different context. In the study of the International Typographical Union, Lipset, Trow, and Coleman found that the small union shops were much more likely to show unanimity in their approval or disapproval of a political party than larger shops. The stronger ties between the members in small shops were seen as preventing any strong political cleavage. See S. M. Lipset, M. A. Trow, and J. S. Coleman, *Union Democracy* (Glencoe, Ill.: Free Press, 1956), esp. pp. 166 ff. The same study has also established the existence of a strong tendency on the part of small locals to support the incumbent administration of the I.T.U., due to stronger attachments to it in terms of communication and interests (see *ibid.*, chap. xvii, esp. pp. 364–82).

19. Since the variation in the votes may be expected by chance alone to be greater in small than in large towns, the observed variation might be the result of that. However, even a turnout as low as 225 voters would still account for less than 7 per cent of the variation two-thirds of the times. Since this is a higher limit and since the variation observed in the data are greater than that, the results cannot be explained this way. A similar remark could have been made with regard to Table 1 above.

20. See W. Kornhauser, *The Politics of Mass Society* (Glencoe, Ill.: Free Press, 1959), pp. 163 ff., and references cited therein.

21. In a largely unemployed community, Jahoda and Zeisel found that during the depression "subscriptions to a very low-priced workers' political publication dropped by almost 60 per cent; whereas subscriptions to another publication which had the same political direction [but was] more concerned with entertainment than with politics . . . declined only by about 27 per cent, in spite of its higher price" (Marie Lazarsfeld-Jahoda and H. Zeisel, *Die Arbeitslosen von Marienthal* [Leipzig: Hirzel, 1932], pp. 35–37; quoted from S. M. Lipset, *Political Man* [Garden City, N.Y.: Doubleday & Co., 1960], p. 187).

22. $N = 75$ and 83, respectively. a_1 (effect of unemployment) $= .12$; $P(a_1^* \leq 0) = .06$.

23. To be sure, the kind of attachments to which an indicator such as the level of unemployment refers is of somewhat different character than the kind represented by other indicators such as the method of decision or the size of the communities. The latter are pointing to attachments through *common* sets of values shared by a group, while the last indicator rather points to attachment of a group to another through a set of interests *particular* to that group. But, as stated previously, the concept of attachment is taken to cover these different aspects, since the consequences of attachments, not their bases, are of interest here.

24. Migrants to cities have apparently always been found to be particularly prone to join mass movements when deprivations and a lack of social integration characterize their situation. For some indication of this process during the late Middle Ages see Norman Cohn, *The Pursuit of the Millennium* (London: Secker & Warburg, 1957), pp. 22 ff.; see also Kornhauser, *op. cit.*, pp. 143 ff., and Lipset, *op. cit.*, pp. 68–71, 171.

25. Areas of depopulation in France were shown to have been particularly sensitive to Poujade's appeals against the established order (see Stanley Hoffmann, *Le Mouvement Poujade* [Paris: Librairie Colin, 1956], pp.

12–13, 197 ff.). Similarly, Angell found that communities with a high degree of population movement (in- and out-migration) were less socially integrated than the others (Robert C. Angell, "The Social Integration of American Cities of More Than 100,000 Population," *American Sociological Review*, 12 [1947], 335–42).

26. The population of continental United States increased from 1940 to 1950 by 14.5 per cent. This offers a rough indicator of what would be the natural increase by birth rate of a community (see U.S. Bureau of the Census, *op. cit.*, Part 1, *U.S. Summary*, p. 18).

27. [Green and Briggs] *Op. cit.*, pp. 3 ff. They did not distinguish in- and out-migration from natural increase, but established only a rank order with regard to growth. An approximation to the present analysis can be obtained by dividing their rank data into three groups. This gives the following proportions of favorable communities (from the largest decrease to the largest increase): 35 per cent $(N = 17)$, 50 per cent $(N = 18)$, 67 per cent $(N = 18)$. Thus only the last group does not meet our expectations. The writer is indebted to S. S. Kegeles, who offered this reanalysis in a written communication.

28. [Gamson and Irons] *Op. cit.*, p. 72.

29. Samples with a total N of 53, 64, and 56 communities, respectively, and "not wholly independent" (*ibid.*, pp. 67–68). It should be noted, as suggested by Paul, that Green and Briggs's results might have been spurious: "Further analysis reveals that in our series rapid growth meant an influx of predominantly younger people, an influence favoring fluoridation" (Paul, *op. cit.*, p. 5).

30. With the exception of the out-migration subgroup in the case of high turnout, based on nine cases only.

31. Since it was established that the fluoridation of water supplies is an effective way to prevent tooth decay among children, it is not surprising to find that communities in which there is a high proportion of children are more likely to accept the project. It points at self-interest as another factor of fluoridation outcome. For similar findings see Gamson and Irons, *op. cit.*, p. 69.

32. A further test to see whether the association between rate of growth and outcome was not due to the direct association between size and growth (small communities experienced less growth) showed that this was not the case either. Both factors are independently related to the outcome.

33. This last aspect of the findings indicates that there is some truth in Rossi's comment that fluoridation controversies in the cases of rapidly growing communities might be inter-

preted as an expression of "the malaise of the older residents in communities experiencing rapid growth" (see Peter H. Rossi, "Community Decision Making," *Administrative Science Quarterly*, 1 [March, 1957], 441).

34. See, e.g., Everett C. Hughes, *French Canada in Transition* (Chicago: University of Chicago Press, 1943), pp. 86–87.

35. Strikingly, a pattern of very low turnout is found in the South: while only 25 per cent of the communities in the other three regions combined have a very low turnout (a turnout of less than 20 per cent), 72 per cent of the communities in the South are in this category ($N = 109$ and 25, respectively) (P [a_1^* $\leq 0 = .0001$]).

36. Note that in the deviant case (North Central) and in the case with no relationship (West), the ethnic homogeneity is rather complete: only 7 per cent and 14 per cent of the communities in these two regions, respectively, are less than 85 per cent native white, compared to 35 per cent and 74 per cent for the Northeast and the South, respectively. One should therefore not expect the ethnic composition in the former two to have any effect.

37. As in the case of the relationship between regions and outcome, a more accurate control variable here would probably be the turnout, since as we should expect, it is much lower in the less homogeneous communities. Such a control again revealed the expected direct association between degree of ethnic homogeneity and positive outcome. But since for many cases the turnout is not known, this expected relationship is already present in the remaining data, even without a control, so that the test remains inconclusive. For a similar pattern of zero-order relationships between ethnic heterogeneity and referendum outcome or turnout (on a metropolitan sewer district referendum), see W. C. Kaufman and S. Greer, "Voting in a Metropolitan Community: An Application of Social Area Analysis," *Social Forces*, 38 (1960), 196–204. However no control by turnout is presented in this last study.

38. By middle-class or lower-class communities, we mean here those which have a relatively high or low proportion of the gainfully employed men in the upper-middle class (the professional and managerial occupational groups).

39. See, e.g., B. Mausner and J. Mausner, *Scientific American*, 192 (1955), pp. 35–39.

40. See Simmel, *op. cit.*, Tables 1 and 3; and other findings reported in W. A. Gamson and C. G. Lindberg, "An Analytic Summary of Fluoridation Research: With an Annotated Bibliography" (Cambridge, Mass.:

Social Science Program, Harvard School of Public Health, 1960; pp. 1–3. (Mimeographed.)

41. Gamson and Irons, *op. cit.*, pp. 70–72; a result consistent with the hypothesis is reported in W. C. Kaufman and S. Greer, *op. cit.*

42. For two such controls, see Tables 11 and 12.

43. Calculated on the basis of four occupational groups: 1. professional and managerial; 2. clerical and sales; 3. skilled and semiskilled; 4. service and unskilled.

44. See, e.g., Table 12.

45. Studies of community power structures have increasingly been aware that these structures may be more or less monolithic, although this does not necessarily imply factions or divisions within the elites (see Delbert C. Miller, "Decision-Making Cliques in Community Power Structures: A Comparative Study of an American and an English City," *American Journal of Sociology*, 64 [1958], 299–310, esp. pp. 307 ff.; Peter H. Rossi, "Power and Community Structure," in E. C. Banfield [ed.], *Urban Government* [New York: Free Press of Glencoe, 1961], pp. 419 ff.). Neither of them, however, suggests that the size of the elites may lead to different power structures; Rossi on the contrary writes that "homogeneous middle class communities . . . will tend to have monolithic power structures, since the class basis for countervailing political power does not exist" (*Ibid.*, p. 421).

46. Again, a similar finding was made in the study of the I.T.U.: the smaller the size of the locals, the less likely they were to have an institutionalized opposition, or even any opposition at all (see Lipset, Trow, and Coleman, *op. cit.*, p. 179, n. 2).

47. Such an interpretation is suggested by analogous findings in the study of immigrant communities, where an association was found between a proportionately small professional elite and a lower degree of outgroup relations among other members of the communities. This finding was shown to be due to the fact that "when the professional elite is small, more people become concerned with the social life of the community [and] a more diversified group of people assumes leadership positions in the ethnic community . . . producing a high degree of cohesiveness in the group" (see Raymond Breton, "Ethnic Communities and the Personal Relations of Immigrants" [unpublished doctoral dissertation, Johns Hopkins University, 1961], pp. 147–55).

48. This relationship is not due to the fact that lower-class communities would be more concentrated in the small-size category; the opposite is actually true.

49. If there is a low proportion of upper-middle-class citizens and a high variance, this indicates that the class structure is heavily skewed toward the lower-class end, thus resulting in a small *and* isolated social elite. Conversely, the combination of a high proportion of upper-middle-class people with a low variance gives a large non-isolated elite. The other combinations lead to two intermediate types; a small non-isolated elite and a large isolated one.

50. The statistically minded reader may be bothered by the small attention paid to the significance tests presented. These allow him, however, to reach different conclusions if he so pleases. It is nevertheless contended that the strength of the demonstration presented in this paper does not rest on these tests, but rather on the diversity of the analysis carried, including the verifications by inference. On this see Lipset, Trow, and Coleman, *op. cit.*, Appendix I, B.

51. One could raise an objection to some of the findings of this paper by maintaining that the variables used here are more indicative of differential degrees of education than of differential degrees of attachments, and that these findings simply show that a higher degree of education is more conducive to approval of a fluoridation project. Many facts, however, are inconsistent with this interpretation. It should be stressed that, while some of the findings might be possibly interpreted in this way, others clearly cannot, while all of them fit the attachment hypothesis. The above argument cannot account, e.g., for the findings that the projects are more likely to be approved in small communities. The same argument holds with regard to the consideration of growth as an indicator and, above all, for the analysis bearing on the pattern of extreme versus moderate outcomes. Finally, it should be stressed that education, although it may produce a greater rationality, is also likely to be conducive to greater attachments in the same way and with the same qualifications made above with regard to occupation.

52. For a review of that literature see Lipset, Trow, and Coleman, *op. cit.*, pp. 13–16 and pp. 73–82, and Kornhauser, *op. cit.*

53. See, e.g., Kornhauser, *op. cit.*

The Distribution of Community Power: Structural Bases and Social Consequences[1]

Michael Aiken

The purpose of this study is twofold: (1) to identify some of the structural attributes of communities that are associated with the dispersion of community power; and (2) to explore some *consequences* that variations in community decision-making structures have on a community's ability to mobilize its resources in attempting to confront some of its problems, i.e., mobilization for community action. Specifically, the study examines participation in several federal self-help programs designed to fight poverty and urban blight. But before discussing the methods and findings of the study, some discussion of the study of community power historically is appropriate.

In 1953 Floyd Hunter published *Community Power Structure*, his landmark study of Atlanta, Georgia, and set off a controversy characterized more by its acrimonious debate than its elucidation of the issues that were raised. The debate reflected to a large degree some basic differences in the assumptions and philosophies of the disciplines of sociology and political science. It continued until approximately 1966 when John Walton published two articles which sought to put the various findings into perspective.[2] The polarities of this controversy were the pluralists—Dahl, Wolfinger, Wildavsky, and Polbsy—versus the elitists—Hunter and his followers—and the reputational versus the decision-making

An original article written for this volume.

approaches. While a number of insightful and sometimes provocative studies emerged from this debate—Robert Dahl's *Who Governs?*,[3] Schulze's study of Cibola,[4] Agger and his colleagues' comparative study of four communities,[5] and Freeman and his colleagues' procedurally sound study of Syracuse[6]—the student who carefully reads this literature would hardly gain a clear perspective of those structural features of communities that are associated with one type of power structure as opposed to another. Nor would he confront very often the question of how the general welfare of a community is affected, if at all, if power and other resources are highly dispersed or narrowly concentrated.

The first aim of this study is by no means unique. Several scholars have hypothesized relationships between community attributes and the type of community decision-making structure,[7] and several researchers besides Walton have examined structural attributes of communities and their association with various aspects of the community decision-making structure.[8] The second purpose of this study leads to areas less trampled over by researchers, although there have been several comparative studies and discussions that have attempted to link the decision-making structure of communities with various aspects of community welfare.[9]

There are a number of important aspects of the community decision-making structure that could logically be examined in a comparative framework: the degree to which power is centralized or dispersed, the number of participants in these issues, the degree of issue specialization, the number of reputational leaders and degree of consensus about them, the degree of overlap among reputational, positional, and decision-making leaders—to name a few of the more salient ones in the literature on community power. To study most of these in a comparative framework would require systematic and comparable studies of a sizable number of communities, but the resources to do such a study would be quite exorbitant. However, some understanding of these community characteristics that are associated with variations in community decision-making structures can

be obtained by using as data the findings from various studies of community decision-making. That is the strategy taken here.

A number of schemes have been proposed for classifying community power structures. Delbert Miller, for example, has suggested the categories of autocratic pyramidal structures, slightly more dispersed pyramidal structures, stratified pyramidal structures, ring or cone models, and segmented power pyramids.[10] Peter Rossi has suggested four categories: pyramidal, caucus rule, polylith, and amorphous;[11] and Robert Dahl has proposed still a third scheme.[12] What is common to these classificatory schemes is that each implies a scale that runs from concentration of community power and resources (elitist model) to dispersion of community power and resources (pluralist model).[13] Thus, a continuum is conceived with highly elitist arrangements—with a single center of power that controls most decisions—on one end and highly pluralistic arrangements—with diverse and competing centers of power and influence—on the other. Walton's four category classification scheme (pyramidal, factional, coalitional, and amorphous) is used in this study because it is representative of concentration-dispersion scales and because it maximizes comparability with previous research of this type.[14]

This study is divided into five sections. In the first section (and in Appendix B), the methodology is described. This is followed by an examination of the relationships between some economic, political, social, and other attributes of communities and the degree of diffusion of community power. Next we examine relationships between the type of power structure and various mobilization "outputs," after which there is some discussion of the representativeness of the cities in the study. To conclude, there is a brief summary and discussion of some of the implications of the study.

Methodological Procedures

Fifty-seven communities that have been the subject of community decision-making studies are included in the analysis made for this study. Forty-three of these were included in Walton's article, although twelve others that he included have been omitted here.[15] Some of the fourteen additional communities included here are from unpublished studies; others were not specifically studies of community power, but studies for which sufficient information about community decision-making was available to classify the type of decision-making structure. A complete list of the communities, the type of decision-making structure of each, and the source from which each was taken can be found in Appendix A.

As stated previously, only one aspect of a community's decision-making structure, the degree of diffusion of power, is included in this study, and Walton's classificatory scheme, which is shown above, is used. These categories can be construed to form a scale of the degree of diffusion of power. The scale runs from a low number meaning concentration of power to a high number meaning diffusion of power.

To provide the reader with a better understanding of the coding scheme that was used here, several examples are presented. Both Alpha and Amory (see Appendix A) are classified as having a highly concentrated—"pyramidal"—power arrangement. In the case of Amory, the author actually classified the community in that way, and he described the existence of a small and well-integrated "clique" of influential people who dominated the community. Alpha was classified as pyramidal because the researchers in this study described how a set of middle class interests continually dominated the decision-making in that city. Algona as well as Cornucopia (see Appendix A) are categorized as having "factional" decision-making structures. In the case of Algona the researcher

identified two major decision-making factions in the community: an "old guard" with conservative interests and a "new clique" of new businessmen and younger men. In the case of Cornucopia, before a new plant was introduced into the community, the researcher identified two major factions: one headed by a banker and the other by a local businessman. Some examples of communities classified as having "coalitional" decision-making structures are Arcadia and Atlanta (see Appendix A). In each case the judgment is made that leadership varies from issue to issue and that fluid coalitions characterize the participation in most issues. For example, in Arcadia the original call for a new municipal building, public housing, and urban renewal most often came from professional administrators, but the final outcomes involved the creation of coalitions which were neither permanent nor utilized for other issues. In the restudy of Atlanta the researcher reported that coalitions of actors, organizations, and institutions tended to prevail in most community issues, not one homogeneous elite. "Amorphous" decision-making structures are defined as those in which there is the absence of any persistent pattern of leadership or power. Seven communities—Big Town, Easterntown, Miami, Milton, Norwood, Oretown and Petropolis—are so classified (see Appendix A). In the case of the latter two, the researcher described the communities exactly in these terms. In Big Town as well as the other communities, there seemed to be no consistent pattern of leadership, and thus these communities are categorized as having the greatest diffusion of community power.

The main statistical procedure used in this study is correlational analysis, although the chi-square test of significance is used with

Concentration ↑

1. Pyramidal: A monolithic, monopolistic or single cohesive leadership configuration.

2. Factional: At least two durable factions that compete for advantage.

3. Coalitional: Leadership varies with issues and is made up of fluid coalitions.

Diffusion ↓

4. Amorphous: The absence of any persistent pattern of leadership or power.[16]

contingency tables. While most of the variables utilized in this study are interval scales, the measure of diffusion of community power is at best an ordinal scale and does not meet the assumptions of this statistical model. At the same time it was felt that the use of correlational analysis was justified in order to simplify the data presentation and in order to be able to control for the effect of third variables on relationships without a loss of cases. Hopefully, there is some gain in this compromise.

Some check on the use of this measure was obtained by constructing two dummy variables from the diffusion variable:[17]

a. Presence (1) or absence (0) of concentrated decision-making structures (i.e., pyramidal power structures are coded "1" and other types are coded "0").

b. Presence (1) or absence (0) of diffused decision-making structures (i.e., coalitional and amorphous power structures are coded "1" and others are coded "0").

The utilization of a dummy variable as a dependent variable also violates the assumptions of the classical regression model. The regression model assumes that the expected value of the dependent variable is a linear *unbounded* function of the independent variable and that the variances of the dependent variable for each value of the independent variables are equal (homoscodasticity). Dummy variables meet neither of these assumptions.[18] It was felt that the gain from having a check on the four-point diffusion scale

would justify these violations of the regression model, but the reader should consider such compromises in interpreting the results.

The .10, .05, and .01 levels of significance are shown for all correlation coefficients, and probabilities are shown for contingency tables although tests of significance are appropriate for none of these data if one uses a very rigorous application of these statistical models. That is, the fifty-seven case studies, or subsets of these case studies, hardly constitute a random sample. Some other findings included here are based on the universe of all the 423 American communities that are non-suburbs and of size 25,000 or more. While use of tests of significance under such circumstances is open to debate, it was felt that in the absence of any other criteria for deciding what relationships were significant and meaningful, probability levels could be helpful.

The actual names of cities with pseudonyms were obtained from authors and other sources in order to identify the true name of each community. Social, economic, political, and other characteristics of these cities were then obtained from various volumes of the *Municipal Yearbook*, the 1960 Census of Population, the 1966 *City-County Data Book*, and other such sources. Data on the economic structure of cities was obtained through a complex and protracted, data-gathering procedure that is described in Appendix B.

Forty-four of the fifty-seven case study communities were of size 10,000 population or more in 1960. Thirty-two of these were of size 25,000 population or more and twelve were in the range of 10,000–24,999 popula-

TABLE 1. *Population Size and Metropolitan Status of the Sample of Fifty-seven Communities and the Universe of Cities of 10,000 Population or More in 1960*

	METROPOLITAN STATUS					
	Central or Independent Cities		Suburbs		All Cities	
POPULATION SIZE	Case Studies	Universe	Case Studies	Universe	Case Studies	Universe
25,000 or more	31	423	1	253	32	676
10,000 to 24,999	5	515	7	463	12	978
Less than 10,000	8	*a*	5	*a*	13	*a*

*a*The number of cities under 10,000 population was unavailable.

tion (see Table 1). These forty-four cities are taken from the universe of 1,654 incorporated urban places of size 10,000 population or more in 1960. The remaining thirteen cities had populations of less than 10,000 in 1960, but information about the number of cities in the universe from which these are taken was unavailable.

There is considerable variation among the fifty-seven case study cities not only with respect to population size, but also with regard to metropolitan status (Table 1). Thirty-one, or 7.0 percent, of the 423 central or independent cities (i.e., nonsuburbs) of size 25,000 population or more in 1960 are included among these case studies. Only one suburb (Salem, Massachusetts) from among the 253 suburbs in that size category is included among these fifty-seven case study communities. Among the 978 medium-sized cities in the size range 10,000–24,999 population in 1960, only twelve cities (or 1.0 percent) are included, and over half of these are suburbs. In a later section of this paper we compare the relationships between community characteristics and mobilization outputs among some of these case study cities and cities in the universe from which they are taken. Since the rate of mobilization outputs is considerably less in suburbs and in cities under 25,000 population, we shall concentrate primarily on relationships between various community attributes and type of decision-making structure among the thirty-one case study cities that are of size 25,000 population or more and are not suburbs. Henceforth, we shall refer to these thirty-one cities as Subset A.

Information about the size of firms, absentee or local control, type of industry, and other characteristics of the economic structure refer only to the manufacturing sector of the community. Information on other kinds of economic establishments was unavailable. The description of the data gathering procedure used in constructing these measures of economic structure is described in Appendix B. Since the measures of economic structure refer only to the manufacturing sector of the community, all analyses of economic structure are limited to manufacturing cities, i.e., those having at least 20 percent of their labor force engaged in manufacturing in 1960. The 20 percent cutoff point was used because it is comparable to the procedures utilized in a previous study.[19]

Among the fifty-seven case studies, thirty-three had at least 20 percent of the labor force engaged in manufacturing (see Table 2). Henceforth, these thirty-three communities will be referred to as Subset B. Of these thirty-three communities, eighteen were also in Subset A, i.e., they were nonsuburbs of size 25,000 population or more. We shall henceforth refer to these eighteen cities as Subset AB since they can be said to be the intersection of Subsets A and B, i.e., they belong to both sets. Salem, Massachusetts is the only suburb included among the nineteen manufacturing cities of size 25,000 population or more shown in Table 2 but not included in Subset AB.

To summarize, there are four sets of these case study cities that are referred to throughout this paper:

Total Set: All fifty-seven case study cities.

Subset A: Thirty-one cities from the total set that have a population size of 25,000 or more and are not suburbs.

TABLE 2. *Population Size and Degree of Manufacturing of the Fifty-seven Case Study Communities*

POPULATION SIZE	AT LEAST 20 PERCENT MANUFACTURING	LESS THAN 20 PERCENT MANUFACTURING	TOTAL
250,000 or more	2	2	4
25,000 to 249,999	17	11	28
10,000 to 24,999	8	4	12
Less than 10,000	6	7	13
All Cities	33	24	57

Subset B: Thirty-three cities from the total set that have at least 20 percent of the labor force in manufacturing.

Subset AB: Eighteen cities that have a population size of 25,000 or more, are nonsuburbs, and have 20 percent of the labor force engaged in manufacturing.

The thirty-one cities in Subset A are taken from the universe of 423 nonsuburbs of size 25,000 or more in 1960. In the analysis of urban renewal decisions, only twenty-six of these cities are included, since the other five cities are located either in states which were quite late in enacting laws which make participation in the urban renewal program possible or in states that still have not enacted such legislation. Sixty-five of the 423 cities are located in these states, meaning that the twenty-six cities in Subset A used for urban renewal decision analysis are taken from a universe of only 358 cities. Similarly, because some states did not have state enabling legislation permitting cities to enter the low-rent housing program, cities in several states have been omitted, meaning the thirty-one cities in Subset A come from a universe of 389 cities for this issue.

Discipline and Methodology of the Research

Both the discipline of the researcher and the methodological procedures employed have been shown to have an effect on the findings of community power studies. Walton reasons that the causal link is as follows: sociologists are more prone to select only the reputational technique and use of the reputational technique alone is more likely to yield a pyramidal power structure.[20]

To determine whether the discipline of the researcher and the methodology employed have an effect on the results of the study, two dummy variables were constructed. The first, discipline of the research, was constructed as follows:

1   Researcher is a sociologist.
O   Researcher is not a sociologist (most of these are political scientists, however).

The second variable, type of methodology, was constructed in the following manner:
1   Only the reputational technique was used.
O   Other techniques, or a combination of techniques, were used.

Our findings are quite similar to those of Walton, as one would expect. There is a very strong inclination for sociologists to use only the reputational technique ($r_A = .77$), and there is a relatively strong relationship between using only the reputational technique and finding a pyramidal power structure ($r_A = .38$). It logically follows from these findings that sociologists should be more prone to "discover" pyramidal power structures than researchers in other disciplines, and they are ($r_A = .22$) as shown in Table 3.

TABLE 3. *The Degree of Diffusion of Community Power by Discipline of Researcher and Methodological Procedure Employed*

DISCIPLINE AND METHOD	DIFFUSION OF POWER		PRESENCE OF PYRAMIDAL POWER STRUCTURE		PRESENCE OF COALITIONAL OR AMORPHOUS POWER STRUCTURE	
	Subset A $N=31$	Total Set $N=57$	Subset A $N=31$	Total Set $N=57$	Subset A $N=31$	Total Set $N=57$
Researcher is a sociologist	−.27	−.16	.22	.17	−.37†	−.18
Reputational Method alone was used	−.47‡	−.32†	.38†	.31†	−.48‡	−.30†

*$p < .10$.   †$p < .05$.   ‡$p < .01$.

None of these relationships is as strong among the fifty-seven cities in the total set as among the thirty-one cities in Subset A, however.

The subsequent findings of this paper could be substantially affected by this kind of bias. Therefore, this bias should be considered in interpreting the findings of this study. In a later section of this paper we shall systematically consider the effects of methodological technique and the researcher's discipline on many of the findings that are discussed below.

Community Characteristics and the Diffusion of Community Power

As noted earlier, the numerous case studies and limited comparative studies of community power have provided little systematic understanding of the structural features of communities that are related to different types of community decision-making arrangements. One of the greatest problems for the student of community power has been that of drawing any coherent conclusions from the plethora of case studies that abound in the sociological and political science literature, although there have been some efforts to draw meaningful conclusions from these studies. The approach here differs from the efforts of Walton[21] and Gilbert[22] since their data about cities were taken from content analyses of various studies. The data about cities in this study, other than the measure of dispersion of community power, were taken from a variety of secondary, but official, sources.

A great number of community attributes that affect or are associated with the distribution of power in communities has been suggested by numerous writers. For example, the degree to which economic firms are absentee controlled has often been suggested as a structural characteristic contributing to the dispersion of community power. Similarly, some have argued that the diversity of the population—heterogeneity in terms of ethnicity, religion, or race—is a structural characteristic that is likely to be found in cities with more decentralized configurations of power.

In this section we shall discuss these various factors under five rubrics: (1) location, size, age, and growth of communities; (2) economic characteristics; (3) political structure; (4) social structure; and (5) other measures of community power. The hypothesized relationship between various community attributes and dispersion of power, as well as a rationale for each expected relationship, will be discussed as each factor is introduced.

Location, Size, Age, and Growth of Communities

Just how do such factors as location, size, age and growth of communities affect the distribution of community power? Looking first at the region in which the community is located, we see that twenty-five of the fifty-seven cities in the total set are located in the South (i.e., cities in the three Southern regions defined by the Bureau of the Census); the remaining thirty-two are located in Northern or Western states. There are several reasons to hypothesize that Southern cities will have more concentrated power arrangements than Northern cities. First, Southern cities are more likely to have conservative value systems, rigid class structures, and one-party political systems.[23] Further, the anti-Negro racial attitudes which buttress a one-party political system undoubtedly support the entrenchment of an old ruling class. In addition, Southern communities have less ethnic and religious heterogeneity and are less likely to have undergone industrialization, especially those located in the Deep South and Southwest. This means that there simply have not been sufficient structural transformations to dislodge the older elites. The hypothesis of greater centralization of power in Southern than in Northern cities seems reasonable considering these factors.

Slightly more Southern cities than Northern cities do have concentrated power structures. Forty-four percent of the twenty-five Southern cities have pyramidal power structures while only 22 percent of thirty-two Northern cities have such concentrated arrangements (Table 4). Among the thirty-one larger cities in Subset A, 41 percent of the seventeen Southern cities as opposed to 14 percent of the fourteen Northern cities have pyramidal power structures. The correlation coefficients in Table 5 (for which Southern cities are assigned the value of one and Northern cities zero) show similar results.

Older cities have slightly more diffused power structures than younger cities. The measure of age of city used here is the census year that the city first reached 10,000 population. The two oldest cities in Subset A are New Haven, Connecticut, which reached

10,000 population in 1830, and Syracuse, New York, which reached the 10,000 mark in 1850. Both have diffused power structures. The youngest city among the thirty-one cities in Subset A is Burlington, North Carolina, which did not reach the 10,000 mark until 1940; Burlington has a pyramidal power structure. The correlation coefficients between the measures of diffusion of power and the age of the city are shown in Table 5 (a high number on age means a young city). The measure of diffusion of power using the dummy variable of presence or absence of

TABLE 4. *Type of Community Power Structure by Regional Location of Cities Among the Fifty-seven Cities in the Total Set*

| | TYPE OF STRUCTURE | | | | |
CITY IN	Pyramidal	Factional	Coalitional or Amorphous	TOTAL	N
North	22%	34%	44%	100%	32
South	44%	20%	36%	100%	25
All Cities	32%	29%	40%	101%	57

*p < .20, chi-square test of significance.

TABLE 5. *The Degree of Diffusion of Community Power by Selected Contextual Characteristics of Communities*

COMMUNITY CHARACTERISTIC	DEGREE OF DIFFUSION OF POWER[a]		PRESENCE OF PYRAMIDAL POWER STRUCTURE[b]		PRESENCE OF COALITIONAL OR AMORPHOUS POWER STRUCTURE[c]	
	Subset A $N=31$	Total Set $N=57$	Subset A $N=31$	Total Set $N=57$	Subset A $N=31$	Total Set $N=57$
Located in South	−.22	−.15	.30	.24*	−.23	−.08
Age of city (census year reached 10,000 population)	−.25		.22		−.31*	
Population size, 1960 (natural logarithm)	−.17	.17	.29	−.01	−.04	.25†
Population increase, 1950–1960	−.28	−.02	.31*	.07	−.31*	−.01

* p < .10.
† p < .05.
[a]The types of power structures are assigned the following values:
   1 Pyramidal
   2 Factional
   3 Coalitional
   4 Amorphous
[b]The values are as follows:
   1 Pyramidal
   0 Other
[c]The values are as follows:
   1 Coalitional or Amorphous
   0 Other

either a coalitional or an amorphous power structure has a stronger relationship with the degree of dispersion of power than the other measures.

Among the cities in Subset A, larger cities have more concentrated power structures than smaller cities, but among the total set of cities, the relationship between size and the degree of diffusion of power is just the opposite. One would expect larger cities to have more diffused power structure than smaller cities because of the greater probability of mutiple centers of power and structural differentiation in the larger cities. The larger the size of the city, the more difficult it should be for any single center of power to exert control over other power centers. Thus, our expectation is that power should be more dispersed in larger cities than in smaller cities. This would suggest that the finding among the cities in Subset A may be anomalous since each of the largest cities in our sample, Dallas and Pacific City, was categorized as having a pyramidal power structure. One of these cities is located in the Far West, the other in the Southwest. These two cities are hardly representative of the sixteen cities of size 500,000 or more in the United States in 1960, suggesting that the relationship between city size and degree of dispersion of community power among the cities in Subset A may be anomalous. The positive relationship between size of city and diffusion of community power among the total set of cities is more understandable and in the expected direction. The question of representativeness of these various cities will be discussed in a later section of this paper.

Finally, growing cities are more likely to have *concentrated* power configurations, while stagnant and declining cities are more likely to have diffused power structures. This also appears to be counter to the expectation that growing cities are more likely to be undergoing structural differentiation, and, thus, a loosening of the older configurations of power. On the other hand, the growing cities in our sample are younger, Southern cities which we have previously shown are more likely to have concentrated power arrangements. It is the older, Northern

central cities that are undergoing either decline or limited growth that are most likely to have greater decentralization of community power. It is also these communities, as will be shown later, that have greater degrees of ethnic and religious heterogeneity, and consequently greater diffusion of community power.

Economic Structure

Many of the writings about and studies of community power structure have linked aspects of the economic substructure with the type of power configuration. One of the more often made observations is that cities which are dominated by absentee-controlled companies are likely to have dispersed power structures.[24]

Not only the degree of absentee control, but a number of other aspects of the economic structure of cities, such as the degree of manufacturing, the degree of concentration of employment, and the degree of industrial diversity, are here related to the type of decision-making structure.

We would expect industrialized cities to have more diffused power arrangements than nonindustrialized cities.[25] Industrialization brings about greater structural differentiation, which means that new centers of power and countervailing elites are likely to be created. Further, the more industrialized cities are those in which the population is likely to be heterogeneous—both ethnically and religiously. These cities are more likely to have become industrialized during the period of American history in which large numbers of immigrants crowded into our urban centers. Such factors as these would provide structural bases for greater dispersion of community power.

The cities in our study vary greatly in their degree of industrialization. Some cities such as Dorado and Service City have only a few, small industrial firms, and have less than 5 percent of the labor force engaged in manufacturing. Others such as Lorain and Stackton are industrial centers with large steel producing firms with over 50 percent of the labor force employed in manufacturing.

The greater the degree of industrialization, the more dispersed is community power (see Table 6). Among the cities in the total set, there is a correlation coefficient of .14 between the four-point diffusion scale and the percent of the labor force engaged in manufacturing. There is a similar relationship among the thirty-three cities of Subset B ($r_B = .23$).

One could hypothesize that cities with greater absentee control of the manufacturing sector will have more diffused power structure. The reasoning behind this assertion is that the managers of absentee-controlled firms have their careers in the corporation, not in the community.[26] This means that they are likely to be geographically mobile and thus stay in a community for only a limited period of time. With few ties to the community and with exigencies in their corporate careers that provide neither the incentives nor potential rewards to become community leaders, they are less likely to initiate projects and follow them through to their completion. In this "power vacuum," in which those with potential economic power choose not to utilize it fully, other centers of power may be activated, with the result of a more decentralized decision-making arrangement.

An excellent illustration of this point is made by French in his study of Cornucopia. He did a longitudinal study of the power structure of a community in which a large, absentee-owned automobile assembly plant was located. He found that the community

TABLE 6. *The Degree of Diffusion of Community Power by Characteristics of the Economic Structure*

Economic Characteristics	Degree of Diffusion of Power		Presence of Pyramidal Power Structure		Presence of Coalitional or Amorphous Power Structure	
	Subset AB $N=18$	Subset B $N=33$	Subset AB $N=18$	Subset B $N=33$	Subset AB $N=18$	Subset B $N=33$
Industrialization Percent of labor force in manufacturing	.16	.23	−.13	−.22	.23	.26
Absentee Control Percent of manufacturing labor force in absentee firms	.40	.31*	−.52†	—.41†	.21	.15
Economic Concentration Percent of manufacturing labor force in firms of size 500 or more	−.16	.26	−.03	−.35†	−.21	.18
Average size of firms (or establishments)	.07	.09	−.10	−.22	.05	.02
Percent of manufacturing labor force in largest firm	.04	−.05	−.05	−.05	−.03	−.14
Low Industrial Diversity Percent of manufacturing labor force in main industry	−.14	−.11	.06	.05	−.22	−.20

*$p < .10$.
†$p < .05$.

power structure was more dispersed two years after the establishment of the plant than before.[27]

Absentee control is defined by whether the home office of a plant or firm is located inside or outside the community. In the former case, a firm would be defined as locally controlled; in the latter, it would be absentee controlled. (See Appendix B for further discussion of the measurement of this variable.) There is considerable variation in the degree of absentee control among the cities in this study. For example, only 16 percent of the manufacturing labor force of Red Wing is employed in absentee firms, but 95 percent of the manufacturing labor force of Edgewood works in such firms. The average percent of absentee control is 52 percent among the thirty-three manufacturing cities in Subset B.

There is a positive relationship between the degree of absentee control and the degree of dispersion of community power ($r_B = .31$). These results are presented in a slightly different form in Table 7. New Haven is particularly noteworthy in this table because

it is the only city in the low absentee-control category (less than 32 percent) that has a coalitional or amorphous power structure.

The relationships among economic concentration and diffusion of power are ambiguous and inconsistent. Three measures of economic concentration are employed here: the percent of the manufacturing labor force employed in firms of size 500 or more, the average size of manufacturing firms, and the percent of the manufacturing labor force employed in the largest firm. There is considerable variation among these cities on each of these three dimensions. For example, there are no firms of size 500 or more in the cities of either Bakersville or Bennington, while almost 90 percent of the manufacturing labor force of both Lorain and Edgewood is employed in firms of size 500 or more. The average size of manufacturing firms varies from a low of fifty-one employees per establishment in Northville to 339 per establishment in Stackton. While the largest firm employs only 12 percent of the manufacturing labor force in both New Haven and Norwood, in Easterntown and Stackton the largest firm

TABLE 7. *Type of Community Power Structure by Absentee Control of Manufacturing Sector of the Community among Thirty-three Manufacturing Cities*

DEGREE OF ABSENTEE CONTROL OF THE MANUFACTURING SECTOR	TYPE OF POWER STRUCTURE		
	Pyramidal N = 9	Factional N = 12	Coalitional or Amorphous N = 12
Low (0%–31%)	Pacific City Dallas Bakersville Metroville Salem	Red Wing Brunswick Riverview	New Haven
Medium-low (32%–48%)	Burlington Alpha Farmdale	Community A	Norwood Gamma Beta
Medium-high (49%–67%)		Gretna Sardis Bennington	Syracuse Delta Oretown Xton
High (68%–93%)	Northville	Wheelsburg Lorain Cornucopia Cibola Edgewood	Petropolis Milton Easterntown Stackton

employs 75 percent of the manufacturing labor force.

The most plausible argument for linking concentration of employment with the type of community power structure is that cities with concentrated economic structures should have more concentrated power arrangements. The reasoning is that concentration of economic resources provides a structural basis for concentration of political power. Those who control large economic resources are likely to utilize these resources in the political arena.[28]

The data relating the degree of economic concentration to the degree of diffusion of power is inconsistent. The findings among the cities in Subset B (see Table 6) show direct relationships between the measure of percent of employees in firms of size 500 or more and diffusion of power; among the eighteen larger cities (Subset AB), the relationship between this variable and dispersion of power is reversed. It is noteworthy that the cities in Subset AB are almost all Northern cities (only five are Southern cities). Thus, this smaller sample may not be representative of all cities. Among the cities of Subset B, the cities with greater concentration have more *diffused* power arrangements. This, of course, is contrary to our expectation. But, large firms in American cities are usually absentee controlled, and, therefore, cities with a high degree of absentee control are cities with a high degree of economic concentration. For example, there are direct relationships between the degree of absentee control and the proportion of the manufacturing labor force in firms of size 500 or more ($r_B = .45$), the average size of firms ($r_B = .57$), and the percent working in the largest firm ($r_B = .40$). These findings make the positive relationship between the first measure of economic concentration and diffusion of power more intelligible. On the other hand, most of the relationships between measures of economic concentration and diffusion of power are neither very strong nor very consistent. We conclude that there are very ambiguous, and weak, relationships between measures of economic concentration and the degree of dispersion of community power.

Our last measure of the economic structure of communities is the degree of industrial diversity. The measure of industrial diversity used here is the percent of the manufacturing labor force employed in the main industry, that is, the standard industrial classification (SIC) categories. The degree of industrial diversity varies considerably among these cities. While New Haven and Norwood have less than 20 percent of the manufacturing labor force employed in the main industry, Oretown and Farmdale have approximately 95 percent of the manufacturing labor force employed in a single industry. One could hypothesize that cities with greater industrial diversity (a low proportion of the labor force in the main industry) would have more diffused power structures. The dispersion of a community's economy across a number of different industrial sectors is likely to mean the creation of more power centers, even within the economic sphere, and hence greater diffusion of power generally. Cities with more industrial diversity do indeed have less concentrated power structures ($r_B = -.11$), but the relationship is weak.

There is another important aspect of the economic structure of communities, the degree of industrial unionism, but we were unable to obtain systematic data about it. One would expect cities with greater industrial unionism to have more diffused power arrangements.[29] Historically, labor leaders represent new types of elites, and a strong labor organization can be the basis for an important power center in a community. While we have no empirical evidence about unionization and the degree of diffusion of power, several types of inferential evidence can be utilized to support this contention. To begin with, unionization of workers is greater in highly industrialized cities than in cities with less industrialization, and we noted earlier that the greater the degree of manufacturing, the greater the degree of diffusion of community power. Second, unionization is greater in the North than in the South, and we noted that Northern cities had more diffused power structures. Third, the studies of Lorain, Stackton, and Sardis examine the role of labor unions in the community decision-making structure, and each supports our contention that active labor organization can provide a structural basis for diffusion of community power.[30] While such inferences as these do not constitute proof, they do provide some support for the contention that labor unions are probably stronger in cities having dispersed power structures.

We conclude that the only measure of economic structure that has been shown to be strongly and unambiguously related to the degree of diffusion of community power is the degree of absentee control, although the data suggests that other factors—industrial diversity and economic concentration—are also more likely to be structural attributes of communities with diffused power arrangements. While no data was presented, we have argued that the degree of industrial unionism is also probably greater in communities in which power is dispersed.

Political Structure

Is there any relationship between the formal political structure of city government and the type of community power structure? Are cities with reformed or nonreformed city governments more likely to have dispersed power arrangements? The reform movement envisioned a form of local government which would eliminate corruption, maximize efficiency, and increase the opportunity of democracy at the local level. Banfield and Wilson argue that this ideal emerged from an Anglo-Saxon Protestant, middle-class ethos of "public regardingness" in which local politics was seen as a mechanism of moralizing life and "serving" the public. The political mechanisms that would accomplish these objectives are council-manager form of government, nonpartisanship, elections-at-large, small size councils, a strong executive with a long term, a merit system for city employees and city planning.[31] A number of studies have shown that homogeneous, middle-class communities are more likely to have these various elements of reform government.[32] One could thus argue that the cities with reformed city governments are those in which political resources are less likely to be dispersed and, therefore, are those more likely to have concentrated power structures.

The data in Table 8 suggest that this is indeed the case. Cities with reformed governments are more likely to have concentrated power structures; nonreformed cities are more likely to have diffused power structures. That is, cities with diffused decision-making structures are more likely to have a mayor-council form of government, direct elections of mayor, large councils, and elections by ward or district. Cities having pyramidal power structures are more likely to have a city manager form of government, indirect election of mayor, small councils and at-large elections.

Similarly, the cities with concentrated power structures have strong executives— indicated by the mayor having veto power and by the presence of a civil service commission. Cities with diffused power structures have weaker executive power.

Cities with concentrated power structures also have more bureaucratized city governments, implying that they have greater administrative efficiency as measured by the presence of a full-time personnel officer and the presence of in-service training. Cities having more diffused power structures are less likely to have these indications of efficient city government.

Cities with more concentrated power structures also have fewer city employees per 1,000 population than cities with diffused power structures. At first, this may seem inconsistent with the previous discussion of bureaucratization, but it is quite consistent. While cities with dispersed community power are more likely to have proportionately larger city bureaucracies, they are probably not highly efficient. In the nonreformed cities the municipal bureaucracy is likely to become a source of political patronage. In such cities many more demands are made for city services, resulting in a proportionately larger, but not necessarily more efficient, city government.

Finally, cities with decentralized power structures are more likely to have a politically

TABLE 8. *The Degree of Diffusion of Community Power by Characteristics of the Community Political Structure*

POLITICAL CHARACTERISTICS	DEGREE OF DIFFUSION OF POWER		PRESENCE OF PYRAMIDAL POWER STRUCTURE		PRESENCE OF COALITIONAL OR AMORPHOUS POWER STRUCTURE	
	Subset A N = 31	Total Set N = 57	Subset A N = 31	Total Set N = 57	Subset A N = 31	Total Set N = 57
Reform Government						
City manager government	−.24	−.03	.26	.12	−.30	−.02
Nonpartisan elections	−.03	.08	−.06	−.02	−.05	.09
Direct election of Mayor	.25	.15	−.23	−.17	.18	.02
Number of councilmen	.25	.25*	−.23	−.24*	.26	.27†
Percent elected at-large	−.25	−.13	.31*	.19	−.27	−.12
Strong Executive						
Veto Power of Mayor[a]	−.21		.24		−.22	
Presence of Civil Service Commission, 1967[a]	−.22		.35*		−.13	
Bureaucratization of City Government						
Full-time personnel officer[a]	−.22		.24		−.15	
Presence of in-service training[a]	−.21		.36†		−.17	
Number of city employees per 1,000 population	.32*		−.22		.31	
Party Preference						
Voted Democratic, 1960 Presidential election	.30		−.20		.30	

[a]These correlation coefficients are based on less than thirty-one cases because of missing data.
*p <.10.   †p <.05.

liberal electorate. The indicator of political values used here is a measure based on the percentage of the vote that was cast for the Democratic and Republican candidates in the 1960 presidential election. A high number means a Democratic plurality while a low number means a Republican plurality. Cities with pyramidal power structures were more likely to have voted Republican while those with amorphous or coalitional power struc-

tures were more likely to have voted Democratic in 1960.

These findings provide a relatively clear and unambiguous portrait. Cities with a number of competing, and perhaps conflicting, centers of power not only have decentralized elite structures, but also have a number of political mechanisms that contribute to that decentralization. This is not to suggest that either the political structure or the type of power structure caused the other; the important point is that they were probably caused by the same process, but they do become mutually reinforcing in the dynamics of city life.

While the relationships presented in Table 8 are fairly consistent (with the exception of the variable of nonpartisan elections that showed no relationship with the degree of dispersion of community power), these relationships are not particularly strong. In spite of this limitation, it seems appropriate to conclude tentatively that cities with decentralized decision-making arrangements tend to have political structural characteristics associated with nonreformed municipal government.

Social Structure

In the previous sections we have examined a number of characteristics of the political and economic structure of communities and their relationships with the degree of dispersion of community power. There are also several aspects of a community's social structure that we shall now consider: the degree of social heterogeneity, the socioeconomic status of the community, and the incidence of economic dependency.

In the discussion of community political structure two aspects of the social structure were noted: ethnic composition and socioeconomic status of the community. Banfield and Wilson maintain that ethnic heterogeneity and lower socioeconomic status lead to a "private-regarding ethos" with repect to city politics, while Anglo-Saxton Protestant (i.e., homogeneous) and middle-class cities are more likely to have a "public-regarding ethos" and reform politics.[33] Therefore, if these factors are related to formal political structures, we could similarly expect them to be associated with informal political structures. This line of reasoning would lead us to expect the ethnically heterogeneous and working-class communities to have diffused power structures and homogeneous, middle-class communities to have concentrated decision-making arrangements.[34]

Three measures of community heterogeneity are utilized here: the percent of the native population that is of foreign or mixed parentage, the percent of the total population that is nonwhite, and the percent of elementary school children in private schools. The first measure is an indicator of ethnicity; the second of the racial mix of the community; and the third is a crude, but reasonable, indicator of the Catholic influence in a community. We assume here that children enrolled in private schools are more likely to be Catholic, although there are obviously other denominations that also have private schools.

Heterogeneous cities, i.e., those with a high proportion of foreign stock and a high proportion of Catholics, have more diffused power structures (see Table 9). Conversely, the more homogeneous the population of a city as indicated by these two measures, the more likely it has a pyramidal power structure. The proportion of the population that is nonwhite has no relationship with the degree of diffusion of power, however. Undoubtedly, the shift in the nonwhite population from Southern to Northern and Western cities in recent decades is a factor that confounds this relationship.

High-status cities are more likely to have concentrated power structures than low-status cities (Table 9). That is, cities with a higher proportion of high school graduates, more white-collar workers, and higher median income have more concentrated power structures. Conversely, cities with diffused decision-making arrangements have more citizens of lower socioeconomic status as measured by these indicators.

On the other hand, only one measure of economic dependency—percent unemployed in 1960—is related to the type of decision-making structure. The cities with higher rates of unemployment have more decentralized decision-making arrangements. There is no apparent relationship between either the incidence of poverty families or limited educational attainment of the adult population (less than five years education) and the type of decision-making structure.

Both the heterogeneity and socioeconomic status of a community are factors that are related not only to whether the city has a

TABLE 9. *The Degree of Diffusion of Community Power by Characteristics of the Community Social Structure*

SOCIAL CHARACTERISTICS	DEGREE OF DIFFUSION OF POWER		PRESENCE OF PYRAMIDAL POWER STRUCTURE		PRESENCE OF COALITIONAL OR AMORPHOUS POWER STRUCTURE	
	Subset A $N=31$	Total Set $N=57$	Subset A $N=31$	Total Set $N=57$	Subset A $N=31$	Total Set $N=57$
Heterogeneity						
Percent foreign stock	.30*		−.26		.33*	
Percent of elementary school children in private schools	.30*		−.28		.34*	
Percent nonwhite	.07	.12	−.09	−.05	−.02	.15
Socioeconomic Status						
Percent four years of education	−.25	.06	.29	−.02	−.16	.17
Percent white collar	−.17	−.17	.25	.18	−.04	−.08
Median income	−.15	.06	.15	−.11	−.06	.05
Economic Dependency						
Percent of families with less than $3,000 annual income, 1959	.08	.21	−.06	−.24*	.00	.12
Percent of adults of age 25 or older with less than five years education	.04		−.01		.00	
Percent unemployed, 1960	.32*		−.22		.25	

*$p < .10$.

reformed or nonreformed city government, but also the degree of dispersion of community power. Decentralized power structures and nonreformed municipal administrations are more likely to be found in cities that have a high degree of ethnicity, many Catholics, and a large working class. Homogeneous, middle-class communities are more likely to have reform city governments and centralized decision-making structures.

Other Measures of Community Power

In 1963 Amos Hawley published an article in which he used the proportion of managers, officials, and proprietors in the civilian labor force (MOP Ratio) as a measure of community power.[35] He reasoned that cities with a high MOP Ratio were cities in which power was diffused among different community subsystems while cities with a low MOP Ratio were cities in which community power was more concentrated. He also argued that cities with concentrated power would have a higher probability of success in activities affecting the collective welfare, and he used urban renewal success as his measure of a collective welfare decision. He was able to demonstrate that cities with low MOP Ratios (concentration of community power) had greater urban renewal success than cities with high MOP Ratios (diffusion of community power). While this study has had its vigorous critics,[36] the MOP Ratio has been accepted by some researchers as a crude, but reasonable, indicator of the degree of diffusion of community power.

The relationship between the diffusion of community power and the MOP Ratio is shown in Table 10. Based on Hawley's reasoning, we should expect a *positive* relationship between the MOP Ratio and our measure of diffusion of community power. That is, a high MOP Ratio (diffusion of communtiy power) should be associated with a high number on our scale of dispersion of power (coalitional or amorphous), but, as shown in Table 10, the relationship is *negative*. The MOP Ratio evidently measures just the opposite of what Hawley proposed.[37]

Part of the problem is undoubtedly involved in the definition of the MOP Ratio. While Hawley intended to include only "Managers, Officials, and proprietors, not elsewhere classified," all managers, officials, and proprietors were actually included.[38] The MOP census category contains numerous occupations in retail trade (which "MOP, n.e.c." would have excluded). This means that cities that are high on retail trade and low on manufacturing are more likely to have a high MOP Ratio. There is a very strong negative relationship between percent of the labor force in manufacturing and the MOP Ratio

$(r_A = -.76)$. Thus, cities that are high on MOP Ratio are probably retail trade centers and more often located in the South $(r_A = .71)$. As we have argued previously, cities that have not undergone extensive industrialization, i.e., Southern cities, are more likely to have concentrated power structures. Thus, it is reasonable that cities with dispersed power structures should be those cities with a low MOP Ratio and a high degree of manufacuring and located in the North. Pyramidal cities are most likely to be retail centers and located in the South. Even an examination of the data in Hawley's article will show that the cities with low MOP Ratios have the characteristics that we have shown above to be associated with dispersed configurations of power. Since Southern cities are less industrialized and have higher MOP Ratios, it could be that the relationship between MOP Ratio and the degree of diffusion of community power is simply an artifact of the large number of Southern cities that were studied. This raises the question of the representativeness of the cities in this study, but that will be discussed in a later section of this paper. Barring the possibility that this is a highly unusual and biased sample of cities, we can conclude that a high MOP Ratio is more likely to be a characteristic of a city with *concentrated* power, not dispersed power as Hawley has argued.

TABLE 10. *The Relationship Between the Degree of Diffusion of Community Power and the MOP Ratio*

COMMUNITY CHARACTERISTIC	DEGREE OF DIFFUSION OF POWER		PRESENCE OF PYRAMIDAL POWER STRUCTURE		PRESENCE OF COALITIONAL OR AMORPHOUS POWER STRUCTURE	
	Subset A $N = 31$	Total Set $N = 57$	Subset A $N = 31$	Total Set $N = 57$	Subset A $N = 31$	Total Set $N = 57$
MOP Ratio (Percent of labor force that are managers, officials, or proprietors)	$-.37\dagger$	$-.25*$	$.35\dagger$	$.24*$	$-.38\dagger$	$-.20$

$*p < .10.$
$\dagger p < .05.$

Controls for Discipline of Researcher and Type of Methodology
In an earlier section of this paper the type of methodology and to a lesser extent the discipline of the researcher were found to be related to the type of community power structure. That is, researchers who used only the reputational technique more often reported a concentrated power structure than did those who used other, or a combination of other, techniques. Sociologists were more prone to use only the reputational technique and sociologists more often found concentrated power arrangements.

Findings such as these raise serious questions about many of the relationships just discussed. Since there is such a strong relationship between the use of the reputational method and finding a pyramidal power structure, it could well be that some previously discussed findings are actually spurious. That is, they may exist simply because the reputational method was used in cities that happen to have some particular attribute. It is therefore necessary to examine these relationships after controlling for the effects of the methodological procedure and the discipline of the researcher. We do this through the use of partial correlational analysis. The partial correlation coefficients between the various community attributes and the degree of diffusion of community power, controlling separately for both the methodological procedure and the discipline of the researcher, are shown in Table 11. Use of only the reputational technique was assigned a value of one; use of any other method or a combination of methods was assigned a value of zero. Similarly, if the discipline of the researcher was sociology, a value of one was assigned; other disciplines (most of the other researchers were political scientists) were assigned zero.

Most of the partial correlations are based on the thirty-one cities in Subset A; in the case of economic characteristics, the correlations are based on the thirty-three cities in Subset B. Subset A was used rather than the total set in order to simplify the presentation of data and because data about community

characteristics for the fifty-seven cities in the total set was unavailable for all cities.

Controlling for the methodological procedure reduces the magnitude of some of the previously noted findings, although some are actually increased. Controlling for the researcher seldom affects any of these relationships, however. Among the relationships between contextual characteristics and the type of power structure shown in Table 5, only the relationship between age of city and diffusion of power is substantially altered by controlling for the methodological technique utilized by the researcher. The reputational technique was evidently more often employed in younger cities (undoubtedly, Southern cities), but there is no apparent causal connection between age of city and type of methodology utilized. Controlling for discipline has no effect on the relationships between age of city and degree of dispersion of power.

The relationships between various aspects of the economic structure and the degree of dispersion of power shown in Table 6 are changed little when the effects of methodology and discipline are separately removed.

Some of the relationships between characteristics of the political structure and the degree of diffusion of power are considerably reduced when the type of methodology is controlled, however. For example, the relationships between number of councilmen, percent elected at-large, number of city employees per 1,000 population, as well as Democratic voting and the dispersion of power are considerably reduced when methodology is controlled. Only the first two relationships are removed completely, however. The relationships between the city manager form of government and direct elections and dispersion of power are not substantially altered when these variables are controlled. In fact, the relationship with direct elections is actually increased when these factors are controlled.

Among the social characteristics shown in Table 9 having moderately strong relationships with the diffusion of power—percent foreign stock, children in private schools, high school graduates, and unemployment—the percent in private schools and the percent

TABLE 11. *Partial Correlation Coefficients between Attributes of Communities and the Degree of Diffusion of Community Power Among Thirty-one Cities in Subset A, Controlling for the Methodology and Discipline of the Researcher*

COMMUNITY ATTRIBUTES	PARTIAL CORRELATION COEFFICIENTS CONTROLLING FOR:	
	Methodology (Reputational)	Discipline (Sociologist)
Contextual Characteristics		
Located in South	−.19	−.24
Age of city (census year reached 10,000 population)	−.10	−.21
Population size, 1960 (natural logarithm)	−.16	−.15
Population increase, 1950–1960	−.24	−.26
Economic Structure[a]		
Percent of labor force in manufacturing	.17	.22
Percent of absentee control	.31*	.34†
Percent in firms of size 500 or more	.23	.27
Average size of firms	.06	.12
Percent in largest firm	−.06	−.03
Percent in main industry	−.12	−.10
Political Structure[b]		
City manager government	−.26	−.34*
Nonpartisan elections	−.09	−.10
Direct election of mayor	.37†	.36†
Number of councilmen	.05	.18
Percent elected at-large	−.12	−.21
Number of city employees per 1,000 population	.20	.30
Voted Democratic, 1960 Presidential election	.19	.26
Social Structure		
Percent foreign stock	.26	.33*
Percent of elementary school children in private schools	.16	.28
Percent nonwhite	.03	.01
Percent four or more years education	−.16	−.19
Percent white collar	−.13	−.14
Median income	−.18	−.11
Percent of families with less than $3,000 annual income, 1959	.08	.02
Percent less than five years education	.07	.04
Percent unemployed, 1960	.30*	.31*
Other Measures of Community Power		
MOP Ratio	−.27	−.34*

[a]These partial correlations are based on the thirty-three cases in Subset B.
[b]Some of the community attributes shown in Table 7 are omitted because they were based on less than thirty-one cases.
*$p < .10$.
†$p < .05$.

of high school graduates are reduced considerably by the partialling out method. The other two measures, however, are little affected by the controlling procedure.

Finally, the relationship between MOP Ratio and type of power structure is reduced somewhat when methodology is controlled statistically, but there still remains a moderately strong relationship between these two variables.

The results of controlling statistically for method and discipline are quite mixed. Some relationships were strongly affected when methodology of the researcher was controlled; others were hardly affected at all; in a few cases the strength of relationships was even increased. While some specific relationships were affected, we conclude that the broad outlines of the findings are still the same. None of the relationships we have found are particularly strong, and some of these are reduced when the effect of method is removed statistically. Yet, the general thread remains, i.e., the older cities, those located in regions that were industrialized earlier, those having had a greater influx of immigrants and other minority groups, and those having nonreformed formal political structures, are cities that are more likely to have decentralized decision-making arrangements.

Community Power and Mobilization Outputs

In the preceding analysis we have attempted to draw together data from different studies of community power and determine through a comparative perspective those attributes of communities that are related to the degree of dispersion of power. There are many references in the studies concerned with community decision-making to the structural factors that may be associated with various types of decision-making structures, but seldom have students of community power asked the consequences of such arrangements for community life. The question of what difference it makes whether a community has a pyramidal power structure or a highly amorphous decision-making pattern has seldom been raised. So much of the debate has been overshadowed by ideological overtones that some important questions, such as this one, have been neglected. On the one side are those who are committed to and believe that American cities are characterized by pluralism (more often the political scientists), while on the other side there are those whose more cynical view of the world sensitizes them to conceive of American communities as being run by self-interested, economic cliques (more often the sociologists).[39] The result has been a relatively sterile debate in which the *consequences* of the type of community decision-making pattern on a range of community issues have seldom been examined. One of the exceptions to this generalization is a

study by Belknap and Steinle, who demonstrated the importance of activating the community power structure for achieving adequate community medical services.[40] At the same time, their study was not concerned with the effects of the variations in the power structure on successful mobilization to solve any community problems.

Community mobilization is defined as the demonstrated capacity of a community to reach a threshold level of collective action. We have included as indicators of community mobilization the degree of participation in four issue areas: the war on poverty, urban renewal, public housing, and model cities. The question we seek to answer is what type of community decision-making arrangement is likely to be most successful in *mobilizing* community resources in order to participate in these federal self-help programs. The indicators of community mobilization used here are the degree of participation in each of these federal programs. Each program was designed to channel federal monies into the local community, and for each of these programs, some type of local initiative is necessary in order for a community to participate although the nature of that initiative varies from one program to the other. Our discussion in no way implies that communities have successfully solved, or are solving, the problems toward which these monies are directed. For example, one could argue that poverty programs hardly alter the problems of the poor. One could equally criticize urban renewal for benefiting only certain elements of the middle class while eliminating housing for the poor and destroying viable neighborhoods.[41] At the same time, community participation in each of these programs can be construed as an *effort* to improve the "general welfare" of the total community although this effort may either fail or attain only limited success.[42]

Are cities with pyramidal power structures more successful or less successful in mobilizing the local resources to participate in these various federal programs? One line of reasoning, derived from Hawley's study, would argue that communities with concentrated or pyramidal power structures would be *more* successful than cities with diffused power structures. This position would argue that if power is concentrated in only one, or a few, centers of power, the problems of coordination would be greatly simplified, resulting in greater mobilization success. Of course, this argument makes the implicit assumption that those who command the centers of power in a city place a *positive* value on such participation. It is not inconceivable that two communities could have equally concentrated decision-making arrangements, but one could be dominated by those with relatively liberal political values while the other could be dominated by those having more conservative political values. The former community might have high rates of participation in these federal programs while the latter may not participate at all. Thus, it is difficult to know the probability of participation in these federal programs without knowing the political commitments of the decision-makers in such a concentrated arrangement. The assumption that oligarchy is necessarily conservative seems overly simplified and unjustified. One could argue that decision-makers in cities with concentrated power structures could have higher rates of participation in these self-help programs *if* they so choose. Unfortunately, we do not know what their choices will be.[43]

A different perspective would argue that cities with more diffused power structures would be more successful in mobilizing resources to participate in these programs. If there are many centers of power in a community, especially if there are many demand units that are concerned about such issues— political parties, ethnic neighborhood groups, welfare rights organizations, to name but a few—there is a stronger possibility that the *need* for these various welfare programs will be identified and action initiated to participate in such programs. From this perspective, no community is completely monolithic; almost all communities have multiple centers of power. But it is probably not necessary to activate all of them on a given issue. Numerous studies have documented the degree of issue specialization in communities. This means that some centers will be

activated on a given issue, but others may be completely neglected, or at least avoided. Under conditions of greater diffusion of power, the various interest groups in the community can bring pressure to bear on the various power centers most involved in a given issue such as housing authorities, redevelopment agencies, and the like. Under such conditions of dispersion of power, there will be a higher probability of successful mobilization of the resources of the community on such issues. Thus, dispersion of power would lead to greater participation in these federal programs. This argument has an analogue in organizational studies of innovation in which it has been found that decentralized authority structures are more conducive to the successful implementation of innovation than centralized ones.[44] There is logically a limiting condition to this argument, however. If power is so dispersed that chaos ensues, no collective action is likely to be forthcoming.

The four federal self-help programs that we shall examine here—public housing, urban renewal, the war on poverty, and model cities—involve different procedures in order for a community to participate in them, but, as stated earlier, each requires some initiative by a community and a commitment of some local resources, thus making them excellent indicators of community mobilization. We shall discuss these programs in the order of their historical development.

Public Housing

The first major commitment by the federal government to publicly-financed, low-rent housing came about through the United States Housing Act of 1937, although most public housing that has been built in the United States was a result of the amendments in the Housing Act of 1949.[45] In order for a community to participate in this program it must have, or have the services of, a housing authority, which negotiates with the federal government and which supervises the program in the community. The housing authority must initiate certain actions in order for a city to participate in these programs, and it must obtain the

TABLE 12. *Relationships Between the Degree of Diffusion of Community Power and Community Mobilization Outputs*

MOBILIZATION OUTPUTS	DEGREE OF DIFFUSION OF POWER $N=31$	PRESENCE OF A PYRAMIDAL POWER STRUCTURE $N=31$	PRESENCE OF A COALITIONAL OR AMORPHOUS POWER STRUCTURE $N=31$
Housing			
Presence or absence of participation in the Housing Programs under the Housing Act of 1949[b]	.43†	−.51‡	.34*
Date the first application for a program reservation (under the Housing Act of 1949) was received by the Department of Housing and Urban Development[a]	−.10	.14	−.13
Number of low-rent housing units per 100,000 population constructed under the Housing Act of 1949[b]	.15	−.15	.08
Urban Renewal[f]			
Presence or absence of participation in the Urban Renewal Program under the Housing Act of 1949[c]	.27	−.23	.23
Number of years after 1949 before the city entered the Urban Renewal Program[c]	−.19	.15	−.23
Number of years after state enabling legislation made it possible before the city entered the Urban Renewal Program[f]	.16	−.23	.06
Number of Urban Renewal dollars per capita reserved for the city (natural logarithm)[c]	.43†	−.34*	.39*
Poverty Programs			
Date the city received its first funds from the Office of Economic Opportunity[d]	−.10	.00	−.07
Number of poverty dollars per capita received by the city (natural logarithm)[d]	.30	−.16	.32*
Model Cities			
Presence or absence of applying for a Model Cities Planning Grant (first or second round)[e]	.21	−.07	.24

[a]SOURCE: Unpublished Report S-115, Statistics Branch, Housing Assistance Administration, Department of Housing and Urban Development Washington, D.C.
[b]SOURCE: *Report S-101, Low-Rent Project Directory,* Statistics Branch, Housing Assistance Administration, Department of Housing and Urban Development, Washington, D.C., June 30, 1966.
[c]SOURCE: *Urban Renewal Directory, June 30, 1966,* Department of Housing and Urban Development, Washington, D.C., 1966.
[d]SOURCE: *Information Book as of June 30, 1966,* Office of Economic Opportunity, Washington, D.C., 1966.
[e]SOURCE: *The Journal of Housing,* 24 (April, 1967), 196–198, and files of the Model Cities Administration, Department of Housing and Urban Development, Washington, D.C.
[f]Five cities that were located in states that did not adopt enabling legislation until 1958 or later have been excluded before computing these correlation coefficients.
*$p < .10$.
†$p < .05$.
‡$p < .01$.

approval of the local government at certain stages in the "conventional bid method."[46]

Three measures of participation in the low-rent housing program are used here: (1) The presence or absence of participation in the low-rent housing program between 1949 and June 30, 1966. This measures the *incidence* of the program in a community. (2) The date the first application for a program reservation (under the amendments of the Housing Act of 1949) was received by the Department of Housing and Urban Development. This application, which establishes local need for federally assisted low-rent housing, is the first step a community normally takes in entering this program. The earlier the date, the greater the *speed* with which community mobilization occurred. (3) The number of low-rent housing units per 100,000 population constructed since 1949. The greater the number of low-rent housing units per 100,000 population, the greater the *intensity* of involvement in this program. Since some states still have no state enabling legislation permitting a city to enter the low-rent housing program, cities in these states have been omitted from the analysis here. While none of the cities in Subset A are omitted, the universe of cities from which these thirty-one case study cities are taken (nonsuburbs of size 25,000 or more in 1960) is reduced to 389.

As shown in Table 12, cities with decentralized power structures were more likely to be involved in the low-rent housing program ($r_A = .43$), were more likely to have entered early ($r_A = -.10$), and were more intensely involved in this program as measured by the number of housing units per 100,000 population ($r_A = .15$). It should be noted, however, that only the first of these is statistically significant; the strength of the latter two correlation coefficients is quite weak.

Urban Renewal

The urban renewal program was also established by the Housing Act of 1949, and it too requires the establishment of a local public agency, often called the renewal or redevelopment agency, to carry out these programs. Four measures of a community's

participation in this program, all as of June 30, 1966, are included here: (1) The presence or absence of participation in the urban renewal program under the Housing Act of 1949. (2) The number of years after 1949 before the community entered the urban renewal program. This is a measure of *speed* of community mobilization to enter this program. There is considerable variation in the number of years after 1949 before these cities entered the urban renewal program. Some cities entered the program in 1950, only one year after federal legislation was enacted; other cities, such as Lorain, Ohio, did not enter the urban renewal program until 1965, sixteen years after the 1949 date, although state enabling legislation was present in Ohio from the outset of the federal program. This measure is not entirely satisfactory, however, since states did vary in the dates of their enabling legislation permitting cities to participate in this federal program. Part of this problem is overcome by omitting cities located in states that either had no enabling legislation or enacted enabling legislation for urban renewal after 1958 (Florida, Louisiana, Maryland, Mississippi, Montana, New Mexico, Oklahoma, South Carolina, Utah, and Wyoming). Even among the states retained in the analysis, some did not get enabling legislation until as late as 1957. Once the state enabling legislation was enacted, many cities immediately entered the urban renewal program. To take this into account, the third measure of urban renewal success was constructed. (3) The number of years after state enabling legislation was enacted before a city entered the urban renewal program takes variations in the dates of state enabling legislation into account. This is also a measure of *speed* of mobilization. If a city never entered the urban renewal program, it was scored seventeen years, i.e., the number of years between 1949 and June 30, 1966. After cities in the above eleven states are omitted, the size of Subset A is reduced to twenty-six cities, and the size of the universe of nonsuburbs of size 25,000 or more from which these cities are taken is reduced to 358. (4) The number of urban renewal dollars per capita reserved for the city is a measure of *intensity* of involvement in the program. The average number of dollars per capita per city reserved for urban renewal projects was $108. Seven of the twenty-six cities for which urban renewal data is present had either never been in the program or had dropped out—Algona, Amory, Burlington, Centralia, Dallas, Delta, and El Paso. At the other end of the distribution, New Haven had received $790.25 per citizen, by far the highest amount of urban renewal dollars per citizen for any city in the United States. Norwood was next highest among these cities with $351.80 per citizen. Because of such a highly skewed distribution, it was necessary to transform the values of this variable to the natural logarithm in order to reduce the extreme skewness at the upper end of this scale.

Cities with diffused power structures were more likely to enter the urban renewal program ($r_A = .27$), and they took *fewer* years to enter the program than did cities with concentrated power structures ($r_A = -.19$). On the other hand, the cities with concentrated power structures took *fewer* years to enter the urban renewal program when the number of years is calculated on the basis of when the state enabling legislation was enacted ($r_A = .16$). What this suggests is that it took cities with concentrated power structures *longer* to enter the urban renewal program than cities having diffused power structures, but cities with concentrated power structures were more likely to be located in states in which enabling legislation was not enacted until several years after the Housing Act of 1949. Finally, the cities with diffused power structures also had greater success in obtaining urban renewal dollars than did cities with concentrated power structures ($r_A = .43$) as shown in Table 12. It should be noted that only the relationship between this last measure and the power dispersion variable is statistically significant.

It could be argued that the relationship between type of power structure and urban renewal dollars may occur only because cities with diffused power structures are older cities, which means they probably have more dilapidated housing and thus a greater need for urban renewal. When the percent of

the housing that was dilapidated in 1950 is controlled, however, the relationship remains virtually unchanged ($r_A = .44$). Cities with diffused power structures do have more old houses, that is, houses built before 1930, ($r_A = .51$). But, having older housing does not imply a higher degree of dilapidated housing; in fact, just the opposite. Among these case study cities, those with more recently built housing structures had *more* dilapidated housing units in 1950 than cities with a high proportion of housing built prior to 1930 ($r_A = .52$). Similarly, younger cities as measured by the year the city reached 10,000 population (a recent year meaning a young city), had more dilapidated housing than older cities ($r_A = .38$).[47]

Poverty Program

The various programs in the war on poverty were established by the Economic Opportunity Act of 1964. Two measures which reflect participation in this program are used here: (1) The date the city received its first funds from the Office of Economic Opportunity, a measure of *speed* of entry into the program. (2) the number of poverty dollars per capita received by the city during the first two years of the program, i.e., from the time the bill was signed by President Lyndon B. Johnson on August 20, 1964, until June 30, 1966, the cutoff date for the purposes of this study.[48] The variations in per capita poverty dollars among the cities in this study are considerable. Among the thirty-one cities in Subset A, the mean was $6.50 per capita. Three communities—Center City, Delta, and Watertown—had obtained no poverty dollars at all, while New Haven had received $36.25 per citizen in poverty funds. Only Kansas City, Missouri, had more poverty dollars per capita among the 676 cities of size 25,000 or more in 1960. Because of the highly skewed distribution on this variable, the natural logarithm was utilized in computing correlation coefficients.[49]

Cities with diffused power structures took less time to enter the war on poverty ($r_A = -.10$) and were able to get more poverty dollars per capita than cities with concentrated power structures ($r_A = .30$) as shown in Table 12.

Model Cities

The Model Cities program was established by the Demonstration Cities and Metropolitan Development Act of 1966. Its purpose was to demonstrate how the living environment and general welfare of people living in slum and blighted neighborhoods could be improved. The measure of participation in this program is whether or not the city applied for a planning grant to participate in this program during either the first round (first four months of 1967) or the second round (first four months of 1968).[50] Application for a planning grant is construed to indicate a demonstrated capacity for collective action, ·i.e., community mobilization.

As shown in Table 12, cities with diffused decision-making structures were more likely to apply for a model cities planning grant than were cities with pyramidal power arrangements ($r_A = .21$), although this relationship does not attain statistical significance.

Each of the mobilization outputs—low-rent housing, urban renewal, the war on poverty, and model cities—tends to be greater in cities with diffused power structures than in cities with more concentrated power structures. These findings provide support for the rationale that under conditions of diffusion of power, greater pressure to solve local welfare problems is likely to occur, with the result of higher rates of participation in these federal self-help programs.

Generalizations from these findings to other types of issues seem questionable at this point, however. Each of the above issues involved the mobilizing of local leadership to obtain resources from *outside* the local community, i.e., from the federal government. It may well be that issues about the reallocation of *internal* community resources may not reflect the same patterns.

The Problem of Sampling: The Representativeness of These Cities

How typical are these case study cities of all cities of comparable size and location in the

United States? If we can demonstrate that these cities, which by no means constitute a random sample of cities, are typical of comparable cities in the United States, then we can draw the tentative conclusion that the results of this study are valid for other cities. If these cities are shown to be highly unrepresentative of the universe from which they were taken, then the findings here may have little meaning. While we cannot completely establish the representativeness of these case study cities, there are some ways of making inferences about their representativeness. Two types of data will be discussed; first, comparisons of some characteristics of these cities with the universe from which they were taken; and second, comparisons of the relationships between various economic, political and social attributes of communities and the four types of mobilization outputs among the thirty-one case study cities in Subset A and among the cities in the universe from which they were taken (nonsuburbs of size 25,000 or more in 1960).

In Table 1 we showed that a majority of the fifty-seven cities in the total set were central or independent cities of size 25,000 or more in 1960. Only one of the 253 suburbs in this size range (0.4 percent) was included, while thirty-one (Subset A) of the 423 nonsuburbs (7.3 percent) had been the subject of a community power study. However, only twelve of all the 978 cities of size 10,000—24,999 population in 1960 (1.2 percent) had been the subject of a community power study. We do not have the data to determine the representativeness of the thirteen cities with populations of less than 10,000 in 1960. The forty-five cities of size 10,000 or more are, therefore, clearly unrepresentative of the 1,654 cities in the universe from which they were taken in terms of population size and metropolitan status. It is for this reason that we have restricted most of our discussion to the thirty-one cities in Subset A.

But how representative are these thirty-one cities of the universe of cities of comparable size? Looking first at the regional location of these cities, we see that these cities are overrepresentative of the South (see Table 13). While only 38 percent of the

TABLE 13. *Comparisons of the Region, Size, and Age of Thirty-one Cities in Subset A and the Universe of 423 Nonsuburban Cities of Size 25,000 Population or More in 1960*

	PERCENT DISTRIBUTION		NUMBER OF CASE STUDY CITIES		
COMMUNITY CHARACTERISTIC	Subset A $N = 31$	Universe $N = 423$	Actual Cases	Expected Cases	Difference
Regional Location					
North	45	62	14.0	19.2	−5.2
South	55	38	17.0	11.8	5.2
Total	100	100	31.0	31.0	
			$P < .10$		
Population Size					
25,000–49,999	16	47	5.0	14.5	−9.5
50,000–99,999	39	26	12.0	7.9	4.1
100,000 or more	45	28	14.0	8.6	5.4
Total	100	101	31.0	31.0	
			$p < .01$		
Age of City (census year reached 10,000 population)					
1790–1870	19	30	6.0	9.4	−3.4
1880–1890	42	25	13.0	7.8	5.2
1900–1910	13	21	4.0	6.5	−2.5
1920–1960	26	24	8.0	7.4	.6
Total	100	100	31.0	31.1	
			$p < .20$		

423 cities in the universe are located in the South, 55 percent of the thirty-one sample cities are Southern cities. If the thirty-one sample cities were distributed by region as are the 423 cities, we would expect only 11.8 Southern cities among the sample cities, but, as shown in Table 13, the actual number of sample cities is seventeen. These case study cities, then, are overrepresentative of the South.

The case study cities are also overrepresentative of larger cities, especially cities of 100,000 or more, and highly underrepresentative of cities in the 25,000–49,999 range (see Table 13). Forty-five percent of the cities in Subset A are of size 100,000 or more, but only 28 percent of the universe of 423 cities are of that size. Similarly, there are slightly more medium-size cities (50,000–99,999) in Subset A than in the universe. Finally, only 16 percent of the case study cities are in the 25,000–49,999 population range, but 47 percent of the 423 cities in the universe are of that size. Larger cities are

overrepresented; smaller cities are highly underrepresented among these case studies of community power. There is less of a difference between the case study cities and universe cities in the distribution of the age of city. We conclude that the cities in Subset A are therefore biased in favor of larger cities and Southern cities.

Another way to examine the representativeness of these case study cities in Subset A is to compare relationships between various social, economic, and political characteristics of cities and the mobilization outputs among the 423 cities in the universe (where appropriate) and the thirty-one cities in Subset A. Relationships between selected mobilization outputs and structural attributes of communities are shown in Table 14. In general, relationships among the case study cities tend to be of a higher magnitude than relationships among cities in the universe, although not necessarily of greater statistical significance. Approximately 80 percent of the pairs of relationships are in the same direction and

TABLE 14. *Comparisons of Correlation Coefficients Between Selected Community Characteristics and Mobilization Outputs Among Case Study and Universe Cities*

COMMUNITY CHARACTERISTIC	PUBLIC HOUSING Date of First Application for a Program Reservation		URBAN RENEWAL Urban Renewal Dollars Per Capita (natural logarithm)		WAR ON POVERTY Poverty Dollars Per Capita (natural logarithm)		MODEL CITIES Presence or Absence of Model Cities Application	
	Subset A $N=31$	Universe $N=389$	Subset A $N=26$	Universe $N=358$	Subset A $N=31$	Universe $N=423$	Subset A $N=31$	Universe $N=423$
Age, Size, and Growth								
Age of city	−.01	.26§	−.53‡	−.39§	−.15	−.30§	−.47‡	−.41§
Population size (Log n)	−.40†	−.31§	−.15	.29§	.25	.37§	.16	.53§
Population increase	−.15	.20§	−.48†	−.36§	−.25	−.20§	−.28	−.28§
Political								
City manager government	−.05	.02	−.26	−.10*	−.38†	−.07	−.26	−.10†
Nonpartisan elections	.19	.00	−.25	−.19§	−.32*	−.08	−.22	−.09*
Percent elected at-large	.13	−.07	−.20	.00	−.15	−.04	−.41†	−.02
Number of councilmen	−.17	−.22§	.40†	.14‡	.10	.19§	.47‡	.22§
Number of city employees per 1,000 population	−.30	−.22§	.23	.15‡	.33*	.16§	.28	.13‡
Social								
Percent foreign stock	.20	.01	.18	.17‡	.26	.18§	.34*	.22§
Percent of elementary school children in private schools	.38†	.08	.11	.14‡	−.04	.11†	.14	.17§
Percent nonwhite	−.53‡	−.36§	.21	.18§	−.01	.03	.08	.11†
Percent four or more years of high school education	.12	.30§	−.14	−.25§	.05	−.06	−.25	−.17§
Percent white collar	−.07	.16§	−.07	−.12†	−.07	.01	−.14	−.07
Median income	.58§	.26§	.15	.03	.19	−.01	.20	.06
Percent of families with less than $3,000 annual income, 1959	−.60§	−.29§	−.10	−.05	−.22	−.03	−.25	−.05
Percent with less than five years education	−.62§	−.34§	−.27	.06	.08	.06	−.12	.07
Percent unemployed	.27	−.13†	.10	.12†	.05	.09*	−.02	.12
Other Measures of Community Power								
MOP Ratio	−.24	.12†	−.62§	−.34§	−.45†	−.23§	−.47‡	−.24§

*p < .10. †p < .05. ‡p < .01. §p < .001.

in many cases the magnitude of relationships are not greatly dissimilar. These findings provide some justification for the inference that while the case study cities are overrepresentative of larger and Southern cities, they are not completely unrepresentative of the universe from which they were taken.

Summary and Conclusions

In this paper we have attempted to do two things: (1) to identify some of the structural attributes of communities that are associated with variations in the diffusion of power in communities and (2) to explore some consequences of variations in the dispersion of community power on the mobilization of community resources in order to participate in several federal self-help programs.

With regard to the first objective, we have identified a number of seemingly diverse, but actually consistently interrelated, community attributes that are more often found in communities with decentralized arrangements of power. For example, there is a tendency for the older Northern cities to have decentralized power structures. Among the economic characteristics, we noted that cities with a high degree of absentee control also had greater dispertion of power. And the various indicators of nonreformed city government were more often found in these cities with decentralized power arrangements, although we noted that a large city bureaucracy—probably a reflection of a substantial patronage system—was also more frequently found in such communities. Finally, cities with dispersed power structures were likely to be more heterogeneous—with more citizens of foreign descent and more children in private schools (an indicator of Catholic influence)—and likely to have a larger working class than cities with concentrated power structures. There is some tendency for these characteristics to coexist together, although it is only a tendency, suggesting that an adequate explanation of these findings must include some explanation of all these factors.

We also found that the MOP Ratio (which

Hawley has argued is an indicator of a highly decentralized power system) was found in the cities with concentrated power structures, indicating that it evidently measures just the opposite of what Hawley thought. In any event, it does not appear to be a good surrogate measure of the nature of the community power structure, at least not in the way Hawley has suggested.

With regard to the second objective, we found that it is the cities having decentralized power configurations that have been more successful in mobilizing local resources in order to participate in several federal self-help programs—low-rent housing, urban renewal, the war on poverty, and model cities. It should be noted, however, that each of these four issues concerns the acquisition of resources external to the community, not the reallocation of internal community resources, such as a community chest decision would involve.

Further, we have only examined one aspect of a community's decision-making structure—the degree of dispersion of community power. There are a number of other aspects of the decision-making structure that are important, and perhaps more important, than this global, and highly subjective, measure. For example, the number of active participants in various community decisions, the degree of issue specialization, the number of consensual leaders, the degree of consensus about reputational leaders, the degree of overlap of reputational, positional, and issue leaders, as well as the nondecisions of the community are also important dimensions of community power arrangements. While the measure used here is crude, and subject to many ·distortions because of differences both in methodology and intellectual perspectives of researchers, it nevertheless provides a basis for some tentative understanding about the structural attributes associated with the diffusion of community power and the consequences of that power dispersion for this range of decisions. These findings can only be considered tentative, however, because of the many methodological compromises that the nature of the available data required in doing this study.

One of the more salient findings of this study is that few of the correlation coefficients between structural attributes, degree of diffusion, or mobilization outputs are particularly strong, neither among the case study cities nor among the universe of cities. This suggests the following interpretations.

First, contemporary American communities are not "tight" social systems such as large-scale organizations, but are fairly "open" social systems in which some subsystems may be largely independent of others. The "loss of community autonomy" or "vertical patterns," as described by Warren, is one factor contributing to the modern American community being a relatively "open" social system.

Second, only a multi-causal model can capture the complexity of the modern American community. Mono-causal models, while seductive in their simplicity, simply ignore too many important aspects of the dynamics that inhere in any community process.

And third, only a model of community dynamics that builds in an historical perspective can adequately capture the subtleties of community life. That is, the many attributes of community structure that we have measured here are cross-sectional representations of the current community structure. But, many of these crudely reflect the vestiges of earlier historical structures and processes, although with considerable loss of accuracy. Hence, the low magnitude of relationships among these variables are less distressing when seen from this perspective.

This third point requires greater clarification, however. There emerges from these data the suggestion that communities having the most dispersed power arrangements are the older, now stagnant or declining, cities that are located in the industrial states of the Northeast and Middle West. While some New England cities experienced the impact of industrialization in the middle of the nineteenth century, many of these cities, especially those in the Middle West, became industrialized in the latter part of the nineteenth century and early part of the twentieth century. That industrialization coincided with radical changes in the economic organization of first Northern, and later Southern, Europe. These industrial centers, especially those in the Northeast, became the destination of diverse immigrant groups, meaning that these cities developed heterogeneous social structures that, in an attenuated form, still exist today. These older cities are still more likely to have nonreformed municipal governments since this political arrangement is more consistent with the private interests of such groups. Such cities have, in comparison to many Southern cities, especially those in the Deep South and Southwest, not only greater structural differentiation but also greater heterogeneity of interest groups. With many competing centers of power, it is not surprising that our findings should suggest that these cities have more diffused decision-making arrangements, even using the crude measure employed here. The process in which absentee control increasingly comes to characterize the economic arrangements of American cities, especially in the Middle West, further contributes to this process of diffusion of power. The industrialization of other regions will undoubtedly have the effect of diffusing political power, but it is unlikely that the process will be completely duplicated since a different set of forces are at work. For example, the new "immigrants" to Southern industrial cities are largely rural whites, although there are also many Negroes. This is likely to mean a persistence of conservative, racially-oriented attitudes and is likely to buttress the hold of conservative elites, not to undermine it. The effect of absentee control is also likely to be different in these communities since it will often mean that a major American corporation will build a new plant rather than take over an existing one (since few exist). Such a completely new center of power is less likely to challenge the controlling elites because of the participation patterns by top staff of absentee-controlled firms previously discussed and because these firms are likely to adopt patterns of accommodation to existing local values and customs.

But there are other implications of these findings that are also important. If these findings are valid, and the discussion of the representativeness of the case study communities does not open these results to serious question, then any theory about community mobilization must somehow be able to explain why community outputs, at least the range of community outputs considered here, are higher in more decentralized communities. In other words, what kind of processes occur in decentralized communities that make them more successful in such mobilization efforts? What are the dimensions of community structure that help to account for these variations?

It seems clear from these findings that the nature of community power structure is by no means the most important or only factor affecting community mobilization and, therefore, is probably not the most effective or appropriate theoretical framework for trying to understand these phenomena. There is obviously a cluster of factors that must be considered in order to understand adequately the processes that lead to these collective outcomes. That is, in Table 14 there are a number of factors such as age of city, city size, number of city employees per thousand, to name some of the stronger ones, that are importantly related to these outcomes in the universe of cities.

Perhaps a framework that considers *all*

communities to be decentralized, that is, made up of diverse and competing centers of power, would be more productive. One important dimension of such a framework would be the number, nature of, and quality of "interfaces" among the various power centers. The size of a city could be considered as a gross indicator of the number of power centers—the larger the city, the greater the number of power centers—and the age of the city might be a crude indicator of a high degree of interface activations in the past—both in terms of number of interfaces with other established power centers and number of times each interface channel has been utilized. From this perspective, the greater the residue of "actuarial" knowledge in such a community system, the higher the probability of a successful collective action. It is not the purpose here to explore in depth what such a model might look like, but rather to suggest that the field of comparative community studies, especially that part which is concerned with variations in community system outputs, is badly in need of a more adequate theoretical framework. It seems apparent from the results here that the community power perspective, as it now exists, is simply not the most appropriate model to use.

Appendix A. Type of Power Structure and Sources of Fifty-seven Sample Cities

NAME OF COMMUNITY	TYPE OF POWER STRUCTURE	SUBSET	SOURCE
Algona	Factional	A	Ernest A. T. Barth, "Community Influence Systems: Structure and Change," *Social Forces*, 40 (October, 1961), 58–63.
Alpha	Pyramidal	AB	Oliver P. Williams and Charles R. Adrian, *Four Cities—A Study in Comparative Policy Making* (Philadelphia: University of Pennsylvania Press, 1963).
Amory	Pyramidal	A	Barth, *op. cit.*
Arcadia	Coalitional	A	Benjamin Walter, "Political Decision-Making in Arcadia," in F. Stuart Chapin, Jr., and Shirley F. Weiss (eds.), *Urban Growth Dynamics* (New York: Wiley, 1962), 141–187.
Atlanta	Coalitional	A	M. Kent Jennings, *Community Influentials: The Elites of Atlanta* (New York: Free Press, 1964).
Bakersville	Pyramidal	B	A. Alexander Fanelli, "A Typology of Community Leadership Based on Influence and Interaction within the Leader Sub-system," *Social Forces*, 34 (May, 1956), 332–338.
Bennington	Factional	B	Harry M. Scoble, "Leadership Hierarchies and Political Issues in a New England Town," in Morris Janowitz (ed.), *Community Political Systems* (New York: Free Press, 1961), 117–145.
Beta	Coalitional	AB	Williams and Adrian, *op. cit.*
Big Town	Amorphous	A	Roland J. Pellegrin and Charles H. Coates, "Absentee-Owned Corporations and Community Power Structure," *American Journal of Sociology*, 61 (March, 1956), 413–419.
Brunswick	Factional	B	Lincoln Smith, "Political Leadership in a New England Community," *Review of Politics*, 17 (July, 1955), 392–409: "Power Politics in Brunswick: A Case Study," *Human Organization*, 22 (Summer, 1963), 152–158.
Burlington	Pyramidal	AB	Charles M. Bonjean, "Community Leadership: A Case Study and Conceptual Refinement," *American Journal of Sociology*, 68 (May, 1963), 672–681.
Center City	Factional	A	Gladys M. Kammerer, *et. al.*, *The Urban Political Community: Profiles in Town Politics* (Boston: Houghton Mifflin, 1963).
Centralia	Pyramidal	A	Ivan Belknap and John Steinle, *The Community and Its Hospital: A Comparative Analysis* (Syracuse: Syracuse University Press, 1963).
Cerebrille	Coalitional	A	Delbert C. Miller, "Town and Gown: The Power Structure of a University Town," *American Journal of Sociology*, 68 (January, 1963), 432–443.
Cibola	Factional	B	Robert O. Schulze, "The Role of Economic Dominants in Community Power Structure," *American Sociological Review*, 23 (February, 1958), 3–9; "The Bifurcation of Power in a Satellite City," in Janowitz (ed.), *op. cit.*, 19–80.
Community A	Factional	AB	David A. Booth and Charles R. Adrian, "Power Structure and Community Change: A Replication Study of Community A," *Midwest Journal of Political Science*, 6 (August, 1962), 277–296.
Cornucopia	Factional	B	Robert Mills French, "Cornucopia in Transition" Unpublished Ph.D. dissertation, University of Wisconsin, 1967.

Appendix A—*(continued)*

Name of Community	Type of Power Structure	Subset	Source
Dallas	Pyramidal	AB	Carol Estes Thometz, *The Decision-Makers: The Power Structure of Dallas* (Dallas: Southern Methodist University Press, 1963).
Delta	Coalitional	AB	Williams and Adrian, *op. cit.*
Dixie City	Coalitional	A	Jackson M. McClain and Robert B. Highsaw, *Dixie City Acts: A Study in Decision-Making* (Birmingham: Bureau of Public Administration, University of Alabama, 1962).
Dorado	Coalitional	Other	Kammerer *et al., op. cit.*
Eastbourne	Pyramidal	Other	Kammerer *et al., op. cit.*
Easterntown	Amorphous	AB	Arnold M. Rose, "Communication and Participation in a Small City as Viewed by Its Leaders," *International Journal of Opinion and Attitude Research,* 5 (Fall, 1951), 367–390.
Edgewood	Factional	B	Robert Presthus, *Men at the Top: A Study in Community Power* (New York: Oxford University Press, 1964).
El Paso	Coalitional	A	William V. D'Antonio and William H. Form, *Influentials in Two Border Cities: A Study in Community Decision Making* (Notre Dame: University of Notre Dame Press, 1965).
Estiva	Factional	Other	Kammerer *et al., op. cit.*
Farmdale	Pyramidal	B	Robert E. Agger, Daniel Goldrich, and Bert E. Swanson, *The Rulers and the Ruled: Political Power and Impotence in American Communities* (New York: Wiley, 1964).
Floriana	Factional	Other	Kammerer, *et al., op. cit.*
Gamma	Coalitional	AB	Williams and Adrian, *op. cit.*
Gretna	Factional	AB	Barth, *op. cit.*
Hiberna	Factional	Other	Kammerer *et al., op. cit.*
Lorain	Factional	AB	James B. McKee, "Status and Power in the Industrial Community: A Comment on Drucker's Thesis," *American Journal of Sociology,* 58 (January, 1953), 364–370.
Metroville	Pyramidal	AB	Agger, *et al., op. cit.*
Miami	Amorphous	A	Edward Sofen, "Problems of Metropolitan Leadership: The Miami Experience," *Midwest Journal of Political Science,* 5 (February, 1961), 18–38; Thomas J. Wood, "Dade County: Unbossed, Erratically Led," *Annals of the American Academy of Political and Social Science,* 353 (May, 1964), 64–71.
Micro City	Pyramidal	Other	Ritchie P. Lowry, *Who's Running This Town? Community Leadership and Social Change* (New York: Harper & Row, 1965).
Milton	Amorphous	B	Barth, *op. cit.*
New Haven	Coalitional	AB	Robert A. Dahl, *Who Governs: Democracy and Power in an American City* (New Haven: Yale University Press, 1961).
Northville	Pyramidal	B	Ted C. Smith, "The Structuring of Power in a Suburban Community," *Pacific Sociological Review,* 3 (Fall, 1960), 83–88.
Norwood	Amorphous	AB	Barth, *op. cit.*
Oberlin	Coalitional	Other	Aaron Wildavsky, *Leadership in a Small Town* (Totowa, N. J.: Bedminster Press, 1964).
Orange Point	Pyramidal	Other	Kammerer, *et al., op. cit.*
Oretown	Amorphous	B	Agger, *et al., op. cit.*

Appendix A—(*continued*)

NAME OF COMMUNITY	TYPE OF POWER STRUCTURE	SUBSET	SOURCE
Pacific City	Pyramidal	AB	Delbert C. Miller, "Decision-Making Cliques in Community Power Structures: A Comparative Study of an American and an English City," *American Journal of Sociology* 64 (November, 1958), 299–310.
Pacific Town	Pyramidal	Other	Baha Abu-Laban, "Leader Visibility in a Local Community," *Pacific Sociological Review,* 4 (Fall, 1961), 73-78.
Petropolis	Amorphous	AB	Agger, *et al., op. cit.*
Red Wing	Factional	B	Donald W. Olmsted, "Organizational Leadership and Social Structure in a Small City," *American Sociological Review,* 19 (June, 1954), 273–281.
Riverview	Factional	B	Presthus, *op. cit.*
Salem	Pyramidal	B	Floyd Hunter, Ruth C. Schaffer, and Cecil G. Sheps, *Community Organization: Action and Inaction* (Chapel Hill: University of North Carolina Press, 1956).
Sanford	Pyramidal	A	Barth, *op cit.*
Sardis ˙	Factional	B	James R. Hudson, "Power with Low Prestige: A Study of Labor Unions in a Dependent Community" (Unpublished Ph.D. dissertation, University of Michigan, 1966).
Service City	Coalitional	Other	Robert C. Stone, "Power and Values in Trans-Community Relations," in Bert E. Swanson (ed.), *Current Trends in Comparative Community Studies* (Kansas City, Mo.: Community Studies, Inc., 1962).
Stackton	Coalitional	AB	Warner Bloomberg, Jr., "The Power Structure of an Industrial Community" (Unpublished Ph.D. dissertation, University of Chicago, 1961).
Syracuse	Coalitional	AB	Linton C. Freeman, *et al.,* "Locating Leaders in Local Communities: A Comparison of Some Alternative Approaches," *American Sociological Review,* 28 (October, 1963), 791–798; Linton C. Freeman, *Patterns of Community Leadership* (Indianapolis: Bobbs-Merrill, 1968). Roscoe C. Martin, Frank J. Munger, *et al., Decisions in Syracuse: A Metropolitan Action Study* (Bloomington: Indiana University Press, 1961).
Watertown	Pyramidal	A	Belknap and Steinle, *op. cit.*
Westbourne	Pyramidal	Other	Kammerer, *et al., op. cit.*
Wheelsburg	Factional	AB	Donald A. Clelland and William H. Form, "Economic Dominants and Community Power: A Comparative Analysis," *American Journal of Sociology,* 69 (March, 1964), 511–521.
Xton	Coalitional	B	Melvin L. Reichler, "Community Power Structure in Action" (Unpublished Ph.D. dissertation, University of Michigan, 1963).

Appendix B. Methodology Utilized in Measuring Characteristics of the Economic Structure of Communities

Several measures of the economic stucture of communities are utilized in this study: the degree of absentee control, the percent of the manufacturing labor force in firms of size 500 or more, the percent of the manufacturing labor force employed in the largest firm, the percent of the manufacturing labor force employed in the main industry, and the average size of firms. The procedures used in constructing these measures can be most easily explained by describing first the measurement of the degree of absentee control.

The degree of absentee control of industry is measured by the percentage of the manufacturing labor force that is employed in absentee-controlled plants or firms. A list of manufacturing plants and firms within a three-mile radius of each community, the number of employees, and the standard industrial classification of the principal product manufactured by each was obtained from the local chamber of commerce or comparable agency in each community. This was supplemented with information from state industrial directories. The criterion of including only those firms within a three-mile radius of the community is arbitrary, but it was assumed that this procedure would include the major employers in the community's economic structure.

The control of plants and firms, i.e., whether absentee or local, was based on the *location of the home office of the firm or plant*. Branch plants, wholly owned subsidiaries, or other plants and firms whose home offices were located outside the community were considered to be absentee. All others were classified as local. The home office of each plant or firm was determined by consulting the following national industrial directories: the 1965 *Thomas' Register of Manufacturing*, the 1966 *Standard and Poor's Directory of Manufacturing*, the 1965–1966 *Fortune Plant and Product*

Directory of Plants, and the 1966 *Moody's Industrial Manual*. In the event that the ownership of plants or firms with 100 or more employees could not be established through these sources, additional information was obtained either by contacting the local chamber of commerce or by sending mail questionnaires directly to plants and firms. In addition, mail questionnaires were sent to each plant or firm in this study with 500 or more employees in order to determine their exact employment figures. The larger plants or firms employed on the average over one-half of the manufacturing labor force in each community. All plants or firms whose ownership could not be determined through these procedures were assumed to be local.

To check the validity of these procedures, the control of each manufacturing plant or firm in the thirteen Wisconsin cities in the study was determined by using the above procedure (Method A) and an alternative procedure (Method B).* In Method B, the locus of control was determined by consulting the files of the Secretary of State of the State of Wisconsin to determine the residential location of the members of the board of directors of each plant or firm. Firms or plants for which at least half of the board members lived within the community area were classified as local. If less than half the board members of a firm resided in the local community, the firm was classified as absentee. The net difference in classification of firms based on Method A, which assumed that a firm or plant whose control could not be established was a local firm, and Method B was only 4.8 percent. That is, only seventy of the 1,468 manufacturing plants or firms in these thirteen cities were misclassified by assuming that a firm or plant whose control could not be established through Method A was local. This involved only 1.1 percent of the 151,916 workers in the combined manufacturing labor force of these thirteen communities. Thus, only a small percentage of both employees and plants were misclassified by assuming that the ownership of a plant or firm that

*Method B is essentially the procedure employed by Oliver P. Williams and Charles R. Adrian in their study of four Midwestern cities, *Four Cities: A Study in Comparative Policy Making* (Philadelphia: University of Pennsylvania Press, 1963).

could not be established by Method A was a local plant or firm.

A second possible discrepancy is that Methods A and B may legitimately yield different ownership and control classifications for given plants and firms. The net discrepancy in classification of plants and firms attributable to differences in these two procedures was only .5 percent of the plants and firms in these fourteen communities, and 6.6 percent of the employees in the combined manufacturing work force of these communities. Most of this latter disagreement occurred as a result of the different classifications by Methods A and B of three rather large firms such as the J. I. Case Company and the Johnson Company in Racine and the Parker Pen Company in Janesville. Each of these has its home office in the respective community, but none has a

majority of the members of its board of directors residing in that community. We used Method A in our study because of the inaccessibility of the information used in Method B for other states. A further justification for the use of Method A is a study by Robert Gordon† who concluded that the officers, not the boards of directors, are decision-makers in large corporations. Since officers are usually located in the home office of companies, Method A seemed to be the most appropriate as well as the most feasible procedure.

Once these data had been gathered, it was fairly simple to compute the other four measures, i.e., percent employed in firms of 500 or more, percent in largest firm, percent in main industry, and the average size of firms.

Notes

1. The research for this paper was supported in part through the generous financial assistance provided by the Center for Studies in Vocational and Technical Education and the Institute for Research on Poverty, both of the University of Wisconsin. Neither organization is responsible for the points of view expressed in this paper. I am indebted to Robert R. Alford, Terry N. Clark, Anne Hudson, James R. Hudson, and Paul E. Mott for critical readings and helpful suggestions on earlier versions of this paper.

2. John Walton, "Substance and Artifact: The Current Status of Research on Community Power Structure," *American Journal of Sociology*, 71 (January, 1966), 430–438; and "Discipline, Method and Community Power: A Note on the Sociology of Knowledge," *American Sociological Review*, 31 (October, 1966), 684–689. Also see his article in this reader and "Differential Patterns of Community Power Structure: An Explanation Based on Interdependence," in T. N. Clark (ed.), *Community Structure and Decision-Making: Comparative Analyses* (San Francisco: Chandler, 1968), pp. 441–459. The latter also appears in *Sociological Quarterly*, 9 (Winter, 1968), 3–18.

3. Robert A. Dahl, *Who Governs?: Democracy and Power in an American City* (New Haven: Yale University Press, 1961).

4. Robert O. Schulze, "The Role of Economic Dominants in Community Power Structure," *American Sociological Review*, 23 (February, 1958), 3–9; "The Bifurcation of Power in a Satellite City," in Morris Janowitz (ed.), *Community Political Systems* (New York: Free Press, 1961), pp. 19–80.

5. Robert E. Agger, Daniel Goldrich, and Bert E. Swanson, *The Rulers and the Ruled: Political Power and Impotence in American Communities* (New York: Wiley, 1964).

6. Linton C. Freeman, *et al.* "Locating Leaders in Local Communities: A Comparison of Some Alternative Approaches," *American Sociological Review*, 28 (October, 1963), 791–798; Linton C. Freeman, *Patterns of Local Leadership* (Indianapolis: Bobbs-Merrill, 1968).

7. Compare Peter H. Rossi, "Power and Community Structure," *Midwest Journal of Political Science*, 4 (November, 1960), 390–401; David Rogers, "Community Political Systems: A Framework and Hypothesis for Comparative Studies," in Bert E. Swanson

† Robert A. Gordon, *Business Leadership in the Large Corporation* (Washington, D.C.: The Brookings Institution, 1945), pp. 143–146.

(ed.), *Current Trends in Comparative Community Studies* (Kansas City, Mo.: Community Studies, Inc., 1962), pp. 31–48; and Terry N. Clark, "Power and Community Structure: Who Governs, Where and When? *Sociological Quarterly*, 8 (Summer, 1967), 291–316. Also see Paul E. Mott, "Configurations of Power," in this volume.

8. M. Herbert Dangzer, "Civil Rights Conflict and Community Power Structure" (Unpublished Ph.D. dissertation, Columbia University, 1968); Claire W. Gilbert, "Some Trends in Community Politics: A Secondary Analysis of Power Structure Data from 166 Communities," *Southwestern Social Science Quarterly*, 48 (December, 1967), 373–381; Gilbert, "Community Power and Decision-Making: A Quantitative Examination of Previous Research," in Clark (ed.), *op. cit.*, pp. 139–156; Gilbert, "The Study of Community Power: A Summary and a Test," in Scott Greer, *et al.* (eds.), *The New Urbanization* (New York: St. Martin's Press, 1968), pp. 222–245; Terry N. Clark, William Kornblum, Harold Bloom, and Susan Tobias, "Discipline, Method, Community Structure, and Decision-Making: The Role and Limitations of the Sociology of Knowledge," *American Sociologist*, 3 (August, 1968), 214–217.

9. C. Wright Mills and Melville J. Ulmer, *Small Business and Civic Welfare*, Report of the Smaller War Plants Corporation to the Special Committee to Study Problems of American Small Business, U.S. Senate, 79th Congress, 2nd Session, Document Number 135 (Washington, D.C.: Government Printing Office, 1946); Irving A. Fowler, *Local Industrial Structures, Economic Power, and Community Welfare* (Totowa, N.J.: Bedminster Press, 1964; Fowler, "Local Industrial Structures, Economic Power, and Community Welfare," *Social Forces*, 6 (Summer, 1958), 41–51; Amos H. Hawley, "Community Power and Urban Renewal Success," *American Journal of Sociology*, 68 (January, 1963), 513–526; and Edgar W. Butler and Hallowell Pope, "Community Power Structures, Industrialization, and Public Welfare Programs," paper read at the sixty-first annual meeting of the American Sociological Association, Miami, Florida, August, 1966.

10. Delbert C. Miller, "Democracy and Decision-Making in the Community Power Structure," in William V. D'Antonio and Howard J. Ehrlich (eds.), *Power and Democracy in America* (Notre Dame: University of Notre Dame Press, 1961), pp. 62 ff.

11. Rossi, *op. cit.*, p. 398.

12. Dahl, *op. cit.*, pp. 184–189. Also see Mott, *op. cit.*

13. See William V. D'Antonio and William H. Form, *Influentials in Two Border Cities* (Notre Dame: University of Notre Dame Press, 1965), pp. 229–230, for a comparison of these three schemes.

14. Walton, "A Systematic Survey of Community Power Research," in this volume.

15. *Ibid.* All communities not in the United States (C. Juarez, Tia Juana, English City), communities of 1,000 or less population (Springdale), and all units that were not communities (Midway County, River County, Beach County, and Southern County) were omitted. Twice studied communities (Community A, Regional City, Seattle, and Syracuse) were included only once. Only studies that have been published since 1950 are included. As a matter of interest, only two studies, those of Easterntown by A. M. Rose and Lorain by J. B. McKee, were published prior to F. Hunter's study of Regional City. By limiting the cities included in the analysis to post-1950 studies, the effect of historical shifts in community structure as well as variations in the lexicon and interests of the researchers are hopefully minimized, though obviously not removed.

16. Walton, "Substance and Artifact," *op. cit.* One could argue that only the first three categories form a scale and that "amorphous" is a totally different dimension. Such an approach would suggest renaming these categories as follows:

   Pyramidal: Structured centralist
   Factional: Structured factionalist
   Coalitional: Structured coalitional
   Amorphous: Unstructured

   "Amorphous" may be a poor label for the last category. For the purpose of this study, the few cities categorized as having "amorphous" power structures should be considered simply as having more dispersed configurations of power than cities that are categorized as "coalitional."

17. Daniel Suits, "Use of Dummy Variables in Regression Equations," *Journal of the American Statistical Association*, 52 (December, 1957), 548–551.

18. Arthur S. Goldberger, *Econometric Theory* (New York: Wiley, 1964), p. 249.

19. Fowler, *Local Industrial Structures, op. cit.*

20. Walton, "Discipline, Method and Community Power," *op. cit.* Compare Gilbert, "The Study of Community Power," *op. cit.*; and Terry Clark, *et al.*, "Discipline, Method, Community Structure, and Decision-Making," *op. cit.*, who use Gilbert's data in their study and come to a different conclusion from that of Walton as well as the finding

here. It is difficult to determine just why this is true, but it should be noted that Gilbert included many more communities than either Walton or the study here, some of which were published prior to 1950.

21. Walton, "Discipline, Method and Community Power," *op. cit.*; "Substance and Artifact," *op. cit.*; "Differential Patterns of Community Power Structure," *op. cit.*; and "A Systematic Survey of Community Power Research," in this volume.

22. Gilbert, "Some Trends in Community Politics," *op. cit.*; "Community Power and Decision-Making," *op. cit.*; and "The Study of Community Power," *op. cit.*

23. Rogers, *op. cit.*, p. 39.

24. *Ibid.*; Marshall N. Goldstein, "Absentee Ownership and Monolithic Power Structures: Two Questions for Community Studies," in Swanson (ed.) *op. cit.*, pp. 49–59; Schulze, "The Bifurcation of Power," *op. cit.*; W. Lloyd Warner, *The Social System of the Modern Factory* (New Haven: Yale University Press, 1947); Walton, "Differential Patterns of Community Power Structure," *op. cit.*; M. Kent Jennings, *Community Influentials: The Elites of Atlanta* (New York: Free Press, 1964); Donald A. Clelland and William H. Form, "Economic Dominants and Community Power: A Comparative Analysis," *American Journal of Sociology*, 69 (March, 1964), 511–521; Ted. C. Smith, "The Structuring of Power in a Suburban Community," *Pacific Sociological Review*, 3 (Fall, 1960), 83–88; Robert Mills French, "Cornucopia in Transition" (Unpublished Ph.D. dissertation, University of Wisconsin, 1967); Mills and Ulmer, *op. cit.* Not all studies agree with this observation, however. See Roland J. Pellegrin and Charles H. Coates, "Absentee-Owned Corporations and Community Power Structure," *American Journal of Sociology*, 61 (March, 1956), 413–419. Paul E. Mott, "The Role of the Absentee-Owned Corporation in the Changing Community," in this volume, also has some qualifications about this observation.

25. Rogers, *op. cit.*

26. Compare *ibid.*; Schulze, "The Bifurcation of Power," *op. cit.*

27. French, "Economic Change and Community Power Structure: Cornucopia in Transition," in this volume. The details of his study can be found in "Cornucopia in Transition," *op. cit.*

28. Compare Mills and Ulmer, *op. cit.*, pp. 22–31. Also see Fowler, *Local Industrial Structures, op. cit.*, 145–146, who used the degree of concentration of employment as one of his empirical indicators of monolithic power structures.

29. Compare Rogers, *op. cit.*; and Fowler, *Local Industrial Structures, op. cit.*, pp. 145–146. Fowler also uses the degree of industrial unionism as a measure of pluralism.

30. James B. McKee, "Status and Power in the Industrial Community: A Comment on Drucker's Thesis," *American Journal of Sociology*, 58 (January, 1953), 364–370; Warner Bloomberg, Jr., "The Power Structure of an Industrial Community" (Unpublished Ph.D. dissertation, University of Chicago, 1961); and James R. Hudson, "Power With Low Prestige: A Study of Labor Unions in a Dependent Community" (Unpublished Ph.D. dissertation, University of Michigan, 1966).

31. Edward C. Banfield and James Q. Wilson, *City Politics* (Cambridge: Harvard University Press, 1965), pp. 138–150.

32. John H. Kessel, "Governmental Structure and Political Environment: A Statistical Note about American Cities," *American Political Science Review*, 56 (September, 1962), 615–620; Phillips Cutwright, "Nonpartisan Electoral Systems in American Cities," *Comparative Studies in Society and History*, 5 (January, 1963), 212–226; Robert R. Alford and Harry M. Scoble, "Political and Socioeconomic Characteristics of American Cities," *1965 Municipal Year Book* (Washington, D.C.: International City Managers' Association, 1965), pp. 82–97; and Leo F. Schnore and Robert R. Alford, "Forms of Government and Socioeconomic Characteristics of Suburbs," *Administrative Science Quarterly*, 8 (June, 1963), 1–17.

33. Banfield and Wilson, *op. cit.*

34. There is support for this contention in the works of both McKee, *op. cit.*, and Rossi, *op. cit.*

35. Hawley, *op. cit.* Hawley called this the "MPO Ratio," but we have transposed the letters to reflect the listing of these categories by the Bureau of the Census.

36. Compare Bruce C. Straits, "Community Adoption and Implementation of Urban Renewal," *American Journal of Sociology*, 71 (July, 1965), 77–82.

37. Hawley found that the higher the MOP Ratio (which he interpreted to mean diffusion of community power), the less the urban renewal success. We also find that the higher the MOP Ratio, the lower the degree of urban renewal success, measuring urban renewal success by the per capita urban renewal dollars reserved for the city. Among the twenty-six eligible cities in Subset A the correlation coefficient is −.62 (the relationship among the 358 cities in the universe of cities is −.34). While we find the same direction of relationship as Hawley between the MOP Ratio and our measure of urban

renewal success, the interpretation is different. The relationship between type of power structure, MOP Ratio, and urban renewal success can be more easily visualized with the following illustration:

High MOP Ratio $-.62^c$ Urban Renewal
(diffusion of   Success (high dollars
power for   per capita reserved
Hawley) $\longrightarrow$ for urban renewal)
                              (natural logarithm)

            $+.42^b$ $-.34^a$

                Presence of a
                Pyramidal Power
                Structure

If the number of years it took the city to enter the urban renewal program after 1951 is substituted as the measure of urban renewal success, the results are similar, although the magnitudes of the relationships are attenuated. While our empirical findings about the relationship between the MOP Ratio and urban renewal success are similar to Hawley's, our interpretation of these findings is just the opposite of his.

38. Compare Straits, *op. cit.*, p. 78. My own examination of Hawley's data confirms Straits' assertion that Hawley's measure was the entire MOP category.

39. Compare Thomas J. Anton, "Power, Pluralism and Local Politics," *Administrative Science Quarterly*, 7 (March, 1963), 425–457. Anton argues that differences in basic assumptions of the disciplines also accounts for many of the differences in methods and findings.

40. Ivan Belknap and John Steinle, *The Community and Its Hospital: A Comparative Analysis* (Syracuse: Syracuse University Press, 1963).

41. See, for example, Herbert Gans, *The Urban Villagers* (New York: Free Press, 1962), pp. 305–335; Martin Anderson, *The Federal Bulldozer: A Critical Analysis of Urban Renewal, 1949–1962* (Cambridge: M.I.T. Press, 1964); and Scott Greer, *Urban Renewal and American Cities* (Indianapolis: Bobbs-Merrill, 1965). Of course, there are those who have taken issue with the views of both Gans and Anderson: see George M. Raymond and Malcolm D. Rivkin, "Urban Renewal: Controversy," in Jewel Bellush and Murray Hausknecht (eds.), *Urban Renewal: People, Politics, and Planning* (Garden City, N.Y.: Doubleday, 1967), pp. 484–491. For a more orthodox defense of urban renewal, see Robert Weaver, *The Urban Complex: Human Values in Urban Life* (Garden City, N.Y.: Doubleday, 1964).

42. For a discussion of some of the problems and attainments of the urban renewal program in several different cities, see Peter H. Rossi and Robert A. Dentler, *The Politics of Urban Renewal* (New York: Free Press, 1961; and Harold Kaplan, *Urban Renewal Politics: Slum Clearance in Newark* (New York: Columbia University Press, 1963).

43. The study of William A. Gamson, "Reputation and Resources in Community Politics," *American Journal of Sociology*, 72 (September, 1966), 121–131, is relevant to this point. Gamson found that if the reputational leaders of a community acted in concert on a given issue, they usually had their way. If they were split, however, then it was more likely that the effort to alter the status quo would fail. Thus, the degree of cohesion as well as the value commitments about given issues is important for predicting issue outcomes.

44. Compare Jerald Hage and Michael Aiken, "Program Change and Organizational Properties: A Comparative Analysis," *American Journal of Sociology*, 72 (March, 1967, 503–519; and James Q. Wilson, "Innovation in Organization: Notes Toward a Theory," in James D. Thompson (ed.), *Approaches to Organizational Design* (Pittsburgh: University of Pittsburgh Press, 1966), pp. 193–218.

45. For an historical account of the history of public housing programs in the United States, including the low-rent housing program discussed here, see Jewel Bellush and Murray Hausknecht, "Urban Renewal: An Historical Overview," in Bellush and Hausknecht (eds.), *op. cit.*, pp. 3–16. They have some pessimistic words to say about the effectiveness of housing programs in helping the poor, however. See their "Public Housing: The Context of Failure," *op. cit.* pp. 451–464. Also see Michael Aiken and Robert R. Alford, "Community Structure and Innovation: The Case of Public Housing" *American Political Science Review*, 64 (September, 1970), for a more detailed discussion of this program.

46. Aiken and Alford, *ibid.*, provide greater details about the various stages in the "conventional bid method."

47. If the variable of proportion of older housing, i.e., the proportion built prior to 1930, is partialled out, the correlation coefficient between the degree of diffusion of power and urban renewal dollars is reduced to .15. On the other hand, it seems that the same historical processes were probably responsible for the older cities having more diffused

$^aP < .10$ $^bP < .05$ $^cP < .001$

power structures. Thus, the relationship between type of power structure and urban renewal success is not necessarily spurious.

48. Sargent Shriver, Director of the OEO, announced the first 120 projects on November 24, 1964. During the first two years of the program, a total of approximately $2.6 billion was appropriated by Congress, $.8 billion during fiscal 1965 and $1.8 billion during fiscal 1966. The bill creating the OEO permitted the governor of a state to veto Job Corps camps in his state and those antipoverty projects contracted between the federal government and a *private* agency. The following year, however, the Director of OEO was given the authority to override any veto by a governor. Thus, the state government had little opportunity to affect decisions made in a local community. Job Corps allocations were eliminated from this study since they reflect government initiative rather than initiative by the local community.

49. This procedure was not entirely satisfactory. While the distribution of poverty dollars per capita was highly skewed to the right, the natural logarithm resulted in a distribution skewed to the left for these thirty-one cities. The skewness to the left was less among the 423 cities discussed in the next section. The natural logarithm transformation resulted in slightly higher correlation coefficients with the diffusion of community power variables than did the actual per capita dollar measure.

50. See "Model Cities Program Draws Applications from 193 Cities and Counties," *Journal of Housing*, 24 (April, 1967), 196–198; and "First Model Cities Grant Recipients Named," *Journal of Housing*, 24 (November, 1967), 547–549, for a description of the program, first round applicants, and first round winners.

Selected Bibliography

Articles and Books

ABRAMSON, E., *et al.* "Social Power and Commitment: A Theoretical Statement," *American Sociological Review,* 23 (February 1958), 15–22.

ABU-LABAN, BAHA. "Leader Visibility in a Local Community," *Pacific Sociological Review,* 4 (Fall 1961), 73–78.

————. "Social Origins and Occupational Career Patterns of Community Leaders," *Sociological Inquiry,* 33 (Spring 1963). 131–140.

————. "Self-Conception and Appraisal by Others: A Study of Community Leaders " *Sociology and Social Research,* 48 (October 1963), 32–37.

————. "The Reputational Approach in the Study of Community Power: A Critical Evaluation," *Pacific Sociological Review,* 8 (Spring 1965), 35–42.

ADRIAN, CHARLES R. "Leadership and Decision-Making in Manager Cities: A Study of Three Communities," *Public Administration Review,* 18 (Summer 1958), 208–213.

————, and Oliver P. Williams. *Four Cities: A Study in Comparative Policy Making.* Philadelphia: University of Pennsylvania Press, 1963.

AGGER, ROBERT. "Power Attributions in the Local Community: Theoretical and Research Considerations," *Social Forces,* 34 (May 1956), 322–331.

————, and DANIEL GOLDRICH. "Community Power Structure and Partisanship," *American Sociological Review,* 23 (August 1958), 383–392.

————, DANIEL GOLDRICH, and BERT E. SWANSON. *The Rulers and the Ruled: Political Power and Impotence in American Communities.* New York: Wiley, 1964.

————, and VINCENT OSTROM. "The Political Structure of a Small Community," *Public Opinion Quarterly,* 20 (Spring 1956), 81–89.

————, and VINCENT OSTROM. "Political Participation in a Small Community," in Heinz Eulau, *et al.* (eds.), *Political Behavior.* New York: Free Press, 1957.

————, BERT E. SWANSON, DANIEL GOLDRICH, and MARSHALL N. GOLDSTEIN. "Political Influence Structures: Some Theoretical and Empirical Considerations," in Bert E. Swanson (ed.), *Current Trends in Comparative Community Studies.* Kansas City, Mo.: Community Studies, Inc., 1962.

AIKEN, MICHAEL. "The Distribution of Community Power: Structural Bases and Social Consequences," in this volume, 1970.

ANTON, THOMAS J. "Power, Pluralism, and Local Politics," *Administrative Science Quarterly,* 7 (March 1963), 425–457.

BACHRACH, PETER, and MORTON S. BARATZ. "Two Faces of Power," *American Political Science Review,* 56 (December 1962), 947–952.

————, and MORTON S. BARATZ. "Decisions and Nondecisions: An Analytical Framework," *American Political Science Review,* 57 (September 1963), 632–642.

BAILEY, N. A. "Local and Community Power in Angola," *Western Political Quarterly,* 21 (September 1968), 400–408.

BALTZELL, E. D. *Philadelphia Gentlemen.* New York: Free Press, 1958.

BANFIELD, EDWARD C. *Political Influence.* New York: Free Press, 1961.

————. *Big City Politics.* New York: Random House, 1965.

————, and JAMES Q. WILSON. *City Politics.* Cambridge, Mass. Harvard, 1963.

BARTH, ERNEST A. T. "Community Influence Systems: Structure and Change," *Social Forces,* 40 (October 1961), 58–63.

————, and BAHA ABU-LABAN. "Power Structure and the Negro Sub-Community," *American Sociological Review,* 24 (February 1959), 69–76.

527

————, and STUART D. JOHNSON. "Community Power and a Typology of Social Issues," *Social Forces*, 38, (October 1959), 29–32.

BELKNAP, GEORGE, and JOHN H. BUNZEL. "The Trade Union in the Political Community," *PROD*, 2 (September 1958), 3–6.

————, and RALPH SMUCKLER. "Political Power Relations in A Mid-West City," *Public Opinion Quarterly*, 20 (Spring 1956), 73–81.

BELKNAP, IVAN, and JOHN G. STEINLE. *The Community and Its Hospitals: A Comparative Analysis*. Syracuse: University of Syracuse Press, 1963.

BELL, DANIEL. "The Power Elite-Reconsidered," *The American Journal of Sociology*, 64 (November 1958), 238–250.

BELL, WENDELL, RICHARD J. HILL, and CHARLES R. WRIGHT. *Public Leadership*. San Francisco: Chandler, 1961.

BENSMAN, JOSEPH, and ARTHUR J. VIDICH. "Power Cliques in Bureaucratic Society," *Social Research*, 29 (Winter 1962), 467–474.

BIERSTEDT, ROBERT. "An Analysis of Social Power," *American Sociological Review*, 15 (December 1950), 730–738.

BLACKWELL, GORDON W. "A Theoretical Framework for Sociological Research in Community Organization," *Social Forces*, 33 (October 1954), 57–64.

————. "Community Analysis," in Roland Young (ed.), *Approaches to the Study o, Politics*. Evanston: Northwestern University Press, 1958.

BLANKENSHIP, L. VAUGHN. "Community Power and Decision-Making: A Comparative Evaluation of Measurement Techniques," *Social Forces*, 43 (December 1964), 207–216.

BLOOMBERG, WARNER JR., and MORRIS SUNSHINE. *Suburban Power Structures and Public Education*. Syracuse: Syracuse University Press, 1963.

BOEK, WALTER. "Field Techniques in Delineating the Structure of Community Leadership," *Human Organization*, 24 (Winter 1965), 358–364.

BONJEAN, CHARLES M. "Community Leadership: A Case Study and Conceptual Refinement," *American Journal of Sociology*, 68 (May 1963), 672–681.

————. "Class, Status, and Power Reputation, *Sociology and Social Research*, 49 (October 1964), 69–75.

————, and LEWIS F. CARTER. "Legitimacy and Visibility: Leadership Structures Related to Four Community Systems," *Pacific Sociological Review*, 8 (Spring 1965), 16–20.

————, and DAVID M. OLSON. "Community Leadership: Directions of Research," *Administrative Science Quarterly*, 9 (December 1964), 278–300.

BOOTH, DAVID A., and CHARLES R. ADRIAN. "Simplifying the Discovery of Elites," *American Behavioral Scientist*, 5, 2 (October 1961).

————. "Power Structures and Community Change," *Midwest Journal of Political Science*, 6 (August 1962), 277–296.

————. "Elections and Community Power," *Journal of Politics*, 25 (February 1963), 107–118.

BOUMA, D. H. "Legitimation of the Social Power Position of a Real Estate Board," *American Journal of Economics and Sociology*, 21 (October 1962), 383–392.

BRADLEY, DONALD S., and MAYER N. ZALD. "From Commercial Elite to Political Administrator: The Recruitment of the Mayors of Chicago," *American Journal of Sociology*, 71 (September 1965), 153–167.

BRAMS, STEVEN J. "Measuring the Concentration of Power in Political Systems," *American Political Science Review*, 62 (June 1968), 461–475.

BRESSLER, MARVIN, and CHARLES F. WESTOFF. "Leadership and Social Change: The Reactions of a Special Group to Industrialization and Population Influx," *Social Forces*, 32 (March 1954), 235–243.

BURGESS, M. ELAINE. *Negro Leadership in a Southern City*. Chapel Hill: University of North Carolina Press, 1960.

BUTLER, JAY. "On Power and Authority: An Exchange on Concept," *American Sociological Review*, 25 (October 1960), 731–732.

CARNEY, FRANCIS M. "The Decentralized Politics of Los Angeles," *The Annals of the American Academy of Political and Social Science*, 353 (May 1964), 107–121.

CLARK, TERRY N. "Power and Community Structure: Who Governs, Where and When?" *Sociological Quarterly*, 8 (Summer 1967), 291–316.

————. "The Concept of Power: Some Overemphasized and Underrecognized Dimensions: An Examination with Special Reference to the Local Community," *Southwestern Social Science Quarterly*, 48 (December 1967), 271–286.

————. "Community Structure, Decision-Making, Budget Expenditures, and Urban Renewal in 51 American Communities,"

American Sociological Review, 33 (August 1968), 576–593.

——— (ed.). *Community Structure and Decision-Making: Comparative Analyses.* San Francisco: Chandler, 1968.

———, WILLIAM KORNBLAUM, HAROLD BLOOM, and SUSAN TOBIAS. "Discipline, Method, Community Structure, and Decision-Making: The Role and Limitations of the Sociology of Knowledge," *American Sociologist,* 3 (August 1968), 214–217.

CLELLAND, DONALD A., and WILLIAM H. FORM. "Economic Dominants and Community Power: A Comparative Analysis," *American Journal of Sociology,* 69 (March 1964), 511–521.

COLCORD, FRANK C., JR. "Decision-Making and Transportation Policy: A Comparative Analysis," *Southwestern Social Science Quarterly,* 48 (December 1968), 383–397.

DAHL, ROBERT A. "Hierarchy, Democracy and Bargaining in Politics and Economics," in *Research Frontiers in Politics and Government.* Washington, D.C.: Brookings, 1955.

———. "The Concept of Power," *Behavioral Science,* 2 (July 1957), 201–214.

———. "A Critique of Ruling Elite Model," *The American Political Science Review,* 52 (June 1958), 463–469.

———. "Equality and Power in American Society," in William V. D'Antonio and Howard J. Ehrlich (eds.), *Power and Democracy in America.* Notre Dame: University of Notre Dame Press, 1961.

———. *Who Governs? Democracy and Power in an American City.* New Haven: Yale University Press, 1961.

DAKIN, RALPH E. "Power Structures and Organizing Efficiency: A Comparative Study of Four Areas," *Sociological Quarterly,* 3 (July 1962), 228–250.

DALAND, ROBERT T. *Dixie City: A Portrait of Political Leadership.* Birmingham: University of Alabama, Bureau of Public Administration, 1956.

———. "Political Science and the Study of Urbanism," *American Political Science Review,* 51 (June 1957), 491–509.

D'ANTONIO, WILLIAM V., HOWARD J. EHRLICH, and EUGENE C. ERICKSON. "Further Notes on the Study of Community Power," *American Sociological Review,* 27 (December 1962), 848–853.

———, and EUGENE C. ERICKSON. "The Reputational Technique as a Measure of Community Power: An Evaluation Based on

Comparative and Longitudinal Studies," *American Sociological Review,* 27 (June 1962), 362–376.

———, and WILLIAM H. FORM. *Influentials in Two Border Cities: A Study in Community Decision-Making.* Notre Dame: University of Notre-Dame Press, 1965.

———, WILLIAM H. FORM, CHARLES P. LOOMIS, and EUGENE C. ERICKSON. "Institutional and Occupational Representations in Eleven Community Influence Systems," *American Sociological Review,* 26 (June 1961), 440–446.

DANZGER, M. HERBERT. "Community Power Structure: Problems and Continuities," *American Sociological Review,* 29 (October 1964), 707–717.

———. "A Quantified Description of Community Conflict," *American Behavioral Scientist,* 12 (November-December 1968), 9–14.

DAVIS, ALLISON, BURLEIGH B. GARDNER, and MARY R. GARDNER. *Deep South: A Social Anthropological Study of Caste and Class.* Chicago: University of Chicago Press, 1941.

DEVEREUX, E. C., JR. "Community Participation and Leadership," in J. Harding *et al.* (eds.), "Leadership and Participation in a Changing Rural Community," *Journal of Social Issues,* 16 (1960), 29–84.

DICK, HARRY, R. "A Method for Ranking Community Influentials," *American Sociological Review,* 25 (June 1960), 395–399.

DYE, T. R. "Popular Images of Decision-Making in Suburban Communities," *Sociology and Social Research,* 47 (October 1962), 75–83.

EDWARDS, HAROLD T. "Power Structure and Its Communications Behavior in San Jose, Costa Rica," *Journal of Inter-American Studies,* 9 (April 1967), 236–247.

EHRLICH, HOWARD J. "The Reputational Approach to the Study of Community Power," *American Sociological Review,* 26 (December 1961), 926–927.

———, and M. L. BAUER. "Newspaper Citation and Reputation for Community Leadership," *American Sociological Review,* 30 (June 1965), 411–415.

FANELLI, ALEXANDER. "A Typology of Community Leadership Based on Influence and Interaction Within the Leader Sub-System," *Social Forces,* 34 (May 1956), 332–338.

FISHER, SETHARD. "Community Power Studies: A Critique," *Social Research,* 29 (Winter 1964), 449–466.

FORM, WILLIAM H. "Organized Labor's Place in the Community Power Structure," *Industrial and Labor Relations Review*, 12 (July 1959), 526–539.

———, and WILLIAM V. D'ANTONIO. "Integration and Cleavage Among Community Influentials in Two Border Cities," *American Sociological Review*, 24 (December 1959), 804–814.

———, and DELBERT C. MILLER. *Industry, Labor, and Community*. New York: Harper & Row, 1960.

———, and WARREN L. SAUER. *Community Influentials in a Middle Sized City*. East Lansing, Mich.: Institute for Community Development, 1960.

———, and WARREN L. SAUER. "Organized Labor's Image of Community Power Structure," *Social Forces*, 38 (May 1960), 332–341.

———, and WARREN L. SAUER. "Labor and Community Influentials: A Comparative Study of Participation and Imagery," *Industrial and Labor Relations Review*, 17 (October 1963), 3–19.

FOSKETT, JOHN M., and RAYMOND HOHLE. "The Measurement of Influence in Community Affairs," *Research Studies of the State College of Washington*, 25 (June 1957), 148–154.

FOWLER, IRVING A. "Local Industrial Structures, Economic Power, and Community Welfare," *Social Problems*, 6 (Summer 1958), 41–51.

———. *Local Industrial Structures, Economic Power, and Community Welfare: Thirty Small New York State Cities 1930–1950*. Totowa, N.J.: Bedminster Press, 1964.

FREEMAN, CHARLES, and SELZ C. MAYO. "Decision-Makers in Rural Community Action," *Social Forces*, 35 (May 1957), 319–322.

FREEMAN, LINTON C. *Patterns of Local Community Leadership*. Indianapolis: Bobbs-Merrill, 1968.

———, et al. *Local Community Leadership*. Syracuse: University of Syracuse Press, 1960.

———, et al. "Metropolitan Decision Making" in *Publications Committee of University College*. Syracuse: University of Syracuse Press, 1962.

———, THOMAS J. FARARO, WARNER BLOOMBERG, JR., and MORRIS H. O. SUNSHINE. "Locating Leaders in Local Communities: A Comparison of Some Alternative Approaches," *American Sociological Review*, 28 (October 1963), 791–798.

FRENCH, ROBERT MILLS. "Change Comes to Cornucopia—Industry and the Community,"

in Robert Mills French (ed.) *The Community: A Comparative Perspective*. Itasca, Ill.: F. E. Peacock, 1968.

———. "Economic Change and Community Power Structure: Transition in Cornucopia," in this volume, 1970.

———, and MICHAEL AIKEN. "Community Power in Cornucopia: A Replication in a Small Community of the Bonjean Technique of Identifying Community Leaders," *Sociological Quarterly*, 9 (Spring 1968), pp. 261–270.

GAMSON, WILLIAM A. "Community Issues and Their Outcome: How to Lose a Fluoridation Referendum," in Alvin W. Gouldner and S. M. Miller (eds.), *Applied Sociology, Opportunities and Problems*. New York: Free Press, 1965.

———. "Rancorous Conflict in Community Politics," *American Sociological Review*, 31 (February 1966), 71–81.

———. "Reputation and Resources in Community Politics," *American Journal of Sociology*, 72 (September 1966), 121–131.

GILBERT, CLAIRE W. "Some Trends in Community Politics: A Secondary Analysis of Power Structure Data from 166 Communities," *Southwestern Social Science Quarterly*, 48 (December 1967), 373–381.

———. "The Study of Community Power: A Summary and a Test," in Scott Greer, *et al.* (eds.), *The New Urbanization*. New York: St. Martin's Press, 1968.

———. "Community Power and Decision-Making: A Quantitative Examination of Previous Research," in Terry N. Clark (ed.), *Community Structure and Decision-Making: Comparative Analysis*. San Francisco: Chandler, 1968, 139–156.

GOLDHAMMER, HERBERT, and EDWARD SHILS. "Types of Power and Status," *American Journal of Sociology*, 45 (September 1939), 171–182.

GOLDHAMMER, KEITH. "Community Power Structure and School Board Membership," *American School Board Journal*, 140 (March 1955), 23–25.

GOLDSTEIN, MARSHALL N. "Absentee Ownership and Monolithic Power Structures: Two Questions for Community Studies," in Bert E. Swanson (ed.), *Current Trends in Comparative Community Studies*. Kansas ,City, Mo.: Community Studies, Inc., 1962.

GORE, WILLIAM J., and ROBERT L. PEABODY. "The Functions of the Political Campaign,"

Western Political Quarterly, 11 (March 1958), 55–70.

GREER, SCOTT. "The Social Structure and Political Process of Suburbia," *American Sociological Review,* 25 (August 1960), 514–526.

———. "Dilemmas of Action Research on the 'Metropolitan Problem,'" in Morris Janowitz (ed.), *Community Political Systems.* New York: Free Press, 1961.

———. *Metropolitics: A Study of Political Culture.* New York: Wiley, 1963.

HAER, JOHN L. "Social Stratification in Relation to Attitudes Toward Sources of Power in a Community," *Social Forces,* 35 (December 1956), 137–142.

HANSON, R. C. "Predicting a Community Decision: A Test of the Miller-Form Theory," *American Sociological Review,* 24 (October 1959), 662–671.

HAWLEY, AMOS. "Community Power and Urban Renewal Success," *American Journal of Sociology,* 68 (January 1963), 422–431.

HERSON, LAWRENCE J. R. "In the Footsteps of Community Power," *American Political Science Review,* 55 (December 1961), 817–830.

HUNTER, FLOYD. *Community Power Structure: A Study of Decision Makers.* Chapel Hill: University of North Carolina Press, 1953.

———. *Top Leadership, U.S.A.* Chapel Hill: University of North Carolina Press, 1959.

———, RUTH C. SCHAFFER, and CECIL G. SHEPS. *Community Organization: Action and Inaction.* Chapel Hill: University of North Carolina Press, 1956.

JACOB, HERBERT, and MICHAEL LIPSKY. "Outputs, Structure, and Power: An Assessment of Changes in the Study of State and Local Politics," *Journal of Politics,* 30 (May 1968), 510–538.

JACOB, PHILIP E., and JAMES V. TOSCANO (eds.). *The Integration of Political Communities.* Philadelphia and New York: Lippincott, 1964.

JANOWITZ, MORRIS. "Community Power Structure and 'Policy Science' Research," *Public Opinion Quarterly,* 26 (Fall 1962), 398–410.

———, (ed.). *Community Political Systems.* New York: Free Press, 1961.

JENNINGS, M. KENT. "Study of Community Decision-Making," in Bert E. Swanson (ed.), *Current Trends in Comparative Community Studies.* Kansas City, Mo.: Community Studies, Inc., 1962.

———. "Public Administrators and Community Decision Making," *Administrative Science Quarterly,* 8 (June 1963), 18–43.

———. *Community Influentials: The Elites of Atlanta.* New York: Free Press, 1964.

KAMMERER, GLADYS M. "Role Diversity of City Managers," *Administrative Science Quarterly,* 8 (December 1964), 421–442.

———, and J. M. DEGROVE. "Urban Leadership During Change," *The Annals of the American Academy of Political and Social Science,* 353 (May 1964), 95–106.

———, CHARLES D. FARRIS, JOHN M. DEGROVE, and ALFRED B. CLUBOK. *City Managers in Politics.* Gainesville: University of Florida Press, 1962.

———, CHARLES D. FARRIS, JOHN M. DEGROVE, and ALFRED B. CLUBOK. *The Urban Political Community: Profiles in Town Politics.* Boston: Houghton Mifflin, 1963.

KAMMEYER, KENNETH. "A Comparative Study of Decision Making in Rural Communities," *Rural Sociology,* 27 (September 1962), 294–302.

KAUFMAN, HERBERT, and VICTOR JONES. "The Mystery of Power," *Public Administration Review,* 14 (Summer 1954), 205–212.

KIMBALL, SOLON T., and MARION PEARSALL. *The Talladega Story.* Birmingham: University of Alabama Press, 1954.

———, and MARION PEARSALL. "Event Analysis as an Approach to Community Study," *Social Forces,* 34 (October 1955), 58–63.

KIMBROUGH, EMORY, JR. "The Role of the Banker in a Small City," *Social Forces,* 36 (May 1958), 316–322.

KIMBROUGH, RALPH B. *Political Power and Educational Decision Making.* Chicago: Rand McNally, 1964.

KLAPP, ORRIN, E. "Social Types: Process and Structure," *American Sociological Review,* 33 (December 1958), 674–680.

———, and L. VINCENT PADGETT. "Power Structure and Decision Making in a Mexican Border City," *American Journal of Sociology,* 65 (January 1960), 400–406.

KURODA, YASUMASA. "Psychological Aspects of Community Power Structure: Leaders and Rank-and-File Citizens in Reed Town, Japan," *Southwestern Social Science Quarterly,* 48 (December 1967), 433–442.

LONG, NORTON. "The Local Community as an Ecology of Games," *American Journal of Sociology,* 64 (November 1958), 251–261.

———. "The Corporation, Its Satellites and the Local Community," in E. S. Mason (ed.), *The Corporation in Modern Society.* Cambridge: Harvard University Press, 1959.

LOWRY, RITCHIE P. "Mediating Leadership and

Community Interaction," in Alvin W. Gouldner and S. M. Miller (eds.), *Applied Sociology: Opportunities and Problems*. New York: Free Press, 1965.

———. *Who's Running This Town?* New York: Harper & Row, 1965.

LYND, ROBERT S., and HELEN MERRELL LYND. *Middletown*. New York: Harcourt, Brace & World, 1929.

———, and HELEN MERRELL LYND. *Middletown in Transition*. New York: Harcourt, Brace & World, 1937.

McCLAIN, JACKSON M., and ROBERT HIGHSAW. *Dixie City Acts: A Study in Decision Making*. Birmingham: University of Alabama, Bureau of Public Administration, 1962.

McKEE, JAMES B. "Status and Power in the Industrial Community: A Comment on Drucker's Thesis," *American Journal of Sociology*, 58 (January 1953), 364–370.

———. "The Power to Decide," in Meyer Weinberg and Oscar Shabet (eds.), *Society and Man*. Englewood Cliffs, N.J.: Prentice-Hall, 1956.

MARCH, JAMES G. "An Introduction to the Theory and Measurement of Influence," *American Political Science Review*, 49 (June 1955), 431–451.

MARTIN, ROSCOE C. *Government and the Suburban School*. ("The Economics and Politics of Public Education, 2.") Syracuse: Syracuse University Press, 1963.

———, FRANK J. MUNGER, *et al. Decisions in Syracuse: A Metropolitan Action Study*. Bloomington: University of Indiana Press, 1961.

MAYER, KURT B. *Class and Society*. New York: Random House, 1955.

MERELMAN, RICHARD M. "On the Neo-Elite Critique of Community Power," *American Political Science Review*, 62 (June 1968), 451–460.

MERTON, ROBERT K. "Patterns of Influence: Local and Cosmopolitan Influentials," in *Social Theory and Social Structure*. New York: Free Press, 1957.

MEYERSON, MARTIN, and EDWARD C. BANFIELD. *Politics, Planning and the Public Interest*. New York: Free Press, 1955.

MICHEL, JERRY B. "The Measurement of Social Power on the Community Level: An Exploratory Study," *American Journal of Economics and Sociology*, 23 (April 1964), 189–196.

MILLER, DELBERT C. "The Seattle Business Leader," *Pacific Northwest Business*, 15 (February 1956), 5–12.

———. "The Prediction of Issue Outcome in Community Decision Making," *Proceedings of the Pacific Sociological Society*, Research Studies of the State College of Washington, 25 (June 1957), 137–147.

———. "Industry and Community Power Structure: A Comparative Study of an American and an English City," *American Sociological Review*, 23 (February 1958), 9–15.

———. "Decision-Making Cliques in Community Power Structures: A Comparative Study of an American and an English City," *American Journal of Sociology*, 64 (November 1958), 299–310.

———. "Town and Gown: The Power Structure of a University Town," *American Journal of Sociology*, 68 (January 1963), 432–443.

———. "Community Power Perspectives and Role Definitions of North American Executives in an Argentine Community," *Administrative Science Quarterly*, 10 (December 1965), 364–380.

———, and JAMES L. DIRKSEN. "The Identification of Visible, Concealed, and Symbolic Leaders in a Small Indiana City: A Replication of the Bonjean-Noland Study of Burlington, North Carolina," *Social Forces*, 43 (May 1965), 548–555.

MILLER, N. "The Jewish Leadership in Lakeport" in A. W. Gouldner (ed.), *Studies in Leadership and Democratic Action*. New York: Harper & Row, 1950.

MILLER, PAUL A. "The Process of Decision-Making within the Context of Community Organization," *Rural Sociology*, 17 (1952), 153–161.

———. *Community Health Action*. East Lansing: Michigan State College Press, 1953.

MILLS, C. WRIGHT, and MELVILLE J. ULMER. *Small Business and Civic Welfare*. Report of the Small War Plants Corporation to the Special Committee to Study Problems of American Small Business. U.S. Senate, 79th Congress, 2d Session, Document Number 135. Serial No. 11036. Washington, D.C.: Government Printing Office, 1946.

MINAR, DAVID W. "The Community Basis of Conflict in School System Politics," *American Sociological Review*, 31 (December 1966), 822–835.

MOTT, PAUL E. "The Role of the Absentee-Owned Corporation in the Changing Community," in this volume, 1970.

———. "Configurations of Power," in this volume, 1970.

———. "Power, Authority, and Influence," in this volume, 1970.

NIX, HAROLD L., JENNIE MCINTYRE, and CHARLES J. DUDLEY. "Bases of Leadership: The Cultural Ideal and Estimates of Reality," *Southwestern Social Science Quarterly*, 48 (December 1967), 423–432.

NORRIS, T. L. "Decision-Making Activity Sequences in a Hacienda Community," *Human Organizations*, 12, 3 (1953).

NUTTALL, RONALD L., ERWIN L. SCHEUCH, and CHAD GORDON. "On the Structure of Influence," in Terry N. Clark (ed.),*: Community Structure and Decision-Making Comparative Analyses*. San Francisco: Chandler, 1968.

OGDEN, JEAN. *Small Communities in Action.* New York: Harper & Row, 1946.

OLMSTED, DONALD W. "Organizational Leadership and Social Structure in a Small City," *American Sociological Review,* 19 (June 1954), 273–281.

OTTENBERG, S. "Leadership and Change in a Coastal Georgia Negro Community," *Phylon,* 20 (March 1959), 7–18.

PARENTON, V. J., and ROLAND J. PELLEGRIN. "Social Structure and the Leadership Factor in a Negro Community in South Louisiana," *Phylon,* 17 (March 1956), 74–78.

PARKER, JAMES H. "Moral Leadership in the Community," *Sociology and Social Research,* 53 (October 1968), 88–94.

PARSONS, TALCOTT. "The Distribution of Power in American Society," *World Politics,* 10 (October 1957), 123–143.

PARTRIDGE, P. H. "Some Notes on the Concept of Power," *Political Studies,* 11 (June 1962), 107–125.

PELLEGRIN, ROLAND J., and CHARLES H. COATES. "Absentee-Owned Corporations and Community Power Structure," *American Journal of Sociology*, 61 (March 1956), 413–419.

PFAUTZ, HAROLD W. "The Power Structure of the Negro Sub-Community: A Case and a Comparative View," *Phylon,* 23 (Summer 1962), 156–166.

PINARD, MAURICE. "Structural Attachments and Political Support in Urban Politics: The Case of Fluoridation Referendums," *American Journal of Sociology*, 68 (March 1962), 513–526.

POPE, LISTON. *Millhands and Preachers.* New Haven: Yale University Press, 1942.

POLSBY, NELSON W. "The Sociology of Community Power: A Reassessment," *Social Forces,* 37 (March 1959), 232–236.

———. "Three Problems in the Analysis of Community Power," *American Sociological Review,* 24 (December 1959), 796–803.

———. "How to Study Community Power: The Pluralist Alternative," *Journal of Politics,* 22 (August 1960), 474–484.

———. "Power in Middletown: Fact and Value in Community Research," *Canadian Journal of Economics and Political Science,* 26 (November 1960), 592–603.

———. "Community Power: Some Reflections on the Recent Literature," *American Sociological Review,* 27 (December 1962), 838–840.

———. *Community Power and Political Theory.* New Haven: Yale University Press, 1963.

PRESENT, PHILLIP EDWARD. "Defense Contracting and Community Leadership: A Comparative Analysis," *Southwestern Social Science Quarterly,* 48 (December 1967), 399–410.

PRESS, CHARLES. *Main Street Politics: Policy Making at the Local Level.* East Lansing, Mich. Institute for Community Development, 1962.

PRESTHUS, ROBERT. *Men at the Top: A Study in Community Power.* New York: Oxford University Press, 1964.

PRICE, H. D. "Review of *Who Governs? Democracy and Power in an American Community*," *Yale Law Journal,* 71 (July 1962), 1589–1596.

ROGERS, DAVID. "Community Political Systems: A Framework and Hypothesis for Comparative Studies," in Bert E. Swanson (ed.), *Current Trends in Comparative Community Studies.* Kansas City, Mo: Community. Studies, Inc., 1962, pp. 31–48.

ROGERS, E. M., and D. G. CARTANO. "Methods of Measuring Opinion Leadership," *Public Opinion Quarterly,* 26 (Fall 1962), 435–441.

ROSE, ARNOLD M. *The Power Structure: Political Process in American Society.* New York: Oxford University Press, 1967.

ROSENBERG, MORRIS. "Power and Desegregation," *Social Problems,* 3 (April 1956), 215–223.

ROSSI, PETER H. "Community Decision Making," *Administrative Science Quarterly,* 1 (March 1957), 415–443.

———. "Theory, Research, and Practice in Community Organization," in Charles R. Adrian (ed.), *Social Science and Community Action.* East Lansing: Michigan State University Press, 1960.

———. "Power and Community Structure,"

Midwest Journal of Political Science, 4 (November 1960), 390–401.

———. "Power and Politics: A Road to Social Reform," *Social Service Review*, 35 (December 1961), 359–369.

———, and PHILLIPS CUTRIGHT. "The Impact of Party Organization in an Industrial Setting," in Morris Janowitz (ed.), *Community Political Systems*. New York: Free Press, 1961.

———, and ROBERT A. DENTLER. *The Politics of Urban Renewal: The Chicago Findings*. New York: Free Press, 1961.

SANDERS, IRWIN T. "The Community Social Profile," *American Sociological Review*, 25 (February 1960), 75–77.

SAYRE, WALLACE S., and HERBERT KAUFMAN. *Governing New York City*, New York: Russell Sage, 1960.

SCHULZE, ROBERT O. "The Role of Economic Dominants in Community Power Structure," *American Sociological Review*, 23 (February 1958), 3–9.

———. "The Bifurcation of Power in a Satellite City," in Morris Janowitz (ed.), *Community Political Systems*. New York: Free Press, 1961, 19–80.

———, and LEONARD U. BLUMBERG. "The Determination of Local Power Elites," *American Journal of Sociology*, 63 (November 1957), 290–296.

SCOBLE, HARRY. "Leadership Hierarchies and Political Issues in a New England Town," in Morris Janowitz (ed.), *Community Political Systems*. New York: Free Press, 1961.

SEIDMAN, JOE, JACK LONDON, and BERNARD KARSH. "Political Consciousness in Local Unions," *Public Opinion Quarterly*, 15 (Winter 1951–52), 692–702.

SIMON, HERBERT A. "Notes on the Observation and Measurement of Political Power," *Journal of Politics*, 15 (November 1953), 500–516.

SMITH, CHRISTOPHER. "Social Selection in Community Leadership," *Social Forces*, Vol. 15 (1937), 530–535.

SMITH, LINCOLN. "Political Leadership," *Social Science*, 29 (June 1954), 147–154.

———. "Town Meeting Government," *Social Science*, 30 (June 1955), 174–185.

———. "Political Leadership in a New England Community," *Review of Politics*, 17 (July 1955), 392–409.

———. "Unrequited Quest for City Status—A Case Study of 100 Years," *Rural Sociology* (June 1961), 170–186.

———. "Power Politics in Brunswick: A Case Study," *Human Organization*, 22 (Summer 1963), 152–158.

SMITH, TED C. "The Structuring of Power in a Suburban Community," *Pacific Sociological Review*, 3 (Fall 1960), 83–88.

SMUCKLER, R. H., and G. M. BELKNAP. *Leadership and Participation in Urban Political Affairs*. Governmental Research Bureau, Political Research Studies No. 2, East Lansing: Michigan State University, 1956.

SOFEN, EDWARD. "Problems of Metropolitan Leadership: The Miami Experience," *Midwest Journal of Political Science*, 5 (February 1961), 18–38.

———. *Miami Metropolitan Experiment*. Bloomington: Indiana University Press, 1963.

SPEIGHT, JOHN F. "Community Homogeneity and Consensus on Leadership," *Sociological Quarterly*, 9 (Summer 1968), 387–396.

SPINRAD, WILLIAM. "Power in Local Communities," *Social Problems*, 12 (Winter 1965), 335–356.

STEWART, FRANK. "A Sociometric Study of Influence in Southtown," *Sociometry*, 10 (February 1947), 11–31.

STONE, GREGORY, and WILLIAM H. FORM. "Instabilities in Status: The Problem of Hierarchy in the Community Study of Status Arrangements," *American Sociological Review*, 18 (April 1953), 149–162.

STONE, ROBERT C. "Power and Values in Trans-Community Relations," in Bert E. Swanson (ed.), *Current Trends in Comparative Community Studies*. Kansas City, Mo.: Community Studies, Inc., 1962.

SWANSON, BERT E. (ed.). *Current Trends in Comparative Community Studies*. Kansas City, Mo.: Community Studies, Inc., 1962.

THOMETZ, CAROL ESTES. *The Decision-Makers*. Dallas: Southern University Press, 1963.

THOMPSON, DANIEL C. *The Negro Leadership Class*. Englewood Cliffs, N.J.: Prentice-Hall, 1963.

TRUMAN, DAVID B. "Theory and Research on Metropolitan Political Leadership: Report on a Conference," *Social Science Research Council Items*, 15 (March 1961).

UNDERWOOD, KENNETH W. *Protestant and Catholic: Religious and Social Interaction in an Industrial Community*. Boston: Beacon Press, 1957.

VIDICH, ARTHUR J., and JOSEPH BENSMAN. *Small Town in Mass Society*. Princeton: Princeton University Press, 1958.

———, Joseph Bensman, and Maurice Stein. *Reflections on Community Studies.* New York: Wiley, 1964.

Walter, Benjamin. "Political Decision-Making in North Carolina Cities," *American Behavioral Scientist,* 3 (May 1960), 18–21.

———. "Political Decision Making in Arcadia," in F. Stuart Chapin, Jr., and Shirley F. Weiss (eds.), *Urban Growth Dynamics.* New York: Wiley, 1962, 141–187.

———. "On the Logical Analysis of Power-Attribution Procedures," *Journal of Politics,* 26 (November 1964), 850–866.

Walton, John. "Substance and Artifact: The Current Status of Research on Community Power Structure," *American Journal of Sociology,* 71 (January 1966), 430–438.

———. "Discipline, Method, and Community Power: A Note on the Sociology of Knowledge," *American Sociological Review,* 31 (October 1966), 684–689.

———. "The Vertical Axis of Community Organization and the Structure of Power," *Southwestern Social Science Quarterly,* 48 (December 1967), 353–368.

———. "Differential Patterns of Community Power Structure: An Explanation Based on Interdependence," in Terry N. Clark (ed.), *Community Structure and Decision-Making.* San Francisco: Chandler, 1968. Also in *Sociological Quarterly,* 9 (Winter 1968), 3–18.

———. "A Systematic Survey of Community Power Research," in this volume, 1970.

Webb, Harold V. *Community Power Structure Related to School Administration.* Laramie: University of Wyoming Press, 1956.

White, James E. "Theory and Method for Research in Community Leadership," *American Sociological Review,* 15 (February 1950), 50–60.

Whitten, Norman, E., Jr. "Power Structure and Sociocultural Change in Latin American Communities," *Social Forces,* 43 (March 1965), 320–329.

Wildavsky, A. "Analysis of Issue-Contexts in the Study of Decision-Making," *Journal of Politics,* 24 (November 1962), 717–732.

———. *Leadership in a Small Town.* Totowa, N.J.: Bedminister Press, 1964.

Williams, Oliver P. and Charles R. Adrian. "A Typology for Comparative Local Government," *Midwest Journal of Political Science,* 5 (May 1961), 150–164.

Wilson, E. K. "Determinants of Participation in Policy Formation in a College Community," *Human Relations,* Vol. 7 (1954), 287–312.

Wolfinger, Raymond E., "Reputation and Reality in the Study of 'Community Power,'" *American Sociological Review,* 25 (October 1960), 636–644.

———. "A Plea for a Decent Burial," *American Sociological Review,* 27 (December 1962), 841–847.

Wood, Thomas J. "Dade County: Unbossed, Erratically Led," *Annals of the American Academy of Political and Social Science,* 353 (May 1964), 64–71.

Wrong, Dennis. "Who Runs American Cities?" *New Society,* 1 (April 1963), 16–17.

———. "Some Problems in Defining Social Power," *American Journal of Sociology,* 73 (May 1968), 673–681.

Yager, J. W. "Who Runs Our Town?" *National Civic Review,* 52 (May 1963), 255–259.

Young, James N., and Selz C. Mayo. "Manifest and Latent Participators in Rural Community Action Programs," *Social Forces,* 38 (December 1959), 140–145.

Dissertations

Acker, Roy Dean. "The Influentials in a Selected County and Their Involvement in the Decision-Making Process" (Unpublished Ed.D. Dissertation, University of Florida, 1963).

Agger, Robert E. "The Dynamics of Local Political Participation: Empirical Research and Theoretical Inquiry" (Unpublished Ph.D. Dissertation, University of Oregon, 1954).

Andrews, Wade H. "Some Correlates of Rural Leadership and Social Power Among Intercommunity Leaders" (Unpublished Ph.D.

Dissertation, Michigan State University, 1956).

Ashley, Thomas J. "Power and Politics in Community Planning: An Empirical Analysis of Four Selected Policy Decisions Made in Anaheim, California Between 1945–1960" (Unpublished Ph.D. Dissertation, Claremont Graduate School and University Center, 1962).

Auerbach, Arnold J. "The Pattern of Community Leadership in Urban Redevelopment: A Pittsburgh Profile" (Unpublished Ph.D.

Dissertation, University of Pittsburgh, 1961).

BENSMAN, JOSEPH. "Small Town in Mass Society: Class, Power, Religion in a Rural Community" (Unpublished Ph.D. Dissertation, Columbia University, 1958–59).

BITTINGER, BEAU S. "Leadership Systems and Social Change in a Texas City of 100,000" (Unpublished Ph.D. Dissertation, University of Texas, 1967).

BLANKENSHIP, L. VAUGHN. "Organizational Support and Community Leadership in Two New York State Communities" (Unpublished Ph.D. Dissertation, Cornell University, 1962).

BLOME, ARVIN CHRIS. "A Study in the Identification of Community Power Structure and Influence on Public School Issues" (Unpublished Ph.D. Dissertation, State University of Iowa, 1963).

BLUMBERG, LEONARD V. "Community Leaders: The Social Bases and Social Psychological Concomitants of Community Power" (Unpublished Ph.D. Dissertation, University of Michigan, 1955).

BOCKMAN, SHELDON E. "Power and Decision-Making Within and Between Institutional Sectors: The Differential Impact by Issues on Institutional Sectors" (Unpublished Ph.D. Dissertation, Indiana University, 1968).

BONJEAN, CHARLES M. "Community Leadership: A Conceptual Refinement and Comparative Analysis" (Unpublished Ph.D. Dissertation, University of North Carolina, 1963).

BOUMA, DONALD H. "An Analysis of the Social Power Position of the Real Estate Board in Grand Rapids, Michigan" (Unpublished Ph.D. Dissertation, Michigan State College, 1952).

CARPENTER, D. B. "Some Factors Associated with Influence Positions in the Associational Structure of a Rural Community" (Unpublished Ph.D. Dissertation, University of Washington, 1951).

CARSTENSON, BLUE ALLAN. "A Method for Studying How People Perceive Power Structure in Their Communities as Tested in Five Michigan Communities" (Unpublished Ph.D. Dissertation, University of Michigan, 1956).

CUYUGAN, RUBEN DARIO SANTOS. "Decision-Makers in a New England Community: A Study of Social Influence and Social Power" (Unpublished Ph.D. Dissertation, Harvard University, 1958–59).

D'ANTONIO, WILLIAM. "National Images of Business and Political Elites in Two Border Cities" (Unpublished Ph.D. Dissertation, Michigan State University, 1958).

DANZGER, HERBERT M. "Civil Rights Conflict and Community Power Structure" (Unpublished Ph.D. Dissertation, Columbia University, 1968).

ERICKSON, EUGENE C. "The Reputational Technique in a Cross-Community Perspective: Selected Problems of Theory and Measurement" (Unpublished Ph.D. Dissertation, Michigan State University, 1962).

FRENCH, ROBERT MILLS. "Cornucopia in Transition" (Unpublished Ph.D. Dissertation, University of Wisconsin, 1967).

GALBO, CHARLES JOSEPH. "Personality and Influence in a Community Power Structure" (Unpublished Ph.D. Dissertation, University of Arizona, 1962).

GALLO, VINCENT A. "A Comparative Study of Occupational Prestige and Social Associations Among Community Leaders" (Unpublished Ph.D. Dissertation, University of Oregon, 1968).

GETTEL, GERHARD FREDRICK. "A Study of Power in a North Central State Community" (Unpublished Ph.D. Dissertation, Michigan State University, 1956).

GILBERT, CLAIRE W. "Community Power Structure: A Study in the Sociology of Knowledge" (Unpublished Ph.D. Dissertation, Northwestern University, 1966).

GOLDRICH, DANIEL. "Parties, Partisanship and Local Politics in Two Oregon Communities" (Unpublished Ph.D. Dissertation, University of North Carolina, 1959).

GOURLEY, HAROLD V. "Patterns of Leadership in Decision-Making in a Selected County" (Unpublished Ed.D. Dissertation, University of Florida, August 1962).

GRISWOLD, LEONARD E. "The Community as a Social System: A Study in Comparative Analysis" (Unpublished Ph.D. Dissertation, University of Kentucky, 1956).

HARPER, JOE W. "A Study of Community Power Structure in Certain School Districts in the State of Texas and Its Influence on Bond Elections" (Unpublished Ed.D. Dissertation, North Texas State University, 1965).

HOLDEN, MATTHEW. "Decision-Making on a Metropolitan Government Proposition: The Case of Cuyahoga County, Ohio, 1958–59" (Unpublished Ph.D. Dissertation, Northwestern University, 1961).

HUDSON, JAMES R. "Power with Low Prestige: A Study of Labor Unions in a Dependent Community" (Unpublished Ph.D. Dissertation, University of Michigan, 1965).

JENKINS, QUENTIN A. L. "Community Actors' Perceptions of Community Power Structure" (Unpublished Ph.D. Dissertation, University of Iowa, 1966).

JENNINGS, M. KENT. "Political Statuses and Political Roles in Community Decision-Making" (Unpublished Ph.D. Dissertation, University of North Carolina, 1961).

JOHNSON, ROGERS P. "Community, Democracy and Power: A Study of Conflicting Themes in the Sociological Conception of Community" (Unpublished Ph.D. Dissertation, Brandeis University, 1968).

JOHNSTON, RAY E. "A Comparative Analysis of Demand Articulation in Three Western Communities" (Unpublished Ph.D. Dissertation, University of Oregon, 1967).

JONES, JOSEPH H., Jr. "A Comparative Analysis of Community Leaders and Non-Leaders in a North Central Kentucky Community" (Unpublished Ph.D. Dissertation, University of Kentucky, 1956).

KIMBROUGH, RALPH B. "The Operational Beliefs of Selected Leaders in a Selected County" (Unpublished Ed.D. Dissertation, University of Tennessee, 1953).

KLEIN, HENRY LOUIS. "Community Organization Leadership in Philadelphia" (Unpublished Ed.D. Dissertation, Temple University, 1965).

LARSON, CALVIN J. "Economic and Ecological Factors in Relation to Community Leadership Structure: A Comparative and Historical Analysis of Two Oregon Communities" (Unpublished Ph.D. Dissertation, University of Oregon, 1965).

LIGHT, KENNETH HENRY. "Community Power Structures and School District Reorganization" (Unpublished Ph.D. Dissertation, University of Colorado, 1964).

LONGSTRETH, JAMES W. "The Relationship of Beliefs of Community Leaders, Teachers and Voters to School Fiscal Policy and Typology of Community Power Structure" (Unpublished Ph.D. Dissertation, University of Florida, 1967).

LOWRY, RITCHIE P. "Who Runs This Town? A Study of the Quality of Public Life in a Changing Small Community" (Unpublished Ph.D. Dissertation, Department of Sociology, University of California, Berkeley, 1962.

MASSE, BERARD. "A Comparison of the Relationship of Influentials to Schools in High and Low Financial Support Communities" (Unpublished Ph.D. Dissertation, University of Michigan, 1964).

MATTHEWS, THOMAS. "The Lawyer as Community Leader: One Dimension of the Professional Role" (Unpublished Ph.D. Dissertation, Cornell University, 1953).

MEREDITH, WILLIAM V. "Comparisons of Liberal-Conservative Socio-Economic Value Measurements Between Influentials and Persons Residing in Two Selected Florida Counties" (Unpublished Ph.D. Dissertation, University of Florida, 1963).

MERRILL, EDWARD C. "Communication and Decision-Making Related to the Administration of Education" (Unpublished Ph.D. Dissertation, George Peabody College for Teachers, 1952).

MILLER, KENNETH EDWARD. "The Structural Correlates of Community Power Systems" (Unpublished Ph.D. Dissertation, Duke University, 1965).

MOSER, RUTH. "Correlates of Decision-Making in Eighteen New England Communities" (Unpublished M.A. Thesis, Department of Sociology, University of Chicago, 1968).

MULFORD, CHARLES LEE. "Some Relationships Between Formal Organizations, Community Problems, and Leadership" (Unpublished Ph.D. Dissertation, Iowa State University of Science and Technology, 1962).

PERKINS, LARRY MANSON. "Leadership in a New York Rural Community" (Unpublished Ph.D. Dissertation, Syracuse University, 1963).

PHILLETT, SERENA. "An Analysis of Community Influence: Some Conceptual and Methodological Considerations" (Unpublished M.A. Thesis, University of Alberta, Edmonton, Canada, 1963).

POWERS, RONALD CLAIR. "Social Power in a Rural Community" (Unpublished Ph.D. Dissertation, Iowa State University of Science and Technology, 1963).

PRESTON, JAMES D. "A Typology of Community Leadership" (Unpublished Ph.D. Dissertation, Mississippi State University, 1967).

REICHLER, MELVIN LITWACK. "Community Power Structure in Action" (Unpublished Ph.D. Dissertation, University of Michigan, 1963).

RHYNE, EDWIN H. "Party Politics and the Decision Making Process: A Study at the County Level" (Unpublished thesis, University of North Carolina, 1957).

ROGERS, ROBERT BURTCH. "Perception of the Power Structure by Social Class in a California Community" (Unpublished Ph.D.

Dissertation, University of Southern California, 1962).

SASTRODININGRAT, SOEBAGIO. "Some Dimensions of Power and Influence in Relation to the Power Structure Data in Two Cities" (Unpublished Ph.D. Dissertation, Indiana University, 1964).

SCAGGS, WILLIAM F. "The Influentials in a Selected County School Administrative Unit: Their Norms and Resources" (Unpublished Ed.D. Dissertation, University of Florida, 1963).

SCHULZE, ROBERT O. "Economic Dominants and Public Leadership" (Unpublished Ph.D. Dissertation, University of Michigan, 1956).

SCHULTZE, WILLIAM A. "Public Leadership in Charter Revision: Case Studies in Four New Jersey Municipalities" (Unpublished Ph.D. Dissertation, Rutgers University, 1967).

SCOBLE, HARRY. "Yankeetown: A Study of Community Decision-Making Processes" (Unpublished Ph.D. Dissertation, Yale University, 1957).

SHIBLES, MARK R. "Community Power Structures and District School Organization Relationships: An Exploratory Analysis of Input Functions" (Unpublished Ph.D. Dissertation, Cornell University, 1968).

SINGH, AUTAR. "Leadership Patterns and Village Structure: A Study of Six Indian Villages" (Unpublished Ph.D. Dissertation, Mississippi State University, 1967).

SPIESS, JOHN A. "Community Power Structure and Influence: Relationships to Educational Administration" (Unpublished Ph.D. Dissertation, University of Iowa, 1967).

WALTER, BENJAMIN. "Communications and Influence: Decision-Making in a Municipal Administrative Hierarchy" (Unpublished Ph.D. Dissertation, Northwestern University, 1959–60).

WALTON, JOHN T. "An Analysis of Methods and Findings in Studies of Community Power Structure" (Unpublished Ph.D. Dissertation, University of California, Santa Barbara, 1966).

WELLMAN, FREDERICK L. "Interrelationships and Operational Patterns of Leaders in the Power Structure of a Selected County", (Ed.D. Dissertation, University of Florida, 1963).

WILEY, NORBERT FRANCIS. "Class and Local Politics in Three Michigan Communities" (Unpublished Ph.D. Dissertation, Michigan State University, 1962).

WILKINSON, KENNETH P. "A Behavioral Measure of Community Leadership" (Unpublished Ph.D. Dissertation, Mississippi State University, 1965).

WILSON, JAMES Q. "Negro Leaders in Chicago" (Unpublished Ph.D. Dissertation, University of Chicago, 1959).

WILSON, L. CRAIG. "Community Power Pressure and Control in Relation to Education in a Selected County" (Unpublished Ph.D. Dissertation, George Peabody College for Teachers, 1952).

Contributing Authors

BAHA ABU-LABAN is an Associate Professor, Department of Sociology, University of Alberta, Edmonton, Canada.

MICHAEL AIKEN is an Associate Professor in the Department of Sociology, University of Wisconsin, Madison, Wisconsin.

THOMAS J. ANTON is an Associate Professor in the Department of Political Science, University of Michigan, Ann Arbor, Michigan.

PETER BACHRACH is a Professor in the Department of Political Science, Temple University, Philadelphia, Pennsylvania.

EDWARD C. BANFIELD is the Henry Lee Shattuck Professor of Urban Government at Harvard University and a member of the Joint Center for Urban Studies of the Massachusetts Institute of Technology and Harvard University, Cambridge, Massachusetts.

MORTON S. BARATZ is a Professor and Chairman of the Department of Economics, Boston University, Boston, Massachusetts.

ERNEST A. T. BARTH is a Professor in the Department of Sociology, University of Washington, Seattle, Washington.

L. VAUGHN BLANKENSHIP is an Associate Professor and Chairman, Department of Political Science, State University of New York, Buffalo, New York.

WARNER BLOOMBERG, JR., is a Professor in the Department of Urban Affairs, University of Wisconsin, Milwaukee, Wisconsin.

LEONARD U. BLUMBERG is a Professor in the Department of Sociology, Temple University, Philadelphia, Pennsylvania.

CHARLES M. BONJEAN is an Associate Professor in the Department of Sociology, University of Texas, Austin, Texas.

DONALD H. BOUMA is a Professor of Sociology, Western Michigan University, Kalamazoo, Michigan.

DONALD S. BRADLEY is an Assistant Professor, Department of Sociology, Emory University, Atlanta, Georgia.

DONALD A. CLELLAND is an Assistant Professor, Department of Sociology, University of Tennessee, Knoxville, Tennessee.

CHARLES H. COATES is an Assistant Professor in the Department of Sociology, University of Maryland, College Park, Maryland.

ROBERT A. DAHL is Sterling Professor of Political Science, Yale University, New Haven, Connecticut.

WILLIAM V. D'ANTONIO is a Professor in the Department of Sociology and Anthropology, Notre Dame University, Notre Dame, Indiana.

M. HERBERT DANZGER is an Assistant Professor, Department of Sociology, Herbert Lehman College of the City University of New York, New York.

EUGENE C. ERICKSON is an Associate Professor in the Department of Rural Sociology, Cornell University, Ithaca, New York.

THOMAS J. FARARO is an Associate Professor, Department of Sociology, University of Pittsburgh, Pittsburgh, Pennsylvania.

WILLIAM H. FORM is Research Professor in the Department of Sociology, Michigan State University, East Lansing, Michigan.

IRVING A. FOWLER is currently a Professor in the School of Social Work, University of Connecticut at West Hartford, Connecticut.

LINTON C. FREEMAN is a Professor in the Department of Sociology, University of Hawaii, Honolulu, Hawaii.

ROBERT MILLS FRENCH is an Assistant Professor, Department of Sociology, Florida State University, Tallahassee, Florida.

WILLIAM A. GAMSON is a Professor in the Department of Sociology, University of Michigan, Ann Arbor, Michigan.

AMOS H. HAWLEY is a Professor in the Department of Sociology, University of North Carolina, Chapel Hill, North Carolina.

FLOYD HUNTER is currently a social science research consultant in Berkeley, California.

STUART D. JOHNSON is an Associate Professor, Department of Sociology, University of Manitoba, Winnipeg, Canada.

VICTOR JONES is a Professor in the Department of Political Science, University of California, Berkeley, California.

539

HERBERT KAUFMAN is a Senior Fellow, Governmental Studies Program, The Brookings Institution, Washington, D.C.

LEWIS M. KILLIAN is currently a Professor in the Department of Sociology, University of Massachusetts, Amherst, Massachusetts.

JAMES B. MCKEE is currently a Professor in the Department of Sociology and Anthropology, Michigan State University, East Lansing, Michigan.

MARTIN MEYERSON is currently Professor of Policy Sciences and President of the State University of New York at Buffalo, New York.

DELBERT C. MILLER is a Professor in the Department of Sociology and Business Administration, Indiana University, Bloomington, Indiana.

C. WRIGHT MILLS was a leading spokesman for radical sociology and made many important contributions in the fields of social stratification and political theory before his untimely death on March 20, 1962, at the age of forty-five.

PAUL E. MOTT is an Associate Professor in the Department of Sociology, Wharton School of Finance and Commerce, University of Pennsylvania, Philadelphia, Pennsylvania.

DAVID M. OLSON is an Associate Professor in the Department of Political Science, University of Georgia, Athens, Georgia.

ROLAND J. PELLEGRIN is a Professor of Sociology and Director, Institute for Community Studies, University of Oregon, Eugene, Oregon.

MAURICE PINARD is currently an Associate Professor of Sociology, McGill University, Montreal, Canada.

NELSON W. POLSBY is currently a Professor of Political Science, University of California, Berkeley, California.

PETER H. ROSSI is Chairman of the Department of Social Relations, Johns Hopkins University, Baltimore, Maryland.

ROBERT O. SCHULZE is a Professor of Sociology (on leave), Brown University, Providence, Rhode Island, and currently Executive Director, The Thomas J. Watson Foundation, Providence, Rhode Island.

CHARLES U. SMITH is currently a Professor and Chairman, Department of Sociology, Florida Agricultural and Mechanical University, Tallahassee, Florida.

MORRIS H. SUNSHINE is currently an Associate Professor in the Department of Sociology, Kent State University, Kent, Ohio.

STEPHAN THERNSTROM is Professor of Urban History, University of California, Los Angeles, California.

MELVILLE J. ULMER is a Professor in the Department of Economics, University of Maryland, College Park, Maryland.

JOHN WALTON is an Assistant Professor, Department of Sociology, Northwestern University, Evanston, Illinois.

WILLIAM F. WHYTE has a joint appointment as a Professor in the New York School of Industrial and Labor Relations and as a Professor of Sociology, Cornell University, Ithaca, New York.

RAYMOND E. WOLFINGER is an Associate Professor in the Department of Political Science, Stanford University, Stanford, California.

MAYER N. ZALD is a Professor in the Department of Sociology and Anthropology, Vanderbilt University, Nashville, Tennessee.